The Ethics and Conduct of Lawyers in England and Wales

ANDREW BOON and JENNIFER LEVIN

Second Edition

·HART·
PUBLISHING
OXFORD AND PORTLAND, OREGON
2008

Published in North America (US and Canada) by
Hart Publishing
c/o International Specialized Book Services
920 NE 58th Avenue, Suite 300
Portland, OR 97213-3786
USA
Tel: +1 503 287 3093 or toll-free: (1) 800 944 6190
Fax: +1 503 280 8832
E-mail: orders@isbs.com
Website: www.isbs.com

Hart Publishing, 16C Worcester Place, OX1 2JW
Telephone: +44 (0)1865 517530 Fax: +44 (0)1865 510710
E-mail: mail@hartpub.co.uk
Website: http://www.hartpub.co.uk

British Library Cataloguing in Publication Data
Data Available
ISBN: 978-1-84113-708-7

Typeset by Forewords, Oxford
Printed and bound in Great Britain by
TJ International Ltd, Padstow, Cornwall

PREFACE

It is nine years since the first edition of this book was published, a long time in any field of law, but especially so in relation to our subject matter, the legal profession of England and Wales. In that edition we said that the ethics of the professions had, until recently, been a largely neglected area of study. This has changed considerably over the last decade, mainly because of the enormous changes that have affected the profession. These include the complete revamping of civil procedure, the introduction of a new legal aid regime, major change in the way the professional bodies do their work, in particular how they deal with complaints, and a new Code of Conduct for solicitors and legislation—the Legal Services Act 2007—which will affect the whole legal services market. The last of these events will see significant inroads into, and arguably even the end of, self-regulation of lawyers. Its impact on professional ethics may not, however, be quite as devastating as has been predicted or that might be imagined.

The field has undergone many developments in its own right. Within a year of our first edition, Donald Nicholson and Julian Webb made a huge contribution with *Legal Ethics: Critical Interrogations*, a volume complementary in many ways to our own. Whilst ours takes an overtly socio-legal approach, Nicholson and Webb bring to the English literature, in the tradition of US luminaries on legal ethics such as Luban, Simon, Postema and Wasserstrom, a rigorous application of moral philosophy to the issues that confront the profession. English academic literature has also benefited immensely from the success of the journal *Legal Ethics* which, under the editorship of Kim Economides and with the active support of Richard Hart, has both established itself and generated a body of significant work. This book is intended to provide a stimulating analysis of the field of legal ethics for all interested or concerned with the subject, whether legal practitioners, teachers, academics or students. In particular, we hope that it will encourage the adoption of professional ethics throughout legal education, a step which, whilst consistently encouraged in the various official reports into the profession, has still to be achieved. Many people have helped us in producing this edition, but, needless to say, any errors are our own. We have endeavoured to state the position as at 31 December 2007.

Andrew Boon (London) and Jenny Levin (Swansea)
Christmas 2007.

ACKNOWLEDGEMENTS

We acknowledge a debt to both the increasing number of academic commentators and also those in the professions, particularly Sir Mark Potter, Mark Stobbs, Sue Nelson, Chris Maguire and all the criminal solicitors and others involved in the training of police station solicitors at Cardiff University Law School, who, in ways they may not even have realised, convinced us that this is not just a worthwhile venture, but an important one. We are grateful to the many commentators on the first edition—Nigel Duncan, Richard Tur and particularly Alan Hutchison, whose review in the *Journal of Law and Society* is one to treasure—for encouragement and the criticism that helped us to develop our thinking. In compiling this second edition, we are conscious of the debt owed to these and others in the community of scholars contributing to the development of this field in the UK and abroad.

We have also accumulated more specific debts. We thank Richard Hart and all at our publishers and the colleagues who have generously read and commented on chapters: Reza Banaker (Ideals), John Flood (Power and Culture), Mark Stobbs (Employment, Litigation and Advocacy) and Susan Nash (Litigation). We thank Valerie Shrimplin, Cordelia Lean and Oliver Hanmer for details of the Bar Standards Board. Last, but certainly not least, we are grateful to Avis Whyte for research assistance throughout the period, Blanca Mamutse for her research assistance in the final stages and for her efforts in checking and formatting the final text, and Sam King and Victoria Bougouneau for secretarial support. Andy is grateful to John Flood and Julian Webb for collaborations furthering his understanding of the legal profession.

CONTENTS

ABBREVIATIONS

ABA	American Bar Association
ADR	Alternative Dispute Resolution
APIL	Association of Personal Injury Lawyer
BITC	Business in the Community
BPBU	Bar Pro Bono Unit
BVC	Bar Vocational Course
CABx	Citizens Advice Bureaux
CCBE	Council of the Bars and Law Societies of the European Union
CCS	Consumer Complaints Service
CEO	chief executive officer
CFA	Conditional Fee Agreement
CLSA	Courts and Legal Services Act
CPD	continuing professional development
CPR	Civil Procedure Rules
CPS	Crown Prosecution Service
DCW	designated case worker
ECHR	European Convention on Human Rights
FRU	Free Representation Unit
IBA	International Bar Association
ILEX	Institute of Legal Executives
LCO	Local Conciliation Officer
LCS	Legal Complaints Service
LLPs	limited liability partnerships
LPC	Legal Practice Course
LSC	Legal Services Commission
LSCC	Legal Services Complaints Commissioner
LSO	Legal Services Ombudsman

MNP	multi-national partnership
NCC	National Consumer Council
NCIS	National Criminal Intelligence Service
OSS	Office for the Supervision of Solicitors
PACE	Police and Criminal Evidence Act
PSC	Professional Skills Course
QC	Queen's Counsel
RFL	Registered Foreign Lawyer
SCB	Solicitors' Complaints Bureau
SDT	Solicitors Disciplinary Tribunal
SEAL	Solicitors' Estate Agency Ltd
SEC	Securities and Exchange Commission
SPBG	Solicitors' Pro Bono Group
SRA	Solicitors Regulation Authority

TABLE OF CASES

TABLE OF STATUTES

Part I

PROFESSIONAL ETHICS

Lawyers, together with clerics and doctors, formed the original triumvirate of learned professions in England and Wales. These occupations enjoyed considerable control over entry into their ranks and the discipline of their members. Their traditions took centuries to evolve, a rich mix of historical accident, high ideals and political necessity. These practices were collectively referred to as 'professional ethics', a term investing them with a moral quality. Analysing these sources is an important in developing a 'critical morality' whereby 'received culture' is examined, assessed, revised or rejected.[1]

In this book we define the legal profession as comprising traditional twin branches: solicitors and barristers. This is not intended to be disrespectful to other providers of legal services.[2] It is, however, beyond the scope of this book to consider the full range of legal services providers. Part I considers the sources and significance of professional ethics through the lenses of professional ideals, organisation, power and culture. Professional ethics will, we hope, be seen more clearly from these foundations,[3] but certain themes run through each of the chapters.

Professions have long been associated with distinctive presentation, values and norms, some of which seem to run counter to what might be called the ordinary morality of society. How do these differences come about and why are they preserved, sometimes from age to age? The idea of professional ethics is intelligible only if one understands professions, their aspirations and their challenges. They are also more comprehensible if one understands the way the profession sees itself, its ideology. In the case of lawyers in England and Wales, ideology was very clearly articulated in one of the many official reports by lawyers, on lawyers:

> In certain respects the legal profession occupies a position which differs from that occupied by other professions. Lawyers must always act in their clients' best interests and must refuse to act if a conflict of interest occurs; lawyers have a duty to the court; they are sometimes required to represent clients in unpopular causes; they have a duty to uphold the rule of law; for all these reasons the ordinary commercial considerations cannot be decisive if the traditional character and functions of an independent legal profession are to be preserved.[4]

[1] P Selznick, 'The Idea of a Communitarian Morality' (1987) 75 *California Law Review* 445, 461.

[2] Notably, the Institute of Legal Executives, which has a long and distinguished history of its own. AM Francis, 'Legal Executives and the Phantom of Legal Professionalism: the Rise and Rise of the Third Branch of the Profession?' (2002) 9 *International Journal of the Legal Profession* 5.

[3] R Terdiman, 'Translator's Introduction to Bordieu, P. "The Force of Law: Toward a Sociology of the Juridical Field"' (1987) 38 *The Hastings Law Journal* 805.

[4] Lady Marre CBE, *A Time for Change: Report of the Committee on the Future of the Legal Profession* (London, General Council of the Bar and Council of The Law Society, 1988) para 6.1.

Critics say that such statements show that professionalism is self-serving; privilege protecting privilege. What is happening to the professional ethics of lawyers now, and what is likely to happen in the future, is comprehensible only if professions are also seen as significant others—clients, consumers and governments—see them. The image thus perceived explains the legal profession's current uneasy relationship with the state.

1

IDEALS

Well, I don't wanna be a lawyer mama, I don't wanna lie[1]

Introduction

Durkheim thought that no social function could exist without moral discipline,

> otherwise, nothing remains but individual appetites, and since they are by nature boundless and insatiable, if there is nothing to control them they will not be able to control themselves.[2]

Professional ethics represents a form of moral discipline. Although some elements are contained in regulations, and may be enforced, others are merely an aspiration to high moral standards. Yet, if professional ethics is conceived of as a distinct stream of social rules, it surely draws on and complements the mainstream. An enquiry into the professional ethics of lawyers begins with an analysis of the distinctive features of professionalism, from self-regulation to the source of professional values. This grounding makes explicit the connections between the rules of professional conduct, the values they represent and how they serve the public good. The sources of legal professional ethics are diverse and sometimes obscure; ideas from history and philosophy vie with the pragmatism of workplace practices, court judgments and individual altruism. Indeed, professionalism itself is a nebulous construct with different faces.

Professions

Professions are self-regulating occupations controlling a socially important area of work, defining consumer needs and determining the way in which those needs are met. Many writers have sought to define more closely the traits of professionalism. They identify intangibles such as the esoteric knowledge they control, their mystique, social prestige and autonomy. More concrete indicators include their stringent entry requirements,[3] demanding educational programmes and ethics codes. Greenwood argued that all professions have five

---

[1] J Lennon, 'Don't Want to be a Soldier' from *Imagine* (Parlophone, 1971).

[2] E Durkheim, *Professional Ethics and Civic Morals*, trans C Brookfield, (London, Routledge 1992) 11.

[3] TJ Johnson, *Professions and Power* (London, Macmillan Press, 1972) 23; CO Houle, *Continuing Learning in the Professions* (San Francisco, CA, Jossey-Bass, 1980); CW Wolfram, *Modern Legal Ethics* (St Paul, MN, West Publishing, 1986); E Schein, *Professional Education: Some New Directions* (New York, McGraw-Hill, 1972); MD Bayles, *Professional Ethics* (Belmont, California, Wadsworth Publishing, 2nd edn, 1989) 14.

features: systematic theory, authority, community sanction, ethical codes and a professional culture.[4] Most authors identify the fact that they deploy generalised and systematic knowledge in the community interest, rather than in their individual self-interest as a defining feature.[5] This is a self-imposed burden, albeit the quid quo pro of privilege, manifest in professional ethics.

Some sociologists identify this orientation to the public good as one of the key 'functions' of professions, which works for the benefit of society beyond the professional sphere.[6] The functionalist's benign construction of professions envisaged a commitment to exemplary performance that was internalised in the process of work socialisation and reinforced by voluntary associations of members and rewards, both monetary and symbolic, for achievement.[7] This altruistic orientation was reflected in voluntary commitment to the highest moral standards, both personally and in relation to work. Recent analyses are hostile to this professional commitment to the public interest, seeing 'professionalization' as the aggressive pursuit of market monopoly.[8] Critics argue that, far from serving the public good, professional protectionism and exclusion of competition forces up the price of work, resulting in incompetent service.[9] Within the framework of this analysis, professional ethics are seen as little more than a smokescreen for a conspiracy 'against the laity'.[10] A more realistic assessment is that professions' moral commitments lie somewhere between these extremes, professional ethics holding '. . . in uneasy juxtaposition the two faces of professionalism—the one monopolistic, even narcissistic, and the other benign, even altruistic'.[11]

It is legitimate to ask whether the tension between monopoly and public interest is still satisfactory and, therefore, whether professionalism offers the best way of organising services of fundamental social importance. Johnson identified alternatives to the self-regulation that defines professionalism, such as state or community control.[12] The argument for self-regulation is that members of the profession understand the issues involved in delivering a service, and have strong interests in delivering those services well and in making and enforcing rules for all members. Professional bodies coordinate and

---

[4] E Greenwood, 'Attributes of a Profession' [July 1957] *Social Work* 45. For more sophisticated attempts, see M Burrage, K Jarausch and H Siegrsit, 'An Actor-based Framework for the Study of the Professions' in M Burrage and R Torstendahl (eds), *Professions in Theory and History: Rethinking the Study of the Professions* (London, Sage, 1990) 203; H Siegrist, 'Professionalization/Professions in History' in *International Encyclopedia of the Social and Behavioral Sciences.* (Amsterdam, Elsevier Science, 2002).

[5] Durkheim, above n 2; R Pound, *The Lawyer from Antiquity to Modern Times: with Particular Reference to the Development of Bar Associations in the United States* (St Paul, MN, West Publishing, 1953) 95.

[6] T Parsons, 'The Professions and Social Structure', in *Essays in Sociological Theory* (New York, Free Press, revised edn, 1954) 34.

[7] Johnson, above n 3, 38.

[8] MS Larson, *The Rise of Professionalism: A Sociological Analysis* (Berkeley CA, University of California Press, 1977); RRL Abel, *The Legal Profession in England and Wales* (Oxford, Basil Blackwell, 1988); A Abbott, *The System of Professions: An Essay on the Expert Division of Labour* (Chicago, IL, University of Chicago Press, 1988).

[9] R Moorhead, A Sherr and A Paterson, 'What Clients Know: Client Perspectives and Legal Competence' (2003) 10 *International Journal of the Legal Profession* 5; R Moorhead, A Sherr and A Paterson, 'Contesting Professionalism: Legal Aid and Non Lawyers in England and Wales' (2003) 37 *Law and Society Review* 765.

[10] GB Shaw, *The Doctor's Dilemma* (Harmondsworth, Middx, Penguin Books Ltd, 1911) Act 1; see also I Illich *Disabling Professions* (London, Marron Boyars, 1977).

[11] TC Halliday, *Beyond Monopoly: Lawyers, State Crises, and Professional Empowerment* (Chicago, IL, University of Chicago Press, 1987) 3.

[12] Johnson, above n 3.

update this knowledge in the interests of all, devising rules of civility and etiquette that minimise interpersonal and group conflict within the profession and standards to govern all.[13] Government, which cedes self-regulatory power to professions, appears increasingly sceptical of this rationale, yet continues to see professionalism as the solution to abuse of power in relationships with consumers.[14]

Professional norms

Groups of people inevitably develop behaviour patterns described as norms. There are various descriptions of norms, such as the 'characteristic spirit and beliefs of community, people, system . . . or person'.[15] Some norms are simply descriptive of standard behaviour—customs, for example—while others are injunctive, concerned with what people ought to do.[16] Durkheim argued that complex societies accommodate a range of different normative systems parallel to those of wider society. He conceived of professional ethics as one of the most developed examples,[17] the distinctive moral orientation emerging from the way that individuals do their work and from the values emerging from the coalition of interests of the occupation generally. It can be argued, however, that there is no substantial difference between occupational norms and those of wider society. Bayles explored four possibilities for the relationship between social norms and professional norms.[18] The first is that professional norms are the same as ordinary norms of behaviour; the second is that they specify how professionals must relate ordinary norms to the situations in which they find themselves; the third is that they take into account the role of the professional in applying ordinary norms; and the fourth is that they are completely independent of ordinary norms.

Each of the possibilities identified by Bayles can be justified to some extent, and more so by selecting examples. For example, we expect lawyers to be honest, just as we expect everybody to be, so the first position is true. We expect them to be honest in situations ordinary people do not necessarily find themselves in, like handling other people's money, so the second position is true. We expect them to hold their client's money separately from their own, so that it cannot be confused, so the third position is also true. Finally, we expect them to conceal suspicions of their client's dishonesty, thus undermining their own claims to being honest and validating the view that professional norms are different from ordinary norms. Ordinary citizens, for example, should let the authorities know the details of a crime and may be obliged by law to cooperate, whereas a lawyer must not divulge knowledge of a client's crime. Therefore, each of Bayles's propositions can be true, depending on the

---

[13] AC Grayling, 'The Last Word on Civility', *The Guardian*, 15 April 2000.

[14] M O'Hara, 'Licensing and Code of Ethics Urged to Stamp Out Rogue Estate Agents', *The Guardian*, 29 April 2004, 7.

[15] Or 'behaviour accepted within a group or to the statistical average of characteristics' (Bayles, above n 3, 16), or 'unorganised but persistent behavioural regularities' (EA Posner, *Law and Social Norms* (Cambridge, MA, Harvard University Press, 2000)).

[16] G Sumner, *Folkways: A study of the sociological importance of usages, manners, customs, mores and morals* (Boston, MA, Ginn & Co, 1906).

[17] Durkheim, above n 2.

[18] Bayles, above n 3, 16–17.

circumstances. Often, professional ethics require more than society does. Most people, for example, think that charities should be supported, but would resent an obligation to provide services free, or *pro bono publico*, which lawyers often accept as a natural incidence of their role in providing legal services. While there are arguably significant differences in the norms of different groups, they tend to influence each other. Professional norms may be more influential than some other types, since they often help to define or change law, and law is sometimes used to change professional norms.

Professional codes

A distinction is often drawn between descriptive norms, those that people follow unthinkingly, and those that have more social force.[19] Aristotle, Plato and Hart distinguished positive law, legal rules made by humans based on community norms, from the 'natural law' of ethics.[20] Another distinction between law and other norms are that law is enforced by the state, while other norms are often enforced informally by gossip, disapproval, ostracism and even violence.[21] Professional ethics crosses the boundary between law and morals, providing formal sanctions for rules not made directly by the state, but under its authority. This does not happen immediately, but during the course professionalisation. When certain occupations initially form, their moral consensus is strong and mutually enforced but, with growth and diversity, informal compliance mechanisms become unreliable[22] and there is pressure to make explicit the expectations of group membership. Codes of behaviour are often seen as the final stage of professionalism,[23] representing both the point when the professional community is sufficiently defined to be represented in writing and when its ethical commitments can form the basis of a contract with society for the provision of services.[24]

The legal profession enacted formal codes relatively recently. The Bar Code resulted from a recommendation of the Benson Commission in 1979,[25] although it drew extensively on a small book by Sir Malcolm Hilbery, first published in 1946,[26] which, ironically, contended that the bar's code of honour was 'incapable of being stated or written out in full like a Legal Code'.[27] The Law Society's *Guide to the Professional Conduct of Solicitors* dates from 1960,[28] steadily growing, with the incorporation of much legislative material, accounts rules

---

[19] This sharp distinction can be questioned; law draws on moral principles and can also help to change conceptions of what is right or good (Sumner, above n 16).

[20] HLA Hart, *The Concept of Law* (Oxford, Clarendon Press, 1961); LL Fuller, *The Morality of Law* (New Haven, CT, Yale University Press, 1964); R Dworkin, *Law's Empire* (Cambridge, MA, Harvard University Press, 1986).

[21] Rules are useful in enforcing the natural law rights of minority groups facing informal social sanctions: EA Posner, *Law and Social Norms* (Cambridge, MA, Harvard University Press, 2000).

[22] Posner, *ibid*, 17.

[23] Johnson, above n 3, 28; Larson, above n 8; Abel, above n 8, 29.

[24] AM Carr-Saunders and PH Wilson, *The Professions* (Oxford, Clarendon Press, 1933).

[25] The Benson Commission was surprised to find that the Bar had no code of conduct and urged it to develop one (The Royal Commission on Legal Services Final Report (1979) Cmnd 7648).

[26] The Hon Sir Malcolm Hilbery, *Duty and Art in Advocacy* (London, Stevens and Sons, 1946).

[27] *Ibid*, 7.

[28] Sir Thomas Lund CBE, *A Guide to the Professional Conduct and Etiquette of Solicitors* (London, The Law Society, 1960).

and periodic revision,[29] until replaced by the trimmer Solicitors' Code of Conduct 2007. The late arrival of codes is partly explained by outside pressure to introduce them, reflecting the fact that such documents generally serve one of two purposes. Codes of ethics tend to be outward facing, articulating professional values for a range of interested parties. Codes of conduct are likely to be internally focused, setting out restrictions and providing guidance on behaviour. The legal profession's codes are a compromise between these possibilities, providing regulation for members and addressing a wider audience by articulating values. They court criticism for containing little genuine ethical material, or little that is enforceable as opposed to 'aspirational'.[30]

In reality, codes of conduct are not exhaustive statements of professional responsibility. They often contain bland statements of the obvious, statements of etiquette[31] and 'mere regulation'. The reason for this may be that regulation reconstitutes professional ethics, either as a subordinate form of state law or as a system of law quite distinct from that of the state.[32] Since professional rules are made under delegated state authority, and therefore are a species of law, there is an increased likelihood that they will be used as evidence of professional liability for negligence or other harms. Therefore, negative obligations are more likely to be included in codes than positive ones, and positive obligations are more likely to be expressed as aspirations rather than requirements.[33] What is in codes is not the sole determinant of ethics. It has been argued that ethical behaviour considers the position of others, is not purely self-interested and can be justified independently of the role held.[34]

Many argue that professional codes of conduct represent only 'a single piece of a larger mosaic of considerations that are morally relevant to a lawyer's conduct'.[35] Professionals must aspire to standards of integrity and service beyond those required by detailed rules,[36] act morally where rules of conduct do not expressly cover a situation[37] and consider the impact of personal behaviour on their profession.[38] This wider obligation embraces a

[29] A Crawley and C Bramall, 'Professional Rules, Codes and Principles Affecting Solicitors (or What Has Professsional Regulation to do with Ethics?)' in R Cranston (ed), *Legal Ethics and Professional Responsibility* (Oxford, Clarendon Press, 1995) 99, 100.

[30] See also D Nicolson, 'Mapping Professional Legal Ethics: The Form and Focus of the Codes' (1998) 1 *Legal Ethics* 51.

[31] Eg rules concerning referrals, consultations, acquiring and receiving clients, recompensing sponsors and relating to peers, supervisors and subordinates (Johnson, above n 3, 56).

[32] In *Johnson v Bingley, Dyson and Furey* (1997) PNLR 392 QBD it was held that professional codes were relevant to issues of foreseeability and reasonableness in negligence but not conclusive. Having read the Solicitors' Guide to Professional Conduct, Hytner QC, sitting as a deputy High Court judge, said, 'It is clear that it is a comprehensive Code of Conduct for solicitors. It embraces the conduct expected of a normally careful and skilful solicitor by his or her governing body. I have, however, come to the conclusion that a breach of the Guide cannot ipso facto and of necessity be negligence.' See also R Cotterrell, *Law's Community: Legal Theory in Sociological Perspective* (Oxford, Clarendon Press, 1995) 28.

[33] For example, *pro bono publico* (see chapter 15) is absent from the codes of the profession in England and Wales but present as an aspiration in American Bar Association, *Model Rules of Professional Conduct* (Chicago, IL, ABA, 2006).

[34] P Singer, *How Are We To Live?* (London, Mandarin, 1994) 174; see generally J Rawls, *A Theory of Justice* (Oxford University Press, 1971).

[35] TW Giegerich, 'The Lawyer's Moral Paradox' (1979) 6 *Duke Law Journal* 1335.

[36] R Cranston, 'Legal Ethics and Professional Responsibility' in R Cranston (ed), *Legal Ethics and Professional Responsibility* (Oxford, Clarendon Press, 1995) 1.

[37] *Ibid*, 5.

[38] See Solicitors Practice rule 1 and *In re G Mayor Cooke* (1889) 5 *Times Law Reports* 407.

philosophical enquiry into 'how the world should be, what will make it better, how one ought to live'.[39] Lawyers, like philosophers, should pose questions such as 'What are good acts?', 'What is a good motive?' or 'What makes a good person?' In this way, professionals have a chance of remaining an ethical community, rather than slavish followers of rules. Circumstances frequently change, and each professional generation must consider ethical revision and renewal. The possibility that professional rules and ethical theory may produce different answers to everyday ethical problems reflects the conflict of different values. While these are sometimes contradictory or overlapping,[40] they offer useful tools for analysing some issues.

Professional values

A recent president of the Law Society asserted that the core values of the solicitors' profession are independence, integrity and confidentiality.[41] Observers of legal professions sometimes argue that they should prioritise different values. Some argue that the first goal of legal professionalism should be public service, assumed to be a public good since antiquity[42] and long part of the rhetoric of Anglo-American lawyers. [43] Public service is particularly important in England and Wales, where, with the doctors absorbed into the National Health Service, the lawyers are the only great profession embracing private enterprise. Yet this emphasis may seem a little anachronistic when many of the largest and wealthiest law firms have little or no contact with the general public. Therefore, another candidate for a prime professional value is promoting the moral autonomy of clients. The main goal of the liberal state is the pursuit of human emancipation from exploitation, inequality and oppression, which is why primary importance is attached to institutions promoting justice, equality and participation.[44] The paternalistic professional ethos of the hierarchical and authoritarian societies of the nineteenth and early twentieth centuries is inconsistent with contemporary society's quest to organise collective life in a way that people can find 'morally justifiable forms of life that will promote self-actualisation in the context of global interdependence'.[45]

A value asserted in all lawyer codes, but with particular resonance today, is independence. By independence the legal profession usually means exercising judgement free from the influence of others, particularly clients but also the state. Anglo-American lawyers are often suspicious of the power of the state and regard themselves as bulwarks against oppression. This spirit is carried through into the judiciary, which, being drawn from practising lawyers,

[39] PA Facione, D Scherer and T Attig, *Values and Society: An Introduction to Ethics and Social Philosophy* (Englewood Cliffs, NJ, Prentice Hall, 1978) 11.

[40] See, eg D Morgan, 'Doctoring Legal Ethics: Studies in Irony' in R Cranston (ed), *Legal Ethics and Professional Responsibility* (Oxford, Clarendon Press, 1995) 203; see criticism in D Nicolson and J Webb, 'Taking Lawyers' Ethics Seriously' (1999) 6 *International Journal of the Legal Profession* 109, 123; see also D Nicolson and J Webb, *Professional Legal Ethics: Critical Interrogations* (Oxford University Press, 1999) ch 2.

[41] P Williamson, 'When Core Values Matter' (July 2003) *Young Solicitors Group Magazine* 8.

[42] Eg by Lord Krishna in Bhagavad Gita: 'One must perform his prescribed duties as a vocation, keeping in sight the public good'. See OP Dwivedi, 'Ethics for Public Sector Administrators: Education and Training' in RM Thomas (ed), *Teaching Ethics: Government Ethics* (London, HMSO, 1996) 339, 345.

[43] Pound, above n 5.

[44] A Giddens, *Modernity and Self-identity: Self and Society in the Late Modern Age* (Cambridge, Polity Press, 1991) 212.

[45] *Ibid*, 215.

is steeped in the rhetoric. While the independence of judges is seen as fundamental to good government,[46] it is often taken for granted. It springs naturally from an independent legal profession, but it is no coincidence that, in many countries, both an independent profession and an independent judiciary are lacking.[47] An interesting conflict of interest is therefore created by an increasing numbers of lawyers employed not in private practice but in private companies and by the state. With a growing number of public sector legal careers, can the independence of lawyers from the state be preserved[48] or will the codes be diluted and the will to resist state power decline?

The final candidate for a defining value of lawyers is the pursuit of justice, a fundamental concern of the legal process and of those working within it. Justice, like other potential core values, has many faces, for example, substantive, procedural and social. Rawls's work expresses the social dimension in two key principles: that offices and positions must be open to everyone under conditions of fair equality of opportunity; and that they are to be of the greatest benefit to the least-advantaged members of society. Both have indirect relevance to lawyers in relation, for example, to recruitment to the profession and to the kinds of work they do. Another relevant conception of justice is natural justice, referring to 'the principles which must be followed in the application of rules, whatever their content, to particular cases'.[49] Jackson identifies two principles necessary to ensure that the law is applied impartially and objectively: 'that no man should be judged without a hearing and that every judge should be free from bias'.[50] The less attractive side of this coin is that lawyers are particularly identified with legalism, the demand that due process is observed.[51] The negative connotations come from those picking up the bill, particularly clients or government. The guidance to the solicitors' new rule 1 states that, where core duties conflict, 'the public interest in the administration of justice takes precedence'.[52] The 'public interest' is sometimes difficult to pin down,[53] but it is likely, since these rules were approved by government, that it means 'the common good of the community',[54] comprising respect for the law and system of government, and respect for persons, integrity, diligence and economy and efficiency.[55]

None of these core values are unique to lawyers; professionals in general aspire to them in different measure. Beauchamp and Childress, writing on biomedical ethics, propose widely accepted criteria for judging the ethicality of actions. Their four principles are respect for individual autonomy, non-maleficence (not doing harm), beneficence (doing good) and justice.[56] All are clearly relevant to lawyers, although justice in this schema is

---

[46] 'Commonwealth principles on the accountability of the relationship between the three branches of government' (2004) 96 *Commonwealth Legal Education* 7, principle IV.

[47] P Eigen, 'Fighting Corruption Through an Independent Judicial System' (Spring 2002) *Law in Transition: South Eastern Europe* 10.

[48] C Sampford, 'What's a Lawyer Doing in a Nice Place Like This?' (1998) 1 *Legal Ethics* 35 at 48.

[49] P Jackson, *Natural Justice* (London, Sweet & Maxwell, 1979) 5.

[50] Jackson *ibid*, 6.

[51] TC Halliday, *Beyond Monopoly: Lawyers, State Crises, and Professional Empowerment* (University of Chicago Press, 1987) 369.

[52] Para 3.

[53] P De Jersey, 'Public Interest and Public Policy: Unruly Horses Alike?' (2003) 6 *Legal Ethics* 16.

[54] A Demack, 'Public Interest or Common Good of the Community?: Bringing Order to a Dog's Breakfast' (2003) 6 *Legal Ethics* 23.

[55] *Ibid*. See also Queensland's Public Sector Ethics Act (1993).

[56] TL Beauchamp and JF Childress, *Principles of Biomedical Ethics* (New York, Oxford University Press, 4th edn, 2001) 12.

more about fairness than a specific association with courts. As with any such model, it may be important to identify the dominant value in situations of conflict. Beaumont and Childress point out that these principles apply differently in different contexts, where efficiency and institutional rules reorder priorities. They suggest, however, that the increasing emphasis on the individual in contemporary society is projecting the moral autonomy of individuals into the position of dominant value. An obvious implication for lawyers is that they should explore options with clients, including ethical issues, but encourage them to make their own moral choices. This, however, is not an emphasis that leaps out from the codes.

The codes of both branches of the legal profession espouse basic professional values. The Law Society's new code of conduct lists the following:

1. You must act with integrity.
2. You must uphold the rule of law and the proper administration of justice.
3. You must not allow your independence to be compromised.
4. You must act in the best interests of clients.
5. You must provide a good standard of service to your clients.
6. You must not behave in a way that is likely to diminish the trust the public places in you or the profession.[57]

The Bar Code of Conduct contains similar general prescriptions, stating, for example, that:

A barrister must . . . not:

(a) engage in conduct whether in pursuit of his profession or otherwise which is:
     (i)   dishonest or otherwise discreditable to a barrister;
     (ii) prejudicial to the administration of justice; or
     (iii) likely to diminish public confidence in the legal profession or the administration of justice or otherwise bring the legal profession into disrepute;
(b) engage directly or indirectly in any occupation if his association with that occupation may adversely affect the reputation of the Bar or in the case of a practising barrister prejudice his ability to attend properly to his practice.[58]

The ethical codes of lawyers in general employ similar statements. The Code of the International Bar Association seeks members' commitment to 'the highest standards of honesty and integrity',[59] serving 'the interests of justice', observing the law, maintaining ethical standards[60] and maintaining sufficient independence to allow them to give their clients unbiased advice.[61] Such lists can be controversial,[62] but the Law Society claims that its core duties serve a number of purposes.[63] They define the values shaping professional character and displayed in professional behaviour; form an overarching framework within which the more detailed

[57] Solicitors Regulation Authority, Solicitors' Code of Conduct 2007, r 1.
[58] Bar Standards Board, Code of Conduct of the Bar of England and Wales (London, BSB, 8th edn, 2004) para 301.
[59] [Summer 1995] *International Bar News* 23, r 1.
[60] *Ibid*, r 2.
[61] *Ibid*, r 8.
[62] Nicolson and Webb, *Professional Legal Ethics*, above n 40, 13–21.
[63] Solicitors Code of Conduct 2007, guidance to r 1, para 2–3.

and context-specific rules in the rest of the Code can be understood, thus illuminating the nature of those obligations and aiding compliance; and assist in navigating through those situations not covered in the detailed rules. The Law Society warns that the core duties are fundamental rules, breach of which may result in the imposition of sanctions. Finally it provides that, where two or more core duties come into conflict, the factor determining precedence must be the public interest, and especially the public interest in the adminis-tration of justice.

The application of the espoused values of the legal profession to concrete situations is often problematic. A recent story in the press tells of a solicitor bringing claims for wage arrears, due under equal pay legislation, on behalf of 13 female care workers against their local authority employer.[64] The cases were conducted on a 'no win, no fee' basis under which each client paid 25% of their damages to the solicitors. The solicitors were also suing the trade union to which the women belonged for having agreed local deals with employers that were less than their entitlement, threatening it with financial ruin. Based in Newcastle upon Tyne, the solicitors were working their way south, suing council after council, and had reached the Midlands. The employers and unions were united in their condemnation, saying that the lawyers' actions were 'clogging up' tribunals, 'causing severe delays to claims and costing taxpayers more money in bureaucracy' and, by reducing the resources of local authorities, threatening the jobs of the clients they were purporting to help. These express and implied criticisms of lawyers, stirring up litigation, lack of regard for wider conse-quences and profiteering, all have ethical connotations. Yet these lawyers defended the rights of members of a disadvantaged section of the community, offering them access to justice. As one of the women said:

> The union said we were rocking the boat. They told us they would sort it out, that we'd lose our jobs [if we went ahead], but they never did sort it out. Yes, we paid [the solicitor]. He deserved every penny. Without him they would have wiped the floor with us.

Therefore, while we may deplore the circumstances, the behaviour of which the lawyers were accused is quite consistent with the values the profession professes, particularly given the overarching commitment to clients.

The social role of lawyers

Below the level of abstract principles and values lies the actual work of a profession. It is in the social construction of the professional role where, in many eyes, the espoused profes-sional values of honesty and integrity are compromised.[65] The social role of any profession reflects the society and institutions it serves, developing as a 'coherent and complex form of socially established cooperative human activity'.[66] It is implicit that the role achieves a

---

[64] D Brindle and P Curtis, 'Fight for Equality that Could Put Jobs at Risk' *The Guardian*, 2 January 2008, 11.
[65] D Nicolson and J Webb, 'Public Rules and Private Values: Fractured Profession(alism)s and Institutional Ethics' (2005) 12 *International Journal of the Legal Profession* 165.
[66] *Ibid*, 187.

social benefit or 'good',[67] and it is usually assumed that justice is the social good pursued by the legal profession. There is no consensus around what justice is,[68] but, in the common law system, justice is intimately connected with courts and trials. Most of the distinctive ethical obligations of lawyers, and their adversarial orientation, are traceable to the medieval era, when the British state centralised power, replacing blood feuds, trials by combat and appeals to divine judgement by judicial authority.[69] One reason why the professional ethics of lawyers are distinctive and controversial are that they are bound up with these origins in adversarial court advocacy rather than the everyday work of dealing with clients' ordinary affairs.

The adversarial ethic

The adversarial trial is often compared to a battle, but a joust is possibly a more apposite metaphor. The conflict may have very serious consequences, but it is in the nature of an exercise or game. Each side has a powerful champion, an advocate, so that there is equality of arms. The judge acts as an umpire, a passive role, deciding the case based on the evidence and argument presented.[70] This gives the parties' lawyers a very significant role, with wide discretion in deciding what investigations to conduct, what evidence to present in court proceedings and how to conduct the case. It also carries distinctive moral responsibilities, since every stage requires an ethical approach. The system relies on lawyers to interview witnesses before the trial and decide which witnesses to produce. It is important that this process does not influence witnesses, leading to the distortion of evidence.[71] How to present the case also involves moral decisions, for example, whether to accuse a witness of lying. The opportunities and temptations to subvert justice make lawyers' ethics more important in an adversarial process than in other judicial systems.[72] The model of the adversarial trial creates a set of obligations that are usefully characterised as a 'standard conception' of the lawyer's role, based on the core principles of partisanship, neutrality and the duty to the court. This standard conception, Luban argues, denies the lawyer's 'personal moral responsibility for role acts by appealing to the fact that the role itself is good'.[73]

---

[67] TL Beauchamp and JF Childress, 'Virtues and Conscientious Actions' in A Flores (ed), *Professional Ideals* (Belmont, CA, Wadsworth Publishing Co, 1988) 27.

[68] Pluralist culture cannot weigh competing claims to justice, eg the justice of taxation versus the justice of income redistribution; they are incommensurable and theories support either view, eg Robert Nozick's emphasis on entitlement or Rawls's on needs, ie maximum liberty consistent with the liberty of others and equality of opportunity subject to priority given to need (Rawls, above n 34, 60–7).

[69] Prior to the development of the legal profession, God was believed to be the judge of guilt or innocence and the clergy was involved in early methods of proof, eg performance of oaths, until the Lateran Council of 1215. EE Sward, 'Values Ideology and the Evolution of the Adversary System' (1989) *Indiana Law Journal* 301, 321.

[70] Except in serious criminal cases when the issues of fact are left to a jury. In the inquisitorial systems of civil law countries the judge exercises more control over the development of the case. Sward, *ibid.*

[71] See EF Loftus, *Eyewitness Testimony* (Cambridge, MA, Harvard University Press, 1996); Sward, above n 69, 312.

[72] In an inquisitorial system, for example, lawyers can suggest those witnesses to be interviewed but generally have no access to witnesses before trial.

[73] See, eg D Luban, *Lawyers and Justice: An Ethical Study* (Princeton University Press, 1988) 129.

Core principles of the standard conception

Partisanship

The standard conception sees the lawyer's role in an adversarial system as partisan. The lawyer is not there to ensure a fair result, to seek the truth, to arbitrate or to explore the possibility of compromise between the parties; the layer's role is the defence of the client's rights. The partisan lawyer must take the client's side even when she considers the client to be morally wrong, and oblivious of the impact that this has on others.[74] This position was most strongly expressed in the early nineteenth century, when Queen Caroline faced a charge of adultery brought against her by the king. Caroline's counsel, Brougham, threatened to expose the king's own adultery and other moral shortcomings as part of her defence. His speech defending his position is sometimes seen as an extreme expression of the advocate's duty, but remains the starting point of any discussion. Brougham claimed:

> An advocate, in the discharge of his duty, knows but one person in all the world, and that person is his client. To save that client by all means, and expedients, and at all hazards and costs to other persons, and among them, to himself, is his first and only duty; and in performing this duty he must not regard the alarm, the torments, the destruction which he may bring upon others. Separating the duty of a patriot from that of an advocate, he must go on reckless of consequences, though it should be his unhappy fate to involve his country in confusion.[75]

It is suggested that the obligation to zealously defend the client's rights means that a lawyer must both present the client's case in the best possible light and ensure that the other party's case is seen in the worst possible light. It may also mean that a lawyer must pursue the client's every preference, provided that it is not an illegal purpose and does not require illegal means. Some of the basic principles of lawyers' ethics, rules protecting clients against conflicts of interest and protecting client confidentiality, are the natural corollary of partisanship.[76] Brougham's conception of the role of advocacy is not now widely shared, mainly because of the importance attached to a balancing obligation to assist courts in administering justice.[77] Nevertheless, some version of partisanship is at the root of a lawyer's duty to her clients and its limits continue to be hotly debated.

---

[74] This view is strongest in the American literature, and particularly in M Freedman, 'Professional Responsibility of the Criminal Defence Lawyer: The Three Hardest Questions' (1966) 64 *Michigan Law Review* 1469. See also T Schneyer, 'Moral Philosophy's Standard Misconception of Legal Ethics' [1984] *Wisconsin Law Review* 1529, who argues that this is because the primary purpose of professional ethics is to guard against lawyers' cooperation with, or cooptation by, third parties, and J Leubsdorf, 'Three Models of Professional Reform' (1982) 67 *Cornell Law Review* 1021).

[75] J Nightingale (ed), *Trial of Queen Caroline* (1821), quoted in ME Frankel, 'The Search for Truth: An Umpireal View' (1975) 123 *University of Pennsylvania Law Review* 1031, 1036; GC Hazard, 'The Future of Legal Ethics' (1991) 100 *Yale Law Journal* 1239, 1239.

[76] *Annesley v Anglesey* 17 How St Tr 1140, 1223–6, 1241 (Ex 1743) is an example of the root of the privilege of confidentiality, viz: '(1) A "gentleman of character" does not disclose his client's secrets. (2) An attorney identifies with his client, and it would be "contrary to the rules of natural justice and equity" for an individual to betray himself. (3) Attorneys are necessary for the conduct of business, and business would be destroyed if attorneys were to disclose their communications with their clients'. JT Noonan, 'The Purposes of Advocacy and the Limits of Confidentiality' (1966) 64 *Michigan Law Review* 1485.

[77] D Pannick, *Advocates* (Oxford, Oxford University Press, 1992) 105.

Neutrality

The second key principle in an adversarial system is neutrality. One aspect of this is the duty not to select between clients on moral grounds. The most famous example of this is the English bar's cherished 'cab-rank rule', requiring a barrister to accept briefs in the order that they are received. The importance of this principle flows from the imperative of representation in the adversarial system; it ensures that every person has a champion. The consequence of having to accept clients is that lawyers must argue a case that they do not believe in or pursue ends they do not agree with. Neutrality, therefore, encourages lawyers to take unpopular clients and increases social goods such as civil liberties, human rights and access to welfare provision in individual cases, as well as producing legal precedents that establish rights for the general population. The combination of the principles of neutrality and partisanship creates a morally ambiguous role for lawyers. It seems that lawyers must do everything possible within the limits of the law to protect the rights of people that they do not care for and for causes with which they do not agree.

The second element of neutrality requires that lawyers are not only morally neutral, but also emotionally detached from their client's purposes. They are interested only in 'the facts', divested of all emotional elements and all that does not fall within the legal rule.[78] This ensures that they can offer dispassionate advice, resisting emotional involvement with the client and focusing on the legal merits of the case.[79] Lawyers are also supposedly indifferent with regard to the final outcome of litigation. If lawyers are not morally neutral about their clients' causes there is a risk that they will be excessively zealous and self-righteous,[80] which may work against the clients' interests. The mind that is independent of ties and conflicting interests can see the whole picture objectively and is therefore more likely to offer wise advice.[81] It also allows lawyers to reconcile their duty of partisanship with their potentially conflicting duty to the court.

The duty to the court

In an adversarial system partisanship is counterbalanced by a wider duty to the system. In the case of advocacy, this is expressed as a duty to the court. This may involve no more than an obligation not to deliberately mislead, although the modern trend is to cast the obligation to the court more widely than this. Balancing the duties of partisanship and neutrality with the duty to the court demands a complex set of responsibilities, described by the Master of the Rolls at the end of the nineteenth century as follows:

> A professional man, whether a solicitor or a barrister, is bound to act with the utmost honour and fairness with regard to his client. He is bound to use the utmost skill for his client, but neither a solicitor nor a barrister is bound to degrade himself for the purpose of winning his client's case. Neither of them ought to fight unfairly, though both are bound to use every

---

[78] V Denti, 'Public Lawyers, Political Trials and the Neutrality of the Legal Profession' (1981) 1 *Israel Law Review* 20.

[79] Johnson, above n 3, 36.

[80] RE Rosen, 'On the Social Significance of Critical Lawyering' (2000) 3 *Legal Ethics* 169, 170.

[81] AT Kronman, *The Lost Lawyer: Failing Ideals of the Legal Profession* (Harvard, Belknap Press, 1993) 144.

effort to bring their client's case to a successful issue. Neither has any right to set himself up as the judge of his client's case. They have no right to forsake their client on any mere suspicion of their own or on any view they might take as to the client's chance of ultimate success. The duty of a solicitor to his client arises from the relationship of solicitor and client. A solicitor has no relation with his clients' adversaries giving rise to any duty to them. His duty is, however, not to fight unfairly, and that arises from his duty to himself not to do anything which was degrading to himself as a gentleman and a man of honour.[82]

The complex task of balancing these competing obligations puts lawyers under considerable moral pressure. It has been suggested that the role that lawyers must fill in an adversarial system requires a distinctive morality that is necessary for the system to operate, but which courts hostile public opinion.

Role morality

It is sometimes said that lawyers' ethics require them to do things for other people that would be considered immoral if they did them for themselves. Lawyers must defend people whom they believe committed heinous crimes. They must keep confidences that may prevent harm or end the suffering of others, for example, when they know the location of murder victims. They must help people to do things that may be harmful to others or to society, for example, represent racketeers, polluters and antisocial individuals. Aggressive presentation of client wishes appears shallow and unprincipled. Lawyers are often cast as amoral technicians and skilful manipulators of legal rules in their clients' legal interests,[83] who must suppress their own moral convictions. The pursuit of a client's causes, right or wrong, places the underlying ethos of lawyers at odds with that of other professions, including other professions working in fields involving personal conflict.[84] Role morality is justified by the demand of the adversarial system for the even-handed analysis of legal rights and duties. But can the role morality of lawyers be justified only in terms of the system's needs or, or is there an independent moral justification?

Fried has argued that role morality is justified on the grounds that a lawyer's relationship with a client is akin to friendship; ordinary morality accepts that people do things for friends that they would not do for anyone else.[85] This argument, that a lawyer is a 'special purpose friend', proved difficult to sustain.[86] Unswerving loyalty is reserved for people we are very close to, family members or close friends. It is not usually given to acquaintances and strangers and it would not be given by lawyers, say cynics, were they not paid. Moreover, lawyers often have little opportunity to foster the genuine concern for their client's interests that grows out of interpersonal relationships.

---

[82] *In re G Mayor Cooke*, above n 38, 408.

[83] ED Cohen, 'Pure Legal Advocates and Moral Agents: Two Concepts of a Lawyer in an Adversarial System' in Flores, above n 67, 87.

[84] D Rueschemeyer, 'Doctors and Lawyers: A Comment on the Theory of the Professions' [1964–5] *Canadian Review of Sociology and Anthropology* 17.

[85] C Fried, 'The Lawyer as Friend: The Moral Foundations of the Lawyer-Client Relation' (1976) 85 *Yale Law Journal* 1060.

[86] EA Dauer and AA Leff, 'Comment on Fried's Lawyer as Friend' (1976) 85 *Yale Law Journal* 573.

Recently, there have been concerns that the legal role, including role morality, may be harmful to lawyers themselves. The emphasis on the consistent application of rules known in advance blocks an empathetic response by lawyers, including judges,[87] to the human issues raised by legal problems.[88] Feminist and critical scholars argue that lawyers trained to equate logic with reason are led to deny the value of feeling and imagination, which means they appear cold and uncaring. The dissonance between personal beliefs and values, and the partisanship and neutrality demanded by adversarialism, may cause lawyers to suffer from 'debilitating psychic tension'.[89] It has been suggested that legal education and training has negative affects on individual personalities, encouraging an obsession with formal rationality.[90] This has been advanced as the reason for the unusually high rates of drink and drug abuse among lawyers detected in the US.[91] The possibility that lawyers' role morality may cause individual lawyers harm raises the question of whether the professional ethics of lawyers should contribute to lawyers achieving a 'good life'[92] and, if so, how.

The extent of the problem of balancing personal morality and system values is contested. It is arguable that neutrality is seldom a problem because lawyers very quickly specialise. As criminal defence lawyers or prosecutors, they seldom need to represent a side they find unsympathetic, acting consistently with their personal values most of the time.[93] Nevertheless, it is accepted that professional roles are too complex to be governed purely by fixed rules. Postema proposes that professional roles are 'recourse roles' that expand or contract depending on the underlying institutional objectives the role is designed to serve.[94] Within this conception, the lawyer should not identify so strongly with the professional role that personal morality and responsibility is excluded. Lawyers have discretion to disobey,[95] by reference to active consideration of the rule and the functional objectives of the role—what Postema calls 'engaged moral judgement'.[96] This is the position that solicitors may be working towards by providing that, where rules conflict, the determining factor is the public interest, and especially the public interest in the administration of justice.[97] Some writers, however, advocate a change in lawyers' ethics to align with personal values, leading to advocacy of 'moral activism' as a guiding principle of lawyers' ethics.[98] They make the case

[87] LH Henderson, 'Legality and Empathy' [1986–7] 85 *Michigan Law Review* 1574.

[88] TM Massaro, 'Empathy, Legal Storytelling, and the Rule of Law: New Words, Old Wounds?' [1988–9] 87 *Michigan Law Review* 2099.

[89] LE Fisher, 'Truth as a Double-Edged Sword: Deception, Moral Paradox, and the Ethics of Advocacy' (1989) 14 *The Journal of the Legal Profession* 89.

[90] But see T Campbell, 'The Point of Legal Positivism' (1998–9) 9 *The King's College Law Journal* 63.

[91] P Goodrich, 'Law-induced Anxiety: Legists, Anti-lawyers and the Boredom of Legality' (2000) 9 *Social and Legal Studies* 143; see also Nicolson and Webb, *Professional Legal Ethics*, above n 40, 175.

[92] Bayles, above n 3, 11.

[93] RE Rosen, 'On the Social Significance of Critical Lawyering' (2000) 3 *Legal Ethics* 169; A Boon, 'Cause Lawyers and the Alternative Ethical Paradigm: Ideology and Transgression' (2004) 7 *Legal Ethics* 250.

[94] GJ Postema, 'Moral Responsibility in Professional Ethics' (1980) 55 *New York University Law Review* 63, 83; where rules conflict with each other, see RS Tur, 'The Doctor's Defense' (2002) 69 *The Mountsinai Journal of Medicine* 317, 327.

[95] S Kadish and M Kadish, *Discretion to Disobey* (Stanford, CA, Stanford University Press, 1973) 31.

[96] Above n 94.

[97] Solicitors Code of Conduct 2007, guidance to r 1, note 3.

[98] D Nicolson, 'Afterword: In Defence of Contextually Sensitive Moral Activism' (2004) 7 *Legal Ethics* 269.

that the bar should forsake the cab-rank rule so that barristers could refuse clients they did not like,[99] a move that others see as deprofessionalisation.[100]

Evaluating professional ethics

Systems

Different legal systems reach different conclusions on the ethics of similar issues. The American, Commonwealth and European systems, despite similar antecedents, developed different responses.[101] In the Netherlands, lawyers have only recently made clients the centre of their ethical obligations;[102] in Germany, the 'duty to the court' is relatively underdeveloped;[103] and almost every European country has a different rule on confidentiality.[104] In France, an *avocat* is bound to keep secret from his own client communications with another *avocat*, placing the virtue of independence above loyalty to clients.[105] This contrasts sharply with the Anglo-American tradition, where information is seen to be the client's, not the lawyer's.[106] There is no reason, therefore, apart from tradition, why professional ethics cannot change. Indeed, it is quite possible that a fundamental shift in the system of courts could bring about a seismic shift in lawyers' ethics. Signs of such a shift occurred with recent reform of civil justice, targeting the alleged excesses of lawyers, formerly legitimised by the adversary system. Increasing the control of litigation by judges, strengthening lawyers' obligations to promote the administration of justice and promoting mediation as an alternative to trial-based dispute resolution are all measures signalling a desire for change. But what has changed?

Sward argues that adversarial legal culture springs from an individualistic society in which personal rights are prioritised over collective rights and where creativity, autonomy and reward for effort are priorities. Even historically, the adversarial system was potentially

[99] A Hutchison, 'Taking it Personally' , in D Nicolson and J Webb, *Lawyers Ethics: Critical Interrogations*, above n 40, 215.

[100] Postema, above n 94, 81.

[101] LE De Groot-van Leeuwen, 'Polishing the Bar: The Legal Ethics Code and Disciplinary System of the Netherlands, and a Comparison with the United States' (1997) 4 *International Journal of the Legal Profession* 14; H Ader, 'Differences and Common Elements in Legal Ethics in France and the United States' in JJ Barceló and RC Crampton (eds), *Lawyers' Practice and Ideals: A Comparative View* (The Hague, Kluwer Law International, 1999) 351.

[102] In the Netherlands, 1986 legislation shifted focus on the core of regulations from the 'honour of the order of lawyers' to 'the interests of the client'. Meanwhile, confidentiality was reinforced in the 1992 Dutch code—possibly because it confers a competitive advantage (*ibid*).

[103] *Arthur JS Hall & Co (a firm) v Simons, Barratt v Ansell and others (trading as Woolf Seddon (a firm), Harris v Scholfield Roberts & Hill (a firm) and another* [2000] 3 All ER 673.

[104] See generally the ECBE Code and A Boon and J Flood, 'The Globalisation of Professional Ethics: The Significance of Lawyers International Codes of Conduct' (1999) 2 *Legal Ethics* 29.

[105] Lawyers can have a duty of partisanship in an inquisitorial system (M Taruffo, 'The Lawyer's Role and the Models of Civil Process' (1981) 16 *Israel Law Review* 5; J Leubsdorf, 'The Independence of the Bar in France: Learning from Comparative Legal Ethics' in Barceló and Crampton, above n 101. In the Eastern European communist states the lawyer was not bound solely by client loyalty but by loyalty to the state. They were under a duty to dissuade clients from proceedings conflicting with the interests of the community or society. See M Bohlander, M Blacksell and KM Born, 'The Legal Profession in East Germany—Past, Present and Future' (1996) 3 *International Journal of the Legal Profession* 255.

[106] In England, privilege can only be waived by a client, expressly or by implication (*Lillicrap v Nalder & Co* [1993] 1 All ER 724), although barristers, in common with *avocat*, have a notion of confidence between themselves.

inefficient and promoted negative values,[107] but its survival after the Middle Ages owes much to its alignment with capitalism. Despite recent emphasis on individualism and commercialism,[108] and counter to trends such as the Human Rights Act 1998 and a significant reduction in eligibility for legal aid, the long-term move in Western society is towards welfare states and a more communitarian ethic.[109] Movement away from the individualistic ethic associated with adversarialism is complemented by shifting values. It is therefore possible for social analysts to assert that the 'conspicuously virtuous things we all praise—cooperation, altruism, generosity, sympathy, kindness, selflessness—are concerned with the welfare of others' and arise out of a cooperative and reciprocal society.[110] So, what are the arguments for an adversarial legal culture?

Adversarial justice has many justifications. First is the case that the presentation of conflicting theories and evidence, as in the adversarial trial, is an effective way to test facts and to arrive at the truth. Second, and linked to the first, is the argument that the distance and impersonal nature of adversary processes, necessary in order to police the conflict of argument, offers the best protection of individual dignity and autonomy and provides a key safeguard for legal values.[111] Legalism embraces legal clarity and certainty, together with insistence that government powers and immunities are subject to rules and rights.[112] The key role of lawyers in the adversarial system underpins their structural independence, including judges, from the machinery of the state. In this way, it can be argued, the adversarial system is the platform for the institutional separation of powers[113] and, therefore, for the rule of law[114] and the modern liberal state. Thirdly, and more recently, it has been argued that the positivist tradition that accompanies the common law and adversarial system encourages blindness to issues such as the social impact of the rules.[115] This indifference of law to social position legitimises centralised state control of societies with pluralistic values, such as those in the Western democracies.[116]

In order that groups in highly pluralistic societies can share a concept of 'the good' they must adopt neutrality as a political ideal and as a framework for institutions and practices. In the absence of a common conception of justice, for example, we agree on procedures for

---

[107] Prest observes that 'going to law in early modern England was often rather a means of expanding and continuing conflicts than bringing them to an end': WR Prest, *The Rise of the Barristers: A Social History of the Bar 1590–1640* (Oxford, Clarendon Press, 1986) 300.

[108] Giddens, above n 44.

[109] See D Kennedy, 'Form and Substance in Private Law Adjudication' (1976) 89 *Harvard Law Review* 1685; Sward, above n 69.

[110] M Ridley, *The Origin of Virtue* (Harmondsworth, Penguin, 1996).

[111] See further Cotterrell, above n 32, 156.

[112] N MacCormick, 'The Ethics of Legalism' (1989) 2 *Ratio Juris* 184.

[113] See generally TC Halliday and L Karpik, *Lawyers and the Rise of Western Political Liberalism* (Oxford, Clarendon Press, 1997).

[114] TC Halliday and L Karpik, 'Politics Matter: A Comparative Theory of Lawyers in the Making of Political Liberalism' in Halliday and Karpik, *ibid*, 15, 21 and 30.

[115] Positivism provides 'mandatory rules of such clarity, precision and scope that they can be routinely understood and applied without recourse to contentious moral and political judgments'. T Campbell, 'The Point of Legal Positivism' (1998–9) 9 *The King's College Law Journal* 63, 66.

[116] D Phillips, 'Some General Thoughts on the State of the Republic and the Obligation of the Legal Profession to it', from an address to a conference of the Fourth Judicial Court of the United States at Hot Springs, VA, 27 June 1969, cited in JF Sutton and JS Dzienkowski, *Cases and Materials on the Professional Responsibility of Lawyers* (St Paul, MN, West Publishing, 1989) 12.

selecting officials, judges and governments. Neutrality, therefore, is the proper disposition for lawyers because it facilitates pluralism.[117] The degree of partisan commitment or neutrality that is essential to the adversary process is, however, debatable. It is difficult to see why the system requires extreme forms of partisanship when lawyer zeal is always constrained to a degree. Whether a total commitment to either partisanship or neutrality is the answer hinges on the purpose of the justice system, a matter on which disagreement is likely. The overriding purpose of criminal justice may be securing freedom by securing order and reducing crime and fear of crime,[118] whereas civil justice has rather different goals.[119] Similarly, the legal profession might regard a lawyer's ultimate duty within an adversarial system not to protect clients from 'the oppressive power of the state'[120] but 'to administer and to facilitate the operation of law'.[121]

There is a clear link between the underlying purposes of the justice system and lawyers' ethics, although the relationship may be out of step. Hazard argues that the professional ideology of lawyers as 'the fearless advocate who champions a client threatened with loss of life and liberty by government oppression' supports the key ethical obligations of loyalty, confidentiality and candour to the court, and balances the legal profession's two basic affiliations, to clients and to the judiciary.[122] In England and Wales this conception of the legal role is challenged. The government has focused on ways in which the present system exacerbates problems of access to law and argues, compellingly, that without access to courts the protection of law and lawyers is illusory. It argues that procedures must be compromised to make justice affordable, and that defence of the existing system reflects a vested interest in legalism[123] and an ideological commitment to established traditions and perceptions. Lawyers must clearly take such criticism seriously, but they should be cautious of abandoning the commitment to the adversarial system or the ethical principles derived from it. At the same time lawyers must continually ask fundamental questions, such as:

— Does the profession maximise the public good?
— Does it increase the autonomy and the autonomous decision making of individuals?
— Does it create a culture independent of political influence and resistant to corruption?

Analysing professional roles

There are a host of perspectives from which to analyse and evaluate professional ethics.[124] The most significant theoretical distinctions are between approaches that assert a duty to

---

[117] T Dare, 'Mere Zeal, Hyper-zeal and the Ethical Obligations of Lawyers' (2004) 7 *Legal Ethics* 24.

[118] R Young and A Sanders, 'The Ethics of Prosecution Lawyers' (2004) 7 *Legal Ethics* 190.

[119] L Webley, 'Divorce Solicitors and Ethical Approaches—the Best Interests of the Client and/or the Best Interests of the Family?' (2004) 7 *Legal Ethics* 231.

[120] J Weinstein, 'On the Teaching of Legal Ethics' (1972) 72 *Columbia Law Review* 452; Sutton and Dzienkowski, above n 116, 3.

[121] Giegerich, above n 35.

[122] GC Hazard, 'The Future of Legal Ethics' (1991) 100 *Yale Law Journal* 1239,1243; Bayles, above n 3, 18–19.

[123] TC Halliday, *Beyond Monopoly: Lawyers, State Crises, and Professional Empowerment* (University of Chicago Press, 1987) 369.

[124] One theory that fits broadly within a feminist perspective, for example, is Gilligan's. Men, she argues, have an ethic of justice based on equal treatment while women's notion of justice is geared to avoiding harm, an 'ethic of care' (see C Gilligan, 'In a Different Voice: Psychological Theory and Women's Development' (Cambridge MA,

behave ethically—deontic ethics, and consequentialism, which assess actions by their results—and those that depend on character—the aretaic or virtue ethics. These approaches to ethics are both evaluative and practical; they have implications for areas of professional activity from education, through entry to the presentation of the codes themselves.[125] The philosophy adopted determines, for example, whether professional disciplinary strategies aim to provide detailed rules, rigorously enforced, or focus on the character of those entering the profession, or both.[126] Deontological approaches posit that certain actions are right in themselves, conferring a duty to behave accordingly.[127] Among the best known of the examples of this is Kant's suggestion that it is wrong to lie, even when a murderer seeks the location of a victim.[128] Deontological evaluation is concerned with the internal logic and morality of rules and value systems, but its main rival, consequentialism, holds that the rightness of an act be assessed in the light of its result.[129] Recognising that there are many affects of some acts, utilitarianism, the best-known form of consequentialism,[130] advocates actions that seek the overall or average well-being of people.[131]

Contrasting the conclusions of deontological and consequentialist analysis can be interesting, but it is important to recognise the suitability of the tools to different levels of analysis. Deontology is best for examining 'micro' issues, such as individual rules or relationships, while consequentialism suits the 'macro' level, looking at overarching principles, theories or systems.[132] The approaches may also be used in tandem to examine overarching theories or systems, deontology identifying the philosophical disposition of the totality of systems and rules, and consequentialist approaches incorporating sociological analysis of lawyers' actions and political analysis of legal institutions.[133] No method of evaluation is infallible and some questions can only be resolved by value judgements. For example, if professional ethics must promote the greatest good for the greatest number, how

---

Harvard University Press, 1993); Nicolson and Webb, *Professional Legal Ethics*, above n 40, 34–8). Postmodernism asserts that all theories must pay attention to the particular circumstances of social milieu (AC Hutchinson, 'Doing the Right Thing? Toward a Postmodern Politics' (1992) 4 *Law and Society Review* 773, 779).

[125] J Webb, 'Being a Lawyer/ Being a Human Being' (2002) 5 *Legal Ethics* 130.

[126] D Nicolson, 'Making Lawyers Moral? Ethical Codes and Moral Character' (2005) 25 *Legal Studies* 601.

[127] Derived from the Ancient Greek *deon*, meaning 'binding duty'. J Pearsall and B Trumble (eds), *The Oxford English Reference Dictionary* (Oxford, New York, Oxford University Press, 1995); see also D Luban, 'Freedom and Constraint in Legal Ethics: Some Mid-course Corrections to Lawyers and Justice' (1990) 49 *Maryland Law Review* 424, 424–8.

[128] C Korsgaard, 'Kant on Dealing with Evil' in JP Sterba (ed), *Ethics: The Big Questions* (Oxford, Blackwell Publishing, 1998).

[129] This can be further refined; act-consequentialism evaluates the rightness of each act by appraising its consequences, while rule-consequentialism evaluates the rightness of each act by appraising the consequences of general rules requiring or permitting such acts—a distinction made by J Rawls, 'Two Concepts of Rules' (1955) 64 *Philosophy Review* 3. See also D Luban, 'Freedom and Constraint in Legal Ethics: Some Mid-course Corrections to Lawyer and Justice' (1990) 49 *Maryland Law Review* 424, 438; R Posner, 'Utilitarianism, Economics and Legal Theory' (1979) 8 *Journal of Legal Studies* 103.

[130] Nicolson and Webb, 21–9.

[131] This involves (i) ranking the outcome of actions solely according to how much welfare (ie pleasure or pain or satisfaction of human preferences) they produce and (ii) determining total welfare by summing the welfares of all affected individuals by reference to intensity, duration, propinquity and extent. Luban, above n 129; Facione *et al*, above n 39.

[132] But see Morgan, above n 40, who suggests that microethics concerns relations between individuals, macroethics concerns relations between groups and mesoethics concerns administrative decision making.

[133] B Freedman, 'A Meta Ethics for Professional Morality' (1977–8) 88 *Ethics* 1.

can the competing claims of clients, as consumers, third parties affected by the delivery of professional services[134] or citizens demanding good governance by law,[135] including minorities, be balanced?[136]

Even using both deontology and consequentialism as tools of analysis leaves questions unanswered. To determine what are 'right actions' or 'good consequences' one must have criteria and decide what weight one attaches to each. For example, deontological analysis may hold that it is wrong to lie, whatever the circumstances, but distinguish between big and small lies. A consequentialist might argue that a lie to protect someone's feelings might be morally justified, whereas one that tries to create trouble is not.[137] A lie to protect someone's feelings might meet the deontologist's definition of a small lie, so both approaches would reach the same conclusion. A deontologist would be forced to condemn a big lie that avoids an environmental disaster affecting the livelihood of thousands. A consequentialist might find such a lie justified, even though it causes financial disaster to a few. However, both might struggle to describe a liar as a 'good person',[138] thus creating arguments for approaches such as 'virtue ethics' that focus on the character of the person making the ethical decision.

This focus on virtue is consistent with an ethical tradition, traceable to Aristotle, which perceives that it is the possession of inner traits, or character, that make an individual's actions right. It finds favour with those commentators on professional ethics advocating personal responsibility in moral choice rather than reliance on rules,[139] but also with those with an opposing perspective who argue that professional role morality is consistent with virtue.[140] Aristotle conceived of virtue normatively, as the mean between extremes of behaviour,[141] reflecting social goods promoted in order that human society achieves its ends, or *telos*. The human *telos* was a good society achieved through 'intellectual virtue', the ability to think and reason, and moral actions for their own sake,[142] a separation between intellect and morality that has proved enduring. Virtue becomes a habit, so the virtuous individual reacts naturally and morally correctly in response to each new situation. In this sense, virtue can be linked to conscience.[143]

Ancient virtue ethics identified four cardinal virtues: temperance, justice, courage and wisdom. In the Middle Ages, Christian philosophers added faith, hope and charity. More recent efforts have identified 18 virtues that are distinct from one another: politeness, fidelity, prudence, temperance, courage, justice, generosity, compassion, mercy, gratitude,

---

[134] Bayles, above n 3, 3. See also Rawls, above n 34, discussed by SG Kupfer, 'Authentic Legal Practices' (1996) 10 *Georgetown Journal of Legal Ethics* 33, 77–81.

[135] They can act so as to avoid penalties, to rely on the conduct of others and to act as they wish so long as this does not infringe upon other values. In a liberal society individuals are entitled to protection from injury, equality of opportunity, privacy in terms of the control over the personal information which others have access to and welfare, as manifest in a minimum standard of living (Bayles, *ibid*, 11).

[136] Rawls, above n 34, argues that utilitarian analysis might achieve maximum benefit by ignoring minority rights.

[137] S Bok, *Lying: Moral Choice in Public and Private Life* (New York, Vintage Books, 1999).

[138] C Fried, *Right and Wrong* (Cambridge, MA, Harvard University Press, 1978) 54.

[139] Eg the postmodern ethics of alterity. Nicolson and Webb, 46–9.

[140] J Oakley and D Cocking, *Virtue Ethics and Professional Roles* (Cambridge University Press, 2001).

[141] For example, Greek society valued courage, the median point between cowardice and rashness.

[142] A Flores, 'What Kind of Person Should a Professional Be?' in Flores, above n 67, 1.

[143] J Hospers *Human Conduct: Problems of Ethics* (San Diego, CA, Harcourt Brace Jovanovich, 1982) 5–9.

humility, simplicity, tolerance, purity, gentleness, good faith, humour and love.[144] These 'excellences' are each unique aspects of human potential, the realisation of which makes one person more human, more excellent, than another. Interestingly, justice is the only one of these virtues that is an absolute good in its own terms: a tyrant can have courage, but a just tyrant is a contradiction in terms.[145] Virtues are relevant to all, but the pre-eminence of justice among the virtues render them of particular interest to lawyers. Oakley and Cocking, for example, argue that professional roles are generally, in themselves, a good, and that such roles should be upheld, except where this produces a gross violation of justice.[146] Therefore, the requirement to be just provides a template for ethical action in legal practice, requiring that lawyers put themselves in the place of the other in assessing the ethicality of an act.

Alistair MacIntyre followed a similar line in seeking to reconcile morality with social structure,[147] to the social role that an individual performs and to the practices central to the performance of that role.[148] He argued that everyone can achieve virtue through performing their social role well, seeking what he calls the 'internal goods' of that role rather than external goods, such as fame, fortune and prestige. For example, a player who cheats at chess may acquire the external goods of fame or fortune but will not achieve the internal goods of the game, which come only to those who play honestly, according to the rules, and with knowledge and skill. The goods internal to practices can be achieved only by 'subordinating ourselves within the practice in our relationship to other practitioners',[149] a view consistent with the professions' long education and apprenticeship systems. It is also consistent with professionals' determination to resist 'the tidal pull of the profit motive'.[150] According to this view of professionalism, service, rather than extrinsic reward, is the crucial element of being a 'good lawyer'[151]—a view expressed in Hilbery's description of the advocate's art:

> The sure way then to great advocacy, is to act only, and at all time, according to the highest standards of professional honour and integrity. And let the work be done, not for the mere gain, but as the artist works, for the satisfaction of making each piece of work as consummate a piece of craftsmanship as you can. It is worth while. Not only is it that way the greatest satisfaction lies. But the work of an advocate is part of the administration of Justice, and in no other spirit can Justice be served.[152]

Finding the 'good life' through carrying out our own ethical responsibilities the best we can is a theme that virtue ethics shares with Eastern philosophy, whereby ethical behaviour is enlightened self-interest.[153] The values of the profession are reflected in expectations of virtuous conduct, for example, that solicitors have the 'level of honesty, integrity and

---

[144] A Comte-Sponville, *A Short Treatise on the Great Virtues: The Uses of Philosophy in Everyday Life* (London, Heinemann, 2002).
[145] *Ibid.*
[146] Above n 140.
[147] Aristotle's *polis*, or city state, pursued 'friendship' between citizens and the common pursuit of the good society. AD Macintyre, *After Virtue: A Study in Moral Theory* (London, Duckworth, 1985) 148.
[148] *Ibid*, 127.
[149] *Ibid*, 191.
[150] WM Sullivan, 'Calling a Career: The Tensions of Modern Professional Life' in Flores, above n 67, 41.
[151] Kronman, above n 81, 367.
[152] The Hon Sir Malcolm Hilbery, *Duty and Art in Advocacy* (London, Stevens & Sons, 1946) 35.
[153] Singer, above n 34, 189–92.

professionalism expected by the public and members of the profession'.[154] Aspiring lawyers must declare any matters, including acts of plagiarism, and failure to disclose is itself sufficient to cast doubt on whether they possess the 'character and suitability'[155] to be admitted. Virtue ethics does not exclude the possibility that practice is informed by principles and values or presented in codes. Rather, these approaches to building an ethical community inform and complement each other.

Conclusion

The professional ethics of lawyers draw on a rich philosophical tradition, yet its study requires subjecting systems, ideologies and traditions to examination. Professional ethics ought to ensure that the practice of law achieves the social good of justice—a goal that is mired in controversy. On the one hand, lawyers work within an adversarial court system that prioritises individual rights and defines their ethic. On the other hand, they aspire to high values, to personal virtue. Emerging priorities, such as access to justice, may cut across the adversarial ethic as traditionally conceived. This raises fundamental questions, such as, is the lawyer's ultimate duty within an adversarial system to protect clients from 'the oppressive power of the state'[156] or 'to administer and to facilitate the operation of law'?[157] The adversarial system itself may exacerbate tensions in the lawyer's role by placing the interests of clients and the demands of the system in sharper conflict than do other systems. This brings the adversarial ethic of lawyers into potential conflict with personal virtues such as honesty and integrity, leading some to argue for the alignment of professional ethics with wider social values. The study of professional ethics is increasingly concerned both with narrow questions about rules of conduct and their application and with wider issues, such as the underlying functions of justice systems, and of professions and their rules.

---

[154] Solicitors Regulation Authority, Guidelines on the Assessment of Suitability and Character (2007).

[155] Originally imposed by the Solicitors Act 1974, the responsibility is now on the SRA (ibid).

[156] J Weinstein, 'On the Teaching of Legal Ethics' (1972) 72 Columbia Law Review 452; see also Sutton and Dzienkowski, above n 116, 3.

[157] Giegerich, above n 35.

2

ORGANISATION

Arising from the proposal that lawyers with different professional qualifications should be permitted to work together as equals, the first and most important issue is to ensure that there is a high level of ethical standards within the legal practice.[1]

Introduction

The organisation of the legal profession and its relationship to the market for legal services is important in understanding professional culture and professional ethics, particularly in a professional community with diverse work. The wide variety of organisational structures that can be adopted by legal practitioners of all kinds is considerable, and will increase exponentially once the Legal Services Act 2007 is in force.[2] The organisation of legal practice is a significant determinant of the culture and the ethics of the profession. There are many aspects of organisation that have changed over the years, but many are recurring. Thus, writing of the US in the 1950s, Pound, commenting on the threats to the professionalism dangers of the day, noted the 'increasing bigness of things in which individual responsibility as a member of a profession is diminished or even lost', the exploitation of young lawyers producing pressures to organise in trade unions and the desire of the service state to replace professional services with administrative bureaux.[3] Organisational diversity is often seen as a threat to professional cohesion and professional norms. This chapter is therefore a foundation for chapters 3 and 4, where we deal with the power of the legal profession, particularly in relation to the state, and its culture.

The monopolies of solicitors and barristers

One of the major accusations levelled at the legal profession is that it maintains a monopoly in relation to legal work and protects it with vigour in order to advance professional interests. Obviously the existence and extent of this monopoly and the way it is protected will have a considerable influence on both the organisation and the ethos of the professions, and so is central to any account of the organisation of the profession. It must first be stressed that,

---

[1] D Clementi, *Review of the Regulatory Framework for Legal Services in England and Wales—Final Report* (London, Legal Services Review, 2004) para 25, 111.

[2] The Act received the Royal Assent in October 2007.

[3] R Pound, *The Lawyer from Antiquity to Modern Times: with Particular Reference to the Development of Bar Associations in the United States* (St Paul, MN, West Publishing, 1953) 354.

whatever the popular wisdom, the provision of legal advice is not, and never has been, a monopoly of the legal profession; anyone can offer legal services to the public, either free or for a fee, without currently being registered in any way or subject to the regulation of a professional body or to any rules about methods of practice, provided they do not trespass on the areas that are exclusive to solicitors or barristers.[4] It is important at the outset, therefore, to be clear what legal services are exclusive to the currently regulated professions. The monopolies exclusive to practising solicitors were and still are laid down in the Solicitors Act 1974 as amended. Those of barristers, advocacy in the higher courts, were traditionally enforced by the courts and not the subject of statutory regulation. Advocacy rights now are governed by the Courts and Legal Services Act 1990 as amended by the Access to Justice Act 1999.

The work which is seen as exclusive to solicitors[5] was laid down in sections 22 and 23 of the Solicitors Act 1974 and is often referred to as 'reserved services'.[6] The areas of work are, broadly, conveyancing, probate, preparation for litigation, lower court advocacy and various notarial acts. However, in most of these fields, solicitors now share the work with other authorised practitioners and the fields are now known as reserved services in the sense that they cannot be provided for gain by unauthorised personnel. Thus, originally, only solicitors could for gain[7] prepare transfers of and documents relating to land for registration with the Land Registry. This work is now also available to licensed conveyancers. Similarly, only solicitors could prepare documents relating to grants of probate or letters of administration. This monopoly was first extended to barristers and then, from November 2004, to banks, insurance companies, members of the Institute of Legal Executives (ILEX) and licensed conveyancers, with certain consumer safeguards.

Advocacy in lower and other courts is obviously shared with barristers, but also increasingly with members of approved bodies such as the ILEX[8] and other, more specialised groups such as the Institute of Patent Agents.[9] Advocacy and the preparation of documents for litigation can be done for gain only by 'authorised litigators' under the Courts and Legal Services Act 1990, section 28. This right can be conferred by an authorised body such as the Law Society, Bar Council, ILEX or the Institute of Patent Agents. Authorised litigators owe a duty to the court to act independently and in the interests of justice.[10] This does not apply

---

[4] A recent exception to this concerns claims companies dealing in personal injury and similar claims, generally via conditional fee agreements. They do now have to be registered under the Compensation Act 2006, which came into in force 30 April 2007.

[5] The solicitor must have a practising certificate from the Law Society and comply with the other conditions, eg in relation to insurance cover.

[6] This is the phrase adopted in the Legal Services Act 2007, which defines them in s 12 and sch 2.

[7] Anyone can do their own legal work in these areas, and a third party could help them provided they did not charge a fee.

[8] ILEX members can obtain advocacy rights in the magistrates' and county courts. They can do some criminal work, such as committal hearings, bail applications and trials in the magistrates' and youth courts. ILEX has about 22,000 members.

[9] The latest group to obtain such rights is the Association of Costs Draftsmen; see 157 NLJ 718, 25 May 2007. Certain designated case workers (DCWs), who are paralegals employed by the Crown Prosecution Service, will be given extended rights to prosecute in summary cases and bail applications under the Criminal Justice and Immigration Bill 2007, pt 5. This development is being vigorously opposed by the Law Society on the ground that DCWs are inadequately trained, are not subject to a regulatory code of conduct and are not officers of the court. See D Hudson (chief executive of the Law Society), 157 NLJ 1625, 23 November 2007.

[10] CLSA 1990, s 28(2A).

to other professionals involved in preparation for litigation. The Bar and Law Society has an obvious interest in ensuring that these statutory provisions are strictly interpreted. Thus, in a case relating to costs, *Agassi v Robinson*,[11] both professional bodies intervened and successfully submitted that a client briefing a barrister directly was a litigant in person. As such, the client could not obtain an order for the costs in relation to the services of his accountants who had, quite properly under the direct access rules,[12] briefed the barrister on the client's behalf. This was because the accountants were not authorised litigants. Any other decision, as Lord Justice Dyson fully understood, would

> allow a litigant in person [to] be able to recover the . . . fees of any person who provides general assistance in litigation

and this in turn would allow

> ample scope for any unqualified and unregulated person to provide general assistance in litigation secure in the knowledge that the litigant in person, if successful, would recover the cost of that assistance as a disbursement.[13]

It is also an offence for an unqualified person to act as a solicitor, or to 'wilfully pretend to be' or imply that he or she is a solicitor.[14] Equally, as is explained in more detail below, a solicitor cannot provide legal services to the public other than through a solicitors' firm or as an employed solicitor, in accordance with the rules governing employed solicitors. Therefore, whilst it is true that anyone can set up in business giving legal advice, they will not be able to act on behalf of their clients in relation to the conduct of litigation before courts.[15] Moreover, certain legal activities, such as conveyancing, probate and the running of a claims company, require the practitioner to be separately qualified or registered.[16] Solicitors used to share with barristers an exclusive right to undertake legal work paid for through the legal aid fund. Now, however, the Community Legal Service can award legal aid contracts to both solicitors and advice agencies in the not-for-profit sector, such as Citizens Advice Bureaux and other advice centres. However, the advice agencies will not be able to provide the monopoly services listed in the Solicitors Act unless, of course, they employ a solicitor to provide them.

Advocacy rights, traditionally the preserve of barristers, are now governed by the Courts and Legal Services Act 1990, as already noted. Barristers[17] alone are still the only group who have automatic rights of audience (including the right to prepare documents in relation to litigation) in all courts. Everyone else, including solicitors in relation to the higher courts, must acquire an advocacy qualification in accordance with the provisions of the Act. These provisions are dealt with in more detail in chapter 19. A recognised body must provide a

---

[11] [2006] 1 All ER 900, CA.

[12] On which see p 30 below.

[13] [2006] 1 All ER 900, para 81. Any other decision would have created a red letter day for non-solicitor claims companies as they would have been able to undertake the whole of a client's case and not have to instruct solicitors for cases involving litigation.

[14] Solicitors Act 1974, ss 20 and 21, as amended.

[15] Tribunals are not included in this prohibition.

[16] Reserved areas are listed in the Solicitors' Code of Conduct 2007 (London, Solicitors Regulation Authority, 2007) (hereafter Solicitors' Code) paras 9–10 of the guidance to rule 20.0. A full explanation of the position is to be found in the report by Clementi, above n 1.

[17] As with solicitors, barrister must be admitted and have a practising certificate from the Bar. See p 29 below.

recognised qualification process. The Law Society is such a body, and provides a recognised qualification process leading to higher court advocacy rights for those solicitors who pass it. At present, 3600 solicitors have such rights. The Law Society is currently consulting on the possibility that solicitors, like barristers, should automatically have full advocacy rights on qualification.[18]

The organisation of professional legal practice

Barristers and solicitors have always been restricted in the way they can offer their services to the public. The basic principle behind these restrictions has been the perceived need to ensure that there was no division between the ownership of a legal practice and its management. As we have seen, independence is a cherished ideal of the legal profession and one enshrined in codes of ethics. Not only must lawyers endeavour to maintain their independence from the state, they must also do so in their relationships with any non-lawyer professionals or managers that they work with. A lawyer in private practice must not be beholden to a manager or 'boss' who is not also bound by the same ethical code and controlled by the same professional body as that of the lawyer. A non-lawyer should not be able to control the work that is done for the client. Indeed, even barristers and solicitors cannot practice jointly as partners (although barristers can be employed by solicitors' firms now): the two professions are separated. A more cynical view on the effect of these rules is that, by preventing anyone other than practising lawyers from being involved in the provision of legal services, the profession ensured that competition was constrained. In other words, market control was the aim rather than the promotion of independence or ethical conduct.[19]

In accordance with these ideas, the traditional and accepted method of organising a solicitors' practice was the partnership. All of the partners[20] had to be solicitors, and they were all responsible for the activities for the practice and personally liable for its debts. Working capital was raised either from the partners themselves or by means of loans from banks. No other person or body could contribute capital and thus buy into the partnership profits. Profits were distributed to each partner according to the share laid down in the partnership agreement. The idea that the solicitor must accept personal responsibility for his or her work also meant that no corporate business structure or limited liability could be used. This latter rule has now been considerably modified, as can be seen below, and other rules, such as the rule against multidisciplinary practices, are currently under attack.[21]

Barristers

Barristers have always worked under even fiercer constraints than solicitors—they cannot even form partnerships—and it appears that less than a quarter of them wish to see any

---

[18] See 157 NLJ 118 and www.higher-rights.org.uk.

[19] See R Abel, *English Lawyers Between Market and State* (Oxford University Press, 2003) ch 6.

[20] The number of partners was limited to 20 until 1967, a rule which limited the growth of solicitors firms considerably.

[21] The Legal Services Act 2007 will considerably modify these rules when it comes into force, see further p 41.

change in this.[22] There are about 11,500 barristers in independent practice (and 2,500 employed barristers). About 70% practise in London. Barristers can only practise as such if called to the Bar by one of the four Inns of Court (Gray's Inn, Lincoln's Inn, Inner or Middle Temples) after having satisfied the Bar's educational requirements and kept the requisite terms in their Inn.[23] Those who have completed the Bar Vocational Course (BVC) and have been called to the Bar are entitled to use the title 'barrister' even though they have not completed pupillage. In these circumstances they have not completed their training, cannot acquire a practising certificate and therefore cannot practise as barristers.

Non-practising barristers may undertake legal work on the same basis as a layperson but must make clear that they are non-practising barristers.[24] This was instituted to alert the public to the fact that a non-practising barrister had not completed pupillage, was not subject to continuing professional development requirements and might not be insured against professional negligence. In 1995 the Bar ratified the policy that call should be deferred until the completion of pupillage,[25] but its implementation stalled amid fears of a challenge on the ground of discrimination. Subsequently there was further debate on the possible negative impact of deferring call on the flow of students from overseas common law jurisdictions to the BVC,[26] and the consequent diminution of the influence of the English Bar overseas.[27] A review of the regulation of legal services cited the tortuous deliberations as illustrating the overcomplexity of the Bar's regulatory structure.[28] Finally the Bar Standards Board reversed the decision to defer call, suggesting that it would be an inappropriate and disproportionate response to the risk of consumer confusion.[29]

Until 2005, once a barrister was fully qualified to practise, there was no further process of renewal of that right similar to the annual grant of a practising certificate needed by solicitors. Now, however, it is necessary for barristers to have a practising certificate. The need to impose some continuing quality control was first recognised by the Bar Council in 1997, when a limited requirement for post-qualification continuing education was imposed. Barristers must also be insured for professional negligence through the Bar Mutual Indemnity Fund in accordance with terms approved by the Bar Council from time to time.[30]

Barristers must practise as sole practitioners and cannot offer their services to the public

---

[22] See MORI survey, 'Perceptions of Barristers', reported in 157 NLJ 1671, 30 November 2007.

[23] The Inns' powers are now recognised by statute—Courts and Legal Services Act 1990, s 41(3). See further chapter 8. Keeping terms means dining in the Inn together with other barristers and judges. Twelve dinners are normally required, but there are provisions which soften this requirement, such as counting attendance at residential advocacy weekends. The rationale for all this is to induct the intending barrister into the ethos and collegiality of the profession.

[24] Bar Code, para 808.4.

[25] There was some debate about whether this should be after six months or a year of pupillage.

[26] Many jurisdictions recognise call to the English Bar as a part of their own qualification regimes. It was on this ground that a number of specialist Bar associations, ie The Commercial Bar Association, London Common Law and Commercial Bar Association and the Chancery Bar Association, objected to deferral of call.

[27] D Matthews, *Deferral of Call: A Review* (London, Bar Council Education and Training Committee, 2005).

[28] Clementi, above n 1, para 22.

[29] Bar Standards Board, *Deferral of Call: Report of Provisional Conclusions* (June 2007) para 50.

[30] Code of Conduct for the Bar of England and Wales (London, Bar Standards Board, 8th edn, as amended, 2004) (hereafter Bar Code) para 204(b). There are some exceptions for those called before 2000: see para 206.1.

through any organisation, such as a partnership or limited company. According to the Bar Code, barristers must be

> completely independent in conduct and professional standing as sole practitioners . . . to act as consultants instructed by solicitors and other approved persons.[31]

Groups of barristers do, however, combine in chambers and thus share the costs of rent and other services, such as marketing and staff training, but this arrangement cannot constitute a formal business partnership. Each set of chambers is normally headed by a Queen's Counsel (QC), but this is not compulsory. A set will normally contain several QCs, but the majority of its members will be junior counsel (ie career barristers who have not yet been appointed QC). In addition, there will be some pupil barristers in training and maybe some 'squatters' and door tenants, who have the right to practise but who are not formally members of the chambers and do not contribute to the running costs. There are about 300 sets of chambers, with an average membership of 30, although some chambers comprise over 100.

Members of chambers share the costs of employing clerks,[32] secretaries, bookkeepers and maybe other non-qualified staff. Traditionally the clerk organises the day-to-day running of chambers and allocates work between members. Nowadays, in addition to a senior barrister having general management responsibilities, many chambers also employ a professional chambers manager. It is not essential now to practise in chambers; barristers of over three years' call can practise from their home, and about 250 do this. In London before 1987 chambers had to be situated in an Inn of Court, but pressure on space led to the abandonment of this rule. Barristers still have to be a member of an Inn, however, in order that they have access to their library and other facilities, and also to encourage the collegiate ethos. Provincial barristers also have to be members of an Inn and are also encouraged to join one of the six circuits throughout England and Wales for the same reason, though this is not compulsory.

A major restriction on the way that barristers could offer their services to the public was the rule that they could be briefed only by solicitors, not by the client directly.[33] This was the *quid pro quo* extracted by solicitors for the barristers' advocacy monopoly in the higher courts. It was also justified by the bar on the more substantive ethical ground that it ensured that the client received independent advice on their case from a professional whose views would not be clouded by a continuing personal or business relationship between them. The barrister thereby preserved his or her objectivity and independence from the client. However, as the respective monopolies of the two professions became eroded throughout the 1980s and 1990s, so did this rule. Direct professional access to barristers was first permitted by the Bar Council in 1989, when members of certain professions, such as accountants and surveyors, were permitted to go direct to barristers. This was gradually extended to other professions or employees of public bodies throughout the 1990s and was known as Bar Direct.

---

[31] Bar Code, para 104(a)(i) and (ii).

[32] For a study of the traditional clerking system in chambers see J Flood, *Barristers' Clerks: The Law's Middlemen* (Manchester University Press, 1983).

[33] The rule is not of great antiquity, having been introduced in 1888 for contentious matters and extended to most other matters in 1955.

In 2004 a more general direct access to barristers by members of the public was introduced, called Licensed Access.[34] There are, however, conditions. Only barristers of over three years' call can be directly briefed by the public and they must have done a training course.[35] Direct access barristers must be registered as such with the Bar Council. Certain issues are excluded from the scheme—immigration, asylum, family proceedings and crime. Barristers are not bound by the 'cab-rank rule' where directly approached, so they can refuse a client but must not discriminate unlawfully. Moreover the barrister should refuse a case if it is in the interests of the client or of justice that a solicitor should be instructed.

There are in fact many obstacles in the way of direct access. For example, barristers cannot hold client monies, cannot conduct the preliminaries of litigation such as writing letters to the other side, and they cannot issue proceedings or serve documents. Barristers are therefore not on the court record as being the client's representative. If the client is unable to do these tasks, or get them done by someone else, in effect as a litigant in person, then the barristers will be unable to take the case on.[36] However, where the client is simply interested in getting a legal opinion, direct access could prove to be the speediest and most economical route. The barrister will be able to draft documents, such as letters before action or offers to settle, for the client to send out. Despite the restrictions, this change in the Bar's working arrangements means that the differences between solicitors and barristers in the work that they can do are now considerably diminished and direct access constitutes a major step towards the de facto fusion of the professions. There will undoubtedly be further pressure to reduce the restrictions as the new system develops.

After a decade or more of practice, the next step in the career ladder for practising barristers is to apply for and obtain 'silk', that is, become a QC. Most senior judges were, and still are, recruited from the ranks of QCs, as are government counsel. QCs get higher fees and no longer do lower level work or paperwork. In the more difficult cases they are usually instructed with a junior, a non-QC barrister. The appointment process used to be obscure and depended on 'secret soundings' amongst the judiciary. It was unjustifiably discriminatory and certainly offended all the normal recruitment or promotion policies common in industry or the public service. In 2003 the Lord Chancellor announced that the system would cease and the appointment of QCs was suspended.[37] It was then decided to allow the QC title to continue but that appointment to it would be subject to a merit-based system of open competition.

From July 2005 the system for appointing QCs has changed. Applicants for silk must now apply anonymously and include references from judges and clients. Applications are made to the Ministry of Justice but are determined by an interview panel consisting of a lay chair,

---

[34] In rules made by the Bar Council and approved by the Lord Chancellor. The move was a response to a report from the OFT in which the old rule was criticised as an unjustifiable restrictive practice. It was accepted by the Bar Council as a response to their own Kentridge Report of January 2002. See the Licensed Access Recognition Regulations and Licensed Access Rules 2004.

[35] It is only a one-day course provided by the College of Law, and deals mainly with the need to keep records of work done and with the money laundering rules.

[36] It has been accepted by the courts that such clients are in the position of litigants in person and this has costs implications. See *Agassi v Robinson* [2006] 1 All ER 900 CA discussed previously at p 27.

[37] He had set up a committee to look into the issue, chaired by Sir Leonard Peach, which reported in 2001. The Law Society was vociferously against the system which discriminated against solicitor advocates. For an account of the controversy up to 2002, see Abel, above n 19, 190*ff.*

three other laypersons, two solicitors and barristers, and one retired judge. They work to an agreed set of competences and have the advice of a human resources professional. The cost of the new system is met by the fees paid by the applicants, set at £1,800 plus VAT. On appointment a further fee of £2,250 plus VAT is payable. The first appointments under this system were made in July 2006 and the numbers of female applicants (68) almost doubled over those applying in 2003 (39), as did their success rate at nearly half the applicants (it had been under a quarter in 2003).[38] Ten applicants from ethnic minorities and four solicitors were also appointed.

About 2,500 barristers are described as employed barristers, meaning that they are employed by a company or other body, such as a solicitors' firm or public authority. Such employed barristers can work only for their employer; they cannot offer their services to the general public or other solicitors.[39] However, a barrister who is employed by a solicitors' firm can provide legal services to the clients of the firm and can thus act for the public.[40] Such a barrister cannot become a partner in the firm, however. If the proposal for legal disciplinary practices, floated by Sir David Clementi and now embodied in the Legal Services Act under the guise of the proposed alternative business structures discussed below, are adopted, then this latter rule would disappear. This would remove the final bar to the fusion of the two professions.

Solicitors

All qualified practising solicitors must have a practising certificate issued by the Solicitors Regulatory Authority (SRA) and renewed annually. They must provide all necessary information to the SRA in relation to this—for example, details of insurance and continuing education compliance.[41] There are powers to issue a conditional practising certificate in certain circumstances, for example where there has been a lapse of over 12 months in taking out a certificate or where there has been a late delivery of an accountant's report.[42] It is an offence to practise or hold out to be a solicitor without such a certificate under the Solicitors Act 1974 sections 20 and 21. The cost of a practising certificate in 2006 was £1,020, having risen steeply from £430 in 1999. Much of this rise was to provide the complaints service of the Law Society with additional funds to deal with chronic backlogs.[43] Solicitors must take out indemnity insurance under the Solicitors' Indemnity Insurance Rules 2001. Such insurance used to be arranged by the Law Society itself, but since 2001 has been provided under approved commercial schemes. Solicitors who have qualified, which includes the period of traineeship in a firm, but do not have a practising certificate may call themselves solicitors but not act as such for reward.

---

[38] See (2006)156 NLJ 1186.

[39] Bar Code, paras 205 and 501.

[40] Employed barristers employed by the Legal Services Commission, a legal advice centre or acting *pro bono* may similarly act for the public, See Bar Code, para 502.

[41] Solicitors' Code, rr 20.01 and 20.03.

[42] Solicitors Act 1974, ss 10 and 12.

[43] For more on this, see chapter 7. The fee must be set in order to cover only those costs approved by the Lord Chancellor, such as regulation, training and developing, and disseminating professional guidance. Some law reform work related to the profession and human rights work can also be included in fixing the cost of the practising certificate. Access to Justice Act 1999, s 46(2)(b).

The rules on how solicitors' firms may be organised have undergone considerable changes in the past decade. The current rules provide that solicitors can practise as conventional unlimited partnerships, as limited partnerships, as limited companies[44] or, of course, as bona fide employees of these organisations. There are complex rules, which are not detailed here, designed to ensure that all the partners, directors or shareholders are solicitors. In addition, all solicitors' firms must have at least one principal or director of at least three years' standing, who is basically responsible for the work of the practice and compliance with the regulations.[45] In reality, modern firms adopt a variety of management structures, some using chief executives who are not lawyers and others adhering to the traditional model of a senior managing partner who must be a lawyer. Firms can freely employ non-lawyers and increasingly do so, in particular as practice managers, trainers, librarians and paralegals, such as members of ILEX.

The basic principle is still that a practising solicitor cannot share professional fees with anyone other than another solicitor and that therefore only another practising solicitor can be a partner, shareholder or director of the company.[46] There is now an exception to the ban on fee sharing in the 2007 Solicitors' Code of Conduct that was originally introduced in February 2004. This is designed to make it easier for firms to raise working capital or acquire services such as computing packages. The rule now permits solicitors to make fee sharing arrangements with non-solicitors provided:

— the arrangement is solely to facilitate the introduction of capital or the provision of services;
— the arrangement does not allow the fee sharer to constrain the solicitor's professional judgement in dealing with clients, either in terms of the agreement or because of the amount of capital introduced under it;
— the arrangement does not in fact create a prohibited partnership;
— the solicitor provides the SRA with details of the agreement if so asked; and
— there is no breach of the referral rules.[47]

It is, therefore, now possible for solicitors' firms to obtain loans the repayment of which is calculated by reference to a percentage of the gross profits of the firm, or to obtain computing goods or other services in return for paying the supplier a percentage of the profits. The Solicitors' Code's guidance warns against the inadvertent creation of a prohibited partnership and also the danger that an arrangement might create a conflict of interest with clients. In particular, the SRA is likely to be concerned if a fee-sharing agreement extends to more than 15% of the gross fees of the firm. The reason for this concern is that, if it were

---

[44] Incorporation has been possible since 2001. See now Solicitors' Code, r 14. Limited liability has also been made available since 2000 (as a result of Limited Liability Partnerships Act 2000, c 12), subject to various safeguards in relation to client liability insurance to compensate for the loss of personal liability. According to the *Law Society Gazette* of 29 April 2004 it is anticipated that about one-third of the top 100 firms will have converted to limited liability partnerships by 2005. Incorporation has been slower to take off.

[45] Solicitors' Code, rr 5.01 and 5.02. All the principles or directors of the firm are so responsible.

[46] The term solicitor in this context embraces also registered foreign and European lawyers. See Solicitors' Code, rr 14.03 and 14.04. Fees can also be shared with solicitor employees and retired partners.

[47] Solicitors' Code, r 8.02. There is also an exception to the fee sharing prohibition in favour of charitable advice-giving bodies such as CABx and Law Centres, whose managing trustees are not normally solicitors. See r 8.01(i).

larger, the solicitors might be tempted to adjust the way they sought or dealt with clients in order to suit the fee-sharer's interest in maximising profits rather than the clients' interests in getting an appropriate level of service. Of course, the solicitors themselves may well be concerned to maximise their firm's profits rather than act in their clients' best interests, but is there really a significant added danger of unethical conduct where third parties are involved in the business?

The reason that the Law Society is so anxious to keep the basic prohibition of fee sharing is, probably, that without these rules it would be possible for any business to offer the full range of legal services to the public; this competition might spell the end of the traditional solicitor's practice. For example, a supermarket might want to enter the market and offer a standardised range of legal services to the public—often dubbed 'Tesco-law'.[48] Certainly the RAC, which already offers some legal services to its members, is interested in this type of development. This will be allowed, with conditions, under the Legal Services Act 2007, as noted at the end of this chapter. In anticipation of this, both the Co-operative and Halifax Banks have already set up legal services departments, ready to expand their activities once the Act comes into force.[49] These developments will require changes to the rules on employed lawyers as well as the rules on fee sharing.

A solicitor's firm, whether a partnership or incorporated, can only carry on the business of providing 'professional services such as are provided by individuals practising as solicitors'.[50] A solicitor's firm cannot, therefore, offer both legal services and other services, such as estate agency or accountancy services, unless they do it through a separate business which complies with the requirements of the Solicitors' Code of Conduct 2007, rule 21.01. The aim of this rule is to ensure that the two businesses are kept separate and that the public are not misled into thinking that the SRA regulates the non-solicitor business simply because it is owned or managed by a qualified solicitor. Moreover, a practising solicitor can offer legal services to the public only through a regulated solicitors' practice.

Under these rules, a solicitor running a separate business as an estate agent cannot offer conveyancing services through that estate agency. The estate agency can, however, refer its clients to that solicitor's practice for conveyancing services, but the client must be informed personally and in writing of the interest of the solicitor in the two businesses. The client must consent to the firm so acting and the conveyancing work must not be undertaken by the same solicitor who has dealt with the sale of the property for the estate agency. These rules are, obviously, designed to manage the conflict of interest that arises if the same person or business receives a fee for both arranging the sale of a property and for doing the legal work, such as checking title to it, making local and other searches and doing all the other conveyancing work which is designed to ensure that the buyer receives a good title to the property. A solicitor with a commercial interest in closing the sale might be tempted to conceal from the client adverse results from searches or defects in title.

---

[48] Tesco launched an online service in June 2004 offering to make and store wills and give advice on a variety of legal issues, including DIY divorce, rights at work and starting a business. This does not require any change in the practising rules as none of the work is within the reserved categories of legal services noted in the text below. See 154 NLJ 947, 25 June 2004.

[49] See (2006) 156 NLJ 694 and (2007) 157 NLJ 134; *Law Society Gazette*, 2 November 2006.

[50] Solicitors' Code, r 14.02.

Whether the rules requiring separate businesses are adequate to protect clients from conflicts of interest in all cases may be doubted. The recent rise of claims companies dealing with personal injury actions (prompted by the relaxation of the rules on conditional fees in 2001) led to very close relationships between these firms and the solicitors' firms to whom they referred business. In many cases the claims companies were and are operated by solicitors as separate businesses. Whether the rules have been broken is difficult to say, but is clear that it is very difficult for the SRA to keep up with this ever-changing field of business and the complex relationships that exist between the claims companies and solicitors' firms.[51] The clients themselves are often confused as to who is managing the case at any one time and what the status of that person is. There have been many cases reported to Citizens Advice Bureaux and other bodies in which clients have been exploited by claims companies and possibly by associated solicitors. They have been encouraged to bring cases of low value to the client but of considerable value, in terms of fees and other commercial benefits such as interest, commissions and insurance premiums, to the companies and the solicitors. Frequently clients have to pay some costs or fees despite being told that there will be no fee if the case is not won, and they end up, after considerable time and effort, with very little or no financial benefit. The Compensation Act 2006 should curb these companies, but it is too early to know what success it will have.

While a practising solicitor can offer legal services to the public only through a solicitors' firm regulated by the SRA, there is nothing to prevent anybody offering and being paid for legal advice and services provided they do not trespass on the reserved services that are exclusive to solicitors. These are laid down in the Solicitors Act 1974, sections 22 and 23, as noted above. The main reason why claims companies who deal in personal injury cases have to employ solicitors' firms is the work preparing for litigation, which non-solicitors cannot do for gain. There is no prohibition on the claims company charging for giving legal advice, negotiating with the other side or their insurance company, gathering evidence or providing any other service short of litigation. What they cannot do is prepare documents for litigation, lodge them in court and act as a representative of the client in court proceedings.

Currently there are some 104,543 solicitors with practising certificates, of whom over 77% work in private practice in 8,926 firms. Eighty-seven per cent of these firms have up to four partners. Although 46.3% of these firms are sole practitioners, such firms employ only 8.2% of solicitors, and 22.8% of firms have only two to four partners. Only 1.3% of firms have over 26 partners, but such firms employ 39% of solicitors. Only 25 firms have more than 81 partners, most of which are situated in London; in fact, 42.2% of all firms are situated in London or the South East.[52] The numbers of firms using the more recently available forms of organisation are few. About 941 are incorporated and 1,288 have formed limited partnership.[53]

---

[51] Claims companies must now be registered under the Compensation Act 2006, which makes it an offence for a solicitor to have dealings with an unregistered claims company. The Act came into force on 30 April 2007. Solicitors have been warned by the SRA that dealing with an unregulated company is a disciplinary offence as well as carrying the risk of criminal prosecution, (2007)157 NLJ 567.

[52] B Cole, *Trends in the Solicitors Profession: Annual Statistical Report 2006* (London, Law Society, 2006), available at www.lawsociety.org.uk/secure/file/163874/e:/teamsite-deployed/documents/templatedata/Publications/Research%20Publications/Documents/trendsasrreport06_v1.pdf (accessed 3 August 2007).

[53] See *Law Society Gazette*, 5 April 2007, 1 and 17 May 2007, 16.

There is a considerable variety of ways in which solicitors' firms actually organise their work, and any attempt to classify them would almost certainly oversimplify. McConville et al describe four main kinds of firm engaged in criminal defence work: classical, managerial, political and routine.[54] These descriptions apply to the organisation of criminal defence within larger units, but they are also useful in describing many firms operating in other fields. Firms often represent a combination of the features of one or more of these ideal types. We briefly outline the essential features of these types before considering two more 'ideal types': large firms, often operating in the corporate/ commercial field, and boutique firms.

Classical

The classical model is broadly coextensive with the traditional partnership noted above and that promoted by professional bodies. The firm is organised around solicitors who handle a relatively low volume of cases. The solicitors are therefore able to be centrally engaged in all the legal tasks: research, interviewing clients and advocacy. In addition, the solicitor inducts trainees and non-qualified staff, and allocates and supervises their work. The staff are loyal, there is rarely a high turnover, and the firm is therefore cohesive and stable. Such a firm also often has a relatively stable client base.

Political

The political firm is organised around personal commitment to particular types of clients. This kind of work has recently been characterised as 'cause lawyering'. The law is used politically in order to highlight injustice or bring about political change. The firm's members empathise with poor and disadvantaged clients in their disputes with the state, corporations or employers.[55] These firms attract highly motivated staff who are committed to providing quality services. Such firms are often keen to change the law in the interests of their client group by pursuing test cases, a course which has been given a considerable boost with the introduction in 2000 of the Human Rights Act 1998. Such firms will often specialise in disaster litigation, such as that arising from road or rail accidents, class actions concerning drugs or tobacco, or political cases involving clients alleged to be involved in terrorism.

Managerial

Firms with a strong managerial structure have responded to competition and reduced funding by introducing systems and procedures aimed at reducing administration and delay. This has the effect of routinising procedures, for example, for time recording and billing, training and the delegation of work.

Routine

Routine firms comprise the majority in McConville et al's study and, to some extent, their work describes some of the work in other firms; it is routine, physically demanding, repetitive

---

[54] M McConville, J Hodgson, L Bridges and A Pavlovic, *Standing Accused: The Organisation and Practices of Criminal Defence Lawyers in Britain* (Oxford, Clarendon Press, 1994) ch 2.

[55] See S Sheingold and A Sarat (eds), *Cause Lawyering: Political Commitments and Professional Responsibilities* (New York, Oxford University Press, 1998).

and unending. Because of this, there is likely to be frequent 'poaching' of qualified and non-qualified staff either for advocacy or for their local connections, which leads to instability in firms and variable service to clients. In all of the firms described in McConville et al's research, staff perceived themselves to be providing a public service in poor working conditions and for relatively low pay. Despite this, they felt they lacked the respect of the public. The same story would probably be heard from lawyers working primarily in civil as well as criminal legal aid or doing other small civil work. These pressures result in the clients of some of these firms receiving perfunctory or discontinuous service, and contrasts markedly with the service received by clients instructing large corporate commercial firms. Large firms will rarely deal with a criminal case unless it is corporate crime. Such firms are, by virtue of their size alone, subject to different but powerful forces which have also led them to depart from the classical model.

Large firms

The increasing numbers of large firms, and the concentration of legal resources within them, is one of the most significant developments in the legal professions of the US, Canada and Britain. They have grown faster than the profession as a whole and receive a larger proportion of the money spent on legal services, mainly from their business clients.[56] While in the US large firms have been a feature of the landscape since the before the turn of the century, in the UK partnerships of solicitors were not permitted to exceed 20 until the passing of the Companies Act 1967.[57] This opportunity for expansion was fuelled by the 'Thatcher revolution' in the 1980s, which led to the 'big bang' in the City of London and the deregulation and re-regulation of financial services.[58] This created substantial work for solicitors' firms and the opportunity to play a part in a growing international market for corporate and commercial legal services.[59] The firms organised around four broad categories of work—corporate and commercial; property; litigation; and tax—but their principal focus was on corporate/ commercial work.[60] Within a short time, large firms transformed the way legal work was conducted and the way in which the legal profession was perceived. Table 1 lists the largest firms, their personnel and their financial profiles.

---

[56] M Galanter, 'Law Abounding: Legalisation Around the North Atlantic' (1992) 55 *Modern Law Review* 5. Lady Marre CBE, *A Time for Change: Report of the Committee on the Future of the Legal Profession* (London, General Council of the Bar and Council of the Law Society, 1988), noted that between 1984 and 1986 the number of firms with more than 11 partners increased by 8% and the number of principals in those firms increased by 12% (para 5.22).

[57] S 120(1)(a). Corporation law practice had emerged in the US by the turn of the twentieth century. It became 'a business' in its own right, stressing high-quality service and demanding large staff, a high degree of organisation, a high overhead and more intense specialisation. The 'law factory' emerged with the mass of work performed by the ablest product of the best law schools. The partners lent their name to this work but were principally business getters and the repository of the goodwill of the corporate clientele. See K Llewelyn, 'The Bar Specialises: With What Results?' [1933] *Annals of the American Academy* 176 and M Galanter and T Palay, *Tournament of Lawyers: Transformation of the Big Law Firm* (University of Chicago Press, 1991).

[58] See J Flood, 'Megalaw in the UK: Professionalism or Corporatism?: A Preliminary Report' (1989) 64 *Indiana Law Journal* 569. Other factors encouraging expansion may have included the abandonment of fee regulation in England and Wales. (See E Skordaki and D Walker, *Research Study No 12, Regulating and Charging for Legal Services: An International Comparison* (London, Research and Policy Planning Unit, The Law Society, 1994) para 3.6.

[59] This prospect led to the merger of Coward Chance and Clifford Turner, creating Clifford Chance, which in 1988 had 168 partners, 386 assistants and 123 articled clerks.

[60] Flood, above n 58.

Table 1: Large law firm finances

No	Firm	Turnover (£m)	Profits per equity partner (£K)	Revenue per lawyer (£K)	Total no. of lawyers	No. of equity partners
1	Clifford Chance	1030.0	810	424	2432	382
2	Linklaters	935.0	1062	451	2072	353
3	Freshfields Bruckhaus Deringer	882.0	830	438	2013	521
4	Allen & Overy	736.0	788	418	1760	342
5	Lovells	396.0	572	293	1353	232
6	DLA Piper	366.4	604	233	1573	135
7	Eversheds	323.0	422	223	1448	157
8	Slaughter and May	321.0	1120	557	576	121
9	Herbert Smith	296.0	839	374	791	120
10	Simmons & Simmons	227.0	470	388	585	146
11	Ashurst	214.0	701	357	600	130
12	Norton Rose	210	445	268	785	140
13	CMS Cameron McKenna	181.3	476	297	611	130
14	Pinsent Masons	172.0	400	230	749	113
15	Adelshaw Goddard	161.2	472	285	566	110
16	S J Berwin	155	711	338	459	83
17	Denton Wilde Sapte	147.5	375	290	509	88
18	Berwin Leighton Paisner	145.0	630	375	387	74
19	Taylor Wessing	142.5	393	274	520	131
20	Hammonds	132.6	328	213	623	95

This table was constructed using figures taken from *The Lawyer UK 100 2006*; the full table is available at www.thelawyer.com/uk100/2006/tb_1-25.html#, accessed 3 August 2007.

The resources of large firms stand in stark contrast to those of most other solicitors,[61] reinforcing a dichotomy, already established in the US,[62] between wealthy firms serving corporate/commercial clients and smaller 'general practice' firms handling lower value work on behalf of individual clients.[63] Most of the firms are located in the City of London and

---

[61] It became accepted that 100 firms, having more than 20 partners, could earn one-fifth of the income of the whole solicitors' branch of the profession. C Glasser, 'The Legal Profession in the 1990s—Images of Change' (1990) 10 *Legal Studies* 1.

[62] Large firms were well established in the USA by the early twentieth century. Galanter and Palay, above n 57.

[63] J Heinz and E Laumann, *Chicago Lawyers: The Social Structure of the Bar* (New York: Russell Sage Foundation, 1982).

provide legal expertise in solving complex problems on a massive scale.[64] Like their American forerunners, large firms in the UK are adept at 'custom work',[65] solving the multitude of problems raised by complex commercial transactions.[66] In order to do this they organise large teams of lawyers, accountants, economists and architects; in reality, therefore, they provide a multidisciplinary approach to legal practice.

Large firms were and are considerably more commercially orientated and entrepreneurial than solicitors firms had been in the past. Emerging in response to the enterprise culture fostered by government policy in the 1980s and having close contact with business and financial institutions, the large firms absorbed the ethic of that period.[67] The firms, and the individuals working within them, were 'becoming more corporate, more specialist, more competitively aware, and more orientated to economic productivity'.[68] As a response to these changes, large firm lawyers were more concerned with technique to the exclusion of the traditional professional virtues.[69] Indeed, Stanley has argued that such firms had begun to place industry, initiative, responsibility and success over the traditional virtues of benevolence and altruism, and even concerns about justice.[70] Manifestations of this changing professional ethos were said to be found in the commodification of legal services, in overcharging and in subservience to client demands.[71]

It would be surprising if such firms did not exercise powerful effects on the profession. Some of these are negative. They attract corporate commercial work away from smaller firms which, therefore, become less viable. They present a powerful image of legal practice which influences the perception of the public and policy makers. They attract the most able entrants to the profession.[72] They can change professional relationships and influence the policies of professional bodies.[73] Examples have occurred in relation to legal education and

---

[64] The denationalisation of publicly owned companies also created new areas of work for lawyers which continued as ambiguous drafting, and the discretionary decisions of new regulators for these industries created fresh legal problems to solve. C Stanley, 'Enterprising Lawyers: Changes in the Market for Legal Services' (1991) 25 *Law Teacher* 44.

[65] See Skordaki and Walker, above n 58, paras 2.5.4, 2.9.1 and 2.10.1.

[66] See generally M Galanter, 'Mega-law and Mega-lawyering in the Contemporary United States' in R Dingwall and P Lewis (eds), *The Sociology of the Professions: Doctors, Lawyers and Others* (New York: The Macmillan Press, 1983) 166.

[67] Firms located in the City of London, for example, were major beneficiaries of the work produced by the policy of denationalisation and became identified with enterprise economics.

[68] EH Greenebaum, 'Development of Law Firm Training Programs: Coping with a Turbulent Environment' (1996) 3 *International Journal of the Legal Profession* 315, 322.

[69] So, for example, Galanter and Palay, above n 57, observe that by the 1950s in the USA 'efficiency, accuracy and intelligence' were the only values sought in large firm lawyers.

[70] Stanley, above n 64, relates this to the conditions in which the UK firms developed, but others have suggested that the structure of the work of large firms places them on 'a collision course with humanistic values such as truthfulness and altruism'. See HT Edwards, 'A Lawyers Duty to Serve the Public Good' (1990) 65 *New York University Law Review* 1148.

[71] Stanley, above n 64.

[72] See MJ Powell, *From Patrician to Professional Elite: The Transformation of the New York City Bar Association* (New York, Russell Sage, 1989) and note that the American television programme 'LA Law', a glamorous representation of life in a corporate commercial law firm, is credited with increasing the demand to enter the legal profession in both the UK and US.

[73] As long ago as 1933, Karl Llewellyn observed that large law firms in the US had attracted the profession's 'best brains [and] most of its inevitable leaders': Llewellyn, above n 57, 176. For the impact on the relationship with the Bar, see J Flood, above n 58, 574 and 578; M Humphries, 'An Artificial Divide That's Had Its Day', *The Lawyer*, 21 November 1995, 12. The Law Society itself grew out 'intimate links with elite City firms': D Sugarman, 'Bourgeois

the regulation of legal services.[74] The influence of large firms can also be positive. Large firms offer a democratic and meritocratic environment for employees, providing better opportunities for the advancement of women and ethnic minorities. This is because, as large organisations, they are more likely to absorb the current norms and standards of public life.[75] They are more likely to have dedicated personnel functions and to be proximate to the public sector, where such norms are most strongly expressed. The salaries earned by city lawyers can dwarf those offered by High Street practices—at the top level they can exceed £2 million per year, and even newly qualified recruits can earn £100,000.[76] They boost national productivity with their work for international clients and can also afford to take a lead in activity such as *pro bono publico*.[77]

From the wider professional perspective, however, large firms present three further problems. First, their growth has made the solicitors' organisational and ethical model increasingly irrelevant. This is not purely a question of scale; it arises from the bureaucracy necessary to run such firms and the attendant changes brought about in their cultures.[78] Further, the cultures of large commercial firms were seen to be as diverse as their management structures, making it difficult to find a model of education or regulation equally acceptable to all.[79] Finally, despite the relatively small number of large firms, they offer a large proportion of solicitor traineeships.[80] To the extent that large firms offer a commercial alternative to traditional professionalism, their influence is bound to grow. The evidence as to whether large firm lawyers are more ethical than their counterparts in general practice is inconclusive. It is not clear, for example, whether professional disciplinary procedures treat the transgressions of large firm lawyers with the same rigour with which they treat those from small and sole practices.[81]

Boutique firms

Boutique firms also represent a high degree of organisational specialisation. They are smaller than typical large and medium firms, with a narrow area of highly specialist work, albeit

Collectivism, Professional Power and the Boundaries of the State: The Private and Public Life of the Law Society 1825–1914' (1996) 3 *International Journal of the Legal Profession* 95, but only 5% of Law Society Council seats are filled by City lawyers. They are keen to be involved when they perceive that the Law Society is acting against their interests, as was shown in the lobbying on the new conflict rules now embodied in the Solicitors' Code r 3. City firms were anxious to obtain exceptions to the basic rule drafted as widely as possible so as to retain as much work as possible. Smaller firms thought they were simply trying to prevent any other firms gaining the clients and thereby the expertise.

[74] A Sherr, 'Of Super Heroes and Slaves: Images and Work of the Legal Profession' (1995) 48 *Current Legal Problems* 327.

[75] WW Powell, 'Fields of Practice' (1996) 21 *Law and Social Inquiry* 956.

[76] *The Guardian*, 23 August 2007, 28.

[77] See chapter 15.

[78] M Burrage, 'From a Gentleman's to a Public Profession: Status and Politics in the History of English Solicitors' (1996) 3 *International Journal of the Legal Profession* 45, 69.

[79] Greenebaum, above n 63.

[80] The largest 5% of firms employ 40% of solicitors and offer the majority of training contracts. A Sherr and L Webley, 'Legal Ethics in England and Wales' (1997) 4 *International Journal of the Legal* 109, 113; see also R Abbey, 'The Crisis in Solicitor Training', *New Law Journal*, 17 December 1993.

[81] CE Reason and C Chappell, 'Crooked Lawyers: Towards a Political Economy of Deviance in the Profession' in T Fleming (ed), *The New Criminologies in Canada: Status, Crime and Control* (Toronto, Oxford University Press, 1985) 221.

work crossing different areas of legal practice.[82] They may specialise in one aspect of a larger field, such as medical law, child care work or immigration cases. Boutique firms, however, often closely overlap the work of large firms or do work which is ancillary to large firm work, such as intellectual property or entertainment law. In the field of public-funded work, the development of such firms has been encouraged by the introduction in 2000 of contracting for legally aided work. Firms must be able to demonstrate to the Legal Services Commission (who awards the contracts) that they are reasonably specialised if they are to win a contract in crime or family work, for example, and such work will only become financially viable if it is done in a reasonable volume. In some cases, in particular in relation to criminal defence work, solicitors have to acquire separate qualifications in order to get the contracts. Such firms can be organised along the lines of the classical, managerial or political models.

Proposed changes to organisationof the profession

It can be seen from the above that solicitors practice under considerable restraints in developing their practices and competing with other businesses offering similar services. Barristers are even more constrained, and there have been many calls to relax the rules so as to allow the legal professions to compete more effectively with others, such as accountants and paralegals of various kinds. Indeed, allowing solicitors to incorporate in 2001, giving them the benefits of running a business within a corporate structure, was a response to some of this criticism. Similarly, limited liability, first allowed in 2001, enabled solicitors to practise like other business persons, protecting their personal property from being used to pay business debts. In 2001 the Office of Fair Trading issued a report recommending the elimination of unjustified restrictions on free competition within the professions. After further consultation, the government appointed Sir David Clementi to carry out an independent review into the provision of legal services which covered, inter alia, the restrictive nature of the business structures delivering the services. His report in 2004 was followed by a Government White Paper and, in 2006, by the Legal Services Bill, now the Legal Services Act 2007, which followed most of Clementi's recommendations but modified those in relation to business structures.[83]

An issue of major concern to Clementi in his report was the restrictive nature of the structures within which legal services were delivered. He considered that choice and therefore competition was severely restricted by them, both for the consumer and for the deliverer of those services. Certain lawyers see a conflict between lawyers as professionals and lawyers as business people, he wrote, but he disagreed:

> access to justice requires not only that the legal advice given is sound, but also the presence of business skills necessary to provide a cost-effective service in a consumer-friendly way.[84]

---

[82] The development of technology assists these firms as they are not now dependent on any particular locality for their business. There is, for example a firm that specialises in dental law (the Dental Law Partnership, www.dentallaw.co.uk) whose client come from all over the country, although their office is in Nantwich.

[83] OFT 2001, *Competition in the Professions—A Report by the Director General of Fair Trading*; DCA, 2003, *Competition and Regulation in the Legal Services Market—A Report Following the Consultation 'In the Public Interest?'*; Clementi, above n 1; White Paper, DCA 2005, *The Future of Legal Services—Putting Consumers First*, Cm 6679.

[84] Clementi Report, 5.

This perspective reflected shifting attitudes to multidisciplinary practices (MDPs), which the Benson Report concluded, in 1979, were not in the public interest.[85] The 1990 Courts and Legal Services Act permitted the Law Society to retain restrictions on solicitors entering unincorporated associations with other professionals.[86]

The possibility that MDPs might be the pattern established in the UK was enhanced when, in 1993, Arthur Anderson, a multinational accounting firm, established a law practice. This practice rapidly developed, operating separately from but alongside the accounting business, employing 100 lawyers and with projected income of £22 million.[87] Such arrangements avoided the Law Society's ban on fee splitting by the maintenance of separate accounts.[88] The Law Society originally resisted MDPs on the ground that it was not satisfied that the public's need for independent legal advice could be properly achieved in an MDP and that further safeguards would be needed if they were permitted.[89] The Bar's response to the Green Papers of 1989 expressed anxiety at reduced entry and the potential loss of independent barristers to MDPs, the loss of cross monitoring of the work of solicitors and barristers by each, the loss of small local solicitors practices through unfair competition with larger units[90] and the loss of the public benefit of the cab-rank rule.[91] Recognising the inevitability of MDPs the Law Society formally ended its opposition and their arrival in the mainstream of corporate/commercial work seemed inevitable.[92] It considers, however, that a change in the primary legislation is required in order for them to be introduced under the Code of Conduct.

The potential attraction of MDPs is that they would provide flexible 'one-stop shops' for clients requiring a variety of professional services. However, there might well be conflicts of interest and professional duties between the professionals. There is also a danger that, if the same firm were to be employed by a client for both legal and accountancy services, the professionals involved might lose their independence and objectivity. This was a feature of the collapse of the multinational firm Enron, based in the US, which provided both tax advice and auditing services. In that case, it was clear that neither the lawyers nor the accountants working for either the corporation or the accountants firms employed by it adhered to their traditional values of integrity or independence. Rather, they simply facilitated the dishonest and ultimately illegal activities of the managers of the business, designed to maximise their returns from the business and deceive the investing public as to its true financial position.

Whilst Clementi was sympathetic to the idea of MDPs, he did not go so far as to recommend them. His preferred option was the legal disciplinary practice (LDP), a practice

---

[85] Report of the Royal Commission on Legal Services (1979) Cmnd 7648 at 401.

[86] S 66(2).

[87] Wolfram, The Lawyer, 27 May 1997, 18.

[88] Solicitors' Practice Rules 1990, r 7.

[89] Law Society, 'Striking the Balance: The Provisional Views of the Council of the Law Society on the Green Paper' (London, Law Society, 1989) 4 and 17.

[90] The General Council of the Bar, The Quality of Justice: The Bar's Response (London, Butterworth, 1989) para 2.35.

[91] Ibid, para 2.57.

[92] 'Medium Sized City Partners Accept Need for MDPs', The Lawyer, 11 February 1997, 48. S Parker, 'Introduction to Legal Ethics and Legal Practice' in S Parker and C Sampford (eds), Legal Ethics and Legal Practice (Oxford, Clarendon Press, 1995) 1. A Law Society Consultation Paper on MDPs is currently out for discussion.

offering only legal services to the public, but whose members or partners could consist of all types of legal practitioner—solicitor, barrister, conveyancer and legal executive, for example. It also could involve other practitioners, such as IT experts or management personnel. All could be equally involved in the management of the firm and also participate in its profits, but the services offered would be exclusively legal services. It could also be possible for the management of such a firm to be separate from the persons who owned it, but lawyers should be in the majority. As the Consultation Paper pointed out, this is the model followed by law centres, which are run by a trustee board or management committee who do not work in the centre and who may not be lawyers or even professionally qualified persons of any kind. However, a more systematic method of regulation would be needed if such practices were to be developed as commercial profit-making organisations. A single regulator of the firm would have to be adopted, either by choosing one of the existing professional bodies or by introducing a new 'public' regulator such as the Legal Services Board (LSB) as provided in the Legal Services Act 2007. The LDP, it is suggested, would facilitate savings in costs and provide a more flexible service for the public.[93]

The model accepted by the Government and provided for in the Legal Services Act 2007[94] is called an Alternative Business Structure (ABS). An ABS can consist of lawyers of all types, and also non lawyers, and will be able to offer all legal services, reserved and unreserved, and other related services, such as insurance or surveying (assuming that other professional organisations allowed this). The Government envisages 'one stop shops' for consumers. No details of the conditions governing ABSs are contained in the Act. This will be for the LSB to decide when granting the necessary licences for ABSs. The regulatory body will be either the proposed LSB or a body (such as the SRA) approved by the LSB. The reasons for the proposals are stated to be to improve consumer choice, reduce prices, improve services and provide better access to justice. For lawyers the advantages are said to be greater access to capital and finance, greater flexibility and more choice for legal professionals, including better rewards for non-legal staff. It is anticipated that Clementi's LDPs will first be licensed in 2009 and the full ABS regime will be available from 2011. He envisaged that there

> should be a Code of Professional Practice for the Legal Disciplinary Practice, to which all lawyers in the practice would need to adhere

agreed by the professional bodies represented in the type of practice.[95]

As already noted, commercial providers of legal services are already anticipating the liberalisation proposed in the Legal Services Act. The RAC, already providing legal advice on motoring matters to its members, is likely to extend this work, both in scope and to non-members. The Co-operative Society is planning a similar service, and the Halifax Bank has set up 'Halifax Legal Solutions' to provide everyday legal products at lower fees than most solicitors to members who will pay a joining fee of £89 per year and then set fees for

---

[93] Not everyone agrees with this, however. Moving advocacy in-house probably does not allow for economies of scale, and both client choice and lawyer independence may be compromised. See J Webb, 'Commentary' (2005) 8 *Legal Ethics* 185.

[94] In pt 5 of the Act, s 71 onwards.

[95] Clementi, above n 1, 111.

services used.[96] At the moment these services cannot include the reserved areas of practice, but if the organisations comply with the regulations of the LSB when it is set up they will be able to do so. The concern of many solicitors is that large corporations such as the Halifax will, in effect, swallow up all the standard and lucrative legal work, leaving the High Street practice with only the low-paid legal aid work, or the difficult non-standard client who is also unable to pay fully for the service required. They predict that many smaller firms will go out of business.

Conclusion

In the past decade possible changes in the way legal firms and chambers are organised, such as the use of incorporation, have not been adopted with any speed, although firms have become increasingly managerial and commercial. There has been a move to greater speciali-sation, encouraged by agencies such as the Legal Services Commission through its contracting system and requirements for monitoring and auditing. It is now pressing legal aid firms to amalgamate and increase in size so that fewer firms will get contracts and those that do will, hopefully, provide economies of scale. This is hastening the decline of the idea that a small High Street firm can deal as general practitioners with all legal issues and moves toward a more commercial, market-driven model of legal practice. The Legal Services Act aims to provide, through the operation of market forces, a high degree of choice in legal services for both the consumer and the provider.[97] The pressure for the formal fusion of the solicitors and barristers branches of the profession may become more intense as a result, especially as the changes in legal aid have made it, and will continue to make it, much more difficult for young barristers to make a living at the Bar. Equally, it may be argued that, while a de facto fusion already exists where it is in demand, it will be accelerated by these reforms. Yet there will always be a need for a body of specialist legal consultants and advocates, and the Bar will therefore probably continue but at a smaller and higher, more specialist level. It will be a profession not for the new graduate, but for the experienced practitioner.[98]

This may well be achieved, say many lawyers, at the expense of ethicality and genuine regard for the clients' best interests. Instead of self-regulation under the old pattern—that is, regulation by the professions themselves—a new bureaucracy, the LSB, will be set up, uncontrolled by the professions and possibly too close to Government. The response of those in favour of the new proposals, reflected in the research done by a number of econo-mists for the Clementi review, is that the old regime did not in fact promote either ethicality or a good service to the public.

Sole practitioners and small unlimited partnerships have always faced acute conflicts of interest between achieving short-term financial gains and providing a decent service for their clients. Increased choice of ways of delivering legal services will increase public access

---

[96] See 156 NLJ 694 and the *Law Society Gazette*, 2 November 2006, 1.

[97] 'The review favours a regulatory framework which permits a high degree of choice: choice both for the consumer in where he goes for legal services, and for the lawyer in the type of economic unit he works for' (Clementi, Final Report, 5).

[98] The Bar itself, however, is still keen to attract new graduates, especially from less privileged backgrounds, as can be seen from the report of the working party on Entry to the Bar, November 2007, www.barcouncil.org.uk.

to the services they actually want rather than those which the current profession wishes to provide and will thereby increase quality.

Bigger firms devote more resources to IT, personnel procedures, quality management and similar quality enhancements, developing a 'brand' they are keen to protect. Consumers will like their services. A somewhat similar argument is made in the context of legal aid. The Carter Report, which supports fixed fees and competitive tendering for contracts in legally aided work, is actually titled 'Legal Aid—A Market-based Approach to Reform'.[99] These arguments are common nowadays amongst economists, but many consumers of existing large corporate services, such as banks, insurance, transport, utility and phone companies, may have a different experience to report. They might prefer to be the client of a smaller firm of lawyers with a deeply embedded professional ethos. Equally, the larger commercial law firms of the future, such as the Co-op or Halifax noted above, may well 'cherry pick' the easiest and most straightforward cases, leaving the difficult cases for others who will not be able to undertake them as a commercial proposition. These cases are likely to be those of the most disadvantaged in society, who are therefore likely to have little or no choice in accessing justice. The question for the future is whether firms serving their interests will be able to survive the Carter-inspired reforms of legal aid and the Clementi-inspired reforms of the legal services market.

---

[99] Published by the LCD in July 2006 and currently the subject of much debate and even strikes by criminal lawyers. For a critique of Carter, see also, *Implementation of the Carter Review of Legal Aid*, House of Commons Select Committee Report May 2007, HC 223.

3

POWER

In *The Conflict of Faculties*, Kant noted that the 'higher disciplines'—theology, law and medicine—are clearly entrusted with a social function. In each of these disciplines, a serious crisis
must generally occur in the contract by which this function has been delegated before the
question of its basis comes to seem a real problem of social practice. This appears to be happening today.[1]

Introduction

There are various dimensions of professional power, in the relationships with clients, with
other occupations and with the state. At times in their history, relations between the branches
of the profession have been tense, but their rivalry has been superseded by competition with
the state. A profession's relations with the state reflect the circumstances of its creation.
Where the state creates professions, the civil service becomes the cultural and social exemplar
of occupational and social success, but where professions emerge independently 'from below',
they become the exemplar of success.[2] Legal professions, independent, corporately and
privately organised occupations,[3] emerged from below in Anglo-American society,[4] but their
unique position of privilege is protected by the social capital, political influence and status
accumulated over centuries. Perkin suggests that, from the nineteenth century, they have
been part of a wider movement towards professional society, constituting the third great
revolution of social relations.[5] He perceives a wide range of specialised occupations, selected
by merit and trained expertise, excluding the unqualified and using human capital, the
capitalised value of education, training and experience to command increasing share of
resources. As experience on the Continent demonstrates, professions like the Anglo-Saxon
models in law are not inevitable. While professional society in general continues in dominant

---

[1] P Bordieu, 'The Force of Law: Toward a Sociology of the Juridical Field' (1987) 38 *The Hastings Law Journal* 805,
819.

[2] H Siegrist, 'Professionalization as a Process: Patterns, Progression and Discontinuity' in M Burrage and R
Torstendahl (eds), *Professions in Theory and History: Rethinking the Study of the Professions* (London, Sage, 1990) 177.

[3] E Freidson, 'The Theory of Professions: State of the Art' in R Dingwall and P Lewis (eds), *The Sociology of the
Professions* (London, The Macmillan Press, 1983).

[4] In the rest of Europe the state prescribes education and status is derived from membership of the educated class.
Law graduates tend to enter a range of occupations, each with additional qualifications. The private practitioner is
not 'the core of any notional legal profession' because members of civil law legal occupations do not see themselves
as part of a wider 'profession'. R Abel and P Lewis (eds), *Lawyers in Society, Vol 2. The Civil Law World* (Berkeley, CA,
University of California Press, 1988).

[5] H Perkin, *The Third Revolution: Professional Elites in the Modern World Since 1945* (London, Routledge, 1996), H
Perkin, *The Rise of Professional Society: England Since 1980* (London, Routledge, 1989).

mode, the state appears determined to roll back the occupational evolution of the legal profession, with negative implications for their ethical regimes.

Historical context

Although lawyers played a significant role in building the medieval state, as courts moved to rational systems for resolving disputes based on evidence and rules of logic[6] their political rise coincided with capitalism and the evolution of the modern state system.[7] With industrialisation and democracy, lawyers assisted the efficient resolution of new types of dispute, created by changing economic systems and modes of enterprise[8] and the emergence of an increasingly powerful middle class.[9] The emergence of a legal profession was underway in England by the thirteenth century, when professional pleaders known as narrators emerged[10] and evolved into serjeants-at-law, from which group judges were chosen. By the later Middle Ages, the serjeants were equal in rank to knights and presided over the Bar hierarchy comprising the benchers and readers of the Inns of Court, the Utter-Barristers and the inner barristers or students.[11] From at least 1609 the lawyers occupied the Inner and Middle Temples, acquired by the Crown on the dissolution of the Order of the Templars.[12] Each Inn provided its own education, separate, 'yet closely welded together by ties of similar education, similar interests and similar pursuits, into one great profession of the law'.[13]

The solicitors' earliest antecedents were the attorneys, originally appointees under royal grant to appear for another in royal courts.[14] Their appearance in court was treated as that of their client, a great benefit to landowners and ecclesiastical bodies who did not then have to appear personally. By the reign of Edward I (1272–1307) their use had become so frequent that attorneys had emerged as a professional group. They were regulated by the same ordinance as pleaders, though prevented from acting as such.[15] Though less likely to become judges than serjeants, some attorneys achieved this distinction and, in 1403, they become thoroughly professionalised when judges were given power to admit and remove

[6] MJ Saks and R Van Duizend, *The Use of Scientific Evidence in Litigation* (Williamsburg, VA, National Centre for State Courts, 1983) 5.

[7] D Rueschemeyer, 'Professions Cross-nationally: From a Profession Centred to a State-centred Approach' [1986] *American Bar Foundation Research Journal* 415.

[8] Democratisation led to 'softening social mores', but also 'unseemly scrambling, for divisive jealousies and resentments resulting from massive social displacement'. D Phillips, 'Some General Thoughts on the State of the Republic and the Obligation of the Legal Profession to it', from an address to a conference of the Fourth Judicial Court of the United States at Hot Springs, VA, 1969; JF Sutton and JS Dzienowski, *Cases and Materials on the Professional Responsibility of Lawyers* (St Paul, MN, West Publishing, 1989) 12.

[9] Societies lacking a legal profession often do not have a dominant middle class majority producing a sufficient volume of distinctive work. LM Friedman, 'Lawyers in Cross Cultural Perspective' in R Abel and P Lewis (eds), *Lawyers in Society* (Berkeley, CA, University of California Press, 1995).

[10] The legal profession was formative in the reign of Edward I. See generally R Pound, *The Lawyer from Antiquity to Modern Times: With Particular Reference to The Development of Bar Associations in the United States* (St Paul, MN, West Publishing, 1953) particularly at 78.

[11] W Holdsworth, *A History of English Law* (London, Methuen, 1924) vol VI, 431 and 486.

[12] *Ibid*, vol II, 501.

[13] *Ibid*, 485.

[14] It is probably for this reason that attorneys were treated as officers of the court. *Ibid*, 318.

[15] TFT Plucknet *A Concise History of the Common Law* (Boston, MA, Little Brown, 1956) 315–31.

attorneys and began to exclude the 'ignorant'.[16] The current configuration and work roles of the legal profession result from the emergence, disappearance and amalgamation of a jumble of groups performing different legal jobs during the Middle Ages.[17] During the latter part of the sixteenth century and the seventeenth century barristers and attorneys became more distinct and new groups, pleaders, conveyancers and solicitors, took over different legal roles. Pleaders and conveyancers approximated to barristers while solicitors were closer to attorneys,[18] being originally a kind of agent for purposes ancillary to litigation that an attorney could not carry out.[19] Two distinct roles were consistently maintained throughout this history; the distinction between a person who conducts litigation and one who appears in court—the advocate—was consistent,[20] as was the right to appoint someone to conduct litigation. Both roles have always enjoyed superior status,[21] and ethical principles associated with these roles, like client confidentiality,[22] accrued gradually over time.

The original rationale for the roles of barristers and attorneys gradually became secondary to differences in qualification, discipline, class background and education.[23] The education of barristers was primarily by mooting, discussion, reading and reporting, while that of attorneys was by 'apprenticeship' to a practitioner.[24] This difference between a theoretical and a practical education gradually separated the attorneys, with their procedural focus and close contact with clients, from barristers, with their deep knowledge of legal doctrine and forensic skills.[25] The process was reinforced by the move to written pleadings, which tended to be prepared by attorneys. Barristers had ceased to have direct client contact by the end of the reign of Elizabeth I.[26] In 1614 the benchers of the Inns declared the attorneys 'but ministerial persons and of an inferior nature', and from the middle of the sixteenth century they began to be excluded from the Inns of Court[27] into the subordinate Chancery Inns, which were eventually dissolved. The discipline and education of the Inns was often lax, yet the nobility and gentry regarded call to the Bar as preparation for other careers, notably entering the House of Commons,[28] providing influential allies on professional issues. By the eighteenth century aristocratic entry had declined at the Bar. It was predominantly, and the attorneys almost exclusively, drawn from the gentry and 'middling wealthy'.[29]

---

[16] *Ibid*, 505.

[17] Eg the serjeants at law were in decline for hundreds of years, until their eventual demise in the nineteenth century, their position eroded by the rise of King's Counsel.

[18] Holdsworth, above n 11, vol VI, 432; people who 'conducted business on behalf of someone else without being an attorney or a barrister' (Pound, above n 10, 107).

[19] Solicitors may have originally been servants of the litigants or of the attorneys conducting the litigation. However, they began to be recognised as a category of legal personnel and, by the end of the seventeenth century, were treated similarly to attorneys (Holdsworth, above n 11, 448–50).

[20] *Ibid*, 432.

[21] Attorneys entitled to conduct litigation were originally treated separately from other attorneys, probably being better educated and enjoying the privilege of belonging to an Inn.

[22] In the sixteenth century, attorneys were granted immunity from giving evidence about client confidences.

[23] Holdsworth, above n 11, vol VI, 433.

[24] *Ibid*, vol II, 506.

[25] *Ibid*, vol VI, 437.

[26] *Ibid*, 440.

[27] *Ibid*, 440–1.

[28] E Cruikshank, 'Building a Profession', 125 *Law Society Gazette*, 26 June 2003, 32.

[29] D Sugarman, '"A Haven for the Privileged": Recruitment into the Profession of Attorney in England, 1709–1792' (1986) 11 *Social History* 197.

Unlike barristers, who were subject to the control of their Inns, attorneys were regarded as officers of the court and subject to its fierce control.[30] This was partly because the main courts had their own staffs of attorneys and required that attorneys were separately admitted to each. During the seventeenth century, however, concerns about discipline led judges to make repeated calls for attorneys to be admitted to Inns. This was one of the factors causing the establishment of the Society of Gentleman Practisers in the Courts of Law and Equity by elite attorneys and solicitors around 1739.[31] The Society's development into the Law Society in the nineteenth century began the process of establishing a profession comprising two branches. The Law Society,[32] first mooted in 1823, incorporated in 1831 and granted its Royal Charter in 1833, greatly increased the influence of the solicitors' branch. Almost immediately, it acquired significant political influence by offering disinterested comment on technical and public interest aspects of law reform.[33] Trust in the Law Society was so great that it was asked to draft the Solicitors Act 1844 and other legislation,[34] and assisted in establishing the new Royal Court of Justice on the Strand.[35] By the end of the nineteenth century, the Law Society had achieved unparalleled influence in law reform,[36] made possible by government dependence on 'elite consensus seeking and co-optation', the blurring of the public and private spheres and the assumption that technical issues were best left to experts.[37]

In addition to their legislative work, the solicitors pursued three major policies which were also identified within the Bar's success: controlling entry and training,[38] exclusive jurisdiction over work and self-government.[39] Artificial restrictions on membership[40] were eventually abandoned, ensuring that the Law Society could speak with authority on behalf of solicitors, although financial restrictions on entry remained.[41] As to jurisdiction, the Law Society was bequeathed by the Society of Gentleman Practisers a monopoly of

---

[30] Holdsworth, above n 11, vol VI, 433.

[31] D Sugarman, 'Bourgeois Collectivism, Professional Power and the Boundaries of the State: The Private and Public Life of the Law Society 1825 to 1914' (1996) 3 *International Journal of the Legal Profession* 81.

[32] The original royal charter in 1831 was to 'The Society of Attorneys, Solicitors, Proctors and others not being Barristers, practising in the Courts of Law and Equity of the United Kingdom'. The Law Society is still constituted under a replacement charter granted in 1845 but did not change its name by supplemental deed to 'The Law Society' until 1903 (P Reeves, 'Case History—A Look Back to the 18th Century to Find the Origins of the Law Society and the Changes over 150 Years', 92 *The Law Society Gazette*, 22 February 1995.

[33] In the 1830s, it set up a committee to lobby on proposed legislation, often using solicitor MPs.

[34] In 1838 the Law Society drafted the Solicitors Act 1844, creating the office of Registrar of Attorneys and delegating it to the Law Society. This led to consultation by the Attorney General on other legislative measures, since the civil service was relatively small and the Law Society subsequently prepared the Acts of 1860 and 1870. Sugarman, above n 31, 97 and 101.

[35] A solicitor, Edward Wilkes Field, led the effort to concentrate the dispersed London courts and the Royal Courts of Justice on the Strand (just behind the Law Society Hall) were completed in 1882. Reeves, above n 32; Sugarman, above n 31, 93–4, 96.

[36] Sugarman, *ibid*, 105.

[37] *Ibid*, 119–20.

[38] Prior to 1877 when the Law Society was given authority by statute, judges controlled examinations for solicitors. Reeves, above n 32.

[39] Unlike the bar, which operated from the Inns of court, the Law Society, organised nationally, needed statutory support in order to implement these policies. *Ibid*, 51.

[40] The cost of membership was originally pitched at a price beyond the reach of ordinary practitioners.

[41] The premium paid by clerks for articles could run to several hundreds of pounds in 1903, when average industrial earnings were £60 per annum. Clerks also had to pay stamp duty of £80 and would receive no pay for five years. Cruikshank, above n 28.

conveyancing,[42] then both high status and extremely lucrative work. A proposal by the Gentlemen Practisers that they should take responsibility for discipline was not taken up by Parliament but, by 1834, the Law Society initiated its first disciplinary proceedings and began to compile and publish 'best practice' on issues of etiquette and costs,[43] often supporting a hard line over solicitor infractions.[44] In 1941 the Law Society completed its structures of self-regulation when it acquired powers to inspect the accounts of practitioners and created a compensation fund.[45]

By emulating the Bar, solicitors achieved the autonomy and independence from the state that had been the Bar's legacy from the 'Glorious Revolution' of 1688 and the accession of William and Mary. The guarantees wrung from the new regime protected diverse groups from the interference by the state, finally establishing the pre-eminence of the rule of law and the independence of judges.[46] Among the groups thus protected, the Bar had further benefited from the lack of definition of their power in the 'unwritten constitution' and status provided scope for the expansion of professional autonomy. Indeed, Weber noted that the English Bar was a strong and organised guild which protected its corporate economic interests, having 'a measure of power which neither King nor Parliament could have easily brushed aside'.[47] Although the social order did not offer English lawyers the same political influence as their US counterparts enjoyed,[48] increasing industrial and commercial society afforded lawyers great business opportunities. In the second half of the nineteenth century, the rise of the urban middle class produced an increased demand for technical services. The solicitors held a powerful position through historic associations with aristocratic members and patrons[49] and a wide client base. Firms and individuals also had considerable social and political connections, through lawyer politicians, lobbying and other work for clients.[50] Solicitors took a lead in formulating, articulating and binding together the great middle-class revolution of the nineteenth century.[51] It was not until 1973, however, that

[42] In the late 1700s Pitt the younger imposed a tax on the annual practising certificates of solicitors and attorneys to finance the Napoleonic Wars, but conceded to the Gentleman Practisers a clause for a bill limiting the right to conduct conveyancing to practising certificate holders. Sugarman, above n 32, 89.

[43] By the Solicitors Acts of 1888, 1910 and 1919, the Law Society's disciplinary committee was given power to discipline, including suspension and removal from the roll. Cruikshank, above n 41; M Burrage, 'From a Gentleman's to a Public Profession' (1996) International Journal of the Legal Profession 45, 94.

[44] The Law Society supported harsh penalties for solicitors, like the Larceny Act 1901. One solicitor was sentenced to 4 years' penal servitude despite having returned money taken from client account. Cruikshank, ibid.

[45] Ibid, 50.

[46] Burrage, above n 43, 60–4. In 1610 Coke CJ asserted that the King had no extra-legal or personal prerogative and should not judge cases personally because he was not versed in the 'artificial reason and judgement of the law'. See Sugarman, above n 31, 83–4. Under the 'balanced constitution', (i) English law was based on customs which were slow to change and, therefore, not amenable to change by legislation; (ii) 'freedom' was guaranteed by law; and (iii) the judiciary must be independent. Sugarman, ibid, 84; see also M Burrage, 'Mrs Thatcher Against the "Little Republics": Ideology, Precedents, and Reaction' in TC Halliday and L Karpik (eds), Lawyers and the Rise of Western Political Liberalism (Oxford, Clarendon Press, 1997) 124, 148.

[47] M Weber, 'Economy and Law (Sociology of Law)' in G Roth and C Wittich (eds), Economy and Society (Berkeley, University of California Press, 1978) 794.

[48] Lawyers in the US are a 'natural aristocracy', mingling with democratic elements of society and serving as intermediaries between property and poverty. GC Hazard, 'The Future of Legal Ethics' (1991) 100 Yale Law Journal 1239, 1272; see also Hazard's discussion of A De Tocqueville's Democracy in America, ibid, 1267.

[49] TJ Johnson, Professions and Power (London, Macmillan Press, 1972).

[50] D Sugarman, 'Simple Images and Complex Realities: English Lawyers and Their Relationship to Business and Politics, 1750–1950' (1993) 11 Law and History Review 257, 281–4.

[51] Ibid, 288.

status differences officially disappeared and the Bar and the Law Society made a statement affirming their equality.[52]

It is arguable that professional separation supports the professional power of lawyers in the UK. The Bar had long established rights, and solicitors, despite having firms of great power in the City of London,[53] also achieved a large democratic mass. The formidable front presented by these two groups may explain the reluctance of government to pursue directly the question of fusion, which has long been on the agenda. Government first proposed fusion in the period of reconstruction after the First World War with a view to solicitors later transferring to the Bar, but the profession refused and the government backed down, as it also did following a minority opinion of the Evershed Committee in 1953 that fusion was in the public interest.[54] The profession has generally opposed closer ties, despite elements of common training being mooted periodically. Differences in the main work of solicitors and barristers were always an impediment, even to this.[55] Since the Courts and Legal Services Act 1990, the government appears to have sought fusion by stealth, gradually allowing and encouraging each branch to do the other's traditional work. Under the Legal Services Act 2007. They will be able to work freely together in jointly owned and controlled legal firms, bringing the eventual victory of the solicitors, or at least of their organisational and business model.

Theories of professional power

The regulative bargain

The professions' 'bargain with society' is the receipt of financial and other prestige rewards in return for subjugating self-interest to the public good.[56] This involved the profession regulating its own members and, in the case of solicitors, indemnifying the public against loss caused by them. The idea of a regulative bargain was consistent with early sociological analysis of professions, known as functionalism, which saw professions as altruistic communities working for the common good and swimming against the tide of materialism.[57] They improved social cohesion and civil society, were a counterweight to state power[58] and a cushion against the fragmentation of the traditional moral order brought about by the division of labour.[59] In a changing intellectual climate economists focused attention on the

---

[52] Burrage, above n 43, 59.

[53] J Slinn, 'The Histories and Records of Firms of Solicitors' (1989) 58 *Business Archives* 22.

[54] Cruikshank, above n 28.

[55] Benson conceded there were problems, but the Law Society, in *Lawyers and the Courts: Time for Change* (1987), advocated it. E Cruikshank 'Surviving Hard Times' (2003) 100 *Law Society Gazette* 22.

[56] D Cooper, T Puxty, K Robson and H Wilmot, 'Regulating the UK Accountancy Profession' (ESRC Research Conference, Policy Studies Institute)' cited in Department for Education and Skills, *Literature Review in Relation to 'Gateways to the Professions'* (London, DfES, 2005) note 5.

[57] RM Rich, 'Sociological Paradigms and the Sociology of Law: An Overview' in CE Reasons and R Rich (eds), *The Sociology of Law: A Conflict Perspective* (London, Butterworth, 1978) 147, 148.

[58] This adopts Durkheim's premise that structures and institutions can contribute to maintenance of social order. See AM Carr-Saunders and PH Wilson, *The Professions* (Oxford, 1933); Johnson, above n 49, 12–14; RL Abel, *The Legal Profession in England and Wales* (Oxford, Basil Blackwell, 1988) 5–6, 26–30.

[59] WH Simon, 'The Ideology of Advocacy' (1978) 29 *Wisconsin Law Review* 38, quoting AM Carr-Saunders, (1934) 12 *Encyclopaedia of the Social Sciences* 476.

monopolistic nature of professional labour, the perpetual struggle between occupations to control the work and exclude competitors,[60] while sociologists articulated constructions of social interaction based on conflict.[61] According to the new critical analysis, professions are joint enterprise aimed at securing material rewards and prestige,[62] their commitment to public service and ethics a sham and ideological propaganda.[63] This damning analysis coalesced with policy makers' doubts that professions operated in the public good and the efficacy of the 'social contract' with them.

The theory of professionalisation posits a struggle for power and professionalism as no more or less than the ability to control a market for services.[64] Abbott's historical analysis notes that, in addition to the usual trappings of institutionalisation, education and licensing, professions establish three jurisdictions—workplace, public and legal—by appeals to different audiences.[65] The workplace defines professional work, first in interactions with clients and then by negotiation of settlement with other occupations on who has the right to perform sets of tasks.[66] Public jurisdiction concerns the profession's authority in the field. Outsiders' perceptions of the profession are shaped by codes of conduct, reports by the professional body, advertising and education.[67] Having established their expertise and legitimacy, professions seek legal jurisdiction, protection by law and privileges such as self-regulation. Abbott argues that these moves depend on the professions' ability to construct their work so that it is 'impermeable', that is, that no outsiders can do it. Others have shown that professions control markets not just through market closure, that is, monopoly, but through social closure, limiting the supply of their services by controlling entry to the profession.[68] Abbot shows that, even in the 1880s, the state created government

---

[60] MS Larson, *The Rise of Professionalism: A Sociological Analysis* (Berkeley CA, University of California Press, 1977), C Harrington, 'Outlining a Theory of Practice' in M Cain and C Harrington (eds), *Lawyers in a Postmodern World: Translation and Transgression* (Buckingham, Open University Press, 1994); A Abbott, 'Jurisdictional Conflicts: A New Approach to the Development of the Legal Professions' (1986) 2 *American Bar Foundation Research Journal* 187; RL Abel, 'Towards a Political Economy of Lawyers' [1981] *Wisconsin Law Review* 112.

[61] Sociologists increasingly saw society as based on conflict and focused on the role of power in the arrangement of social roles and social organisation. Rich above n 57, 148–9.

[62] A Giddens, *Sociology* (Cambridge, Polity, 5th edn, 2006).

[63] H Jamois and B Peloille, 'Changes in the French University-Hospital System' in J Jackson (ed), *Professions and Professionalisation* (Cambridge, Cambridge University Press, 1970) 117; Johnson above n 49, 57. This calls into question the whole notion of 'profession': P Bordieu and L Wacquant, *An Invitation to Reflexive Sociology* (University of Chicago Press, 1992) 242.

[64] Abel, 'The Decline of Professionalism?' (1986) 49 *Modern Law Review* 1, 1, suggests that professionalism is 'a specific historical formation in which the members of an occupation exercise a substantial degree of control over the market for their services, usually through an occupational association'.

[65] A Abbott, *The System of Professions: An Essay on the Expert Division of Labour* (University of Chicago Press, 1988).

[66] *Ibid* and above n 60, 191. This is just as the Bar and the solicitors did in the last century, when each agreed not to compete over each others monopolies over advocacy and conveyancing.

[67] Abbott, above n 60, 196. See also Johnson, above n 49, 55: 'legends, symbols and stereotypes operate in the public sphere to formulate public attitudes to the profession'. Bordieu argues that this must be seen further as the attempt of sub-groups within the professional hierarchy to impose their internal norms on the wider field; to establish the legitimacy of their own self-conceptions and interpretations of that field: R Terdiman, 'Translator's Introduction to Bordieu, P. "The Force of Law: Toward a Sociology of the Juridical Field"' (1987) 38 *The Hastings Law Journal* 805.

[68] Johnson, above n 49, ch 2, sees the regularisation of recruitment and practice as the key feature of the professionalising process. See also Abel, above n 58, 4.

offices and procedures that would deliver legal services without the need for lawyers.[69] Thus, he concludes, while US lawyers competed with major corporations over the legal market, the chief competitor of English lawyers was always the state, a conflict that may be fuelled by professionals within the civil service.

While there are many who query whether self-interest is really the motive underlying the professional project,[70] the appearance of self-interest certainly undermines it. Ruling elites lose their social mandate if they extract too much from their position of power. According to Perkin, in successful capitalist countries, such as France and Germany, stakeholding is built into the structure of society, so that business stakeholders cooperate and elites balance their own interests with the public good. English society had no entrenched system of stakeholding and Labour governments in the 1990s sought to create one. Its attempted dialogue with the legal profession, on the issue of *pro bono*, for example, was often resisted. The domination of the public sector by the private sector[71] was reflected in the declining success of the advocacy of the welfare professions, and the increasing power and wealth of corporations. This exposed the schism in the legal profession between the commercial lawyers, linked to the corporate sector, and the legal aid lawyers, linked to the public sector.[72] To the extent that the regulative bargain had broken down, the English profession had no common platform from which to renegotiate.

Knowledge

Theories of professionalisation have knowledge at their core.[73] Among the factors that affect aspiring occupations, the existence or otherwise of a distinctive field of knowledge, preferably a university discipline, is the main determinant of status.[74] And, of course, esoteric knowledge carries considerable mystique.[75] Law is firmly established in the academy, but is unusual among professions in having a social science rather than pure science base. This tends to make legal monopolies vulnerable because some level of legal sophistication can be achieved without exceptional intellect or a taxing education. It is not, however, monopoly or even superior knowledge of the law that forces a client to depend on professionals, or allows the professional to control the relationship. Professional knowledge has a technical component and an element of 'indeterminacy', demanding the application of professional judgement.[76] This gives professional work a craft dimension which, together with profes-sional prestige and status, creates a social and economic distance between lawyers and their clients.

---

[69] Jurisdictional Conflicts, 218.

[70] CO Houle, *Continuing Learning in the Professions* (San Francisco, CA, Jossey-Bass, 1980); CW Wolfram, *Modern Legal Ethics* (St Paul, MN, West Publishing, 1986); E Schein, *Professional Education* (New York, McGraw-Hill, 1972); MD Bayles, *Professional Ethics* (Belmont, CA, Wadsworth Publishing, 2nd edn, 1989).

[71] Perkin, above n 5.

[72] *Ibid*, 14.

[73] E Freidson, *Professional Powers: A Study of the Institutionalization of Formal Knowledge* (University of Chicago Press, 1986).

[74] RA Barnett, RA Becher and NM Cork, 'Models of Professional Preparation: Pharmacy, Nursing and Teacher Education' (1987) 12 *Studies in Higher Education* 51, 61.

[75] MJ Osiel, 'Lawyers as Monopolists, Aristocrats and Entrepreneurs' (1990) 103 *Harvard Law Review* 2009, 2023.

[76] Above n 49, 43; H Jamous and B Pelloille, 'Changes in the French University Hspital System' in JA Jackson (ed), *Professionalization* (London, Cambridge University Press, 1970).

Professionalism is a system of occupational control whereby producers define both the need and the best way of providing the service. Ethics is a central component here, because self-control must be institutionalised, embedded in the structure and culture of the profession and socialised into new entrants. If professionalism works, it is a rational market solution.[77] Although professionalism is an imperfect way of controlling important knowledge, the alternatives have weaknesses. For example, patronage systems allow powerful clients to define their own needs and the services they require, but offer insufficient curbs on improper behaviour by the patron's lawyers. Additionally, patronage control does nothing to provide legal assistance to the less powerful. Of the other alternatives, communal control, whereby consumer organisations control occupations or state mediation, would be inflexible. Such systems would suppress initiative and occupational responsibility, encouraging legal occupations to act in their own economic interest.[78]

Authority

Authority is the culturally legitimised organisation of power,[79] including the ability to influence policy, for example, in law reform work.[80] Indeed, the authority of organisations can be measured by their ability to shape social institutions and public policy. Halliday argues that the degree of legitimacy of the professional view depends on the conjunction of its authority in relation to particular type of issues and the sphere of influence in which it is operating. The legal professions have considerable legitimacy in their areas of technical expertise—the conduct of litigation—and in their primary institutional sphere—the operation of the legal system. Even so, moral authority is contingent, so that attempts to influence public policy to the profession's advantage may undermine legitimacy.[81] Further, the fact that the legal profession's knowledge base is primarily normative, like the clerics, rather than scientific, like the natural and biological sciences,[82] means that legal technical opinion is more easily contested by other disciplines. The growth of disciplines such as sociology since the heyday of direct legislative influence in the nineteenth century may have undermined the legal profession's authority, but the Law Society claims recent successes in influencing government policy, for example, on mental health[83] and fraud trials.[84]

In addition to degrees of expert and moral authority and spheres of primary influence, professions also have spheres of secondary influence, where the weakness of its disciplinary

---

[77] D Rueschemeyer, 'Doctors and Lawyers: A Comment on the Theory of the Professions' (1964–5) *Canadian Review of Sociology and Anthropology* 17.

[78] Above n 49, 46, 65 and 86.

[79] RK Merton, *Social Theory and Social Structure* (New York, The Free Press, 1957).

[80] R Cranston, 'Legal Ethics and Professional Responsibility' in R Cranston (ed), *Legal Ethics and Professional Responsibility* (Oxford, Clarendon Press, 1995) 1.

[81] Obviously, a profession is more likely to be heeded when its position on an issue is not self-interested. Koehn cites the example of the campaign waged by dentists for the fluoridisation of water, even though this would decrease their work. D Koehn, *The Ground of Professional Ethics* (London, Routledge, 1994) 178.

[82] TC Halliday, *Beyond Monopoly: Lawyers, State Crises, and Professional Empowerment* (University of Chicago Press, 1987) 32.

[83] Law Society press release, 'Huge Success in Long-running Law Society Campaign', 23 March 2006.

[84] Law Society press release, 'Government Climb Down over Abolishing Juries in Fraud Trials', 14 March 2006.

base becomes strength. Normative issues, moral and ethical questions, are relevant to public policy and to everyday issues of practice. The normative professions therefore have 'a broad mandate to range extensively over moral terrain',[85] and a legitimate view on social issues beyond their narrow area of technical competence. Lawyers colonise secondary institutional spheres like politics, where they have always been disproportionately represented, although their technical expertise and moral authority is more marginal.[86]

Ethics

Professional ethics is a key part of the regulative bargain. It is also a vital component of professional knowledge, the guiding hand behind its use and the precondition for the trust underpinning professional authority. The common lawyer's ethical commitment is inextricably bound up with commitment to the adversarial system, as the best guarantee of the rule of law, and to the ethical emphasis on partisanship and neutrality. This professional ideology has deep roots,[87] but was evident relatively recently in the Marre Committee's[88] assertion that:

> the rights which can give rise to the strongest feelings usually concern a principle or cause, or involve a real or perceived oppression or abuse of power, either by the state or by a person or corporation which is more powerful and influential than the injured citizen. It is in these circumstances that the public needs an independent lawyer to ensure that justice is achieved . . .[89] [and] The public interest which requires that citizens are free to have access to, and protection for, their legal rights may transcend the interests even of government where those rights conflict with the wishes and interests of government.[90]

Abbott, Abel and others see ethics as so inextricably linked to professional jurisdiction that the failure of market control will cause the inevitable decline of professionalism and a retreat from ethical commitments.[91]

The crisis of legal professionalism

The future of professionalism in England and Wales is uncertain. In the middle of the twentieth century, two of the three great medieval prototypes, the clerical and medical professions, suffered relative decline, leaving the lawyers alone in securing the expansion of their empire. The idiosyncratic circumstances of the other two, secularisation and the creation of the National Health Service respectively, left open the question of whether the age

---

85 Halliday, above n 82, 36.

86 *Ibid*, 41–7.

87 In the 1880s the Law Society advanced solicitors as a counterweight to state authoritarianism, 'officialism', the growth of the bureaucratic machinery of the modern state and 'state socialism'. Sugarman, above n 31, 111.

88 The Committee was established by the Bar and Law Society to review the needs of the public for legal services, where changes in structure practice and education might be in the public interest, to make recommendations to the professional bodies on such changes.

89 Lady Marre CBE, *A Time for Change: Report of the Committee on the Future of the Legal Profession* (London, General Council of the Bar and Council of the Law Society, 1988) para 6.8 (the Marre Report).

90 *Ibid*, para 6.7.

91 See generally Johnson, above n 49.

of professionalism was dead. Towards the end of the twentieth century, conditions became inhospitable to the legal profession. Following the Second World War there was a massive expansion in the demand for legal services, attributable to changing patterns of ownership (including personal ownership of real property or national ownership of industry), the increased regulation of social life and the development of technology.[92] The growth in the personal resources of the employed and the advent of legal aid brought the services of lawyers within the scope of more people.[93] Between the 1960s and 1980s the solicitors' branch tripled in size,[94] fuelled by a higher education boom and the wide availability of legal aid.[95] In the 1980s, the search for increased international competitiveness, a more commercially orien-tated society and a growing rights culture turned attention on the cost of legal services. Lawyers' fees were a drain on economic prosperity and social development, a fact brought home to the government by the soaring cost of legal aid to the Exchequer. Most analyses suggest that the growth of the legal profession sowed the seeds of declining market control, but they were undoubtedly nurtured by the high cost of legal services and the detrimental affect this had on access to justice in the growing rights culture.

A number of groups—academics, consumers and the government—combined to reduce confidence in the legal profession's public jurisdiction and particularly its ethical claims. Since the 1960s there has been increasingly close academic attention to the legal profession and, latterly, its ethics. This scrutiny found a professional ideology that had become inward looking and outdated. Legal professional ethics were based on adversarial litigation, and particularly on criminal practice. They ignored the reality that both branches of the legal profession conduct a large amount of non-contentious work,[96] and that the largest and most powerful solicitors firms were not built on litigation at all but on company and commercial work. Another ethical totem which received thorough critique was the attitude to clients revealed in the English code. This reflected a paternalistic attitude to clients, with the commitment to neutrality and partisanship either unclear or incoherent. While the dogged defence of unsympathetic but wealthy clients was undoubted, there was alleged neglect of adversarial values in Magistrates' Court proceedings.[97] The period was also

---

[92] Ramsay identifies a range of factors which influence demand: increasing the need to regulate the relations of individuals and corporations; the organisation of legal business, eg by creating or reinforcing monopolies; inter-nationalisation of legal work, bringing together geographically remote parties; population diversity, requiring normative ordering, changing demographics, wealth levels, levels of complexity in life; increasing bureaucratisation of society and growth in the range and use of administrative remedies; changes in production of goods and services; transactions affecting the allocation of resources; andcomplexity in business transactions and financial innovation, changing technologies. IM Ramsay, 'What Do Lawyers Do? Reflections on the Market for Lawyers' (1993) 21 *International Journal of the Sociology of Law* 355; see also Abel, above n 58, 20.

[93] Funding work which arises particularly from increases in the levels of crime, family breakdown and debt. Marre Report, above n 89, paras 3.14–3.31.

[94] Between 1961 and 1986 the numbers of lawyers in England and Wales increased by 147%. In the US and Canada the number of lawyers increased by 129 and 253%, respectively. M Galanter, 'Law Abounding: Legalisation Around the North Atlantic' (1992) 55 *The Modern Law Review* 1, 4.

[95] C Glasser, 'The Legal Profession in the 1990's: Images of Change' (1990) 10 *Legal Studies* 1.

[96] Until the 1980s domestic conveyancing was the bedrock work of most solicitors' firms.

[97] M McConville, J Hodgson, L Bridges and A Pavlovic, *Standing Accused: The Organisation and Practices of Criminal Defence Lawyers in Britain* (Oxford, Clarendon Press, 1994). The Australian judge, Mr Justice Kirby, noted that miscarriages of justice arise 'from the way in which operators of the present system at every level allow it to be manipulated, pre-trial, trial and on appeal, with too much attention to rules and procedures and insufficient concern about the risk of injustice'. M Kirby, 'Miscarriages of Justice: Our Lamentable Failure?', public lecture delivered on 4 June 1991 at the Inns of Court School of Law, London, 6.

marked by a shift in judicial attitudes to the link between professional privileges and ethics. In 1967 the House of Lords held that abolishing advocates' immunity from actions in negligence would discourage barristers from taking awkward clients and was therefore a threat to the cab-rank rule.[98] In 2003, in *Hall v Simons*, the court roundly rejected this argument and abolished the immunity.[99]

Public awareness and attitudes to professions became more critical. Increased claims consciousness[100] led consumers to challenge the necessity for professional interventions and their cost and effectiveness.[101] A survey of consumer attitudes in the UK suggested that people saw the legal system as 'out of date, slow, too complicated and easy to twist'.[102] Only a quarter of respondents believed that the legal system was something to be proud of. Middle income groups, ineligible for legal aid but not rich enough to fund litigation, were the most likely to be dissatisfied with the legal help available to them. Although many lawyers were not rich,[103] high levels of consumer demand for change in the delivery of legal services coalesced with a general loss of confidence in professions.[104] The situation was ineptly dealt with by the profession itself.[105] The National Consumer Council,[106] consistent critics of the legal profession,[107] argued for a consumer voice in professional regulation[108] and for the expansion of the advice sector through legal aid funding.[109] These factors strengthened the government's resolve to undermine the professional monopoly[110]—a

---

[98] Lord Pearce claimed in *Rondel v Worsley* [1969] 1 AC 191, 275: 'it would be tragic if our legal system came to provide no reputable defenders, representatives or advisers for [those who are unpleasant, unreasonable, disreputable and have an apparently hopeless case]; and that would be the inevitable result of allowing barristers to pick and choose their clients. It not infrequently happens that the unpleasant, the unreasonable, the disreputable and those who have apparently hopeless cases turn out after a full and fair hearing to be in the right'.

[99] Lord Hutton in *Arthur JS Hall & Co (a firm) v Simons, Barratt v Ansell and others (trading as Woolf Seddon (a firm), Harris v Scholfield Roberts & Hill (a firm) and another* [2000] 3 All ER 673, 729.

[100] WF Felstiner, RL Abel and A Sarat, 'The Emergence and Transformation of Disputes: Naming, Blaming, Claiming . . .' (1980–1) 15 *Law and Society* 631.

[101] The Marre Report, above n 89, para 3.52, observed that 'More members of the public are now inclined to complain about poor quality or costly services . . . are no longer deferential to those who provide professional services and will no longer tolerate secretiveness . . . consumers are less willing to accept uncritically the authority which used to be attached to professional people'.

[102] National Consumer Council, *Seeking Civil Justice* (London, NCC, 1995) 8.

[103] In 1972 the median income of the 4000-strong Bar was £2,300 a year and 30% earned less than £1,000. Cruikshank, above n 55.

[104] Civil servants used research by legal academics, media and consumer groups undermined its claim to act in the public interest. Burrage, above n 46, 68.

[105] Burrage, above n 46, 69, suggests that the Law Society's inept handling of accusations of chronic overcharging by one of its own leading members (The Glanville Davies affair) helped to create the climate for the political onslaught in the 1980s.

[106] The NCC assesses goods and services against criteria such as access, choice, information, quality and value for money, safety and representation. See C Ervine, *Settling Consumer Disputes: A Review of Alternative Dispute Resolution* (London, NCC, 1993).

[107] See, eg the following NCC publications: *Making Good Solicitors: The Place of Communication Skills in their Training* (London, NCC, 1989); *Professional Competence in Legal Services: What is it and How do you Measure it?* (London, NCC, 1990); *Eligibility for Civil Legal Aid: Response to the Lord Chancellor's Department* (London, NCC, 1991); *Out of Court: A Consumer View of Three Low-Cost Arbitration Schemes* (London, NCC, 1991); *Court Without Advice: Duty Court-Based Advice and Representation Schemes* (London, NCC, 1992) *Seeking Civil Justice: A Survey of People's Needs and Experiences* (London, NCC, 1995).

[108] NCC, *Ordinary Justice* (London, HMSO, 1989) 3.

[109] NCC, *Civil Justice and Legal Aid* (London, NCC, 1995).

[110] The exercise of consumer power has not been limited to the UK legal profession. Galanter, above n 94, 3, suggests that the populations in the UK, US and Canada have, since the 1960s, became more educated and enjoyed

resolve underpinned by a counter-ideology and a faith in markets. National Consumer Council surveys showed public confidence in solicitors at 'rock bottom'.[111] It welcomed the Legal Services Bill, demanding that the proposals for independent complaint handling not be watered down.

Market control

The profession's loss of control over the market for legal services began with the prosaic issue of the solicitors' conveyancing monopoly. The sinecure offered solicitors by an archaic system of land transfer continued despite the 1925 property legislation.[112] By 1968, 55.6% of solicitors' income, but only 40.8% of expenses, came from conveyancing, leading to investigations by competition authorities in 1966, 1970 and 1974. The abolition of conveyancing scale fees in 1973 combined with a property slump to produce strong competition. Consumer pressure rose with the growth of owner occupation,[113] fuelled by the Thatcher government's policy of selling council houses.[114] In 1983 legislation allowed competition for conveyancing and stimulated unprecedented competition and price cuts far greater than necessary.[115] This success greatly encouraged the Thatcher government, but further progress against the legal monopoly was halted in its early years by Lord Hailsham, the Lord Chancellor, who was sympathetic to professions and their 'arcane ethics', and believed the independence of the judiciary was a more valuable prize than laissez faire.[116] Hailsham's departure began a period in which successive governments, both Tory and Labour, began an assault on the lawyers' legal jurisdiction over work.

Abel's account of the assault on the legal professions' jurisdiction over the market for legal services focuses on the resources that the various actors brought to the struggle, and in particular their rhetorical resources.[117] Under the banner of competition, the government demanded that the profession justify restrictions on competition in the public interest.[118] A committee was established by the branches of the profession in 1987, under Lady Marre, to consider the issue of rights of audience in higher courts. The committee was the last chance

---

higher incomes. The economies of these countries greatly expanded, becoming more service driven and more internationalised.

[111] 'Legal Profession Set to Improve' [July 2006] *Which* 71.

[112] The Solicitors' Remuneration Act 1881 caused unrealistically high conveyancing fees, leading to the Law of Property Act 1925 and a simpler system. This was supported by the Law Society, which secured concessions ensuring that there was still fees to be made from land transfer. Cruikshank, above n 28.

[113] Glasser, above n 95.

[114] Owner-occupied dwellings increased from around 7 million in 1961 to over 14 million in 1986. Marre Report, above n 89, paras 3.16–3.17.

[115] With licensed conveyancers (Administration of Justice Act 1986) and banks and building societies (Building Societies Act 1986). Between 1983 and 1986, however, solicitors reduced their conveyancing fees by an average of 30%. S Domberger and A Sherr, 'Competition in Conveyancing: An Analysis of Solicitors' Charges' (1987) 8(3) *Fiscal Studies* 17; A Sherr, 'Coming of Age' (1994) 1 *International Journal of the Legal Profession* 3. Conveyancing provided less than 30% of solicitors' gross income. Despite this, most high street firms still derive more than half of their income from that source. C Glasser, 'The Legal Profession in the 1990's: Images of Change' (1990) 10 *Legal Studies* 1.

[116] R Abel, *English Lawyers between Market and State: The Politics of Professionalism* (Oxford, Oxford University Press, 2003), 14.

[117] See generally *ibid*, 14.

[118] General Council of the Bar, *The Quality of Justice: The Bar's Response* (London, Buttwerworths, 1999).

for the profession to agree a resolution that might satisfy government, but it failed to do so. The report argued:

> it is not possible, when considering the legal profession and the need for change, to be guided solely by considerations of price, cost and convenience. Considerations which may be appropriate to the sale of goods, or to the supply of other services, are not always relevant to the supply of legal services . . . the raison d'être of an independent legal profession is, and should remain, its ability to fulfil [its duties as traditionally conceived] and any change which would derogate from those duties should not be encouraged.[119]

The Courts and Legal Services Act 1990 swiftly followed, allowing bodies other than the Bar to seek the right to accredit their members in the exercise of advocacy rights, and bodies other than the Law Society to accredit members to conduct litigation. Solicitors lost the exclusive right to brief barristers when other professions were granted 'direct professional access',[120] but the Bar resisted seeking permission to conduct litigation alone.

Advice agencies were allowed to claim legal aid for clients and to compete with solicitors for legal aid franchises. In 1987 the administration of the Legal Aid Scheme was transferred from the Law Society to the Legal Aid Board.[121] It is worth looking at franchising in particular. The 1995 Green Paper and the 1996 White Paper proposed a system whereby solicitors and advice agencies would bid for, and be contracted to conduct, a fixed number of cases at set prices.[122] In the contracting process, price would not be the only consideration; the quality offered would also be significant.[123] The quality of providers was to be measured by a range of indicators, such as the result of the case, the length of time taken, client satisfaction and the accuracy of predictions of success.[124] Such mechanisms are likely to be powerful determinants of lawyer behaviour, perhaps even more influential than professional regulation.[125] By January 2006, however, the Law Society was driven to issue press statements citing examples of the risks run by those instructing unregulated advisors, like will writers and claims farmers.[126]

Access to justice

Access to justice is an aspect of market control, since a surplus of lawyers should make legal services cheaper, at the cost of their power and prestige. During the twentieth century

---

[119] Marre Report, above n 89, para 6.9.

[120] Eg patent agents, parliamentary agents, local authority-employed lawyers.

[121] In 1987 the Legal Aid Board (Since 2000 the Legal Services Commission) assumed responsibility from the Law Society of the legal aid scheme.

[122] *Legal Aid: Targeting Need,* Cmnd 2854 (London, HMSO, 1995); see also E Gilvarry, 'Mackay Taken by Fundholding', *Law Society Gazette* 7 September 1994, 3; and *Solicitors Journal,* '550 firms Offered Franchises', *Solicitors Journal* 29 July 1994, 755.

[123] T Goriely, 'Debating the Quality of Legal Services: Differing Models of the Good Lawyer' (1994) 1 *International Journal of the Legal Profession* 159.

[124] By 1995 over 100 offices were approved for welfare work. T Goriely, 'Law for the Poor: The Relationship Between Advice Agencies and Solicitors in the Development of Poverty Law' (1996) 3 *International Journal of the Legal Profession* 215, 240.

[125] P Abrams, A Boon and D O' Brien, 'Access to Justice: The Collision of Funding and Ethics' (1998) 3 *Contemporary Issues in Law* 59.

[126] Law Society press release, 'The Risk of Unregulated Advisors', 19 January 2006.

demand forced up numbers, a situation the legal profession was ambivalent about. It accepted jurisdiction over low status work to fend off competition.[127] The Law Society was convinced when the Lord Chancellor considered giving waivers to solicitors to work in advice agencies following the Legal Aid and Advice Act 1972.[128] In the late 1980s the decline in residential conveyancing forced solicitors into legal aid work,[129] particularly the newly introduced Magistrates' Courts duty solicitor scheme.[130] The government was forced to cut eligibility rates for civil legal aid to prevent the legal aid budget spiralling out of control. This threatened the post-war promise of access to justice, a necessary precondition of the rule of law,[131] and intensified the government's campaign to curb the lawyers' power. The government's position was that the public interest demanded justice, expeditiously and at the lowest practical cost.[132] The profession's response was to propose that, when justice is in question, there is little compromise with cost. The government encouraged reduced reliance on the private legal profession,[133] employing criminal prosecution and defence lawyers direct, setting up the Community Legal Service and encouraging competition with the established profession.[134]

The perception that the cost of bringing ordinary cases to court was too high led to sustained tinkering with rules of court to reduce unpredictability and risk. The process culminated in the more substantial changes proposed in the Woolf Report 1998, which reduced lawyer control over litigation by introducing pre action protocols, increased judicial control and incentives to settlement.[135] Woolf also shared the government's enthusiasm for alternative methods of dispute resolution, like mediation, which offered claims processing without the cost of ordinary court proceedings. At the same time the government introduced conditional fee arrangements, popularly known as 'no win, no fee', to replace legal aid in a wide range of cases. It also aimed to reduce costs by reforms of legal aid that allowed advice agencies to compete for franchises with solicitors. Franchise arrangements ensured, sometimes overzealously,[136] that legal aid cases were handled within a tight costs framework.

The escalating cost of criminal legal aid in particular, possibly caused by government changes to the system,[137] led to a review by Lord Carter of Coles. Under his proposals,

---

[127] Goriely identifies a four stage process by which the legal profession accepts low status work: denial of the need for legal services in the particular area; second, having accepted a need, devising a plan but doing nothing about it; the advice sector develops the area of work and involves local solicitors; the profession defends the market that has been established. Goriely, above n 124, 216.

[128] Cruikshank, above n 55.

[129] M Hope, *Expenditure on Legal Services* (London, Lord Chancellor's Department, 1997) 7.

[130] Cruikshank, above n 55.

[131] AV Dicey, *An Introduction to the Study of the Law of the Constitution* (London, MacMillan, 10th edn, 1959); *R v Sec of State for Home Department ex p. Pierson* [1998] AC 539.

[132] TD Morgan, 'The Evolving Concept of Professional Responsibility' (1977) 90 *Harvard Law Review* 702.

[133] A common way by which states expand access to professional services. Johnson, above n 49, 79.

[134] On announcing new rights of audience for legal executives under the CLSA, Lord Irvine welcomed the Institute of Legal Executives as a 'fully-fledged part of the profession'. AM Francis, 'Legal Executives and the Phantom of Legal Professionalism: the Rise and Rise of the Third Branch of the Profession?' (2002) 9 *International Journal of the Legal Profession* 5.

[135] See chapter 17.

[136] P Rohan, 'High Court Rules LSC Legal Aid Embargo was Unlawful', *Gazette* 98/31, 9 August 2001, 5.

[137] E Cape and R Moorhead, 'Demand Induced Supply? Identifying Cost Drivers in Criminal Defence Work' (2005), available at www.lsrc.org.uk/publications.htm (last accessed 26 March 2008).

franchisees were forced to accept fixed and graduated legal aid fees in replacement of hourly rates or they would cease to be eligible to perform legal aid work.[138] The Constitutional Affairs Select committee expressed severe reservations about the scope and pace of the reforms, and the threat to the quality of complex work and to the supplier base generally,[139] concerns dismissed by the government.[140] Over 90% accepted the unified contract, with the Legal Services Commission implementing the changes, but a spokesman for one of London's leading legal aid firms said:

> This is an abusive contract with a future of slavery and gradual strangulation and decline. So far as I am concerned we're out of it.[141]

The Court of Appeal subsequently restricted the LSC's power to unilaterally amend the contract,[142] but this was a relatively minor impediment to the reforms.

Self-regulation

Successive governments' willingness to interfere with the legal profession was not limited to issues of jurisdiction, but extended to regulatory matters generally. Prior to the Courts and Legal Services Act 1990, procedures, statutory rules and regulations governing solicitors were drafted by Law Society committees and approved by Council prior to approval by the Master of the Rolls under section 31 of the Solicitors Act 1974. Rules and regulations relating to incorporated practices were approved under procedures set out in section 9 of the Administration of Justice Act 1985, prior to their submission to the Master of the Rolls for approval under the 1974 Act. Most of the practice rules at that time were based on common law case outcomes and were amended by the Law Society Council to conform to case law.[143] There was no requirement to involve other senior judges, the Office of Fair Trading (OFT) or the Lord Chancellor in the regulatory process. After the Act, proposed rule changes were scrutinised by the Lord Chancellor's Advisory Committee for Education and Conduct (ACLEC),[144] which had

> the general duty of assisting in the maintenance and development of standards in the education, training and conduct of those offering legal services[145]

and then approved by the Lord Chancellor. The Law Society's response to the Green Papers proposing these changes objected that

---

[138] Lord Carter of Coles, *Legal: Aid: A market-based approach to reform* (London, Lord Chancellor's Department, 2006).

[139] R Miller, 'The Rush to Reform' (2007) 157 *New Law Journal* 645, M Zander, 'Carter's Wake' (2007) 157 *New Law Journal* 872.

[140] *Implementing Legal Aid reform: Government Response to the Constitutional Affairs Select Committee Report*, Cm 7158 (Norwich, HMSO, 2007).

[141] C Dyer, 'Poor Likely to Suffer in Fees Dispute as Some Legal Aid Firms Hold Out', *The Guardian*, 2 April 2007.

[142] *Law Society v Legal Services Commission* [2007] EWCA Civ 1264.

[143] We are grateful to the Law Society for the information.

[144] See s 19(1) of the Courts and Legal Servises Act 1990 and, for the composition of the committee, see s 19(2) and (3).

[145] *Ibid*, s 20(1). However, note that the Legal Services Act also preserves areas of independence. For example, the Legal Services Ombudsman established by s 21 does not have powers to investigate matters 'which is being or has been determined by . . . (ii) the Solicitors' Disciplinary Tribunal; (iii) the Disciplinary Tribunal of the Council of the Inns of Court'.

the proposals represent a dangerous accumulation of power in the hands of a government minister . . . the government should not take control over the very profession that has a duty to act for the citizen against government power and state prosecution.[146]

In fact, ACLEC was soon abandoned amid the government's apparent disillusion with the pace of progress, but the Lord Chancellor's powers remained.

Further interference with professional structures was threatened by the Competition Act 1998, chapter 1 of which prohibits

agreements between undertakings, decisions by associations of undertakings or concerted practices which may affect trade within the United Kingdom or have as their object or effect the prevention, restriction or distortion of competition.

The providers of legal services are 'undertakings', their professional associations are 'associations of undertakings' and their codes of conduct are 'decisions by an association of undertakings'. The profession, having not sought exemption from the chapter 1 prohibition in relation to any of their rules, was caught. In 2000 the OFT launched a long-promised review of competition in professions and in a consultation paper considered the professions of law, accountancy and architecture.[147] The report, *Competition in Professions*, identified rules, practices and customs with anti-competitive effects and put the onus of proof on their proponents to 'demonstrate strong justifications for them in terms of consumer benefit'.[148]

The professions concerned were invited to make changes in the identified areas within a reasonable time, or within a year, in default of which the OFT threatened to use its own powers to remove the restrictions.[149] The Law Society was told to remove restrictions on multidisciplinary practice,[150] employed solicitors acting for third parties,[151] seeking business by telephone and comparative fee advertising[152] and receiving payment for referrals,[153] and to stop issuing fee guidance for conducting probate work. The General Council of the Bar were told to remove restrictions on barristers forming partnerships, barristers having direct access to clients, comparative advertising[154] and employed barristers conducting litigation. The report also made passing comment about a number of other arrangements. It suggested that the separate roles of solicitors and barristers may add unnecessarily to costs,[155] that the QC system was of dubious value to consumers,[156] that there should be an extension of professional privilege to accountants providing tax advice[157] and that particular auditing requirements may stand in the way of multidisciplinary practice.[158] These matters are not subject to any professional rules and are not included in any timetable for change.

---

[146] The Law Society, *Striking the Balance: The Final Response of the Council of the Law Society on the Green Papers* (London, The Law Society, 1989) para 1.4.

[147] The review was conducted under the Fair Trading Act 1973, s 2.

[148] Director General of Fair Trading, *Competition in Professions*, OFT328 (2001) paras 3 and 11.

[149] Para 50.

[150] Specifically in Solicitors' Practice Rules 4 and 7.

[151] Employed Solicitors' Code 1990 and Solicitors' Practice Rule 4.

[152] Solicitors' Publicity Code.

[153] Solicitors' Practice Rule 3.

[154] Including fees, success rates and comparisons with other barristers.

[155] Para 49.

[156] Para 46.

[157] Para 47.

[158] Para 48.

The Bar's response to the OFT proposals was contained in a committee report which accepted that barristers, subject to safeguards, should be allowed to accept instructions direct from clients and to advertise fee comparisons.[159] However, it rejected the proposals that barristers should be able to advertise success rates, enter partnership or conduct litigation. The report also asserted that the QC system was of value to consumers, and would provide useful information of quality if direct access were permitted. It suggested that there was no justification for expanding legal professional privilege to non-lawyers. The OFT admitted that there was force in the Bar's arguments against advertising success rates[160] and announced that it did not intend to pursue the point.[161] It was not convinced, however, that a split profession was in the public interest, or that abandoning it would create regulatory difficulties. It rejected the Bar's arguments against allowing barristers to conduct litigation and promised further detailed consideration of the Bar's arguments against partnership.[162] The OFT did not accept that handling clients' money would impinge on barristers' capacity to specialise in, and maintain excellence at, advocacy,[163] or that partnership would limit choice, increase overheads and undermine the cab-rank rule. The Law Society successfully argued against the cold-calling of non-business clients,[164] but otherwise set about amending or reviewing the offending rules. The OFT was inclined to allow it to continue its 'programme of reform . . . so long as self-deregulation is proceeding effectively, public action is not immediately necessary'.[165]

Government attacks on the legal profession's monopolies and practices were frequently accompanied by attacks on lawyers' conduct and ethics. This usually involved impugning their public service, for example by highlighting the extreme wealth and salaries of the big firms, barristers' claims against the legal aid fund or the profession's lack of *pro bono* work. The most serious failing, however, was delay in dealing with the backlog of complaints against solicitors, which attracted government attention. In 2003 the Department of Constitutional Affairs published a report that concluded that the regulatory framework for legal services was 'outdated, inflexible, over-complex and insufficiently accountable or transparent'.[166] Sir David Clementi, who was then asked to undertake a review of the regulatory framework for legal services, added to this list that they were 'inconsistent'.[167]

Clementi's consultation paper, issued in March 2004, floated the idea that the regulatory functions of the professional bodies, entry standards, rule making, monitoring and enforcement, complaints and discipline should be placed with a single regulator, leaving

---

[159] Sir S Kentridge (Chair), *Competition in Professions* (General Council of the Bar, January 2002).

[160] Kentridge had argued that advertising success would provide a disincentive to accepting difficult cases, that winning cases did not correlate with 'success' and that such rates might therefore be misleading (Kentridge Committee Report, para 5.3).

[161] OFT, *Competition in Professions: Progress Statement*, OFT 385 (April 2002) para 3.24.

[162] M Gerrard, 'Lifting the Bar to Progress', *Gazette* 99/36, 19 September 2002, 26.

[163] OFT 385, paras 3.25–3.31.

[164] OFT 385, para 3.15.

[165] Para 3.18.

[166] Department for Constitutional Affairs, *Competition and Regulation in the Legal Services Market* (2003) para 70.

[167] 'Review of the Regulatory Framework for Legal Services in England and Wales: A Consultation Paper 2004. See also the description of the 'regulatory maze' by R Baldwin, K Malleson, M Cave and S Spicer *Scoping Study for the Regulatory Review of Legal Services* (2003), 16.

them with only representative functions on behalf of their members. The government accepted the recommendations of the Clementi Report that proposed a compromise separation of functions and the increase in lay representation on the profession's regulatory committees. It also accepted the idea that oversight of all regulatory functions should be given to a Legal Services Board, a proposal contained in the Legal Services Bill of 2006. The Law Society broadly welcomed the changes, which were much less stringent that predicted at the start of the process.[168] It warned, however, that the government must not be allowed to make its own appointments to positions of power over the profession or change regulatory objectives through secondary legislation.[169]

De-mystification of legal knowledge and craft

The final factor in the crisis of legal professionalism concerns legal knowledge. Law's lack of a scientific base makes it particularly vulnerable to deconstruction. Medical science assists the physician in diagnosis and prediction, whereas at the heart of legal work is the exercise of discretion, 'how it is invoked, confined, and yet ever elastic'.[170] In the US the legal realists theorised a gap between the law in books and the law in action, suggesting that practical legal analysis inevitably involves extralegal decisions and actions.[171] Socio-legal scholarship produced evidence to prove this proposition, showing that lawyers could be an impediment to just outcomes. Professional judgement itself was seen as more technical and routine, and achievable without the intervention of professions. Even advocacy, the ineffable skill, declared by earlier generations of barristers to be innate or achieved only through experience, underwent demystification. There was compelling research data showing that expertise rather than legal education is the key to success,[172] solicitors declaring there to be 'no magic to advocacy'[173] and litigants advised to bring their own cases.[174] New methodologies of peer review claimed to be able to accurately assess legal competence, and to control the flow of work to legal aid providers accordingly.[175] The need for legal professionalism, which hinged on the indeterminacy of the tasks performed, was inevitably weakened.[176] The information revolution, and particularly the internet, threatens to reduce the need for expert advice,[177] raising questions about the need for lawyers, or at least lawyers provided on a professional model.

---

[168] Law Society press release, 'Clementi Review Let Loose', 1 August 2003; Law Society press release, 'Balancing Act', 21 November 2003.

[169] Law Society press release, 'Legal Profession must be Truly Independent', 23 January 2006.

[170] SS Silbey, '"Let Them Eat Cake": Globalisation, Postmodern Colonialism, and the Possibilities of Justice' (1997) *Law and Society Review* 207, 231.

[171] *Ibid.*

[172] HM Kritzer, *Legal Advocacy: Lawyers and Nonlawyers at Work* (Ann Arbor, MI, University of Michigan Press, 1998).

[173] J Edwards, 'Revolution: Solicitors March on Bar's Territory' [March 1995] *Legal Business* 46.

[174] M Randle, 'The DIY Defence', *The Guardian*, 26 September 1995.

[175] A Sherr and S Thomson, 'Professional Competence: Some Work in Progress' (2006) 49 *Socio-Legal Newsletter* 8.

[176] Johnson, above n 49, 47; Abel, above n 58, 10.

[177] R Susskind, *The Future of Law: Facing the Challenges of Information Technology* (Oxford, Clarendon Press, 1998).

Post-professionalism?

There has much speculation on the future of the legal profession. De-professionalisation of large areas of work, and the exclusion of those working in these areas from professional groupings, is certainly possible. It is not the path that the legal profession has shown signs of taking, but there has been increasingly despairing talk of a possible move to trade unionism and strike action by groups affected by low rates of legal aid.[178] Yet recent commentators stress the resilience of professionalism.[179] Even the most basic attack, such as limiting the ability to achieve social closure of the market, can be overcome, in the short term, by internal closure within firms themselves.[180] By stratification within the legal services market and by organisational closure, professional elites may preserve their position at the expense of junior members and at the expense of collegiality. While such strategies may preserve the power of elites, the legitimacy and influence of professions will suffer, making it easier to undermine professionalism. The most profitable path for legal profession is, arguably, an ethical line that justifies professional organisation.

It is ironic that the state's deconstruction of the legal profession should coincide with a revival of interest in the social benefit of professionalism. Neo-functionalists now attempt to fill the void in their predecessors' argument, suggesting ways that professions function for the benefit of civil society. Sciulli argues that, in addition to fiduciary responsibility to advance client well-being and, by extension, the well-being of identifiable local communities, they bear a further structural responsibility for institutional design that is inherent in the governance, regulation and activities of any structured situation in civil society.[181] Fidelity to these two fiduciary duties makes it necessary to establish and maintain ongoing deliberation, to

> ceaselessly scan their environments for any changes in their knowledge base or in client needs that bear on the positional interests of anyone in their entrenched position of power.[182]

Collegial organization is evidence of this ongoing process, which is quite distinct from the processes of other expert organisations. Finally, they provide their services consistently with prevailing standards of truth and with an orientation of disinterest, opposing positional power, including their own power over clients. Therefore, Sciulli argues, the collegial form and ongoing deliberation not only affect the direction of social change, they are the essence of professions.

---

[178] C Dyer, 'Lawyers Threaten Strike over Low Pay', *The Guardian*, 6 June 2005.

[179] H Kritzer, 'The Professions are Dead, Long Live the Professions: Legal Practice in a Postprofessional World' (1999) 33 *Law and Society Review* 713; E Freidson, *Professionalism: The Third Logic* (Chicago, IL, University of Chicago Press, 2001); A Boon, J Flood and J Webb, 'Postmodern Professions? The Fragmentation of Legal Education and the Legal Profession'(2005) 32 *Journal of Law and Society* 473.

[180] D Muzio and S Ackroyd, 'On the Consequences of Defensive Professionalism: Recent Changes in the Legal Labour Process' (2005) 32 *Journal of Law and Society* 615.

[181] D Sciulli, 'Continental Sociology of Professions Today: Conceptual Contributions' (2005) 53 *Current Sociology* 915.

[182] *Ibid*, 936.

Conclusion

In recent years the state has challenged the assumption that professionalism is the best way to control services important to society, demanding that the legal profession justifies its traditional ways of working. Despite the incremental loss of the trappings of professional power, monopoly and self-regulation, jurisdiction over work in the workplace, the key to professional power, remains. The aggressive international performance of English firms is something the government does not want to lose. Such considerations may bring the state into a new compromise with the legal profession, although continued sponsorship of professional power undoubtedly depends on the profession's guarantee of ethical behaviour in a new social role. Independence may be the new warrant of professionalism, meaning that lawyers will be required to balance more effectively client demands and the social harm involved in fulfilling them. Far from being redundant, ethics could hold the key to the future of legal professionalism.

4

CULTURE

... ideology is both interested and distorted, but also practical and lived.[1]

Introduction

Sociologists regard culture as the way of life of a society[2] whereby language conveys ideas, attitudes and values through socialisation, the process of social shaping that occurs through families and other institutions. Culture is also represented by artefacts, places of work, recreation and worship, symbols and institutions[3] revered as manifestations of common cultural identity and passed from generation to generation. In complex societies, groups may also be said to have distinctive cultures. Professions are archetypes of such groups,[4] and the legal profession of England and Wales is unique in the richness of its traditions, the original purpose of which are sometimes obscure.[5] As the legal profession comes under increasing pressure to conform to a business model of operation, and as memberships diverge in terms of wealth and standing, can professional culture bind lawyers together as a community, providing status for individuals and organisations?[6] If so, professional ethics, the formal representation of a common culture, must provide the normative glue.

Legal and professional culture

If there is a distinctive legal professional culture it is part of a wider legal culture. The idea that there is a distinctive legal culture is, however, controversial.[7] Friedman described legal culture as having an external dimension, popular attitudes towards law and legal institutions,

---

[1] J Laws (ed), *Power, Action and Belief: A New Sociology of Knowledge?* (London, Routledge & Kegan Paul, 1986) 4.

[2] A Giddens, *Sociology* (Cambridge, Polity Press, 3rd edn, 1997) 18.

[3] H Becker, *Doing Things Together: Selected Papers* (Evanston, Northwestern University Press, 1986); C Geertz, 'Thick Description: Toward and Interpretative Theory of Culture' in C Geertz (ed), *The Interpretation of Cultures* (New York, Basic Books, 1973). Culture can therefore be seen as 'conventional understandings made manifest as act and artefact': R Redfield, *The Folk Culture of Yucatan* (University of Chicago Press, 1941) 132.

[4] E Greenwood, 'Attributes of a Profession' [July 1957] *Social Work* 45, 52.

[5] TJ Johnson, *Professional Power* (London and Basingstoke, Macmillan, 1972) 47. An analogy is anthropological studies, with 'taboo' rules: A Macintyre, *After Virtue: A Study of Moral Theory* (London, Duckworth, 1985) 112.

[6] E Friedson, 'The Theory of Professions: State of the Art' in R Dingwall and P Lewis (eds), *The Sociology of the Professions* (London, The Macmillan Press, 1983).

[7] D Nelken (ed), *Comparing Legal Cultures* (Aldershot: Dartmouth Publishing Company, 1996).

and an internal dimension, the perspective of lawyers.[8] The external dimension is shaped by the projection of law in contemporary media, and how it is understood and experienced.[9] The internal dimension is shaped by the sources and practices of legal reasoning, and by the values, ideologies and politics of lawyers, by processes such as legislation and judicial decisions, and by the aims of the legal system, like providing certainty, validity and flexibility. The criticism that legal culture is inseparable from general culture[10] has some truth, since all fields of activity absorb wider social, political and economic influences,[11] but it is arguable that the work, institutions, community and values of the legal profession differ sufficiently from the mainstream to constitute distinctive culture.[12] It is therefore necessary to explore the prospective elements of professional culture.

Work

Legal work is organised around markets for legal services and these often have a large impact on the behaviour of lawyers.[13] Some of these markets are hidden, for example those determined by the structure of business, but the court system is the public face of law. In the common law world that face is adversarial. Advocates are fierce intellectual adversaries during the case but colleagues, if not best of friends, afterwards. The court system is identified with the recognisable artefacts of the profession—the court clothes, wigs and gowns[14] of judges and barristers—as well as the distinctive language of law. As the earlier profession, the Bar monopolised advocacy and supplied the judges, thereby securing access into elite social strata. The exclusion of the attorneys from membership of an Inn reinforced the superior status of the Bar and entrenched the divided legal profession.[15]

By the second half of the seventeenth century, barristers eradicated direct relationships with lay clients. Receiving instructions only from attorneys and looking to them for payment of fees obviated the need to hold clients' money. Arrangements for briefs, including fees, were negotiated by barristers' clerks, elevating barristers above 'trade'. The Bar distinguished between their professional clients, solicitors, to whom they acted as consultants, and lay clients. The settlement of professional boundaries was cemented in the nineteenth century, with solicitors gaining the exclusive right to conduct conveyancing, probate and primary legal advice and referral, while barristers provided advocacy and specialist advice. This satisfied the status aspirations and preferences of solicitors and barristers, and continued to mould their character. Solicitors were seen as safe, unambitious

---

[8] LM Friedman, *The Legal System: A Social Science Perspective* (New York, Russell Sage Foundation, 1975).

[9] R Cotterrell, 'Law in Culture' (2004) 17 *Ratio Juris* 1.

[10] Cotterell prefers the term legal ideology to legal culture. It describes the ideas, beliefs, values and attitudes embedded in and shaped by practice, particularly the practices of developing interpreting and applying legal doctrine. R Cotterrell, *Law's Community: Legal Theory in Sociological Perspective* (Oxford, Clarendon Press, 1995) 36; R Cotterrell, 'The Concept of Legal Culture' in Nelken, above n 7, 13.

[11] GC Hazard, 'The Future of Legal Ethics' (1991) 100 *Yale Law Journal* 1239, 1241.

[12] Cotterell, above n 9.

[13] See, eg J Van Hoy 'Markets and Contingency: How Client Markets Influence the Work of Plaintiffs' Personal Injury Lawyers' (1999) 6 *International Journal of the Legal Profession* 345.

[14] Wigs were considered a regency affectation even in the 1700s (C James, *Curiosities of Law and Lawyers* (London, Low, Marston, Searle and Rivington,1882)), but confirms special status and fraternity; JG McLaren, 'A Brief History of Wigs in the Legal Profession' (1999) 6 *International Journal of the Legal Profession* 241.

[15] WR Prest, *The Rise of the Barristers: A Social History of the Bar 1590–1640* (Oxford, Clarendon Press, 1986) 9.

office lawyers, portrayed in fictional media as the reader of wills of the deceased to hopeful beneficiaries. Barristers had the more risky but glamorous task of advocacy.

The division of roles between solicitor and barrister gives rise to different ethical priorities, most obvious in the lawyer and client relationship. Solicitors handle clients on a day-to-day basis and are therefore often under direct pressure. Barristers might see lay clients only once before a court hearing, even in serious cases, making it easier to observe a primary loyalty to the court. The expertise of solicitors in the process of settlement is complementary to the advocacy expertise of barristers, thus supporting different roles and ethical priorities.[16] Despite the erosion of distinctions, these patterns are deeply embedded. Solicitors outside the large firms used to be ambivalent about higher rights of audience, and to fusion of the branches of the profession generally, because they relied on the Bar to provide specialist advocates in any area.[17] Barristers sought to preserve their distinctiveness by defending their established ethic, for example, accepting instructions only from solicitors. Now that barristers can receive instructions direct, the most distinctive ethical principle of the Bar is the cab-rank rule.

The cab-rank rule

Barristers, as advocates, must accept a case unless they have a reason, which the Bar's Code of Conduct recognises as valid, for not doing so.[18] A separate rule obliges them to comply with the 'cab-rank rule', requiring that they accept any brief to appear before a court in which they profess to practice.[19] The rule is so called because they must also accept briefs in the order they arrive and, having accepted a brief, cannot withdraw from a case because a preferred case comes along except in specific circumstances[20] and subject to specific requirements for return of the brief.[21] Solicitors are not subject to a similar rule in their day-to-day work. Many assert that they would not act for certain types of client,[22] and others that the cab-rank rule is outmoded,[23] although it is argued that they should accept the cab-rank rule when acting as advocates. The rational basis of the cab-rank rule is that it ensures that any solicitors' firm can instruct any private practice barrister on behalf of any client, maximising equal access to justice.

---

[16] Advocates argue wholeheartedly one side of the case whereas negotiators must see both sides to compromise. J Flood, A Boon, A Whyte,. E Skordaki, R Abbey and A Ash, *Reconfiguring the Market for Advocacy Services: A Case Study of London and Four Fields of Practice* (London, University of Westminster, 1996) 99.

[17] *Ibid*, 58.

[18] A barrister who supplies advocacy services must not withhold those services: (a) on the ground that the case is objectionable to him or any section of the public; (b) on the ground that the conduct opinions or beliefs of the prospective client are unacceptable to him or to any section of the public; or on any ground relating to the source of financial support . . . (Bar Code, para 601). Reasons for refusal would include being professionally embarrassed within the meaning of para 603 (including lack of experience, professional commitments, conflict of interest) and are also provided for specific groups, like employed lawyers, in paras 604–606.1.

[19] Bar Code, para 602.

[20] If he is satisfied that his brief or instructions have been withdrawn, his professional conduct is being impugned or there is some other substantial reason for so doing. Bar Code, para 609.

[21] The barrister must not, for example, cease to act or return a brief or instructions without having first explained to his professional client his reasons for doing so, or return a brief or instructions to another barrister without the consent of his professional client or his representative, Bar Code, para 610.

[22] Christian Khan, solicitors, reputedly refused to act for the National Front, Hitler's deputy and Saddam Hussein. N Hanson, 'Matter of Principle', *Law Gazette*, 19 August 2004.

[23] G Bindman, 'Lies, Lawyers and Ethics', *The Times*, 1 May 2001.

The cab-rank rule also provides formal protection for advocates from identification with their clients in the minds of members of the public.[24] Rather than offering convoluted justifications of how they can represent murderers and rapists, barristers can say that their professional rules require them to do so. This is perfectly consistent with the principle of presumed innocence before conviction. There are examples of cases where advocates have attracted criticism by agreeing to act[25] and some where the cab-rank rule was compromised.[26] For the Bar it is emblematic, although its use as a market control device[27] raises suspicion about underlying motives. Although the Courts and Legal Services Act provides that the rules of conduct of an approved body must make 'satisfactory provision' to ensure neutrality in client selection, it does not require a full cab-rank rule. The Law Society did not adopt a cab-rank rule when drafting its code for advocacy.

The Courts and Legal Services Act requires someone offering advocacy services not to withhold them on the ground that the nature of the case, or the conduct, opinions or beliefs of the client, is objectionable or unacceptable to him or to any section of the public or any ground relating to funding of the legal services.[28] The Solicitors' Code of Conduct 2007, like the Bar Code, provides that solicitors must not refuse cases objectionable to them, or where the conduct opinions or beliefs of prospective clients are unacceptable to them.[29] However, unlike the Bar Code, it has no rule referring to the cab-rank principle. Therefore, contrary to the intentions of Lord Alexander, who introduced this section as an amendment to the 1990 Act during its progress through Parliament,[30] solicitors appear not to be bound by a cab-rank rule.[31] The affect is that they can decline to act for clients when acting as advocates in the same manner that they can on other occasions, as long as the reasons are not proscribed in their code or by the Act. The Law Society repealed its Code for Advocacy in its new Code of Conduct[32] and with it detailed guidance, similar to the Bar's, on refusing briefs for reasons of professional embarrassment. The only reasons now provided relate to not being offered a proper fee.[33]

There may not be much difference in solicitors' and barristers' observance of the cab-rank rule since it is said that barristers' observance is patchy. If the Bar Code's many exceptions do not avail, barristers might 'discover' prior obligations in order to refuse a brief. The argument that the cab-rank rule was a reason that barristers should not be liable

---

[24] Reducing, says Geoffrey Robertson QC, a leading barrister, 'the excrement through the letter box': G Robertson, *The Justice Game* (London, Chatto & Windus, 1998) 377.

[25] For some examples, see D Pannick, *Advocates 92* (Oxford University Press, 1992)143.

[26] From the sixteenth century, barristers took retainers from magnates and corporations: D Sugarman, 'Simple Images and Complex Realities: English Lawyers and their Relationship to Business and Politics, 1750–1950' (1993) 11 *Law and History Review* 257, 268. Robertson above n 24, 379, alleges that the Bar Council prevented English barristers defending the accused in the Nuremberg Trails, that 21 QCs turned down briefs for the Old Bailey bombers in 1974 and that he was advised by a judge to do so or risk 'joining the alternative bar'.

[27] Eg in seeking to deny barristers working for the Crown Prosecution Service the opportunity to gain higher rights of audience. M Zander, 'Rights of Audience in the Higher Courts in England and Wales Since the 1990 Act: What Happened?' (1997) 4 *International Journal of the Legal Profession* 167, 186–8.

[28] Courts and Legal Services Act 1990, s 17(3)c(i)–(iii).

[29] Solicitors' Code of Conduct 2007, r 11.04.

[30] Pannick, above n 25 136.

[31] Pannick disagrees on this point. *Ibid*, 145.

[32] R 25.01.

[33] R 11.04(2).

to clients for negligence in the conduct of litigation was rejected by Lord Steyn in *Hall v Simons*. He observed that solicitor advocates did not have a cab-rank rule but still claimed that immunity. As to the impact of the rule itself he believed:

> ... its impact on the administration of justice in England is not great. In real life a barrister has a clerk whose enthusiasm for the unwanted brief may not be great, and he is free to raise the fee within limits. It is not likely that the rule often obliges barristers to undertake work which they would not otherwise accept.[34]

The ethical basis of the cab-rank rule is that justice is served only if every person can secure representation. The relevance of this argument diminishes with increasing numbers of solicitor advocates with higher rights, although finding advocates at the right level or in remote areas may still prove difficult. The other consideration is securing representation for unpopular clients. Some argue that this need not be problematic,[35] while others compare the English situation favourably with other jurisdictions, such as the US, where there is no equivalent rule.[36]

Institutions

The term 'institution' is identified with established and respected organisations, with deep-rooted habits and customs, and often with impressive buildings. The Bar embodies all of these. The four Inns of Court were grouped together in a single square mile of London, enhancing the Bar's standing and sense of identity.[37] The first Inn, the Temple, occupies 20 acres of land, originally the English base of the Knights Templar and containing the Temple church. It contains many artefacts, including a hatch cover from Sir Francis Drake's ship *The Golden Hind*, on which Middle Templars sign the roll of members called to the Bar. The chambers let to groups of barristers in the Inns allow nothing other than a tight-knit community. The physical identity of the Inn, the requirement of belonging to an Inn before training for the Bar commences, the tradition of communal dinners, reinforces the idea of a collegial group.[38] This also provided a framework for effective informal discipline. Although the Inns of Court, and later the Senate of the Inns of Court and the Bar Mess of the six Circuits, had responsibility for discipline, the Bar often relied on more informal mechanisms, such as reporting infractions to the Heads of Chambers. Although the Bar was rooted in London, it served circuits around the country, and barristers followed judges around those circuits. The Circuit Mess and its Grand Council were given disciplinary powers over the travelling Bar.[39] Although there are now small local Bars in some larger cities, barristers

---

[34] *Arthur J S Hall & Co (a firm) v Simons, Barratt v Ansell and others (trading as Woolf Seddon (a firm), Harris v Scholfield Roberts & Hill (a firm) and another* [2000] 3 All ER 673, 680e.

[35] See D Nicholson and J Webb, *Professional Legal Ethics: Critical Interrogations* (Oxford, Oxford University Press, 1999); D Nicholson, 'Afterword: In Defence of Contextually Sensitive Moral Activism' (2004) 7 *Legal Ethics* 269.

[36] R Cranston, 'Legal Ethics and Professional Responsibility' in R Cranston (ed), *Legal Ethics and Professional Responsibility* (Oxford, Clarendon Press, 1995) 1, 28–9.

[37] This was reinforced when the Supreme Court, built in the nineteenth century, was placed in the centre of the Inns on the Strand.

[38] The serjeants, then the senior advocates, addressed each other as 'brother'. R Pound, *The Lawyer from Antiquity to Modern Times: with Particular Reference to the Development of Bar Associations in the United States* (St Paul, MN, West Publishing, 1953) 13.

[39] Pound, *ibid*, 12.

continue to travel from London to courts in the regions, their practices often based on geographical considerations. Their concentration in a few centres gives barristers opportunities to participate in communal professional activities, such as educational activities, and their London base gives most the opportunity to participate in committees and other activities.

While Bar discipline was informal, the attorneys felt the difference sorely when they were excluded from the Inns, because control by the judiciary proved less effective.[40] When the Law Society was created in the nineteenth century, it sought a distinctive physical identity in Law Society Hall in Chancery Lane,[41] next to the Supreme Court. The Hall, an impressive building built with members subscriptions, had its own library, meeting rooms, dining rooms, a large members' room and an atmosphere like a gentlemen's club. The Victorian vogue for public bodies linking learning, science and public interest through public lectures was also adopted. In contrast to barristers, however, many solicitors have only a fleeting acquaintance with the Law Society Hall. They are more linked to a locality, because this is convenient for their clientele, whether corporate or private, and local law societies are more likely to be the hub of professional activity for those outside London. While it lacks artefacts of the same antiquity as that of the Bar, the Law Society holds many historically significant documents.

Community

Hierarchy is integral to legal professionalism in England.[42] The Bar has an internal status hierarchy, with judges, Queen's Counsel, benchers, readers and heads of the Inns. The Law Society, with fewer official degrees of hierarchy, has an unofficial elite in the long-established and high-status firms established in major cities, particularly London. Both branches also have elites within the professional body, officers answering to elected councils and a president, rotated annually. Hierarchy is arguably important in disciplinary terms, because elites dictate standards accepted by all in return for the esteem bestowed by professional status and association with the elite reference group.[43] Professional socialisation and culture,[44] status and distinction are all incentives to conformity, small compensations for the lack of more material rewards. Hierarchy also defined the relationship between solicitors and barristers, the latter being seen as the 'superior' branch of the profession. This was partly down to chronology, but solicitors' reliance on barristers as consultants perpetuated their hegemony.[45] This was reflected in the etiquette of the profession, whereby solicitors took

---

[40] W Holdsworth, *A History of English Law* (London, Methuen, 1924) vol VI, 448.

[41] D Sugarman, 'Bourgeois Collectivism, Professional Power and the Boundaries of the State: The Private and Public Life of the Law Society 1825 to 1914' (1996) 3 *International Journal of the Legal Profession* 81, 91.

[42] C Glasser, 'The Legal Profession in the 1990's: Images of Change' (1990) 10 *Legal Studies* 1.

[43] MS Larson, *The Rise of Professionalism: A Sociological Analysis* (Berkeley CA, University of California Press, 1977) 227.

[44] RL Nelson and DM Trubeck, 'New Problems and New Paradigms in Studies of the Legal Profession' in RL Nelson, DM Trubeck and RL Solomon (eds), *Lawyers' Ideals/Lawyers' Practices: Transformations in the American Legal Profession* (Ithaca, NY, Cornell University Press, 1992) 1, 17.

[45] 'Even in litigious matters, the solicitor instructs the barrister, makes all preliminary enquiries and prepares all the preliminary papers needed for a brief. It is he who is constantly in touch with the client' (JO Orojo, *Conduct and Etiquette for Legal Practitioners* (London, Sweet & Maxwell, 1979) 5). The reliance was such that it is reflected in the legal principle

clients to barristers' chambers for advice in conference, but also in the backgrounds of those entering each branch. Although, during the 1980s and 1990s, the large solicitors' firms began to command a more equal share of the most sought-after graduates, barristers continued to be seen as socially and intellectually superior.

Another signifier of professional community is collegiality. Durkheim identified etymological roots in the Roman *collegia*,[46] which collected dues from members, had distinctive feasting rituals, claimed 'ties of brotherhood'[47] and engaged in common employment or pursuit. He described the primary motivation of such organisation as:

> just to associate, for the sole pleasure of mixing with their fellows and of no longer feeling lost in the midst of adversaries, as well as for the pleasure of communing together, that is, in short, of being able to lead their lives with the same moral aim.[48]

Pound observed that early professional constitutions had the aim of cultivating 'a spirit of friendship and good will toward each other.'[49] Collegiality, he wrote,

> enables them to contest with their professional brethren all day in the forum, and meet outside on the friendliest terms and with respect for those with whom they have been engaged in the strife of litigation.[50]

In recent usage, 'collegiality' describes both a model of occupational control, of which professionalism is an example,[51] and the mutually supportive relations between members of the producer class.[52] Working closely with colleagues may make the idea of foregoing short-term interests for the common good easier to accept.[53]

The English Bar has an archetypal collegial structure, the regulatory impact of which is the envy of other professions. Arthurs, for example, observes that:

> For the Canadian legal profession, the real (or imagined) culture of the English bar is the point of reference (not to say reverence) . . . Indeed, if there is any legal profession whose culture can be identified with some precision, it is surely this one. Accordingly, in the case of the English bar, culture can be seen as an important vehicle for the transmission of values and the regulation of behaviour.[54]

The Bar has needed to foster collegiality, however, in order to support discipline. One reason

---

that solicitors could plead reliance on counsel as a defence to negligence actions in areas where they are not experienced. See *Manor Electronics v Dickson* (1990) 140 *New Law Journal* 590.

[46] *Collegia* were craft organisations membership of which carried duties and privileges and provided a focus of loyalty for members said to rival loyalty to their own families. The medieval European guilds were similar: E Durkheim, *Professional Ethics and Civic Morals* (trans C Brookfield) (London, Routledge & Kegan Paul, 1957) 19).

[47] *Ibid*, 21.

[48] *Ibid*, 25.

[49] Above, n 38, 15.

[50] *Ibid*, 127.

[51] Johnson, above n 5, 45.

[52] Ihara defines collegiality as support and cooperation between colleagues, a reciprocal respect for colleagues' ability to further professional ends through their knowledge and skills, a commitment to common professional values and goals, a willingness to have confidence in colleagues as responsible autonomous agents, a sense of 'connectedness', or sharing with others the bond of being part of a larger independent whole: CK Ihara, 'Collegiality as a Professional Virtue' in A Flores (ed), *Professional Ideals* (Belmont, CA, Wadsworth Publishing, 1988) 56.

[53] PF Camenisch, 'On Being a Professional: Morally Speaking' in Flores, *ibid*, 14.

[54] HW Arthurs, 'Lawyering in Canada in the 21st Century' [1996] *Windsor Yearbook of Access to Justice* 202, 223.

for the exclusion of attorneys from the Inns in the sixteenth century was that many Bar students were forced to live outside the Inns, weakening control over them. Combined with the fashion for gentlemen joining Inns for social rather than professional reasons, the resulting decline in standards led to the requirement that barristers 'dined' at their Inn as a symbol of residence, thus creating one of the strongest surviving rituals of the English legal profession.[55] While, today, it is acknowledged that collegiality is essentially the professional ideal in law offices and other professional organisations, it is only now being investigated in depth.[56]

Values

Motivations and values are often difficult to divine and, perhaps more than any other area of culture, often ideological in character. What is deemed a worthy value to declare depends on the spirit of the time. The example of the Bar influenced the aspirations of the Law Society in 1825 and its concern with status and social standing.[57] The forerunner of the Law Society, The Society of Gentlemen Practisers, formed in 1739, expressed this in its aim of:

> supporting the honour and independence of the profession [and the] moral elevation of its members, [who] being placed under the constant observation of the whole body, the least tendency to ungentlemanly conduct or dishonourable or illiberal practice will be immediately noticed and checked.[58]

For the leaders of the solicitors, honour, and maybe even moral elevation, were closely connected with status. For this, they sought a protected market for a narrow range of preferred, high-status work, for which strong organisation and representation were necessary.[59] Independence was probably also seen in institutional terms, referring to similar powers of self-regulation and organisation then enjoyed by barristers. In ethical terms, judged by contemporary criteria, barristers often failed to achieve independence.[60]

While honour and independence may have meant different things to lawyers in the nineteenth century than they mean today, they are enduring values in professional ideology. The idea of institutional independence continues to be important,[61] but the emphasis in professional ethics has shifted more to formal independence, for example avoiding conflicts of interest. The shift of concern to the individual has brought personal qualities like

---

[55] Pound, above n 38, 109. Student barristers are still required to take the required number of dinners in their Inn before call.

[56] E Lazega, *The Collegial Phenomenon: The Social Mechanisms of Cooperation Among Peers in a Corporate Law Partnership* (New York, Oxford University Press, 2001).

[57] M Burrage, 'From a Gentleman's to a Public Profession' (1996) *International Journal of the Legal Profession* 45, 89–90; Sugarman, above n 41, 88; Pound, above n 38, 105.

[58] Burrage, *ibid*, 49.

[59] When provincial solicitors sought county court rights of audience in the nineteenth century, the Council of the Law Society rejected the proposal because 'gentlemen did not frequent the county court'. Sugarman, above n 26, 98 and 109.

[60] Barristers, for example, were often on retainers from magnates in the sixteenth and seventeenth centuries. *Ibid*, 268.

[61] Independence from the state is still seen as 'fundamental to upholding the rule of law and the independence of the judiciary'. 'Commonwealth Principles on the Accountability of and the Relationship between the Three Branches of Government' (2004) 96 *Commonwealth Legal Education* 7.

judgement and responsibility, to the fore.[62] The image of the professional as a 'the solitary, disciplined, highly educated, and deeply ethical practitioner dealing with clients one by one' is strongly identified with sole practice in law,[63] the norm for barristers and common for solicitors until recently. Even partnership, the dominant business form for solicitors, has individualistic aspects—each partner having personal responsibility for all partnership debts, for example.[64] In the classical solicitors' firm, synonymous with the partnership model, the focus of activity is the professional practitioner around whom everything is organised.

While independence and honour are long-standing professional values, respect for diversity is a more recent addition to professional values. While the profession has been committed to equal opportunities in terms of gender and ethnicity from the early 1990s, transition from a profession of largely homogeneous membership of white, middle-class men has been less smooth. Both branches publish codes designed to promote good practice. Practitioners are persuaded that it is in their interests to promote diversity and offered guidance on how to achieve it.[65] It may be that as a result of the process of sensitisation to personal diversity issues, diversity in general is more likely to be accommodated. A notable recent example of this is the Bar's recognition of employed barristers.

Pressures on professional culture

Diversity

The legal services market has a multitude of sites in which different norms proliferate. Many developments are alien to the existing professional culture but, for various reasons, must be accommodated by it: for example, modes of practice. English legal professionalism is based solidly on private practice,[66] yet a growing numbers of lawyers find themselves working outside solicitors' firms or barristers' chambers, in corporations, the civil service, local government, the Crown Prosecution Service and law centres.[67] The professional bodies had to decide between accommodating employed lawyers within existing structures and rules and creating two-tier membership, a route with potential for conflict and resentment. Doubt about whether employed professionals could truly be as independent as those in private

---

[62] Johnson, above n 5, 13 and 53.

[63] The sole practitioner is arguably the most ethically powerful lawyer because only he or she can make an autonomous decision on how to represent—most other lawyers are constrained by the policy and bureaucracy of organisations. L Sheinman, 'Looking for Legal Ethics' (1997) 4 *International Journal of the Legal Profession* 139, 151. Negligence actions are typically against three- to –five-partner firms rather than sole practitioners. Sole practitioners are more likely to be guilty of fraud, but the largest claim against the Compensation Fund in respect of fraud, £13 million, was committed by the senior partner of a 35-partner practice. A Sherr and L Webley, 'Legal Ethics in England and Wales' (1997) 4 *International Journal of the Legal Profession* 109, 130.

[64] R Greenwood and CR Hinings, 'Understanding Radical Organisational Change: Bringing Together the Old and the New Institutionalism' (1996) 21 *Academy of Management Review* 1022, 1027.

[65] Bar Council, *Equality and Diversity Code for the Bar* (London, Bar Council, 2004).

[66] RL Abel, *The Legal Profession in England and Wales* (Oxford, Basil Blackwell, 1988) 306.

[67] Employed lawyers increased from around 3,000 in 1966 to 15,000 in 1996. Lady Marre CBE, *A Time for Change: Report of the Committee on the Future of the Legal Profession* (London, General Council of the Bar and Council of the Law Society, 1988) paras 5.24–5 and 6.8.

practice appeared justified by employed lawyers' questioning of their own ability to be the corporate conscience, let alone have a professional conscience.[68] Others questioned whether government-employed lawyers bringing or defending criminal proceedings could be independent of the state.[69] In the event, the profession opted for integration of the private and employed ethics regimes,[70] creating exceptions for incompatible principles like the cab-rank rule.[71]

At the level of the private practitioner, there were differences in lawyers' work, financial rewards and structures. The classical firm, for example, has a flat structure wherein managerial tasks are shared and fee-earners do similar work.[72] The traditional 'lockstep' system for partnership pay, rewarding experience, seniority and length of service, reinforces collegiality. The vast majority of solicitors' firms, including the medium-sized, generalist High Street firms, still employ some version of this model. The cultural values of this kind of organisation once covered all types of private practice solicitor, but they continue to be typified by 'cause lawyers'. This umbrella term covers a range of organisations dedicated to single causes[73] or with a radical or critical perspective. They are not overtly driven by profit and more concerned to reflect egalitarian values internally.[74]

In contrast to the classical firm, the large London-based firms that now dominate legal indicators such as partnership size, training places and gross fees have centralised and bureaucratic management structures.[75] Although disparity of income was always a feature of legal professional life,[76] the increasing prosperity of large firms has opened up a large pay gap between the commercial firms and the rest. The atmosphere of such firms is more like a business than the 'gentlemen's clubs' of old[77] and their size supports specialist functions like

---

[68] An employed lawyer was quoted as saying: 'On the one hand the in-house legal counsel is supposed to be the corporate conscience, and on the other hand they're supposed to assist the company in achieving its commercial objectives. Sometimes these requirements clash'. 'Ethics on Agenda at in-house Conference', *The Lawyer*, 14 November 1995.

[69] This is a debate already well established in the US and Israel. It is often argued, for example, that the obvious role of public service lawyers should be to assist the judge reach a wise decision rather than to be partisan. M Taruffo, 'The Lawyer's Role and the Models of Civil Process' (1981) 16 *Israel Law Review* 5.

[70] Note that, in 1995, the Bar Council removed the rule which prevented employed barristers from being elected Chairman or Vice Chairman of the Bar so as to address the perception that employed barristers were inferior and to enable the Bar Council to claim that it represented all barristers equally. 'Employed Barristers Eligible for Office', *New Law Journal*, 3 February 1995, 134.

[71] Employed lawyers cannot be subject to the full cab-rank principle, for example (but see Bar Code, para 604).

[72] This contrasts with 'ordinary lawyering' in a number of ways, including the detail of organisation, span of operation, relation to clients and operating style. L Bishop, 'Regulating the Market for Legal Services in England: Enforced Separation of Function and Restrictions on Forms of Enterprise' (1989) 53 *Modern Law Review* 326.

[73] A Boon, 'Cause Lawyers and the Alternative Ethical Paradigm: Ideology and Transgression' (2004) 7 *Legal Ethics* 250.

[74] Radical lawyers are likely to have a client base of organisations seeking to change basic social structures but their organisational culture may appear fairly conventional. Critical lawyers, however, work to undermine hierarchical social, family and workplace relationships and this will almost inevitably be reflect in their organisational cultural values. S Scheingold and A Bloom, 'Transgressive Cause Lawyering: Practice Sites and the Politicization of the Professional' (1998) 5 *International Journal of the Legal Profession* 209, 220.

[75] See chapter 2. Contrast the position in France, where, following the *avocats* and *conseil juridiques* (lawyers specialising in non-contentious commercial work), salaried *avocats* must have a written contract guaranteeing, inter alia, autonomy in the organisation of working time. See JL Leubsdorf, 'The Independence of the Bar in France: Learning from Comparative Legal Ethics' in JJ Barceló and RC Crampton (eds), *Lawyers' Practice and Ideals: A Comparative View* (The Hague, Kluwer Law International, 1999).

[76] Sugarman, above n 26, 270.

[77] C Stanley, 'Enterprising Lawyers: Changes in the Market for Legal Services' (1991) 25 *Law Teacher* 44.

finance, marketing, personnel, library, information technology and training, performed by non-lawyers.[78] They are less collegial and increasingly entrepreneurial, competitive and meritocratic, favouring pay policies that reward effort, billing and client attraction and retention.[79] Surrendering lucrative private client work, like personal trusts and tax advice, to smaller firms,[80] they also have little contact with the concerns of individuals, even wealthy ones. Llewellyn feared that such a retreat into corporate specialisation might produce expert practitioners with a technocratic outlook, narrow vision and a 'trained incapacity for social responsibility',[81] but others have argued that such organisations have an inevitable impact on ethical principles,[82] whereby the rewards overshadow ethical principles.[83] So, for example, commercial clients, because they bring high-paying, repeat business, dominate their lawyers, whereas private client lawyers are less likely to be in the thrall of clients.[84]

There is also increasing diversity in the make-up of the profession. This is most marked in terms of gender, fuelling speculation about the impact on the culture and ethics of the workplace. Most of the discussion has centred on the theory that men and women use different moral languages and approaches in solving problems.[85] The cultural norms of legal professionalism—'instrumental rationality, ambition, competitiveness, aggression'—are seen to be masculine dispositions, contrasting with a feminine preference for 'empathy, care or compassion'.[86] Men, it is said, adopt a rights or justice orientation to a problem, ignoring the impact of decisions, whereas women approach problems with empathy, seeking solutions

[78] EH Greenebaum, 'Development of Law Firm Training Programs: Coping with a Turbulent Environment' (1996) 3 *International Journal of the Legal Profession* 315, 322.

[79] See chapter 16. See also M Galanter and T Palay, 'Public Service Implications of Evolving Law Firm Size and Structure' in RA Katzmann, *The Law Firm and the Public Good* (Washington, DC, The Brookings Institution, 1995) 19 (size is coextensive, with increased rationalisation, specialisation, hierarchy, meritocracy and market orientation); KI Eisler, *Shark Tank: Greed, Politics and the Collapse of Finley Kumble, One of America's Largest Law Firms* (New York, Plume, 1990).

[80] J Currie 'Reversal of Fortune', *The Lawyer*, 8 July 2002.

[81] Llewellyn argued that the absence of the 'poor man's case' would have a negative ethical impact: '. . . any man's interests, any man's outlook, are shaped in greatest part by what he does. His perspective is in terms of what he knows. His sympathies and ethical judgements are determined essentially by the things and people he works for and on and with. Hence the practice of corporation law not only works for business men towards business ends, but develops within itself a business point of view toward the work to be done, toward the value of the work to the community . . .': K Llewellyn, 'The Bar Specialises: With What results?' (1933) *Annals of the American Academy* 177.

[82] Johnson, above n 5, 16–17 and at 90: 'practitioners subject to corporate patronage . . . will exhibit beliefs, attitudes ideologies which diverge from and sometimes conflict with those exhibited by practitioners subjected to meditative or collegiate forms of control'. See also Gordon, who argues that commercial firms are tainted by commercialism, to the detriment of 'their lofty professionalism': R Gordon, 'The Independence of Lawyers' (1988) 68 *Boston University Law Review* 63; and HF Stone, 'The Public Influence of the Bar' (1934) 48 *Harvard Law Review* 1.

[83] See M Regan, *Eat What You Kill: The Fall of a Wall Street Lawyer* (Ann Arbor, MI, University of Michigan Press, 2006) for a cautionary tale of a leading US bankruptcy attorney.

[84] Lawyers in general 'serve those clients they are likely to see and who occasionally bring them the cases they prize': JP Heinz, 'The Power of Lawyers' (1983) 17 *Georgia Law Review* 891, 900. Whereas, in relation to clients, corporate sector lawyers are said to be timid and weak, personal service sector lawyers are arrogant and imperialistic: A Sarat, 'Lawyers and Clients: Putting Professional Services on the Agenda of Legal Education' (1992) 41 *Journal of Legal Education* 43, 44.

[85] C Gilligan, *In a Different Voice* (Cambridge, MA, Harvard University Press, 1982).

[86] R Collier, '"Nutty Professors", "Men in Suits" and "New Entrepreneurs": Corporeality, Subjectivity and Change in the Law School and Legal Practice' (1998) 7 *Social and Legal Studies* 2.

that 'avoid pain' by meeting the needs of all those affected by a problem and attempting to minimise disruption of relationships.

The ethical difference between men and women has been characterised as a male preference for an 'ethic of rights' and a female preference for an 'ethic of care'. Menkel-Meadow summarises the implications of the ethic of care as the move towards less confrontational, more mediational approaches to dispute resolution and greater sensitivity to clients' needs and interests, as well as the needs and interests of other affected relation-ships, such as clients' families or employees. She speculates that women practitioners might apply different moral and ethical sensibilities, employ fewer hierarchical management styles and have social justice or altruistic motives, seeking greater integration between their work and family lives.[87] These orientations could be a considerable force behind innovations such as consensual representation, participatory lawyering and non-trial-based methods of dispute resolution.[88]

Gender stereotypes identifying males with the values of independence, autonomy and universalistic principles and women with intimacy, relationships and care can only operate as broad generalisations. They ignore overlap in the propensities of males and females, and the affect of changing expectations, aspirations and opportunities on the gender-differen-tiated behaviour of men and women. Therefore, phenomena detected in early studies of gender difference may already be dissipating, while assumed differences may be used to justify workplace discrimination.[89] The impact of greater numbers of women practitioners on work place and professional cultures is difficult to identify empirically. Organisationally, it may be that women make connections through membership of a network of lawyers where communication is open and empathetic.[90] This seems unlikely to affect the long hours and client service orientation in large commercial firms, which appear to be the main reasons for high rates of female attrition.[91]

The impact that the presence of women in greater numbers has on legal work is also contentious, partly because it is difficult to establish definitively how professionals interact with clients,[92] but also because there is no convincing evidence that men are competitive and women cooperative. Indeed, it is likely that legal socialisation affects men and women in similar ways, intellectually, emotionally and psychologically,[93] so that men and women are defined more by their profession than gender. The idea that an increasingly equal gender balance will change the way work is performed may, therefore, be misplaced. Organisational culture and a competitive environment represent great pressure to conform. Entrants to well-established structures tend to adapt to those structures and changing them is beyond the capacity of new entrants to the profession, although longer-term change on gender lines cannot be ruled out. The largest firms were shown to indirectly discriminate against

---

[87] C Menkel-Meadow, 'Portia Redux: Another Look at Gender Feminism, and Legal Ethics' in *Legal Ethics and Legal Practice: Contemporary Issues* (Oxford, Clarendon Press, 1995) 24, 34.

[88] C Maughan and J Webb, *Lawyering Skills and the Legal Process* (London, Butterworths, 1995) 116–20.

[89] See above n 87, 29–34.

[90] *Ibid.*

[91] L Duff and L Webley, *Equality and Diversity: Women Solicitors*, vol II (London, Law Society, 2004).

[92] See B Danet, K B Hoffman and N C Kermish, 'Obstacles to the Study of Lawyer Client Interaction: The Biography of a Failure' (1980) 14 *Law and Society Review* 905.

[93] JM Hedegard, 'The Impact of legal Education: An In-depth Examination of Career-relevant Interests, Attitudes, and Personality Traits among First-year Law Students' (1979) 4 *American Bar Foundation Research Journal* 791.

working class and ethnic minority solicitors, and did little to further the career progression of women.

Competition and specialisation

Competition in the legal services market has eroded established markets and patterns of work. One of the most observable impacts on professional culture is the move from generalist, 'full service' units to greater specialisation. Since the 1980s, when the Thatcher government decided that the legal profession was anti-competitive, competition offered a way of containing legal costs. With the conveyancing market declining, solicitors moved into legal aid.[94] Successive Labour governments sought increasing competition in the legal services market to force down costs, culminating in the Carter Review proposals to limit legal aid.[95] The fiercer market for legal services probably spurred greater specialisation, as firms sought a niche. Large firms became increasingly focused on their prime markets and 'boutique practices' grew around small but remunerative markets.[96] In parallel moves, precipitated by allegations of incompetence in generalist solicitors, the Law Society introduced specialist panels to articulate ethical principles in a number of areas, for example, what constitutes competence.[97] By 2005 many panels were operating accreditation schemes, and 18% of solicitors belonged to one or more.[98] Sections of the Bar were also badly affected by the squeeze on legal aid[99] and many barristers also began to specialise more narrowly. Far more significant for the Bar was the success of the Law Society's campaign for rights of audience in higher courts. This paved the way for a concerted attack by leading large firms on the advocacy monopoly of the Bar and for large provincial firms to compete for referral work from solicitors in their area.

Specialisation and competition affected the relationship between solicitors and barristers. Some large firms were determined to offer advocacy in-house, because clients expected a 'one-stop shop' and they felt that instructing barristers called their own competence into question. As solicitors focused on narrower fields of work, they were confident in tackling work for which they previously instructed barristers, like drafting pleadings, appearing in interlocutory hearings in chambers and advising,[100] undermining the barrister's command of decision making in commercial cases.[101] The large commercial firms began using teams to handle large transactions, representing different kinds of legal expertise and even

---

[94] In 1975 solicitors derived 6% of their income from legal aid work, but this had risen to 15% by the 1990s. Glasser, above n 42.

[95] For the latest attempt, see Lord Carter of Coles, *Legal: Aid: A Market-based Approach to Reform* (London, Lord Chancellor's Department, 2006) and chapter 3.

[96] R Lee, 'From Profession to Business: The Rise and Rise of the City Law Firm' in P Thomas (ed), *Tomorrow's Lawyers* (Oxford, Blackwell, 1992) 31.

[97] The personal injury panel was introduced in 1992 and there were five panels at 31 July 1996. Medical Negligence had 100 panel members, Children 1,597, Personal Injury 2,233, Planning 197 and Mental Health Review Tribunals 367. There are now panels for Local Government, Licensed Insolvency Practitioners, Rights of Audience in Higher Courts and Qualified to Conduct Discrete Investment Business. See further Sherr and Webley, above n 63.

[98] http://www.lawsociety.org.uk/professional/accreditationpanels.law (accessed 23 December 2005).

[99] By the 1990s barristers were receiving half of their income from the state in the form of legal aid especially in criminal cases (above n 42).

[100] R Hill, 'Higher Aspirations' (1995) *Solicitors Journal* 14 April 340.

[101] Above n 16, 115.

professionals from other disciplines. If counsel was instructed, he or she was expected to be 'part of the team' and was chosen with compatibility with the team, or even compliance, in mind.[102] The shifting balance of power between the large firms and the Bar was reflected in recruitment, with elite chambers going to greater extremes to compete with City solicitors for sought-after candidates. Competition between solicitors and barristers also spilled over into disputes over cultural symbols. Solicitors feared that barristers' wigs and gowns conferred a competitive advantage, leading to their declining use in some courts and proposals that judges abandon wigs in civil trials.[103] Solicitors argued that they should have the benefit of court attire, 'to command respect and authority and bestow on the wearer gravitas and anonymity'.[104] They were granted their wish and will don full court dress from October 2008.[105]

Although competition cuts cost, there was concern that reducing income would have a deleterious effect on standards. Firms forced to perform more work cheaply risk cutting corners, poor service standards and dishonesty. The market leaders claiming high fees had different ethical risks, with disruption to the delicate balance between ethics and client loyalty.[106] When client satisfaction becomes top priority, shady deals may be the cost of keeping business.[107] Those who consider collegial, non-hierarchical structures the best support for ethical commitments found the most disturbing feature of competition was drift away from the classical solicitors' firm. The first steps were by the elite solicitors' firms, where small partnerships were the norm until the mid 1950s.[108] The Companies Act 1967 removed the ceiling of 20 on partnership numbers and paved the way for mega-firms, for whom scale was an important indicator of capacity and where thousands of employees had small hope of even knowing each other.

A hierarchical structure and managerial approach was necessary for the mega-firms, but it also suited a shift at the other end of the market, where work was more specialist and routinised.[109] By 1990, 70% of the solicitors' branch claimed to be moderate or extreme specialists[110] and barristers and chambers reduced the areas of work offered,[111] leading to smaller numbers of lawyers regarded as competent to do work in certain fields. Government criteria of expertise and efficiency in awarding legal aid franchises forced solicitors to

---

[102] Greenebaum, above n 78, 321.

[103] R Burns, 'When will we be rid of this Hairy Affectation?', *The Times*, 11 May 2004; C Dyer, 'Civil Court Judges Prepare to Cast Aside their Wigs after 300 Years', *The Guardian*, 5 January 2007, 5.

[104] S Allen 'Solicitor-advocate Begins Wig Campaign', *Gazette* 98/07, 15 February 2001, 3.

[105] From 2 January 2008 solicitors have been able to wear wigs in court when barristers are allowed to do so.

[106] LR Patterson, 'On Analyzing the Law of Legal Ethics: An American Perspective' (1981) 16 *Israel Law Review* 28, 31.

[107] CE Reason and C Chappell, 'Crooked Lawyers: Towards a Political Economy of Deviance in the Profession' in T Fleming (ed), *The New Criminologies in Canada: Status, Crime and Control* (Toronto, Oxford University Press, 1985) 212.

[108] In 1937 Linklaters was the largest City partnership, with 11 partners, and Freshfields usually had three. See above n 26, 265 and 266.

[109] T Goriely, 'Debating the Quality of Legal Services: Differing Models of the Good Lawyer' (1994) 1 *International Journal of the Legal Profession* 159, 163, citing L Bridges, B Sufrin, J Whetton and R White, *Legal Services in Birmingham* (Birmingham, Birmingham University, 1975) and suggesting that some legal aid firms handled high volumes of work in a routinised way.

[110] G Chambers and S Harwood, *Solicitors in England and Wales: Practice Organisation and Perceptions, First Report* (London, Research and Policy Planning Group, The Law Society, 1990) 150.

[111] Above n 16.

further narrow areas of work.[112] The increasing demand for efficiency tipped firms towards managerialism, increasing internal differentiation and a culture of surveillance.[113] Specialisation, and a technological revolution in the office,[114] encouraged compartmentalisation of cases and transactions, with qualified staff reserved for more complex elements or overseeing several junior staff or paralegals. Such arrangements arguably contribute to the de-skilling of all, since no one performs the whole transaction, and increase the risk of error.[115]

Whatever was going on under the surface of legal practice, competition had an immediate and obvious impact on the Law Society code when the prohibition of advertising was abandoned. Advertising was previously deplored as unprofessional conduct,[116] because it symbolised the distinction between professions and business. Permitting advertising forced lawyers from the high ground, where clients seek professional advice and professionals do not seek out clients. Stopping practitioners claiming individual distinction forces them to channel their effort into collective control and promotion,[117] supporting professional collegiality and community, and encouraging the modest demeanour associated with professionalism.[118] The abandonment of these principles in 1984 in anticipation of the turf war with licensed conveyancers[119] resulted in a loss of mystique, with advertisements in trade sections of local papers[120] vying with upmarket but controversial offerings for tastelessness.[121] By the end of the decade, even the Bar had

---

[112] A Boon, 'Ethics and Strategy in Personal Injury Litigation' (1995) 22 *Journal of Law and Society* 353.

[113] H. Sommerlad, 'Managerialism and the Legal Profession: a New Professional Paradigm' (1995) 2 *International Journal of the Legal Profession* 159; H. Sommerlad 'The Implementation of Quality Initiatives and the New Public Management in the Legal Aid Sector in England and Wales' (1999) 6 *International Journal of the Legal Profession* 311.

[114] Word processing, photo-reproduction, computerisation, online data services, overnight delivery services, electronic mail and fax machines. M Galanter, 'Law Abounding: Legalisation Around the North Atlantic' (1992) 55 *The Modern Law Review* 1, 6.

[115] This may explain why cost cutting in conveyancing work has caused a massive increase in claims for negligence. Glasser, above n 43; S Domberger and A Sherr, 'The Impact of Competition on Pricing and Quality of Legal Services' (1989) 9 *International Review of Law and Economics* 41 (it was the collapse of the conveyancing market in 1988 that most affected the profession, not the cuts in costs which occurred between 1983 and 1986).

[116] Boulton, 'it is contrary to professional etiquette for a barrister to do .. anything with the primary motive of personal advertisement': WW Boulton, *A Guide to Conduct and Etiquette at the Bar* (London, Butterworths, 6th edn, 1975) 55; and Orojo, '[i]mproper attraction of business will include all those acts which tend to give an unfair advantage in obtaining legal business, because such acts lower the prestige of the profession and, therefore, constitute unprofessional conduct': JO Orojo, *Conduct and Etiquette for Legal Practitioners* (London, Sweet & Maxwell, 1979). Since lawyers were permitted to produce promotional brochures in 1984, virtually all have done so: J Flood, 'Megalawyering in the Global Order: The Cultural, Social and Economic Transformation of Global Legal Practice' (1996) 3 *International Journal of the Legal Profession* 169.

[117] D Rueschemeyer, 'Doctors and Lawyers: A Comment on the Theory of the Professions' (1964–5) *Canadian Review of Sociology and Anthropology* 17.

[118] In the US advertising was said to have 'changed the image of lawyers from professionals who deplored self-laudation into that of aggressive self -promoters'. Hazard, above n 11, 1256.

[119] Restrictions on advertising were also lifted in the Netherlands in 1990. See LE De Groot-van Leeuwen, 'Polishing the Bar: The legal Ethics Code and Disciplinary System of the Netherlands, and a Comparison with the United States' (1997) 4 *International Journal of the Legal Profession* 14.

[120] A relatively mild form is 'Have you suffered an accident? We are specialists in personal injury. Free initial consultation'.

[121] A divorce specialist generated national news coverage with advertising banners reading 'Ditch the bitch' and 'All men are bastards' in the national press aimed at 'City-based clients'. F Callister, 'Split Decisions', *The Lawyer*, 4 June 2001, 17.

capitulated to advertising.[122] The issue is ever present, however, with concern about whether television advertising compromises professional gravitas[123] and European competition law supporting ever deeper incursions into limitations on advertising.[124]

Solicitors' firms and barristers' chambers had always had different areas of expertise. Competition, specialisation and their consequences, such as advertising, heightened a sense of difference, and increasing divergence, among lawyers. Aspects of professional ideology began to melt away. The vision of sole practice as an idealised ethical form, for example, gave way to a realisation that busy sole practitioners, acting for individuals in conveyancing, estates and litigation, are the most likely subjects of complaints.[125] There was also growing realisation that the large and elite firms ran the risk of being, like their US counterparts, 'flawed by a lack of concern for comprehensive and dedicated service, by a marked self-interest, and by incompetent performance'. [126]

Segmentation of the legal profession was accompanied by the formation of groups promoting sectional interests.[127] The implications of diversity for the codes of the respective branches was realised in the growth of professional sub-groups expounding norms that threatened the established ethical consensus.[128] This process began when the Law Society's panels issued their own codes or recommended the codes of associated bodies.[129] In some areas, this process went beyond the recognised panels. The Association of Personal Injury Lawyers (APIL), an association for solicitors and barristers representing personal injury plaintiffs, developed its own code for members.[130] While it was only 11 paragraphs long, drawing substantially on the Law Society Guide,[131] there was controversy over a proposed clause prohibiting members from charging referral fees. This went beyond the Law Society's own regulations and was designed to prevent 'ambulance chasing', but complaints by members led to its amendment.[132]

---

[122] Barristers were allowed to advertise in 1990, but usually use subtle forms (see *Practice Management for the Bar—Standards and Guidelines for Barristers and Chambers* (London, General Council of the Bar, 1995 (reviewed 2006)).

[123] S Ward, 'As Seen on TV', *Gazette* 97/36, 21 September 2000, 26.

[124] P Stanley 'European Briefing', *Solicitors Journal*, 1 June 2001.

[125] Disbarred sole practitioners shared a profile: typically 10 year qualified, average law school performance and predictable life problems of family debt, children and business commitments. Many had been the subject of previous disciplinary proceedings. above Reason and Chappell, n 107, 206; see also Arthurs, above n 54.

[126] Houle observes that the association of professionalism and sole practice was always overidealised and over generalised, and that it is increasingly atypical: CO Houle, *Continuing Learning in the Professions* (London, Jossey Bass, 1980).

[127] Eg medical negligence defence lawyers set up a group (Healthcare Lawyers Association) to give them a 'balancing voice' in legal debates traditionally dominated by plaintiff's groups. N Hilborne, 'New Voice for Defendants' Solicitors', *Law Society Gazette*, 13 November 1996, 1.

[128] T Schneyer, 'Professionalism as Politics: The Making of a Modern Legal Ethics Code' in Nelson *et al*, above n 44, 95.

[129] See chapter 20 ADR.

[130] See APIL Code of Conduct (1996). APIL is a pressure group 'dedicated to the improvement of services provided for victims of accidents and disease'. The objectives of the Association are to promote and develop expertise in the practice of personal injury law, campaign for improvements in the law, gain wider redress for personal injury, promote safety and alert the public to hazards wherever they arise.

[131] In para 1, for example, 'APIL members will act in the best interests of clients' replicated Practice Rule 1(c), (R Taylor (ed), *The Guide to the Professional Conduct of Solicitors* (London, The Law Society, 1996) 1.

[132] C Fogarty and A Laferla, 'Protests Force APIL to Relax Ambulance-chasing Clause', *The Lawyer*, 21 January 1997.

The interpretation of professional body rules by bodies with different levels of official status suggested a way that the profession might cope with segmentation. The potential is for a hierarchy of codes, starting with the broad principles espoused by the profession but developed into increasing levels of detail by groups of practitioners closest to the area of work. It also suggested that there was potential for schisms on fundamental ethical issues to break out. The obvious source was the growing economic and social gap between members of the profession. This had already led to calls for the Bar to abrogate the cab-rank rule, because legal aid fees were not 'adequate in all cases'.[133] The financial crisis of legal aid firms meant that they often could not afford to offer traineeships, forcing the Legal Services Commission to sponsor trainees' wages through a Training Grants scheme. This suggested an existential problem, raising issues about the professions control of education and training for those sectors.

If homogeneity is a significant factor building common culture, the increasing diversity of business forms is a threat. The alternative business structures permitted by the Legal Services Act 2007 will challenge the conventional structure of private practice. The multi-disciplinary partnership, a 'one-stop shop', offering professional services from solic-itors, accountants and merchant (investment) bankers to chartered surveyors and stockbrokers, is contentious in many jurisdictions.[134] The main concerns surround the compatibility of the work of the different professions and whether the regulatory arrange-ments can span the different ethical regimes within one organisation. Government has pursued the idea, despite avenues of escape being offered by European courts,[135] because it sees cost benefits for consumers. Both branches of the legal profession were concerned that financial and management integration of the different professions would impinge on the necessary independence of lawyers in MDPs. Do they pursue their own occupational ethics, are the different ethics integrated into one code or, if neither of these, which professional rules prevail? The solution is to adopt a business framework of incorporation and limited liability with external regulation.[136] This raises further questions about the place of ethics in increasingly commercialised practice.

A common professional culture?

The fragmentation thesis and other 'crises of professionalism' evoke the spirit of the golden ages[137] where lawyers shared a common culture. Although crises were also a feature of

---

[133] J Malpas, 'Bar Council to Confront Cab-rank Rule', *The Lawyer*, 16 July 1996.

[134] MDPs receive support from some European governments and the World Trade Organisation. Protectionist provisions in the ABA code might restrict them in the US, placing American lawyers at a global competitive disad-vantage but limiting encroachment of European MDPs in US markets. CW Wolfram, 'Comparative Multi-disciplinary Practice of Law: Paths Taken and Not Taken' (2002) 52 *Case Western Law Review* 961.

[135] ECJ held in Case C–309/99 *Wouters/Nova* [2002] that Holland's ban on MDPs was appropriate where necessary for the proper practice and functioning of a profession. A primary concern was that the supervisory activ-ities of accountants might not be compatible with the advisory capacities of lawyers.

[136] Above n 56.

[137] RL Solomon, 'Five Crises or One: The Concept of Legal Professionalism, 1925–1960' in Nelson *et al*, above n 44, 114.

bygone times,[138] the existence of a current issue is undeniable, the question being its seriousness. Even 10 years ago Burrage saw that:

> The solicitors' branch is becoming a more public profession than its predecessors . . . more educated and heterogeneous, less concerned with its corporate honour, more market-oriented and competitive, with others and amongst themselves, and therefore less secure . . . all these things make it more unruly and fractious, more unethical and disloyal.[139]

Scope for division is increased when lawyers from large, commercial firms and small, private client firms are so different.[140] Even if the regulatory structure can find the flexibility to accommodate such diversity,[141] coping with divergence on ethical issues is problematic. If the ethics code represents the view of one interest group, other groups may struggle to conform. If professional elites, like large firms,[142] draft ethics rules,[143] they may set standards of competence that cannot be met by others[144] because they take no account of the economic and other realities in which others operate.[145] This risks the profession breaking into interest groups and falling apart.[146] Rules governing the many different roles that lawyers fulfil are too unwieldy.[147] Rules that are general, embracing all kinds of practice, are likely to be aspirational, providing little practical guidance[148] and fulfilling a legitimating function at best.[149] This may be the only viable form for ethical rules that must span diverse professional

---

[138] The Law Society was frequently accused of elitism in the nineteenth century and saw off several attempts to set up competing provincial associations. In 1870 only a quarter of solicitors were members (Sugarman, above n 26, 294). Pound, above n 38, 362, wrote of the profession in the US in a vein that is echoed in contemporary debates: 'Integration of the Bar has [become], therefore, a mission of the first importance. By keeping the followers of the different specialities of practice, the different groups into which the lawyers in the large cities of today tend to regroup themselves, conscious of a higher organization of which they are members and to which, as the profession itself, they are responsible, it can stand fast against the disintegrating tendencies which, threatening professions, threaten ultimately the law'.

[139] M Burrage, 'From a Gentleman's to a Public Profession' (1996) *International Journal of the Legal Profession* 45, 75.

[140] J Heinz and E Laumann, *Chicago Lawyers: The Social Structure of the Bar* (New York, Russell Sage Foundation, 1982) 905.

[141] A Boon, J Flood and J Webb, 'Postmodern Professions? The Fragmentation of Legal Education and the Legal Profession' (2005) 32 *Journal of Law and Society* 473.

[142] Above n 128; see also the discussion in this chapter.

[143] Above n 5, 67–8.

[144] Corporate lawyers, with secure goodwill, can demand the highest ethical standards and attack 'the ambulance chasing evil'. Abel argues that this conceals elite self interest. Advertising, for example, is resisted by those with an established client base. New firms need to advertise. See extracts from the speech of Senator John V Tunney, Chairman, Senate Judiciary Committee's Subcommittee on Constitutional Rights, (July/August 1975) 5 *Juris Doctor*, cited in JF Sutton and JS Dzienkowski, *Cases and Materials on the Professional Responsibility of Lawyers* (St Paul, MN, West Publishing, 1989) 11: 'The economically marginal lawyer[s] . . . are precisely the ones who do not have certifiable specialities, who cannot meet rigid trial practice criteria, and who can be most easily replaced by paraprofessionals . . . [and while] [t]echnological advances and their application to legal practice are generally considered to be good . . . [f]or the small practitioner, they are vaguely threatening.'

[145] Goriely, above, n 109, 161, argues that the franchising standards tacitly recognise that legal aid solicitors will have a lower standard than large city solicitors.

[146] In the case of the Law Society, it is the large firms that might feel tempted to break away. As one large firm lawyer observed, 'firms of our size would not rely on the Law Society to represent our interests . . . we recognise that we've got to look after ourselves'. 'Law Soc Damned by Members' (1997) 11 *The Lawyer*.

[147] This was the discovery of the Kutak Commission in the US (see chapter 6).

[148] R Abel, 'Why Does the ABA Promulgate Ethical Rules?' (1981) *Texas Law Review* 639.

[149] RL Nelson and DM Trubeck, 'Arenas of Professionalism: The Professional Ideologies of Lawyers in Context' in Nelson *et al*, above n 44, 177, 196.

sub-cultures, provide common educational requirements[150] and balance competing interests.[151]

The survival of professional ethics depends on the ability and commitment of professional bodies to perform the role of 'instructing, mentoring, censuring, defending, nurturing and regulating, their members'.[152] Success depends, however, on the commitment to professional goals of the organisations in which professionals work. The culture of institutions and organisations shapes the behaviour of individuals. Like individuals, organisations respond to rituals, norms, shame and the desire for legitimacy.[153] Large organisations have the resources to explore new ways of engaging with ethical agendas, like corporate social responsibility. In some jurisdictions large firms employ 'compliance professionals', responsible for ensuring regulatory observance. Compliance officers tend to work within the culture of the firm, trying to harmonise demands on the organisation rather than forcing choices.[154] They frequently employ strategies such as building corporate citizenship, using support from outside networks.

Nosworthy sees the relationship between internal and external influences in large firm culture as a series of concentric circles, with ethics the central concern.[155] The next ring represents the structure and culture of the firm and the third the relationship between partners and governance in general, including relationships between partners and staff. In the outer ring lie relationships with the outside world. Nosworthy argues that the relationships between partners and staff determine the ethical culture of the firm. Partners therefore have particular responsibility to ensure that they lead by example and ensure that their mutual dealings are characterised by respect, courtesy, equity and trust.[156] There are examples of large firms promoting their own distinct values and cultures, and holding even senior members to account if they fail to measure up.[157] The continuing relevance of this theory was illustrated in 2002, when a survey was published showing that the New York office of Clifford Chance, one of the largest and richest law firms in the world, was ranked worst in the country for associate satisfaction. Associates' complaints included pressure to 'pad bills', poor communication, partner indifference and discouragement of *pro bono*

---

[150] Attempts to include a universalistic approach to management issues for solicitors three years into qualification (via 'The Best Practice Course') failed, in part, because of the divergence of experience of young lawyers in different parts of the profession. A Sherr, 'Professional Legal Training' (1992) *Journal of Law & Society* 163, 171.

[151] For example, under threat from large law firms who wanted to offer their own LPC training, the Law Society has fundamentally changed the patterns of study in the LPC, dropping Wills and Probate as a subject assessed as part of the core and increasing the component of Business Law and Practice so that it contributes a maximum of 40% to the overall assessment.

[152] Above n 54, 225.

[153] MC Suchman and LB Edelman, 'Legal Rational Myths: The New Institutionalism and the Law and Society Tradition' (1996) 21 *Law and Social Inquiry* 903.

[154] Parker notes that in some jurisdictions in-house counsel, with other professions, have this role, trying to create 'virtuous cultures'. Without such interventions, she suggests, ethical agendas do not penetrate organisational culture. C Parker 'The Ethics of Advising on Regulatory Compliance: Autonomy or Interdependence' (2000) 28 *Journal of Business Ethics* 339.

[155] E Nosworthy, 'Ethics and the Large Law Firm' in S Parker and C Sampford (eds) *Legal Ethics and Legal Practice: Contemporary Issues* (Oxford, Clarendon Press, 1995) 57.

[156] *Ibid*, 66–9.

[157] One firm adopted six behavioural values—being straightforward, team working, mutual respect, accountability, continuous improvement and being client centred—with dire warnings for partners who did not subscribe. J Cahill 'Eversheds Partners and Staff Told to Shape Up to New Values or Ship Out', *The Lawyer*, 27 October 2003.

work,[158] and Clifford Chance responded with new criteria for promotion reflecting a strong ethical orientation.[159] This demonstrates that the relationship between individuals and organisations, and the profession and its constituent organisations, are reciprocal,[160] or reflexive. Professional norms and ethics inevitably reflect this fact.

Conclusion

Professional culture is a mixture of traditions, symbols and understandings about the profession and its role. Legal professionalism culture has been based on hierarchy, homogeneity and adversarialism, which are challenged by new values like diversity. Older values, like independence and collegiality, are under pressure because of developments in the legal services market, particularly the advent of competition. Collegiality, for example, is threatened by institutional pressures towards bureaucratisation and profit,[161] which tend to marginalise traditional virtues and the structures that support them.[162] The vision of the lawyer as an isolated and committed general practitioner, working alone or in a small partnership or chambers, has been overtaken by the increasing size of firms, and the diversity and distinctiveness of the profession. This raises questions about the possibility of a common professional culture, when diversification and stratification has weakened the similarity of work and interests.[163] While we should not idealise the historical homogeneity of the profession, common culture is assisted by modest scale and frequent interaction.[164] The legal profession must work harder to build a common professional culture, and perhaps even to convince the public that it is worth preserving.[165]

---

[158] http://financialtimes.

[159] Respect and mentoring, quality of work, excellence in client service, integrity, commitment to diversity, performance of *pro bono* work and contribution to the firm as an institution. N Rovnick 'Clifford Chance New York Puts Pro Bono on Associates' Agenda', *The Lawyer*, 3 February 2003, 3.

[160] Above n 158.

[161] Gordon, above n 87; CK Ihara, above n 57.

[162] See Macintyre's argument (chapter 1) that practices are sustained by institutions but that institutions, paradoxically, prioritise external goods. Without the virtues, practices cannot withstand the corrupting power of institutions. The conflict between internal goods, such as the development of virtues, and external goods, such as fame, fortune and power, are exacerbated by a disjunction between the values of professional practitioners and the institutions through which they practice (eg the firm or the courts). The rich rewards at one end of the profession and the poor living to be had at the other provides little incentive for young lawyers to prioritise the public nature of their calling rather than their personal self interest: 'Why be a virtuous person in one's professional role if the goods that are regarded as most important are the external goods the institution emphasises?' A Macintyre, *After Virtue: A Study of Moral Theory* (London, Duckworth, 1985) 194.

[163] Johnson, above n 5, 80.

[164] 'when the group is small, the individual and the society are not far apart; the whole is barely distinguishable from the part, and each individual can therefore discern the interests of the whole at first hand, along with the links that bind the interests of the whole to those of each one.' Durkheim, above n 46, 15.

[165] M Brown, 'Temple Opens Door to Mark 400 Years of Autonomy', *The Guardian*, 27 December 2007.

Part II

PROFESSIONAL STRUCTURES

Professions are organised through professional bodies, initially groups of an occupation sharing a common interest. As professional bodies grow in organisation and confidence they take on the task of representing their membership to society and often acquire powers over the membership delegated by the state. These powers include the power to make rules binding on members and to enforce them through disciplinary machinery. This latter power is arguably the essential component of professional ethics because, without prescription or sanction, rules are unlikely to work.[1] There are also reasons other than sanctions why rules do work, and collective action, through the professional group as a whole, provides a counter-balance to pressures militating against the observance of professional norms.

The machinery supporting professional ethics, the disciplinary, educational and other mechanisms controlled by the profession, is known as self-regulation. It is frequently argued that self-regulation serves the best interests of clients because only professionals can effectively review professional performance. Self-regulation was necessary historically because the art of the professional practitioner was impermeable and external regulation was therefore seen as impracticable. In part I we considered why that view has been challenged. In part II we see the implications for professional self-regulation.

Professional bodies have also been the means by which the interests of the occupational group are protected. Lawyers operate in a market for their services, which in England and Wales is more overtly commercial than that in which most other professions operate. It is increasingly more fluid, competitive and differentiated. While there is a need for enforceable standards of regulation, this diversity often makes detailed regulation difficult and discipline problematic. Therefore, beyond issues of enforcement, some expectations of professionals might only be realised through the process of education and training.[2]

In part II we work through these issues by looking in turn at the governance of the profession through its professional bodies, how regulation is managed through codes of conduct, the operation of the current disciplinary framework, legal education and training, and the role of ethics in the preparation of law students for professional life. The themes that run through these chapters are the formation, promulgation and revision of professional norms, together with the changes to these processes that have occurred over the past 20 years and that will be wrought by the Legal Services Act 2007, many of which are already underway. Despite the inroads that have been made in, and planned for, self-regulation, it will be seen that the two major regulatory powers that are essential for meaningful professional ethics—education and discipline—remain in the hands of the profession.

[1] R Baldwin 'Why Rules Don't Work' (1990) 53 *Modern Law Review* 321.
[2] JF Sutton and JS Dzienkowski, *Cases and Materials on the Professional Responsibility of Lawyers* (St Paul, MN, West Publishing, 1989) 2.

5

GOVERNANCE

Be strong, be supple; that is the way to rule.[1]

Introduction

This chapter considers the acquisition and exercise of powers of self-regulation and the role of the professional bodies, first as representatives of their members and second as their regulator. This dual role, maker and enforcer of regulation, will be fundamentally affected by the Legal Services Act 2007, although the profession has tried as far as possible to create governance structures that will harmonise with the new regulatory regime. The literature developing the principles of governance largely relates to corporations, but the principles of accountability and ethics that characterise it are of general relevance.[2] A detailed study of management roles and responsibilities with the profession is beyond the scope of this book. Here we are more concerned with how governance structures affect regulation, and particularly the systems used to develop standards and promote ethical practice. The professional bodies have complex structures that employ a permanent executive, administrative and secretarial structure to run operational aspects of the organisation. This structure services a plethora of committees that formulates policies for approval by a council. This committee structure draws extensively on the professional membership. This involvement of members in policy and regulation offers recognition and status, but is also a manifestation of collegiality and public service.

The evolution of self-regulation

Professions are distinguished from other occupations because the regulations governing their conduct are self-imposed, rather than being imposed by governments or employers. These powers of self-regulation are exercised by their professional bodies, which have traditionally acted in both a representative and a regulatory capacity. The development of self-regulation has a long history. Prior to the sixteenth century, discipline was maintained by the judiciary

---

[1] From 'Crouching Tiger, Hidden Dragon' (Dir: Ang Lee), United China Vision Inc (2000).

[2] See further, RSF Eells, *The Meaning of Modern Business: An Introduction to the Philosophy of Large Corporate Enterprise* (New York, Columbia University Press, 1960); J Charkham, *Keeping Better Company: Corporate Governance Ten Years On* (Oxford University Press, 2005), Office of Government Commerce, available at http:www.ogc.gov.uk/delivery_lifecycle_governance.asp.

for the whole profession, which comprised a number of different categories: barristers, attorneys (advisers in law suits) and solicitors (who specialised in real property). From the sixteenth century, barristers became more differentiated from the others, offering formal education in the Inns of Court[3] and exercising disciplinary authority over their own members. Discipline was often rather perfunctory and the sanctions informal. They tended to be imposed for breaches of etiquette and used threats to status as the main means of exerting control.[4] The creation of the Law Society provided an opportunity to take a firmer hold of disciplinary issues and even to overtake the Bar, which did not adopt a code until the Benson Report noted the lack of such in 1979.[5] The General Council of the Bar (Bar Council) was founded in 1894 to represent the interests of barristers, but, among an array of other responsibilities, acquired the task of maintaining and enhancing professional standards and maintaining effective complaints and disciplinary procedures.[6]

The relatively late emergence of the Law Society in 1836 began the process of self-regulation for solicitors, commencing with maintaining the roll of solicitors. In 1839 the Law Society was allowed to appear in court when solicitors were accused of disciplinary offences for which they might be struck off the roll. A solicitors' disciplinary committee was established under the Solicitors' Act 1888, but it had no power to impose sanctions.[7] In 1874 the Law Society was permitted to conduct preliminary investigations before disciplinary proceedings[8] and in 1907 it was given the power to investigate solicitors' accounts and to issue annual practising certificates.[9] The Law Society began to organise disciplinary tribunals with power to impose sanctions only in 1919. On many issues the Law Society came into conflict with the political and legal establishment. Advertising, for example, was regarded as unprofessional conduct by the Law Society but, during the nineteenth and early twentieth centuries, judges were not supportive of the Society's attempts to suppress either advertising or touting by solicitors.[10] The Law Society did not acquire the power to make

---

[3] Education at the Inns can be traced to the Middle Ages. D Sugarman, 'Bourgeois Collectivism, Professional Power and the Boundaries of the State. The Private and Public Life of the Law Society 1825 to 1914' (1996) 3 *International Journal of the Legal Profession* 81, 85.

[4] A good example of this is provided by R Pound, *The Lawyer from Antiquity to Modern Times: With particular reference to The Development of Bar Associations in the United States* (St Paul, MN, West Publishing 1953), 127. In early time barristers who had progressed to the point that they could not conveniently carry their briefs were permitted exclusively to carry a purple brief bag. This had to be presented by King's Counsel. The Circuit Grand Court preferred an indictment against one barrister who received a purple bag from a King's Counsel to whom he was related by marriage; the terms of the indictment were that he carried 'one purple bag wholly collapsing by reason of emptiness'. It will be noted that the unfortunate holder of the purple bag had not broken a specific rule but that he, and the donor of the bag, had ignored norms of behaviour. The indictment was a rebuke to them both for engaging in nepotism and a warning to others that similar conduct risked exposure.

[5] The Royal Commission on Legal Services Final Report (1979) Cmnd 7648 (Benson). The Bar did have a small book of etiquette and conduct distilled from authoritative sources published since 1895 but, although it was compiled by the former secretary of The Senate, the preface was at pains to point out it was not an official publication. WW Boulton, *A Guide to Conduct and Etiquette at the Bar* (London, Butterworths, 6th edn, 1975).

[6] It comprises 115 barristers who are elected or who represent the Inns, Circuits and other interest groups and meets seven times a year.

[7] See further R Cranston, 'Legal Ethics and Professional Responsibility' in R Cranston (ed), *Legal Ethics and Professional Responsibility* (Oxford, Clarendon Press) 3.

[8] M Burrage, 'From a Gentleman's to a Public Profession' [1996] *International Journal of the Legal Profession* 45, 56.

[9] Sugarman, above n 6, 106.

[10] *Ibid* See also L Sheinman, *The History, Form and Functions of the Law Society's Early Rules of Conduct*, PhD Thesis (London, IALS, 2003) 51.

binding rules until 1933, so in this respect their self-regulatory powers are in fact of quite recent origin.

Despite the impressive acquisition of powers, the level of control that professions exercise over members is debatable. Arthurs, for example, states:

> Governing bodies are formally responsible for the regulation of professional practise: within the scope of their statutory authority they admit and disbar, they educate and exhort; they legislate and speak as the official voice of the profession. But it would be foolish to pretend that no sparrow falls without the knowledge of the governing body, that no norms of conduct exist save for those they proclaim, that no system of sanctions or rewards influences lawyers' conduct except those which bear an official imprimatur. To the contrary: it is the governing body which occupies a marginal role in directing professional behaviour, albeit a role which does become more central at the defining moments of entry to and exit from practise.[11]

Since this was written, self-regulation has arguably declined. Criticism of the Law Society by consumer groups led to the appointment by the Lord Chancellor of the Legal Services Ombudsman in 1990 to deal with those complaints that the professional body had failed to deal with adequately. In 2004 a Legal Services Complaints Commissioner was appointed by the Lord Chancellor to monitor and set targets for complaints handling by the Law Society.

The Lord Chancellor's Department's oversight powers on both conduct rules and education were first introduced with the creation of the Lord Chancellor's Advisory Committee on Education and Conduct (ACLEC) in 1990. They have continued since then with the requirement, under the Access to Justice Act 1999, to obtain the Lord Chancellor's consent to changes in the Rules, which he deals with via the Legal Services Consultative Panel. These moves involved the progressive involvement of lay people in regulation of the profession.[12] This long-term trend towards external oversight of regulation is also emerging in other countries[13] and will be continued with the Legal Services Act 2007. Although self-regulation will be compromised by the Act, governance of the profession will remain in the hands of the professional bodies. The fact that Arthurs's statement was made over 10 years ago, and that the profession's grip on self-regulation has been progressively weakened in that time suggests that, by now, that grip should be feeble. This is not the case, however, because one of the consequences of stripping away of formal powers appears to be that the profession strives harder to be in more effective control of what remains.

Governance structures

All institutions are concerned with using resources to solve conflicts and make decisions. Governance is concerned with how organisations are directed and controlled, and where

---

[11] HW Arthurs, 'Lawyering in Canada in the 21st Century' (1996) 15 *Windsor Yearbook of Access to Justice* 202, 223.

[12] It is via membership of ACLEC that for the first time lay persons were given a role in defining the responsibility of lawyers: AA Paterson, 'Professionalism and the Legal Services Market' (1996) 3 *International Journal of the Legal Profession* 137, 153. On the Legal Complaints Commissioner's powers see p 135 and on ACLEC see chapters 3 and 8.

[13] A number of Australian Law Societies are no longer self-regulating: A Evans, 'Professional Ethics North and South: Interest on Clients' Funds and Lawyer Fraud. An Opportunity to Redeem Professionalism' (1996) 3 *International Journal of the Legal Profession* 281, 283; C Parker 'Lawyer Deregulation via Business Deregulation: Compliance Professionalism and Legal Professionalism' (1999) 6 *International Journal of the Legal Profession* 175.

accountability and responsibility are located within them; where the power to take action is located; and how the organisation structures its units and groupings in order to manage change. Governance is usually managed through policies and processes, although an executive usually enacts policies where action, like publishing documents or issuing press releases, is required. While corporate governance concerns shareholders, managers and boards of directors, the professions usually have a member as a nominal head, or president, who holds office for a year. A permanent administration services committees of members. The concerns of these groupings are the formulation of strategies and policies over a wide range of activities. They affect the relationships with stakeholders in the profession, the distribution of central and local authority, the ways in which services are provided and the enforcement of standards.

Although self-regulation is still seen as appropriate in the formulation of professional norms, under the Legal Services Act 2007 the process will be overseen and possibly controlled by the Legal Services Board, on which there will be a majority of lay people. The Board will be responsible, not to the professions, but to Parliament. In anticipation of the Act and in order to integrate as far as possible with the framework that it will introduce, the profession has implemented changes to its governance structures. The regulatory functions of the Bar Council have been taken over by the Bar Standards Board, just as those of the Law Society have been taken over by the Solicitors Regulation Authority. These developments will inevitably accelerate the tendency to centralisation of power round the professional bodies and the growth of bureaucracies charged with carrying out and enforcing policy. Such bureaucracies already exist in nascent form, but are relatively underdeveloped, given the scale of the regulatory and representative tasks facing the profession.

Solicitors

The Law Society, which is a statutory body, governs solicitors. The everyday business of the Law Society is managed by the Chief Executive. A number of post-holders, permanent employees, report to him, including Directors of Communications, of Legal Policy and of Governmental Relations (see Figure 1).

The policy of the Law Society is approved by the Council, consisting of 105 members, including five laypersons. The members are elected by the membership, and most represent constituencies throughout England and Wales, along with some members representing specialist groups. The Council presides over a number of committees, from which it receives reports and recommendations for policy (see Figure 2).

In anticipation of the changes to be brought forward in the Legal Services Act 2007, which in turn had been recommended in the Clementi Report of 2004, the Law Society split its regulatory and representative functions in January 2006. Only if the regulatory and representative functions were adequately separated would the proposed Legal Services Board be able to approve the Law Society as a frontline body exercising regulatory functions. The referendum vote in favour of the Council's proposal to do this was, however, close, with 7909 in favour and 7175 against, giving a majority of only 734.[14]

---

[14] *Law Society Gazette*, 15 September 2005, 4. A total of 123,000 solicitors were entitled to vote, which means that only 12.2% did so.

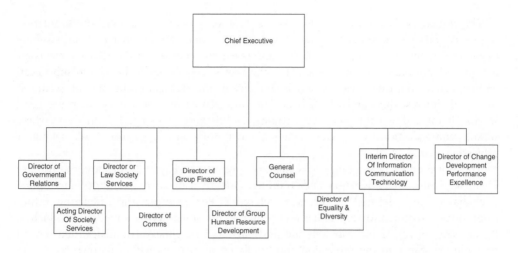

Figure 1: Law Society management structure, representation and central services.

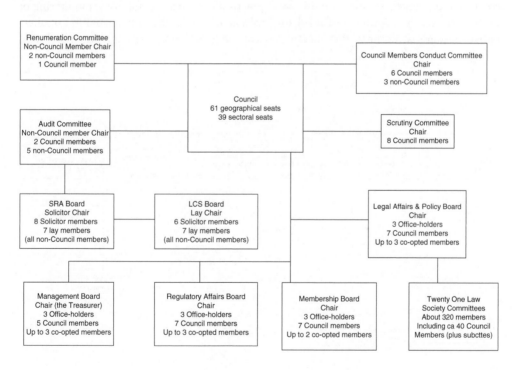

Figure 2: Law Society governance structure.

The regulatory functions for solicitors are now the province of a Solicitors Regulation Authority (SRA),[15] although the SRA Board (SRB) is one of a number of boards subordinate to Council. There are nine solicitor and seven lay members of the SRB and the chair is Peter Williamson, a previous president of the Law Society. None of the SRB members can be members of the Law Society Council. The aim of the SRA is to promote and secure in the public interest the standards of behaviour and performance necessary to ensure good service. It must deal with policy and strategy in all these areas apart from those where statute requires action by the Law Society Council, for example, in the actual making of professional conduct rules.

The SRB presides over a range of regulatory committees (Figure 3), including Consumer Financial Protection, Education and Training, Quality Assurance, and Rules and Ethics. Each has a remit defined by terms of reference. For example, the Rules and Ethics Committee is required to keep under review all matters potentially relating to rules, such as the decisions of courts and tribunals and the Solicitors Disciplinary Tribunal, with a view to providing guidance to the profession and public on all matters within its own remit and that of the Solicitors Regulation Board. The Compliance Committee has a broader brief: to advise the SRB on developing principles of risk-based and proportionate regulation. This role includes oversight of many aspects of regulatory activity, including investigation of conduct and regulatory issues, imposition of practising certificate conditions, monitoring of practice standards, assessment of regulatory risks arising from the implementation of alternative business structures, the effectiveness of rules and proposals for amendment. It

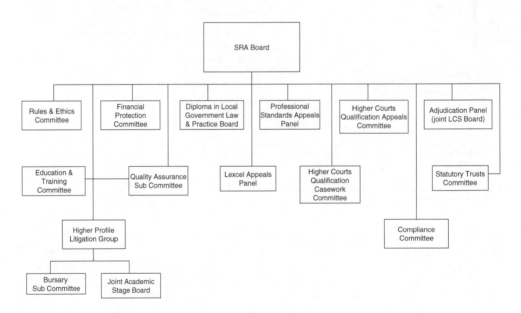

Figure 3: Solicitors Regulation Authority committee structure.

---

[15] So named from January 2007. Previously known as the Regulation Board.

appears therefore that, while the work of the Rules and Ethics Committee and the Compliance Committee overlap, it is the latter that has the role of anticipating change and the former that implements appropriate and detailed changes.

There is also the Consumer Complaints Board, which runs the Consumer Complaints Service described in chapter 7. These committees have delegated decision-making powers, insofar as these are lawful. Again, changes in the Rules can be effected only by the Council. The SRA also has an executive structure, with a number of permanent post-holders reporting to a chief executive (Figure 4).

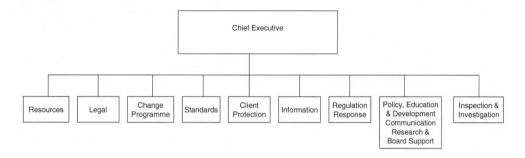

Figure 4: Solicitors Regulation Authority management structure.

Barristers

The Bar has a more complex governance structure than solicitors because the Bar's ancient seats of governance were the Inns of Court. Their influence and residual power is strong yet uncertain, since much of what the Bar Council enacts by way of policy is negotiated with the Inns. Clementi thought that the real power of the Inns of Court derives from their property holdings and their contribution to the Bar Council's finances. He concluded, however, that

> it would be hard for any reviewer to conclude that it is clear where regulatory authority, and hence responsibility, lies between the Bar Council and the Inns.[16]

Practising barristers must still be members of one of the Inns, which are mainly concerned with providing training, a library and the chambers from which many barristers practice, but which also have some disciplinary powers. In exercising the latter, the Inns have agreed to be bound by the policies laid down by the Bar Council, which regulates barristers, both practising and employed. Its current structure dates from 1985, and it has 120 members and three officers. All the members are elected from the Bar; none are laypeople. The Council was not set up by any statute, as was the Law Society, but its existence is recognised by statute in the Courts and Legal Services Act 1990 (CSLA), section 31 in relation to its power to make rules on rights of audience. Its structure is set out in Figure 5, which shows the major

---

[16] D Clementi, *Review of the Regulatory Framework for Legal Services in England and Wales*, (London, Department for Constitutional Affairs, 2004) ch B, para 23.

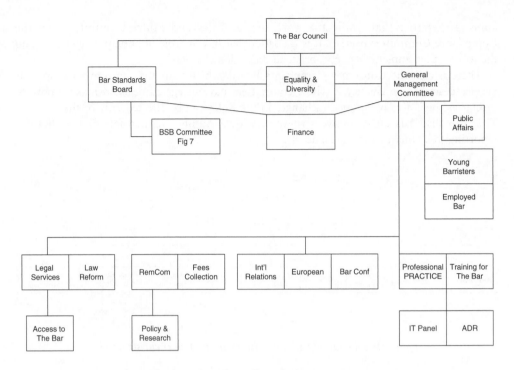

Figure 5: Bar Council governance structure.

organisational change that took place in 2006 when the Bar Council separated its representative from its regulatory functions, ceding the latter to the Bar Standards Board (BSB).

The BSB was created in anticipation of the changes to be brought forward in the Legal Services Act 2007, which in turn had been recommended in the Clementi Report of 2004. It is not elected and neither can any of its members be members of the Bar Council. The BSB consists of seven barristers (with, currently, a majority of QCs), six laypersons and a lay chair, Ruth Evans. The BSB is funded by the Bar Council. It has set up two oversight committees chaired by laypersons: the Consumer Panel and the Performance and Best Value Committee. Five working committees report to the BSB, concerned with education and training, qualifications, standards, quality assessment and the Complaints Committee. The committees make recommendations to the BSB. Most of the committees are advised by a number of sub-committees covering the different areas of their remit. For example, the Education and Training Committee has three sub-committees covering the Bar Vocational Course, Pupillage and Continuing Professional Development. Despite the fact that the BSB is virtually an independent entity within the Bar Council, it is still the function of the Bar Council to change its rules of practice.

The representative functions—defending the Bar's interests to government, in the press or before commissions and inquiries, and exercising a trade union function in relation to fees and legal aid—are the concern of the General Council, as the Bar's representative body. Figure 6 shows how the representative and regulatory sides overlap on important issues,

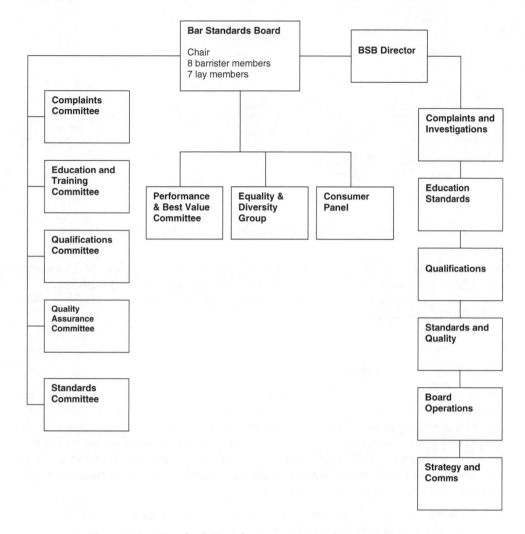

Figure 6: Bar Standards Board management and committee structure.

with the work of the BSB's Education and Training Committee reflected in the representative side's Training for the Bar Committee. The BSB also has a director controlling a number of functions, such as Complaints and Investigations, and a complex of committees, such as a Complaints Committee, reporting to it (see Figure 6).

Like the Law Society, the Bar Council has an administration and a secretariat, headed by a Director of Representation and Policy, supporting the representative side (Figure 7).

The Law Society and the Bar Council have very similar basic structures, including committee and management networks. These are hierarchical, elaborate and complex. The large amount of work performed within these structures would be difficult to sustain without the contributions of large amounts of time contributed by their members. One of

Figure 7: Bar Council representation and central services.

the key justifications of self-regulation is the 'ownership' of regulation that this engenders. The changes proposed by the Legal Services Act 2007 will allow the profession to sustain this involvement despite the move towards greater lay representation on the regulatory side of the profession's operations.

The Legal Services Act 2007

The Clementi Report criticised the way that practice rules were made by the professions. For example, it considered that the Bar Council and the Law Society were often held back by their members in making desirable changes to the rules, and this had in the past restricted both competition and innovation in the professions. Changes were often forced on the professions by outside pressures that they could no longer resist, such as the new rules on direct access to the Bar (and, indeed, the recent division of the professional bodies into representative and regulatory branches). Clementi concluded that

> issues such as changes in the practice rules should be examined, not against the wishes of the membership, but against the test of public interest.[17]

However, Clementi did not recommend that all rule-making powers should be taken away from the professions: day-to-day rule making should be left to them as they have the necessary knowledge and expertise to do it. Moreover, it is desirable that practitioners should be committed to high standards, and this is more likely to be achieved if they see that the rules are formulated by their own profession and are therefore to be obeyed rather than regarded as a 'constraint to be circumvented'.[18] Clementi was also anxious to preserve the profession's independence. Accordingly he recommended that the proposed Legal Services Board (LSB)[19] should be 'an oversight regulator', exercising the powers currently exercised by the Lord Chancellor in relation to the approval of rules of conduct.

[17] *Ibid*, para 13.
[18] *Ibid*, para 29.
[19] See chapter 6 at p 128 on this.

The Legal Services Act 2007 will change the way professional rules are approved but probably not the way they are initially produced by the professions. Under the Act the LSB, a non-departmental public body which will be at arm's length from government, will have the power to approve regulators. These are the bodies referred to by Clementi as 'front line regulators' and in the Act as Approved Regulators. Certain existing regulators are automatically approved under Schedule 4 part I, and these include the Law Society and the General Council of the Bar. They are therefore authorised to continue to make practice and conduct rules.[20] Their rule-making powers must be exercised with regard to the regulatory objectives governing activities and also those of the LSB itself, which are noted below. It is likely, therefore, that the LSB will rely heavily on the professions to propose new rules or amend old ones, as is now the case with the Lord Chancellor.

The 'regulatory objectives' are set out in section 1 of the Act and are:

(a) protecting and promoting the public interest;
(b) supporting the constitutional principle of the rule of law;
(c) improving access to justice;
(d) protecting and promoting the interests of consumer interests;
(e) promoting competition in the provision of services (that is, those services provided by authorised bodies);
(f) encouraging an independent, strong, diverse and effective legal profession;
(g) increasing public understanding of the citizen's legal rights and duties; and
(h) promoting and maintaining adherence to the professional principles.

The protection of the good repute of the professions, so beloved of the existing professional codes, does not as such feature here. The 'professional principles' noted in (h) above are elaborated in section 1(3). They are independence, integrity, maintaining proper standards of work, acting in the best interests of clients, and confidentiality. In addition, those exercising rights of audience or who conduct litigation must comply with their duty to the court to act independently and in the interests of justice.

The LSB must act in accordance with these objectives 'so far as is reasonably practicable' in all its activities, not just rule making or approving.[21] Its activities must also be 'transparent, accountable, proportionate, consistent and targeted'.[22] Detailed rules on how the LSB will work are not yet available, but it may be presumed that any rule change proposed by the professions will normally have to undergo a public consultation process wider than that traditionally undertaken by the professions and also a consultation process with the Board. This would probably include the views of a consumer panel, also provided for under the Act, which will consist of business and individual consumers of legal services who were not otherwise involved in providing legal services themselves or were members of any approved regulator such as the Law Society or bar.

Approved regulators are required by the Act to have governance rules which enable those undertaking regulatory functions to make representations to and be consulted by the LSB, the consumer panel and other approved regulators, and to act independently of those

[20] Legal Services Act 2007, s 21.
[21] Legal Services Act, s 3(2).
[22] *Ibid*, s 3(3).

exercising representative functions. Indeed, the regulators must be able to 'notify the Board where they consider that their independence or effectiveness is being prejudiced'.[23] If regulators do not act in accordance with the regulatory objectives or contravene the provisions separating regulatory and representative functions, then the Board has a range of enforcement provisions. These range from setting performance targets and monitoring, making directions (failure to comply can result in an application to the High Court), publishing a statement censuring the regulator, imposing fines and direct intervening in the regulator's functions when the Board itself can act as an approved regulator instead of the original regulator.[24] The ultimate sanction is to ask the Lord Chancellor to cancel a regulator's approval.[25] The power of the Master of the Rolls to approve Law Society rules is abolished.[26]

It is difficult to predict what will be the effect of the new procedure when it comes into force. It will certainly be more open and easier for laypersons both to find out what is proposed by regulators and also have an input. It is not currently clear whether it is proposed that the Bar's rules should have binding force as currently applies to solicitors. This would only be the case if the rules were to be formally made by the LSB itself, which appears to be possible. The professions will undoubtedly lose whatever remains of their autonomy to make their own rules, but since most of the important rules are already subject to the approval of the Lord Chancellor, that autonomy has not in reality existed since the 1999 Access to Justice Act. Both professions currently consult fairly widely, especially among other government bodies such as the Office of Fair Trading, when proposing a rule change. A considerable advantage of the new system relates not so much to control by the LSB of professional rule-making autonomy, but to the loss of that control by the Lord Chancellor. He will lose his powers under the 1999 Act and the professional bodies will be controlled in a much more regulated and open way by the LSB, a body not under his direct control. As the Lord Chancellor is a politician and a member of the government and cabinet, this in fact represents an advance for the independence of the professions and their freedom from political influence.[27]

Representation

One of the key purposes of the Legal Services Act 2007 was to force the profession to separate its regulatory and representative functions. The principle behind this is that the revenue from compulsory charges on practitioners, such as practising certificate fees, should be used for regulating the profession, not for its political purposes. It is therefore necessary to consider what role representation plays in the governance of the profession. Professional organisations

---

[23] *Ibid*, s 30(3)(b).
[24] *Ibid* ss 31–44.
[25] *Ibid*, s 45(3).
[26] *Ibid*, sch 16.
[27] This is even more the case since June 2007. The Lord Chancellor does not have to be a lawyer or a member of the House of Lords, but is a member of the House of Commons and a cabinet member, heading the Ministry of Justice. The current and first Lord Chancellor of this type is Jack Straw, who has had a number of other ministerial posts in the past, such as Home Secretary and Leader of the House of Commons.

are the main means through which professions seek to influence public policy, especially in relation to its own working practices. Here, professions must choose how they claim legitimacy for their views. A large and inclusive professional group confers a degree of legitimacy on the professional body and, therefore, allows it to speak with authority. But the more inclusive professional membership becomes, the wider the range of views which must be represented. This often makes it difficult for the profession to come to a common view on any issue. Small exclusive bodies can more effectively mobilise their membership, but their problem is that they may lack legitimacy and, therefore, influence. An organisation with a large membership may have legitimacy, but will find it difficult to take effective collective action. There is more risk with a large and diverse organisation that members pursue sectional advantage at the expense of the higher goals the profession may set itself.

Professional bodies have historically had a key role in defining, sustaining and promoting the professional ethic. At times when the membership has common values this may be achieved without much participation by the membership. The role of members is often seen to be to obey the rules, not to make them. But this expectation is built on very fragile foundations:

> For the effective enforcement of a professional ethic, it is not necessary that all members of the profession adhere to it with total commitment . . . But . . . there must be excellent leadership and good morale. The leadership is necessary to provide definition and application of the professional ethic in constantly changing circumstances; and morale is necessary if this leadership is to be effective. The ordinary members of the profession must respect the leaders according to their criteria of skill and success, and be prepared to accept their guidance and control. Also, they must have some degree of commitment to doing good work, so that a consensus can operate against those who betray the good name of the profession. Otherwise the enforcement of a professional ethic is impossible.[28]

Effective leadership and consultation are important because the observance of rules depends on the support of members. This support is easier to achieve when the members share a common purpose and common values and have a lively interest in the development of the profession.[29] It is more difficult when the membership has only an occasional interest in governance. Law Society elections traditionally have a poor turnout, and its consultations produce disappointing numbers of responses. Moreover, the difficulty of providing effective leadership is exacerbated by the declining influence of the professional body on the government. A realisation of this fact—and the increasing intervention by the government into the affairs of the profession—may explain why, after 40 years of uncontested elections for senior positions in the Law Society, there were four contested and acrimonious elections in the 1990s. This increase in democratic participation was, however, short lived. Nevertheless, the professional bodies have been forced more openly by their members into the role of 'trade union' negotiator and lobbyist.

---

[28] JR Ravetz, 'Ethics in Scientific Activity' in A Flores (ed.), *Professional Ideals* (Belmont, CA, Wadsworth Publishing, 1988) 147, 153.

[29] Although professional bodies assume responsibility for the ethics of a profession, individual professionals must also accept responsibility, not only for their own performance, but for the performance of fellow professionals. Membership of professional bodies and local associations is perhaps indicative. In a survey of solicitors it was found that over 50% of respondents were not involved with the Law Society or their local law societies: 'Law Soc Damned by Members' (1997) 11(22) *The Lawyer* 1.

Combining the representative or 'trade union' and regulatory roles presented the profession with three problems which hampered its commitment to professional ethics. First, it made it difficult to maintain either the reality or the image of objectivity in investigating and pursuing disciplinary issues. Secondly, there is a conflict between providing protection to consumers whilst also promoting individual responsibility among members.[30] Thirdly, there is the problem of representing a diverse constituency and the various factions within it. These problems, along with clear indications from the government that the two functions could no longer be combined in one professional organisation, led both the solicitors and the Bar to divide the roles from January 2006. Now the Law Society takes on the 'trade union' and representative role under the direction of its Council and the regulatory role is undertaken by the SRA. The SRA is funded by the Law Society but not controlled by its Council. A similar split has been introduced by the Bar. The regulatory function has been taken over by the BSB, which is separate from (though funded by) the Bar Council. How far this change will increase public trust in the regulation of the profession is yet to be seen and, in any case, they may well be overtaken by the schema of the Legal Services Act 2007. However, the task of representing an increasingly diverse membership will remain, and it is to this problem that we now turn.

The task of the professional bodies in dealing with these problems is complicated by the fact that one of their key tasks is to articulate the membership's demands for autonomy in the way that they conduct their work.[31] In chapter 1 we considered the legitimacy of professional norms of behaviour in terms of wider social norms. We noted that acceptance of the legitimacy of rules depends on acceptance by practitioners of the legitimacy of the authority making the rules. They may accept the rules because they are consistent with the actor's own purposes, because the rules are believed to be worthy in their own right, because they accord with the actor's feelings or emotions or because observance is traditional or habitual.[32] However, one way of securing legitimacy is through participation by the objects of regulation, in this case, members of the profession, in the creation of the regulations. This needs mutual interpersonal trust between the members of the professional community—that is, the professional body must be an appropriate repository of this trust[33] between the various groups in the professional community. As we saw in chapter 2, the increasing differentiation of the legal profession creates tensions between the so-called professional elites, whose interests tend to dominate professional bodies, and the bulk of the membership. There are increasing pressures for professional leaders to be made more accountable to the rank and file.[34] Inter-professional conflict is by no means new. Examples of these tensions have occurred throughout the history of the solicitors' branch.

---

[30] This is often problematic because financial consequences are spread through insurance. The weakness of compensation funds is that the whole professional group take responsibility for individual misbehaviour.

[31] MD Bayles, *Professional Ethics* (Belmont, CA, Wadsworth Publishing, 2nd edn, 1989) 8. Many critics suggest that this is all that professional bodies achieve and that 'what is done is largely trivial or irrelevant, what needs to be done is left unaccomplished': JC Payne, 'The Weakness of Bar Associations' (1977) *The Journal of the Legal Profession* 55.

[32] R Cotterrell, *Law's Community: Legal Theory in Sociological Perspective* (Oxford, Clarendon Press, 1995) particularly at 140, discussing Weber's theory of legitimate domination.

[33] See chapter 1 and Cotterrell, *ibid*, particularly at 330 and references to Giddens in ch 1.

[34] R Owen, 'The Governance of the Bar: Constitutional Reform' [May/June 1997] *Counsel* 3.

During the periods 1840–1850 and 1880–1914 tensions between the London-dominated Law Society and provincial solicitors became severe, particularly when the Law Society was thought not to be defending the conveyancing monopoly or other work sufficiently strongly. Various alliances of provincial law societies threatened the control of the Law Society but failed to gain a significant foothold.[35] As the Law Society increasingly promoted the idea that it advanced the public interest, it became diffident in defending the profession's interests against the government. The ultimate humiliation occurred when country solicitors' opposition to a land transfer bill forced the government to back down even though the Law Society had already agreed its terms. Thereafter the Law Society was forced to become more vocal in protecting its members' interests.[36] In the debates regarding the legalisation of trade unions in the late nineteenth century the Law Society increasingly saw its representative role as both legitimate and necessary.

The strains of articulating the views of an increasingly diverse membership also became quite severe in the 1990s. As noted above, in 1995 the election of the President of the Society was contested for the first time since 1954. In an acrimonious election campaign, Martin Mears was elected on a populist ticket to represent the interests of the 'ordinary' practitioner. His themes were the damage done to standards of conveyancing by the ending of the solicitors' monopoly, the oversupply of lawyers and the bureaucracy of the Law Society. His period in office highlighted the tension between the elite and the rest of the profession, and his challenge to the liberal establishment both within and outside the Law Society excited much disagreement about its role.[37] A lawyer in a large personal injury firm commented:

> The Law Society under Mears regards itself as a Trade Union to make sure that lawyers earn enough. It isn't actually looking at how we serve the public. If someone doesn't start looking at that someone is going to take it away from us.[38]

This proved to be an accurate prophecy, since the Legal Services Act 2007 will take away much of the public protection function from the profession and vest it in the LSB. However, the contested election reflected deeper problems. One of these was loss of confidence, reflected in the fact that solicitors felt they had fallen in public esteem. Many criticised the Law Society for this. An independent survey conducted for the Law Society in 1997 established that only 8% of solicitors in private practice felt that the Law Society was doing a good job of promoting the profession to the public and only 21% thought that it was doing a good job of representing the views of the profession to decision makers and Parliament.[39]

The Law Society's reaction to its falling credibility was to emphasise that it could not

---

[35] Sugarman, above n 3, 103.

[36] *Ibid*, 115.

[37] Henry Hodge, the official Council candidate, was defeated by over 3,000 votes (*The Guardian*, 11 April 1995). Mears proposed a reduction in powers of the Secretary General at a Council Meeting (*The Independent*, 11 September 1995). In October 1995 Mears excited adverse press reaction with attacks on the Equal Opportunities Commission and the Commission for Racial Equality (Lawtel doc z51024 10/10/95).

[38] J Flood, A Boon, A Whyte, E Skordaki, R Abbey and A Ash, 'Reconfiguring the Market for Advocacy Services: A Case Study of London and Four Fields of Practice' (Research Report for the Lord Chancellor's Advisory Committee on Legal Education and Conduct, 1996) 55.

[39] Above n 29. A similar survey in 1989 had found that 32% of solicitors thought that the Law Society was good at promoting the profession and 53% that it was good at representing the profession.

accept full responsibility for the fortunes of the profession. A spokesperson for the Law Society said

> I fully accept that the Law Society must bat more strongly. Individual solicitors must do so too. The Law Society cannot single-handedly guard and promote the reputation of the profession.

One cause for concern in terms of participation and legitimacy therefore is that so few solicitors vote on issues of fundamental importance to the profession.[40] For example, in 1996 less than 30% of the membership voted on the issue of whether the Law Society should separate its representative and regulatory roles.[41] Even fewer, 12.2%, voted in 2005, when the change was finally approved by a mere 734 votes. The change, introduced in 2006, was not sufficient to deter the government from keeping to its decision to vest regulatory oversight of the profession, and other bodies providing legal services, in the Legal Services Board. Few solicitors participate in Law Society decision making, yet over 70% believe that the LSB will have too much power over the profession. It is difficult not to conclude that, if true, this is partly their own fault.[42]

The nature of the representative task has itself changed. It is no longer accepted by the public or government that lawyers are in reality servants of public need. The Law Society has had to counter a flood of research and opinion which undermines the profession's image of ethicality. In doing this, it has developed its own research capability and has become more

> conscious of the need to justify its policies publicly and to demonstrate how the public and professional interest may be reconciled.[43]

The multiple tensions in its role are thus exposed for all to see. As Sugarman observed:

> the strength and weakness of the Law Society (and the profession) has stemmed from its propensity to express several contradictory tendencies side by side: its claim to act in the general interests of society; its much asserted independence and relative autonomy from external influence, notably that of the state; its 'gentlemanly' character, in part sustained by the image of the barrister, its 'national' character; its claims to act as an effective pressure group and trade union on behalf of its membership; and its inherent dependence upon and imbrication within the state.[44]

As the spotlight has been turned on the professions, they have to work harder to be more effective advocates of their own value to society and to find the structures and mechanisms that can help them achieve this.

---

[40] Only 23,000, of over 65,000 solicitors eligible to vote did so in the election in the 1995 presidential elections (*The Times* 11 July 1995), and only 8,881 (29.8%) voted on the proposal to separate the Law Society's disciplinary and representative function. See N Hilborne, 'Voters Reject Split Society', *Gazette* 93/38 16 October 1996, 1.

[41] The vote was rejected and was therefore seen as a desire to retain self-regulation, although 40% voted for the division of functions (Hilborne, *ibid*).

[42] Survey reported in *New Law Journal*, 1 September 2006.

[43] Burrage, above n 8, 75.

[44] Above n 3.

Conclusion

The governance of the profession has become increasingly centralised with the need for effective regulation. In the case of the Bar, for example, power has shifted from the Inns to the Bar Council. Both professional bodies have powerful bureaucracies supporting their memberships in formulating policy and in enacting it. This reflects the coming to pass of Burrage's prediction that, as the work of the profession becomes more diverse, and the status and circumstances of solicitors become more differentiated, the problems of governance will become more extreme.[45] The separation of regulatory and representative functions should make governance in the public interest a little more straightforward, but there are limits to the extent that the professional bodies can adapt their governance system in response to increasing divergence in the interests of the membership. The remaining vestiges of self-regulation represent a last chance for the profession to demonstrate the efficacy of its structures in supporting ethical professions.

---

[45] Burrage, above n 8, 73.

6

REGULATION

But one who is intended coming to the profession might ask where is this code to be found, and how is to be learnt? The answer to the first question is in the traditions of the profession. The answer to the second is in the Schools of the profession, its ancient craft guilds, called the Inns of Court, where all matters of professional conduct are freely and daily discussed, and where the transgressor is answerable for his misconduct. It is, of course, incapable of being stated or written out in full like a Legal Code.[1]

Introduction

The aim and process of regulation is a systematic attempt to restrict fluctuations in behaviour. In the case of professional ethics, making the behaviour of professionals conform to a norm is managed through professional codes, although other mechanisms, like education, play a part. Codes of conduct are now the repository of the legal profession's ethical commitments and therefore the principal mechanism of ethics regulation. The status of the codes, the processes of rule making and the nature of those rules are important in understanding the ways in which changing social, economic and political conditions create the need for new kinds of rules. The precise operation of these mechanisms is, however, unknown. Rules clearly respond to changing national circumstances, for example, but we do not know whether professional bodies in different countries influence each other, although it seems likely.[2] There are many possible models for regulating legal practice. Despite the pre-eminence of rules in the regulatory strategy of the professions, many argue that codes are an ineffective means of achieving ethical compliance. This chapter concludes with a consideration of some of the alternative models for regulation.

The nature and status of the codes

Codes of conduct are a relatively recent innovation. Both the Bar, through the Bar Standards Board, and the Law Society, through the Solicitors Regulation Authority (SRA), consider, revise and publish their own codes of conduct. As noted in the previous chapter, they have

---

[1] M Hilbery, *Duty and Art in Advocacy* (London, Stevens & Sons, 1946) 7.

[2] The attempts of the American Bar Association (ABA) to establish a common code for State Bar Associations is an of professions expand the influence of their own ethical codes. R Pound, *The Lawyer from Antiquity to Modern Times: With Particular Reference to The Development of Bar Associations in the United States* (St Paul, MN, West Publishing, 1953) 270.

committees the sole purpose of which is to oversee these functions. The rules are frequently changed as new circumstances arise, such as when the Bar adapted its code to recognise the position of employed barristers. Another strong influence is the courts. While we think of professional ethics as conduct imposed upon them by their professional body, many of the rules of professional conduct are in fact to be found in the ordinary law, such as that on contract, agency or trusts. Increasingly, we might expect the courts to influence the rules, if not always determine them. The profession does not necessarily fall in line with every decision of the courts, but may issue guidance on how it interprets recent judicial decisions or pronouncements on ethical or conduct issues.

Solicitors

Until 2007 the Law Society did not have a comprehensive and binding body of principles and rules, so might be said to have not had a code of conduct. The Solicitors' Practice Rules 1990, which preceded the 2007 Code, were made under the Law Society's delegated powers but did not claim to constitute a complete code. In particular, they omitted any rules on confidentiality and conflict, a gap which was remedied only in 2005 in anticipation of the introduction of the 2007 Rules. The Law Society also made the Solicitors' Accounts Rules under their delegated powers; these still exist and are binding on practitioners. The Solicitors Code of Conduct 2007[3] represents an attempt to provide a genuine and complete code of conduct of professional practice. As delegated legislation in the form of Solicitors' Practice Rules made by the Law Society under their powers in the Solicitors' Act 1974,[4] they are legally binding on the profession.

The SRA has the power to waive many of the rules in individual circumstances, a significant self-regulatory power which is however rarely used.[5] Apart from this power of waiver, it might be thought that the rules would be binding in the same way as any other delegated legislation provided they are intra vires. However, the courts have not always followed this line. First, it has been held that the fact that the Solicitors' Practice Rules prohibit a practice does not, by itself, mean that the practice is illegal.[6] In *Giles v Thompson*,[7] Lord Mustill stated that the rules (or at least those banning contingency fees) were simply rules of professional conduct. Secondly, Lord Justice Millett, in *Thai Trading Co v Taylor*, stated that the rules are based on a perception of public policy derived from judicial decisions. In that case he overturned those judicial decisions on public policy grounds and so, in effect, he also declared the relevant Solicitors' Practice Rule to be also inapplicable.[8]

---

[3] *Solicitors' Code of Conduct 2007* (London, Solicitors Regulation Authority, 2007). This can be accessed on the SRA website and will be regularly updated. A paper copy is also available, published for the SRA by the Law Society, June 2007.

[4] Ss 31–4.

[5] There is no power to waive the core duties or the basic rules on conflict or confidentiality. See Solicitors' Code of Conduct 2007, rr 3.23,4.06 and 22(2).

[6] See *Picton Jones & Co v Arcadia Developments Ltd* [1989] 1 *EGLR* 43 and *Thai Trading Co v Taylor* [1998] 3 All ER 65, 69.

[7] [1993] 3 All ER 321.

[8] [1998] 3 All ER 65. In this case the relevant rule was r 8 of the 1990 Rules, relating to contingency fees. For further details of the case and the issues raised, see chapter 12.

In contrast, it was implied in *Garbutt v Edwards*[9] that the rules were binding but not necessarily all the guidance or supplementary codes issued under the rules. Therefore, the Client Care Code of 1999 or the Solicitors' Publicity Code had a debatable legal status and conventionally would not be regarded as legally binding.[10] However, in common with the many other varieties of guidance that now proliferate, adverse legal consequences may well follow for those who disregard them. The Law Society seemed to consider that any of its guidance, whether in the form of a formal code or simply that attached as commentary on the rules, is authoritative. As the 1999 version of the Law Society Guide firmly noted, Law Society guidance

> is treated as authoritative by the Compliance and Supervision Committee (now the Consumer Complaints Board), the Solicitors' Disciplinary Tribunal and the Court.

'Authoritative' does not necessarily mean binding, and these bodies could conclude that such guidance was contrary to law. Breach of the guidance could clearly be the basis of, or evidence of, a complaint or disciplinary allegation, but is not conclusive of the issue.[11] Guidance on conduct can also be sought from the actual decisions made by the Disciplinary Tribunal, which tends to follow its own precedents. This analysis of the legal status of the old rules and guidance will, presumably, also apply to the new 2007 Rules, but there is as yet no judicial guidance.

Before 2007 the novice had difficulty in finding a way through this morass of material, as the Legal Services Ombudsman pointed out.[12] The 1999 Guide itself spoke of the rules being sometimes 'based on a common law ethical requirement'.[13] The latter is an odd phrase, implying that the common law creates ethical rules as opposed to some other form of rule. Ethical considerations, broadly conceived, may, of course, form the basis of common law rules, but their binding force derives from their accepted legality as the common law and not from any assumed ethical basis. Some of the non-statutory guidance issued by the Law Society was also stated to be based on 'an interpretation of statutory rules'.[14] On normal principles, such interpretation could be challenged in the courts.

Even more confusing, some of the content of the 1999 Guide simply provided good advice or factual information that had no legal status at all. The 1999 Guide also stated that the rules of professional conduct should not be 'confused with the requirements of the general law of contract or tort or . . . criminal law'.[15] But many of the rules stated in the Guide were, and are, part of that general law as applied in the particular context of solicitor and client. This law is, of course, constantly changing and growing, so that rules which may well have been regarded originally as being in some way based on ethical principles rather than legal requirements have now become incorporated into the law. An example of this can be seen in the developing law on confidentiality and legal privilege. Crawley and Bramall,

---

[9] [2005] All ER (D) 316.

[10] See HWR Wade, *Administrative Law* (Oxford, Clarendon, 1994) 857.

[11] R Taylor (ed), *The Guide to the Professional Conduct of Solicitors* (London, The Law Society, 1996) para 1.03. See below on the definition of 'conduct unbecoming' in the context of disciplinary proceedings.

[12] See both the 1995 and 1996 Annual Reports.

[13] Above n 11, 1999 edn, para 1.03 note 3.

[14] *Ibid.*

[15] *Ibid.*

who worked in the Professional Ethics Division of the Law Society, pleaded for a broad approach, arguing that

> The codes of conduct . . . .should not be treated as if they were tax statutes to be scrutinised for loopholes. They establish rights and responsibilities that must be viewed broadly and in the spirit.[16]

This approach is essential if the codes are to be properly regarded as embodying ethical, as opposed to legal, obligations.

By the late 1990s it was obvious that a comprehensive code of conduct for solicitors, with a clearly binding legal status and capable of being fairly enforced, was needed. In 1999 the Law Society set up a regulation review working party to make proposals for such a code. After an extensive consultation exercise,[17] the new rules were passed by the Law Society Council and submitted to the Lord Chancellor for the approval process. This was finally received at the end of 2006 and the rules came into force in July 2007 as the Solicitors' Code of Conduct 2007.[18] It is now published by the SRA, not the Law Society, and the SRA will keep it updated.[19] One of the aims in introducing the 2007 Code was to clear away the confusion on the legal status of the rules, codes, guidance and other material that appeared in the 1999 Guide. The 1999 Guide had become

> a mix of mandatory and non mandatory conduct requirements and best practice information which sometimes left the reader unable to identify the relevant regulatory obligations

amongst a morass of material.[20]

The 2007 Code is much shorter than the equivalent sections of the old 1999 Guide, which ran to over 800 pages. It consists of 25 basic sections, each of which contains the rules on a particular topic and also guidance on the rules. It is written as far as possible in plain English, bearing in mind that the extensive consultations required a fair amount of compromise, and is meant to be understandable by the layperson as well as the lawyer. It consists of only 207 pages, although it does not include the accounts and indemnity insurance rules, or other rules relating to client compensation and financial services that are not superseded by the new Code. It replaces not only the 1990 Solicitors' Practice Rules, but also a variety of specialist rules, such as the Incorporated Practice Rules, the Overseas Practice Rules and the Solicitors' Anti-Discrimination Rules. It also replaces the specialist Codes that had grown exponentially in the previous two decades, such as the Employed Solicitors' Code, the Solicitors' Publicity Code and the Solicitors' Costs Information and Client Care Code.

---

[16] A Crawley and C Brammall, 'Professional Rules, Codes and Principles Affecting Solicitors (or What has Professional Regulation to do with Ethics?)' in R Cranston (ed), *Legal Ethics and Professional Responsibility* (Oxford, Clarendon Press, 1995) 99, 103.

[17] See *Rules for the Twenty-First Century, Regulation Review Working Party Final Consultation* (London, The Law Society, 2004).

[18] It should be noted that the new rules do not and were not intended to replace the more detailed rules governing the organisation and management of solicitors' firms, such as the Accounts, Investment Business or Incorporated Practice Rules.

[19] Indeed, it has committed to doing so on its website every three months.

[20] Introduction to the 2007 Code, ix (above n 3). The 1990 version of the *The Guide to the Professional Conduct of Solicitors* contained 600 pages, whereas the 1999 edition was 860 pages.

The Law Society, not the SRA, has published a companion to the Code, by Peter Camp,[21] which is mainly concerned to provide practitioners with help in finding when they are bound by each rule and how, if at all, the rules have been substantively changed from the principles and rules laid out in the 1999 Guide. Obviously this work does not claim to be authoritative, in the sense of being binding. It does not claim to offer strong guidance that it would be dangerous or negligent to ignore, any more than any other legal treatise. It does not, therefore, have whatever binding force was attributed to the 1999 Guide. As Camp notes, because the 2007 Code does not purport to cover all the material in the 1999 Guide, especially the statutory obligations on solicitors, the old Guide still contains material useful to solicitors. The Law Society also continues to give advice to solicitors on their obligations, for example in relation to their money-laundering duties, guidance on confidentiality and disclosure, and guidance on confidentiality and reporting terrorism. This is not binding and possibly does not now have the same authority as it did when the Law Society combined the regulatory and representative functions. Currently, there is no further guidance issued by the SRA on the new Code.

Basic content of the rules

One of the main problems with the old rules and principles of professional conduct governing solicitors was that there was no clear statement on the basic principles which underlay ethical practice. There was no short summary, capable of being understood by the lay client as well as the professional, on the basic duties. The 1999 Law Society Guide claimed that they were contained in the old rule 1 of the 1990 Solicitors' Practice Rules, which 'sums up the basic principles of practice' governing solicitors and even goes so far as to claim that 'it is arguable that no further rules or guidance are required'.[22] Old rule 1 simply provided that solicitors should not do anything that compromised their duty to act with independence and integrity, to allow freedom of choice of solicitor, to act in the best interests of the client, to preserve the good repute of the profession, to provide a proper standard of work and to preserve their duty to the court. How can anybody deduce from this list the more detailed rules relating, for example, to the rules on confidentiality, advertising, referral fees or conflicts in conveyancing transactions? The claim that rule 1 embodied a complete code of ethical conduct was simply fanciful and served only to reveal the absence of such a code. Many of the 1990 Rules were clearly aimed primarily at preserving jurisdiction and preventing competition rather than requiring ethical practice. Moreover, two of the most basic rules of ethical practice, relating to confidentiality and conflict of interest, did not appear in the Rules at all until 2005, when they were added in anticipation of the introduction of the new 2007 Code.

The structure adopted in the 2007 Code is to start with rule 1, containing a set of six 'core duties' which are intended to be a statement of the basic ethical duties of solicitors and which are legally binding. Deriving from these core duties is a set of more detailed practice rules which are also binding. Attached to each rule is guidance which is not binding. However, as the introduction to the Code notes,

---

[21] P Camp, *Companion to the Solicitors' Code of Conduct 2007* (London, The Law Society, 2007).
[22] Above n 11, para 1.02(4).

Although the guidance is not mandatory, solicitors who do not follow the guidance may be required to demonstrate how they have nevertheless complied with the rule.

The Working Party also sought to comply with certain basic criteria for rule making. Rules should be necessary, clear, fair, enforceable, proportionate, targeted and consistent. Some of these aims may be controversial. For example, the need for the rules to be enforceable, in particular by the SRA when dealing with complaints and also by the Disciplinary Tribunal, means that they may well be regarded as modest in their scope. They are not intended to be overly aspirational[23] or to encourage expectations in clients that cannot be reasonably met by any enforcement mechanism. They are also intended to be proportionate—that is, proportionate to the risks concerned and not over-burdensome on either the solicitor or the regulator.

The reference to proportionality reflects the government's own attitude to regulation expressed by the Better Regulation Task Force, but one person's reasonable protection is usually another's overregulation, hence the controversy that some of the proposed rules encountered. Perhaps the most striking change in the 2007 Code as compared with the old Guide is that it is shorter and much less detailed and prescriptive. Solicitors are now expected to exercise their own discretion as to how to act, using the general ethical principles set out in the Code and in particular the core duties; they are no longer thought to require detailed legalistic regulation on every issue. The history of the solicitors' rules has been one of modest beginnings leading to the confusing and overblown attempt to control all contingencies that characterised the Law Society Guide in the 1980s and 1990s. The solicitors have returned to a shorter and more straightforward Code, leaving many detailed decisions to the discretion of the practitioner. This follows to some extent the model of ethical rule making proposed by many commentators, discussed in the previous chapter. They favour 'more general statements of principles which operate as professional aspirations' rather than detailed conduct rules. The reason for this is that detailed ethical codes are said to undermine ethical evaluation, replacing it with mindless conformity to rules. However, the 2007 Code has been expressly designed to be enforceable through disciplinary sanctions, an objective that on the whole does not seems to be advocated by these commentators.[24] Insofar as more is now left to the discretion of the solicitors, it becomes even more important that they should receive training in their ethical duties.

The new core duties require solicitors to act with integrity, not allow their independence to be compromised, act in the best interests of each client, provide a good standard of service to clients and not to behave in a way that is likely to diminish the trust the public places in you or the profession. These duties constitute rule 1 and are therefore binding.[25] They are intended to embody the basic duties of solicitors to both clients and society, the latter's interest being upholding the rule of law and the administration of justice. They embody the traditional lawyerly virtues of integrity, independence, acting in the best interests of clients, proper service standards and upholding the dignity of the profession.

---

[23] See chapter 4.

[24] For a survey of these approaches see D Nicolson, 'Mapping Professional Ethics: The Form and Focus of the Codes' 1 *Legal Ethics* 51, 66.

[25] The Working Party proposed 10 core duties, the 10 commandments, but these were reduced to six somewhere along the prolonged approval process in the Department of Constitutional Affairs.

They do not deal with competence and the proper management of a practice as such, nor with any detail on how to deal with clients; these issues are all left to the detailed rules. As the Guidance states, a breach of a core duty can by itself constitute misconduct, but it is more likely that a breach will related to one of the more detailed rules made under these 'overarching principles'. It is not the intention of either the core duties or the rules made under them to embody all the principles and precepts laid down in the old 1999 Guide to Professional Conduct, many of which were, in any case, simply rules of law (such as the statutory rules on costs or the solicitors' lien) or had no particular ethical content, such as advice on paying counsels' fees.

Many of the rules do, however, reflect or restate rules of law, such as the rules on confidentiality and conflict which have been the subject of much case law in recent years. Obviously solicitors have an obligation to obey the law and can be sued for any breach like any other person. But embodying these laws in the Code, and possibly extending their scope, means that there is no doubt that their breach can also form the basis for disciplinary proceedings and disciplinary penalties. A breach of the ordinary law is not by itself a justification for disciplinary action, otherwise every solicitor who filled in a form incorrectly or incurred a parking fine would be vulnerable to it. However, a breach of the law which is also a breach of the Code would justify some form of discipline, depending, of course, on its seriousness.

Barristers

Status of the Code

The latest version of the Bar Code of Conduct made by the Bar Council is the eighth edition of 2004, which is set out, as subsequently amended, on the Bar website.[26] This is not a statutory code, unlike the Solicitors' Code of Conduct, but it is subject to the approval process laid down in section 31 of the Courts and Legal Services Act 1990 as amended by the 1999 Access to Justice Act. Insofar as the Code replicates the common or statutory law, it is of course binding on both barristers and others. But the force of the Bar Code itself lies in the fact that it has to be adhered to by barristers or they risk disciplinary sanction. This can range from a small fine to being barred from practising at all, either because of a regulatory failure, for example a failure to acquire a valid practising certificate, or because of being struck off by the disciplinary tribunal for a major breach, such as breach of confidentiality. Like the Law Society, the Bar Council has the power to waive any part of the Code 'either conditionally or unconditionally'.[27] This is a considerable self-regulatory power and would presumably now be exercised only after advice from the Bar Standards Board.

Content of the Code

The Bar Code is much shorter than both the new and old versions of the solicitors' code. This is not surprising as it is much younger and has not so long to develop as had the old

---

[26] *Code of Conduct of the Bar of England and Wales* (London, Bar Standards Board, 8th edition, as amended, 2004). The Bar embarked on a three-year review of its Code in June 2007 to be ready for the introduction of the Legal Services Act. See Bar Standards Board, *Initial Consultation Paper on the Review of the Code of Conduct* (June 2007).

[27] Bar Code, para 108.

solicitors' Guide. Moreover, barristers do not have the same variety of functions. In particular, they do not handle a client's business affairs, prepare for litigation or hold client money.[28] Their traditional role is to deal with solicitors and other professional clients and not with lay clients directly. The aim of the Bar Code is to provide a basis for practice and also for enforcement of the rules by the appropriate disciplinary machinery. There is no overarching statement of the basic ethical principles, as there is now for solicitors in the 2007 core duties. Part 1 of the Code, however, states that the general purpose of the Code is to provide requirements and rules and standards of conduct appropriate in the interests of justice, and in particular:

> (a) in relation to self-employed barristers to provide common and enforceable rules and standards which require them: (i) to be completely independent in conduct and in professional standing as sole practitioners . . .; (ii) to act only as consultants instructed by solicitors and other approved persons (save where instructions can be properly dispensed with); (iii) to acknowledge a public obligation based on the paramount need for access to justice to act for any client in cases within their field of practice;

> (b) to make appropriate provision for employed barristers taking into account the fact that such barristers are employed to provide legal services to or on behalf of their employer.[29]

The third obligation of (a) is, of course, a reference to the cab-rank rule, and not an obligation to take *pro bono* cases. Quite what is the meaning of the words 'public' and 'acknowledge' in the rule is obscure. It seems to be more rhetoric than enforceable obligation. It is also notable that the Bar Code says virtually nothing about the fees that barristers may charge the public—and the cab-rank rule applies only where the prospective client offers the appropriate fee.

These general principles are augmented by part 111 of the Code, which lays down some 'fundamental principles' for barristers expressed as prohibitions. Barristers must not engage in conduct which is 'dishonest or otherwise discreditable to a barrister'. They must not do anything prejudicial to the administration of justice or that is

> likely to diminish public confidence in the legal profession or the administration of justice or otherwise bring the legal profession into disrepute.[30]

This creates the unfortunate impression of concern to protect the 'image' of the profession rather than protect the client. However, it is also stressed that the barrister has an overriding duty to the court and must not 'knowingly or recklessly mislead' it.

The details of the Code, like that of the old solicitors' rules and principles, then, consist of a mixture of practising regulations with little, if any, ethical content and rules of a more fundamental ethical character, such as those on confidentiality and conflict. For example, part 111, after laying down the 'fundamental principles', goes on to prescribe an odd mixture of duties and prohibitions, ranging from the barrister's duty to the Legal Services Commission, to the duties not to discriminate unlawfully and not to give or accept loans from clients or receive or handle money other than remuneration. There are many annexes

---

[28] Above n 24.
[29] Para 104.
[30] Bar Code, para 301. Although not very long, the Bar Code is rather wordy.

to the Code dealing with the details of, for example, a barrister's contractual relationship with a solicitor, the direct access rules and the complaints procedure. Standards of professional work are dealt with in a separate section 3 added to the Code. This is not regarded as setting mandatory standards, but is advice. However, failure to adhere to the advice can be cited in complaints or disciplinary proceedings. It is, in general, difficult to read and navigate the Code and its annexes, and it is certainly not written in plain English or aimed at the lay reader.

The Bar Code is, in fact, ripe for revision, and this is currently being undertaken. Not only has it not been subject to a comprehensive review for many years (apparently not since it was first compiled in 1981), but there is a need to respond to the provisions of the Legal Services Act 2007. The Office of Fair Trade (OFT) has criticised some of the Bar Code provisions on the ground that they are uncompetitive. The initial consultation issued by the Bar Standards Board[31] also notes that it is drafted very legalistically and inconsistently, some rules being very detailed and others being very general with little added guidance. They favour adopting the core principles and plain English approach of the 2007 Solicitors' Code. The review is expected to take at least three years and the first subjects to be tackled will be business structures, core principles, cab-rank rules and client care. The review will conclude with complaints and discipline.

Making the rules

The autonomy of both professions in making or changing their practice rules was first limited under the Courts and Legal Services Act 1990, which set up the Lord Chancellor's Advisory Committee on Legal Education and Conduct (ACLEC), a body consisting of both lawyers and laypersons.[32] This required that any proposed changes in the rules relating to rights of audience and the conduct of litigation had to be approved by the Lord Chancellor and four designated judges after having taken advice from ACLEC. This was the first time the professions had to submit their rule changes to outside scrutiny and comment. In fact this was a compromise solution, as the government had wanted the power to approve all the professional rules to be given to the Lord Chancellor.[33] By 1998 ACLEC was under attack from the Lord Chancellor, who thought that it had not furthered the objectives of the 1990 Courts and Legal Services Act to develop new means of providing legal services, but had upheld the status quo. One of his concerns was the amount of time it took to obtain approval to any change, so he changed the rules to require the consent of the Lord Chancellor only. Following the Access to Justice Act 1999, the Lord Chancellor must approve any rule changes concerning audience rights and rights to conduct litigation, and also has the power to call in any rules he considers unduly restrictive. He may take advice from the designated judges and from the newly formed Legal Services Consultative Panel, but the final decision is his alone.[34] Consultation on rule changes is also required, where relevant, with the OFT and the Financial

---

[31] Above n 26.
[32] See further chapter 3.
[33] Above n 16, 101.
[34] Consultation Paper, *Rights of Audience and Rights to Conduct Litigation: The Way Ahead* (London, Lord Chancellors Department, June 1998) ch 4.

Services Authority (FSA). In addition, as has always been the case since it acquired rule-making powers in 1933, the Law Society's rules have to be approved by the Master of the Rolls. The government was still not satisfied, however, that the professions were making rules in the public as opposed to their own interests. It therefore enacted the Legal Services Act 2007, the impact of which is explained at the end of this chapter.

Promulgating and enforcing ethical norms

The most obvious way in which self-regulating professions reflect and disseminate professional norms is through codes of conduct. Codes of conduct are a normal, though not a necessary, part of professional disciplinary machinery. They are not necessary because discipline is usually imposed for actions or neglect which are either illegal in any event or are clear breaches of professional standards. Codes of conduct, while they deal with such instances, also generally contain aspirations to high standards. Not all of these aspirational principles are intended to have disciplinary force. This ambiguous role of codes gives rise to two views of their significance. On the one hand, they are seen as indications of professionalisation and symbolic of the evolution of the role of the profession.[35] On the other, they are also seen as a part of a profession's attempts to justify a monopoly position and to control its market. What evidence is there to support either of these views? Four areas can be considered. First, the commitment to create codes can be seen as a manifestation of the commitment to effective self-regulation. Secondly, the nature of the content of the codes and other regulations governing the profession can be indicative of either high ideals or market control. Thirdly, how far are disciplinary mechanisms actually used to enforce the norms in the codes or are they a sham? Fourthly, how far are the ethical norms which do not carry sanctions actually observed in practice?

Codes and self-regulation

The adoption of formal codes by the professions in the UK was a fairly late development and the formal enforcement of those codes was even later. An early account of 'etiquette' for the bar was published in 1875,[36] but it did not prescribe standards and so could not be seen as a disciplinary code.[37] The Royal Commission on Legal Services 1979 recommended that the Bar adopt written standards. This recommendation resulted in the publication of the Code of Conduct for the Bar of England and Wales in 1981.[38] The Law Society, albeit at first

---

[35] See also LH Newton, 'Lawgiving for Professional Life: Reflections on the Place of the Professional Code' in A Flores (ed), *Professional Ideals* (Belmont, CA, Wadsworth Publishing, 1988) 47.

[36] R Abel, *The Legal Profession in England and Wales* (Oxford, Basil Blackwell, 1988) 133. In fact the first attempt to publish a code of ethics for the bar was in 1645 by John Cooke, who prosecuted Charles I (see G. Robertson, *The Tyrannicide Brief* (Chatto & Windus, 2005)), but it was doomed to obscurity with the restoration of Charles II and the execution of Cooke.

[37] The first formal code of ethics in the US was adopted by the Alabama State Bar Association in 1887, which served as a model for the ABA's Canons of Professional Ethics in 1908. LR Patterson, 'On Analyzing the Law of Legal Ethics: An American Perspective' (1981) 16 *Israel Law Review* 28.

[38] Report of the Royal Commission on Legal Services (Benson Commission), 1979, vol 1, 310; see also Abel, above n 36, 133.

unenthusiastically, accepted powers to make regulations governing solicitors under the Solicitors' Act 1933. Two reasons overcame the Law Society's unwillingness. The first was the need to pre-empt regulation by the government in the wake of a growing scandal surrounding the embezzlement of client funds by solicitors[39] and the second was the desire to increase the Law Society's credibility in the eyes of the government.[40]

Since then, rule making has increased apace, particularly in the solicitors' branch. Yet many aspects of the professional codes remain undeveloped.[41] The Bar Council's code remains relatively brief.[42] The Law Society's 1999 collection of rules[43] and principles of conduct, *The Guide to the Professional Conduct of Solicitors*, was more comprehensive and grew rapidly in the last few years of the twentieth century. It did not, however, aspire to be a 'code' and there were problems with its enforceability, leading to the introduction of the new Solicitors' Code of Conduct 2007.[44] This Code is much shorter than the old Guide. It aims to deal only with the fundamental principles governing practice as a solicitor, and not with all the technical rules relating to accounts and the like. On this evidence, therefore, the legal profession has not, historically, been particularly energetic in developing codes of conduct with effective sanctions. It is now attempting to do so, a reaction to the pressures outlined in part I of this book, ironically just as is about to lose a large portion of its powers of self-regulation.

The substance of the rules of conduct

In general terms, the professional obligations found in codes of conduct can be classified into three distinct types.[45] First, 'standards' set by the professional body usually set out such virtues as honesty and competence. Secondly, 'principles' prescribe general responsibilities and allow a degree of discretion in interpretation and implementation. Thirdly, 'rules' prescribe specific conduct and leave little room for interpretation. Disciplinary sanctions are normally imposed for breaches of rules rather than for breaches of principles. Therefore, in creating a rule, it must be quite clear that the conduct involved is recognisably wrong and capable of being enforced by a disciplinary sanction. In revising the rules prior to the promulgation of the Solicitors' Code of Conduct 2007, the Law Society was keen to stress that the rules should be necessary, fair and enforceable.[46] Where codes are most detailed,

---

[39] L Sheinman, 'Looking for Legal Ethics' (1997) 4 *International Journal of the Legal Profession* 139. See C Maughan and J Webb, *Lawyering Skills and the Legal Process* (London, Butterwoths, 1995) 92 note 4. The problem remains significant and is not limited to the UK. Evans recounts that one firm in Wellington, New Zealand defrauded clients of NZ$60 million, bankrupting the New Zealand fidelity fund. Thefts of A$10 million are 'not uncommon' in Australia, according to A Evans, 'Professional Ethics North and South: Interest on Clients' Funds and Lawyer Fraud. An Opportunity to Redeem Professionalism' (1996) 3 *International Journal of the Legal Profession* 281.

[40] Hence, the Law Society improved its prospect of taking control of the infant Legal Aid scheme in 1949. C Glasser, 'The Legal Profession in the 1990s: Images of Change' (1990) 10 *Legal Studies* 1.

[41] J Levin, *An Ethical Profession?* (Swansea, University of Wales, 1994) 8.

[42] As Nicolson, above n 24, points out, this is partly a consequence of its comparative youth—'codes become increasingly detailed over time' and the fact that solicitors are subject to far more statutory regulation.

[43] It consisted of 860 pages, compared with the Bar's just under 200 pages. The new 2007 Rules are much shorter but, of course, do not include much of the regulatory and statutory material contained in the 1999 Guide.

[44] Which came into force in July 2007.

[45] MD Bayles, *Professional Ethics* (Belmont, CA, Wadsworth Publishing, 1981) 22.

[46] See *Rules for the Twenty-First Century*, above n 17, iii.

traditionally in the area of professional etiquette such as advertising or referral rules, they were enforced so as to reinforce legal jurisdiction. Other detailed rules, such as the accounts rules, are also more easily subject to disciplinary processes than the principles or standards, and in the main they are clearly aimed at upholding ethical conduct in handling money.

What of the rules concerning ethical practice as opposed to administrative regulations? It has been argued that such rules of conduct rarely place lawyers at a commercial disadvantage and are also so vague that they do not set clear boundaries for professional behaviour.[47] This is not, however, always the case. For example, the rules on conflict of interest frequently act to the disadvantage of lawyers as they require them to refuse clients. Big city firms have been notorious in seeking to circumvent them at times because of this. As to the vagueness of professional codes, this is not necessarily deliberate, but is inevitable. Aspirational standards are unsuitable as a basis for imposing sanctions but should form the basis of legal education and training. Unfortunately the professions record here is patchy at best.[48] Professional self-regulation and ideology are not inevitably or always a charade. However, professionals often need to be alerted to their self-serving tendencies when drafting their rules. There are areas of practice which clearly involve the public interest where the codes are silent. For example, the codes say nothing about whistle-blowing obligations or the needs of clients who have no funds, or run out of funds, to obtain or keep representation.[49] There is virtually nothing on the relationship between lawyers and corporate clients.[50] Scrutiny of rule making by an independent body not dominated by lawyers, such as the proposed Legal Services Board, might redress these omissions.

The nature and use of disciplinary machinery

The third area for consideration, disciplinary mechanisms, has often been a focus of criticism. The complaints and disciplinary procedures run by the professions have often been slow and provide inadequate redress to the consumer. There is a suspicion of lack of rigour and independence. For example, Abel's analysis of complaints against barristers suggests that, since 1957, the majority of complaints have been dismissed before reaching the Senate.[51] The senate rejected a recommendation of the 1979 Royal Commission that it should interview all complainants, a measure that might have improved the success rate.[52] Of the complaints reaching the Bar Disciplinary Tribunal, less than 3% led to disbarment and only 1% in suspension.[53] More recently, however, the Legal Services Ombudsman has found the Bar complaints machinery to be reasonably competent,[54] although there remains the problem

---

[47] See works by R Abel, above n 36, 30; 'Why Does the ABA Bother to Promulgate Ethical Rules?' (1981) *Texas Law Review* 639; and 'The Decline of Professionalism?' (1986) 49 *MLR* 1, which cites the report of the KUTAK Commission (see below) in support of the proposition that it is impossible to come to grips with the intrinsic problem of enforcing professional rules.

[48] See chapter 6.

[49] Above n 21, 65.

[50] See further chapter 14.

[51] Abel, above n 36.

[52] *Ibid*, 135–6.

[53] *Ibid*, 136.

[54] Annual Report of the LSO 2003–2004, 65–6. The LSO was satisfied with the Bar's handling of complaints in nearly 87% of the cases referred to her. D Clementi, *Review of the Regulatory Framework for Legal Services in England and Wales—Final Report* (Department of Constitutional Affairs, 2004) ch C, para 23.

that it is not perceived by clients to be independent of the Bar. It is noteworthy that the Legal Services Act contains proposals to change radically the complaints procedures but not the disciplinary procedures of the professions, which the Clementi Report considered work appropriately.[55]

Solicitors have been less successful in convincing consumers and others of their dedication to dealing with complaints competently and fairly, as can be seen from virtually all the annual reports of the Legal Service Ombudsman and also the Clementi Report. Major criticisms concern delay in dealing with complaints and unhelpfulness in relation to clients trying to understand the complexities of the system. This failing has provided a major impetus towards the creation of an independent complaints service under the Legal Services Act 2007.[56] The professions have a conflict of interest in pursuing sanctions against members. One aim is to maintain public confidence, and ensuring that complaints are properly handled is a key part of this aim. But, by dealing with complaints and discipline openly and publicly, professions also highlight their inadequacies. This threatens, rather than enhances, not only their powers of self-regulation but also their other professional privileges.[57] From this point of view it is sensible for professional bodies to use disciplinary sanctions in the clearest cases only and instead rely on informal measures whenever possible.[58] It follows that formal disciplinary procedures are likely to be used only in cases where offences are likely to become public anyway.[59]

The voluntary observance of norms

An effective commitment to ethics requires practitioners and the professional bodies to take both observance and enforcement seriously. Are norms and standards observed in areas in which sanctions do not operate? We have already noted that where rules are ambiguous or do not relate to specific practice contexts there is scope for interpretation. Where the rules fail to recognise the economic and practical realities of practice there is an incentive for non-observance. Unsurprisingly, only very limited hard evidence is available on this. Carlin's study of the New York City Bar in the 1970s suggested that ethical standards were differently accepted by lawyers, depending on the status of the field in which they operated.[60] Carlin analysed the acceptance of ethical norms by status of firm and found that a large majority of lawyers in all firms accepted certain basic standards, usually pertaining to lawyer client relations,[61] but only

---

[55] *Ibid*, ch C para 84.

[56] See chapter 7.

[57] Abel, above n 36, 30.

[58] This is evident from the reports of the Bar's Complaints Commissioner, whose appointment was followed by a 30% increase in complaints and a first report which suggested that '. . . a very small percentage of barristers are disciplined as a result of criminal conviction. A slightly larger percentage make mistakes through incompetence or cutting corners. Overwork or laziness leads to mishaps. Arrogance and self-importance result in rudery and bombast. Sometimes these can cause real disadvantage and distress' ('Barristers Accused of Arrogance and Self Importance', *The Lawyer*, 19 May 1998).

[59] M Burrage, 'From a Gentleman's to a Public Profession' (1996) *International Journal of the Legal Profession* 45, 57.

[60] J Carlin, 'Lawyer's Ethics' in *The Sociology of Law: A Socio-Structural Perspective* (London, The Free Press, Collier Macmillan, 1980) 257.

[61] Carlin, *ibid*, distinguished bar norms proscribing behaviour generally socially unacceptable, eg cheating and bribery. Elite or paper norms proscribe behaviour acceptable in the wider community (he cites the case of advertising or accepting commissions for referring business).

high status, usually large firm, lawyers accepted norms which went beyond wider social norms. Carlin also found that the lower the status of lawyers' clientele, and the lower the status of the courts in which they worked, the higher the rate of violation of ethical standards.[62] Lower status lawyers also reported more frequent pressure from clients to violate professional norms.

In the absence of consensus as to ethical norms, Carlin suggests three possible models: random disagreement, where it was not possible to predict adherence to particular norms; plural standards, where different groups uphold different or opposing norms; and a norm hierarchy, where certain norms are universally upheld, but in relation to which some groups adhere to additional, more demanding norms, such as *pro bono* work. Despite the fact that codes become rigid, outdated or dominated by the values of a particular group within the profession, the notion that they could be abandoned in favour of practitioners developing their own individual moral code is fanciful. As Nicolson observes,

> Given the current dearth of ethical education, the commercial and institutional constraints on lawyers, and their current socialisation into and immoral stance towards their work, the chances of deregulation leading to greater concern for the interests of third parties, the general public and the environment are, at least in the medium term, rather slim.[63]

Review and reform of the conduct rules

In general, the development of the actual rules and principles of professional ethics in England and Wales has proceeded in a piecemeal, way with little debate or consultation with the profession as a whole or with outsiders. The advantages and perils of a more public and comprehensive review of the ethics of a legal profession were discussed in the context of the American Bar Association's (ABA) review of its ethics code in 1977 in the wake of the Watergate scandal. Robert Kutak's review encouraged one section of the profession, mainly comprising personal injury lawyers, to propose the adoption of their own code and, in effect, to challenge the authority of the ABA over the profession.[64] In the result, compromise was reached, but the process was seen by some as intensely political and divisive, presenting an image to the public of a profession at odds with itself, unable to agree on the most funda-mental principles. On the other hand, the process by which the Kutak Commission produced the Model Rules of Professional Conduct has also been described as the 'most sustained and democratic debate about professional ethics in the history of the American bar'.[65] It could therefore be justified on the grounds that it engendered participation, exposed, and helped to reconcile, differences and thereby obtained legitimacy for the rules eventually produced. It is worth considering the process adopted by Kutak in more detail.

The first stage of the Kutak review, beginning in 1977 and ending with the publication of a discussion draft in 1980, operated under conditions of secrecy. This was partially to ensure

---

[62] Carlin, *ibid*, attributed this to the instability of clientele and the temptation offered by personal gain (at 264).

[63] Above n 24, 68.

[64] T Schneyer, 'Professionalism as Politics: The Making of a Modern Legal Ethics Code' in D Nelson, R Trubeck and R Solomon (eds), *Lawyers' Ideals/Lawyers' Practices: Transformations in the American Legal Profession* (New York, Cornell University Press, 1992) 95.

[65] *Ibid.*

that the shape of the new model rules could emerge before interest groups within the profession began to shape them. At this stage, the Commission sought to address academic criticism of existing rules, in particular that they went too far in prioritising client interests over those of third parties. It also garnered lay comment and fostered relations with the press.[66] Early drafts included some radical provisions. These increased accountability to third parties in non-contentious proceedings,[67] including imposing an obligation to warn of the threat of serious bodily injury by clients. They extended the duty to the court by imposing a duty to draw the judge's attention to adverse evidence which would have a substantial impact on a material issue of fact.[68] They also imposed a mandatory *pro bono* obligation.[69]

The leaking of the first draft of the Kutak proposals before the end of the first stage caused uproar and almost persuaded the ABA to abandon the project. A compromise was struck when a nine-month adjournment was agreed so that bar interest groups could consider the proposals. Between the end of the first stage and final stage, Kutak's radical proposals were considerably diluted following fierce debate and political struggle within the profession.[70] The criticism which apparently caused the most damage was made by the small but influential American College of Trial Lawyers. It charged that Kutak's proposals, particularly insofar as they undermined the obligation of confidentiality, were contrary to both the adversarial system and effective legal representation. But neither the process of revision nor the concerns of the Kutak Commission, as might have been expected, were monopolised by elite firms.[71] While this may be taken to challenge the theory that such firms in fact dominate ethical rule formation, it perhaps illustrates something more limited. Given an extensive and overtly democratic process of rule revision, organisations and interest groups representing the views of small firm lawyers could bring considerable pressure to bear. It is not clear how far they can do so within the more secretive and incremental processes of rule revision favoured by the legal profession in England and Wales.

The passage of the Kutak proposals suggests that any legal profession should be very cautious before embarking on a root and branch reformation of its professional ethics. Such a move may be welcomed on the grounds that it would stimulate debate and thought, and force the profession to articulate what it really thinks about ethics; it would be a sign that ethics are at least taken seriously by the legal profession. It could also stir up and exacerbate internal divisions in the profession and invite press criticism and public controversy. For these reasons a compromise process may be preferred whereby the views of practitioners, and other interested bodies such as consumer bodies and Citizens Advice, are sought before any firm drafts are produced. This was the approach of the Law Society in its recent revision of the practice rules. The consultation process lasted over six years, from 2001 to 2007, which was much longer than originally envisaged.

One of the reasons for the protracted review of the solicitors' rules was that the process

---

[66] *Ibid*, 97.
[67] See chapter 8.
[68] See chapter 14.
[69] See chapter 9.
[70] The second stage ended with the presentation of a proposed final draft in 1981 and the final stage with the adoption by the ABA of the model rules in 1983.
[71] Above n 64, 141.

did in fact reveal divisions within the profession. This was particularly the case in relation to the rules on conflict, where the big city firms had very different views from the smaller firms. Also controversial was the issue of referral fees. Many solicitors considered such charges to be beyond the pale, whilst others recognised that to outlaw them would not, in fact, be enforceable.[72] Despite the disappointing level of participation from solicitors in the process of consultation and, unlike in the US, a lack of comment in the lay press, the rules have been revised and given more coherence than the old rules. The Bar's systematic review of the Bar Code, commenced in 2007 and likely to last three years,[73] will again increase the experience of formulating ethics codes under the public gaze. These processes have an educative function that may be built on in future.

The future of regulatory codes

The last 20 years have seen a large increase in activity around the issues of ethics and conduct. The amount of regulation by the profession has increased at the same time as external regulation has increased. This can probably be explained by the increasing complexity of practice, the increasing incidence, or at least appearance, of professional malfeasance, the demand for accountability from government and consumer bodies, and the corresponding desire of the profession to combat these demands by showing that they are willing and able to do it adequately. There is increasing attention to criticism so that, in some vital areas, obligations to clients have been reinforced and in other areas rules and principles have been clarified. Assuming that the volume of regulatory material is increasing, what are the implications for professional ethics? Simon argues that there are two contrasting ethical philosophies typically underlying a profession's approach to the regulation.[74] The first is the libertarian stance under which the lawyers' freedom of conduct is constrained only by duties to clients. A libertarian approach places procedure over substance. Typically, if a particular course of action is permitted by a code of conduct the lawyer can pursue that course of action. Any doubt as to whether or not particular conduct is ethical is resolved by asking whether the conduct is in the client's interest.

One consequence of the libertarian philosophy is that professional norms are placed above ordinary social norms. The fact that the lawyer is acting for another, rather than for himself, is taken to justify the action. The libertarian conception of lawyer responsibility is therefore consistent with the image of the adversarial advocate who places his or her client's cause above every other consideration.[75] Contrasted with libertarianism is a more regulatory philosophy that places the substance of rules over procedure. It is reflected in principles of conduct which are more detailed and allow practitioners less scope for interpretation or discretion. Where this model applies, the professional body may, for example, reinforce its rules of conduct with guidance from its officers in individual cases. The emphasis of the regulatory philosophy is on the public responsibility of the lawyer as a facilitator of

---

[72] See chapter 9, p 179.
[73] Of course, the Bar will have to deal with the Legal Services Board before finalising its new rules.
[74] WH Simon, 'Ethical Discretion in Lawyering' (1988) 101 *Harvard Law Review* 1083.
[75] This is discussed further in chapters 1 and 12.

informed dispute resolution, an officer of the court and the distiller and transmitter of information. This tempers the idea of the lawyer as a partisan advocate and increases the scope of obligation. As the codes of conduct in the legal profession become more explicit we might anticipate that the partisanship of lawyers will be tempered by more explicit obligations to others and to the system of justice. This certainly appears to be the view of the government, and the attitude of the proposed Legal Services Board may well accelerate this trend. This may be a prelude to movement from a libertarian system to a system which is more regulatory in nature.[76]

Alternative models

A number of alternatives to the traditional mode of self-regulation have been suggested. First, reliance could be placed on individual professional autonomy. Secondly, the professional rules could be legalised and enforced via the courts, as in the US, described below. Thirdly, control of professional conduct could be given to the state in the form of a quango or similar arm's-length public body, akin to the Financial Services Authority in financial matters. The argument for professional autonomy is based on the idea that to try to enforce universal norms on the profession is futile but instead a framework should be provided whereby lawyers take greater responsibility for developing their own professional conduct. The second model, legalisation, involves strengthening key principles of conduct by methods of enforcement other than self-regulation. The rules become, in effect, rules of law and give rise to individual rights of action in the ordinary courts rather than in disciplinary tribunals. Legalisation means that the power and publicity of public adjudication is used to ensure professional compliance. The third model, control by a public authority, is the way forward chosen by the government in the Legal Services Act 2007. Obviously a public body could be given a wide variety of powers, ranging from the purely advisory to a high level of exclusive control and regulation of the professions. The proposed model is participatory, but its survival depends on the success of the new regime.

Legalisation

The experience of the Kutak Commission in the USA also offers a cautionary tale of the risk of incremental legalisation of professional ethics. In 1964 a committee was established by the ABA to draft a new professional code of conduct, resulting in the Code of Professional Responsibility (CPR), which replaced the 1908 Canons in 1970.[77] The code comprised a three-tier system of Canons, Ethical Considerations and Disciplinary Rules, the last of which were rapidly adopted by 40 states and recognised by Federal courts in dealing with lawyers appearing in federal litigation.[78] The authority of age-old rules,[79] 'the shared understandings

---

[76] The growth of a regulatory philosophy is also evidenced by the fact that the Law Society encourages solicitors to telephone the SRA's Division of Professional Ethics with ethical queries.

[77] GC Hazard, 'The Future of Legal Ethics' (1991) 100 *Yale Law Journal* 1239.

[78] *Ibid*, 1251 and note 63.

[79] *Ibid*, 1255.

of a substantially cohesive group', was thereby replaced by 'rules of public law regulating a widely pursued technical vocation whose constitutional position is now in doubt'.[80] The Disciplinary Rules were intended to be adopted by State Bars as an enforceable code. The Ethical Considerations were intended as both a statement and aid to the interpretation of the Disciplinary Rules and as guidance to lawyers in 'grey areas', but this model was not entirely successful because courts began to interpret the 'considerations', as well as the Disciplinary Rules, as binding and enforceable.[81]

In 1980, the Kutak Commission was established to revise the 1970 CPR, circulating Model Rules of Professional Conduct intended to replace the Code of Professional Responsibility in 1983. The Model Rules retained the idea that they should be enforceable but substituted commentary as a replacement of the ethical considerations. It has been suggested that the Kutak's Commission proposals, by searching for general unifying principles, settled for lowest common denominators.[82] In any event, many states either adopted only parts of the Model Rules or retained the old Code of Professional Responsibility. Moreover, the attempt by ABA to universalise standards exacerbated problems, exposed differences and encouraged separate bars to go their own ways. While these political ramifications of legalisation are less likely to arise in the more centralised system of England and Wales, other problems experienced in the US are likely to be similar.

The greatest risk is that the legalisation of ethical norms diminishes their ethical status[83] and their diminished moral quality detracts from the personal responsibility of the practitioner.[84] It encourages the attitude that the professional practice rules, like tax laws, are there to be circumvented wherever the letter of the law allows, rather than obeyed in their spirit. The profession must therefore exercise care before going down the route of legalising ethical norms. Not only does legalisation of ethics diminish the lawyer's personal responsibility but, once begun, it is unlikely that there can ever be a return to self-regulation. Legalisation can, by reducing ethical responsibility, also legitimise the use of ethically based rules as unethical tactics in litigation. An example of this arises in relation to rules on conflicts of interest, which can be used by rich corporations to harass the other side by attempting to deprive them of their lawyers after the case has begun.[85] It also gives rise to satellite litigation, which may be in the interest of lawyers' fees but is rarely in the client's best interests. The Kutak Commission argued that compliance with rules depended 'primarily upon understanding and voluntary compliance, the rules of conduct are frequently forgotten'. It favoured

---

[80] *Ibid*, 1279.

[81] Moreover, the schema concentrated on the adversarial process at the expense of office based work and the rules on advertising and solicitation were outdated. LR Patterson, 'The Limits of the Lawyer's Discretion and the Law of Legal Ethics: National Student Marketing Revisited' (1979) 6 *Duke Law Journal* 1251.

[82] Above n 64.

[83] Hazard concludes that the bar in the US will be subject to regulation, common law, public statutes and external disciplinary agencies because it is too large, diverse and balkanised in its practice specialities for the old system of governance (above n 77, 1279). These are the circumstances that are often taken to justify external regulation in the UK. See also TW Giegerich, 'The Lawyer's Moral Paradox' (1979) 6 *Duke Law Journal* 1335.

[84] When the judge admonishes the parties in court for some unethical conduct it is often 'the plaintiff' or 'the defendant' who is criticised rather than their lawyer (above n 37, 32).

[85] They achieve this by instructing leading lawyers from different firms as often as possible so that they cannot appear against them. J Flood, 'The Cultures of Globalisation: Professional Restructuring for the International Market' in Y Dezalay and D Sugarman (eds), *Professional Competition and Professional Power: Lawyers Accountants and the Social Construction of Markets* (London, Routledge, 1995) 139.

'reinforcement by peer and public opinion' rather than coercion although, 'finally, when necessary, by enforcement through disciplinary proceedings'.

Individual moral autonomy

As noted above, moral autonomy, of which the principle advocate is William Simon,[86] is at the other end of the spectrum to legalisation. Rather than operating within a system of formalised ethical rules, lawyers are asked to exercise their own judgement and discretion in deciding what clients to represent and how to represent them. Lawyers exercising moral autonomy would seek to do justice and would be required to consider the merits of a client's claim relative to those of opposing parties and other potential clients.[87] For example, the lawyer might need to consider the resources available to each side in deciding what behaviour may be justified. Further,

> the lawyer must be granted discretion in the representation of a client, sometimes to go beyond the letter of the law, sometimes not to utilise the law to its full extent.[88]

This requires lawyers to analyse the substantive merits of a client's claim and the reliability of standard legal procedures for resolving the particular problem. Under this 'discretionary' approach, rules of conduct are framed as rebuttable presumptions; instructions to behave in a certain way unless the circumstances suggest that the values relevant to the rule would not be served by doing so.

The value of the discretionary approach is that it addresses the central weakness of the regulatory approach, namely that ethical responsibility is simply a question of following rules,[89] and also the central weakness of the libertarian approach, the tendency to limit lawyers' responsibilities to clients only. There are, however, obvious risks. As noted above, the idea is simply not realistic in the context of modern legal practice. There is also the potential harm that the client might suffer where the lawyer fails in practice to prioritise his or her interests and the potential subversion of the client's autonomy. There is a risk that lawyer-power is increased, the client having no clear idea of how the lawyer may choose to interpret his or her ethical obligations. The relationship of trust between lawyers and clients could break down if lawyers were perceived to abuse ethical autonomy. While the adoption of a philosophy of ethical discretion would strengthen the lawyer's own 'ethical autonomy', there is a substantial risk that this kind of ethical regime would cause confusion. It is therefore unlikely to be acceptable to the profession as a whole or to the public. Nevertheless, an adaptation of the notion of moral autonomy is perhaps necessary if ethics, as opposed to regulation, is to survive.

Control by public authority

This is the model favoured by the government for England and Wales, and is contained in the

---

[86] Simon, above n 74.
[87] *Ibid*, 1090.
[88] Above n 37, 35.
[89] J Ladd, 'Legalism and Medical Ethics' in Flores, above n 35, 96.

2007 Legal Services Act. Clementi, in his report on legal services which preceded the Bill, considered two possible models for this type of regulation. Model A involved 'stripping out all regulatory functions from the front-line practitioner bodies and giving them to a legal services authority'.[90] This would leave the professional bodies with representative functions only. It would have a number of advantages, including complete independence from the professions, simplicity, the avoidance of conflict between regulatory bodies and consistency in decision making. In the result, Clementi preferred his Model B, which was to set up a Legal Services Board (LSB) to act in collaboration with the professional bodies in regulating and rule making. Many of the advantages of Model A could be provided for in Model B, which would have the additional advantages of increasing practitioner commitment to regulation. Further, Model B would increase the independence from the government and allow greater flexibility in the rules. Probably the most telling reason for rejecting Model A was, however, the work that would be involved setting up what would be a large and possibly unwieldy organisation covering the regulation of all involved in the delivery of legal services, not just solicitors and barristers.

Model B envisages that the LSB will be a 'non-departmental public body operating at arms length from government'.[91] It will consist of 7–10 members, of whom the chair and the majority of members will be laypersons. The chair and members will be appointed by the Lord Chancellor, a fact that raised concerns about their political independence. The Bar and Law Society did, however, succeed in getting an amendment inserted into the Act that the Lord Chancellor must consult the Lord Chief Justice before appointing any member of the Board,[92] but the consent of the Lord Chief Justice is not required. The chief executive of the LSB will be appointed by the Board members. They will have a fixed term of membership of five years, renewable for a further five years. One of the major functions of the Board will be to approve what Clementi referred to as front-line regulators (FLRs), that is, the professional associations such as the Law Society and the Bar. They will be approved only if they separate their representative from their regulatory functions, hence the separation instituted by both the Law Society and the Bar Council in January 2006.[93]

The idea is that the LSB will delegate the day-to-day rule making and regulation, apart from complaints,[94] to these bodies so as to 'increase the commitment of practitioners to high standards'.[95] However, the approved regulators will act subject to considerable restraints. First, they must adhere to the statutory regulatory objectives laid down in the Bill, which include improving access to justice, protecting consumers and promoting competition in the provision of legal services. Secondly, they are subject to the oversight powers of the LSB. The Board will be able to require information from them, issue guidance to them, set targets and direct them to take certain action or change their arrangements. Where the approved regulator is deemed by the Board to have failed to perform its functions in

[90] Clementi Report, above n 54, ch B, para 5.
[91] See the White Paper, *The Future of Legal Services: Putting Consumers First*, Cm 6679 (October 2005).
[92] Legal Services Act 2007, sch 1, para 1(3).
[93] The Bar has even appointed a consumer panel to help its Standards Board, thus anticipating the consumer panel that will be appointed by the Legal Services Board: see 156 NLJ 1894, 15 December 2006. As a consequence of these changes, the Law Society and the Bar are automatically approved under the Act in sch 4, pt 1.
[94] See chapter 7.
[95] Clementi Report, above 54, ch D, para 29.

accordance with the statutory objectives, then the Board may issue directions to remedy the failure, subject to various obligations to consult, seek advice and warn.

There are also powers for the Board to publicly censure approved regulators and impose financial penalties upon them.[96] There are powers to intervene in the affairs of a regulator and ultimately take over its functions altogether or cancel its approval.[97] The potential for control is therefore very far reaching and could, if firmly exercised, clip the wings of professional self-regulation to a very considerable extent. The government is, however, aware that regulation is only likely to work if the professions are committed to it themselves and that to exercise the powers in too heavy handed a fashion would undermine that commitment. A 'light touch' regulator is frequently referred to by ministers to convince the profession that it can live with these changes. Despite the wide range of possibilities of the new regulatory regime, it is inevitable that it will create 'regulatory space' within and outside organisations. It is quite likely that it will increase organisational incentives for ethical compliance and lead to new occupational groups, compliance professionals, which advise on compliance.[98] It is predictable that the larger firms will appoint their own compliance professionals, thus creating a new source of ethical influence and resource for ethical discourse.

Conclusion

A change brought about by the pressure on the profession to account for itself as a public body is a perceptible shift from a prevailing libertarian philosophy to one which is increasingly regulatory in matters of conduct. There have been considerable efforts, in the solicitors' branch in particular, to revise and enlarge the rules and principles of conduct. There remains scope, however, for future change, particularly in how the rules are shaped and made. While the Law Society's efforts to formulate the Solicitors' Code of Conduct 2007 involved consultation with the membership and with sections of the profession on matters of drafting, there has been little debate with the lay recipients of legal services as to the guiding principles of the profession's ethics. This could make a significant contribution to the development of the professional ethics of lawyers because participation potentially increases the legitimacy of the profession's efforts to regulate itself in the eyes of both its members and the public. It seems that this objective will now be achieved, but only as a result of the loss of many of its powers of self-regulation under the Legal Services Act 2007. A debate on the basic principles of the professions' ethics and how they should be enforced could be an obvious step for the proposed Legal Services Board.

---

[96] There will be a maximum amount set, as yet unknown.

[97] These powers are currently laid out in the Legal Services Act 2007, pt 4.

[98] C Parker, 'Lawyer Deregulation via Business Deregulation: Compliance Professionalism and Legal Professionalism' (1999) 6 *International Journal of the Legal Profession* 175.

7

DISCIPLINE

Bar Associations are notoriously reluctant to disbar or even suspend a member unless he has murdered a judge down town at high noon, in the presence of the entire Committee on Ethical Practices.[1]

Introduction

By discipline we mean orderly behaviour and the training or control that produces it. In this chapter we are more concerned with the mechanisms of control, both external and internal. The legal profession has assumed a self-regulatory role both in relation to complaints against members and also in relation to instigating disciplinary proceedings as a part of the self-regulatory ethos. These powers are comparatively recent. For example, the Law Society has had a proper consumer complaints procedure only since 1986 and the Bar since 1997. Disciplinary powers are older but of more limited scope as they apply to breaches of professional practice rules rather than poor or negligent service. These self-regulatory processes are, of course, additional to the normal civil and criminal legal processes that apply to everyone else. The profession has often claimed that, because of the overlap of general and professional jurisdictions, the public enjoy double protection and the profession endures double jeopardy. Professional standards are thereby effectively upheld. Despite misgivings about the credibility of this argument,[2] the existence of disciplinary processes is generally regarded as a necessary contribution to securing ethical compliance. The right of professions to require obedience, or to consciously socialise members to their norms, is also an ethical issue since it denies another person's autonomy.[3] This, however, is not an issue that generally causes concern in discussions of professional regulation or legal education.

---

[1] SJ Harris, quoted in MT Bloom, *The Trouble with Lawyers* (1968) 157.

[2] This claim would be more impressive were it not the case that, until recently, the profession also claimed immunity from court proceedings in relation to negligence connected to court advocacy. See the next section.

[3] JS Mill and Foucault observed this: 'The web of discipline aims at generalising the *homo docilis* required by "rational", "efficient", "technical society", an obedient, hard working conscience ridden useful creature pliable to all modern tactics of production and warfare . . . discipline thrives on 'normalizing judgement'. JG Merquoir, *Foucault* (London, Fontana Press, 1991) 94. See also J Simons, *Foucault and the Political* (London, Routledge, 1995) 22 and 116–18; M Ridley, *The Origin of Virtue* (Harmondsworth, Penguin, 1996) 183; D Nicolson and J Webb, *Professional Legal Ethics: Critical Interrogations* (Oxford University Press, 1999) 43.

Compliance

Before considering the machinery of control for professions it is worth considering the nature of compliance, which is their main aim. Professional discipline demands a legitimate basis and it is arguable that trust provides this basis.[4] Trust is the key reason why people use professionals, but it is increasingly conditional,[5] fostered by conformity, including apparently superficial aspects of dress and behaviour[6] but dependent on the collective experience of consumers of professional services. The profession's collective interest in nurturing the public perception also depends on trust, this time between members of the profession. Colleagues must believe that each will uphold shared commitments to standards and service and deal with infractions.[7] It seems somewhat contradictory that the rational root of professional ethics is a collective self-interest while professional practice requires foregoing personal self-interest, but it is a basic morality.[8] A profession without effective order is much like a society without order, with, as Hobbes observed, an existence likely to be 'solitary, poor, nasty, brutish, and short'.[9] If professional order can be achieved, however, the great advantage of professional self-regulation is the fact that no one understands potential infractions better than other members of the profession or is in a better position to remedy them.

In addition to identifying a rationale basis for ethical observance, it is necessary to briefly consider the psychology of compliance. A common distinction is between cultures where behaviour is internalised,[10] giving rise to guilt when norms are broken, and those that rely on external sanctions, which induce shame in the person subjected to them. The capacity for guilt and shame clearly coexist in most people, but the cultures of antiquity are sometimes identified as predominately shame cultures while those of Renaissance Europe, under Christian influence, are identified with the notion of guilt. The effectiveness of guilt as a control mechanism was, however, undermined by capitalism and industrialisation, which created systems and institutions undermining reliance on traditional habits, customs and authorities, and, intellectually, by relativism, the notion that there are no universal answers to what is 'good',[11] culturally, aesthetically or socially.[12] Nietsche even argued that moral judgements are no more than the means by which dominant social groups control

---

[4] Trust facilitates trade, a basic form of human interaction, and is emerging as key rationale for professional ethical compliance. Ridley, *ibid*, ch 10; M Little and M Fearnside, 'On Trust' (1998) 2 *The Online Journal of Ethics*, http://www.depaul.edu/ethics/ontrust.html.

[5] 'The idea of holding an *office* . . . confers trust on the office-holder, presumptively, from clients and outsiders just as does professional certification; but it also embodies expectations by the principal, or body conferring the office, of certain standards of behaviour on the part of the agent, or office-holder, which are contingent.' A Dunsire, 'The Concept of Trust' in RM Thomas (ed), *Teaching Ethics: Government Ethics* (London, HMSO, 1996) 335.

[6] EA Posner, *Law and Social Norms* (Cambridge, MA, Harvard University Press, 2000) 13.

[7] Foucault observed that in society, just as in closed communities such as armies or prisons, discipline is fostered by hierarchical, continuous and functional surveillance. M Foucault, *The Foucault Reader* (edited by P Rabinow) (Harmondsworth, Penguin, 1986) 192.

[8] B Jordan, *The Common Good: Citizenship, Morality and Self-Interest* (Oxford, Basil Blackwell, 1989).

[9] T Hobbes, *Leviathan* (edited by M Oakeshott) (Oxford, Blackwell, 1946) ch 13, 82.

[10] Explanations that rely on individual propensities for altruism, envy or conformity or that assume that these propensities flow naturally from socialization. Posner, above n 6, 5.

[11] Kant and Kierkegaard failed to establish universal morality, respectively by reference to reason or to acts of choice between models, eg ethical or aesthetic. Hospers, *Human Conduct* ch 5; Macintyre, *After Virtue*, 47.

[12] Macintyre, *ibid*, 32; AA Leff, 'Unspeakable Ethics, Unnatural Law' (1979) 6 *Duke Law Journal* 1229.

others, 'a creation of individual will in search of power'.[13] In this intellectual climate, breaking rules may not invoke guilt, requiring renewed attention to 'the psychology of acting morally'.[14]

Giddens suggests that there has been another turn in the psychology of compliance. Increasingly, he argues, mastery of the self has become a substitute for the kind of obedience that was once understood as 'morality'.[15] In modern society people construct self-identity around a personal biographical narrative, making sense of who they are and avoiding anxiety about personal adequacy.[16] They are also moral agents capable of making choices, taking responsibility for their behaviour and able to give rational explanations for the way they act. A feature of this transition is that shame has replaced guilt or fear as the main reason for compliance,[17] but shame operates in an individualised way. A person feels psychological pressure to conform only when they feel that they have let themselves down by not conforming to their constructed self-identity, recognition that is sometimes stimulated only by external involvement. The machinery of professional discipline, whether internally or externally imposed, therefore serves several purposes in securing compliance. It provides an exclusion mechanism for those who are a menace to the integrity of the profession, a deterrence mechanism for those who might be tempted and assurance to members of the profession that their mutual commitment to ethics is taken seriously.

Independent controls

Courts

Lawyers are controlled by the courts in various ways. For example, the courts can control lawyers' fees via their powers to assess legal costs and can also order a lawyer to pay any wasted costs. Moreover, the court exercises a general summary jurisdiction controlling the conduct of solicitors who fail to fulfil their duty to the court. The remedy is discretionary and can include an order that the solicitor compensate the applicant in some way. This jurisdiction provides an alternative to suing the lawyer in contract or tort, and has procedural advantages for the applicant.[18] According to Lord Justice Mummery,

> The power is essentially a summary disciplinary one exercised by the court over its own officers to ensure their observance of an honourable standard of conduct and to punish derelictions from duty

and is

---

[13] Macintyre, *ibid*, 258.

[14] D Nicolson, 'The Theoretical Turn in Professional Legal Ethics' (2004) 7 *Legal Ethics* 17, 22.

[15] A Giddens, *Modernity and Self-identity: Self and Society in the Late Modern Age* (Cambridge, Polity Press, 1991) 202.

[16] *Ibid*, 65.

[17] *Ibid*, 153.

[18] See *Myers v Elman* [1939] 4 All ER 484; *Udall v Capri Lighting Ltd* [1987] 3 All ER 262. See also Hon AD Ipp, 'Lawyers' Duties to the Court' (1998)114 *Law Quarterly Review* 63.

flexible and unfettered by any absolute rules and is to be exercised according to the facts of the particular case.[19]

The power is not frequently used because its summary nature makes it difficult to deal with the allegations justly.

There are currently plans to allow judges to dismiss lawyers from representing their clients in very high cost cases where the lawyers cause unnecessary delays, although if the plan is enacted it is likely to be the Legal Services Commission who will undertake this task.[20] Where a barrister fails in his duties to the court the matter will normally be referred by the judge to the Bar for disciplinary investigation. The court can also refer a solicitor to the complaints procedure of the Solicitors Regulation Authority (SRA).[21] There is no information as to how frequently this happens.

Courts also preside over cases involving lawyers, some of which, whether criminal or civil proceedings, arise from the conduct of work. The claim to immunity from actions in negligence[22] was not seriously challenged in any of the reviews of the legal profession taking place between 1969 and 1999, when the immunity was abolished by the House of Lords.[23] The Bar also claimed immunity from contractual liability.[24] Moreover, these immunities were used by the profession to limit the scope of its own internal complaints procedures so as to exclude complaints about advocacy; double jeopardy gave way to no jeopardy at all. Consumers obviously disliked the rule, but it also came under increasing criticism from lawyers and judges. For example, in *Kelley v Corston* Lord Justice Judge commented,

> the immunity of the advocate is not founded on some special protection granted by the court to the legal profession to enable lawyers to avoid justified complaints by dissatisfied clients . . .
> The immunity arises in very limited circumstances when the general public interest prevails against even a meritorious claim. [25]

It was no surprise when the immunity of advocates was swept away by the House of Lords in 1999, despite the misgivings of some in the professions. In *Hall and others v Simons*[26] the House of Lords decided that advocates were no longer immune from liability in negligence in either criminal or civil cases, thus overruling *Rondel v Worsley* and all the cases derived from it. The legal profession is therefore now subject to both the ordinary law on negligence and breach of contract as well as the possibility of professional discipline. It is therefore now true

---

[19] *Taylor v Ribby Hall Leisure* [1997] 4 All ER 760 CA, 768–9.

[20] See *Law Society Gazette*, 7 June 2007 18.

[21] See *Goodwood Recoveries v Breen* [2006] 2 All ER 533 for an example.

[22] Upheld in *Rondel v Worsley* [1967] 1 AC 191. See also *Saif Ali v Mitchell* [1978] 3 All ER 1033; *Kelley v Corsten* [1997] 4 All ER 466; *Atwell v Perry & Co* [1998] 4 All ER 65.

[23] On the contrary, the Courts and Legal Services Act (CLSA) 1990, s 62 extended this immunity to anyone acquiring advocacy rights under the Act. See now *Arthur JS Hall & Co (a firm) v Simons, Barratt v Ansell and others (trading as Woolf Seddon (a firm), Harris v Scholfield Roberts & Hill (a firm) and another* [2000] 3 All ER 673 HL.

[24] The power conferred by the CLSA 1990, s 61 to allow barristers to make binding contracts was initially overridden by the Bar Code of Conduct, under a power also conferred by the CLSA. However, it is now possible for barristers to make binding contracts with solicitors if they so wish and the terms of work are laid out in Annex G2 of the *Code of Conduct of the Bar of England and Wales* (London, Bar Standards Board, 8th edition, as amended, 2004).

[25] [1997] 4 All ER 466, 471.

[26] *Hall v Simon*, above n 23. Solicitors cannot claim payment for negligent work: *Nicholas Drucker & Co v Pridie Brewster & Co* [2005] EWHC 2788.

to say that the legal profession faces more control over its conduct than other commercial undertakings.

Legal services ombudsman

Before 1991, solicitors were subject to the jurisdiction of an official called the Lay Observer, a post established by statute[27] to deal with complaints from the public where complainants did not receive satisfaction from a complaint to the profession. This office was replaced under the Courts and Legal Services Act (CLSA) 1990 by that of the Legal Services Ombudsman (LSO), who must not be a qualified lawyer.[28] The LSO is appointed by the Lord Chancellor to consider complaints which have first been considered by a legal professional body, which includes the Council for Licensed Conveyancers and the Institute of Legal Executives, as well as the Law Society and Bar Council.[29]

The LSO's main task is to investigate the way in which the professional body has dealt with the complaint, but he or she can also investigate the complaint itself. On completing the investigation, the LSO must send a written report to the complainant, the lawyer against whom the complaint was made and the relevant professional body. The LSO can recommend that:

— the professional body reconsider the complaint;
— the professional body initiate disciplinary proceedings;
— compensation be paid to the complainant by the lawyer for loss, inconvenience or distress caused;
— compensation be paid by the professional body for the loss, distress or inconvenience caused by the way it dealt with the complaint; or
— the costs of making the complaint be paid by the professional body or the lawyer complained of.[30]

The report is a public document and absolutely privileged. A failure by the lawyer complained of, or the professional body, to do what the LSO orders within three months may result in that failure being publicised. The costs of that exercise may be borne by the defaulter. The LSO's reports are not directly enforceable in any other way.

The number of new cases reviewed by the LSO in 2004–2005 in relation to solicitors was 1.265, representing just under 7.5% of the total complaints made to the Law Society and an improvement on the 10% common in the late 1990s. The LSO was dissatisfied with the way 38 % of these complaints had been handled. Of the 455 complaints made against barristers, the LSO dealt with 174, but she was satisfied that nearly 79% had been properly handled.[31] In addition to reviewing complaints handling by the professional bodies, the LSO acquired the role of Legal Services Complaints Commissioner (LSCC), set up under the Access to Justice Act 1999, with powers to monitor and set targets for the Law Society complaints

---

[27] Administration of Justice Act 1985, s 3.
[28] See the CLSA 1990, s 21 and Administration of Justice Act, ss 51 and 52.
[29] CLSA 1990 ss 21–6.
[30] See CLSA 1990, s 23(2).
[31] Annual Report of the Legal Services Ombudsman for England and Wales 2004–2005, *Making Sure Your Voice is Heard* (July 2005) 40.

service. Despite the oversight of the LSO, most clients with a complaint about professional services must first use the procedures operated by the professions themselves.

Complaints

The main way by which the profession enforces its ethical and regulatory rules is by receiving, investigating and acting on complaints received from clients or, sometimes, from other solicitors or the courts. This jurisdiction now resides in the regulatory arms of the professional bodies, a situation that will continue until the introduction of the Office for Legal Complaints under the Legal Services Act 2007.

Solicitors

The current complaints system operated by the Law Society was instituted in February 2007 and was developed after decades of criticism from consumer groups and the LSO. It was also instituted in the knowledge that the government was likely to take control of complaints away from the profession and vest them in an independent Office for Legal Complaints, which is contained in the Legal Services Act 2007.[32] Jurisdiction over complaints is vested in the SRA, now separated from the Law Society in its representative capacity. The SRA receives complaints but can also act on its own initiative, and sometimes does so where there is a risk of public scandal. An example is the case of multi-murderer Frederick West's solicitor, who proposed to write a book on his client's case. The Law Society, which was then in control of complaints, took the issue up and instituted disciplinary proceedings for breach of confidentiality. Another example occurred in relation to a proposed takeover of the Co-operative Wholesale Society, where it was alleged that the solicitors for a predator investor had acted on the basis of documents they knew were confidential and stolen.[33]

Development of the system

Until 1986 complaints were dealt with directly by the Law Society. This led to the criticism that the process was concerned more with protecting the profession than protecting the public.[34] In 1986 the Society set up the semi-autonomous Solicitors' Complaints Bureau (SCB), which was very soon accused of being insufficiently independent of the Law Society and also very slow. It would not deal with complaints of negligence, as the Law Society considered that these should be dealt with by the courts. It would, however, deal with shoddy work, but this concept was not defined in written professional standards and clients found it difficult to establish that work was shoddy to the satisfaction of the SCB. Clients found it difficult to perceive the difference between negligence and shoddy work, and even lawyers could not draw a clear line. In any case, clients considered negligence to be just the kind of

---

[32] See every annual report of the Legal Services Ombudsman. This criticism was repeated in the Clementi Review of Legal Services 2005. Even the Benson Royal Commission on Legal Services in 1979 (Cmnd 7648), which was notoriously gentle with the legal profession, made criticisms—see ch 22 of the report. See also the National Consumer Council Report, *Ordinary Justice* (London, HMSO, 1989).

[33] See *The Lawyer*, 6 May 1997.

[34] See M Davies, 'The Regulatory Crisis in the Solicitors' Profession' (2003) 6 *Legal Ethics* 185.

serious conduct that should be dealt with by a profession claiming to be self-regulating, court action being costly, lengthy and wearing to the complainant.

Criticisms of the SCB were not limited to the scope of its jurisdiction. Communications to complainants from the Bureau were legalistic, and often perceived to be evasive and protective of solicitors. Such criticisms showed, according to both the Lord Chancellor's Department and the National Consumer Council, that self-regulation in the profession was not working.[35] Nor was the LSO impressed with the SCB. In his 1996 Annual Report, Michael Barnes noted,

> In . . . 1995 . . . I expressed the view that, unless the professional bodies were able to deliver a higher level of consumer satisfaction with the way that complaints were dealt with, it was unlikely that self-regulatory complaints handling would survive into the next century.[36]

In the 1997 Annual Report the newly appointed LSO, Ann Abraham, warned that poor communication in dealing with complaints

> pervades the dealing of both practitioners and the professional bodies with clients and complainants [which] suggests a . . . significant and deep-rooted introspection which fails to engage with the legitimate expectations of the contemporary consumer of legal services.[37]

Solicitors were not happy with the SCB, which they saw as an expensive public relations disaster which did not protect them but leaned in favour of clients. The SCB cost £13,213 million in 1994–1995, a rise of just over 23% on the previous year.[38]

The SCB was abolished and replaced, in 1996, by the Office for the Supervision of Solicitors (OSS). This was thought to be a last chance to retain a measure of self-regulation for solicitors in the field of complaints.[39] However, the delays and the criticism, especially from the LSO, continued. Targets for dealing with complaints were set by the Lord Chancellor's Office. For example, the OSS was asked to deal with 75% of complaints within six months, but by November 2003 the LSO noted that the OSS was 'currently falling well short of its agreed targets'.[40] Another attempt to remedy the situation was made by the Law Society by appointing its own lay Complaints Commissioner to audit the system, a post that lasted until 2005. In its turn, the OSS was replaced by the Consumer Complaints Service (CCS). As the LSO noted in her 2003–2004 Report, these reorganisations were welcome, but she considered them 'insufficiently robust'.[41] The quality of complaints handling had improved but the speed and quantity had declined since the previous year, and the Law Society continued to fail all but one of the targets on timescales.[42] The immediate response of the government was to utilise a power, originally created by the 1999 Access to Justice

---

[35] See the 1995 *Annual Report of the Legal Services Ombudsman* and the complaint of Conrad Burnham described in the *New Law Journal* March 1997.

[36] *Annual Report of the Legal Services Ombudsman for England and Wales (1996) Conclusion.*

[37] See August 1998 *Legal Action* 8.

[38] Solicitors Complaints Bureau, *Annual Report* 1995, 17.

[39] Complaints rose sharply at the end of 1997 and the delays in dealing with them once again became unacceptable, *The Lawyer* 24 March 1998.

[40] LSO Interim Report, *Breaking the Cycle* (November 2003). See also the LSO's Annual Report 2003–4, *In Whose Interest?* (July 2004), in which the LSO reports that she was satisfied of the Law Society's handling of complaints in only 53% of the cases brought to her, down from 67% the previous year.

[41] 2003–4 Report, *ibid*, 14.

[42] *Ibid*, 13.

Act,[43] to appoint the LSO to the post of Legal Services Complaints Commissioner. From February 2004, the LSO was charged with the task of reviewing the Law Society's performance, setting targets and imposing penalties (of up to £1 million) where needed.[44]

The government had also set up the Clementi Review of the Organisation of Legal Services, with a particular emphasis on complaints handling. In October 2004 this review recommended the setting up of an independent Office for Legal Complaints under the aegis of an equally independent Legal Services Board. Seeing which way the wind was blowing, in the direction of taking complaints away from the profession altogether, the Law Society separated its regulatory and representative functions, placing the latter under an independent Solicitors Regulation Board, now the Solicitors Regulation Authority. Under this was set up a separate Consumer Complaints Board to be responsible for the Consumer Complaints Service. The final change, in 2007, was to rename the CCS the *Legal* Complaints Service (LCS). It has pledged to keep both sides better informed on the progress of complaints and to go online from September 2007.

The current system

Firms' complaints systems

A client who has a complaint against his or her solicitor should first use the firm's own complaints system before approaching the LCS. This requirement was first introduced in 1991 and now comes within the Solicitors' Code of Conduct 2007, which requires every firm to have a written complaints procedure for clients and to ensure that complaints are handled 'promptly, fairly and effectively'.[45] Clients must be told at the outset in writing who to complain to and be given a copy of the procedure on request. They must also be told in writing how the complaint will be handled and within what timescales. Solicitors must not charge for handling complaints. Apart from this, the Code does not prescribe any particular procedure and nor does the guidance suggest any. The guidance does stress, however, that the procedure must be 'in writing, clear and unambiguous', and if a complaint is made to the LCS then compliance by the firm will have to be demonstrated.[46] There should be an agreed timeframe and there must be no unlawful discrimination. Obviously it is desirable that the complaint be dealt with by a member of a firm not directly involved in the client's case. The Law Society has a form[47] which can be used to initiate the complaint, but it is not essential to use this. The solicitor should reply promptly, preferably within 14 days. If a detailed reply has not been received within 28 days, then the client may complain to the LCS. The guidance stresses that there are great benefits in terms of efficiency and client satisfaction if complaints are properly dealt with. It also notes that a material breach of the rule will be evidence of inadequate professional service.

---

[43] Under ss 51 and 52.

[44] The LSCC did fine the Law Society for failing to improve complaints handling sufficiently. A fine of £25,000 was imposed in May 2006, characterised by the Consumer Complaints Board as being 'wholly unreasonable' and 'outrageously disproportionate' in *The Guardian*, 18 May 2006. In the end £30,000 of the fine was remitted when a plan setting targets for the CCS was agreed: *Law Society Gazette*, 9 November 2006, 3.

[45] Solicitors' Code of Conduct 2007 (London, Solicitors Regulation Authority, 2007) r 2.05.

[46] Solicitors' Code of Conduct 2007, r 2, guidance, para 48.

[47] The LCS Resolution Form, which has the approval of the Plain English Campaign. The same form can be used to complain to the LCS.

The Law Society has for some time sought to encourage firms to set up effective complaints systems in order to minimise the number of complaints it has to deal with.[48] It is, however, clear that solicitors have been slow in complying with these requirements. In 1997, 86% of all firms stated that they had a formal complaints procedure, but in the case of single partner firms, only 66% had complied with this requirement. Only 29% of solicitors had received any training in handling complaints.[49] One study of solicitors' complaints handling has shown that very few complaints enter the formal system operating in solicitors' offices. The formal system was felt to be overelaborate and unworkable in small firms. The researchers concluded that it is

> probably a mistake to press solicitors to adopt systems which do not accord with their sense of professional obligation, and which, in the context of their particular practice, do not make economic sense.[50]

In research done for the Clementi Review it was noted that the requirements of the old rule 15 (which preceded rule 2 in the Code) were 'either derided or misunderstood by a sizable proportion of the profession'.[51] Resistance took various forms, including non-compliance and grudging compliance, through 'prolix and incomprehensible client care letters which perverted the aims of clarity and good communication'.[52]

The Legal Complaints Service

The LCS has 400 employees and a chief executive dealing with the business of handling consumer complaints.[53] Whilst it is funded by the Law Society, the LCS is independent in the sense that it does not come within the control of the Law Society Council. It reports to the Consumer Complaints Board (CCB), which has 12 members, of whom seven are lay persons, including the chair. The CCB in turn reported initially to an independent Solicitors Regulation Board, which from 2007 became the SRA. The authority consists of nine solicitors and seven laypersons, and is responsible for laying down policy in the public interest. The chair is a solicitor. The members of the SRA cannot also be members of the Law Society Council. The LCS can normally deal only with complaints from clients about their own solicitors, not those of a third party, for example the other side's solicitor.[54] It also deals with complaints about bills of costs under the procedure for obtaining remuneration certificates.[55]

The time limit for complaints to the LCS require that they are received within six months of the work done by the solicitor or the solicitor's response to the complaint. There is

---

[48] The OSS (predecessor of the Complaints Service) dealt with some 12–20 complaints per 100 solicitors a year (LSO Annual Report 2000–2001, 4).

[49] A client care survey reported in the *Law Society Gazette*, 25 June 1997, 26. The LSO Report, *ibid*, also notes that the Law Society's attempts to encourage proper complaints handling at firm level had largely failed.

[50] See G Davis, C Christensen, S Day and J Worthington, 'The Client as Consumer' [1998] *New Law Journal* 832. They recognise that political pressure forced the complaints system on the Law Society.

[51] Research by R Moorhead, 'Self-regulation and the Market for Legal Services' (2004), quoted in the Clementi Report 2005, ch C, para 59.

[52] *Ibid.*

[53] It replaced the OSS in 2006 and was set up by the Law Society using their powers under the Solicitors Act 1974 and the Law Society Charter.

[54] Third parties can, however, raise complaints about professional misconduct (see below).

[55] On which see chapter 12. The LCS cannot deal with costs where court proceedings are involved—these are a matter for the court.

discretion to extend the time limit in very serious cases or where there is good reason for not adhering to the time limit. Of course, the client may not realise he or she has grounds for complaint about poor service for some time after the service has been completed. In this case the first step is to complain to the solicitor concerned in order to start the clock ticking. The case might be referred to a Local Conciliation Officer (LCO), often a retired solicitor, who will visit the complainant and the solicitor to try to sort the matter out. LCOs are not, however, supposed to give complainants legal advice or act for them. This is meant to be helpful to clients who have a complicated complaint or who have difficulty in reducing it to writing. Their role is therefore rather difficult for complainants to understand. Whether or not the services of an LCO are used, the LCS tries to settle the matter with the solicitor, first by mutual agreement. About 34% of cases are settled. If this cannot be done, the LCS makes further formal investigation and a decision, either that there is no case or that there is a case and a remedy is required.

Complaints are divided into three categories: inadequate professional service, professional misconduct and negligence. Inadequate professional service is the main jurisdiction of the LCS. Professional misconduct can also constitute inadequate professional service and, insofar as it does, a complaint is within the consumer complaint jurisdiction of the LCS. If the conduct does not constitute inadequate professional service, then the matter has to be dealt with under the disciplinary processes described below. Negligence can also be part of inadequate professional service and, as such, falls within the jurisdiction of the LCS.[56] If the complaint is upheld in whole or in part, the LCS can reduce the solicitor's bill, require any corrective work to be done without cost or order compensation of up to £15,000. The most common complaints relate to failure to reply to clients and inform them of the progress of their case. The second most common is delay, the third failure to follow instructions and the fourth failure to keep the client informed on costs. Substantial professional misconduct issues, breaches of confidentiality or conflict of interest result in comparatively few complaints, suggesting that most complaints are about rudimentary and avoidable issues of client care.

The LCS can investigate allegations of professional misconduct and in so doing may receive complaints from another solicitor[57] or a person affected in some way by the misconduct, for example, a client complaining about the other side's solicitor. However, this investigation will be focused on whether there has been a breach of professional conduct rules. If so, and if it is serious enough, disciplinary action against the solicitor will be commenced through the Regulation Compliance Directorate. This is concerned to assess whether the solicitor is likely to repeat the conduct and may decide to advise, reprimand or warn the solicitor about future conduct. The serious cases are referred to the Solicitors' Disciplinary Tribunal, dealt with below. The client has a right to appeal to an appeals committee, but the process does not provide a remedy in the form of compensation for any client or other complainant.

---

[56] Complex negligence cases are not normally dealt with and, in any case, the limit for compensation from the LCS is inadequate for most such cases. Complainants with complex negligence cases are referred to a panel of specialist solicitors and will get one hour's free advice on the viability of the claim in negligence.

[57] Solicitors are under a professional duty to report serious misconduct by another solicitor to the SRA, subject to client consent. See Solicitors' Code of Conduct 2007, r 20.04.

Solicitors are under a professional duty to deal with the SRA and the LCS in an 'open, prompt and cooperative way'.[58] Failure to comply with a request for an explanation of conduct complained of could result in the refusal of a practising certificate or the imposition of conditions on the grant of a practising certificate. Solicitors must not try to hinder anyone who wishes to complain or victimise them for doing so. Nor can they accept any instructions on the basis that the client waives the right to complain, or sue the client in defamation in relation to the complaint, unless malice is alleged. Solicitors have no right to an oral hearing before the LCS, although they may be heard at the latter's discretion,[59] and no right of appeal against its decision. If a solicitor fails to pay any compensation or abide by any other order made, then the complainant or the Compliance Directorate can take the issue to the Disciplinary Tribunal. This can review the order, which, if upheld, becomes enforceable. No other enforcement method is permitted.[60] The only other possibility for the aggrieved solicitor is judicial review, but applications tend to fail.

Complaint handling by the LCS is improving, but is still not up to the standard required by the LSO. The service deals with upwards of 18,500 complaints a year now. In April 2007 the Board agreed with the LSO that at least 67% of complaints should be closed within three months of receipt in 2007–2008 and that there should be no more than 65 files open for more than 12 months. The LSO was still critical of complaints handling in the year 2006–2007, reporting herself satisfied with the way they had been dealt with in 68% of the 1,680 referred to her. She recognised that this represented an improvement over previous years, but considered that the service was 'still well short of where a modern, customer focussed organisation should be'.[61] The SRA is currently consulting on whether to publish the complaints records of solicitors for the information of the public. Whilst not being keen on 'league tables', the Chair of the LCS does want to provide 'complaints records [which] differentiate at a glance between those firms with a good record and those with a bad one'. The main concern is that such a move might make firms risk adverse in taking on 'difficult' clients.[62]

SRA intervention powers

The Law Society's regulatory arm, the SRA, is responsible for the exercise of intervention powers under the Solicitors Act 1974, schedule 1, part 1 of which specifies the circumstances that call them into operation. They are often exercised where there is evidence that action is urgently needed to protect clients, for example, where dishonesty is suspected, where the solicitor is bankrupt, has been imprisoned or is otherwise incapacitated, or where he or she is practising without a current practising certificate. They are also exercisable where there has been a breach of certain practice rules, in particular where the Solicitors' Indemnity Insurance Rules or Solicitors' Accounts Rules have been breached. A client complaint against

---

[58] Solicitors' Code of Conduct 2007, r 20.03(1).

[59] See 2007 Code, r 20.03 and guidance thereon and *R(Ex parte Thompson) v Law Society* [2004] 2 All ER 113, para 109*ff*. See also *White v OSS* [2001] EWHC Admin 1149, para 26.

[60] Solicitors Act 1974, sch 1A, para 5(1). See also *R(Ex parte Thompson)*, *ibid*, paras 98 and 99 and *R (on the application of White) v Law Society* (2002) 152 NLJ 21.

[61] *Law Society Gazette*, 21 June 2007, 1. There is some concern amongst solicitors that the LSO herself has a conflict of interest in that she both sets the targets for complaints handling and also investigates and penalises failures by the profession to reach those targets.

[62] *Law Society Gazette*, 25 November 2007, 14.

a solicitor per se will not justify an intervention unless it also shows that one of the circumstances listed in schedule 1, paragraph 1(1) exists. However, if a solicitor has failed to deal with a complaint of undue delay and fails to reply to the LCS about the complaint after at least 8 days of the request, then the intervention powers may be exercisable. These wide powers enable officials of the SRA to constrain a firm from operating freely. For example, documents can be possessed and finances effectively frozen and subjected to SRA control if the Council passes a resolution to this effect. Solicitors' practising certificates can be suspended where there is a suspicion of dishonesty.[63]

The SRA conducts some 50–60 interventions a year, a figure which has been going down in recent years. The vast majority are made in sole practitioner firms.[64] The SRA must give the firm notice in writing of the intention to intervene and the firm or solicitor then has eight days to object. The solicitor can apply to the High Court for an order to withdraw intervention. For example, in *Sheikh v Law Society*,[65] a case under the old regime, a solicitor applied on the ground that, although she had committed some breaches of the Solicitors' Accounts Rules, there was no evidence of dishonesty and the breaches were not serious enough to merit intervention. At first instance she succeeded, but the Court of Appeal was more circumspect. It stressed that the Law Society could exercise its intervention powers if it had a suspicion of dishonesty or had other grounds, such as a failure to comply with the Solicitors' Accounts Rules. It could also take into account past regulatory history in deciding whether future compliance was likely if the intervention powers were not exercised. If there was no reason to suspect dishonesty, then the Law Society should carefully consider whether the issue could be dealt with by using powers short of intervention. The court should be slow to substitute its own views for those of the Law Society. The Court of Appeal recognised that the use of the intervention powers could have potentially catastrophic consequences to the solicitor and for existing clients.

Barristers

Until April 1997 there was no effective complaints system for barristers' clients. Insofar as a system did exist, its function was to alert 'the Professional Conduct Committee to possible breaches of the Bar's code of conduct'.[66] There was no indication in the Bar Code of Conduct as to what should be done if a client or solicitor wished to complain, although it did set out, in an appendix, details of the workings of the Professional Conduct Committee. About 400 complaints were received by this committee each year. After lengthy and often acrimonious negotiations[67] the Bar Council launched a new complaints system dealing both with matters of discipline and also with inadequate professional service. The system has been modified since 1997, in particular with the setting up of the Bar Standards Board in 2006.[68] It is on

---

[63] Solicitors Act 1974, s 15(1A), as inserted by the CLSA 1990, s 91(2).

[64] Sole practitioners accounted for 88% of such interventions in the years 1993–1996. M Davies, 'The Solicitors' Accounts Rules: How safe is Clients' Money?' (2000) 3 *Legal Ethics* 49.

[65] [2005] 4 All ER 717 at first instance; [2006] EWCA Civ 1577 [2007] 3 All ER 183 on appeal. See also *Sritharan v Law Society* [2005] 4 All ER 1105.

[66] See 1996 Report of the Legal Services Ombudsman, above n 36, para 3.23.

[67] For a summary, see M Zander, *Cases and Materials on the English Legal System* (London, Butterworths, 7th edn, 1996) 578.

[68] Full details of it are to be found in the Bar Council website and in Annexe J of the Bar Code.

first glance a complex system. The account of the procedure runs to 71 lengthy paragraphs with numerous sub- and sub-sub-clauses,[69] which makes it less than user friendly at best and confusing at worst.[70] The actual operation of the bar complaints system seems to work quite well, according to both the LSO and the Clementi Report. A review of the bar complaints system by the lay Complaints Commissioner, who is appointed by the Bar Council,[71] concluded that it is a basically good system in which the strengths outweigh the weaknesses, but that it needs reform to make it more responsive to the needs of complainants, less complex, more independent and more accessible.[72] The report recommends use of plain English for procedures, the creation of one tribunal to replace the current four, greater use of laypersons and a dedicated phone line to deal with complaints. He hopes the new system can be implemented by Spring 2008, which is probably optimistic.

All chambers are expected to have a complaints procedure and it is the responsibility of the Head of Chambers to ensure that it is set up and operated properly. If the complainant is not satisfied after having used this system, he or she may use the bar complaints system, which, from 2006, has been managed by the Bar Standards Board. Complaints must be made to the Board within six months of the action complained of, although there is discretion to extend this time limit.[73] The complaint will be dealt with first by the lay Complaints Commissioner, who makes an initial investigation and obtains the views of the barrister complained about,[74] as well as expert advice from other barristers if required. He can decide there is no substance in the complaint if there is no prima facie case or if the matter is obviously trivial. He can also try to conciliate the matter providing the complaint does not raise an issue of unprofessional conduct. He can also recommend that the barrister apologise, even where he finds there is no prima facie case of poor service or misconduct, or report the barrister to his Inn. If he considers there is a prima facie case, he will refer the case to the Professional Conduct and Complaints Committee of the Bar Standards Board.

The Professional Conduct and Complaints Committee (the Committee) consists of barristers and laypersons appointed by the Commissioner. As with solicitors, complaints are divided into three categories: professional misconduct, inadequate professional service and negligence. Negligence which is serious and not a part of inadequate professional service will not normally be dealt with as the client is expected to use the courts. The Committee will then consider the complaint, postpone consideration if it is reasonable to do so or take no further action on it. They can dismiss it only if the majority of lay members agree. If they consider the complaint justified there are four possible outcomes: reference to an adjudication panel, an informal hearing, reference to a summary procedure panel and a disciplinary hearing.

Issues of inadequate professional service can be referred to an adjudication panel consisting of a lay chair, two barristers and a layperson. If the panel finds the complaint

---

[69] Annex J, *ibid.*

[70] There are simpler guides provided for laypersons.

[71] V Cowan, 'Great Scott? Not Quite but Showing Promise', *The Lawyer*, 9 June 1998, 7.

[72] R Behrens, *A Strategic Review of Complaints and Disciplinary Processes* (London, Bar Standards Board, July 2007), and see Bar Standards Board, *Complaints and Disciplinary Paper* (London, Bar Standards Board, 2007).

[73] The complaint will not be considered if relevant legal proceedings are still continuing.

[74] Which he will send to the complainant.

proved on the balance of probabilities it can order the barrister to apologise, to repay fees and to pay compensation of up to £15,000 to the client. Compensation will be ordered only if it would also be recoverable under the ordinary law. The barrister, but not the client, can appeal from this adjudication to a panel consisting of a QC as chair, a barrister and two laypersons. Issues of professional misconduct may have three possible outcomes, depending on severity. The first level is to hold an informal hearing before two barristers and one layperson. If the complaint is upheld, this panel can advise the barrister on his conduct, admonish him or her about it or order compensation to the client for any element of inadequate professional service that is also involved up to £15,000. More serious cases can be dealt with by a summary procedure panel consisting of one QC, a barrister and a layperson. This panel has all the powers available to the panel of an informal hearing and can also fine the barrister or order up to three months' suspension from practice. The final stage is the Bar Disciplinary Tribunal (BDT), to which the Conduct Committee can remit the case. This procedure is dealt with below.

Complaints against barristers rose by 25% after the introduction of the new system in 1997. Of the 551 complaints in 1997, 140 were referred to the Professional Conduct and Compliance Committee.[75] There were 667 in 2004 and 877 in 2005. In 2006–2007, 166 cases were referred from the bar complaints system to the LSO, and she was satisfied that 84% had been satisfactorily dealt with.[76] There has been no significant increase of complaints due to the introduction of the direct access rules. The Bar introduced an additional system in 2007, whereby poorly performing barristers will be referred to an advisory panel for help. The referrals will come from solicitors, barristers or judges. This is not a part of either the complaints or the disciplinary procedures but is intended to be helpful.

Disciplinary procedures

There is, as we have seen, some overlap between complaints processes and disciplinary procedures in that disciplinary action may arise from a complaint. However, disciplinary action can arise independently of complaints from clients, for example, following a reference by a court. It is therefore necessary to deal with disciplinary proceedings as a separate issue.

The Solicitors Disciplinary Tribunal

Discipline is dealt with by the SDT, which is constituted under the Solicitors Act 1974, section 46.[77] The SDT is independent of, though funded by, the Law Society. The solicitor chair and the twenty one legal members of the SDT are appointed by the Master of the Rolls and eleven lay members are appointed by the Ministry of Justice. Three members, including one lay person, sit for each hearing, usually in public. Anyone may apply to the Tribunal in relation

---

[75] See *Law Society Gazette*, 20 May 1998.

[76] LSO Annual Report and Accounts 2006–7, *Delivering Excellence* (LSO, June 2007) ch 5, 40.

[77] As amended by the Administration of Justice Act 1985 and the CLSA 1990. The Law Society started to deal with discipline in 1888.

to an allegation of conduct unbefitting a solicitor, including that arising prior to admission,[78] although cases are usually brought by the SRA. Only the latter may make the application where the issue relates to breaches of the rules, such as the Accounts Rules or those relating to practising certificates. The Tribunal has powers to compel attendance[79] and evidence is given on oath. Its decisions can be appealed to the Divisional Court of the Queens Bench Division or, in the case of applications for restoration to the Roll, to the Master of the Rolls.[80] A solicitor complained about cannot take his or her own case to the Tribunal, which they might want to do by way of appeal from the LCS.[81] The issue could be raised in the Tribunal, however, if the solicitor fails to abide by an order of the LCS and the matter is referred by the SRA or the complainant for ratification and enforcement.

The Tribunal adopts the criteria for unbefitting conduct laid down in *Re A Solicitor*.[82] Mere negligence is not enough; conduct must be 'such as to be regarded as deplorable by his fellows in the profession' or 'a serious and reprehensible departure from the proper standards of a solicitor as a professional'.[83] The primary issue is usually whether there has been a violation of the Solicitors' Code of Conduct or of the Solicitors' Accounts Rules, although this test is neither exhaustive nor conclusive. The old Law Society Guide was said to be 'a Highway Code' for solicitors,[84] but what was considered unbefitting conduct 20 years ago might not be so today. Normally an element of culpability is required, but 'impecuniosity will not excuse failure to discharge a professional liability'.[85] Honest and genuine decisions by solicitors on questions of professional conduct do not give rise to a disciplinary offence, but if the decision is one no reasonable solicitor would make, then the only conclusion is that the solicitor did not address the issue and that is a disciplinary matter.[86]

The Tribunal makes its own procedural rules, currently the Solicitors' (Disciplinary Proceedings) Rules 1994, with the consent of the Master of the Rolls.[87] The proceedings are public, formal and court-like, and proof is required beyond all reasonable doubt,[88] although the Tribunal will not normally reopen any finding of dishonesty already decided in a civil court or proceedings.[89] The Tribunal has the power to make 'such order as it thinks fit',[90] including

— striking a solicitor off the roll;
— suspension from practice indefinitely or for a fixed period;

---

[78] *Re A Solicitor* (Co/2860196) [1997] *Current Law* 421.

[79] See the Solicitors' (Disciplinary Proceedings) Rules 1994 and Solicitors Act 1974, s 46(11).

[80] Further details of the jurisdiction and procedure of this Tribunal can be found in a guide by a former President of the SDT: B Swift, *Proceedings Before the Solicitors' Disciplinary Tribunal* (London, The Law Society, 1996); see also L Haller, 'The Public Shaming of Lawyers' (2004) 10 *International Journal of the Legal Profession* 281.

[81] *R(on the application of White) v Law Society* (2002) 152 NLJ 21. Judicial review might be available. See *R (ex parte Thompson) v Law Society* [2004] 2 All ER 113 CA.

[82] [1972] 2 All ER 811.

[83] Swift, above n 80, 12.

[84] *Ibid*, 13.

[85] *Ibid*, 17.

[86] *Connolly v Law Society* [2007] EWHC 1175 (Admin).

[87] These are not considered in detail here, but it should be noted that new rules are expected in 2007.

[88] See *Re A Solicitor* [1992] 2 All ER 335, *Campbell v Hamlet* [2005] 3 All ER 1116.

[89] *Conlon v Simms* [2006] 2 All ER 1024.

[90] Solicitors Act 1974, s 47.

— a fine of up to £5,000 for each established allegation;
— the imposition of conditions on the issue of a practising certificate;[91]
— exclusion from legal aid work permanently or for a fixed period;
— the issue of a reprimand; and
— an order for payment of costs.

As regards imposing conditions on the issue of a practising certificate, the SRA can do this quite apart from any decision of the Tribunal or the LCS,[92] for example, where a solicitor has failed to provide an explanation of his conduct after having been requested so to do by the SRA. Oddly, appeals from this decision go to the Master of the Rolls and the hearing is in public.[93] The power to award costs is not normally used against the Law Society or Regulator in the absence of proof of dishonesty or lack of good faith.[94]

There is a rough tariff of penalties according to the significance of the offence, with striking of the roll of solicitors, which means they may no longer practise, the most serious.[95] Cases of dishonesty usually lead to striking solicitors off the roll while breaches of the accounting rules involving substantial sums normally results in either striking off or suspension. In *Bolton v The Law Society*,[96] the Court of Appeal noted that the most serious charges against solicitors involved dishonesty and

> in such cases the tribunal almost invariably, no matter how strong the mitigation, ordered that the solicitor be struck off.

Where no dishonesty was found,

> it remained a matter of very great seriousness in a member of a profession whose reputation depended on trust. A striking off order might, but would not necessarily, follow.

The Tribunal should be concerned fundamentally to maintain the reputation of the profession as one in which every solicitor can be completely trusted. In addition to dishonesty and accounts offences, solicitors have also been struck off for grossly misleading clients, failing to honour undertakings, failing to comply with court orders and knowingly employing a struck off or suspended solicitor.

The fines imposed by the SDT range from £200–300 to at least one of £25,000, imposed on a solicitor who had written to leaseholders demanding ground rents of £6.50 and threatening forfeiture for the arrears and £250 for his costs. This was considered conduct unbecoming a solicitor by making an improper demand, seeking to take an unfair

---

[91] Established *in R (on the application of Camacho) v Law Society* [2004] 4 All ER 126. Until this decision the Tribunal had simply recommended that the Law Society impose conditions, but the court considered this not to be in the public interest. The Tribunal should impose the conditions and the Law Society should then to enforce them. See 131e.

[92] Solicitors Act 1974, s 12. See also s 13A for the conditions in invoking this power.

[93] D Clementi, *Review of the Regulatory Framework for Legal Services in England & Wales* (DCA, 2004) ch C, para 84, recommended that such appeals should be made to the High Court.

[94] *Baxendale Walker v Law Society* [2007] 3 All ER 330. According to Sir Igor Judge P at para 39, 'For the Law Society to be exposed to the risk of an adverse costs order simply because properly brought proceedings were unsuccessful might have a chilling effect on the exercise of its regulatory obligations, to the public disadvantage', so there is no assumption in these proceedings that costs follow the event.

[95] Swift, above n 80.

[96] *The Times*, 8 December 1996.

advantage, sending a misleading letter and seeking irrecoverable costs.[97] In 2005–2006, from a total of 187 applications against solicitors were made to the Tribunal, a drop of 10% on the previous year. In relation to these cases, 63 solicitors were struck off, 39 suspended, 64 fined amounts between £500 and £15,000 and 16 reprimanded. Over half the cases relate to breaches of the Solicitors' Accounts Rules or the misappropriation of client funds.[98] Total fines levied in 2005–2006 amounted to £257,500, compared with £433,000 in 2004–2005 and £93,000 in 2003.[99]

The Bar Disciplinary Tribunal

The Bar Disciplinary Tribunal consists of a judge, two barristers and two lay representatives nominated by the President of the Bar. The charges are laid before the Tribunal by the Professional Conduct and Complaints Committee. The hearing is normally in public, but it can be in private if desirable.[100] The standard of proof is criminal for professional misconduct and civil for inadequate professional services. If the charge is found to be proved, the main powers of the Tribunal are:

— disbarment;
— suspension for a prescribed period;
— a fine of up to £5,000;
— an order to forgo fees;
— a reprimand by the treasurer of the barrister's Inn;
— admonishment by the Tribunal;
— advice from the Tribunal on future conduct;
— an order for the reduction or cancellation of legal aid fees; or
— exclusion from legal aid work.

The Tribunal can make such order for costs as it thinks fit, and may also order compensation to the complainant of up to £15,000.[101] An appeal may be made to the Visitors, High Court judges appointed by the Lord Chief Justice. One or three will hear the appeal, depending on the issue involved. The reports of decisions, where there is an adverse finding against the respondent, are sent to a variety of persons and bodies, including the Bar Council. They can publish the report if they think fit, unless the hearing was in private.

---

[97] See R Colbey, *New Law Journal*, 11 January 2002; L Haller, 'Disciplinary Fines: Deterrence or Retribution?' (2002) 5 *Legal Ethics* 152..

[98] M Davies, 'The Solicitors' Accounts Rules: How Safe is Clients' Money?' (2000) 3 *Legal Ethics* 49.

[99] SDT Annual Report 2004–5 and 2005–6 (www.solicitorstribunal.org.uk).

[100] This rarely happens. See Haller, above n 80, 298.

[101] For full details of the procedure see the Disciplinary Tribunal Regulations 2005, to be found in the Bar Code, Annex K.

Compensation for clients

Solicitors

Since the primary aim of disciplinary proceedings is not the compensation of clients, they may often feel aggrieved that their, often considerable, efforts have not produced a personal return. The results of disciplinary proceedings may, however, have a beneficial affect on compensation, for example, from related liability and insurance claims. Apart from an order of the LCS, compensation for clients for losses connected with the work done by their solicitors comes from two other main sources: the solicitor's own indemnity insurance, which is a requirement of practice and must comply with the Solicitors' Indemnity Insurance Rules 2001; or the Solicitors' Compensation Fund (SCF), which is run by the SRA.

Indemnity insurance

This used to be organised by the Law Society itself, but the premiums were not appropriate to all types of practice and, after much debate, it was decided that insurance should be negotiated on an individual firm basis. This proved a sensible decision since competition has in fact pushed average premiums down, by 14% in 2006 alone.[102] All solicitors must obtain 'qualifying' insurance from a qualified insurer with cover of up to £1 million. Limited companies and limited partnerships must also have additional cover, normally of £2 million. Where firms have failed to acquire insurance they are assigned to an assigned risk pool, which is funded by the qualifying insurers to ensure that all firms are covered. They will have to pay a premium by default, which will exceed the premiums charged by qualifying insurers. Such firms are in breach of the rules and there are other penalties, including being monitored by the LCS. Only 17 firms were in the assigned risk pool in 2006. The main cause of claims is commercial and residential conveyancing, which represents 46% of claims according to one insurer, whereas litigation gives rise to only 22% of claims.[103]

Solicitors' Compensation Fund

The SCF is administered by the Solicitors' Regulation Authority. It is a 'discretionary fund of last resort',[104] meaning that applications are entertained only where there is no other source of compensation from insurance or elsewhere.[105] Claims must normally be made within six months of the date of the loss or the applicant's knowledge of it. The SCF makes grants to those who have suffered loss as a result of a solicitor's dishonesty or failure to account for money that is due. The claimant does not necessarily have to be a client of the defaulting solicitor, but the dishonesty must be proved by establishing that there has been a conviction for, or a civil finding of, fraud or by presenting evidence leading to the 'inevitable presumption' of theft.[106] The SCF does not normally pay sums in excess of

---

[102] *Law Society Gazette*, 16 November 2006, 1.

[103] Report of Zurich Professional 2005–6.

[104] See E Skordaki and C Willis, *Default by Solicitors* (London, The Law Society, 1991).

[105] It was set up in 1942 and is administered by the profession according to the Solicitors' Compensation Fund Rules 1995.

[106] *Ibid*, schedule, para 4.

£1 million, inclusive of the legal costs of the application, or cover certain kinds of losses, namely:[107]

— losses which are not part of the fraud even though caused by it;
— losses 'tainted with the applicant's own dishonesty"
— losses contributed to by the applicant's own acts or omissions, including the applicant's own professional negligence; and
— losses caused by a solicitor's failure to honour an undertaking.[108]

This fund is run by the SRA and contributions of about £300 per year currently are made to it by all practising solicitors holding client monies under the Solicitors Act 1974, section 36.

The majority of the defaulters whose clients are compensated from this fund are sole practitioners.[109] This is not unexpected, in view of the fact that the indemnity fund will not provide compensation for fraud in multi-partner firms unless all the partners are involved in the fraud. Although defaulters do not appear to be a homogeneous group, common factors include a history of submitting late accounts to the Law Society and personal problems at the time of the default. Major claims were made on the fund in the 1980s in connection with mortgage fraud, fuelled by the collapse of the property market. The discretionary powers of the Law Society in compensating for such frauds were the subject of litigation in the case of *R v Law Society, ex parte Mortgage Express Ltd*,[110] a test case, behind which lay claims by lenders of up to £25 million. The case concerned inflated valuations made of properties about which the solicitor failed to warn the mortgage lender (the solicitor represented both borrower and lender, on which see chapter 10). As a result, when the borrowers defaulted, the lenders lost a considerable amount of money. The Law Society's policy that compensation from the fund would be refused where the dishonest solicitor did not commit the fraud for his own benefit was upheld by the Court of Appeal. Lord Bingham considered that the profession was not called upon to make good every loss caused by a solicitor's dishonesty.[111] This case was subsequently applied in *R v Law Society, ex parte Ingram Foods*,[112] where the Law Society was held to be entitled to reduce the compensation that would otherwise have been ordered by 100% because of the applicant's own reckless conduct in accepting an undertaking in relation to a $5 million deposit from a sole practitioner without any documentation or other checks.

Barristers

Barristers must be insured against claims for professional negligence with Bar Mutual

---

[107] *Ibid*, schedule, para 3.

[108] However, if the solicitor gave the undertaking dishonestly in order to obtain funds and the applicant reasonably relied on this undertaking, the applicant's right to compensation would be 'considered'.

[109] Forty-six of the 49 defaulters were sole practitioners in 1988 (above n 104).

[110] [1997] 2 All ER 348.

[111] 'The Law Society has always . . . made clear that they regard the fund as, first and foremost, a source from which to replace money which has been taken by dishonest solicitors for their own benefit'. *Ibid*, 360.

[112] [1997] 2 All ER 666.

Indemnity Fund (BMIF) in accordance with the terms approved by the Bar Council from time to time.[113]

The Legal Services Act 2007

Dissatisfaction with the system of complaints against lawyers, and in particular solicitors, has been the subject of criticism for decades. In his report on the legal services market, Sir David Clementi said:

> I do not believe that the current system delivers sufficient independence from the legal practitioner, nor that it provides appropriate levels of consistency and clarity.[114]

He recommended the creation of an independent complaints process under the control of the Legal Services Board (LSB). His criticisms were directed at the complaints procedures and not the disciplinary tribunals, to which he proposed virtually no changes. He considered that a single Office for Legal Complaints (OLC) would provide a single entry point into the system for consumers, independence from the profession, and greater consistence and clarity. He also thought that it would be a more flexible system, capable of accommodating the varieties of business structures delivering legal services in the future. His proposals were accepted in the Government White Paper that followed in October 2005[115] and are embodied in the Legal Services Act 2007.

Under part 6 of the Act an independent complaints handling body, to be known as the Office for Legal Complaints (OLC), will be established deal with all consumer complaints against members of 'approved regulators', including the Law Society and Bar Council. The costs of the service will be met by a levy on legal services providers on the principle that the 'polluter pays'.[116] As the professional bodies will no longer be dealing with complaint against their members, the need to police the system will disappear, so the current LSO and Commissioner posts will be abolished. Confusingly, however, the whole OLC service is referred to as an ombudsman service and the OLC will appoint a chief ombudsman.[117] The OLC will report to the LSB and also make an annual report to Parliament.

The LSB will appoint the members of the OLC, including its lay chair, in consultation with the Lord Chancellor. The OLC will appoint its staff and also the LSO, who must be a layperson. The LSB is also responsible for setting performance targets for the OLC and monitoring its performance, but the OLC will make its own rules on the handling of complaints to be approved by the LSB. It must specify time limits for complaining and also that the complainant should first use the respondent's own complaints procedure. It will become a statutory obligation to have such a procedure in the sense that the Act requires approved regulators to make rules requiring its members to establish and enforce such procedures. Moreover, beyond the point where clients complain to the provider of services, approved regulators are forbidden to make their own provision for consumer redress, thus

---

[113] Bar Code, para 302.
[114] Clementi Report, n 93 above, ch C, para 33.
[115] *The Future of Legal Services: Putting Consumers First*, Cm 6679 (DCA, October 2005).
[116] Legal Services Act 2007, s 173.
[117] It also has a power to appoint assistant ombudsmen. See Legal Services Act 2007, s 122.

ensuring that all consumer complaints go through the OLC. No contract or agreement can seek to prevent access to the OLC.

There are wide powers requiring either party to the complaint to produce documents or specified information, although these powers cannot infringe legal professional privilege. The OLC must make a decision which is fair and reasonable in all the circumstances of the case and may direct that the provider of services, the respondent, apologises to the complainant, rectifies any error at his own expense, reduces or remits fees, whether or not already paid, pays compensation of up to a specified amount (likely to be £20,000) or takes 'such other action in the interests of the complainant' as may be specified in the direction.[118] The total value of any directions made must not exceed £30,000. The decisions of the OLC will be given in writing and contain reasons. Once accepted by the parties the decision is final and binding, and enforceable through the civil courts. Provision may be made for awarding costs against the respondent in favour of the OLC where the respondent loses. However, such costs must be waived if the respondent wins and the OLC is satisfied that the respondent took all reasonable steps to resolve the complaint under its own procedures.[119] There will be no cost to the complainant in bringing a complaint to the OLC since the cost will be met by a general levy on legal service providers.

Once these provisions are in force the complaints procedure will be more transparent and open, and the system will not be subject to the perception that it is pro-lawyer. It will also be easier for the public to get information on how the system is working and the types of complaint made. Whether it will be more efficient and speedy remains to be seen. The Child Support Agency is a government agency which sought to provide a better and speedier service than the courts in enforcing maintenance orders in relation to children. Its record is, and has always been, disastrous and it is soon to be abolished. A similar experience with the OLC would give the professions the last laugh. The LSO has reservations about the proposed reforms because of their cost and also because of the likelihood that most of the SRA complaints staff are likely to transfer to the OLC. Her chief objection, however, is that her own role will disappear—a fact that fuels her doubt that consumers will be better served under the new regime.[120]

Conclusion

It is arguable that the profession's powers over complaints are far less significant to ethics than its control of education and training, which, as yet, it retains. Emphasis on self-identity in cultivating virtue leads to the inevitable conclusion that it is education rather than discipline that is the precondition of an ethical profession. While disciplinary machinery, as the data reveals, is necessary to control a minority of extreme cases, education provides knowledge, understanding, interpretation and application of ethical rules. It is also the best

---

[118] Legal Services Act 2007, ss 137–8.

[119] *Ibid*, s 136.

[120] See Legal Services Ombudsman Annual Report and Accounts 2006–7, *Delivering Excellence*, foreword and 14–15.

opportunity of entrants to the profession internalising values and accepting their fundamental importance and legitimacy.[121] The modern professional, it must be assumed, will
respond reflexively to reasons for behaving in a certain way, because rational behaviour is
more likely to be absorbed as part of the individual's self-identity. While we cannot be sure
that education will make moral practitioners, there is an impact, for better or worse, of moral
messages.[122]

---

[121] 'The question is why, in the value or meaning sense, should I conform to the rules, should I conform to the
expectations of the others with whom I interact? What in other words is the *basis* of right? Is it simply that some
authority says so without further justification? Is it some religious value, or is it that I and the others have some
natural rights it is wrong to violate? What is the basis of *legitimation*?' T Parsons, 'The Law and Social Control' in
WM Evan (ed), *The Sociology of Law: A Social-structural Perspective* (New York, The Free Press 1980) 60.

[122] Economics students, told that self-interest is natural, became markedly more selfish. Ridley, above n 3, 260.

8

EDUCATION

I always was of opinion that the placing a youth to study with an attorney was rather a prejudice than a help. We are all too apt by shifting on them our business, to encroach on that time
which should be devoted to their studies. The only help a youth wants is to be directed what
books to read, and in what order to read them.[1]

Introduction

Education and training are traditionally at the heart of professionalism, knowledge being the
foundation of professional power. On the European continent, the universities created the
modern law of Europe, whereas in England it was created by the judiciary and the profession
in the Inns of Court.[2] Institutionalised legal education not only consolidates, expands and
theorises the knowledge base in universities, it is also symbolically important,[3] the length of
education and training signifying the intrinsic difficulty of assimilation and mastery, and the
commitment to perfection. Since the profession and academy negotiate the curriculum, it is
surprising that, until recent times, ethics had no part, even at the vocational stage. This
results from the historical relationship between the main stakeholders and others, like organs
of the state.[4] As the profession and academy are increasingly called to account for the
outcomes of legal education, pressure is growing for a different legal education curriculum,
and a role for professional ethics within it.

Compulsory education and training for lawyers currently has four stages: the initial stage,
the vocational stage, the training stage and Continuing Professional Development (CPD),
which continues after qualification. The main routes are a three-year full-time law degree or
a non-law degree followed by a one-year 'conversion course', called a graduate diploma in
law, and/or by qualifying as a fellow of the Institute of Legal Executives, then taking the
solicitors' vocational course. The vocational stage is a one-year full-time course, followed by
a period of work-based learning under the guidance of an approved practitioner.[5] The

---

[1] T Jefferson, Letter to Thomas Turpin, 5 February 1769, in *Papers of Thomas Jefferson* 1:24 (edited by JP Boyd)
(Princeton, NJ, Princeton University Press, 1950).

[2] B Hepple, 'The Renewal of the Liberal Law Degree' (1996) 55 *Cambridge Law Journal* 470.

[3] After its royal charter was granted in 1831, the Law Society instituted a programme of public lectures in 1833.
See D Sugarman, 'Bourgeois Collectivism, Professional Power and the Boundaries of the State: The Private and
Public Life of the Law Society, 1825 to 1914' (1996) 3 *International Journal of the Legal Profession* 81.

[4] See generally M Young (ed), *Knowledge and Control: New Directions for the Sociology of Education* (London,
Collier-Macmillan Publishers, 1971).

[5] This comprises one year's pupillage for barristers and a two-year traineeship for solicitors. Practising solicitors
and barristers are subject to compulsory professional development (CPD) requirements. See chapter 16.

structure offers a progression from theory to practice, known as the 'partnership model' of professional preparation,[6] using varying degrees of the three modes of learning—inquiry, instruction and performance—that are assigned to the stages.[7] Inquiry is the province of the academy, instruction the province of the professional school and performance, including the development of skills in a practical context, that of the employer. The professional bodies prescribe a core curriculum for qualifying degrees by a joint announcement and largely prescribe the content of their respective vocational courses.[8]

The core of the qualifying degree in law, allowing holders to progress to the vocational stage, currently comprises the 'Seven Foundations of Legal Knowledge'. This fills approximately one half of a three-year degree and a rather overfull year for a graduate diploma. The subjects are contracts, torts, crime, land law, equity and trusts, public law, and European law. While there is acceptance of the 'Seven Foundations', methods of law teaching have been contentious since the 1960s. Much of the criticism derives from law teachers' intellectual dissatisfaction with the positivist tradition of legal scholarship. This holds that the law can be understood by extracting governing principles from legislation and cases[9] without any reference to any social, political or moral context. The numerous criticisms of the 'black letter' law[10] approach includes suggestions that, although it purports to be value neutral, it is essentially conservative and sterile.[11] The technical and substantive focus of university law teaching leaves students struggling to understand the practical impact or potential of law for lawyers, clients or society. How did this situation come about?

Historical context

Legal education has a long but sometimes inglorious history. The medieval Bar required attendance at lectures and debates led by senior practitioners, participation in moots[12] and taking notes in court as a condition of call,[13] and provided what Holdsworth identified as a superb technical training in law and a social and moral education.[14] Subsequent periods of decline led to criticisms of low standards and unqualified practice. In the nineteenth century

---

[6] RA Barnett, RA Becher and NM Cork, 'Models of Professional Preparation: Pharmacy, Nursing and Teacher Education' (1987) 12 *Studies in Higher Education* 51, 61.

[7] CO Houle, *Continuing Learning in the Professions* (London, Jossey-Bass Publishers, 1980).

[8] This 'core' is negotiated with university law schools and published in a joint announcement by the branches of the profession. See 'Announcement on Qualifying Law Degrees', issued jointly by the Law Society and the Council of Legal Education, January 1995, 6.

[9] The institutionalisation of approach is attributed to the Harvard law professor Christopher Columbus Langdell, who, in 1887, asserted that 'Law is a science, and that all the available materials of that science are contained in printed books': see 'Harvard Celebration Speeches: Professor Langdell' (1887) 8 *The Law Quarterly Review* 123.

[10] The term 'black letter law' derives from the presentation of basic legal principles in bold type in traditional texts. AC Hutchinson, 'Beyond Black-letterism: Ethics in Law and Legal Education' (1999) 33 *Law Teacher* 301.

[11] See Hutchinson, *ibid*.

[12] Established lawyers debated for periods of several hours either side of a communal dinner and were judged by senior barristers.

[13] R Pound, *The Lawyer from Antiquity to Modern Times: With Particular Reference to the Development of Bar Associations in the United States* (St Paul, MN, West Publishing, 1953) 90.

[14] Fifteenth-century Inns were collegiate, with conditions of life similar to those of modern Oxford or Cambridge universities, attracting many not intending to practise. W Holdsworth *A History of English Law* (London, Methuen, 1924) vol II, 509–10.

the profession began to use educational requirements, particularly examinations, to control entry,[15] formulating firmer 'vocational stage' requirements in the twentieth century.[16] By contemporary standards the profession sailed under a cloud of suspicion on issues of access, clearly demonstrated by the record on women.[17] Perhaps the most significant change in the latter part of the twentieth century was that by the 1960s the 'university route'[18] finally overtook the five-year Articles of Clerkship as the most popular way to qualify. The Law Society later accepted the Ormrod Report proposal that, by 1980, legal education should comprise a law degree, a one-year course and two-year articles, the current blueprint for education and training.

As legal education developed in the twentieth century, university law schools clung to the scientific pretensions of positivism, manifest in the doctrinal approach to law study.[19] The case method of US legal education, though not the Socratic aspect, evolved in England in the nineteenth century under the influence of a largely Oxford-based elite, including Anson, Salmond, Dicey and Pollock. The 'classical period' in the development of the 'black letter' law tradition[20], between 1850 and 1907, prioritised the systematisation, exposition and analysis of legal doctrine,[21] creating an area of autonomy between the university, the profession and the state. The organising concept of this domain was the rule of law.[22] This reification of doctrine at the expense of social, political or moral perspectives was the bedrock of English legal education, but it was, as Sugarman says, a narrow ledge. Practitioners remained masters of the relation between law and facts. On their ledge,

> Law dons were masters of the principles of law. To assert that law was principled and internally coherent seemed to require that facts and reality were kept at a safe distance.[23]

Academic lawyers took a conservative and static role.

In the mid-1800s a select committee urged the development of law in the universities,

---

[15] The Law Society instituted examinations in 1836 to control unqualified practice. The Solicitors Act 1860 introduced a three-tier examination at the beginning, middle and end of articles. The preliminary examination included Latin. Formal training for the Bar began in 1852, when the Inns of Court standardised training by creating the Council of Legal Education, but examinations were not introduced until 1872. Passing an examination became compulsory in 1872, but the process leading to it was haphazard. E Cruikshank, 'Building a Profession' 100/25 *Law Society's Gazette*, 26 June 2003, 32.

[16] By 1925 the Inns of Court School of Law was responsible for vocational preparation for the Bar under the Council of Legal Education, but full-time staff were not appointed until 1968. The Law Society acquired the private law tutors Gibson and Weldon in 1961 and established the College of Law. E Cruikshank, 'Surviving Hard Times' 100/32 *Law Society Gazette*, 23 August 2003, 22.

[17] In 1903 the Benchers of Gray's Inn refused to admit Bertha Cave as a law student. Four female graduates sued the Law Society in 1913 for refusing to register them for its examinations. In *Bebb v Law Society* [1914] 1 Ch 286 the Court of Appeal held that it was justified, citing medieval authority that 'the law will not suffer women to be attorneys, nor infants nor serfs'. After the First World War, the Law Society revised its view, supporting the Sex Disqualification (Removal) Act 1919. Helena Normanton began practice as the first woman barrister and Carrie Morrison qualified as the first woman solicitor in 1922. Cruikshank, above n 15.

[18] In 1756 the Bar introduced a two-year exemption from the qualification period for entrants with a university degree to attract higher-status entrants. The Law Society did so in 1821.

[19] This took different forms in different jurisdictions. Under Langdell's (above n 9) 'Socratic method', students were expected to state the facts of the case, the outcome and whether it was 'good' law.

[20] Above n 10.

[21] D Sugarman, '"A Hatred of Disorder": Legal Science, Liberalism and Imperialism' in P Fitzpatrick (ed), *Dangerous Supplements: Resistance and Renewal in Jurisprudence* (London, Pluto Press, 1991) 34.

[22] *Ibid*, 36.

[23] *Ibid*, 41.

but identifiable law programmes, which at their best combined philosophy, theory, practice and reform, only emerged at Oxford, Cambridge and London towards the end of the nineteenth century.[24] When, at the turn of the century, they began to develop in provincial universities, the programmes were often developed in collaboration with local law societies and, being taught by local practitioners, reflected their practical approach.[25] In 1913 the Haldane Commission promoted the combination of theory and practice,[26] again excluding social, political or moral context,[27] gaining support from the academic establishment.[28] Others, notably Gower, argued for lawyers versed in economics, political science and sociology as early as 1950, and orthodoxy came under sustained pressure. Later critics argued that the pedagogy of the case method stimulates competitiveness, orthodoxy and conservatism, turning students away from whatever public service orientations stimulated their interest in law.[29] Positivism fell out of favour with many academics from the 1960s onwards and the addition to the joint announcement by the Law Society and Bar Council that law should be taught in its contexts encouraged increasing multi-disciplinarity.[30] The context of legal education began to change with the 1960s' expansion of higher education and the creation of polytechnics in the 1970s. The recruitment as academics of substantial numbers of qualified lawyers and practitioners coincided with the growth of socio-legal research in the universities, breaking the stranglehold of conventional legal analysis.[31] This opened the door to a broader approach to law.

Ethics and conduct in legal education

Between 1970 and 1990 three major reports considered legal education. None recommended including professional ethics in the initial stage. The Ormrod Report in 1971 acknowledged that lawyers needed to 'grasp . . . the ethos of the profession' but saw a problem in reconciling the demand for a "learned" profession with instruction in the skills and techniques essential to legal practice.[32] The Benson Report in 1979 enquired into changes to 'the structure,

---

[24] M Partington, 'Academic Lawyers and "Legal Practice" in Britain: A Preliminary Reappraisal' (1988) 15 *Journal of Law and Society* 374.

[25] B Abel-Smith and R Stevens, *Lawyers and the Courts: a Sociological Study of the English Legal System 1750–1965* (London, Heinemann, 1967) 182.

[26] Hepple, above n 2, 474.

[27] Partington, above n 24.

[28] The president of the Society of Public Teachers of Law in a post-war review of legal education said that legal education should be based on precedent, not legislation. Criticising law and discussing law reform was dangerously like sociology, and impinged on the objectivity necessary for legal study.

[29] D Kennedy, 'How the Law School Fails: A Polemic' (1971) 1 *Yale Review Journal of Law and Social Action* 71; CC Stanley, 'Training for the Hierarchy? Reflections on the British Experience of Legal Education' (1988) 22 *The Law Teacher* 78; S Matambanadzo, 'Fumbling toward a Critical Legal Pedagogy and Practice' (2006) 4 *Policy Futures in Education* 90.

[30] See the Hon Mr Justice Ormrod (Chairman), *Report of the Committee on Legal Education*, Cmnd 4595 (1971) para 109; ACLEC, para 2.4; K Economides, 'Legal Ethics—Three Challenges for the Next Millenium' in *Ethical Challenges to Legal Education and Conduct* (Oxford, Hart Publishing, 1998) xxxii.

[31] This constituted a form of knowledge that was not found in practice and was valuable in law reform, as evidenced by the establishment of the Law Commission in 1965. Partington, above n 24.

[32] Ormrod, above n 30, para 100.

organisation, training, regulation of and entry to the legal profession' that were desirable in the public interest[33] and stated that:

> It is essential that throughout their training students should be impressed with the importance of maintaining ethical standards, rendering a high quality of personal service, maintaining a good relationship with clients, providing information about work in hand for clients, avoiding unnecessary delays, maintaining a high standard in briefs and preparation for trial, promptly rendering accounts with clear explanations and attending to other matters mentioned elsewhere in this report.[34]

Benson considered, however, that the time to bring together theory and practice was at the vocational stage.[35] The Marre Committee Report in 1989[36] endorsed the shift to a more practically orientated legal education and proposed a split between skills suited to the academic and vocational stages. Those skills with an ethical dimension[37] were confined to the vocational stage. The list also included 'an adequate knowledge of professional and ethical standards',[38] but this was not assigned to either stage. The Marre report was published during the planning of the more practically orientated Bar Vocational Course (BVC), a development that it welcomed enthusiastically. The success of the university route to qualification had left a deficit in the professional preparation of lawyers, which the vocational courses had failed to fill.

Vocational preparation for professions generally seeks a balance between 'scientific knowledge' ('knowing that') with client interaction skills ('knowing how'),[39] but, until the 1990s, the vocational courses were bastions of 'knowing that'.[40] The new BVC in 1989 and the Legal Practice Course in 1993 were precipitated by a crisis of confidence in professional knowledge,[41] and demands for competence, flexibility and adaptability from graduates.[42] They were influenced by developments in other common law countries,[43] shifting the

---

[33] Benson, *The Royal Commission on Legal Services Final Report*, Cmnd 7648 (1979) vol 1, vi.

[34] *Ibid*, vol 1, para 39.47 and see vol 1, para 3.40.

[35] *Ibid*, vol 1, 629, para 39.4.

[36] The committee was organised by the legal profession to resolve the dispute over advocacy, but undertook a wide review of regulation. The Committee on the Future of the Legal Profession (The Marre Committee), *A Time for Change* (London, General Council of the Bar and the Law Society, 1988).

[37] Eg 'an ability to help clients understand the options available to them so that they can make an informed choice of action or direction'. *Ibid*, para 12.21, no 18.

[38] *Ibid*, 12.21, no 15

[39] Barnett *et al*, above n 6.

[40] Remodelled in 1980, the LSF was based on preparation for the typical firm, a 'four partner firm in Oldham' but, by 1992, 70% of trainees worked in large firms dealing with commercial law. A Sherr, 'Professional Legal Training' (1992) 20 *Journal of Law & Society* 163, 164.

[41] 'The fixed person for fixed duties, who in older societies was such a godsend, in the future will be a public danger'. Whitehead (1926), quoted in Houle, above n 7.

[42] The Law Society stated that the reasons for the change to a more practical curriculum were '. . . the continuing needs to improve the quality of entrants to the profession and to increase the system's ability to respond flexibly to changes in demand for solicitors' services': Law Society Training Committee, *Training Tomorrow's Solicitors: Proposals for Changes to the Education and Training of Solicitors* (London, The Law Society, 1990) para 1.2. The climate had also changed with the growth of the clinical movement in law schools, the development of the philosophy of 'lifelong learning' in higher education and by a short-lived but worrying recruitment crisis. See *The Recruitment Crisis: a Report by the Training Committee of the Law Society* (London, The Law Society, 1988); J Randall, *Review of Legal Education: An Alternative Approach* (London, The Law Society, 1989) 5.

[43] The US, Canada and Australia had already incorporated clinical or skills components in the education and training of lawyers.

balance from instruction to performance by introducing the 'DRAIN' skills—drafting, research, advocacy, interviewing and negotiation—taught through the 'transactions' of legal practice and small group work.[44] The new courses had broad aims, aspiring to provide students with such knowledge, skills and attitudes to prepare them for pupillage and future practice,[45] and

> to inculcate a professional approach to work and to develop in students a respect for the prin-
> ciples of professional conduct.[46]

Presented as central, but in fact marginal, the delivery of professional conduct was often idiosyncratic and banal, with outcomes that were uncertain at best.

On the new vocational courses ethics was 'hidden' in the curriculum as a 'pervasive' topic rather than as a subject in its own right.[47] It had neither substantive content nor focus, presenting the problem of how best to deliver and assess. Most providers opted for a few introductory lectures, the dispersion of rudimentary conduct points throughout the course and assessment through other subjects.[48] The approach risked confusing ethics with regulation and 'good practice',[49] so that, for example, procedures like participative decision making were presented as mandatory[50] rather than a counsel of perfection that might sometimes be unrealistic.[51] Students might therefore perceive that the ethics taught were not attainable, leading to their ethics teaching losing credibility. Although the new vocational courses gained general approval, continuing complaints from practitioners about the defective knowledge of pupils and trainees[52] forced the professional bodies to reintroduce more substantive material, reducing time for practical work.[53] In the more frank analyses, both skills and ethics became increasingly marginal.[54]

During the 1990s ethics moved higher up the agenda, due largely to the efforts of the Lord Chancellor's Advisory Committee on Education and Conduct (ACLEC),[55] created to advise the Lord Chancellor on legal education and conduct under the Courts and Legal

---

[44] The BVC focused on civil and criminal litigation and evidence while the LPC had Business Law and Practice, Litigation and Evidence, Conveyancing and Wills and Probate. Both had a third term of option subjects.

[45] The course would 'emphasise the importance of being able to practice in a culturally diverse society, communicate effectively with everyone involved in the legal process, and of recognising the role of other professionals and their expertise'. General Council of the Bar Validation Steering Committee, *Application Procedure to be Validated to Offer the Bar Vocational Course: Course Specialisation Guidelines* (London, General Council of the Bar, 1995) 3, para 1.1.

[46] *Ibid*, para 1.1(2)(6).

[47] The Inns of Court School of Law, for example, had three lectures and three tutorials on ethics in its BVC. The Inns of Court School of Law, *Bar Vocational Course Handbook, Full Time Studies 1997–98*, para 4.7.

[48] Most students are assessed on ethical issues planted in four skills assessments, reflecting the way that ethical issues arise in practice. Although more realistic than formal examination, the issues tend to be either obvious and easily 'spotted' or so obscure that high failure rates are courted.

[49] A Sherr, 'Lawyers and Clients: The First Meeting' (1986) 49 *Modern Law Review* 323, 324.

[50] The written standards for the LPC require that students 'advise the client on the legal consequences of his or her proposals . . . agree a [case preparation] strategy with the client'.

[51] A Boon, 'Client Decision-making in Personal Injury Schemes' (1995) 23 *International Journal of the Sociology of Law* 253.

[52] S Nathanson, 'The Real Problem with the Legal Practice Course' *New Law Journal*, 24 May 2002.

[53] EH Greenebaum, 'How Professionals (Including Legal Educators) "Treat" Their Clients' (1987) 37 *Journal of Legal Education* 554.

[54] H Brayne, 'LPC Skills Assessments—A Year's Experience' (1994) 28 *Law Teacher* 227.

[55] ACLEC, *First Report on Legal Education and Training* (London, ACLEC, 1996) paras 2.3–2.8.

Services Act 1990. ACLEC's first report in 1996 decried the rigid separation of the initial and vocational stages, advocating that legal education should imbue 'the standards and codes of professional conduct'[56] and that the curriculum should go beyond 'a familiarisation with professional codes of conduct and the machinery for enforcing them'.[57] None of ACLEC's main proposals for legal education were adopted, and it was later disbanded by the Lord Chancellor. Implementing the vision was considered only in outline, the report providing a discussion point rather than a template. The key points, however, are that the initial stage must take more responsibility for delivering ethics, a position that threatened a complicated and possibly fraught negotiation with the academy.

Stakeholders in legal education and training

ACLEC's 1996 report endorsed Twining's observation that legal education reflects three entrenched spheres of influence: the universities, the Bar and the Law Society.[58] Vocational education is dominated by a private sector comprising the professions' former schools of law, the College of Law, the Inns of Court School of Law and BPP Law School,[59] although many universities offer vocational courses. The main tension between the profession and providers is over the content of qualifying law degrees. The degree of resistance to change in the university sector largely reflects a status hierarchy determined by the date of designation as a university. The older universities tolerate the 'Seven Foundations' because the 'qualifying degree' guarantees students, but they resist expansion of the core, demand autonomy in delivering the curriculum and are hostile to 'vocationalism'.[60] While the old universities cling to the Ormrod view that the role of the liberal law degree is to educate rather than to train, the polytechnics' original mission was to increase access to higher education, offering vocational subjects and a more practical approach. The former polytechnics are heavily represented among the providers of the vocational courses[61] and are generally more receptive to change. While ACLEC anticipated negative reaction to its proposals from all university law schools,[62] in the event both the profession and university law schools were unreceptive to its report,[63] possibly stirring government resolve to exercise stakeholder rights on its own behalf and on behalf of students[64] and employers.

[56] *Ibid*, paras 1.10 and 1.21.

[57] *Ibid*, para 1.19.

[58] W Twining, *Blackstone's Tower: The English Law School* (London, Stevens & Sons/Sweet & Maxwell 1994) ch 2, note 47 and 53, and ch 3, 162–6.

[59] Although the Inns of Court School of Law formally became part of City University in 2001 it retains its name and location.

[60] J Webb, 'Inventing the Good: Prospectus for Clinical Education and the Teaching of Legal Ethics in England' (1996) 30 *The Law Teacher* 270, 271 and notes 4 and 6.

[61] A number of universities were authorised to offer the new BVC—Cardiff, Manchester Metropolitan, Northumbria, Nottingham Trent and West of England—as were the private providers College of Law and BPP. 'The Providers' [May/June 1997] *Counsel*, 12. Over 30 providers, including these, offer the LPC.

[62] Para 2.5.

[63] 'Earthworks against ACLEC', *SPTL Reporter*, Spring 1996.

[64] See the response to Nigel Bastin, Chief Education Officer of the Bar, that the degree should shoulder more of the burden of professional preparation so as to reduce student debt: N Wikeley 'The Law Degree and the BVC' [Spring 2004] *The Reporter* 23.

The profession and the academy have divergent interests. While the profession's main concern is competent lawyers, the academic law schools seek academic respectability, as reflected in the movement toward multi-disciplinarity.[65] The Ormrod view that the aim of higher education is producing 'not mere specialists but rather cultivated men and women'[66] is consistent with the old belief that the 'vision, range, depth, balance and rich humanity' of ethical practitioners are fostered by the study of law as a liberal art,[67] with morality at its core.[68] Ormrod welcomed the 'practically useful' on law degrees so long as it was 'taught in such a way as to promote the general powers of the mind'. This could justify almost any curriculum, and degree courses have followed diverse paths, from the traditional diet of 'black letter' law, through the interdisciplinary perspectives of sociology, politics and economics, and even the practical. Therefore, although the period since the 1960s took most law schools further from the profession,[69] 'clinical legal education', that is, work by students on real cases, made inroads into the curriculum of many law schools over the period. Generally favoured by the new universities but rare in the elite universities, it did not become universal, being relatively expensive and distracting staff from research,[70] and was resisted as vocational preparation or even 'indoctrination'.[71]

Students welcomed the practical orientation of the vocational courses and the integration of skills and ethics. [72] The old course had not dealt with some of the most basic ethical issues[73] and the emphasis on dealing with clients, and other professionals, relieved students' anxiety about what they may face in work.[74] Undergraduates also generally like a practical flavour to law degree studies, although only 60% of law graduates go into practice.[75] Student reviews of their educational experiences are often mixed. Most choose law for intellectual interest, security of income and future employment prospects and

[65] Twining, above n 58, 2, conceived of this as 'a tug of war between three aspirations: to be accepted a full members of the community of higher learning; to be relatively detached, but nonetheless engaged, critics and censors of law in society; and to be service-institutions for a profession which is itself caught between noble ideals, lucrative service of powerful interests and unromantic cleaning up of society's messes'.

[66] *Report of the Committee on Higher Education*, Cmnd 2154 (1963) (The Robbins Report) paras 24–6; Ormrod, above n 30, para 106.

[67] K Llewellyn, 'The Study of Law as a Liberal Art' (1960), reprinted in *Jurisprudence: Realism in Theory and Practice* (University of Chicago Press, 1962) 376. See also the discussion by Twining, above n 58, ch 4, note 42.

[68] Twining, *ibid*, 159–62.

[69] HT Edwards, 'The Growing Disjunction between Legal Education and the Legal Profession' (1992) 91 *Michigan Law Revue* 34. Twining, above n 58, 141–2.

[70] Law is in the lowest funding bracket per student of the undergraduate disciplines, its traditional teaching methodology being cheap 'chalk and talk'.

[71] See generally Twining, above n 58, ch 7 and note 54.

[72] V Johnston and J Shapland, *Developing Vocational Legal Training for the Bar* (University of Sheffield, Faculty of Law, 1990).

[73] *Ibid*, 42–7.

[74] More than half of the barristers responding to the Bar study reported ethical difficulties encountered through naivrty. J Shapland and A Sorsby, *Starting Practice: Work and Training at the Junior Bar* (University of Sheffield, Institute for the Study of the Legal Profession, 1995).

[75] The Law Society cohort study found that more than 50% of home law students had, at age 16, seriously considered a career as a solicitor and 33% per cent had considered a career as a barrister (D Halpern, *Entry into Legal Professions: The Law Student Cohort Study* (London, The Law Society, 1994) ch 7). By the second year of their undergraduate course, the percentage of home students thinking about becoming a solicitor had jumped to 75%, while those considering the Bar had fallen to 14% (*ibid*, 46).

independence,[76] and there is a noticeable absence of ethical reasons for such study, like the opportunity for public service.[77] Students seek degree courses that are consistent with their career aspirations, prioritising technical mastery over broad goals such as personal development, understanding the social context of law, law reform and preparation as policy makers.[78] While the vocational courses are seen by some as a good grounding for practice, others criticise them as insufficiently practical, as intellectually undemanding spoon-feeding or as exam-orientated money-makers for course providers.[79]

The government is primarily concerned that students secure value for money from legal education, allied to a concern about access to a legal profession still seen as the preserve of a self-perpetuating[80] and privileged elite.[81] Although more part-time, mature and often disadvantaged students obtain law degrees, and there is considerable student diversity at the initial stage,[82] this presence is not always reflected in the profession. The ethical issues raised include locating the responsibility for informing students of the realities of professional recruitment[83] and that of the profession in addressing the problem. Greater diversity also presents challenges such as the assessment of interpersonal and presentational skills. Early indications of a problem arose with allegations of discrimination at the Inns of Court School of Law. This led to the establishment of a Committee of Enquiry in March 1994 to investigate differential pass rates for white and ethnic minority students. The Committee concluded that, although there was no direct discrimination, there was, perhaps, a deeper problem:

---

[76] According to A Sherr and J Webb, 'Law Students, the External Market, and Socialisation: Do We Make them Turn to the City?' (1980) 16 *Journal of Law and Society* 225, 233, motivations were, in descending order: interest in subject matter, desire for intellectual stimulation, desire for professional training, desire to practise law, prospects of above average income, enjoyment of debating and arguing, desire for independence, expectation of a stable, secure future and the prestige of the profession. A large US study found that students chose law because they thought it offered future independence, correlating it with the desire for varied work, handling others' affairs and interest in the subject matter: R Stevens, 'Law Schools and Law Students' (1973) 59 *Virginia Law Review* 551.

[77] Careers in Government Legal Service are presented as a form of public service in which financial benefits are surrendered in order to work in the public good: J Currie, 'For Queen and Country' [June 2002] *Lawyer 2B* 50. Stevens found that restructuring society or working with the underprivileged came around the middle of the range of motivations: R Stevens 'Law Schools and Law Students' (1973) 59 *Virginia Law Review* 551.

[78] Halpern, above n 75, 21; Sherr and Webb, above n 76; but see C Glasser, 'The Legal Profession in the 1990's: Images of Change' (1990) 10 *Legal Studies* 1, arguing that professionalism gives Anglo-American entrants a high sense of 'calling'; A Boon 'From Public Service to Service Industry: the Impact of Socialisation and Work on the Motivation and Values of Lawyers' (2005) 12 *International Journal of the Legal Profession* 193 (desire for public service may surface later).

[79] N Fletcher, *Equality, Diversity and the Legal Practice Course: Research Study 49* (London, The Law Society, 2004) 83.

[80] Whereas 6% of pupils are at independent schools, 18% of new university, 26% of other university and 45% of Oxbridge law students were at independent schools at the age of 14. One in five law students had a close relative in the profession and, among home students, there is a 10 times higher number than would be expected by chance. *Ibid,* ch 5.

[81] The Royal Commission on Legal Services found that 54% of university law students had fathers with professional or managerial positions and 16% had working class fathers, compared with 50 and 30% in the general university student population respectively (Benson, above n 33). In 1994 only 18% of law students had working class backgrounds (Halpern, above n 75, 21).

[82] According to *Trends in the Solicitors' Profession: Annual Statistical Report* (London, Law Society 2003) Table 9.4, approximately 20% of students accepted for a first degree in law were from ethnic minorities and over 50% were women. Most ethnic minorities are better represented on law degrees and conversion courses than the proportion they represent in that age group in the general population (Halpern, *ibid,* 18–19).

[83] The general issue is dealt with in chapter 16.

the school and the course were designed to reproduce the model English barrister, who is white, male and upper class. Anyone who does not conform and has no wish to, or is unable to, may feel uncomfortable. This is equally so of pupillage, tenancy and further eminence at the Bar but it is less noticeable then because those who have reached the later stages will already have successfully conformed.[84]

Later research conducted for the Law Society found that ethnicity did not affect performance on the Legal Practice Course (LPC), but that some ethnic groups pushed children to seek legal qualification who were not personally motivated to do so.[85]

Another group with a direct interest in legal education and training is legal employers. Many solicitors' firms criticised trainees for having inadequate writing skills, research skills or knowledge of law. The loudest voices were among the commercial firms, many of which paid prospective trainees' LPC fees. A group of elite law firms therefore negotiated with three providers and the Law Society to validate a 'City LPC', delivering a curriculum suited to their mode of practice.[86] Lord Woolf used his Upjohn lecture to point out that hiving off the most able students would not only affect the quality of other courses and the importance of 'lawyers emerging into practice regard[ing] themselves as one profession'.[87] In 2004 the 'City five' dropped two of the three providers, which then, together with College of Law, began to offer bespoke courses for individual firms with enough trainees, tailored to their specific requirements.[88] Competitors described the development as divisive and unhealthy,[89] but no concerns were raised about basic ethics teaching being prescribed by employers.

Proposals for change

In 1998 the profession adopted the ACLEC view that the law degree should stand as an independent liberal education not tied to any specific vocation,[90] a move consistent with assessing transferable skills rather than legal skills in higher education.[91] The profession also endorsed the position that students should acquire knowledge 'of the social economic political, historical, philosophical, moral, ethical, cultural and comparative contexts in which law operates'. No specific content was prescribed beyond the core, and it is doubtful that there is systematic coverage of these perspectives or that ethics appears anywhere except in a handful of courses. Amid international movement towards ethics curricular,[92] the Law Society consulted on a new training framework in 2001, promising that ethics would join

[84] *Equal Opportunities at the Inns of Court School of Law: Final Report of the Committee of Inquiry into Equal Opportunities on the Bar Vocational Course* (The Barrow Report, 1994) 99, para 8.10.

[85] Fletcher, above n 79, 32.

[86] A Mizzi, 'The City Generation', *Gazette* 99/34, 5 September 2002.

[87] A Mizzi 'Lord Woolf Criticises City Law Firms for Launching 'Elite' Training Consortium', *Gazette* 97/25, 22 June 2000.

[88] In 2006 a firm launched an LPC in collaboration with the College of Law for only 25 students studying over a single semester. J Parker, 'Fast Train to London Bridge', *The Lawyer*, 13 March 2006, 16.

[89] G Charles, 'A Revolution in Legal Education', *The Lawyer*, 22 March 2004.

[90] The Law Society and the General Council of the Bar, *A Consultation Paper on the Revision of the Joint Announcement on Qualifying Law Degrees* (September 1998).

[91] J Bell, 'General Transferable Skills and the Law Curriculum' (1996) 2 *Contemporary Issues in Law* 1.

[92] G Powles, 'Taking the Plunge: Integrating Legal Ethics in Australia' (1999) 33 *Law Teacher* 315.

knowledge and skills as the core elements of solicitors' education and training 'from the cradle to the grave'.[93] Respondents to a consultation gave almost universal approval to the central role conceived for ethics[94] and the Law Society convened a group, the Training Framework Review Group (TFRG), to develop the concept.

The TFRG began by identifying what a newly qualified solicitor should know and be able to do before proposing that regulation should focus on assessing these outcomes, rather than courses or other processes. The conventional stages of the partnership model would finally be abandoned, providing greater flexibility in delivering education and training. The only course requirement would be an honours degree, the common currency of European education and professional entry under the Bologna Declaration.[95] A two-year period of work-based learning, completed under the supervision of a solicitor, would also be required. The review took place amid growing awareness that cost may hinder access by those from poorer backgrounds[96] and it was proposed that students would not be required to attend a course before taking vocational examinations. The training contract would be abolished so that students would be able to complete their training with a period of work-based learning in organisations other than a firm of solicitors.

The TFRG's proposals mapped onto the existing structure of legal education and training, although not perfectly.[97] The first of six groups of 'day one outcomes' re-works the 'Seven Foundations' of the initial stage. The second group, intellectual, analytical and problem solving skills, underpins the whole of education and training. Reflecting the content of the LPC, the third group comprises transactional and dispute resolution skills, and the fourth, legal, professional and client relationship knowledge and skills. The fifth group, personal development and work management skills, and the sixth group, professional values, behaviours, attitudes and ethics, overlap the LPC and work-based learning. None of the content was tied to a particular stage, however, and creation of a multiplicity of routes to qualification was an explicit aim of the framework.[98] This was not welcomed by providers of the LPC, their course threatened by the intended flexibility, nor by some firms, who feared declining standards.[99] The Chief Executive of the Law Society robustly defended the proposals, arguing that they would increase access to the profession.[100]

The TFRG proposals attempted to address concerns about 'non-standard' applicants by reducing the costs of qualification and removing potential bottlenecks in the qualifying

---

[93] Law Society, *Consultation: Training Framework Review* (London, Law Society, 2001).

[94] A Boon and J Webb, *Consultant's Report on the Training Framework Review Consultation* (London, Law Society, 2002).

[95] J Webb, 'Academic Legal Education in Europe: Convergence and Diversity' (2002) 9 *International Journal of the Legal Profession* 139, 142.

[96] C Sanders, '£40,000 Bill before you Get Near the Bar', *Times Higher Education Supplement*, 3 October 2003, NA Bastin, 'Why I Think Legal Training Has to Change', *Times Higher Education Supplement*, 3 October 2003, 16.

[97] The current version is on the SRA website http://www.sra.org.uk.securedownload/file/229.

[98] *Ibid*, para 38. Therefore, degrees and conversion courses for non-law graduates might incorporate the 'vocational stage' outcomes, vocational courses might incorporate work-based learning and some of the larger firms might incorporate the 'vocational stage' outcomes in the period of work-based learning.

[99] C Sanders, 'Law Revamp Could Hit Coffers', *The Times Higher*, February 2005; B Malkin, 'Market Slams Law Soc Plans to Abolish Vocational Training', *Lawyer 2B*, February 2005, 1; N Johnson, 'The Training Framework Review—What's all the Fuss About?' (2005) 155 *New Law Journal* 341.

[100] C Sanders, 'Profile: Janet Paraskeva, Chief Executive, Law Society' *The Times Higher*, February 2005.

process.[101] They respond to internationalisation of practice by recognising the need for qualification regimes to be more flexible, a message reinforced by the European Court decision in *Morgenbesser*[102] that held that European legal professions must consider the equivalence of qualifications and experience gained in other member states when deciding whether to enrol their lawyers, rather than insist on specified qualifications. Assessment of *Morgenbesser* applications would be easier under the new training framework, a matter of matching qualifications and experience to outcomes, as would considering the work experience of UK students for similar credit. This is important because, while there is no requirement to treat domestic applicants in the same way as those of other European countries, fairness, and ultimately the courts, may dictate otherwise. The framework was also a response to specialisation, offering the possibility of a more efficient allocation of time and effort between generalist pre-qualification and specialist post-qualification programmes.

It is not clear how the TFRG's proposals deliver the promise to make ethics central from cradle to grave. The first group of outcomes, echoing ACLEC, includes 'the jurisdiction, authority and procedures of the legal institutions and the professions that initiate, develop and interpret the law', 'the rules of professional conduct' and the 'values and principles on which professional rules are constructed'. The fact that these outcomes map onto the initial stage suggest that a substantial programme of ethics could become part of qualifying degrees, but how much time would be spent on each outcome, what activity might be involved or how the profession would check whether the outcomes are met were unresolved, and acknowledged by the chair of TFRG as being problematic.[103] The 'Seven Foundations' could be revised to reduce the old content and introduce some new, but because of the lack of detail, even academics broadly supportive of the proposals are reserving judgement.[104]

The Bar announced a review of its education and training framework in 2004 by the Bell Working Party. Its remit was to consider the vocational stage, constantly criticised for its high cost against the low chance of pupillage and tenancy.[105] The working party did not take the TFRG's iconoclastic approach and its consultation proposed little substantive change. The review process became marooned during the creation of the Bar Standards Board, but, once this was complete, another review group was established to consider the

---

[101] Sir Alan Langlands, *Gateways to the Professions: A Consultation Paper* (Department for Education and Skills, January 2005); A Fuller and L Unwin, 'Vocational Guidance', *Education Guardian*, 29 March 2005.

[102] *Christine Morgenbesser v Consiglio dell'Odine degli avvocati di Genoa* [2003] ECR I–13467, [2003] All ER (D) 190 (Nov).

[103] S Nelson 'Reflections from the International Conference on Legal Ethics from Exeter' (2004) 7 *Legal Ethics* 159.

[104] J Webb and A Fancourt, 'The Law Society's Training Framework Review: On the Straight and Narrow or the Long and Winding Road' (2004) 38 *Law Teacher* 293; A Boon, J Flood and J Webb, 'Postmodern Professions? The Fragmentation of Legal Education and the Legal Profession' (2005) 32 *Journal of Law and Society* 473.

[105] The BVC currently has validated numbers of 1,594 and total students of 1,709, whereas the LPC had over 8,273 places and 6,837 enrolments for 2004–2005. In the year ending 31 July 2003 there were 5,650 new traineeships registered with the Society, representing an increase (4.9%) on the previous year's registrations of 5,385 (*Trends in the Solicitors' Profession: Annual Statistical Report* (2003) para 8.6). The number of pupillages offered fell from 853 to 572 between 2000–2001 to 2003–2004 ('Bar Special: An Educated Risk' *Legal Week Student*). The average fees for both courses approach £10,000, with the BVC tending to be slightly more expensive.

numerous issues that surrounded the course.[106] When this group was in its early stages, a comprehensive report on the role of all stages in the preparation of barristers was published, aimed at improving access by the less privileged and raising standards.[107] Among 57 wide-ranging recommendations, including the introduction of a module on law and lawyers to the National Curriculum in schools, 14 related to the BVC. These included retaining the length of the course and the policy of open entry, but arranging matters so that students knew in advance whether or not they had pupillage. The most radical proposals were the introduction of a national final examination and a recommendation that the Bar Standards Board investigate the impact of introducing the requirement of an upper second degree. No recommendations specifically related to ethics.

The place of ethics in legal education and training

The aims of an ethics curriculum

Ethics is at the point of a potentially important breakthrough into legal education and training, but the nature of this breakthrough is unclear. Many directions are possible, yet the most profitable may be obvious once purpose is clarified. The underlying purpose of the government and the profession is, presumably, to increase the prevalence of ethical behaviour in legal practice. The possibility of achieving this and the means of doing so are contentious. It is ambitious to expect education to raise standards of morality[108] and notable that major disciplinary infractions often occur well after legal education.[109] This is no reason not to try, particularly since there is some evidence that curriculum affects student motivation and values. The fifth survey of the cohort study showed a close relationship between subject interest and intended work areas. Students had a strong orientation to social welfare subjects, including personal injury, commercial law, family and childcare, criminal law, European Community law, employment and human rights.[110] Consistent with earlier studies,[111] however, many students did not intend to work in such areas because of poor pay or lack of status, or because there were known to be too few jobs.[112] Whether these subject preferences are consistent with altruistic motivation is unclear since these areas of work also offer considerable control over the conduct of work and clients, aims that are consistent with the basic

---

[106] The BVC Review Working Party, chaired by Derek Wood QC.

[107] Lord Neuberger of Abbotsbury, 'Entry to the Bar Working Party' (2007), available at http://www.barcouncil.org.uk/search/ (last accessed 25 March 2008).

[108] J Weinstein, 'On the Teaching of Legal Ethics' (1972) 72 *Columbia Law Review* 452, note 2. But see Webb, above n 60, 281.

[109] S Arthurs, 'Discipline in the Legal Profession in Ontario' (1970) 70 *Osgoode Hall Law Journal* 235, shows that 80% of serious disciplinary proceedings in Canada involve lawyers who have been qualified for eleven years or more.

[110] E Duff, M Shiner, A Boon and A Whyte, *Entry into the Legal Professions: The Law Student Cohort Study Year 6* (London, The Law Society, 2000) 32–3 and 60.

[111] See P McDonald, '"The Class of '81"—A Glance at the Social Class Composition of Recruits to the Legal Profession' (1982) 9 *Journal of Law and Society* 267.

[112] Human rights and EU law had a disproportionately high level of interest compared with numbers of trainees who expected to find work. Commercial areas, including commercial property and business and commercial affairs, had low levels of interest compared with numbers expecting to work in them (Cohort Study 5th Survey).

motivations of many students for studying law.[113] Although job possibilities steer many law students away from public service type work, many retain altruistic intentions towards it and some participate in *pro bono publico* and similar work.[114]

The socialising impact of legal education is difficult to test. Although most observers agree that it has an effect,[115] the dominant view is that it is negative ethically. Law school teaches formality, neutrality and objectivity, rejecting the personal, and hence bias, passion and commitment.[116] The impact is also negative in terms of attitudes to public service work like helping the socially disadvantaged, which is often considered indicative of orientation.[117] A consistent criticism of the conventional method of law teaching, the 'black letter' approach, is that narrow, doctrinal study, instils in law students the values of individualism, competitiveness, legalism and authoritarianism.[118] These critics suggest that teaching and assessing rule-handling techniques encourages lawyers to uncritically accept established power relationships, creating 'responsible' jurists who become zealous promoters of hierarchy.[119] These critics are lecturers, and hence former students of law, but research confirms their view that legal education has a generally negative effect on students' moral reasoning,[120] and shifts attitudes and values towards a conservative view of the legal role, away from idealism towards instrumentalism[121] and career intentions away from legal aid, public service or government work.[122] The evidence, largely from the US, is often limited, [123]

---

[113] Steven's study found that the desire for independence is the prevalent reason for choosing legal careers and that control is an important underlying issue for intending lawyers. He speculates that features of control, the legitimation of verbal aggression, concern for justice and curiosity about others' lives are central to the work of lawyers. AS Watson, 'The Quest for Professional Competence: Psychological Aspects of Legal Education (1968) 37 *University of Cincinatti Law Review* 91, 101.

[114] Boon, above n 78.

[115] 'Students are absorbing . . . a sense of what the functions of the profession are and what their individual role is to be in that profession': Weinstein, above n 108. See also JF Sutton and JS Dzienkowski, *Cases and Materials on the Professional Responsibility of Lawyers* (St Paul, MN, West Publishing, 1989) 3.

[116] P Goodrich, 'Law-induced Anxiety: Legists, Anti-lawyers and the Boredom of Legality' (2000) 9 *Social and Legal Studies* 143, 151; P Schlag, *The Enchantment of Reason* (Durham, NC, Duke University Press, 1998) 126.

[117] D Schleef, 'Empty Ethics and Reasonable Responsibility: Vocabularies of Motive among Law and Business Students' (1997) 22 *Law and Social Inquiry* 619; Sherr and Webb, above n 76.

[118] J Webb, 'Ethics for Lawyers or Ethics for Citizens? New Directions for Legal Education' (1998) 25 *Journal of Law and Society* 134.

[119] Above n 29.

[120] TF Willging and TG Dunn, 'The Moral Development of the Law Student: Theory and Data on Legal Education' (1982) 32 *Journal of Legal Education* 306.

[121] Schleef, above n 117, found that US degree students shifted from extreme self-interest or altruism towards a mid-point consensus, whereby a desire to 'help the poor' transformed into support for zealous advocacy and *pro bono* representation. Gender does not seem significant to this shift: J Taber, MT Grant, MT Huser, RB Norman, JR Sutton, CC Wong, LE Parker and C Picard, 'Gender, Legal Education, and the Legal Profession: An Empirical Study of Stanford Law Students and Graduates' (1988) 40 *Stanford Law Review* 1209.

[122] S Homer and L Schwartz, 'Admitted but Not Accepted: Outsiders Take an Inside Look at Law School' (1989–90) *Berkeley Women's Law Journal* 1, 42; R Granfield *Making Elite Lawyers* (New York, Routledge, 1992); HS Erlanger and DA Klegon, 'Socialisation Affects of Professional School: The Law School Experience and Student Orientations to Public Interest Concerns' (1976) 13 *Law and Society Review* 11; JM Hedegard, 'The Impact of Legal Education: an In-depth Examination of Career-relevant Interests, Attitudes, and Personality Traits among First-year Law Students' (1979) 4 *American Bar Foundation Research Journal* 791, 805.

[123] Many US studies are snapshots of a single cohort or longitudinal studies of changes of a small number of institutions. Hedegard's study (*ibid*), for example, is of the law school at a Mormon college, Brigham Young University, with an exclusively Mormon intake, raising issues of reliability. Schleef's (above n 117) was a small-scale longitudinal study.

but an English study of Warwick University law degree students found a similar shift,[124] attributed partly to career choices.

Accepting the difficulty of guaranteeing attitudinal or behavioural change in students, there are presumably some measures that are more likely to achieve beneficial effects than others. These measures concern the structure, content and methods for an ethically based legal education.

Structures

ACLEC's main structural proposal was that the vocational stage should comprise a licentiate common to intending solicitors and barristers for half the vocational year, after which they would follow their own courses,[125] and a master's programme built around 'a more rigorous basic education in common professional values'. The initial stage would contribute ethical education by paying more attention to 'the moral quality of law', with universities deciding what to teach provided they included 'a proper knowledge of . . . legal values and ethical standards'.[126] It envisaged that the profession's power to prescribe a compulsory core should be reduced.[127] The view that the undergraduate stage should cover system ethics and professional ethics appears to enjoy wide support, from the architect of the ACLEC report,[128] the TFRG and leading judges.[129] The TFRG's proposals may satisfy these demands, but the detail is still lacking. This may suggest a need for an overarching body, like the one proposed by the Ormrod Report,[130] to develop a blueprint for professional values, but this gap may be filled by the regulation regime of the Legal Services Act.

Content

ACLEC's 1996 report suggested that legal education should develop students' capacities in five key areas; intellectual integrity and independence of mind, core knowledge, contextual knowledge, legal values and professional skills.[131] Contextual knowledge included 'appreciation of the law's . . . moral . . . contexts' and professional skills included 'learning to act like a lawyer'.[132] ACLEC thought that intending lawyers should 'fully appreciate the essential link between law and legal practice and the preservation of fundamental democratic values'.[133] This was said to entail a number of commitments:

---

[124] Sherr and Webb, above n 76.

[125] The licentiate was to involve an element called 'Professional Responsibility', including 'general principles, with projects in the context of criminal and civil procedure and evidence'. *Ibid*, para 5.14.

[126] ACLEC recommendations 4.2 and 4.4.4; above n 55.

[127] *Ibid*, 4.4.5.

[128] Hepple believed that 'the teaching of professional ethics and conduct cannot simply be left until the vocational courses'. Above n 2, 484.

[129] At an Anglo-American conference on ethics in legal education, Lord Justice Potter argued that the undergraduate curriculum must include the ethics of law and the ethics of practising lawyers: Lord Justice Potter, 'The Role of Ethics in Legal Education' in *Legal Education in the United Kingdom and the United States in the New Millenium* (Chicago, IL, American Bar Association, 2000) 33, 43.

[130] Twining, above n 58.

[131] Above n 55.

[132] *Ibid*, para 2.4.

[133] *Ibid*, para 1.5.

to the rule of law, to justice, fairness and high ethical standards, to acquiring and improving professional skills, to representing clients without fear or favour, to promoting equality of opportunity, and to ensuring that adequate legal services are provided to those that cannot afford to pay for them.[134]

This is consistent with the views of Kronman, who argued that legal education should be underpinned by the ultimate value of democratic individualism,[135] but there is no consensus about what the dominant values of legal education should be. Evans and Palermo's study of Australian law students focuses on personal values such as honesty and moral values such as truth and justice,[136] Cownie emphasises broader educational values, singling out the capacity for critical self-examination,[137] and Webb proposes core values, integrity, loyalty and respect for others.[138]

The report by the American Bar Association task force (The MacCrate Commission) in 1992 proposed four key professional objectives for legal education in American universities, all with explicit ethical context. The objectives were: providing competent representation; promoting justice, fairness and morality; maintaining and improving the profession; and taking personal responsibility for one's own professional development. Law degree students in the US are, however, undertaking three years of legal studies following a first degree and are therefore more committed to legal careers. This explains the vocational flavour of the MacCrate objectives and ACLEC's suggestion that degrees might teach 'legal ethics' rather than professional ethics.[139] There are a number of possibilities for this approach.

Brownsword, one of the earliest academic supporters of teaching ethics on degree courses,[140] highlighted a range of possible approaches.[141] Proponents, he suggested, held a range of theoretical positions. The legal idealist sees law itself as a moral enterprise and legal argumentation as inevitably linked to moral argumentation, although he concedes that it is only viable to teaching from the base of positivist analysis of law. The intersectionist position recognises instances when legal and moral issues intersect and the elasticity of legal argumentation in such circumstances. Contextualism, the position advocated by ACLEC, advocates teaching the context—economic, social, political or ethical—in which the problems addressed by law arise. The liberal position is that legal education should not prepare for a specific vocation, but should produce cultivated individuals with a deep understanding of law and a critical view of social institutions that must be informed by ethical perspectives. Within the consensus thus described, only the contextualist or liberal might consider that the role of lawyers in delivering legal services is an essential part of the broader understanding they seek. The weakness of the theoretical positions is that they

---

[134] *Ibid*, para 2.4.

[135] A Kronman, *The Lost Lawyer* (Cambridge, MA, Belknap Press, 1993).

[136] A Evans and J Palermo, 'Australian Law Students' Perceptions of their Values: Interim Results in the First Year—2001—of a Three-year Empirical Assessment' (2002) 5 *Legal Ethics* 103.

[137] F Cownie, 'Alternative Visions in Legal Education' (2004) 6 *Legal Ethics* 159, 174.

[138] Webb, above n 118, 142–4.

[139] R MacCrate, 'Preparing Lawyers to Participate Effectively in the Legal Profession' (1994) 44 *Journal of Legal Education* 89.

[140] R Brownsword, 'Ethics in Legal Education: Ticks, Crosses and Question Marks' (1987) 50 *Modern Law Review* 529 and 'Where Are All the Law Schools Going?' (1996) 30 *The Law Teacher* 1.

[141] R Brownsword, 'High Roads and Low Roads, Mazes and Motorways' (1999) 33 *The Law Teacher* 269.

provide only a weak response to students whose interests are primarily vocational, or those objecting that they chose to study law, not moral philosophy.[142]

Before the TFRG proposals, speculation about a possible ethics curriculum for the initial stage[143] ranged from incorporating professional ethics[144] to a more gradual progress from 'general system ethics'.[145] The TFRG clarified this by proposing the legal profession, the rules of professional conduct and the values and principles on which professional rules are constructed, as material for the initial stage.[146] Nevertheless, there remains a dilemma, highlighted by Arthurs, concerning the approach to teaching ethics as an academic subject. Arthurs identifies two main approaches: ethics from the 'inside out' or from the 'outside in'. With the first approach, students study the codes in order to master the norms of profes-sional practice, the approach normally taken on vocational courses. This is, however, naive and superficial, often the first response to the demand for an ethics curriculum.[147] A more critical approach, from 'the outside in', is a much better fit with the initial stage, whereby students might explore professions as intermediate bodies in civil society,[148] empirical evidence of workplace studies, the impact of stress, competition, authority, peer and time pressures,[149] using empirical studies of different practice fields and interdisciplinary schol-arship.[150] This seems more in line with the TFRG proposals, but the concern is that it may be counterproductive. Showing the profession's record, warts and all, may be taken to normalise or legitimise unethical behaviour.

The argument that an 'outside in' perspective necessarily encourages unethical behaviour is dubious. An issue that it does raise, however, is whether the ethics curriculum is designed to train lawyers to enter the world as it is or to help them to change it.[151] Handled well, the 'outside in' perspective should encourage an appreciation that professionalism is a worthy tradition, deserving support by each generation,[152] but provide the intellectual tools to help change it. It should also assist students in seeing that professional ethics are not fixed, but susceptible to necessary and beneficial change. The 'outside in' perspective is therefore consistent with 'transformative models' of ethical education, as opposed to 'replicative models' that aim to teach what the codes say without promoting change.[153] The aim must therefore be a balance between the different approaches and the need to promote obser-vance, healthy critique and the capacity for autonomous action. The TFRG's proposal for

---

[142] *Ibid*, 281–3.

[143] Economides, above n 30, xvii.

[144] R O'Dair, 'Recent Developments in the Teaching of Legal Ethics—A UK Perspective' in *Ethical Challenges*, above n 30, 151–2.

[145] J Webb 'Conduct, Ethics and Experience in Vocational Legal Education: Opportunities Missed' in *Ethical Challenges*, above n 30, 272, 292.

[146] Because of the open-ended nature of the framework, students would not have to cover this (or any) material in a degree and could cover it at the vocational stage, though this is hardly ethics from cradle to grave.

[147] S Bundy, 'Ethics Education in the First Year: An Experiment' (1995) 58 *Law and Contemporary Issues* 19, 31, says that US ethics courses tend to be legalistic, stressing the external rather than the internal regulation of lawyers.

[148] HW Arthurs, 'Why Canadian Law Schools Do Not Teach Ethics' in *Ethical Challenges*, above n 30, 105.

[149] DL Rhode, 'Ethics by the Pervasive Method' (1992) 42 *Journal of Legal Education* 31.

[150] A Goldsmith and G Powles, 'Where Now in Legal Education for Acting Responsibly in Australia?' in *Ethical Challenges*, above n 30, 119.

[151] K Economides, 'Learning the Law of Lawyering' (1999) 52 *Current Legal Problems* 392, 410.

[152] C Parker, *Just Lawyers* (Oxford University Press, 1999) 171.

[153] Goldsmith and Powles, above n 150, 416.

grounding students in the work and workings of the legal profession and ethical values is a potential starting point.

Methods

The issue of how to deliver the ethics curriculum has been a topic of debate. In the US discussion has focused on degree-level work and the choice between making ethics a subject in its own right or a 'pervasive' topic. The risk with the subject approach is that students may see ethics as a discrete area for 'moralising' irrelevant to technical law or that it becomes a case of learning rules, with limited assistance to ethical development.[154] In extreme cases, courses may be a training in

> unethics . . . the careful delineation of precisely how far the lawyer can go without disbarment, with copious suggestions on how to do things lawyers ought not to be doing.[155]

The problem with the pervasive method is that ethics is not weighty or developed enough to be taken seriously[156] and is not dealt with properly anywhere, if at all. The obvious answer is to integrate both approaches, with 'system ethics' pervasive and professional ethics taught as a subject. This leaves the substantial criticism of the ethics curriculum, that courses provide a platform of knowledge and understanding of ethical responsibilities, but have little impact on ethical judgement[157] and, indeed, may lead students to approach their professional role with heavy cynicism.[158]

Some think this must be taken further to be part of the 'holistic' development of the law student, whereby individual experience and values are linked to the student's developing skills and knowledge.[159] This is because real-life ethical decision making derives from four distinct capacities of the individual: the recognition of an ethical issue, judgement in identifying ethical actions, motivation to act accordingly and the character to see the action through.[160] The first two of these aims are certainly assisted by a curriculum providing many opportunities for discussion, which the Law Society's own research found to be the most important mechanism of teaching and learning on the LPC.[161] Even character may be built if academic law schools embrace collective or community models of education,

---

[154] Above n 147, 29.

[155] Rhode, above n 149.

[156] 'There is no place in which students and institutions confront in any probing and systematic way, the central ethical concepts, institutional and political understandings and regulatory alternatives that underline all areas of professional ethics and regulation.' Above n 147, 32.

[157] JR Rest, *Moral Development: Advances in Research and Theory* (New York, Praeger, 1986).

[158] A worldwide survey found unanimity among students that lawyers have a lot of prestige (over 70% agreed) and deserve their incomes (over 60% agreed), but there was relatively little confidence that they were trustworthy or ethical (under 30% agreed). M Asimow, S Greenfield, G Jorge, S Machura, G Osborn, P Robson, C Sharp and R Sockloskie, 'Perceptions of Lawyers—a Transnational Study of Student Views on the Image of Law and Lawyers' (2005) 12 *International Journal of the Legal Profession* 407.

[159] See A Boon, 'History is Past Politics: A Critique of the Legal Skills Movement in England and Wales' (1998) 25 *Journal of Law and Society* 151; J Webb 'Developing Ethical Lawyers: Can Legal Education Enhance Access to Justice?' (1999) 33 *The Law Teacher* 284.

[160] This model, proposed by J Rest, 'Background: Theory and Research' in J Rest and D Narvaez (eds), *Moral Development in the Professions: Psychology and Applied Ethics* (Hillsdale, NJ, Lawrence Erlbaum Associates, 1994), is discussed by Webb, *ibid*, 290–2.

[161] Fletcher, above n 79, 58–60.

whereby students are involved in governance and rule making and take positive steps to reject plagiarism and other academic offences.[162] However, more thought is required generally to ensure that existing opportunities are put to best use. A simple example relates to the aspiration of both the profession and its vocational courses to promote diversity. The Law Society research found that good integration was important to the success of group work[163] but that, in some institutions, students from different ethnic backgrounds refuse to work with each other;[164] hardly a platform from which to grasp diversity.

Many academics argue, echoing Aristotle, that all of the virtuous capacities required for ethical action, and particularly motivation and character, are most successfully developed when deployed habitually in role. The most effective ethical training would enable students to absorb ethical theory while performing the actual role under supervision, so that difficulties, dilemmas and temptations can be discussed. If the ideal environment for creating reflective practitioners is the workplace, there remains a need for skilled teachers familiar with ethical issues to ensure that experience is put to best use.[165] This ideal often leads to the conclusion that any serious attempt to develop ethical lawyers must involve some clinical practice from an early stage in their legal education.[166] Such a conclusion harnesses the conventional view that an ethical approach to practice emerges from work experience guided by skilled and ethical practitioners, but locates the experience in the academy rather than the workplace, where outcomes are less certain. A methodology for this approach is provided by Donald Schon, who argued that professional students cannot be taught about professional practice but can be coached, seeing for themselves the relations between means and methods employed and results achieved.[167] Schon's notion of 'reflective practice' is predicated on one-to-one coaching, providing

> an environment in which every aspect of legal work can be the object of the most painstaking planning, reflection and review.[168]

Stimulating reflection is, however, a complex task that cannot be undertaken lightly.[169]

The US experience of linking professional responsibility to law school clinical classes shows that practical experience needs to be supported, certainly by suitable instruction[170]

---

[162] Webb, above n 159, 296–7.

[163] Fletcher, above n 79, 58–60.

[164] *Ibid*, 61.

[165] See P Brest, 'The Responsibility of Law Schools: Educating Lawyers as Counsellors and Problem Solving' (1995) 58 *Law and Contemporary Problems* 5.

[166] Above n 159, 295.

[167] DA Schon, *Educating the Reflective Practitioner: Toward a New Design for Teaching and Learning in the Professions* (London, Jossey-Bass Publishers, 1987) 17 and *The Reflective Practitioner: How Professionals Think in Action* (New York, Basic Books, 1983). For discussion regarding the initial stage, see A Boon, 'Skills in the Initial Stage of Legal Education: Theory and Practice for Transformation' in J Webb and C Maughan (eds), *Teaching Lawyers' Skills* (London, Butterworths 1996).

[168] M Meltsner and G Shrag, 'Scenes from a Clinic' (1978) 127 *University of Pennsylvania Law Review* 1. See also R Barnhiler, 'The Clinical Method of Legal Education: Its Theory and Implementation' (1979) 30 *Journal of Legal Education* 67.

[169] D Boud and D Walker, 'Promoting Reflection in Professional Courses: the Challenge of Context' (1998) 23 *Studies in Higher Education* 191.

[170] RL Doyel, 'The Clinical Lawyer School: Has Jerome Frank Prevailed?' (1983) 18 *New England Law Review* 578, 597.

and possibly extending the discussion to professional policy issues, like access to justice.[171] Kupfer argues that the aim must be to encourage students to subject ethical norms to critical scrutiny, to argue the merits of prioritising practice norms or regulatory structures and to make 'self-determined, responsible, self reflective and critical judgements about themselves and their work'.[172] Her account of working through the ethical dilemmas of her students demonstrates that clinic produces stimulating material for ethical reflection.[173] Condlin warns that clinical instructors must be sensitised to ethical issues, lest they pass on the worst elements of professional interaction.[174] These points are addressed by William Simon, who argues that practitioners must be trained to act as moral agents rather than simply to follow the professional code.[175] Simon links this to his proposal that rules of conduct become advisory rather than regulatory. The approach also links with 'communitarian' ethical models that aim to harmonise the pursuit of rationality, autonomy and self-interest, and a greater social good.[176] Communitarian models build on concepts such as reflexivity to develop understanding of the perspectives of others through dialogue.[177] Their aim is a 'negotiated ethic' offering greater congruence between professional ethics and personally held values.[178]

Some critics doubt that 'communities of virtue' are credible[179] or suspect that 'moral autonomy' of the kind suggested by Simon is an abrogation of regulatory responsibility, both unrealistic and impractical.[180] It is, however, not necessary to make a stark choice between moral agency and traditional ethical regimes. By taking elements of each, a good understanding of ethical codes and the willingness to debate their application, it is possible to construct an ethics curriculum that sensitises receptive students to the issues and sets them on the path of ethical compliance. Conduct rules already require high levels of interpretation and a professional tackling any ethical problem benefits from a sophisticated ethical appreciation. Similarly, even professional rule making would benefit from the communitarian ethos encouraging local discussion and reflective judgement rather than conformity.[181] It is important to realise, however, that even with substantial commitment of resources to law clinics, there is no panacea for 'teaching' professional responsibility.

---

[171] C Menkel-Meadow, 'The Legacy of Clinical Education: Theories about Lawyering' (1980) 29 *Cleveland State Law Review* 555, 573; Economides, above n 30, 415.

[172] SG Kupfer, 'Authentic Legal Practices' (1996) 10:1 *Georgetown Journal of Legal Ethics* 33.

[173] *Ibid.*

[174] RJ Condlin, 'Clinical Education in the Seventies: An Appraisal of the Decade' (1983)33 *Journal of Legal Education* 604.

[175] W Simon, 'The Trouble with Legal Ethics' (1991) 41 *Journal of Legal Education* 65 and 'The Ideology of Advocacy: Procedural Justice and Professional Ethics' [1978] *Wisconsin Law Review* 30.

[176] 'Community . . . implies integration, shared symbolic experience and self regulating activities groups and institutions' (P Selznick, 'The Idea of a Communitarian Morality' (1987) 75 *California Law Review* 445, 449; see also R Cotterrell, *Law's Community: Legal Theory in Sociological Perspective* (Oxford, Clarendon Press, 1995) particularly at 246 and 332–7).

[177] See Kupfer, above n 172, 62–7.

[178] *Ibid.*

[179] See, eg C Douzinas, R Warrington and S McVeigh, *Postmodern Jurisprudence: The Law of Text of Law* (London, Routledge, 1991) 6.

[180] MJ Osiel, 'Lawyers as Monopolists, Aristocrats and Entrepreneurs' (1990) 103 *Harvard Law Review* 2009, 2016); L Sheinman, 'Looking for Legal Ethics' (1997) 4 *International Journal of the Legal Profession* 139, 5.

[181] See further RW Gordon and WH Simon, 'The Redemption of Professionalism' in RL Nelson, DM Trubeck and RL Solomon (eds), *Lawyer's Ideals/Lawyer's Practices* (Ithaca, NY, Cornell University Press, 1992) 230, 236–40.

Conclusion

Despite acknowledgement of the importance of professional ethics in many official reports into legal education and conduct, the subject has only recently gained a foothold in legal education. Introduced into the vocational stage as a pervasive subject in the early 1990s, it has struggled to establish itself, but increasing awareness that education is 'the cement' binding the legal profession together[182] suggests an increased role, traversing the conventional stages.[183] Plans for the expansion of ethics in education and training coincides with growing concern that the cost of legal vocational skews the profession by discouraging the less well off. There will continue to be pressure on the profession to justify or amend its requirements for practice, but it cannot abandon its vocational stage requirements because it cannot be sure that the initial or training stage can bridge the gap. The Law Society proposals are therefore for a relaxation of requirements, opening the door to cheaper paths to qualification that avoid expensive courses. This is potentially problematic because the consensus is that instilling ethical values involves a process of 'habitualisation' rather than rote learning. This points towards a curriculum involving both ethical and clinical elements, but there are problems with such a conclusion. They include the expense of law clinics, the difficulty of locating such programmes in the initial stage and the additional pressure on an already crowded prescribed curriculum.

---

[182] Glasser, above n 78.

[183] A Boon, 'Ethics in Legal Education and Training: Four Reports, Three Jurisdictions and a Prospectus' [2002] *Legal Ethics* 34.

Part III

CLIENTS

Clients are the primary focus of professional ethics generally, and the duties owed to clients are both hard and deep. Like any provider of a service, lawyers must ensure that what they offer is valuable, which means that expertise must be delivered in a form that is both valuable to the client and good value. Lawyers must also be discreet, and scrupulously maintain their professional detachment and neutrality. Therefore, in discharging professional duties to clients, lawyers must avoid conflicts that may arise between the client's interests and those of the lawyer (for example, in relation to fees), and also any conflict between the client's interests and those of the court.

Part III begins with consideration of the nature of the relationship between lawyers and their clients, raising some of the most fundamental questions in professional ethics. The first relates to the fundamental ethical principle of autonomy, crudely expressed by asking 'who is in charge: the lawyer or the client?' Or, if the relationship is more complex than such a question implies, who has moral responsibility for the lawyer's actions on behalf of clients? This raises the issue of how far can, or should, a lawyer depart from his or her own standards of morality, or those standards generally accepted, in advancing the interests of the client? Such issues are particularly important when wrongdoing is potentially cloaked by the lawyer's privilege of confidentiality. And does it matter that confidentiality is not only a founding ethical principle, but also an important market advantage of lawyers?

Examination of these issues reveals a complex interrelationship between the operation of rules of law, both statutory and case law, professional rules and guidance, and general ethical precepts. The divisions between all these sources are fluid. Some ethical principles, which at one point in time may be barely articulated, later became embodied in professional principles. Principles then become practice rules or are referred to in judicial decisions and may become rules of common law. Statutory changes can, of course, cut a swathe through all of these, as has happened with the money laundering provisions, but may fail to articulate precisely what ethical or other principles form their basis. In turn, these new rules may lead to the formulation of new professional principles.

We also see in these situations the tension between professional rules and basic ethical principles. If, for example, the promotion of justice is the fundamental basis for lawyers' ethics, how can the rules on confidentiality be justified where they appear to promote injustice? If it is a fundamental principle that lawyers should act in the best interests of their clients, how can rules relating to fees that operate against those best interests be justified?

9

DILIGENCE

A responsibility of diligence or zeal is closely related to, but distinct from, that of competence. One can be supremely competent but not diligent, or diligent and zealous but incompetent.[1]

Introduction

The nature of the relationship between lawyers and clients is one of the most contested areas of professional ethics. Are lawyers merely instruments of their clients' desires and, if not, how far can they go in placing a moral filter on clients' wishes? Two overarching principles have been fundamental in answering these questions: neutrality (or non-accountability) and partisanship. They are central both to the issue of who lawyers should accept as clients and what they are entitled to do on their behalf. The principle of neutrality requires that lawyers adopt a neutral stance in relation to their client and their client's case. The lawyer's role is to advance that case whatever view the lawyer may have of it. Neutrality requires that lawyers advance causes that they find morally repugnant, but they are not personally, legally, professionally or morally accountable for the means or the ends achieved. The principle of partisanship requires that lawyers 'maximise the likelihood that the client's objectives will be attained'.[2]

Neutrality and partisanship mean that lawyers avoid responsibility for having to assist a client to achieve a purpose about which the lawyer would otherwise have moral qualms. The justification for this 'standard conception' of the lawyer's role is that it reinforces the notion of equality before the law, itself a social good, particularly in a society of pluralistic values. Nevertheless, it also means that, instead of striving to do justice, lawyers must follow rules which may, *or may not*, lead to justice being done.[3] At their worst, these principles can lead lawyers to indulge in 'ingenious and far fetched arguments' in order to 'sprinkle . . . transactions with holy water' of apparent legality when, in reality, the transactions are designed to confuse the public or conceal their true nature.[4] It has proved difficult to forge new principles that effectively balance diligence or 'zeal' in representing clients with fidelity to the ideals of justice or the public good.

---

[1] MD Bayles, 'Trust and the Professional–Client Relationship' in A Flores (ed), *Professional Ideals* (Belmont, CA, Wadsworth Publishing, 1988) 71.

[2] See D Luban, 'Partnership, Betrayal and Autonomy in the Lawyer/Client Relationship' (1990) 90 *Columbia Law Review* 1004 and *Lawyers and Justice* (Princeton University Press, 1998). See also the discussion in chapter 1.

[3] LJ Tapp and FJ Levine, 'Legal Socialisation' in WM Evan (ed), *The Sociology of Law* (London, The Free Press, 1980) 121.

[4] As was the case in the US in relation to the collapse of the Enron Corporation. See RW Gordon, 'Professionalisms Old and New' (2005) 8 *Legal Ethics* 24.

Gaining, refusing and losing clients

The process of gaining clients may have a profound effect on the nature of particular lawyer and client relationships, the basis on which services are provided and the expectations of the client. It affects what information the client receives. Personal contact and word of mouth was the traditional method, a method which favoured lawyers with established clienteles. Rules in relation to methods once regarded as unethical, such as advertising and paying for client referrals, have been relaxed but are still very controversial. Paying for referrals was the subject of two referenda of members of the Law Society in 2004–2005 and is still causing problems for the Solicitors Regulation Authority (SRA). Given that the principle of neutrality prioritises client access to representation, the question of when clients can be refused or existing instructions terminated, and on what basis, is also relevant in this context.

Advertising

Advertising legal services is now permitted, but is regulated by both the Bar and the SRA, though in the case of the latter with a very light touch. Advertising can be a valuable source of information for consumers, enabling them to make an informed choice of advisor. Alternatively it can be a way of concealing problems or inflating virtues. Since 1989 the Bar has permitted barristers to advertise in accordance with the British Code of Advertising and Sales Promotion. Fees and methods of charging can be advertised, but certain other claims are banned. In particular, a barrister may not make comparisons with other barristers, advertise success rates, 'diminish public confidence in the legal profession or the administration of justice' or bring the legal profession into disrepute. Advertising must not indicate that the barrister will restrict the clients who will be represented other than in compliance with the Bar Code.[5]

Solicitors' advertising must comply with the code[6] and any legal requirements, for example in relation to investment advice and services under the Consumer Credit Act 1974 and Consumer Protection Act 1987. Apart from such provisions, the Solicitors' Code of Conduct 2007 Rule 7 permits publicity providing it is not 'misleading or inaccurate'. Publicity on charges must be 'clearly expressed', making clear whether disbursements and VAT are included, and state gross fees not fees discounted by any commission.[7] Solicitors can now claim to be experts in a particular field provided they can justify such a claim, complying with the Advertising Standards Authority (ASA) British Code of Advertising requirement that it is 'legal, decent, honest and truthful'. However, a breach of this Code is not automatically a breach of rule 7.[8] Complaints about solicitor advertising are generally made by other solicitors rather than members of the public, and the SRA recommends that minor breaches are raised with local law societies. The old guidance that publicity should

---

[5] *Code of Conduct of the Bar of England and Wales* (London, Bar Standards Board, 8th edn, as amended, 2004) (hereafter Bar Code) paras 710.1 and 7.02.

[6] R 7.07 states that a firm's letterhead must reveal the names of partners or directors, whether the firm has limited liability and also the words 'regulated by the SRA' to ensure that the client knows who to contact in the event of a complaint.

[7] See *Solicitors' Code of Conduct 2007* (London, Solicitors Regulation Authority, 2007) r 7, guidance, para 8*ff.*

[8] *Ibid*, paras 5 and 6.

not be in 'bad taste' has now gone, the relaxed attitude of the ASA reflected in its acceptance of a solicitor's advertisement that asked 'Do you need more cash this Christmas?', offering prospective personal injury clients £300 on account of compensation within seven days of signing up.[9]

Personal contacts and referrals

There is nothing in the Solicitors Code of Conduct 2007 that prevents solicitors from seeking clients by contacting other solicitors or potential professional connections, for example estate agents or insurance agents. What is not acceptable is 'cold calling', such as going unannounced to old people's homes to offer to make their wills. Rule 7.03 states that 'you must not publicise your practice by making unsolicited visits or telephone calls to a member of the public', but this does not include other lawyers' 'existing or potential professional or business' connections, commercial organisations or public bodies. Paying for referrals used to be completely banned under the old Introduction and Referral Code because it could lead to a conflict of interest between solicitor and client. The solicitor might be more concerned to protect the source of his referrals—such as an estate agent—than to promote the best interests of the client referred. However, the ban was hard to detect unless an aggrieved client found out about it. It was even harder to enforce as many referral fees were concealed behind payments for 'administrative' or 'marketing' services or the like. This was particularly common in the case of claims companies who referred clients to solicitors, as detailed in chapter 12. The Law Society also considered that such fees were not in fact unethical provided clients were aware of their existence and able to take their business elsewhere if they objected to them.

The 2007 Rules permit referral fees provided certain conditions laid down in rule 9.02 are satisfied. These require that the agreement is in writing and subject to SRA inspection; the introducer as well as the solicitor must agree to abide by the rule; and, with regard to publicity, the agreement does not compromise any other duties in the Rules. The agreement with introducers must not allow them to 'influence or constrain' the solicitor's advice to the client. Most important, the rule also requires that the client receives in writing all details of the amount of the referral fee and the business arrangements between the solicitor and the introducer, as well as the details listed above. This rule applies to all payments made to a third party in respect of referrals, even if it is otherwise described, except for 'normal' hospitality. As the guidance states, 'When investigating complaints the SRA will consider the substance of any relationship rather than the mere form'.[10]

Solicitors are also warned that they should not 'become so reliant on an introducer as a source of work that this affects the advice you give to your client', and in monitoring this firms should consider 'the amount and proportion of your firm's income' arising from a particular referrer.[11] How this advice will be policed is not clear, but the danger is clearly solicitors may be hesitant in giving any advice to clients that causes conflict with the referrer. The solicitor has a duty to warn the client of any potential problem in relation to a

[9] See *Law Society Gazette*, 8 April 2004, 4.
[10] See Solicitors' Code of Conduct 2007, r 9, guidance, para 3.
[11] *Ibid*, para 1.

house purchase where an estate agent is the referrer, but this prejudices the solicitor's relationship with the estate agent. The old Referral Code suggested that firms should keep a record of agreements for the introduction of work, and that they should review the situation every six months to ascertain whether or not the provisions of the Code have been complied with and the amount of income that had been earned from such introductions. If more than 20% of a firm's income has been derived from a 'single source of introduction', the firm should 'consider whether steps should be taken to reduce that proportion'.[12] This advice is not repeated in the guidance to the new Rules, but could usefully be used by both the Law Society and firms. The previous Lord Chancellor (Lord Falconer) was reported to dislike the new rules and Mr Justice Lightman commented in a case preceding their intro-duction that 'clients are not merchantable commodities to be bought and sold'.[13] When, in 2006, the Practice Standards Unit visited 135 firms, only 6% fully complied with them, and in 39% of firms the breaches were major. In June 2007 the SRA reported that approximately one-third of the 52 firms inspected had signed referral agreements which 'required the solicitor to act contrary to the client's best interests and may also compromise their ability to act independently'.[14] The SRA has launched a campaign on compliance, threatening that if they are not obeyed referral fees will be banned.[15]

Ceasing to act

Barristers are, in theory, bound to accept clients even if they disapprove of their case or character,[16] but solicitors are not bound by the cab rank rule. Rule 2.01(b) states that a solicitor must refuse or cease to act if 'you have insufficient resources or lack the competence to deal with the matter'. This is aimed at ensuring that solicitors do not act in cases which are beyond their knowledge or expertise, or where they have insufficient support to deal with them. However, in possibly the first judicial decision on the new rules, a solicitor sought to withdraw from representing a criminal defendant because the court had refused an appli-cation for an adjournment needed to prepare for the case. The solicitor (and the barrister) had been retained after previous representatives had had to withdraw because of professional embarrassment. The court decided that the lack of time to prepare was no good reason to withdraw. If they disagreed with the refusal of the court to grant an adequate time to prepare, the proper remedy was to appeal the order. However, once the order had been made, both the solicitor and the barrister owed a duty to the court to comply with the order and 'soldier on'.[17]

Once a client has been accepted, the solicitor must not terminate the relationship except for 'good reason and upon reasonable notice'.[18] Examples of good reason are where there is a breakdown of confidence between the solicitor and the client, or where the solicitor is unable to get proper instructions. This could arise if the client is determined on a course of

---

[12] Introduction and Referral Code, s 2, paras 10–12.
[13] *Mohamed v Alaga & Co* [1998] 2 All ER 720, 724.
[14] *Law Society Gazette*, 28 June 2007, 1.
[15] P Holt, 'Cash for Services', *Law Society Gazette*, 2 November 2006 and 156 NLJ 1859.
[16] See chapter 4.
[17] *R v Ulcay* [2007] EWCA Crim 2379; [2008] 1 All ER 547.
[18] Solicitors' Code of Conduct, r 2.01(2).

conduct to which the solicitor has grave moral objections, if the client fails to make agreed payments on account, or if either the solicitor or the client suffers bankruptcy or mental incapacity. Barristers must cease to act if continuation would cause them professional embarrassment.[19] This phrase embodies all the reasons, such as lack of skill or time, which justify refusing the brief in the first place.[20] As with solicitors, they cannot withdraw simply because the court has made an order which makes it difficult for them to do their best for their client. In *R v Ulcay* Sir Igor Judge said

> The cab rank rule was essential to the proper administration of justice . . . The absence of what [the barrister] would regard as sufficient time for the purpose of preparation did not constitute and exception.[21]

They must also cease to act where legal aid has been wrongly obtained and the client refuses to remedy the situation, and also in circumstances where to continue to act would involve a breach of the law or professional conduct rules.

Free choice of solicitor

The old rule 1 of the 1990 Rules provided that a solicitor should do nothing to restrict a person's freedom to instruct the solicitor of their choice.[22] This was re-emphasised by principle 11.01 in the 1999 Law Society Guide. The aim of the rule was to protect the client from improper influences from third parties or the solicitor. An example given in the guidance to old rule 1 is that of a landlord client who requires his solicitor to ask that a tenant does not use solicitor Y because in the past Y had advised another tenant that the lease contained unfavourable terms. Another example is where a solicitor, in negotiating a settlement, includes a term that the other side's solicitor should not act for other clients against his client in the future. These terms would contravene rule 1. No similar rule appears in the Core Duties or the new Rules. Such a rule may be implied in rule 9.03 on referrals. This states that 'You must not enter into any agreement or association which would restrict your freedom to recommend any particular firm . . .' This does not appear to address the examples noted above, nor is guidance provided on its extent.

Why, therefore, has a fundamental principle, which previously took precedence over the duty to act in the best interests of the client, been abandoned? One reason is likely to be the 2001 decision in *Sarwar v Alam*[23] relating to legal expenses insurance. In its decision, the Court of Appeal held that, while there was a strong public interest in maintaining a client's freedom to retain the solicitor of his choice, this would not override all other considerations, such as cost. In accordance with the philosophy behind the Civil Procedure Rules, costs

---

[19] Bar Code, r 608.

[20] *Ibid*, r 603.

[21] Above n 17.

[22] An equivalent to this rule in the case of barristers is the cab-rank rule (see chapter 4). Free choice of lawyer is abrogated in the case of special advocates (see chapter 14).

[23] [2001] 4 All ER 541. See also *R v Legal Aid Board, ex parte Duncan* [2000] COD 159 DC. There are special regulations on choice of lawyer where legal expenses insurance is involved: Insurance Companies (Legal Expenses Insurance) Regulations 1990, SI 1990/1159. See H Blundell, 'Free to Choose?'[2004] *Journal of Personal Injury Law* 93.

should be reasonable and proportionate, and sometimes that may mean a restriction on the choice of solicitor. Another case which challenged the principle of freedom of choice of solicitor was that concerning the tobacco litigation settlement.[24] An action by lung cancer sufferers alleged that Imperial Tobacco knew of the association of tobacco with cancer long before they revealed it, but the claimants could not continue to litigate and were forced to settle. The solicitors, who were acting under a conditional fee agreement, could not afford to carry on the case. The costs of Imperial Tobacco had reached £7 million. Accordingly a settlement was reached whereby the litigation ceased and Imperial Tobacco agreed not to ask for costs, provided the solicitors agreed not to represent any claimants against the company in a similar matter for 10 years. This prevented the free choice of solicitor for future clients wanting to use a firm with so much expertise on the issue. The settlement was agreed by the court and approved of by the Law Society. The solicitors were under an acute dilemma, but it was obviously in the overwhelming best interests of their existing clients to agree to it.

The idea that the common law requires a free choice of a solicitor, which is the view that was taken before 2000, is now modified. The rule is, however, implicitly recognised in the legislation governing legal expenses insurance, which allows companies to restrict the freedom of choice of solicitor of their members in specified circumstances only.[25] It is also recognised by the courts in the context of cases of conflict of interest, where over-strict interpretation of those rules can result in a denial of choice of solicitor.[26] It may be, therefore, that restricting a client's freedom to choose a solicitor is sometimes against the common law but is no longer a disciplinary matter. Only if such a practice by solicitors could be interpreted as contravening core duty 1.06, not behaving in a way that diminishes trust in the profession, or 1.03, not compromising their independence, could it become a disciplinary issue. Obviously the issue may also involve a conflict of interest, in which case those rules would be enforced. It may also be that this is a matter that, in general, concerns solicitors more than clients—solicitors are concerned to protect their own client base and not be excluded from panels held by insurance companies and the like.[27] Perhaps the rule is not really a fundamental ethical rule after all.

The nature of the lawyer and client relationship

The most basic premise of professional ethics is that the client's interests should take precedence over those of the lawyer.[28] Enlightened self-interest might predispose professionals to act with integrity, because this serves their own long-term commercial interests:

---

[24] Reported, but not on this point, at *Hodgson v Imperial Tobacco* [1998] 2 All ER 673.

[25] See page 214 of the first edition of this book. Insurance companies want clients to choose a solicitor from their approved panels only. See also P Camp, *Companion to the Solicitors' Code of Conduct 2007* (London, The Law Society, 2007) 7.

[26] See chapter 10; *Koch Shipping v Richards Butler* [2002] 2 All ER (Comm) 957 and *Re A Firm of Solicitors* [1995] 3 All ER 482.

[27] A letter in the *Gazette*, where the writer complained that Trades Unions were prepared to fund their members' actions only if they used solicitors on their panels, even if the client already had a solicitor, illustrates this.

[28] Solicitors' Code of Conduct 2007, core duty 1.04.

The client is dependent for his welfare on the accomplishment of the task; but he is not competent to assess the adequacy of the work done; recognised competence in the set of tasks is legally restricted to those certified to have completed a training of a scientific character; and in exchange for the monopoly of practice the group accepts responsibility for the achievement of the purposes of clients. The situation of the professional thus involves an essential fiduciary element; incompetence or malfeasance constitutes a betrayal of the clients' trust. Should this occur, there is a risk of scandal, and the erosion of or loss of the legally enforced monopoly enjoyed by the professional group . . . It is thus in the long term collective interests of the profession to maintain standards of work and to protect the interests of clients . . .[29]

How should the principle of giving priority to the interests of the client be translated into everyday practice? The relationship of all professional persons with their clients, or patients, has been the subject of considerable debate in the last 25 years or so. The modern view is that the relationship with clients should be one that has the capacity to empower them by treating them as individuals and allowing them to reach their own decisions. This is consistent with the contemporary emphasis on individual autonomy as an overarching ethical good.[30] Indeed, the feature which unites professional skills and virtues is precisely the professional commitment to treating clients as individuals. Therefore the professional must hear a client's individual story before deciding what can be done. This sensitivity to human individuality ensures that professionals do not subvert the client's personal values, take over, manage them or do what they do not want.[31]

This participatory approach implies a continual dialogue between lawyer and client. At each stage the progress of work should be evaluated in the light of the client's aims and interests. New agreements are reached on the steps to be taken. The relationship between lawyers and clients should be client centred because:

> Client-centred relationships entail shared decision-making responsibility and mutual participation by lawyer and client. By avoiding the trap of either lawyer or client-dominance, these relationships provide greater opportunities for facilitating wise client decisions in a supportive atmosphere.[32]

In effect, the client has control over decision making and the lawyer is a technical advisor and counsellor. This conception of the lawyer–client relationship can be contrasted with the traditional or paternalistic view. This is that, once the lawyer has been engaged by the client and been broadly instructed on what the client wants to achieve, the lawyer should be left to take the decisions in the best interests of the client. The lawyer, argues the paternalist, has superior knowledge, skills and experience of the matter in hand and therefore knows what is best.[33] The issues involved are far too complicated for clients to understand, hence the need

---

[29] JR Ravetz, 'Ethics in Scientific Activity' in A Flores (ed), *Professional Ideals* (Belmont, CA, Wadsworth Publishing, 1988) 147, 152. Philosophers have long debated whether altruism must have a generous motive as well as a generous act. For a scientific discussion of this issue, see M Ridley, *The Origin of Virtue* (Harmondsworth, Penguin, 1997) particularly ch 1.

[30] See chapter 1.

[31] D Koehn, *The Ground of Professional Ethics* (London, Routledge, 1994) 176.

[32] RD Dinerstein, 'Client-centered Counselling: Reappraisal and Refinement' (1990) 32 *Arizona Law Review* 501, 556.

[33] For further discussion of the concept of paternalism, see D Nicholson and J Webb, *Professional Legal Ethics: Critical Interrogations* (Oxford University Press, 1999) ch 5.

for lawyers. Rhode observes that this view is now 'seldom preached but often practised'.[34] The old Law Society Rules traditionally preached paternalism by stressing that the solicitor should act in the best interest of clients rather than on the basis of the instructions of the client.[35] In contrast, the Code of the American Bar Association does not mention the client's best interest, but stresses the role of the lawyer in doing what the client requires even if this is unwise.[36] David Luban concludes that 'the American model is loyalty to the client's wishes and not his interests'.[37] However, in reality, the paternalistic, and even domineering, lawyer is to be found as much in the US as in the UK. In research conducted in the US it was found that higher levels of participation by clients in their personal injury claims tended to increase the sums that they recovered in damages.[38] This suggests that paternalistic professional relationships are sometimes not even in the best interests of clients.

Some paternalism is unavoidable in many lawyer–client relationships, and the more vulnerable the client the more paternalistic that relationship is likely to be. However, many would prefer to develop a model of the relationship which accords a high level of respect for client autonomy and collaborative working practices. This view is also prevalent in relation to other professional relationships, such as between a doctor or nurse and a patient. The reasons for attacking the paternalistic model are generally based on the notion of personal autonomy. People should be allowed and enabled to make as many decisions as possible for themselves, exercising free will. They should be seen not as passive recipients of advice or assistance, but as consumers. As such, they have a right to obtain what they want in a form which is appropriate to their circumstances. Professional help may be needed, and in some cases may be essential, to achieve this, but sufficient information should be given to allow clients to make their own informed decisions on their own interests.

Many solicitors argue that they should not be passive in the relationship either, that promoting client autonomy is not simply a question of doing what clients say. It may include a responsibility to ensure that clients make ethically defensible decisions. Further, in many cases the slavish pursuit of the client's wishes may produce an unsatisfactory result, for example, where a client's lie is revealed in court.[39] The value of patient autonomy has, in the medical field, led to much discussion of the need to ensure that the patient makes an informed consent to treatment. In many jurisdictions this has led to the abandonment of the *Bolam* test,[40] which states that it is for the doctor's professional judgement to decide what to tell the patient. Instead, the 'prudent patient' test is preferred—what would the prudent patient in his or her particular circumstances need to know about his medical condition in order to decide what treatment to follow? Little of

---

[34] D Rhode, *Professional Responsibility: Ethics by the Pervasive Method* (Boston, MA, Little Brown, 1994) 411.

[35] The Solicitors' Code of Conduct 2007, core duty 1.03, still refers to best interests.

[36] The lawyer should 'abide by a client's decisions concerning the objectives of the representation' (model rule 1.2).

[37] D Luban, 'The Sources of Legal Ethics' (1984) 48 *Rabels Zeitschift* 262.

[38] DE Rosenthal, *Lawyer and Client: Who's in Charge?* (New York, Russell Sage Foundation, 1974), which dates from 1974 and therefore might not reflect current practice. See also A Gutmann, 'Can Lawyers be Taught Virtue' (1993) 45 *Standford Law Review* 1759.

[39] A Boon, 'Assessing Competence to Conduct Civil Litigation: Key Tasks and Skills' in P Hassett and M Fitzgerald (eds), *Skills for Legal Functions II: Representation and Advice* (London, Institute of Advanced Legal Studies, 1992).

[40] *Bolam v Friern Hospital Management Committee* [1957] 1 WLR 582.

this discussion has arisen in the context of lawyer and client; this is ironic, as one of the lawyer's main functions is to facilitate client autonomy.[41] No cases on the issue have come before the English courts, possibly because of the immunity from suit enjoyed until recently by litigation lawyers.

Models of the lawyer–client relationship

One approach to examining the nature of the lawyer–client relationship is by analogy with existing legal relationships. The relationship and its obligations have been compared with agency, contract and trust relationships. These concepts are illuminating in terms of defining the legal nature of the relationship. The ethical approach adopted in relation to key issues such as confidentiality, conflict of interest, the financial relationship between lawyer and client and the nature of the bargaining and advocacy role will be influenced by the model of the lawyer–client relationship adopted by the profession.

Agency

One model is that of the professional as agent for the client. In this model the client directs the professional as to the broad remit of the task but the professional, as an agent, has considerable latitude as to how the task is achieved. There are constraints on the agent but the constraints are often fixed by the general law or by custom and practice. Such constraints are mainly concerned with the duty the agent owes to the principal. Therefore, they largely operate so as to reinforce the fidelity of the agent to the client's prime objective. In the context of legal practice, this model is consistent with visions of the lawyer as a 'hired gun' or the client's mouthpiece.[42] There are two problems with this model. First, it seems to require the lawyer to abandon any moral evaluation of the client's objectives or methods of achieving them. The lawyer is unconcerned with the moral or other worth of the client or with their objectives, since lawyers cannot presume to question the task given to them. Secondly, because the agency relationship permits a reasonably wide implied or ostensible authority to the agent, the lawyer may undertake actions or bind the client/principal in ways that the latter might not really want. The model cannot easily be reconciled with the requirements of both the law and professional conduct codes. It is not consistent with the lawyer's obligation to take into account the interests of justice and the duty to the court.

Contractual relationships

Another model is that of contract: this conception of the relationship sees lawyers and clients as parties to a bargain they have agreed upon in relation to their respective rights and duties.

---

[41] For a good discussion of this idea, see SL Pepper, 'The Lawyer's Amoral Ethical Role' (1986) *American Bar Foundation Research Journal* 613 and reply by D Luban (1987) *American Bar Foundation Research Journal* 637. See also S Spiegel, 'Lawyering and Client Decision Making: Informed Consent and the Legal Profession' (1978) 128 *University of Pennsylvania Law Review* 41.

[42] See chapter 19.

Some of these duties are assumed, that is, they are imposed by the law or professional codes. Obviously many of the terms of the lawyer–client relationship are in fact based on a contractual agreement between them, but, equally obviously, not all of the terms are capable of being agreed. This model presumes an equal relationship which may not exist. The client may be vulnerable, ignorant or poor and at a disadvantage in agreeing terms. Alternatively, a rich and powerful corporate client is capable of dominating the lawyer. The contractual model may incorporate a high degree of lawyer paternalism or alternatively a high degree of client autonomy. What determines this is the respective bargaining power of the client and the lawyer and, where the client has power, the degree to which they wish to be involved in decision making.

The fiduciary model

Under the fiduciary model the superior knowledge and skills of the professional are acknowledged in that he or she is required to take special care to ensure that no advantage is taken of the client, and that there will be no undue influence.[43] This is based on the concept in the law of trusts whereby a trustee is subject to a high degree of responsibility for protecting the interests of the beneficiaries of the trust. There is a presumption that any profit made from dealings arising from the relationship by the trustee is a breach of trust. The fiduciary model often involves a higher level of participation than is inherent in the other models. If the lawyer is expected to act in the client's best interests, clearly the client has to be consulted and counselled so as to establish what exactly their best interests may be. But consultation is only necessary thereafter when vital interests are affected, possibly only at the end of the transaction. So, the fiduciary model does not always conform to the participatory model of decision making.

Under the fiduciary model the lawyer must make every reasonable effort to inform the client and then to obtain his or her authority to act, but the day-to-day conduct of transactions is a matter purely for the lawyer. All kinds of decision, which may or may not affect the client, including ethical decisions, may be taken on their behalf by the professional. The client is expected to trust the lawyer and the lawyer to justify that trust. The courts tend to see the relationship as fiduciary, as illustrated by the decision of the House of Lords in *Hilton v Barker Booth & Eastwood*.[44] In this case a solicitor acted where there was a conflict of interest and sought to argue, unsuccessfully, that an implied term of his contract with his client enabled him to modify his duty to disclose to him all relevant information. This argument had in fact succeeded in the Court of Appeal but was rejected firmly by the Lords. Lord Walker considered that the solicitor's duty to the client was 'primarily contractual', but that it was also a fiduciary relationship. The fiduciary relationship could be 'moulded and informed' by the terms of the contract, but its fundamental basis could not be so modified.

---

[43] For discussion of this model in the American context, see Dinerstein, above n 32.
[44] [2005]1 All ER 651, particularly paras 28 and 38.

Application of the models to practice

As with all models, the three alternatives outlined have limitations in describing what the profession is trying to achieve and what is happening 'on the ground'. They are also restricted in terms of conceptualising the lawyer–client relationship.[45] In different fields of practice or in any particular lawyer–client relationship any one of the models or all three may be in operation. The fundamental difference in the dimensions of problems presented by different kinds of clients and the impact on the relationship is illustrated by a practitioner observing:

> In company/commercial work the client is aware through their own experience and so the solicitor is helped by the client. Also the possible permutations of problems have been explored before. In a High Street firm it can be anything; emotional, legal and quasi-legal problems all need to be unravelled . . .[46]

The relationship between lawyer and corporate client can be very different from that of lawyer and individual client. The role of the individual lawyer in the 'mega-lawyering' context of big corporate or class action litigation as described by Galanter may well be more akin to a cog in a machine rather than that of an autonomous independent professional person. The corporate client involved in heavy strategic litigation may be served by teams of lawyers who provide a customised service for years.[47] This is very different work from the High Street lawyer making a living from a series of individual criminal, civil or matrimonial clients. Representing a child, a confused elderly person or a mental patient may justify a more paternalistic approach than representing a healthy adult. It is nevertheless important not to ignore the shift towards participatory decision making, which is expected by clients and, indeed, by the courts. In *Griffiths v Dawson*,[48] for example, a solicitor failed to oppose a divorce petition based on five years' separation on the ground of financial hardship because he considered such opposition to be 'unsporting', in other words unfair and therefore unethical. The wife lost pension rights as a result. The solicitor was held to be negligent because he should have filed the defence, unless specifically instructed not to do so, and not decide himself on the basis of his own personal views.

The fiduciary model, which is the model we consider to be closest to what the profession is presently trying to achieve, demands more of some weaker clients than they may be capable of or desire. Equally, the powerful clients may wish to insist on an arrangement which is closer to the contractual or agency model. Some clients, those with comparatively simple or routine legal needs, will just want the lawyer to get on with the work efficiently and not bother them with information or alternatives to choose from. Many such clients receive lengthy client care letters from their solicitors which they do not read or understand, or even want to. They just want to be able to trust that the job will be done speedily, efficiently and cheaply by the lawyer and that they will not have to provide much input.

---

[45] For a fuller discussion of these models, see M Bayles, *Professional Ethics* (Belmont, CA, Wadsworth Publishing, 1981).

[46] Above n 39.

[47] This was the case in the US, for example, where litigation involving Braniff Airlines went on for 12 years to try to eliminate competition from lucrative routes. Lloyds of London have produced a code regulating the relationship of Lloyds' Underwriters and their lawyers. The lawyers must justify their fees, provide advance notice of bills, standardise their advice and make greater use of ADR (*Law Society Gazette*, 1 July 1998, 9).

[48] [1993] FL 315.

Funding constraints may also impose limitations on what the lawyer would wish to do. Thus, in one study, a personal injury lawyer said:

> In PI you are getting to the sort of Tesco stage: pile it high and sell it cheap, get turnover moving as quickly as you can. The service that we are going to deliver to our clients in the future will be much less than it is at the moment, you will be saying to clients, 'Don't phone me up; if you do I will charge you. Don't write me letters unless I want something from you . . .'[49]

The model in use must, therefore, respond to the needs and abilities of the client in question, the nature of the work involved and the economic circumstances in which it is done.

There is, however, one issue which is raised by the participative model that perhaps arises less where a lawyer fulfils a more paternalistic role; what is the lawyer to do when the client seeks advice in such a way as to suggest that he intends to break the law? Pepper gives two hypothetical examples.[50] In the first example, a lawyer advising on the drafting of a contract is asked by the client what the consequences would be if he broke the contract three years hence. In the circumstances, the lawyer knows that, in fact, the client will break the contract if the consequences are not financially unfavourable. In the second example, a client asks the lawyer about the legal consequences for someone who participates in consensual euthanasia with a parent who is terminally ill and in immense pain. Pepper speculates that full legal advice would include reference to extra-legal factors—factors which are not strictly legal knowledge but could be relevant to the client's query. The advice could, therefore, include reference to court backlogs, which might encourage the other contracting party to accept a lesser sum in damages than the claim is worth, or the practice of local prosecutors not to bring charges in cases of consensual euthanasia. By giving such information to the client in each of these circumstances, the lawyer could be seen to be counselling the commission of breaches of contract or crimes.

Pepper argues that in civil cases, such as contract or tort, breaches of the law are not prohibited; they merely invoke financial sanctions.[51] Therefore advice on the financial consequences of unlawful conduct is ethical. Where criminal conduct has consequences for third parties, however, he argues that lawyers should not provide advice which may assist in the commission of an offence. Beyond this, the variety of situations that can arise make it difficult to formulate clear rules or even guidelines. He suggests four relevant principles. The first principle is that the client is presumed to have a right to know the law. The second is that the lawyer has an obligation to counsel the client if the client is likely to use the advice in order to violate a significant legal or moral norm. The third is that the lawyer is bound to consider a number of factors regarding the impact of the conduct to which the advice may give rise.[52] Finally, he argues, in addition to using these technical aids to decision making,

---

[49] J Flood, A Boon, A Whyte, E Skordaki, R Abbey and A Ash, *Reconfiguring the Market for Advocacy Services: A Case Study of London and Four Fields of Practice* (A Report for the Lord Chancellor's Committee on Legal Education and Conduct, 1996) 36.

[50] SL Pepper, 'Counselling at the Limit of the Law: An Exercise in the Jurisprudence and Ethics of Lawyering' (1995) 104 *The Yale Law Journal* 1545.

[51] This view would be contested by many contract lawyers, but it is a view promoted by economic theories of law. For an account of these and their relevance to legal ethics, see the symposium in (2005) 8 *Legal Ethics* from 87.

[52] Pepper acknowledges that the kinds of distinctions he draws are highly complex, but the kinds of factors he indicates might be relevant include: the distinction between criminal and civil law; conduct wrong in itself and

lawyers must self-consciously balance the good of providing access to law with their own obligation to their role as a lawyer.

The policy of the professions

The Bar maintains a distance between barristers and lay clients except where the direct access scheme is concerned. A barrister is required by the Bar Code to promote his or her client's best interests fearlessly, but also to

> not permit the intermediary to limit his discretion as to how the interests of the lay client can be best served.[53]

The Law Society's old Rules, developed as recently as 1990 and amended in 1999, were paternalistic in tone, but the 2007 Code encourages a greater flow of information between solicitor and client. On the surface, it appears that the fiduciary model is now favoured, with a reasonably high level of client participation. The 1999 client care regime, to be found in the old rule 15 of the 1990 Solicitors' Practice Rules, seemed to be more concerned with standards of work and with processing client complaints, rather than with promoting a particular model of lawyer–client relationships.

The client care regime was brought into force in 1991 as a result of a number of scandals relating, in particular, to solicitors' charges. It was also linked to the failure of the old Solicitors' Complaints Bureau to convince the public that it could deal fairly with the resultant complaints.[54] Despite public dissatisfaction with the complaints system, it cost the profession a considerable sum to run. And solicitors thought the best way to manage the issue was to try to minimise the numbers of complaints by introducing new rules on client care. An additional pressure was the need to protect solicitors' legal aid work. The government wanted value for money, and made this very clear both in the context of the Legal Aid Efficiency Scrutiny[55] and in its plans for the later development of legal aid contracting.

In the Green Paper *Legal Services: A Framework for the Future*, published in 1989,[56] it was made obvious that if the Law Society was to retain its regulatory powers and protect the economic base of those members who depended on legal aid, it had to do something about standards of work and the treatment of complaints about bad service. This is why the old rule 15 concentrated on fees and complaints rather than constituting a comprehensive client care code. Old rule 1, meant to express the basic principles of a solicitor's practice, still

---

conduct 'merely' prohibited; the extent to which the particular law is enforced; whether the query relates to procedural rules, substantive law or the enforcement of law (eg where a criminal client seeks information relating to police procedures which might be known to lawyer); whether the information is in the public or private sphere; whether the lawyer or client initiated the discussion of the particular issue; and the likelihood that the information will assist unlawful conduct. Above n 50, 1586.

[53] Bar Code, para 303(a), (b). The Written Standards of Work, to be found as pt III of the Bar Code, says very little on the relationship with the client. Para 5.7 suggests that a barrister should ensure that the advice is 'practical', appropriate to the needs of the particular client and 'clearly and comprehensively expressed'.

[54] See the cases of Glanville Davies and Peggy Wood. See O Hansen, 'The Lessons of the Peggy Wood Case' [October 1993] *Legal Action* 9.

[55] *Legal Aid Efficiency Report* (London, Lord Chancellor's Department, 1986).

[56] *Legal Services: A Framework for the Future* (London, HMSO, 1989).

prevailed. This stressed acting in the client's best interests but said nothing about how much information should be given to the client or about the lawyer's responsibility for following the client's instructions. In an experiment reported in 1986 one of the most significant 'failures' of newly qualified solicitors conducting an initial interview was that they recorded what they had to do for the client in their notes but did not share this information with the client.[57]

The new Code shows a change in approach. Core duty 1.03 still requires the solicitor to act in the best interests of the client. This obligation is subject to the duties to abide by professional conduct rules and promote the interests of the administration of justice. Rule 2.02 on client relations, however, specifies that the solicitor must 'identify clearly the client's objectives', provide the client with a clear explanation of the issues involved and the options available, agree on the next steps to be taken and keep the client informed of progress. The appropriate level of service must be agreed at the outset and the responsibilities of both client and solicitor explained. Any constraints on the solicitor–client relationship arising from the solicitor's relationship with a third party, such as a funder or introducer, must be explained to the client. The name of the person handling the matter and his or her supervisor must be given to the client in writing.

On costs, rule 2.03 requires that the best information possible must be provided and also how costs are to be met, including possible liability for the costs of the other side. Similarly, information must be given on any payments the client will or may have to make to others, so-called disbursements. Methods of payment must be investigated, for example the availability of legal aid or insurance. All this information on costs must be 'clear and confirmed in writing' under rule 2.03(2). Conditional fee agreements (CFAs) are subject to additional requirements on information.[58] In sympathy with the objective of the Civil Procedure Rules that costs should be proportionate to the matter in issue, the solicitor must discuss with the client whether 'the potential outcomes of any legal case will justify the expense or risk involved', including the risk of having to pay the other side's costs. The principle behind all these provisions is to ensure that the client is provided with sufficient information to make an informed choice when instructing the solicitor—and also that the solicitor is aware of the client's concerns.

The guidance warns that the rules are not exhaustive; a solicitor must act in the client's best interests and not abuse or exploit the relationship. A failure to abide by these rules (and rule 2.04 on complaints handling) does not 'invariably' mean that the retainer is unenforceable but, rather, that 'the rule will be enforced in a manner which is proportionate to the seriousness of the breach'.[59] This may represent the intention of the SRA, but the attitude of the courts to breaches is yet to be seen. The guidance also advises providing the client information 'in a clear and readily accessible form' and that 'over complex or lengthy terms' of business letters covering many matters may not be the most helpful way of doing it. Some solicitors send out a lengthy standard-form 'client care' letter on being instructed

---

[57] A Sherr, 'Lawyers and Clients: The First Meeting' (1986) 49 *Modern Law Review* 323, 330. It will be noted that this experiment was conducted before the introduction of interviewing on the Legal Practice Course, a move that may have remedied some of the problems identified in the research.

[58] Solicitors' Code of Conduct 2007, r 2.03 (2) and the guidance thereon. For further detail, see chapter 12.

[59] *Ibid*, guidance paras 1 and 2.

which often deal with issues of no concern to the particular client and which, even if the client manages to read it, is more confusing than informative. The guidance stresses the value of good communication, and also making agreements about the level of service from the outset. All these new rules stem from a partnership model of the lawyer–client relationship rather than a paternalistic one. It remains to be seen what effect they will have in actual practice. The very first report of the Solicitors' Complaints Board noted that 'About ninety per cent of complaints are resolved immediately once the client understands what is going on'. Despite this, it has taken a long time to convince many solicitors of the need for change.

There are other provisions, apart from the Code and its guidance, which encourage some solicitors to adopt a more informative and client-friendly approach. Firms who have, or wish to obtain, a legal aid contract must demonstrate certain standards in relation to client care. For example, it is mandatory to record the instructions and requirements of the client, to record the advice given and to comply with the written standards on costs, all of which must be confirmed with the client, normally in writing. The needs for written communications with clients and the use of plain English are stressed. In all cases information about the client's costs liability (for example, in relation to the statutory charge) must be given at least every six months. Similarly, firms who appear on panels run by Insurance Companies or Trades Unions often have to comply with contractual standards relating to client information.

The Code therefore promotes a model of practice which gives freer rein to client's wishes and preferences and this addresses the central problem of the lawyer-client relationship; the paternalistic and disempowering effect of expert authority. It does however, create another problem. If the lawyer is more closely tied to her client's preferences and prejudices, what limits or ethical considerations constrain the lawyer's actions? For, if the fiduciary model strengthens the hand of clients, what of the interests of third parties, opponents in a suit or participants in a transaction, who may be damaged financially, socially or psychologically by what a client requires the lawyer to do in the interests of the client? Is there any counter-vailing force in the lawyer–client relationship to the increasing power of clients? As we have seen, in the US the pursuit of client preferences has been seen as the dominating principle of professional ethics. This leads lawyers to do things for clients which they would feel ashamed to do for themselves. How can this be justified? The justification provided is that the unique role of the lawyer requires a quite distinctive set of norms which are amoral in character; in effect. that the practice of law has its own role morality, a proposition discussed in chapter 1 and in the next section.

The limits of partisanship

A lawyer may sometimes be required to do something for a client that he or she would not feel morally justified in doing for him- or herself, something that conflicts with the moral rules prevailing in the wider society. This conduct may be justified by the lawyer by appealing to the particular demands of the professional role and its distinctive 'role morality'. As described in chapter 1, this approach has been justified, in the UK and the US at least, by the adversarial nature of the court system. Adversarial adjudication gives the parties substantial control over the conduct of their cases and the lawyer acts as the neutral but partisan advocate of the client. Within this model, lawyers are technicians, skilful manipulators of legal rules for the benefit of their clients, suppressing their own moral convictions concerning both the worth and the objectives of the client.[60] Paradoxically, whilst lawyers are expected to act cooperatively, altruistically and ethically when dealing *with* their clients, they are expected to be uncooperative, selfish and possibly unethical in pursuing the objectives *of* their clients. This creates considerable moral strain, but is justified on the grounds that adversarialism protects client autonomy and dignity. Parties decide for themselves what they wish to claim and how they wish to support their claims, and the lawyer facilitates that exercise of autonomy. Lawyers claim that this enables them to do for their client what they would not do for themselves. Indeed, if lawyers were to exercise moral censorship on their clients they could be accused of adopting an unacceptably paternalistic attitude towards them.

Attempts to resolve this dilemma have so far not been successful. In a seminal article on the issue, Wassertrom discusses a number of examples.[61] Should a lawyer draft a will for a client who wishes to disinherit a child because he opposed the war in Vietnam? Should the lawyer represent a corporation which manufactures harmful substances, like tobacco? He assumes that both of these actions would be immoral (which can be disputed) but comes to no conclusion as to what the lawyers should do, recognising the force, in many contexts, of the 'role differentiated way of approaching matters'. At the same time, he is concerned that lawyers will fail to confront the moral dilemmas that these two examples raise by taking refuge in the requirements of the role. A slightly different approach is adopted by Simon,[62] who promotes a 'professional duty of reflective judgement' requiring evaluation of client goals to see if they will promote justice.[63] Even in an adversarial context, Simon argues, the interests of justice should take priority for the lawyer. It is clear that Simon is thinking primarily of the powerful corporate client in putting forward this view. It begs the question as to why clients, corporate or otherwise, should engage the services of a lawyer who seeks to limit their autonomy, impose their values upon them and deny them 'the opportunity . . . to seek vindication of hypothetically legal interests'.[64]

Another attempt to reconcile the role morality of lawyers with ordinary morality comes from Charles Fried,[65] who argues that the lawyer–client relationship is like that of friendship. Friends will typically do things for each other that they would not do for a stranger, and this is regarded as acceptable in the wider society. The basis of this justification is, however, very doubtful and the idea has been subjected to considerable criticism.[66] The idea is of the lawyer as a friendly advocate in an adversarial system could discourage

---

[60] ED Cohen, 'Pure Legal Advocates and Moral Agents: Two Concepts of a Lawyer in an Adversary System' in Flores, above n 1, 82.

[61] R Wasserstrom, 'Lawyers as Professionals: Some Moral Issues' (1975–6) 5 *Human Rights* 1.

[62] See WH Simon, 'Ethical Discretion in Lawyering' (1988) 101 *Harvard Law Review* 1083.

[63] It may be, for example, that a lawyer acting on behalf of a large corporation should not plead the limitation rules if, by so doing, a poor person is unable to enforce a debt which undoubtedly is owing to them. The lawyer should not, in other words, lend assistance to the client who wants to use procedural rules or technical devices to defeat, rather than promote, the interests of justice.

[64] Dinerstein, above n 32, 558.

[65] C Fried, 'The Lawyer as Friend: The Moral Foundation of the Lawyer-Client Relation' (1976) 85 *Yale Law Journal* 1060.

[66] EA Dauer and AA Leff, 'Comment on Frieds' Lawyer as Friend' (1977) 86 *Yale Law Journal* 573.

behaviour conducive to promoting such virtues as truth, justice and honesty. For example, if a pure legal advocate remains silent when a client lies under oath he compromises a commitment to truth and also justice. In interviewing witnesses before trial, which is required in the adversarial but not the inquisitorial system, the lawyers will be tempted to influence their evidence and distort the truth. Add to these pressures the economic interests of the lawyer and the expectations of both clients and peers, and it can be seen that this creates for the individual lawyer a struggle between ethos (in the sense of habit) and ethics.

Professional rules of advocacy can, however, attempt to restrain the more extreme examples of the behaviour apparently allowed to the pure legal advocate, as have the civil procedure rules introduced in England and Wales since 1990. How far does the guidance contained in the current professional codes do this? It can be argued that in both the US and the UK the adversarial ethic and partisanship have been modified, arguably more so in the UK than in the US. In the US, the obligation of partisanship historically flows from a commitment in the American Bar Association's (ABA) code to the notion of 'zealous advocacy' on behalf of the client.[67] As this concept has now been replaced by a duty of diligence, much of the writing on the professional obligation to clients which is based on the concept of zealous advocacy must be treated with caution.[68] There was no corresponding obligation in the UK in either the Law Society Guide or the Bar's Code of Conduct.[69] Even the duty of 'diligence', which was found in the old Guide,[70] closely related to zeal but with less combative connotations, is not found in the new Code.[71] Whereas 'zealous advocacy' implies that lawyers are bound to pursue their clients' every desire, the Marre report reflected a different ethos when it observed that:

> the client is frequently acting under physical, emotional or financial difficulties and may well wish to take every step he can, whether legal or extra-legal, to gain advantage over the other party. In this situation the lawyer has a special duty and responsibility to advise his client as to the legal and ethical standards which should be observed and not to participate in any deception or sharp practice.[72]

This approach is reflected in the practice of a Manchester solicitor who regularly gets drunk drivers acquitted on technicalities. Morally he cannot square this with his conscience, he writes but 'ethically I can. I am a lawyer and my job is to give my clients the best defence I can.' However, he will also take his clients to one side and 'give them a polite ticking off . . . and advise them not [to] transgress again'.[73]

The balance between duties to clients and duties to the wider system varies considerably

---

[67] American Bar Association Code, canon 7. See RJ Condlin, 'Bargaining in the Dark: The Normative Incoherence of Lawyer Dispute Bargaining Role' (1992) 51 *Maryland Law Review* 1, 72.

[68] But for a recent application of the concept, see T Dare, 'Mere Zeal, Hyper-zeal and the Ethical Obligations of Lawyers' (2004) 7 *Legal Ethics* 24.

[69] J Levin, *An Ethical Professional* (Swansea University, 1994) 23.

[70] R 12.11 stated that a solicitor is bound to exercise diligence in carrying out a client's instructions. See R Taylor (ed), *The Guide to the Professional Conduct of Solicitors* (London, The Law Society, 1996).

[71] Indeed, the core duties place justice and the rule of law before the duty to act in the client's best interests.

[72] Lady Marre CBE, *A Time for Change: Report of the Committee on the Future of the Legal Profession* (London, General Council of the Bar and Council of the Law Society, 1988) 6.1.

[73] *The Guardian*, 27 January 2006.

between countries as a result of complex interactions: between different conceptions of the judicial process and its purpose, between theories and ideologies about procedure and substantive justice and between different ideologies relating to the role of the judge and the legal profession.[74] Based on the ABA's code, on the writings of American scholars inter-preting that code and on the guidance in the codes of both branches of the domestic profession, lawyers' ethics are moving further from partisanship, but the balance in England and Wales is tipped more towards the legal system than it is in the US.[75] This is the clear implication for solicitors of the guidance to the Core Duties, which reads:

> where two or more core duties come into conflict, the factor determining precedence must be the public interest, and especially the public interest in the administration of justice.[76]

Barristers are told that they have an 'overriding duty to the court to act with independence in the interests of justice'.[77]

Representing clients to the press

The dealings which a lawyer is entitled to have with the press is a reflection of their wider role. If it was seen as acceptable for lawyers to be aggressively partisan, lawyers could be forgiven for using the media to pursue their clients' ends and, incidentally, to promote their own services. However, if lawyers are expected to retain their neutrality, or professional detachment, then being involved with the press in a kind of public relations capacity would damage that role. The existence of some constraints on the way lawyers are expected to deal with the press suggest that detachment from clients is required. These may be seen as a remnant of the conservatism reflected in rules against advertising, or as a sensible attempt to prevent indiscreet or publicity-seeking lawyers from bringing the profession and legal system into disrepute. Restraints might also be imposed in recognition of the substantial difference between what must be done for clients under the cloak of professionalism and the image of professionalism that should be presented to the public. As Lord Woolf said in *Hodgson v Imperial Tobacco Ltd*:

> The professionalism and the sense of duty of lawyers who conduct litigation of this nature should mean that the courts are able to rely on the legal advisers to exercise great self restraint when making comments to the press, while at the same time recognising the need for the media to be properly informed of what is happening in the proceedings.[78]

Lord Woolf did not recommend any greater restrictions than were already contained in the law on contempt of court.

A lawyer's primary role is to provide legal advice and representation, but many lawyers adopt a wider role as 'men of affairs', assisting generally in promoting the business or other

---

[74] M Taruffo, 'The Lawyer's Role and the Models of Civil Process' (1981) 16 *Israel Law Review* 5.

[75] The idea that obligations of candour to the court and fairness to others significantly qualify loyalty to clients has also gained ground in the US. See L R Patterson, 'The Limits of the Lawyer's Discretion and the Law of Legal Ethics: National Student Marketing Revisited' (1979) 6 *Duke Law Journal* 1251.

[76] Solicitors' Code of Conduct 2007, core duties, guidance, para 3.

[77] Bar Code 2004, para 302.

[78] [1998] 2 All ER 673.

interests of their clients.[79] This work may include lobbying, presentational and educational work. Similarly, it is not unusual for lawyers to give their client's statements to the press, or to comment on their client's position or the adequacy of the law in dealing with the client's particular problem. This is common in high-profile criminal cases and also in test cases or other public interest litigation, where lawyers may hope to mobilise public opinion in the client's favour or correct adverse publicity generated by the press and police. The Law Society's old guidance on press statements, contained in the 1999 Guide, was sparse[80] and the guidance to the 2007 Code, rule 11 adds little, recommending that solicitors exercise their 'professional judgement' in deciding whether it is appropriate to make statements to the media, doing so in the client's best interests with his or her consent[81] and with regard for the law of contempt.[82] Of course, in dealing with the press a solicitor must also be aware of the core duty not to damage the reputation or integrity of the profession.[83] Equally they must beware of the laws on defamation.[84]

Barristers are advised that they must not express a personal opinion to the press or in any public statement on any 'anticipated or current proceedings or mediation' in which they are or expect to be briefed.[85] They can therefore express their client's opinion or offer an explanation of the legal or factual issues involved in the case which does not include a personal opinion. This represents a relaxation of the old position, which prohibited any comment at all on current cases on which barristers had been briefed.

The issue of press comment by lawyers in criminal cases was the subject of a report by the Lord Chancellor's Advisory Committee on Legal Education and Conduct (ACLEC) in 1997.[86] The Committee considered that it was not adequate for the Law Society to rely solely on the law of contempt as a guide, with its requirement of proof of intention and the criminal standard of proof. In criminal cases the Committee considered that a solicitor should not say anything that might prejudice the outcome of the proceedings. He or she should be able to say anything on behalf of the client that the client can lawfully say, such as 'My client denies any involvement with this charge and considers the evidence against him flimsy and unreliable'. The Committee would, however, retain a rule that prohibits an advocate from expressing a personal opinion about the merits of the case whilst it is current and would extend it to solicitors generally.[87] The prohibition should cover the period from

---

[79] As is illustrated in the case of BCCI, [2004] 3 All ER 168 (Court of Appeal); [2005] 1 AC 610 (House of Lords). See also chapter 11.

[80] 'A solicitor who on the client's instructions gives a statement to the press must not become in contempt of court by publishing any statement which is calculated to interfere with the fair trial of a case which has not been concluded.' Law Society Guide, above n 70, 21.18, p 381.

[81] Press statements can be made only with the consent of the client, otherwise there may be a breach of confidence.

[82] Solicitors' Code of Conduct 2007, r 11, guidance, para 10.

[83] *Ibid*, core duty 1.06, on which see chapter 14.

[84] In *Regan v Taylor*, *The Times*, 15 March 2000 CA, it was held that a solicitor was covered by qualified privilege in making defamatory statements on his client's behalf to the press in reply to a defamatory attack on his client by the other side. The reply had to be relevant and proportionate. Ironically the complainant was the editor of a 'scurrilous' journal called *Scallywag*.

[85] Bar Code, para 709.1. This prohibition does not apply to educational or academic comment.

[86] *Lawyers' Comments to the Media* (London, Lord Chancellor's Advisory Committee on Legal Education and Conduct, May 1997). For comment on this, see editorial in (1998) 2 *Legal Ethics* 109.

[87] This has now been adopted into the Bar Code, para 709.1, as noted above.

charge to acquittal or the disposal of any appeal. It would not prevent a solicitor from commenting on issues which did not go to the merits of the case, such as any delay in prosecuting. The same rules should also apply to barristers.

The reasoning behind ACLEC's proposals was the elimination of any risk that personal comments from lawyers on the merits would prejudice the outcome of the proceedings and 'detract from public recognition of the principle that these are matters to be decided by the courts and the courts alone'. They were also concerned that

> lawyers may come under pressure to express views [to the press] that they do not genuinely hold on the merits of their clients' cases.

The Committee did not look in detail at civil cases, but recommended to the profession that it consider adopting the same rules in relation to such cases. Other than a change to the Bar Code, no other changes have been made in response to this report, which was not well received by either the professions or commentators.

Conclusion

The dominant principle of lawyers' relations with clients has been characterised as partisanship. The tendency of lawyers to adopt a partisan perspective in situations where it is inappropriate, in political life for example, can lead to very damaging results.[88] The increasing limits on 'zeal', imposed in the interests of third parties in litigation and advocacy, will drive the profession to a more neutral conception of the obligation to clients, such as diligence. The trend towards limiting what lawyers must do for clients is consistent with the growing demand for more participatory decision making, because it provides scope for ethical discourse with clients about their aims and wishes. The development of a participatory model of client representation, in which ethical discourse plays a part, might tackle the 'discrepant moral reasoning'[89] that lawyers sometimes draw from their professional ethic. It could also provide the key to constructive counselling, build the integrity of individuals and bolster public trust in lawyers as public figures. It would also allow lawyers to present their authentic personalities in their relationship with clients, preventing the fragmentation of personality, or 'false self', sometimes associated with professional roles.[90]

---

[88] One explanation for the involvement of so many government officials, trained as lawyers, in the Watergate scandal is that they brought their 'discrepant moral reasoning' to both the political problem and to their attempts to defend the Nixon administration (Wasserstrom, above n 61).

[89] *Ibid*, 15.

[90] A Giddens, *Modernity and Self-identity: Self and Society in the Late Modern Age* (Cambridge, Polity Press, 1991).

10

CONFLICT OF INTEREST

There can be no betrayal if there is no pre-existing trust.[1]

Introduction

A central tenet of professional practice is that a lawyer should promote the interests of the client and avoid situations where those interests conflict, either with the lawyer's own interests or with those of another client. This, for solicitors, arises from core duty 1.04, to act in the best interests of clients and the conflict rules are contained in rule 3 of the Solicitors' Code of Conduct 2007. This principle is often said to derive from the adversarial nature of common law systems, which requires that each party to a dispute should have someone on their side, and their side alone, whose duty it is 'to advocate its own case and to assault the case of the other' irrespective of the moral or other merits of that client or the case.[2] Whilst the conflict of interest rules, and the related rules on confidentiality discussed in the next chapter, are closely connected with the adversarial process, they can also be justified independently of it.

The main justification is that the rule against conflict protects client autonomy. A lawyer is retained by a client in order to do what the client would have done for him or herself, given the necessary knowledge, skills or time. The lawyer thus provides access to the law and increases the ability of the client to act autonomously.[3] Unless the client can confide absolutely freely in the lawyer, confident that the information will not be used to his disadvantage and confident that any proposed action will not be tainted by a contrary interest of the lawyer, then the client cannot be sure that the lawyer will be either able or willing to act as the client would act. This justification applies just as much to non-contentious business, such as making wills or drafting contracts, as to contentious business. The need for the lawyer to act disinterestedly in the interests of the client alone is as important in such transactions as it is in litigation. Unlike the rules on confidentiality, those on conflict have not attracted academic criticism. Perhaps this is because, all too often, they operate to the commercial disadvantage of lawyers, requiring them to forgo business rather than helping them to acquire it. Lawyers themselves have often sought to restrict the scope of the rules in

---

[1] AC Grayling, *The Meaning of Things: Applying Philosophy to Life* (London, Weidenfeld & Nicholson, 2001) 51.

[2] D Luban, *Lawyers and Justice: An Ethical Study* (Princeton University Press, 1988) xx and 57.

[3] SL Pepper, 'The Lawyer's Amoral Ethical Role: A Defense, A Problem, and Some Possibilities' (1986) *American Bar Foundation Research Journal* 613 and the response by D Luban, 'The Lysistratian Prerogative: A Response to Stephen Pepper' (1987) *American Bar Foundation Research Journal* 637.

order to acquire or hold onto business, as can be seen below in relation to the way City firms clearly disregarded some of the rules in the past, and also the elaborate rules designed to maximise conveyancing business even where, to the lay observer, there is a clear conflict of interest.

The basic rule against conflict might seem to be uncontroversial and obvious. It is not, however, always deeply ingrained in the way the legal profession operates, as can be shown from the rather extraordinary case of *Hilton v Barker Booth & Eastwood*,[4] which had to go to the House of Lords for a decision that many would consider beyond argument. The defendant solicitors had acted for B when he was convicted and imprisoned for fraud and in relation to his bankruptcy. B had contacted Hilton, a small builder eager to get into property development, with a proposal that he should buy some commercial property. Hilton agreed, and also agreed to sell on the property to B once it was developed. B had, at the same time, agreed to sell the property to another. The three contracts were all completed on the same day, the solicitors acting for both B and Hilton. To add to the conflict, the solicitors had lent the deposit to B. All these facts were unknown to Hilton, and the solicitors did not enlighten him. Unsurprisingly, B failed to complete the contracts, resulting in financial disaster for Hilton. Hilton sued the solicitors for breach of contract. In the Court of Appeal he lost on the extraordinary basis that there was an implied term in his contract with his solicitors excusing them from revealing the confidential information they held on B. No suggestion was made that this was a totally unacceptable breach of professional conduct which would justify disciplinary sanctions against the solicitors. The Lords reversed the decision. Giving the leading judgement, Lord Walker said that he found the case 'particularly shocking'. The solicitors could not act for both parties in these circumstances even if they had obtained their informed consent, which they had not done. The Court of Appeal's decision that the solicitors could rely on an implied term limiting their duty of disclosure to their client was, he said, 'contrary to common sense and justice', as well as being contrary to legal principle. However, even Lord Walker did not suggest that the solicitors ought to be reported to the Law Society for unprofessional conduct.

Breaches of the rules on conflict are not always as obvious as in *Hilton*. In practice, there can be difficulties in determining when a breach has occurred. What are the client's and the lawyer's interests? When does a conflict arise? How can avoiding conflict be reconciled with other interests, such as allowing a free choice of lawyer or reducing cost by acting for groups or more than one client where their interests appear to be similar?

The nature of interests

By interests we mean benefits or advantages which a person may wish to acquire, defend or promote, including those relating to personal or business relationships, financial or property

---

4 [2005] 1 All ER 651. Another example of official blindness to conflict is that of the Peggy Wood case in 1993. The Law Society saw no conflict of interest where a solicitor arranged a loan between clients, even though the solicitor had a substantial interest in the loan company. It could not arrive at the same decision today. See O Hansen, 'The Lessons of the Peggy Wood Case' [October 1993] *Legal Action* 19.

interests, or interests in maintaining certain public offices.[5] In reality, of course, it is not possible to eliminate all conflict of interest, and in certain circumstances it may not even be desirable to do so. As is discussed in chapter 9, it may not always be desirable that a lawyer disregard his own moral standards or interests in order to advance those of the client. Can, or should, the lawyer act on behalf of the client in a way which would be regarded as immoral if such actions were done in a personal capacity? There may be a conflict between professional obligations and those of the client, such as the lawyer's duty to act towards all with integrity or not to deceive the court. Quite apart from these more obvious conflicts, however, no human being can act in a manner totally or exclusively concerned with the interests of another. A lawyer always has considerations to take into account other than the interests of clients. These include the exigencies of running an efficient or profitable practice, relationships with partners or other clients, and the lawyer's own conception of the morally acceptable way to behave. It is naive for any professional—whether a doctor, lawyer or social worker—to maintain that they *always* put the interests, or the best interests, of the patient, client or child first.

So far we have assumed that we know who the client is—an individual with interests he or she can articulate. In reality, however, many clients are not individuals but are institutions or corporations made up of many individuals and interests[6]. It may be difficult to identify a client: who is the client of the prosecution lawyer? Is it the Crown, the Crown Prosecution Service? Do either of those bodies have an 'interest' in maximising convictions or in obtaining a particular sentence? If not, what are their interests?[7] Where a lawyer represents a child or an incompetent person it is clear who the client is, but who instructs the lawyer or decides what the best interests of the client are?

These problems are faced daily by practising lawyers and guidance is often needed. A code of professional ethics should advise and also seek to control any avoidable, unacceptable or unreasonable conflicts of interest between lawyers and their clients.[8] It should also indicate the limitations on what clients can expect from their lawyers, such as when the lawyer can refuse to act in a morally repugnant (though legal) manner on behalf of the client. A code should be realistic and not promise what cannot be delivered. This is especially important in the context of conflicts of interest because lawyers are in the uncomfortable position of having to refuse business where a conflict of interest arises.

The basic rules

For barristers the basic rule on conflict is expressed in the Bar Code as one of the accepted exceptions to the 'cab-rank rule'. A barrister may reject instructions

---

[5] Fees can be a source of conflict between lawyer and client, but this issue is dealt with in chapter 12.

[6] On which see WH Simon, 'Whom (or What) Does the Organisation's Lawyer Represent? An Anatomy of Intraclient Conflict' [2003] 91 *California Law Review* 59.

[7] Sir Herbert Stephen wrote that the role of the prosecutor was 'not to get a conviction without qualification, but to get a conviction only if justice requires it'. The CPS *Statement of Purpose and Values 1993* requires prosecutors to treat defendants 'fairly'. See A Ashworth, 'Ethics and Criminal Justice' in R Cranston (ed), *Legal Ethics and Professional Responsibility* (Oxford, Clarendon Press, 1995) 172.

if there is or appears to be a conflict or a risk of conflict either between the interests of the barrister and some other person or between the interests of any one or more clients (unless all relevant persons consent to the barrister accepting instructions).[9]

Similarly, if, when representing multiple clients, there is or appears to be a conflict between them, the barrister must withdraw from the representation unless all parties consent.[10] There is little more guidance in the Code for the Bar. For solicitors the new rule 3 and its guidance is more detailed. With the exceptions in rule 3.02, a solicitor must not act if there is a conflict of interests. This is developed in rule 3.02(2). There is a conflict of interest where either the solicitor or the firm owes separate duties to act in the best interests of two or more clients

in relation to the same or related matters, and those duties conflict, or there is a significant risk that those duties may conflict.

In addition, the solicitor cannot act where there is a similar risk of conflict with the solicitor's own interests in relation to the matter or a related matter. In the latter context, if the matter involves the same property, asset or liability there is always a conflict.[11]

The guidance recognises that the solicitor will have to make a judgment on what matters are related. For example, suppose a solicitor acts for a company in dispute with a garage over the cost of repairs to a car. A potential bidder for the purchase of the company then asks the solicitor to act for them. The work could be accepted as, although the car is an asset of the company being bid for, it is a very minor asset and the two issues are not related.[12] Solicitors are advised that they should get the views of their existing client if that can be done without a breach of confidentiality.

It is sometimes possible for clients to consent to a solicitor or firm acting where there is a conflict, and also for firms to erect information barriers between their employees to enable this to happen. These issues are developed further below. The new Rules have developed this area of the law in order to accommodate City solicitors who have, it appears, long been breaking the previous, more strict principle, which prohibited acting even where the client consented to the conflict.[13] The City firms justified this on the basis that it was what their clients wanted and also that the old Law Society principles were unclear and unenforceable. Conflicts should be 'managed', not prohibited.[14] The introduction of the new rules caused and continues to provoke much opposition, especially from smaller firms who consider that the big firms are attempting to establish an effective monopoly over certain types of

[8] C Wolfram, *Modern Legal Ethics* (St. Paul, Minnesota, West Publishing, 1986) 313.

[9] *Code of Conduct of the Bar of England and Wales* (London, Bar Standards Board, 8th edition, as amended, 2004) (hereafter Bar Code) pt VI, para 603(e).

[10] *Ibid*, para 608.

[11] *Solicitors' Code of Conduct 2007* (London, Solicitors Regulation Authority, 2007) r 3.01(3).

[12] *Ibid*, guidance to r 3, para 4.

[13] See J Griffiths-Baker, *Serving Two Masters; Conflicts of Interest in the Modern Law Firm* (Oxford, Hart Publishing, 2002). According to her research, over 60% of City firms admitted breaking the old rules, doing so for commercial reasons and believing their corporate clients were happy with the practice. See 174. This has even been impliedly accepted by the SRA in its guidance to r 3, para 7(iv). See also H McVea, '"Heard it Through the Grapevine": Chinese Walls and Former Client Confidentiality in Law Firms' (2000)59 *Cambridge Law Journal* 370.

[14] Griffiths-Baker, *ibid*, 163–4. The City was not always successful at 'managing' conflict, as the case of *Marks & Spencer v Freshfields*, discussed below, illustrates.

lucrative business, such as that relating to corporate takeovers and major licensing issues. It has been said that anyone who wishes to sue one of the top five clearing banks will find it virtually impossible to instruct one of the top firms because of the conflict rules. The smaller firms are happy with this; the top firms might well resist the rules in order to get the business unless they are worried about damaging their relationships with the banks.[15]

Conflicts between existing and proposed clients

Where a proposed client consults a solicitor, that solicitor must consider whether there is a conflict with the interests of an existing or previous client. A major risk arising from conflict in this situation is a breach of confidentiality. If a solicitor acts for a client who is suing a former client of the firm, then the solicitor or the firm may have access to useful confidential information about the latter. The solicitor is under a duty to disclose to the new client all relevant information about the case, and to do this would involve a breach of confidentiality to the former client. The conflict therefore relates to confidentiality and not to any other interest. The 2007 rules on confidentiality permit the solicitor to act in these circumstances under the strictly defined conditions in rules 4.04 and 4.05. These are:

— the proposed client knows that the solicitor or firm holds relevant information that cannot be disclosed;
— there is a reasonable belief that both existing and proposed clients understand the issues and have given their informed consent to the firm acting;
— both clients agree to the conditions under which the firm will be acting; and
— it is reasonable in all the circumstances so to act.

If a firm is already acting for a new client and then discovers that it holds relevant confidential information about a former or existing client, then it may be possible to continue so to act even where the latter client does not consent to this. For example, it may not be possible to obtain informed consent from the client whose confidential information needs protection. Indeed, to ask for such consent might in itself be a breach of the confidentiality of the new client. Equally, the existing client may be incapacitated and unable to consent.[16] If this is the case, then under rule 4.05 the firm can continue to act for the new client provided that client understands and agrees that the firm may hold information it cannot disclose and all safeguards required by law are in place (that is, effective 'Chinese walls' preventing any leakage of confidential information, as explained below). It must also be reasonable to so act. The guidance warns that generally it will be only sophisticated new clients, such as corporate bodies with in-house legal advisers, who will be able to give such informed consent.[17] Acting in this way without the consent of the old client is clearly regarded as a last resort and the guidance states at paragraph 38 that 'you should always seek consent when you can reasonably do so'.

---

[15] See *The Lawyer*, 27 September 2004, 1.
[16] At least it may be presumed this is an acceptable reason. Neither the rule nor the guidance mentions this possibility.
[17] Solicitors' Code of Conduct 2007, r 4.05 guidance, para 35.

Before the new rules were introduced in 2005, solicitors obviously considered that they could act in the above circumstances without the consent of the both parties provided they could establish an effective Chinese wall between those members of the firm acting for the two clients. All the judicial decisions on Chinese walls date from before the new Rules, and often do not mention client consent, but they are nevertheless still relevant on the issue as to how to erect such a wall.

The leading case, *Bolkiah v KPMG*,[18] involved a firm of accountants, but it was held that the same rules apply to solicitors. KPMG had acted as the auditors of an agency of the Government of Brunei that was chaired by Prince Jefri. They also acted for the prince in his own commercial affairs and gave advice in relation to litigation similar to that given by solicitors, for which he paid them £4.6 million. After the prince had ceased to chair the government agency, the Government of Brunei wanted KPMG to undertake an investigation into its affairs. KPMG had ceased to act for Prince Jefri 2 months previously and so they accepted the government work. They were aware of the conflict of interest—indeed, it is glaringly obvious—and sought to manage it by erecting a Chinese wall around the staff undertaking the government work. Unsurprisingly Prince Jefri objected and sought an injunction to prevent KPMG acting for the Brunei Government. He won. Lord Millett acknowleged that there was no *absolute* duty not to act against former clients, but, if the client could show that the solicitor held relevant confidential information which was adverse to their interests, then the solicitor could not act without that former client's consent. The ad hoc Chinese wall was insufficient to prevent the possible leakage of information:

> the duty to preserve confidential information is unqualified. It is a duty to keep the information confidential, not merely to take all reasonable steps to do so.[19]

Another recent attempt to retain valuable business in apparent disregard of a clear conflict of interest can be seen in the case of *Marks & Spencer plc v Freshfields Bruckhaus Deringer*.[20] Freshfields, the solicitors, had acted for Marks & Spencer (M&S) in a great deal of its contentious commercial and employment work, and in particular on the renegotiation of a particularly valuable and important contract. M&S was then the subject of a takeover bid by G, and Freshfields agreed to act for G in this. M&S objected on the ground of conflict of interest. Freshfields alleged that there was no conflict in relation to the actual transaction, namely the takeover bid, but that in any case they had erected a Chinese wall to deal with any potential leakage of confidential information. The court held that the solicitors held considerable confidential information about M&S and no effective internal barriers could be put into place to prevent a breach. Freshfields also pleaded that it would be difficult for G to find another solicitor expert in the field able to act for him, to which short shrift was given by Lawrence Collins J:

> I find it hard to accept . . . that there will be no reasonably competent firm in the City able to help [him].

---

[18] [1999] 1 All ER 517.
[19] *Ibid*, 527.
[20] [2004] EWHC 1337 (Ch).

Re A Firm of Solicitors (1992)[21] provides some guidance on how impermeable a Chinese wall should be. A large firm of City solicitors wished to represent a client bringing an action against a company which, some years previously, had been, in effect, a client of the firm. The solicitors went to some trouble to erect a Chinese wall between the staff working on the current case and those on the previous case. Nevertheless, the Court of Appeal upheld the grant of an injunction prohibiting the firm from representing the new client. There was, held the Court, no general rule that a solicitor could *never* act against a former client, but it could not do so if the ordinary man in the street would reasonably anticipate a breach of confidentiality or some likelihood of mischief. In this particular case, it was found that the Chinese wall could not provide an effective barrier against such a risk.

Conflicts of this kind can also arise in the increasingly common situation where firms of solicitors merge or where solicitors move firms. Solicitors may find that their new firm is acting against their own former clients. Again, the firm must cease to act if there is likely to be a leakage of confidential information. In *Re A Firm of Solicitors* (1995)[22] a solicitor who had been employed by a firm acting for a plaintiff in patent litigation moved firms. Some two and a half years later the new firm was retained to act for the defendants in the patent litigation. The individual solicitor had never been involved in the case against these defendants in his previous employment. Moreover, he managed to establish that he had no information relating to the previous litigation that would now be recallable, confidential or relevant, bearing in mind the lapse of time and the complexity of the issues. The injunction to prevent the firm from acting was refused. The judge held, however, that it was for the solicitor to prove that there was no reasonable prospect of a conflict between the two clients, not for the complainant to prove that there was a conflict. He also acknowledged that the American-based plaintiffs in the action were 'genuinely aghast' at the turn of events since, in the US, there would be no question of the solicitor continuing to act. The court had to balance two conflicting principles, namely the protection of client confidence and the freedom of the client to instruct a solicitor of its choice.[23]

In a subsequent case, *Koch Shipping v Richards Butler*,[24] a solicitor employed by a firm representing the applicants to an arbitration left her employment and joined the firm (Richards Butler) acting for the defendants. The applicants sought an injunction to prevent Richards Butler from acting on the ground that their new employee had confidential information about the applicant's case—which she did. The injunction was refused. Richards Butler convinced the Court of Appeal that an effective Chinese wall had been erected between the employee and those working on the case. She was a solicitor of integrity who had given an undertaking not to discuss the case with those handling it and she worked on a different floor of the firm's building. She was the sole employee with the confidential

---

[21] [1992] 1 All ER 353 CA. See also *Rakusen v Ellis Munday and Clarke* [1912] 1 Ch 831; *Supasave Ltd v Coward Chance* [1991] 1 All ER 668; *David Lee & Co v Coward Chance* [1991] 1 All ER 668.

[22] [1995] 3 All ER 482.

[23] The court considered that the same rule applied to barristers. In *Laker Airways Inc v FLS Aerospace Ltd* [2000] 1 WLR 113 it was suggested there was no conflict of interest where an arbitrator was appointed from the same set of chambers as counsel for the defendant. Barristers were said to be sole practitioners working 'on their own papers for their own clients and sharing neither career nor remuneration', *ibid*, 125.

[24] [2002] EWCA Civ 1280 (Comm). See also *GUS Consulting v Leboeuf Lamb Greene* [2006] EWHC 2527 (Comm).

information and therefore the case was not similar to *Bolkiah*, which involved a team of accountants. Lord Justice Tuckey was anxious that clients should not be deprived of their solicitors in the name of preserving confidentiality where 'the risk is no more than fanciful or theoretical'.

Re A Firm of Solicitors (1995) was followed in *Re Schuppan (A Bankrupt)*,[25] the facts of which would cause even greater incredulity amongst American lawyers. The solicitor for the petitioning creditor had also acted for that creditor in litigation against the bankrupt. The solicitor was retained by the trustee in bankruptcy to advise in the administration of the bankrupt's estate. The bankrupt objected on the ground of conflict of interest. The court disagreed. It was held that it was not unreasonable for the trustee to retain the creditor's solicitors who would already be aware of difficulties relating to the tracing of the bankrupt's assets. Separate solicitors had been retained by the creditors to deal with issues that remained to be settled in relation to the litigation, such as a wasted costs application. In relation to an outstanding slander action brought by the bankrupt against the creditor's solicitors, any conflict of interest that might arise by virtue of the fact that they, in their capacity as the trustee's solicitors, might have access to the debtor's documents relating to this litigation could be resolved. One solution would be for the solicitor to give an undertaking not to use those documents without leave of the court. This decision seems to stretch the criteria laid down in *Re A Firm of Solicitors (1995)* much too far. In particular, it fails to apply the criterion that it is for the solicitor to prove that there is no reasonable prospect of conflict.

Maintaining a balance between preventing conflict and protecting confidence on the one hand and maintaining the freedom of clients to instruct lawyers of their choice on the other is difficult. To permit such conflicts of interest undermines client confidence in the integrity of the profession. But where clients consent to a possible conflict because they have a common interest and want to save costs, why should they not employ the same solicitor or firm? Equally, even where there is a clear conflict but both parties want to employ a particular firm with particular expertise, why should they be prevented from doing so by the conflict rules? Rule 3.02, under the heading of confidentiality, originally introduced in 2006, accommodates both desires. In the latter example they are intended to apply only to 'specialized areas of legal services' where 'clients are sophisticated users of those services', such as large companies who, in the words of the guidance, want to use their usual advisors 'in the knowledge that these advisors might also act for competing interests'.[26] The rule is not intended for the unsophisticated client who is incapable of giving informed consent.

Accordingly rule 3.02(1) allows an individual solicitor or a firm to act for two or more clients even if there is a conflict provided the clients all have a substantially common interest and they give informed consent in writing. The conflict must therefore be substantially less important to the clients than their common interest. Thus, under this provision a solicitor can act for a number of family members in relation to family affairs, or a number of people setting up a company. It must, however, be reasonable to act in all the circumstances, and care has to be taken to ensure that the clients are aware of the situation, capable of

---

[25] [1996] 2 All ER 664.
[26] See guidance to r 3, para 7 (a)(iv) .

understanding it and not under any undue influence from other clients. If there is any doubt, separate representation is recommended.[27] It is for the solicitor to show that the representation is reasonable and the test is whether 'one client is at risk of prejudice because of the lack of separate representation'.[28]

Rule 3.02(2) permits a firm (but not an individual solicitor) to act for clients competing for the same asset where there is no other conflict between the parties. The parties must agree to this in writing, and again the solicitor must be satisfied they are of full capacity and understand the issues involved. Again it must be reasonable to act in all the circumstances. This exception is intended to cover 'multi-party complex commercial transactions where sophisticated users of legal services, who have a common purpose', want a single firm to act for two or more parties because this will speed up the transaction or make it more efficient[29]. Examples of where rule 3.02(2) might be used are insolvency cases where a firm acts for more than one creditor or for competing bidders in an auction. The guidance warns that solicitors should 'always exercise caution' when proposing to act in accordance with rule 3.02(2) and be mindful of the reasonableness test. City firms can therefore now carry on what they were doing before the Rules were changed in their favour.

There is an increasing tendency in some commercial cases to use the rules against conflict cynically and unethically as a litigation tactic. There are instances where litigants have sought to deny an opponent access to the lawyer of his choice and run up the costs by initiating such actions where the risk of conflict is very remote. This problem is prevalent in the US[30] and was also noted as an emerging phenomenon in England in the Report of the Solicitors' Complaints Board for 1994. The new Rules and guidance should alleviate this problem, but only if firms institute appropriate conflict detection procedures and fully inform all clients with a view to obtaining consent. In criminal as well as civil proceedings, lawyers are generally precluded from acting against former clients. The criminal courts have not, however, been so particular about spelling out the way the rules should operate in this context. For example, in *R v Ataou*[31] the court stated merely that it was 'at least doubtful' whether a solicitor should continue to act for either client in a case where a conflict might arise between an existing and a former client (the conviction was, however, quashed in this case because of such a conflict). Slightly stronger guidance was given by Lord Donaldson in *Saminadhen v Khan*,[32] who said:

> I can conceive of no circumstances in which it would be proper for a solicitor who has acted for a defendant in criminal proceedings, the retainer having been terminated, to then act for a co-defendant where there is a cut throat defence between the two defendants.

---

[27] See guidance to r 3.02(1), para 7(a)(viii). Particular care should be taken where a couple are re-mortgaging their home—one spouse might need separate advice: *Kenyon-Brown v Desmond Banks & Co* (1999)149 NLJ 1832 CA.

[28] *Ibid*, para 9.

[29] *Ibid*, para 7(a)(iv).

[30] See, eg L Crocher, 'The Ethics of Moving to Disqualify Opposing Counsel for Conflict of Interest' (1979) 6 *Duke Law Journal* 1310.

[31] [1988] 1 QB 798.

[32] [1992] 1 All ER 963.

Where conflict arises between existing clients

The 2007 Rules state that if a solicitor or firm acts for two or more clients and a dispute or conflict arises between them during the course of the conduct of the matter, then the firm may act

> for one of the clients . . . provided that the duty of confidentiality to the other client(s) is not put at risk.[33]

There is no guidance on which client to choose to continue to represent in these circumstances. In the 1999 Guide the Law Society advised that it would be 'prudent' to check that the other party does not object. As this will mean that the other party will have to find another solicitor, it is likely that they will object. A similar situation can arise in relation to matrimonial proceedings, where a solicitor may have previously acted for either or both spouses in relation to house purchase or making a will. Provided the solicitor does not hold confidential information on one spouse, he may choose which to represent in the matrimonial case; if he has such confidential information, he should act for neither.

On the basis of *In Re A Solicitor (1995)*, it is clearly for the solicitor to establish that there is no reasonable prospect that this is so. This is likely to be difficult in the case of small firms of solicitors who normally deal with family matters.[34] It is arguable that the rule is not strict enough, even though the burden of proving the absence of conflict of interest rests on the solicitor. Private clients are normally most upset if 'their' solicitor acts for their opponent. The solicitor will obviously know them, their character, the way they are likely to act under stress, etc. This information may not be regarded as confidential but it will be useful to an opponent. A similar case could be made in relation to acting against an organisation that is either an existing client or a former client. A general knowledge of the culture of a company or public authority and of the way they work will often be very useful in conducting litigation or negotiations with it.

Conflicts between clients arising in the course of the representation arise typically in criminal cases where the solicitor represents co-defendants. Initially there may be no problem, as both clients are telling the same story. If one of them then either changes his story and implicates the other or says something that is inconsistent with the other's story, the solicitor must withdraw from representing both of them because there is now a conflict between the clients and to continue to represent one would involve a breach of confidence of the other. Even if there were no breach of confidence, it would be generally impossible to continue to act for both where one co-defendant pleads guilty and the other not guilty to the same offence based on the same facts. It would be impossible to accept in one case that evidence was probative of a fact that in the other case was contested. Could the solicitor continue to act for one of the clients in such circumstances? In this context, the guidance states that the solicitor should cease to act for one 'and possibly all'.[35] This type of conflict can arise both in the police station when clients are being interviewed as suspects and also

---

[33] R 3.03.

[34] In *Royal Bank of Scotland v Etridge* [1998] 4 All ER 705 the court said it was a matter of 'professional judgement' for a solicitor to decide whether to continue to represent both a husband and a wife where the home was to be charged.

[35] Guidance to r 3, paras 24–36 covers the issue of codefendants and conflict generally.

in court at the trial. Even if both co-defendant clients plead guilty, there may be a conflict when pleas in mitigation are considered, as where one client says the other led him on. The Criminal Defence Service Regulations prefer that one solicitor represent two or more co-defendants as it is more economical, and pressure is often put on solicitors by the court about this. However, the guidance comes down firmly on the side of refusing such representation wherever there is or is likely to be a conflict, and solicitors are reminded that they should not provide details of why they have to withdraw from representation as this itself would be a breach of confidentiality. The Criminal Law Solicitors' Association has firmly resisted any change to the rule, pointing out that it would have Human Rights implications.[36]

Acting for organisations

In acting for a company, partnership or other organisation, a solicitor must be clear who gives the instructions. There is a danger that the solicitor might become involved in conflicts within the organisation, for example, between shareholders and the board of directors or between partners. There is no guidance in the 2007 Code on this. From whom should the solicitor accept instructions where the client is an organisation? Presumably the solicitor should make sure that the relevant governing body, such as the board of directors, has lawfully approved the instructions or authorised the instructor. Where the solicitor has acted for the company and has also acted for the directors in a personal capacity, then, if there is subsequently a dispute between directors and shareholders which leads to litigation, it unlikely that the solicitor would be able to act for either party. A solicitor who has acted for a partnership may act against a partner only if he or she had no confidential information relating to that partner. Again, it follows from the previous section that it is for the solicitor to prove that there is no conflict of interest.[37] In acting for a club or other informal organisation, conflicts of interest may arise and an individual member may need to be advised that separate representation should be sought.

Acting for buyer and seller or lender and borrower

The conflict of interest arising from acting for both sides in a conveyancing matter is so manifest it might be thought that no such joint representation would ever be allowed. This is not the case, although there has in the past been a high level of default related to mortgage frauds in cases where the solicitor acted for both lender and borrower.[38] There are a number of specified situations under the 2007 Code, rules 3.07–3.22, where the solicitor can act for both buyer and seller or buyer and lender. Their length and complexity are a consequence of the fact that, in reality, these joint representations are riven with conflict and the consequent

---

[36] See *Law Society Gazette*, 16 September 2004.

[37] *Re A Solicitor* [1995] 3 All ER 482.

[38] See, eg the case of *R v Law Society, ex parte Mortgage Express Ltd* [1997] 2 All ER 348. This was remedied by the Law Society by permitting standard terms of instructions from lenders which restrict the work that the solicitor is supposed to do. See now the new r 3.19 for the detail.

possibility of unprofessional conduct and negligence claims from clients. On the one hand, if these rules are abolished, solicitors would lose business and fees. On the other, these joint representations are often cheaper for clients: a fine line has to be drawn between these competing priorities, and this requires long, detailed rules and similarly lengthy guidance.[39]

The 2007 Rules replace the old rule 6 of the Solicitors' Practice Rules 1990, which are otherwise largely unchanged in substance. First, if a transaction is not at 'arm's length', then the solicitor can act for both parties, provided there is no actual conflict or significant risk of it. In this context, a transfer is regarded by the Law Society as being not at arm's length if it is between related persons, settlor and trustee, trustee and beneficiary, personal representatives and beneficiaries, or sole traders and their companies and associated companies.[40] Even where the transaction is at arm's length, the solicitor may act for both the buyer and the seller in certain exceptional cases, providing no actual conflict of interest arises. The parties must consent in writing to the joint representation, and the solicitor must not be involved in negotiating the sale of the property, nor in representing the developer of the property. If these conditions are satisfied, then the solicitor can represent both sides to the transaction in the following cases:

— where both parties are established clients;
— where the consideration is less than £10,000; or
— where the parties are represented by different individuals at separate offices or practices in certain conditions.[41]

There are also elaborate and similar rules governing acting as a mortgage broker or as an estate agency (through a SEAL)[42] and also acting for the buyer and seller in rules 3.11–3.13. Again the informed consent of all parties must be obtained in writing, and the parties must be informed of the solicitors and other side's interests in the transactions.

In relation to mortgages, the solicitor can act for both the purchaser and a 'standard'[43] mortgage lender provided there is no actual conflict of interest and provided the lender's instructions do not extend beyond the terms set out in rules 3.16–3.18. Consent is not mentioned in this context, but the solicitor must not so act if there is an actual conflict of interest. Also the instructions to the solicitor must be limited to those listed in rule 3.19. In the case of a private mortgage, a solicitor can act for both, provided the transaction is *not* at arm's length.[44]

---

[39] These rules are currently subject to a consultation by the SRA which may lead to changes in 2008. For an account of the Rules, see L Sheinman, 'Ethical Practice or Practical Ethics? The Case of the Vendor Purchaser Rule' (2000) 3 *Legal Ethics* 27.

[40] Guidance to r 3.08, para 73.

[41] For full details, see r 3.09–10 and the guidance thereon from para 74.

[42] Solicitors can do this only under a SEAL, a Solicitors' Estate Agency Ltd. This is a company consisting of at least 4 practices which undertakes property selling services.

[43] This is defined in r 3.17, and would include building society mortgages and those offered by banks if on standard terms.

[44] These Rules are extensive and complex and it is not proposed to go into them in detail here. The standard instructions are set out in r 3.19 and are restricted to legal matters of title, etc and not those requiring notifying the lender of the true value of the property or of the financial status of the borrower, matters which caused so many problems before the Rules were changed.

It can be seen from this that there is, in fact, considerable scope for acting for both buyer and seller or borrower and lender, and that this has recently been extended by the introduction of SEALS. Much depends on identifying when a conflict of interest actually arises and also, where acting for a buyer and seller is concerned, on the consent of the clients. This is an issue on which clients may well not be fully informed. Again, it is likely that the criterion laid down in the case of *Re A Firm of Solicitors (1995)* will apply, namely that the burden of proving the absence of a conflict of interest is on the solicitor. Representing both borrower and lender has led to heavy calls upon the compensation fund and considerable litigation against solicitors by lenders whose borrowers have defaulted on the repayments. All these cases occurred before the rules were changed in relation to restricting the terms of the instructions from mortgage lenders. As Peter Gibson LJ noted in *National Home Loans Corporation v Giffen Couch & Archer,*

> the recession and the collapse of the housing market at the beginning of this decade, left mortgage lenders, who had vied with each other to obtain business in the 1980's, with defaulting mortgagors and substantial losses which they were unable to recover out of the security they had taken. This has led mortgage lenders to seek ways to recover their losses from others, and actions in negligence against their professional advisers have become only too common.[45]

In *National Home Loans Corporation*, the loan company had lent the borrower over £92,000 on the security of a home which was already subject to another mortgage. On default of repayment, the property was sold for £70,000. The loan company sued for their loss. The company and the borrower had both been represented by the same firm of solicitors, Giffen Couch & Archer. The company maintained that the solicitors should have told them that the lenders were in arrears with their existing mortgage and had been threatened with legal proceedings. They succeeded at first instance. On appeal, however, it was held that, in the circumstances of the case, there was no duty on the solicitors to pass on this information about the borrower to the lenders. The solicitors' duties depended heavily on what they were instructed to do (and were paid for) by the client. In this case they were instructed to report on title and to certify whether there had been a change in circumstances since the loan had been offered. They had to undertake a bankruptcy search. They were not asked to report on the personal creditworthiness of the borrower. The list of standard instructions contained in rule 3.19, which now limits the duty of the solicitor to the lender, does not include the buyer's creditworthiness, although it can include a bankruptcy search.

The *National Home Loans* case can be contrasted with that of *Mortgage Express v Bowerman*.[46] In this case a solicitor acting for both lender and borrower became aware that the lenders had been told that the value of the property was £220,000, whereas in fact the purchaser was buying it for £150,000. In the report on title to the lender the solicitor did not mention this discrepancy. The borrower eventually defaulted on the loan and the property was repossessed and sold for only £96,000. It was held that the solicitors *did* have a duty to pass on information which had a bearing on the value of the lender's security as their duty had not been confined to advising on title alone: the instructions to the solicitors

---

[45] [1997] 3 All ER 808 at 810.
[46] [1996] 2 All ER 836 CA. See also *Bristol & West BS v Fancy and Jackson and others* [1997] 4 All ER 582.

required them to undertake 'the normal duties of a solicitor when acting for a mortgagee'.[47] Lord Bingham considered that

> if, in the course of investigating title, a solicitor discovers facts which a reasonably competent solicitor would realise might have a material bearing on the valuation of the lender's security or some other ingredient of the lending decision then it is his duty to point this out.[48]

Reporting on the purchase price is contained in the standard terms in rule 3.19, so this decision would be the same today as in 1996. However, the solicitor is still bound by confidentiality and so the information can be given only if the borrower/buyer consents.[49] This qualification again shows how problematical this can be. If the buyer client refuses to allow the solicitor to reveal confidential information which the lender has a right to receive under the standard instructions agreed between the lender and the solicitor, then the solicitor must presumably decline to act for either on grounds of professional embarrassment. Not a very satisfactory situation for either client.

Acting for spouses and children

Where both spouses have been clients, a solicitor should not normally agree to act for one spouse against the other, certainly where the solicitor has confidential information unknown to one of the spouses which was acquired during the course of the retainer. But can the solicitor act for *both* spouses in contested matrimonial matters where the parties agree to it and wish for a non-contentious divorce settlement? This is allowed if all the conditions linked to rule 3.02(1) noted above are complied with. There must be a substantial common interest and fully informed written consent. Such clients are rarely particularly sophisticated in this context. It must also be reasonable so to act. In reality, it will be difficult to continue to act if, once the work is begun, conflicts do arise between the parties. Also one spouse may allege that the implications were not fully understood by them, or that some form of undue influence was exerted. As it is clearly for the solicitor to prove a lack of significant conflict, this could lead him or her into considerable difficulties. The savings in costs arising from such joint representation could prove illusory.

The difficulties can be illustrated by a number of cases where charges on matrimonial homes were made as security for a husband's business debts. In *Barclays Bank v Thomson*,[50] the bank obtained such a charge over the home, which was owned by the wife. The solicitors acted for the husband's business, for the wife in relation to the transfer of the home into her name and for the bank in registering the charge. They were also asked by the bank to ensure that the wife fully understood the nature of the charge. In resisting a possession order when the loan repayments were in arrears, the wife attempted to negate the validity of the charge

---

[47] It will be noted that no such general instruction had been included in the case of *National Home Loans Corporation v Giffen Couch & Archer*, above n 132.

[48] *Ibid*, 842.

[49] However, legal professional privilege does not protect purchasers where their solicitor's advice is used to 'further iniquity' by procuring a loan by deception: *Nationwide Building Society v Various Solicitors* [1998] NLJR 241.

[50] [1997] 4 All ER 816.

on the ground, inter alia, that she had not been properly advised by the solicitors of the extent of her potential liability under the charge. She maintained that the bank had constructive knowlege of this deficiency because the solicitors were acting for them. She lost her case on the ground that the bank was entitled to rely on their solicitor's advice that they, the solicitors, had discharged their duty to the wife to warn her of the nature of the charge. Significantly, there was no comment in the judgments of the Court of Appeal on the wisdom or the propriety of one firm of solicitors acting for all the parties despite an obvious conflict of interests.[51]

Solicitors can also act as mediators between the parties in family matters, but should not thereafter act as a solicitor for one of them if a dispute arises.[52] The mediator's role is to help the parties to reach their own solution to the dispute, not to impose a solution upon them. The mediator should be impartial and the process confidential. It is not the role of the mediator to give professional legal advice to the parties, either individually or collectively. This must be difficult to avoid in cases where one or both of the parties does not have a solicitor.[53] However, rule 3.06 states that a solicitor must not act for any party for whom the solicitor or the firm has acted as a mediator or vice versa.

Some have argued for further relaxation of the constraints of the conflict rules in the family context; for example, there are lawyers who feel that the rules against acting for both spouses are unduly restrictive. Thus, Tur argues that

> some reformulation of the conflict-of-interest rules of professional conduct is highly desirable in order to permit family lawyers to act, where appropriate, for and in the best interests of the family rather than solely for one individual member.[54]

There is talk of being a 'lawyer for the family' rather than a representative of an individual member of the family. This might be appropriate under rule 3.02(1), but all the parties must consent and that consent must be fully informed. How can the latter be achieved by one lawyer who also has his or her own interest in retaining the rest of the family as clients? The notion could be dangerous, especially for the members of the family with the least power.

In representing children, the solicitor must be clear who gives instructions. In ordinary civil litigation, such as personal injuries, a minor cannot initiate litigation except by a litigation friend.[55] A parent has the right to act as such a friend. It is for the litigation friend to instruct the solicitor in the best interests of the child, and he or she must not have any interest adverse to those of the child. Any settlement or compromise requires the consent of the court. The solicitor acts for the litigation friend but must be conscious of any conflict of interest between the child and the friend. The solution, if such a conflict does arise, is for the litigation friend to be removed by the court on the application of the solicitor or other

---

[51] The solicitor's fee in this case was paid initially by the bank, but would be added to the borrower's total liability. See also the following similar cases: *Banco Exterior Internacional v Mann* [1995] 1 ALL ER 936 and *Bank of Baroda v Rayarel* [1995]2 FLR 376. In these two cases the court advised the solicitors not to act for the complaining wife if they thought there was a conflict of interest.

[52] See Solicitors' Code of Conduct 2007, r 3.06.

[53] See further chapter 20 on mediation generally.

[54] RH Tur, 'Family Lawyering in Legal Ethics' in S Parker and C Sampford (eds), *Legal Ethics and Legal Practice: Contemporary Issues* (Oxford, Clarendon Press, 1995).

[55] Civil Procedure Rules (CPR) 2007 r 21.2, unless the court so orders under r 21.2(3).

interested person.[56] In family proceedings there is provision for a child to initiate or defend litigation, such as an application under section 8 of the Children Act 1990 in relation to care or contact, without a litigation friend. The solicitor must ascertain if the child has both a sufficient understanding of the issues and the ability to give instructions.[57] If this is the case, then the solicitor can act directly for the child. If expert evidence of what is in the best interests of the child is required, then a social worker from the government agency CAFCASS can be instructed. The court can also appoint a CAFCASS expert. However, a solicitor who forms the view that the child is capable of instructing him must accept those instructions.[58]

This raises the issue of what is in the best interests of the child in these circumstances. In criminal proceedings, which can only involve children over 10 years old, it has never been suggested that the child client needs a litigation friend. It is up to the solicitor to try to make sure that the child understands the legal advice and then accept the child's instructions. In the police station an 'appropriate adult' (AA) should be present when the child is interviewed by the police in order to ensure that the child understands what is going on and generally to protect the child's interests. The AA can be a relative, a social worker or, often, a member of the local Youth Offending Team. However, it is clear that the AA does not represent the child and neither does he or she have the right to give instructions or override the advice of the solicitor. Indeed, the AA is not under the same duty of confidentiality (or professional privilege) as is the solicitor, so it is important that the AA should not be present at the child client's interviews with the solicitor. Therefore if any conflict of interest, or of view as to what should be done in the case, does arise between the AA and the child, the solicitor should follow the instructions of the child—and may have a duty to get the AA replaced by someone else.

A solicitor may well represent a child who cannot really give informed instructions on the case and also cannot legitimately get instructions from any other source. In these circumstances, the solicitor must act in a manner that he or she considers to be in the best interests of the client. The solicitor might also take the view that the best interests of the child are advanced by ensuring that the court has all relevant information on all options so that it can arrive at a decision on the best interests of the child. A full discussion of this issue is beyond the scope of this chapter, but it is clear that a solicitor in this position must beware of presenting the court with his or her own personal views on the best way to bring up children. In the absence of instructions from a litigation friend or a competent child, it is probably best for the solicitor to rely on the court rather than any personal opinions. Such opinions are not expert in the field of family welfare, and may even be quixotic or inappropriate to the particular child and his family.

---

[56] CPR 2007 r 21.7; *Re Taylor's Application* [1972] 2 All ER 873.

[57] Ie is the child Gillick competent; *Gillick v West Norfolk etc AHA and DSS* [1986] AC 112.

[58] See *Re T* [1993] 4 All ER 518, in which the court stressed that while it is basically for the solicitor to determine whether a child is capable of giving instructions, nevertheless the court has the ultimate right to decide the issue either on it own motion or on the application of another because 'there are bound to be some cases . . . where a maverick assessment might be made by a solicitor', Waite LJ at 529. A CAFCASS guardian can be removed by the court, *Mabon v Mabon* [2005] 2 FCR 354.

Acting for groups and representative actions

Major disasters, such as air crashes, adverse reactions to drugs and environmental problems, can affect large groups of people, all or some of whom may want to seek compensation. There may be conflicts of interest between the victims or between them and their lawyers. Some victims may not be aware that litigation is underway or, if they are, may not understand what is happening. The majority of the victims may leave the matter to a small group of representative plaintiffs or even to the lawyers alone. The litigation is therefore often characterised by a 'relative absence of client control'[59] which can leave the lawyers free to follow their own inclinations rather than the instructions of the client.

Two frameworks exist for litigating such group actions. First, all the parties may sue as a group. This requires leave of the court to join all of them as parties and, in theory, all are equally involved in the progress of the case. Secondly, some of the group may bring the action as representatives of the others. This avoids the need to join large numbers of people as plaintiffs, but every person represented is bound by the outcome of the litigation. Representative actions are comparatively rare; the multi-party group action is more usual. Examples of such actions include litigation arising in relation to abestosis, the Dalkon Shield and Opren.[60] The *Opren* case concerned the alleged side effects of the anti-arthritis drug Opren. Two group actions, involving about 1,500 plaintiffs, were launched against the manufacturers, Eli Lilly & Co and were coordinated by a group of solicitors known as the Opren Action Group (OAG). The clients set up an Opren Action Committee (OAC) and the Law Society set up a register of solicitors acting for Opren victims. The management of the case was difficult and fraught with the possibility of conflict between the different groups. In the event, a settlement was reached whereby a lump sum payment was agreed with the defendants and was distributed between the various plaintiffs by the solicitors in the OAG, subject to an appeal to a judge as arbitrator. However, it seems that the solicitors did not discuss the terms of the settlement with the OAC and, moreover, told their clients that if the settlement were not agreed they would cease to act.[61] The case had been further complicated by legal aid. The court ordered that, despite the fact that the action had been brought only by plaintiffs entitled to legal aid, the costs of the action should be shared equally by all of the group involved, including those not legally aided. The unaided parties naturally had a different attitude to the risks of the litigation than those who were legally aided, the latter being unlikely to face any personal liability for the costs of the action.[62]

The actual and potential conflicts inherent in litigation such as the *Opren* case are obvious. The situation can be helped by the involvement of professional bodies in the proceedings.[63] In multi-party actions the parties clearly have to sacrifice some of the protection provided by the conventional conflict of interest rules in order to obtain the

---

[59] Lord Woolf, *Access to Justice: Final Report to the Lord Chancellor on the Civil Justice System in England and Wales* (London, HMSO, 1996) 243, para72 (hereafter Final Report).

[60] M Day and S Moore, 'Multi-party Actions: A Plaintiff View' in R Smith (ed), *Shaping the Future New Directions in Legal Services* (London, Legal Action Group, 1995) 188.

[61] See G Dehn, 'Opren: Problems, Solutions and More Problems' (1989) 12 *Journal of Consumer Policy* 397.

[62] *Davies v Eli Lilly & Co* [1987] 1 WLR 1136. Another successful multi-party action was that against British Coal in respect of miners' lung disease. For details of how this was handled, see *The Lawyer*, 10 February 1998.

[63] The Law Society can help to coordinate multi-party actions, as they did in the Opren case.

benefits, in terms of finance and expertise, that can come from a multi-party action. Without the group they would probably be unable to get any redress, bearing in mind the complexity and costs of the litigation. The *Opren* case, for example, involved investigations and scientific research costing millions of pounds. However, these inherent conflicts must be appropriately managed if justice is to be done equally to all the parties. Lord Woolf addressed some of these issues in his Final Report on Civil Procedure and recommended special procedures for managing group actions. These are now contained in the CPR.[64] The court may, on application or on its own motion, make a group litigation order. This will set up a register establishing the court and judge, the issues and the management of the case.

The solicitors involved in multi-party actions are asked to consult the Law Society's multi-party information scheme and a lead solicitor is appointed. Any judgments or orders are binding in relation to all the claims on the register at the time unless the court orders otherwise. Woolf thought that an application should be made to the court at the outset to certificate a multi-party action and a managing judge should be appointed to control the proceedings. The role of the informed client can be taken by an action group or, where there is no such group, by the appointment of a trustee to undertake this role. All settlements have to be approved by the court so as to ensure that 'the lawyers do not benefit themselves while obtaining minimal benefits for their clients'. Lord Woolf also recommended that the Bar and the Law Society 'give special attention to the ethical problems involved in multi-party litigation'.[65] So far this has not happened, although the Law Society do run the information scheme noted above. Such ethical guidance must, at the very least, ensure that all the parties are fully informed in writing of the nature of the group action and the constraints within which is being conducted, in particular the limited possibilities for the client to give personal instructions. They should have a right to a regular progress report, either in person or in writing, and be informed of the terms of any proposed settlement and how it would affect them. It is essential to inform the client fully from the outset what can be expected from the lawyer because the relationship between lawyer and client in multi-party actions is not the same as in one-to-one relationships.

Conflicts with the solicitors own interests

The Solicitors' Code of Conduct 2007, rules 3.01(1) and (2)(b) state that a solicitor must not act for a client if his or her own interests conflict, or there is a significant risk of conflict, with those of the client. There are no exceptions to this rule. The most obvious example of such conflict is where the solicitor sells, buys or lends money to the client. A startling example of this arose in relation to the trial of Frederick West for multiple murders in 1994. His solicitor was alleged to have been commissioned by a publisher to write a book about the case when it was concluded. The guidance[66] on this states firmly that a solicitor should never enter into any arrangement relating to publication rights with the client *prior to the conclusion of the matter*. There seems to be no problem about such agreements for publication once the case

---

[64] CPR 2007, pt 19 III Group Litigation, rr 19.10–15 and the associated practice direction.
[65] See Final Report, above n 59, ch 17.
[66] At para 42.

has finished, though a solicitor cannot reveal confidential information about a client without the client's consent, and in obtaining that consent the solicitor must ensure that the client has independent advice under the guidance noted below. Equally tempting, and increasingly common in notorious cases, may be the possibility of negotiating with the press on behalf of the client for exclusive interview rights. Again, the solicitor must avoid any conflict of interest, which might arise, for example, where the solicitor obtains a proportion of the interview fee for acting as an agent or where the solicitor gets valuable publicity from such an interview.

More conventional conflicts arise where the solicitor, or his firm, personally buys from or sells or lends to the client, or has a personal interest in any transaction which the client is undertaking.[67] In these cases the solicitor must reveal the interest to the client with 'complete frankness'[68] and the client must receive independent advice from another solicitor or other appropriate advisor such as a surveyor. Only if the client gets such advice can the solicitor continue to act in relation to the transaction. The rule applies also where another member of the firm has such an interest, provided that the solicitor is aware of the fact and that 'it impairs your ability to give independent and impartial advice'.[69]

Are solicitors prohibited from acting for a client with whom they have some personal relationship? Clearly a conflict of interest could arise in such circumstances as neither the solicitor nor the client may always wish to be frank in their professional dealings if this would compromise their personal relationship. The guidance states that if a solicitor is involved in a sexual relationship with a client then interests may conflict and the solicitor must 'consider' whether the relationship impairs the ability to act in the best interests of the client.[70] This guidance seems a little thin. It fails to deal adequately with the risk of abuse of power where personal relationships are mixed with solicitor–client relationships and also the risk that the reputation of all lawyers will be impugned when, as sometimes happens, sordid allegations are made in the press. Normally the solicitor will be in the more powerful position and there may be a risk that the help or advice given may be influenced by the prospect of sexual favours. Arguably professionals must adhere to higher standards than are the norm, and it should be a rule that solicitors and barristers never act for their spouses, cohabitants or lovers. However, this guidance must be read in the context of other rules, in particular core duty 1.04, to treat the interests of the client as paramount.

Where a solicitor discovers that a client may have a claim against him or her, for example for negligence, then the advice is that the client be informed of this and advised to take independent advice. Where the client makes such a claim, then, obviously, the solicitor cannot continue to act.[71] There are also other situations where a close relationship between the solicitor and a particular person or body may lead the client to suspect that the solicitor will not act energetically in his or her best interests. An example of this is a firm of solicitors who had close ties with the local police, one of their partners being an ex-policeman, and who habitually handled divorces and conveyances of officers working in the local police

---

[67] See chapter 12 in relation to commissions.
[68] Guidance to r 3, para 45.
[69] *Ibid*, para 48.
[70] Guidance to r 3, para, 49.
[71] Guidance, para 55, which also makes reference to r 20.07 in dealing with such claims.

station. Arrested suspects who found a member of that firm advising them under the Dut Solicitors' Scheme might well be concerned that conflicting loyalties would inhibit the assistance given to them. However, it is not clear that this is an example of conflict of interest as prohibited by rule 3.

A solicitor must decline to act for a client where the solicitor, or a partner, employee or relative, holds an office which gives rise to a significant risk of a conflict of interest.[72] A number of examples are given in the guidance, such as local councillor, judge, coroner and member of the police authority. Where such roles are held, the solicitor must consider whether the duties or interests of the public role conflict with the ability to provide the client with independent advice. A solicitor, whilst a member of a police authority, 'should not' appear as an advocate in prosecutions brought by the Criminal Prosecution Service in the authority's area. A solicitor who is a recorder, deputy judge or registrar must not sit in a court in which he, she, a partner or an employee regularly practices. Somewhat oddly, this advice applies even where the fact that a solicitor holds a public office could be to the advantage of the client. The guidance states that the solicitor should consider whether to act where there

> is likely to be a public perception that you, or your firm, have been able to obtain an unfair advantage for your client as a result of the office or appointment.

The reason for this advice must relate to the core duty 1.06—not to act in a way which damages or is likely to damage the reputation or integrity of the profession—rather than the conflict rules.

Conclusion

No lawyer can guarantee that there will be no conflict of interest between the interests of the client and other interests. However, one of the most valuable services that a lawyer can offer, in contrast to many other commercial advisers, is disinterested and confidential advice. The client needs to know what this entails and, in particular, what the position is where a conflict can or does arise. This is particularly important where the lawyer is working outside the context of a one-to-one lawyer–client relationship, such as where the lawyer is representing an institution or a group, or is undertaking mediation, conciliation or other non-conventional work. Now that civil procedures are less adversarial as a result of the Woolf reforms, it may be that the rules and principles on conflict of interest should be revised in order to accommodate a more cooperative and facilitative ethos. This is already apparent in many family cases, especially where children are involved. This leads to Tur's proposal that lawyers should act for the family, rather than for individual members of it.

The litigation that has arisen in relation to the joint representation of buyer and seller or mortgagor and mortgagee, instituted with a view to allowing solicitors to offer an efficient and less costly service in a non-contentious situation, should, however, lead to caution. It may be asking too much of anyone that they represent different interests at the same time and are also constantly alive to the possibility of conflict of interest arising. The risk is that

---

[72] R 3.05 and guidance, paras 64–66.

the lawyer who is required to warn a client will possibly lose his or her business, will upset the arrangement or progress already made on the issue and will cause other parties also to incur increased costs. This, is turn, might lead to a claim for wasted costs. It is possible and desirable for the law to encourage a cooperative ethos whilst at the same time recognising that in the majority of cases each party involved in legal matters or litigation should be separately represented by a lawyer whose primary role is to give that party disinterested advice, unconstrained by any conflict of duty to any other party.

11

CONFIDENTIALITY

This principle we take to be this; that so numerous and complex are the laws by which the rights and duties of citizens are governed, so important is it that they should be permitted to avail themselves of the superior skill and learning of those who are sanctioned by the law as its ministers and expounders, both in ascertaining their rights in the country, and maintaining them most safely in courts, without publishing those facts, which they have a right to keep secret, but which must be disclosed to a legal advisor and advocate, to enable him successfully to perform the duties of his office, that the law has considered it the wisest policy to encourage and sanction this confidence, by requiring that on such facts the mouth of the attorney shall be for ever sealed.[1]

Introduction

A fundamental ethical duty imposed on the legal profession is to keep client affairs confidential. Most other professions also adopt this rule. On the face of it, this duty seems easy to justify. It embodies a respect for privacy—a 'right' which many would argue is still inadequately protected elsewhere in English Law but which is increasingly being protected under the developing jurisprudence of the Human Rights Act.[2] In purely professional terms, clients will be loath to consult a lawyer who gossiped about their affairs in the pub or at the PTA meeting, or who wrote a bestseller about their cases. Such conduct would also run counter to other general principles of professional conduct, such as the obligation to act in the client's best interest and not to profit personally from client information. It would also amount to a breach of contract. The doctrine of confidentiality is central to another major ethical rule, namely not to act where there is a conflict of interest between clients. To do so may involve breaching the confidentiality of those clients, as was explained in the previous chapter. Confidentiality 'belongs' to the client and not the lawyer; only the client can waive it, either expressly or, sometimes, impliedly.

Lawyer confidentiality is also justified by many on the more fundamental basis that it safeguards both access to justice and the protection of individual legal rights.[3] In the leading House of Lords case of *Bolkiah* Lord Millett had no doubt of this:

---

[1] L Shaw, *Hatton v Robinson*, 31 Mass (12 Pick) 416, 422 (1834).

[2] See, in the context of legal professional privilege, *Morgan Grenfell v Special Commissioners of the IR* [2002] UKHL 21 and *R v Sec of State for the Home Dept, ex parte Daly* [2001] UKHL 26.

[3] As can be seen in the cases of *Bolkiah v KPMG* [1999] 2 AC 222 and *R v Derby Magistrates' Court, ex parte B* [1995] AC 487, discussed below, and *B v Auckland District Law Society* [2004] 4 All ER 269. See also the cases cited in the previous note and *D v NSPCC* [1977] 1 All ER 589, 606.

It is of overriding importance for the proper administration of justice that a client should be able to have complete confidence that what he tells his lawyer will remain secret. This is a matter of perception as well as substance. It is of the highest importance to the administration of justice that a solicitor or other person in possession of confidential and privileged information should not act in any way that might appear to put that information at risk of coming into the hands of someone with an adverse interest.[4]

In a complex modern society access to justice can be delivered to individuals only with the assistance of a lawyer. Unless the client is confident that the information he or she provides for the lawyer will remain confidential, then the client will not be frank and the lawyer will be unable to do the job of advising or representing the client. Where the client is accused of a crime this is particularly important; without confidentiality the right to silence and the protection from self-incrimination would be negated. The lawyer is seen as being an extension of the client him or herself; their interests are the same:

> this identity of lawyer and client provides the moral foundation for an absolute privilege . . . If we regard them as constituting one conceptual unit then, ex hypothesi, no 'communication', as such, has been made.[5]

Yet many commentators express doubts about the value of the concept of confidentiality and its colleague, legal professional privilege. These doubts are not recent. Jeremy Bentham considered that the privilege could only protect the guilty, the innocent had nothing to fear, a surprisingly sanguine view given Bentham's generally more critical view of the way the criminal justice system actually worked.[6] Both the lay public and philosophers have queried the morality of some of the consequences of lawyer confidentiality, for example that lawyers can never tell the police if a client confesses to having committed a crime. A much-quoted and criticised case is that of *State v Macumber*, in which it was held that two lawyers were prevented by legal privilege from testifying in a capital murder trial in Arizona that their deceased client had confessed the murder to them.[7] Equally, in civil proceedings, is it in the public interest to suppress an expert's report which indicates that the other side is correct?

In England and Wales the idea that civil proceedings are still adversarial is being undermined gradually by the development of the Civil Procedure Rules (CPR), initiated by Lord Woolf.[8] This diminishing adversariality may also undermine the justification for some of the manifestations of the confidentiality rules, in particular in relation to legal privilege. To quote Lord Scott in the House of Lords decision in the *Three Rivers* case:

> civil litigation conducted pursuant to the current CPR is in many respects no longer adversarial. The decision in *Re L*[1996] warrants a new look at the justification for litigation privilege.[9]

---

[4] *Bolkiah, ibid,* 528.

[5] A Paizes, 'Towards a Broader Balancing of Interests: Exploring the Theoretical Foundations of the Legal Professional Privilege' (1989) 109 *South African Law Journal* 109, 120.

[6] J Bowring (ed), *The Works of Jeremy Bentham* (New York, Russel & Russel, 1962) vol 7, 474–5.

[7] 112 Arizona 569,544 PZd 1084 (1976).

[8] For further details of the Woolf reforms, see chapter 17.

[9] *Three Rivers DC and others v Gov of the Bank of England* [2004] UKHL 48, para 29. See below for a discussion of *Re L*.

In a different context, suppose a client admits that he is abusing his child or is unlawfully syphoning off money from a pension fund he controls. Why should the ethical rules relating to legal practice prefer to protect the 'guilty' client rather than seek to protect an 'innocent' third party from injury or injustice?[10] The danger is that the claim to confidentiality can become 'ritualistic and universal', resulting in

> a kind of moral blindness to the real issues of potential conflict and abuse that a broad and unqualified claim to confidentiality can mask.[11]

Similarly, confidentiality can be regarded as protecting

> not only lawyers' pockets but also their egos and social status and to shield them from public scrutiny of the sort of dubious activities which flow from their neutral partisan role.[12]

Others doubt whether 'empirical evidence would lend any support to the rationale of encouraging client disclosure'.[13] Few clients are aware of all the qualifications that attend the rules on confidentiality and research results appear to indicate that there is a low correlation between client frankness and such knowledge.[14] There are, however, many criticisms that can be made of the design of these studies. Certainly most advisers find that clients who seek advice on commercial, criminal or highly personal matters are concerned with the confidentiality of that information. They are similarly concerned when consulting other professionals such as doctors, accountants or even the local Citizens Advice Bureau. Practitioners would agree with Zacharias that 'in routine cases, attorney–client confidentiality is uncontroversial', whether or not clients know or understand the nature and limits of the doctrine. The real issue is not whether client confidentiality should be protected, but how far it should extend and how many exceptions should be allowed.

Many commentators are also sceptical when lawyers claim that privilege and confidentiality belong to the client and not the lawyer. Lawyers benefit considerably from the legal protection that they gain from both concepts, but in particular legal privilege, which applies only to lawyers and their clients. Legal privilege is a 'valuable product' that lawyers, and no other professionals, can sell to their clients.[15] Accountants, for example, consider that lawyer privilege distorts competition between them and lawyers when dealing with tax work. The Chair of the Consultative Committee of Tax Bodies considered that lawyers had an unfair advantage over accountants because the new regime requiring disclosure of certain types of tax schemes was subject to legal professional privilege and to that extent did not apply to lawyers. They called, unsuccessfully, on the government to

---

[10] See R Wasserstrom, 'Lawyers as Professionals; Some Moral Issues' (1975–6) 5 *Human Rights* 1; W Simon, 'Ethical Discretion in Lawyering' (1988) 101 *Harvard Law Review* 1083, 1142. For a fairly extreme attack on lawyer/client confidentiality, see DR Fischel, 'Lawyers and Confidentiality' (1998) 65 *University of Chicago Law Review* 1. For an account from the more recent UK perspective, see D Nicolson and J Webb, *Professional Ethics; Critical Interrogations* (Oxford University Press, 1999) ch 9; HL Ho, 'Legal Professional Privilege and the Integrity of Legal Representation' (2006) 9 *Legal Ethics* 163.

[11] C Wolfram, *Modern Legal Ethics* (St Paul, MN, West Publishing, 1996) 246.

[12] Nicolson and Webb, above n 10, 255.

[13] R Cranston (ed), *Legal Ethics and Professional Responsibility* (Oxford, Clarendon Press, 1995) 9. Equally there is little evidence the other way. Cranston's claim that most clients are ignorant of the privilege seems doubtful, especially of criminal clients; if they are, then their solicitors should tell them of it.

[14] FC Zacharias, 'Rethinking Confidentiality' (1989) 74 *Iowa Law Review* 351.

[15] Wolfram, above n 11, 247; Fischel, above n 10.

remedy this.[16] Privilege and confidentiality can protect the lawyers from public scrutiny,[17] yet lawyers abandon the rhetoric of confidentiality once it 'rubs hard against lawyer self-interest', such as when they are sued by their clients for malpractice.

The professional rules on confidence

The extent and detail of the law on confidence and legal privilege are obviously a matter of common law and legislation. However, both branches of the profession deal with these issues under their respective codes. Thus breaches of the law or the branches' respective codes could lead to both professional complaints or disciplinary proceedings and legal liability to clients, for example breach of confidence or contract.

Barristers, under paragraph 702 of the Bar Code, must 'preserve the confidentiality or the lay client's affairs' and not reveal 'the contents of the papers in any instructions' or any other information entrusted to them without the prior consent of the lay client. They also must not use confidential client information 'to the client's detriment or to his own or another client's advantage'. The Bar Code makes no mention of any possible exceptions to this rule. The refusal of instructions because of a 'significant risk' of a breach of client confidentiality is also one of the exceptions to the 'cab-rank rule'.[18]

For solicitors the rules on confidence are now considerably developed. The duty of confidentiality is contained in the Solicitors' Code of Conduct 2007 at rule 4 (previously confidentiality was contained in a principle and was not enacted in the Solicitors' Practice Rules).[19] This states that a solicitor or firm

> must keep the affairs of clients and former clients confidential except where disclosure is required or permitted by law or by your client.

The solicitor is responsible for ensuring that all the staff in the firm also adhere to the principle. It protects existing clients, previous clients and deceased clients. It also protects potential clients even if, at the end of the day, the solicitor does not act for the client. For example, if a solicitor interviews a prospective client but concludes that he or she cannot act because, for example, there is a conflict of interest with an existing client, the solicitor is under an obligation to keep confidential the information provided by the potential client. The duty of confidence extends to all information about clients, whether or not it is acquired in the context of acting for them or from some other source.[20]

Problems may arise where the solicitor acts for two or more clients jointly, for example acting for husband and wife in the purchase of a property. Generally the solicitor must share

---

[16] See R Baldwin, K Malleson, M Carr and S Spicer, 'Scoping Study for the Regulatory Review of Legal Services' (Lord Chancellor's Department, March 2003) and news item at 154 *New Law Journal* 1463 and 1511 (8 and 15 October 2004). For details of the new rules under the Finance Act 2004 and regulations thereunder, see 154 *New Law Journal* 1608 and see below.

[17] The case of *Medcalf v Mardell* [2002] UKHL 27 on wasted costs, post 281, is an illustration of this.

[18] *Code of Conduct of the Bar of England and Wales* (London, Bar Standards Board, 8th edn, as amended, 2004) (hereafter Bar Code) pt VI, para 603(f); see also para 608.

[19] The rule was briefly added as rule 14 E of the old 1990 Rules in 2005.

[20] *Solicitors' Code of Conduct 2007* (London, Solicitors Regulation Authority, 2007) Solicitors' Coder Solicitors' Code) guidance to rule 4.01, para 4.

all information with both of the clients and neither can expect to be protected from the other by the rules on confidentiality. Suppose the wife tells the solicitor that as soon as the purchase is completed she proposes to institute divorce proceedings. Must the solicitor inform the husband about this? The answer is yes, as the information is relevant to the purchase and the solicitor acts jointly for both. The solicitor should, of course, also tell the wife that the husband will be informed. If the information is irrelevant to the purchase, for example the wife tells the solicitor that she had a lover in the past unknown to the husband, this confidence should not be broken. Acting for joint clients, for both sides to a transaction or for a new client in a matter which is also relevant to the affairs of a previous client can raise acute conflicts between the duty of confidence and the duty of full disclosure to clients. Rule 4.02 states that

> you must disclose to a client all information of which you are aware which is material to that client's matter regardless of the source of the information.

However, at 4.02(a) it also states firmly that 'the duty of confidentiality . . . always over-rides the duty to disclose'. This raises issues of conflict which were developed in chapter 10.

Confidence and legal privilege

In considering these issues, it is necessary at the outset to distinguish between the general professional duty to keep confidences and the narrower concept of legal professional privilege. Much of the criticism previously noted is addressed to the latter rather than the former, although the critics do not always make this clear. Legal professional privilege has developed a rule of evidence[21] under which neither the lawyer nor the client can be ordered to give evidence in court, or elsewhere, of communications between them or of work done by the lawyer in giving legal advice to the client or in preparing for litigation. We now have a statutory definition of this privilege, which is accepted as being applicable to both criminal and civil proceedings, in the Police and Criminal Evidence Act (PACE) 1984, section 10. 'Items' protected by legal privilege are:

1. communications between a lawyer and his client or person representing his client in connection with giving the client legal advice;
2. such communications, including communications with 'any other person', made in connection with or in contemplation of legal proceedings; and
3. items referred to or enclosed with such advice or proceedings in the possession of anyone entitled to them.

'Items held with the intention of furthering a criminal purpose are *not* items subject to legal

---

[21] But not only a rule of evidence, as has been pointed out in a number of recent cases. See, eg *General Mediterranean Holdings v Patel* [1999] 3 All ER 673, where Toulson J stated that privilege was a fundamental basis of the administration of justice which cannot be overridden by general statutory words. The House of Lords has held that legal privilege is a fundamental human right protected by Art 8 of the ECHR in *R v Special Commissioners of Income Tax* [2002] UKHL 21 and *R v Secretary of State for Home Dept, ex parte Daly* [2001] UKHL 26. For an analysis of the concept, see C Tapper, 'Prosecution and Privilege' (1996)1 *International Journal of Evidence and Proof* 5.

privilege' (our emphasis).[22] It will be noted from this definition that *all* communications between solicitor and client are privileged if they concern giving legal advice, whether or not they relate to litigation. This is often known as legal advice privilege.

Communications between solicitors and third parties, on the other hand, are privileged only if they relate to litigation. This is known as litigation privilege. For example, reports compiled by an expert in preparation for litigation would be covered by such privilege. However, a witness who has prepared a report for the solicitor on one side can be subpoenaed to give evidence by the other side, there being no property in a witness. The solicitor could not, however, be required to produce or give evidence of the report.[23] Despite this statutory definition, which, it has been held, embodies the common law,[24] the case law in this field is often ambiguous or confused. Recently professional privilege has been under attack by governments eager to convict criminals or reduce money-laundering or tax evasion. Until very recently the issues have been subjected to little sophisticated analysis by either the judiciary or the legal profession.[25] Guidance is, therefore, thin on the ground.

An illustration of the operation of professional privilege, and a justification for it, can be found in the House of Lords decision in *R v Derby Magistrates' Court, ex parte B.*[26] On arrest B admitted murdering a girl, but before the trial he retracted his confession and implicated the girl's stepfather. B was acquitted. He later again admitted the offence and subsequently retracted the confession. Eventually the stepfather was charged with the murder. B was called as a witness for the Crown. Counsel for the stepfather sought to obtain evidence from B, and also from his solicitor, of B's previous inconsistent instructions relating to his defence to the murder charge.[27] At first instance this succeeded; the public interest in ensuring that all relevant evidence was available to the defence outweighed the interest of confidentiality. B no longer had any recognisable interest in the privilege—having been acquitted of the murder, he could not, at the time, be tried again and a prosecution for perjury was unlikely. It was held by the Lords, however, that B's statements were protected by professional privilege and so immune from production.

In a comprehensive judgment, Lord Taylor, the Lord Chief Justice, examined the history of, and previous cases on, legal privilege. He concluded:

> The principle which runs through all these cases . . . is that a man must be able to consult his lawyer in confidence, since otherwise he might hold back half the truth. The client must be sure that what he tells his lawyer in confidence will never be revealed without his consent. Legal professional privilege is thus much more than an ordinary rule of evidence, limited in its application to the facts of a particular case. It is a fundamental condition on which the administration of justice as a whole rests.

---

[22] Police and Criminal Evidence Act 1984, s 10(2).

[23] *Harmony Shipping Co SA v Saudi Eutope Line Ltd* [1979] 3 All ER 177.

[24] See *R v Bowden* [1999] 4 All ER 43 CA, 48.

[25] An academic analysis recently published which is concerned with the justification or otherwise of privilege is J Auburn, *Legal Professional Privilege* (Oxford, Hart Publishing, 2000).

[26] [1995] 4 All ER 526.

[27] Under the Criminal Procedure Act 1965 ss 4 and 5 and the principles laid down in *R v Barton* [1972] 2 All ER 1192 and *R v Ataou* [1988] QB 798.

Lord Taylor also concluded that legal privilege, *once established,* should be absolute. No exception should be allowed.[28] Were this not to be the law, then solicitors would have to tell their clients that their confidence would be broken if 'in some future case the court were to hold that [they] no longer had "any recognisable interest" in asserting it'.[29]

Lord Nicholls, agreeing with Lord Taylor, considered that if the court were to have a discretion to override privilege it 'would be faced with an essentially impossible task'. What criteria would it use? Would the public interest in the conviction of the guilty always override it? Would the need for evidence in a serious civil claim be a sufficient cause, 'say where a defendant is alleged to have defrauded hundreds of people of their pensions or life savings?'[30] Many would, unlike Lord Nicholls, answer yes to both of these questions and point out that such balancing acts—deciding in individual cases which of two competing public interests (or private interests) should prevail—is just what the courts should be doing.

In a subsequent House of Lords case, *Re L,*[31] concerning child care proceedings, a distinction was made between communications between solicitor and client to which absolute privilege applied and 'other forms of legal privilege', such as reports made by expert third parties on a party to the litigation. In *Re L* it was held that in cases under the Children Act 1989 no privilege attached to such reports and therefore a report made for the mother in care proceedings could be revealed to the police with a view to investigating whether or not she should be prosecuted. This case probably applies only to Children Act proceedings, though even on this basis it is not easily reconciled with the *Derby Magistrates* case (and Lord Nicholls and Lord Mustill considered it could not be).[32]

The analysis in *Re L* led the courts into making the distinction between 'litigation privilege' and 'legal advice privilege' noted above. The former covers all advice and documents prepared for the purposes of conducting litigation, including communications with third parties in this context. Legal advice privilege is not exclusively concerned with preparation for litigation but covers legal advice given to a client by a lawyer in all contexts, for example in making a will, drawing up contracts or undertaking conveyancing. It is in this context that the Court of Appeal recently attempted to rein in what was seen as an attempt to overextend the scope of this privilege. Following *Three Rivers District Council v Bank of England,*[33] many City lawyers were horrified that legal advice privilege was confined to circumstances where a client's dominant purpose in consulting a lawyer was to get advice about legal rights and obligations. It did not extend to all the work that a solicitor might do for a client, and in this particular case it did not extend to the preparation of materials to be presented to an internal Bank of England inquiry into the collapse of the BCCI bank and designed to put the Bank of England in the best possible light.

---

[28] *Ibid,* 542d. Lord Taylor's ruling has been followed by the Privy Council in *B v Auckland District Law Society* [2004] 4 All ER 269, especially at 283. See *Saunders v Punch Ltd* [1998] 1 All ER 234, 244 for a more sceptical judicial view on the need to rule out any exceptions to legal professional privilege. A similar view was expressed, obiter, in the Court of Appeal in *Three Rivers DC v Bank of England* [2004] 3 All ER 168, 182, para 39.

[29] [1995] 4 All ER 526, 541g.

[30] *Ibid,* 545.

[31] [1996] 2 All ER 78. Lord Nicholls, who sat in the *Derby Magistrates* case, above n 26, was one of two dissenters in *Re L.*

[32] For guidance in the Solicitors' Code of Conduct 2007 on this see r 4 guidance, para 15.

[33] [2004] 3 All ER 168 in the Court of Appeal and [2005] 1 AC 610 in the House of Lords.

Lord Phillips was critical of the current wide scope of legal privilege:

> Where . . . litigation is not anticipated it is not easy to see why communications with a solici-
> tor should be privileged. Legal advice privilege attaches to matters such as the conveyance of
> real property or the drawing up of a will. It is not clear why it should.[34]

He called for a review of the law. However, the Court of Appeal decision was overturned by
the House of Lords. The Lords held that solicitors, as 'men of affairs', provided their clients
with a wide variety of advice on their rights, liabilities and obligations. This was covered by
legal advice privilege, and the advice given to the bank in this case was so covered. Legal
advice included, said Lord Carswell at paragraph 59, 'advice as to what should prudently and
sensibly be done in the relevant legal context'. Moreover, it was emphasised that, once information was covered by legal professional privilege, it could not be set aside on the ground of
some higher public interest. As Lord Scott said,

> it is necessary in our society, a society in which the restraining and controlling framework is
> built apon a belief in the rule of law, that communication between clients and lawyers,
> whereby the clients are hoping for the assistance of the lawyers' skills in the management of
> their affairs, should be secure against the possibility of any scrutiny from others.[35]

Nevertheless, Lord Scott also said that he favoured 'a new look at the justification for
litigation privilege' in the light of the CPR and the fact that civil litigation was 'in many
respects no longer adversarial'.

It should be emphasised that *Three Rivers*, *Derby Magistrates* and the other cases noted
above concern privilege, not the general duty of confidence, to which there are recognised
exceptions. They also state that the doctrine of privilege is absolute *once established*. So,
much depends on defining when it is so established and when it is not.

Establishing legal privilege

The definition of legal privilege under the Police and Criminal Evidence Act 1984 has been
noted above. This definition is regarded as embodying the existing common law definition
and covers both solicitor and client communications and third party communications made
in connection with litigation, such as experts' reports.[36] The statute confers privilege on
communications between solicitor and client in connection with giving legal advice. However, the courts have adopted a wider definition. For example, in *Nederlandse Reassurantie
Groep Holding NV v Bacon & Woodrow*[37] assistance provided for the client included advice
given by solicitors on the commercial wisdom of a proposed transaction. This information
was held to be covered by privilege provided it was given in the context of acting as a legal
advisor. This is similar to the reasoning of the House of Lords in *Three Rivers*, noted above.

---

[34] CA Report, 182, para 39.
[35] HL Report, above n 34, Lord Scott's judgment at paras 25 and 34.
[36] It was held at first instance in *R v Egdell*, *The Times*, 14 December 1988, that legal professional privilege did not
extend to experts' reports, which is not consistent with PACE s10. For criticism of this see J V McHale, 'Confidentiality, an Absolute Obligation' (1989) 52 *Modern Law Review* 715.
[37] [1995] 1 All ER 976.

Privilege extends to the client's instructions to the solicitor, instructions to a barrister and the barrister's opinion, documents, and copies of them, created in order to obtain legal advice and which 'betray the trend of the advice which [the solicitor] is giving the client'.[38] The privilege extends to employed lawyers and also to patent agents, licensed conveyancers and 'authorised advocates and litigators'.[39]

The definition in PACE, section 10(2) denies privilege to items held with the intention of furthering a criminal purpose, as in the old case of *R v Cox & Railton*.[40] This issue was considered by the House of Lords in *Francis & Francis v Central Criminal Court*.[41] Mrs G retained a solicitor to assist her in purchasing a house. Unknown to both her and the solicitor, the money for this purchase allegedly came from drug trafficking by a member of Mrs G's family. The police applied for an order requiring the solicitors to deliver up all the files in their possession relating to the transaction, arguing that they fell within PACE, section 10(2). The House of Lords agreed. It did not matter that neither the solicitor, as holder of the records, nor the client of the solicitor intended to further a criminal purpose. As long as someone had a criminal intention in relation to the documents, they fell within section 10(2).[42]

There must be prima facie, and probably strong, evidence of a criminal purpose, which includes civil fraud or 'iniquity' which might not constitute a crime. In *Barclays Bank v Eustice*,[43] it was held that documents created by the client's solicitors for the 'dominant' purpose of prejudicing the interests of the creditor bank were not privileged in subsequent civil proceedings by the bank under the Insolvency Act 1986. It was stressed that there was clear prima facie evidence that this was the intention and also that the purpose of seeking legal advice was not to explain what had been done (or prepare a criminal defence on that basis), but to 'enter into transactions at an undervalue the purpose of which was to prejudice the bank'.[44] Lord Justice Schiemann regarded this purpose as being

> sufficiently iniquitous for public policy to require that communications between [the client] and his solicitor in relation to the setting up of these transactions be discoverable.[45]

How far this decision is consistent with the *Derby Magistrates* case (it was decided at about the same time and not discussed in it) is clearly debatable. It may be that the same rules do not (or should not) apply in civil as in criminal cases, though their Lordships in the *Derby*

---

[38] See A Keane, *The Modern Law of Evidence* (London, Butterworth, 1996) 520–1. See also *Re Barings Plc* [1998] 1 All ER 673 for a comprehensive review of the law by Sir Richard Scott VC. Privilege does not extend to client attendance notes, *R (Howe) v South Durham Justices* [2004] EWHC 362.

[39] Courts and Legal Services Act 1990, s 63. However in relation to EU competition investigations before the European Court of Justice it has been held that legal professional privilege does not extend to employed lawyers and their employer clients, see *Akzo Nobel Chemicals Ltd V EC* [2007] All ER(D) 97 (Eu Ct) and comment on in 157 NLJ 1492. This decision is being appealed.

[40] [1884] 14 QBD 153.

[41] [1989] AC 346.

[42] For a criticism of the correctness of this decision, see L Newbold, 'The Crime/Fraud Exception to the Legal Professional Privilege' (1990) 53 *Modern Law Review* 472.

[43] [1995] 4 All ER 511.

[44] *Ibid*, 524f. The case was followed in *Nationwide Building Society v Various Solicitors* (1998) NLJR 241, which held that procuring a loan by deception fell within the exception to professional privilege where the solicitor's advice furthered the deception, even though the solicitor was unaware of the deception.

[45] See also *Derby & Co Ltd v Weldon No 7* [1990] 3 All ER 161 and *Re Konigsberg* [1989] 3 All ER 289.

case clearly thought that they did.[46] In *Barclays Bank v Eustice*, Lord Justice Schiemann was more than happy to carry out what Lord Nicholls in the *Derby* case considered to be the 'impossible task' of evaluating the balance of public interest. He commented:

> I do not consider that the result of . . . the order in the present case will be to discourage straightforward citizens from consulting their lawyers. Those lawyers should tell them that what is proposed is liable to be set aside and the straightforward citizen will then not do it and so the advice will never see the light of day. In so far as those wishing to engage in sharp practice are concerned, the effect of the present decision may well be to discourage them from going to their lawyers. This has the arguable public disadvantage that the lawyers might have dissuaded them from the sharp practice. However, it has the undoubted public advantage that the absence of lawyers will make it more difficult for them to carry out their sharp practice.[47]

In the light of recent notorious city frauds and sharp financial practices, such as those perpetrated by Robert Maxwell and BCCI in the UK and the Enron collapse in the USA, this was a timely warning for both city financiers and their solicitors. It reflects the thinking behind the government's attempts to prevent and detect money-laundering by clients, described in chapter 14.

Exceptions to privilege or confidentiality

Privilege in cases involving children

A controversial field in which legal professional privilege and confidentiality has been considered relates to proceedings under the Children Act 1989. Here, too, the case law is either vague in extent or conflicting. Debates may be had on whether privilege exists at all in Children Act cases[48] or whether they constitute an exception to the normal operation of privilege, and, if the latter, the extent of that exception. The issue has arisen in a number of cases, starting with *Re A*,[49] in which the effect of the 1991 Family Proceedings Rules, rule 4.23 came to be considered. This provides that, with the leave of the court, documents normally confidential can be disclosed to all parties, *Guardians Ad Litem* and welfare officers. In addition, the general policy of the Children Act that the welfare of the child is paramount has encouraged the courts to take the view that all expert reports, whether prepared for the parents, the local authority or any other party and whether or not actually used in evidence, should be disclosed to the parties and the court. Children proceedings are considered not to be adversarial and therefore there is no scope for claiming legal privilege for these reports. This reasoning makes two rather sweeping assumptions: first, that the proceedings are not experienced in reality as adversarial by the parties, especially the parents; and secondly, that privilege is justified only by reason of adversariality.

---

[46] The same view was taken in the CA decision on money laundering, *Bowman v Fels* [2005]ECWA Civ 226.
[47] Above n 44, 525c.
[48] See R Cross and C Tapper, *Cross and Tapper on Evidence* (London, Butterworths, 1995) 494, for a rather sweeping view.
[49] [1991] 2 FLR 473. See also *Essex CC v R* [1994] Fam 167, *Oxfordshire CC v M* [1994] Fam 151.

The justification for privilege is based only partly on adversariality. It is also based on the need to allow free and frank access by a client to his or her lawyer. The need for such access, and the privilege, covers both litigation and non-litigious matters. The courts have, however, created a general rule which denies the protection of legal privilege to experts' reports in Children Act 1989 proceedings, though the precise extent of this rule is not clear. In 1996 in *Re L* the House of Lords had an opportunity to consider the issue. The mother, a drug addict, had, via her solicitor, commissioned a report by a consultant on how her child had come to take methadone. Clearly the consultant thought that it had been administered by the mother, whereas her story was that the child had swallowed it accidentally. The report was disclosed to all parties in the care proceedings under the normal procedures noted above. The police were not parties to the care proceedings but, when they heard of this report's existence (at a case conference), they sought a copy of it with a view to instituting criminal proceedings against the mother. The mother claimed that the report was covered by legal professional privilege, and also the privilege against self-incrimination. She failed. The House of Lords held by a majority that there was a difference between the privilege attaching to solicitor–client communications and to reports by third parties for the purposes of litigation. The former was absolute, but the latter was not covered by privilege in care proceedings under the Children Act, which were non-adversarial and investigative. Moreover, because the documents were not covered by privilege, there was no need for a judge to undertake a balancing act in order to decide whether it was in the public interest to order their disclosure.[50]

Does this mean that a court order is not needed at all before such disclosure? Logically it should not be, but their Lordships were not clear on this point. Lord Jauncy considered whether solicitors have what he called a 'duty' to make a 'voluntary' disclosure of 'all matters likely to be material to the welfare of the child'.[51] There are cases that indicate that no court order is needed,[52] but Lord Jauncy did not find it necessary to decide the issue. He did, however, say that 'this further development of the practice in cases where the welfare of children is involved [may well be] welcomed'.[53] Here he did not appear to be confining himself to reports by third parties but included communications between solicitor and client also.

If it is argued that there is a duty to disclose in these circumstances, what penalty for non-disclosure is proposed? Non-disclosure could be contempt of court only where there is a breach of a court order. Would failure by the solicitor or barrister to disclose amount to professional misconduct? Clearly there are issues here which have not been explored by their Lordships in *Re L* and the law is in need of clarification.

Lord Jauncy gave the sole judgment for the majority in *Re L*. A powerful dissenting judgment was given by Lord Nicholls, with which Lord Mustill agreed. Lord Nicholl's basic point was that it is nowhere clearly spelled out in the Children Act that legal professional privilege is abrogated and its abrogation cannot be implied from the welfare principle in section 1. This principle, in any case, considerably predates the passing of the Act in 1989,

---

[50] See Lord Jauncy in *Re L*, note 32, 87j.
[51] *Ibid*, 86e.
[52] Eg *Re R* [1994] Fam 167; *Re DH* [1994] 1 FLR 679.
[53] *Re L*, above n 32, 97b.

and it had not been suggested that the privilege did not apply before 1989. If the Children Act had abrogated privilege, then the Family Proceedings Rules 1991, rule 4.23 on disclosure of evidence would not have been required. Lord Nicholls denied that privilege can be split into solicitor and client privilege (which he calls legal advice privilege) and 'litigation privilege' covering third party reports: both are equally privileged. The decision of the majority in *Re L* was contrary to the decision of the House in the *Derby Magistrates* case. But the most fundamental reason for Lord Nicholl's dissent is the importance of the doctrine of legal professional privilege. Parties to family proceedings are also entitled to a fair hearing and the same safeguards enjoyed by parties to other proceedings, and

> it must be doubtful whether a parent who is denied the opportunity to obtain legal advice in confidence is accorded the fair hearing to which he is entitled under Article 6(1), read in conjunction with Article 8, of the European Convention of Human Rights.[54]

This is, of course, a dissenting judgment, but it clearly illustrates the competing issues of public policy that have to be considered.

What advice is given to solicitors by the Law Society on this matter? In *Disclosure of Reports in Childrens' Cases* (1994) the Law Society advised solicitors to consider carefully with their client whether or not to commission an expert's report in the light of the duty to disclose it and the possibility that it might be adverse. It is essential that solicitors obtain all existing medical reports and information before deciding to commission another report, and also ensure that the expert instructed is fully informed. In the guidance to the 2007 Code, rule 4 it is stated that there is a duty to reveal experts' reports as they are not privileged, but that 'the position in relation to the voluntary disclosure of other documents or solicitor client communication is uncertain'.[55] The solicitor is reminded of the general duty not to mislead the court. The rule also encourages the solicitor to get the client to agree to disclosure on the ground that this will enable the solicitor to do a better job, and suggests that failure to reveal adverse information may result in the solicitor being subject to 'severe criticism' by the court! It advises the solicitor to withdraw from the case if the client will not give authority to disclose all relevant information if to carry on would result in a breach of the obligation to the court. Whether the rule in *Re L* covers private, as well as public, proceedings involving children is also unclear. Certainly the justification for the *Re L* rule, that the proceedings are not adversarial, can also be used in private cases.

The Law Society's advice to solicitors does not address what to tell the client about confidentiality in child cases. Arguably the client should be told at the outset that their experts' reports and other information may be revealed to the court and to the police even if not used in the litigation by the client. In other words, confidentiality has very limited scope in these cases. If a solicitor becomes aware that a client (or anyone else) is harming a child sexually or otherwise physically, then, whether that information comes from the child as client or from an adult, the solicitor should 'consider revealing the confidential information to an appropriate authority'. However, the solicitor must be satisfied that the harm is 'sufficiently serious to justify a breach of confidentiality'.[56] A report can, but does not have to be,

---

54 *Ibid*, 90h.
55 Solicitors' Code of Conduct 2007, r 4.02 guidance, para 15.

made to Social Services or the police in these circumstances, but note 'non-serious' abuse is excepted.

Many jurisdictions in the US have 'reporting' statutes in relation to child abuse which require professionals, including lawyers, to break confidence and inform the authorities where they have reason to suspect child abuse. There are no such statutory provisions in this country. The 1999 guidance stated:

> Only in cases where the solicitor believes that the public interest in protecting children out-weighs the public interest in maintaining the duty of confidentiality could the solicitor have a discretion to disclose confidential information.

This very cautious balancing approach is not repeated in the 2007 guidance. These are obviously disclosures made in the public interest, discussed in more detail below.

Disclosure in the public interest

Here we are concerned with an exception to the duty of confidence only, not to privilege. Most professional codes relating to confidence permit breaking it where it would be in the public interest. For example, doctors can breach confidentiality under this head where secrecy would cause serious harm to anyone.[57] The main problem is defining public interest. In an English case concerning a doctor, W v Egdell,[58] the need to protect public safety prevailed over the public interest in confidentiality. Doctor Egdell had prepared a report on W, a patient detained under the mental health legislation, for W's solicitor for the purposes of a hearing before a Mental Health Review Tribunal (MHRT). Dr Egdell strongly opposed W's release from a mental hospital because he considered him to be a danger to the public. W decided to abandon his application to the MHRT in the light of this report and accordingly it was not revealed to the tribunal. Dr Egdell was concerned that the hospital had not been given his report and might release W voluntarily, so he sent it to them, and also to the Secretary of State.[59] W applied for an injunction to restrain further disclosure of the report and also for damages for breach of confidence. He lost. The court held that the public interest required disclosure.[60] A doctor who fears that such a decision will be made on the basis of inadequate information is justified in breaking a confidential relationship.[61]

It has long been accepted that a lawyer can break a client's confidence in order to prevent the commission of certain serious crimes. The Law Society's 1999 Guide advised that where the solicitor is being 'used by the client to facilitate the commission of a crime or fraud' the

---

[56] *Ibid*, para 14.

[57] General Medical Council, *Confidentiality* (London, General Medical Council, 1995). See also the American case of *Tarasoff v Regents of the University of California* (1976) 131 Cal Rpter 14.

[58] [1990] 1 All ER 835.

[59] It should be noted that W had already committed murders and the authorities needed to be sure there was no risk of repetition.

[60] It was accepted by counsel that legal professional privilege did not arise in this case (*ibid*, 846b). The question had been argued in the court below and Scott J had found that expert evidence was evidence of fact and therefore not subject to legal professional privilege. For a criticism of this finding, see McHale, above n 36, 719.

[61] See *W v Egdell*, above n 58, *per* Bingham LJ, 852–3.

solicitor is not bound by confidentiality.[62] This is, of course, in accord with the definition of privilege under PACE. Solicitors are also advised that they can reveal information to prevent the client 'or a third party' from committing a crime where the solicitor has reasonable grounds for believing that it will lead to 'serious bodily harm'. The guidance to the 2007 Code states that solicitors may reveal confidential information if they

> believe it necessary to prevent the client or a third party from committing a crime that [they] reasonably believe is likely to result in serious bodily harm.[63]

Solicitors, therefore, are advised that they may not break confidence and reveal anticipated crimes which do not involve serious bodily harm.[64] The guidance is not totally clear: would it be sufficient, for example, if bodily injury was not the intended purpose of the crime but an incidental risk, for example, in an armed robbery? The solicitor is bound by confidentiality where the client reveals past criminality, however heinous, but is of course restricted in the way he or she may represent that client in relation to that crime.[65] This guidance does not extend to material covered by legal privilege. A solicitor would therefore be in breach of privilege if he or she revealed privileged information in order to prevent a serious harm to another (for example, to prevent an innocent person serving a term of imprisonment). However, it must be remembered that if the anticipated harm amounts to furthering a criminal purpose, then privilege does not exist.

Does the above advice on confidentiality extend to the situation where what is feared is a public danger which may not involve the commission of a crime? Suppose, for example, a client tells a solicitor that he knows that a building owned by his adversary is seriously unsafe but he does not want the information revealed to anyone for tactical reasons connected with the litigation. Should, or may, the solicitor reveal this information in the interest of public safety? The *Derby Magistrates* case, which as we have seen takes a robust 'no exceptions' approach to legal privilege, would suggest that the information should not be revealed. But if the case of *Egdell* is to be extended to solicitors, then the courts might well accept the argument that

> as a matter of public policy . . . the solicitor ought to be entitled, without either being liable to action by his client or to a charge of professional misconduct, to take the necessary steps in the public interest to prevent death or serious injury.[66]

The solicitor does not have an obligation to reveal information to prevent the commission of a crime; he or she may do so. The exception to this is in the money-laundering legislation dealt with in chapter 14, and also in the Terrorism Act 2000.[67] This states that a person who has information which he 'knows or believes might be of material assistance' in either preventing an act of terrorism or securing the apprehension of a person who has committed

---

[62] *Law Society Guide to Professional Conduct of Solicitors* (8th edn, 1999) principle 16.02, para 1, 325.

[63] R 4.02 guidance, para 13.

[64] The US Model Rules extends this to 'substantial injury to the financial interests or property of another'. See r 1.6.

[65] See chapter 19 on this issue in relation to advocacy.

[66] M Brindle and G Dehn, 'Confidence, Public Interest and the Lawyer' in Cranston, above n 13, 122.

[67] S 38B. Two other sections, 19 and 21A, are also specifically stated not to cover privileged information. See Anti-Terrorism Practice Note issued by the Law Society, July 2007.

such an act must reveal it. It is an offence not to do so, so the solicitor has an obligation to reveal it. The advice of the Law Society is that this only applies to solicitors where the information is not covered by privilege. Where it is not, but is covered only by the ordinary rules relating to confidentiality, the solicitor must reveal it or be guilty of an offence. Confidentiality will not be a defence. Normally such confidences can be revealed only to those having a legitimate interest in receiving the information, which would include the police or other relevant enforcement authority, and also the intended victim. Gossiping in the pub about it or informing a tabloid newspaper would not be a disclosure in the public interest.

Where a statute, court or warrant requires the release of confidential information, then the solicitor must comply, but if the solicitor considers that the order or warrant can be challenged legally he or she should discuss with the client the possibility of getting it set aside. In any event, the solicitor should take care to reveal only the information required by the law.[68] This does not apply where the solicitor decides to inform in order to prevent a crime from being committed. Various other exceptions to confidentiality rules are dealt with elsewhere. Money laundering is dealt with in chapter 14. There are now elaborate rules under which lawyers (and many others, such as bank officials and accountants) are obliged to inform the relevant authorities if they suspect a client of laundering the proceeds of crime. This is done without client consent, and the lawyer must not, in certain circumstances, even inform their client that they are going to do this as it may amount to the crime of tipping off. This is clearly a major exception to the confidentiality rules. A proposed exception, requiring disclosure of tax avoidance schemes in advance to the Inland Revenue, has been largely successfully opposed by lawyers and is also dealt with in chapter 14. Required disclosure to the Legal Services Commission, involving exceptions to both confidentiality and privilege, although ostensibly with the consent of the client, is dealt with in chapter 13.

Freedom of Information Act 2000

Under this Act the public has a right of access to certain information held by public authorities, including central and local government, the National Health Service, the police and education authorities, and similar. There are, of course, exemptions, classified as either absolute or qualified exemptions. Where the exemption is qualified, then a balance must be struck between the public interest in maintaining confidence and that of disclosure. The Act treats information held under a legal duty of confidence differently from that covered by legal professional privilege. If disclosure would amount to an actionable breach of confidence, then it is covered by an absolute exemption. However, if it is covered by privilege, it enjoys only qualified exemption.[69] Therefore the privileged material relating to a public authority must be revealed if the public interest in this outweighs the public interest in keeping it confidential. This appears to be the only exception to legal professional privilege on the general ground of public interest recognised by the law. It must be emphasised that it applies only to information held by public bodies, not private lawyers' offices.

---

[68] Guidance to r 4, paras 16 and 17.
[69] See the Act, ss 41 and 42.

Client/solicitor litigation

Where the client sues the solicitor, then confidentiality vanishes in that the solicitor can reveal confidential information from the client in order to establish a defence. This also covers the investigation of a complaint against the solicitor and proceedings of the Solicitors Disciplinary Tribunal.[70] A justification put forward for this in the 1996 edition of the Law Society Guide is not that it constitutes an exception to confidentiality or privilege, but that the client has impliedly waived them. This justification could not therefore apply where the solicitor initiated the proceedings against the client, as where the client is sued by the solicitor for fees.

An example of the operation of these rules is *Lillicrap v Nalder & Son*.[71] The plaintiffs were property developers for whom the defendant solicitors had acted in a number of purchases. In relation to one of them, the plaintiff alleged that the solicitors had been negligent in failing to tell them of a right of way over the land. The solicitors admitted negligence but maintained that the plaintiffs would have gone ahead with the purchase anyway. They sought to base this contention on evidence that in six other transactions in which they had acted for the plaintiffs they had bought property despite having been told of various risks. The plaintiffs considered that this evidence was covered by legal privilege and sought delivery up of the relevant documentation. On appeal it was held that, once the client had instituted proceedings against the solicitors, they had impliedly waived privilege in relation to all documents relevant to the suit.

Waiver

It follows from the previous section that the client can waive his or her right of confidentiality or privilege. Where this is done by the client in the context of a conflict of interest with another client, then the new rules require informed consent to prevent exploitation of the first client.[72] The rules relating to the client's consent are quite strict, and are laid down in rule 4.04. The new client must know that the firm holds relevant information that it cannot disclose, both clients must agree to the conditions under which it is proposed to act, the firm must reasonably believe that they understand the issues and it must be reasonable in all the circumstances so to act. This rule can therefore apply only to 'sophisticated' clients. A firm may continue to act for an existing client under rule 4.05 where a conflict between the duty of confidentiality and that of disclosure arises without consent from the client protected by confidentiality but only if it is impossible to get their consent and it is reasonable so to act. This might occur where two firms merge and the client is either physically unable to consent or cannot be traced. It could also occur where there are sufficient information barriers between the two clients, known as Chinese walls, which were discussed in chapter 10.

Waivers should normally therefore be made expressly, but implied waivers can also arise, such as where the client sues the solicitor, as noted above. Where privileged documents are given to the other side's solicitor, then the privilege will normally have been impliedly

---

[70] Solicitors' Code of Conduct 2007, r 4 guidance, para 19.
[71] [1993] 1 All ER 724 CA.
[72] See further chapter 10 on conflict of interest at p 201.

waived. However, if the documents have been provided by accident or mistake, there is no implied waiver. If, therefore, a solicitor acquires information from the other side which is clearly confidential and came by mistake, then the information must be returned and cannot be used in litigation.[73] This rule must also extend to confidential information that was unlawfully acquired by the client, for to use it would be to profit from the commission of a crime. A case illustrating this involved the solicitors who advised Andrew Regan in his attempt to take over the Cooperative Wholesale Society in April 1997. Stolen documents which were privileged were allegedly used by the solicitors in preparing the predatory takeover. This is not only unethical, but also probably unlawful.[74]

The law on waiver of privilege as opposed to confidentiality is complex and reference should be made to texts on evidence for the detail. In general, once privilege in relation to a document is waived, the privilege in relation to the whole document is waived; the client cannot 'edit' it.[75] However, it is possible to waive privilege in a document for one purpose but retain it in relation to all other purposes.[76] The client's reasons for such limited disclosure are irrelevant. A client can also decide to waive privilege over some documents but not others, but this waiver is subject to a general condition that such partial waiver must be fair. For example, where the documents relate to the same issue and are not severable, then waiver of one may lead the court to order the discovery of the other:

> to allow an individual item to be plucked out of context would be to risk injustice through its real weight or meaning being misunderstood.[77]

Where a report of an expert witness has been given to the other side and the litigation privilege in it thereby waived, then privilege in any background material referred to in the report is also waived. This was held to be the case in *Clough v Thameside and Glossop Health Authority*, where Mrs Justice Bracewell stressed that her decision was also based on the need to make the litigation process more open, in the light of the Woolf Report:

> Although civil litigation is adversarial, it is not permissible to withhold relevant information, nor to delete nor amend the documents of a report before disclosure, as was submitted . . . to be the practice of some firms of solicitors.[78]

At what point in the proceedings is the other party entitled to the additional related documents where there has already been partial disclosure? There is some confusion here. Some authorities consider that the additional documents are not discoverable until those originally waived have been used in court. Others consider this rule illogical. The most recent decision follows the latter line. In *R v Secretary of State for Transport and Factortame and*

---

[73] See Solicitors' Code of Conduct 2007, r 4 guidance, para 21(c). Note also that waiver cannot be implied where documents are handed to the police in order to assist a criminal investigation: *British Coal Corp v Dennis Rye Ltd* [1988] 3 All ER 816. Merely mentioning a privileged document in a witness statement does not automatically mean that privilege is waived: *Expandable v Rubin* [2008] EWCA Civ 59.

[74] See *The Lawyer*, 6 May 1997, 7.

[75] See Keane, above n 38, 537. See also Cross and Tapper, above n 48, 474.

[76] See *B v Auckland District Law Society* [2004] 4 All ER 269.

[77] Mustill J in *Nea Kateria Maritime Co Ltd v Atlantic and Great Lakes Steam-Ship Corp* [1981] Comm LR 138. See C Passmore, 'The Dangers of Waiving Privilege' (1997) 147 *New Law Journal*, 931.

[78] *Clough v Thameside and Glossop Health Authority* [1998] 2 All ER 971, 977.

Others, Auld LJ decided that the additional discovery could be ordered as soon as the documents in relation to which privilege was waived were disclosed.[79] Waiver of confidentiality clearly can sometimes result from the operation of law and is not dependent on either the express or implied consent of the client. In *R v Bowden*[80] the defendant client's counsel cross-examined a police witness for the prosecution in order to establish that the client's silence on police questioning had been on legal advice. It was held that, as a consequence, legal privilege was waived. This waiver was said to be voluntary, but this must be regarded as something of a legal fiction.

Joint retainers

As already noted, where two or more clients jointly instruct a solicitor then all information in relation to that transaction must be given to all of the clients; one cannot claim confidentiality in respect of the other.[81] This is not strictly an exception to the doctrine of confidentiality, but it may appear to be so to the client. In some circumstances they may regret information being given to a co-client, as in *Re Konigsberg*, discussed below. As noted in chapter 10 in relation to conflict of interest, there have been a number of cases on the duty of solicitors to inform a mortgagee of a change in the mortgagor's circumstances where both are being represented by the same solicitor. All joint clients must waive their rights before any confidential information is given to a third party.[82]

Insolvency and bankruptcy

The problem of precisely who is the client, and therefore to whom the duty of confidentiality is owed, can be confusing in the case of corporate or other group clients. Where the solicitor acts (or has acted) for a company, as opposed to an individual director, and the company becomes insolvent, how much information should the solicitor give to the liquidator or similar person? The liquidator has extensive duties and powers to collect information about the company's business dealings and is, in effect, in the same position as the company itself in relation to this information. Liquidator and company are regarded as being the same person. Therefore, the solicitor for the company should provide all the information in his or her possession to the liquidator. This is not, in theory, an exception to these doctrines because of the special status of the liquidator.

Similarly, where an individual client becomes bankrupt, there is an obligation to hand over all the bankrupt's property, including papers and records relating to his estate and affairs, to the trustee in bankruptcy. This can apply to confidential or privileged communications with a solicitor.[83] Again, in theory this does not amount to an exception to confidence or privilege because the trustee in bankruptcy is in the position of the bankrupt. However, this is theory rather than practice. In reality, the bankrupt and the trustee often do

---

[79] *The Times*, 11 September 1997; Passmore, above n 77.
[80] [1999] 4 All ER 43.
[81] *Hilton v Barker Booth & Eastwood* [2005] UKHL 8.
[82] *Buttes Gas & Oil Co v Hammer No 3* [1981] QB 223 CA.
[83] Insolvency Act 1986, s 311.

not have identical interests. The rules in the Insolvency Act are therefore better thought of as exceptions to confidentiality. The guidance to rule 4 impliedly recognises this by advising that solicitors should ensure 'that any disclosure you make is strictly limited to what is required by the law'.[84] This reality is clearly illustrated in the case of *Re Konigsberg*.[85] Mr and Mrs Konigsberg jointly consulted a solicitor in order to transfer property from the husband to the wife. The husband subsequently became bankrupt and the trustee sought to set aside the transfer as being a voluntary settlement and therefore void as against the trustee under the Bankruptcy Act. Mrs Konigsberg objected to the solicitor giving evidence to the trustee on the nature of the transfer on the ground that this information was a communication between solicitor and client and therefore covered by legal privilege. It was held that the communication was properly available to both clients as the solicitor was jointly retained by them. The Trustee in Bankruptcy had to be treated as being in the same position as the bankrupt client and therefore no assertion of legal privilege could be made to prevent his receipt of the communication. A trustee in bankruptcy, said Mr Justice Peter Gibson, 'is no ordinary third party'. All the assets of the bankrupt are vested in him and, as a successor in title, he 'stands in the predecessor's shoes'.[86]

Conclusion

Legal professional privilege and aspects of the doctrine of confidentiality are under increasing attack. Two main justifications for the attack are put forward. The first, made in particular in proceedings relating to children, is that where the proceedings are not really adversarial there is no need to maintain legal privilege. If the non-adversariality of the proceedings alone justifies an abandonment of legal privilege, then it could also apply to many other types of proceeding, for example some tribunal cases, mediations or arbitrations. Lord Woolf's proposals in relation to civil litigation were aimed at reducing the adversarial ethos more generally. These reforms may well justify reducing the scope of professional privilege. Does it have any justification where litigation is not involved at all or where a solicitor is providing services similar to those in the *Three Rivers* case? If it is justifiable only where legal advice is being provided in the context of adversarial litigation, how are these terms to be defined and how can such a rule be reconciled with the idea that privilege is an aspect of the right to privacy and protected under ECHR, Article 8?

The second justification for attacking privilege is the need to protect the public interest. Privilege may, in some cases, have to give way to the need to protect the welfare of a child or the prevention or detection of crimes. The speedy development of the money-laundering legislation to cover all proceeds of crime shows that the government desires to constrain confidentiality in the public interest and, in effect, requires lawyers to act as gatekeepers in order to assist in the detection of this crime. But how far should this be extended? In the case of the money-laundering provisions, there is an additional matter to be taken into account. Money laundering can often be effected only if 'the launderer' engages the services

---

[84] Solicitors' Code of Conduct 2007, r 4 guidance, para 8.
[85] [1989] 3 All ER 289.
[86] *Ibid*, 297a.

of a lawyer under the cloak of secrecy provided by professional privilege. The privilege is therefore being used to allow the client to benefit from the proceeds of his or her unlawful acts and not simply to prepare a defence by being frank with his or her lawyer. How far should this idea be extended? Should it apply where a client asks the solicitor to undertake acts which are unlawful in the civil sense, such as transferring funds from a pension fund unlawfully or assisting with the commission of a tort or breach of trust?[87]

As we have seen, professional privilege, although it may 'belong' to the client, is in fact a valuable commodity that only a lawyer can deliver to a client. It is arguable that society allows this in return for a guarantee of high professional and ethical standards from lawyers when advising clients. Those who argue that lawyers are now simply commercial entrepreneurs and should not be expected to adhere to professional or ethical norms over and above the ordinary law must accept that this argument also undermines the case for privilege. Put at its lowest level, the commercial interests of the profession demand ethical behaviour. Otherwise, this valuable commodity, legal professional privilege, will be lost. This, then, is perhaps a prime example of why the legal profession cannot afford to surrender a claim to ethicality. It is in its own interests as well as providing a protection for clients.

---

[87] Further ideas on the reform of the doctrine con be found in Nicolson and Webb, above n 10, 263*ff.* See also chapter 14 on duties to collective third parties, and in particular in relation to corporate collapses such as that of Enron in the US.

12

FEES

There are three golden rules in the profession [criminal law] . . . the first . . . thoroughly terrify your client. Second, find out how much money he has and where it is. Third, get it. The merest duffer can usually succeed in following out the first two of these precepts, but to accomplish the third requires often a master's art. The ability actually to get one's hands on the coin is what differentiates the really great criminal lawyer from his inconspicuous brethren.[1]

Introduction

Fees are central to the relationship of lawyer and client, including the conditions under which they are negotiated and charged. In most professional relationships the client is often unable to evaluate the amount or type of work that needs to be done. It is essential, if the client's interests are to be protected and prioritised, that there is effective control against overcharging. A separate issue is that of doing more work than is necessary given the nature or value of the case (sometimes known as 'churning'). Even the sophisticated corporate client may find this difficult to control. These issues cannot be left to the operation of the market. Fees are an ethical issue because, in Schaffer's words,

> The distinctive feature of ethics in a profession is that it speaks to the unequal encounter of two moral persons. Legal ethics . . . becomes the study [for lawyers] of what is good . . . for this other person, over whom I have power.[2]

In the context of charging fees, the lawyer has power because he or she has knowledge of the likely costs and benefits of any proposed course of action and the client is, at least relatively, ignorant of this.

Background

Fees and costs are a longstanding[3] and common bar to justice,[4] a basic constitutional right

---

[1] A Train, *The Confessions of Artemas Quibble* (New York, Scribners, 1926) 77.

[2] TL Schaffer, 'Legal Ethics and the Good Client' (1987) 36 *Catholic Universiy Law Review* 319.

[3] M Cook, in *Cook on Costs* (Butterworths, 2001–2002) 77, points out that legislation attempting to control lawyers' costs go back to 1605.

[4] Costs are not only a problem in the UK. In the US George W Bush actually made the issue part of his presidential campaign, saying that 'avarice among many plaintiffs' lawyers has clogged our civil courts' and advocating a

that can be abrogated only by express provision in an Act of Parliament.[5] Lord Woolf was sceptical that controlling costs is a central concern of the profession, concluding in his review of civil justice that 'the present system provides higher benefits to lawyers than to their clients'.[6] The Civil Procedure Rules (CPR) embody his vision of a regime where costs are proportionate to the nature and value of the case.[7] This reflects the fact that complaints about lawyers' charges are among the most common of all complaints received by the Legal Complaints Service and the Legal Services Ombudsman. The latter, in his Report for 1995, specifically noted that legal fees were soaring and that clients generally lacked adequate information. As an example, he gave the case of a builder who lost an action to recover £9,800 and in so doing incurred costs of £26,000, including an expert's fee, to which he had not agreed, of £5,000.[8] In his 1996 Report the Ombudsman noted 'almost wistfully' that he had dealt with solicitors' costs in every annual report since 1991 and that, six years later, 'lack of adequate costs information remains a staple of my work diet'.[9] Once again, in the 2003–4 Report the Ombudsman noted that many complaints concerned cost and that many clients 'complain that they received no cost estimate at all or did not receive a cost estimate in writing'.[10]

Despite their importance, remarkably little attention has been given to fees in texts on legal ethics other than in relation to the perennial debate over contingency fees.[11] The 1999 Law Society Guide provided a fairly brief 40 pages on the topic, including all annexes, containing little that could be described as general principles of an ethical nature. Significantly, the first 'general principle' dealt with in the relevant chapter (14.01) was the power of solicitors to 'require' payments on account from clients! Similarly, the Bar Code says little about fees in relation to clients except to state that a barrister may charge on any basis or by any method he thinks fit.[12] In reality, both the current law and the guidance is more

---

clients' bill of rights on the issue. See HM Kritzer, 'The Fracturing Legal Profession: the Case of Plaintiffs' Personal Injury Lawyers' (2001) 8 *International Journal of the Legal Profession* 225.

[5] *R v Lord Chancellor, ex parte Witham* [1997] 2 All ER 779, where the Lord Chancellor's order withdrawing exemption from court fees to those on income support was declared ultra vires because there was no specific provision in the relevant enabling Act permitting this.

[6] Lord Woolf, *Access to Justice: Interim Report to the Lord Chancellor on the Civil Justice System in England and Wales* (London, Lord Chancellor's Department, 1995) 13. See also P Abrams, A Boon and D O'Brien, 'Access to Justice: The Collision of Funding and Ethics' (1998) 3 *Contemporary Issues in Law* 59.

[7] CPR 2007, r 1.1 states the 'overriding objective' of the rules as being to enable the court to deal with cases justly, and this means that as far as practicable saving expense, putting the parties on an equal footing and dealing with cases proportionately, bearing in mind costs and the financial position of the parties.

[8] Fees were the problem in relation to a major scandal known as the 'Glanville Davies affair', in which the Law Society complaints machinery failed for a long time to deal with an overcharge by the solicitor of £130,000. This was dealt with only after much litigation, a report by the lay observer and also by the Law Society (the Ely Report) in 1984. More recently the fees overcharged by solicitors acting for miners in relation to the miners' compensation scheme generated 1,000 complaints to the Law Society and required the appointment of a dedicated team to deal with them. Law Society press release, 4 April 2006.

[9] 1996 Report of the Legal Service Ombudsman, HC Paper 24, 14.

[10] Report of the Legal Services Ombudsman 2003–4, *In Whose Interest?* (DCA, July 2004).

[11] Deborah Rhode's text, *Professional Responsibility: Ethics by the Pervasive Method* (Boston, MA, Little Brown, 1994), barely mentions fees, for example.

[12] *Code of Conduct of the Bar of England and Wales* (London, Bar Standards Board, 8th edn, as amended, 2004) (hereafter the Bar Code) para 405. Barristers may not change a fixed fee over a fixed period of time irrespective of the amount of work done, nor may they give or receive commissions or loans from clients or intermediaries or pay referral fees. See para 307.

complex than this implies, but the literature still contains little or no commentary or analysis from the ethical point of view, and no clear statement or explanation of the principles underlying it.

In relation to fees there is an inherent conflict of interest between lawyer and client.[13] The lawyer normally wishes to charge more than the client wants to pay. Given a knowledge imbalance in favour of the lawyer, a few general principles suggest themselves. First, and most obviously, the level of the fees cannot be left solely to market forces or individual agreement. Secondly, the client should give an informed and unpressured consent to any agreement made with the lawyer, whether at the beginning of the case or throughout its progress. Thirdly, the client should be aware of any actual or potential conflicts that may arise in relation to any particular funding mechanism, such as conditional fees or costs insurance. Fourthly, the client should be regularly updated on his or her liability for fees and the amount owed. Fifthly, there should be effective, fair and accessible procedures for reviewing fees so as to rectify overcharging or any failure by the lawyer to abide by the above principles.

Permitted fees

In the past, the Law Society sought to control undercutting of fees by solicitors by enforcing fixed fees linked to the value of the transaction involved, for example, with conveyancing before the 1980s.[14] Otherwise the most usual and accepted method of charging was by the hour, though other methods were not proscribed. Certain types of fee were, however, prohibited, and some of the oldest and most arcane rules of legal professional conduct relate to these prohibitions, which mainly applied to contentious matters. Thus the contingency fee (under which the lawyer is not paid if the case is lost, but gets a percentage of the winnings if it is won) has always been prohibited in the UK under the common law relating to champerty.[15] Speculative fees, where the solicitor agrees to be paid only what the losing side is ordered to pay in costs, and arrangements whereby a client's fees are paid by third parties or even by the solicitor himself, were prohibited or affected by the common law prohibiting maintenance.[16]

The traditional American texts on legal ethics confined their discussion of the ethical implications of fee arrangements to these issues, or

---

[13] This is implicitly recognised by the *Solicitors' Code of Conduct 2007* (London, Solicitors Regulation Authority, 2007) (hereafter Solicitors' Code) r 3.01 guidance, para 52, which states that 'You are free to negotiate your terms of business, including costs, with your clients . . . In all these negotiations you are not acting for the client'.

[14] For an account of the history of the issue, see L Sheinman, 'Ethical Practice or practical Ethics: The Case of the Vendor–Purchaser Rule' (2001) 3 *Legal Ethics* 27. *Ad valoram* fees date back to the 1883 Solicitors' Remuneration Order and Practice Rules passed in 1936, which prevented solicitors from acting at less than scale fees fixed by the court or prevailing in the area where they practised.

[15] For a recent statement of the rule, see *Aratra Potato v Taylor Joynson Garrett* [1995] 4 All ER 695 and *Thai Trading Co v Taylor* [1998] 3 All ER 65, which established that speculative fees were lawful. On champerty, see *Factortame v Secretary of State (No 2)* [2002] 4 All ER 97.

[16] The latter is urging others to litigate. See *Hill v Archbold* [1968] 1 QB 686 and *Shah v Karanjia* [1993] 4 All ER 792.

the mysteries of the Macbethian witches of the common law who stirred the law of despised litigation—maintenance, champerty and barratry.[17]

In the UK they were not only unethical and unenforceable arrangements, they were criminal until the passing of the Criminal Law Act 1967, despite being rendered obsolete by case law long before 1967. The principles of these rules still affect the legality of fee arrangements despite inroads made by the statutory changes which permit conditional fees. However, it is instructive to consider the basic ethical concerns which made maintenance, champerty and barratry illegal and unprofessional.

The laws against maintenance and barratry enshrined the principle that persons with no direct interest in a dispute should not intermeddle and encourage spurious litigation, causing grief and possible financial loss to the other side. The same justification was applied to the law on champerty, because lawyers who handled cases on a no-win, no-fee basis, or who were paid a proportion of the winnings, would have a personal interest in stirring up another's litigation. Indeed, many organisations are devoted to the task of encouraging and enabling others to take legal action, including charitable organisations, pressure groups and bodies like insurance companies, motoring organisations and trade unions. The state is the largest maintainer of litigation of all, through legal aid. Participating in such public service provision, *pro bono publico*, is a mark of professionalism. Nowadays, few people consider maintenance to be unethical; access to justice is a more serious concern.

The laws against maintenance and champerty were also based on the ethical principle against conflicts of interest between a lawyer and client. A lawyer who has a personal investment in the proceeds of the client's litigation has an interest other than the best interests of the client. At first sight this may seem to be a curious view. Surely, it may be argued, the contingency fee arrangement ensures that the lawyer and the client have the same interest, namely, winning the case and maximising the damages recovered. In some cases this may not be so. For example, where the issue of liability is clear, it may be in the client's interest to maximise the amount of damages by negotiating long and hard. The lawyer, however, might want to settle quickly for less because the extra amount that he or she could recover for the client by hard bargaining would not compensate for the extra hours that had to be put in to achieve it.[18] Should the lawyer in this situation be allowed to withdraw from the case if the client refuses to authorise the earlier but lower settlement? Conflict of interest also arises in relation to maintenance. If the lawyer is being paid by a third party, then he or she might owe some allegiance to, or be instructed by, that third party rather than by his client. The profession's resistance to the growth of trade union organised legal expenses insurance plans in the US was publicly justified on this basis. In

---

[17] CW Wolfram, *Modern Legal Ethics* (St Paul, MN, West Publishing, 1986) 489. It is suggested by Luban that the strict control of contingency fees in ethics codes in the US reflects the disdain with which high-status lawyers regarded the methods used by low-status lawyers to get access to clients and the courts; see D Luban, 'Speculating on Justice: The Ethics and Jurisprudence of Contingency Fees' in S Parker and C Sampford (eds), *Legal Ethics and Legal Practice: Contemporary Issues* (Oxford, Clarendon Press, 1995) 114.

[18] The empirical evidence on this in the US seems to indicate that in the smaller cases this is what actually happens; see HM Kritzer, *The Justice Broker: Lawyers and Ordinary Litigation* (New York, Oxford University Press, 1990) 108ff; P Danzon, 'Contingent Fees for Personal Injury Litigation' (1983) 14 *Bell Journal of Economics* 213; L Schwartz and DB Mitchell, 'An Economic Analysis of the Contingent Fee in Personal Injuries Litigation' (1970) 22 *Stanford Law Review* 1125.

England some lawyers resisted the introduction of legal aid in the 1940s and 1950s on the ground that the independence of lawyers to act in their clients' best interests would be compromised by their responsibilities to the legal aid fund.[19]

The ethical objection to champerty is the threat to promote the integrity of the legal process and the lawyer's role as an officer of the court. A personal interest in the outcome of a client's litigation might induce the solicitor to encourage perjury or corruption, or attempt sharp practices, which would corrupt the legal process. Moreover, the higher the percentage taken by the lawyer, the higher the damages that are likely to be awarded, it is alleged, and this is unjust to the losing party. In addition, contingency fees in the US are held responsible for a litigation explosion and defensive practices by manufacturers and service providers, which are assumed to have negative social consequences, such as driving up the cost of goods and services.[20]

The problem with all these arguments is that it is never convincingly explained why the hourly paid lawyer does not also have a personal incentive to take on spurious cases, or to seek to win them by sharp practices. Not only does the lawyer thereby increase his income from the case, he pleases his client, who may then be prepared to pay him larger fees, employ him again and recommend him to friends. Whilst contingency fees may sometimes encourage lawyers to minimise the work they do in order to maximise their gain when the case is settled or won, at least such lawyers have an interest in winning their cases. Hourly paid fees can encourage the lawyer to do unnecessary work in order to increase fees, or simply to work more slowly and inefficiently, confident that he or she will be paid whatever the outcome.

> Experience shows that, given a free reign, lawyers (who are normally paid by the hour) will tend to do too much rather than too little work with not always sufficient regard to the relevance of what they are producing.[21]

The client, presented with a choice between these two types of conflict of interest, might well choose that inherent in the contingency fee system, which at the very least offers an incentive to the lawyer to win the case and obtain a reasonable amount in damages because his fees depend on that.[22]

The main constraint on overworking in the English system is assessment of costs by the court after the event, which is explained in more detail below. This constraint is not adequate in itself, particularly in relation to the vast majority of cases which settle, with the fees being agreed between the lawyers. This is because the lawyers advising the client who is paying the other side's costs have an incentive to recommend payment of high fees so that they can justify charging a similarly high fee for their own work. The continued prohibition of contingency fees is difficult to justify in the light of the introduction of conditional fees

---

[19] B Abel-Smith and R Stevens, *Lawyers and the Courts: A Sociological Study of the English Legal System, 1750–1965* (London, Heinemann, 1967), ch 5, note 343. The block funding and franchising of legal aid proposed by the Conservative and Labour governments has led to the same allegations: see Abrams *et al*, above n 6.

[20] Against which argument see M Galanter, 'The Day After the Litigation Explosion' (1986) 46 *Maryland Law Riview* 3 and Luban, above n 17, 89–126.

[21] Stated, admittedly in a slightly different context, in the Report of the Law Society's Civil Litigation Committee on Multi Party Actions, *Group Actions Made Easier* (London, The Law Society, 1995) 3.

[22] In the US this is exactly the choice made by both individual and institutional plaintiffs. See Wolfram, above n 17, 526.

in 1995, and their expansion in 1998 and 2000.[23] The types of fee arrangement currently lawful and ethically acceptable are now considered.

Hourly or fixed fees

Hourly fees are still the normal fee arrangements in the UK, despite increasingly being under attack, especially in commercial and legally aided cases. The solicitor is paid by the hour for the actual work done. In fairly routine transactions, like conveyancing or making wills, a fixed fee is normally negotiated. There is evidence that large commercial clients now prefer a fixed fee for a particular piece of work rather than hourly rates, as the client is thereby enabled to maintain more control over the work done for them.[24] The Legal Services Commission (LSC) also favours fixed fees for criminal work and now, increasingly, civil legal aid litigation. The method used by the LSC to control costs in civil cases is by contracting—solicitors agree to a contract to do a fixed number of case starts per year for a fixed yearly fee. Since 2000 the CPR have also increasingly introduced fixed costs especially for routine or minor steps in litigation.[25] In addition, the Civil Justice Council aims to negotiate set fees with the major players in certain types of litigation. For example, in personal injury cases agreements are being made with insurers, employers and lawyers relating to levels of success fee in conditional fee cases.[26] Practitioners are generally opposed to fixed fees, apparently on the ground that they result in scrimped work.

Barristers normally quote a fixed fee for a particular advice or piece of drafting and a daily rate for court work. They also, however, are paid fixed fees in some civil work, especially family matters, and in legally aided criminal work.[27] Barristers have traditionally attempted to avoid the problems of conflict of interest inherent in fixing fees by denying any interest in the issue. Their fees were negotiated by their clerks and regarded as 'honoraria', giving rise to no legal liability on either side. This was used, inter alia, to justify the immunity of barristers for liability in negligence for court work.[28] Barristers were given the power to enter into binding contracts under section 61 of the Courts and Legal Services Act 1990, and this is now accepted in the Bar Code.[29]

Clients who are surprised by larger than expected legal bills often fail to appreciate the issue of disbursements. These are the payments made by solicitors to third parties on behalf of their clients, such as stamp duties, registration fees, court fees and witness fees, which are

---

[23] These were introduced in 1995 after the publication of the Government Green Paper, *Contingency Fees*, Cm 571 (1989). This rejected US-style contingency fees on the ground that the litigant would be unable to negotiate meaningfully with the lawyer on them; see para 4.9. Speculative fees were legalised in *Thai Trading Co v Taylor* [1998] 3 All ER 65 and recognised in the Rules on Conditional Fee Agreements (CFAs) in 2000.

[24] See, eg G Hanlon, 'A Profession in Transition' (1997) 60 *Modern Law Review* 798, 813.

[25] See, eg CPR 2007, r 45.1, where fixed costs are listed for fast track litigation, such as £500 for cases worth between £3,000–10,000. They have applied in civil road traffic cases since June 2004 and for accidents at work from October 2000.

[26] See, eg 154 NLJ (18 June 2004).

[27] Indeed, some barristers claim that in some cases they are being paid as little as £15 per hour under legal aid and, in June 2004, for the first time went on strike. A similar strike of solicitors went ahead in 2007.

[28] See B Abel-Smith and R Stevens, *Lawyers and the Courts* (London, Heinemann, 1967) 231 for the debate between the professions in 1876 on this issue. This immunity has now gone; see *Arthur JS Hall & Co (a firm) v Simons, Barratt v Ansell and others (trading as Woolf Seddon (a firm), Harris v Scholfield Roberts & Hill (a firm) and another* [2000] 3 All ER 673.

[29] See Bar Code, above n 12 Annex G2, setting out the contractual terms between barristers and solicitors.

added to the final bill. Most clients would accept that these items should be charged separately, though they often complain that they were not warned about them. It is often not clear to the client whether postage, printing and travel costs are disbursements or simply overheads that should be absorbed in the agreed fee. Whatever charging methods are used, there are now no professional rules restraining lawyers from undercutting each other, as existed in the mid-1930s for solicitors. In 1996, Martin Mears, a past president of the Law Society, wanted these rules restored in relation to conveyancing charges, but the Law Society Council managed to avoid making a decision on his proposal.[30] Clearly, undercutting is not an ethical issue but relates to the desire of the profession to maximise its income. Some lawyers claim that the possibility of undercutting encourages 'fee shopping' and low standards of work, and is therefore a proper issue for professional codes of conduct. Similarly, low rates of pay for LSC funded work can make it difficult for lawyers to act in the best interests of the client unless they are prepared to do unpaid work.

Overcharging is, however, more of a problem than undercharging. There is considerable pressure from commercial clients, and also institutional funders like the LSC and insurance companies, for fixed rather than hourly fees. This is aimed at controlling both overwork and overbilling, which many institutions, including the judiciary, see as endemic.[31] Hourly charging encourages inefficiency as well as overcharging. Richard Susskind has even suggested that lawyers will be 'reluctant to become too efficient with technology until there is a move beyond the billable hour'.[32] The reluctance of lawyers to abandon the billable hour was illustrated in 1993, when the Law Society challenged, by judicial review, the decision of the Lord Chancellor to introduce standard fees in legally aided criminal cases. The case was lost. Fees can, of course, be controlled by assessment by the court and other mechanisms, but at some cost and uncertainty.

Conditional and contingency fees

Contingency fees are arrangements whereby the lawyer is paid a fee by the client only if the case is won, in which case the fee will be a percentage of the amount recovered. As already noted, such arrangements, in relation to contentious business, are still unlawful under the common law against champerty and section 59(2) of the Solicitors' Act 1974.[33] As also noted

---

[30] See *The Lawyer*, 19 March 1996, 2.

[31] See, eg *The Guardian*, 18 November 1996. As long ago as 1993, a solicitor in a legal expenses insurance group made a plea for more fixed fees in litigation: *The Lawyer*, 18 May 1993, 12. Lord Woolf also saw fixed fees as essential to the success of his proposed 'fast track' procedure for civil cases up to £10,000. There are already many fixed fees in relation to criminal work, introduced in the teeth of lawyer opposition during the 1980s and 1990s. Large corporate clients now produce detailed codes regulating their relationship with their lawyers. See, eg Lloyds of London, whose code requires lawyers to justify their fees and give advance warning of bills. Lloyds Underwriters are concerned about overmanning in solicitors' firms. See *Law Society Gazette*, 1 July 1998, 9.

[32] R Susskind, *The Future of Law: Facing the Challenges of Information Technology* (New York, Oxford University Press, 1996) 173.

[33] They are also banned under the Solicitors' Code of Conduct 2007, r 2.04 'except as permitted by Statute or the Common Law'. Contingent fees are allowed in respect of non-contentious business, including debt collecting. They are also allowed in employment cases before employment tribunals. See J Levin, 'Solicitors Acting Speculatively and Pro Bono' (1996) 15 *Civil Justice Quarterly* 44, 47 and *Bevan Ashford v Yeandle* [1999] Ch 239. Speculative fees are now lawful in England and Wales: *Thai Trading v Taylor* [1998] 3 All ER 65 and under the regulations covering conditional fees.

above, the ethical principle advanced for this rule is the prevention of conflicts of interest between lawyer and client and to uphold probity in court proceedings by lawyers.[34] The consequences of charging an unlawful contingency fee are, first, that the solicitor will not recover the fee, or even disbursements, from the client.[35] If, however, the client has already paid money over to the solicitor, it cannot be reclaimed, the agreement being unenforceable rather than void or voidable.[36] The loss of champertous fees is not insurable.[37] More serious for solicitors is that they may find themselves liable for the costs of the other side if the case is lost, as occurred in the case of *McFarlane v EE Caledonia*.[38] If the case is won, the question of a costs order against the loser arises. Here there is no direct authority, but it is arguable that, if the liability for costs between solicitor and client is unenforceable, then there is no basis for ordering the losing party to pay such costs unless they have already been paid by the client, as in the *Aratra Potato* case cited above. In addition, the solicitor could be subject to disciplinary proceedings.

The most significant exception to the rules forbidding contingency fees is contained in section 58 of the Courts and Legal Services Act 1990, which legalised conditional fees and came into force in 1995.[39] Under a conditional fee agreement (CFA) solicitors and barristers can agree with the client that a fee will be payable only if the case is won. But, if the case is won, the fee may be increased by up to 100% of the normal fee (known as a success fee), excluding disbursements. Initially these agreements could be made in three types of cases only: actions for personal injury; actions relating to winding up companies or in bankruptcy proceedings; and actions before the European Commission or Court of Human Rights.[40] From July 1998 conditional fees were extended to all civil actions other than matrimonial cases.[41] This coincided with the withdrawal of legal aid in personal injury cases, with the exception of medical negligence. They cannot be used in criminal cases.

Where the case is lost the client will not pay a lawyer's fee but will normally have to pay the disbursements—which can be considerable, especially where expert witnesses are used—and he will normally have to bear the costs of any insurance policy covering the litigation that he had taken out. The losing client is also usually ordered to pay the costs of the winner. When the new CFA law was originally introduced in 1995 the client would have to pay some fees even where the case was won—the lawyer's success fee and also the costs of any insurance he had taken out as these were not recoverable in costs from the other side. It was not surprising, therefore, that the Law Society did not like to use the expression 'no win, no fee' to describe conditional fees. It also meant that clients were hesitant about using the

---

[34] In the US the term 'contingency fee' also covers percentage uplifted fees (our conditional fee) and speculative fees; a US contingency fee is a no win, no fee arrangement of any kind.

[35] *Re Trepca Mines* [1963] Ch 199; *Wild v Simpson* [1919] 2 KB 544. For further details see Levin above n 33.

[36] *Aratra Potato*, above n 15.

[37] *Haseldine v Hosken* [1933] 1 KB 822.

[38] [1995] 1 WLR 366.

[39] As amended by the Access to Justice Act 1999, ss 27 and 29. See now the Solicitors' Code of Conduct 2007, r 2.03(2). For a full analysis of the law, see M Napier and F Bawdon, *Conditional Fees, a Survival Guide* (London, The Law Society, 1995).

[40] Conditional fees cover court proceedings and litigation services generally. The Courts and Legal Services Act 1990, s 58 does not extend to arbitrations, but it has been held, in *Bevan Ashford*, above n 34, that there is no public policy objection to conditional fees in arbitrations in cases similar to those covered by the Act.

[41] Conditional Fees Order 1998, SI 98/1860.

new conditional fees, which were not only complex[42] but also did not always protect them against expenses when the case was won, let alone when it was lost. The prospect of paying the other side's costs was just as much a disincentive to a client as having to pay his own lawyer would have been. It seemed initially that access to justice was not greatly advanced by conditional fees.

The government's determination that conditional fees be successful was fuelled by the desire to abolish legal aid in personal injury cases. The Access to Justice Act 1999 was therefore passed to allow the success fee and the cost of an insurance premium to be recovered in costs from the other side if the case was won. The successful CFA litigant therefore was protected from most costs, and any that might continue to be payable could be easily paid from the damages recovered. The statute and the rules prescribed in some detail what information about the CFA had to be given to the client before the agreement was made, but most clients did not understand it and, in any case, were not interested in it as they were now unlikely to have to pay any of the costs. As Lord Nicholls remarked, CFA 'claimants now operate in a costs-free and risk-free zone',[43] which he said caused him serious concern. Control of costs in these cases now passed to the losing defendant in assessment proceedings and this led to a considerable amount of costs litigation.

The problem of liability for the other side's costs where the CFA client lost the case was 'solved' not by the government but by the insurance industry. Litigants could take out insurance to cover the possibility of being ordered to pay the other side's costs. The first commonly used insurance was arranged by the Law Society itself, and was known as Accident Direct. Clients were offered insurance cover at a reasonably modest premium for their personal injury (PI) cases provided their solicitor agreed to insure all his PI cases with Accident Direct. The policy would also cover the client's disbursements where they were not paid by the other side on winning the case.

Many still disapprove of conditional (and contingency) fees and would agree with Lord Ackner's observation in the House of Lords debate that

the lawyer with a financial stake in the outcome of litigation has a concern to win the case which may distort the advice he gives and may even tempt him into unethical conduct.[44]

Lord Allen, a non-lawyer, put the contrary view, that they look

rather different if one is just an ordinary person who is not poor enough for legal aid and not rich enough to embark upon litigation with equanimity . . . To people like me it seems that at last there is some prospect of access to justice becoming more open.[45]

The development of conditional fees permitted by the 1999 Access to Justice Act, combined with the abolition of legal aid in personal injury cases, opened up great commercial possibilities. The legal expenses insurance industry received an enormous boost. It was now possible for anyone, including the poor and those of moderate means, to litigate personal injury cases and other claims without worrying about cost other than paying the initial insurance premium. That remaining worry could be taken care of by offering the client a loan at the

[42] S Yarrow, *Just Rewards? The Outcome of Conditional Fee Arrangements* (Nuffield, London, 2001).
[43] In *Callery v Gray* [2002] 3 All ER 417, 422.
[44] HL Debs, 1613, 1 November 1994, Col 789.
[45] HL Debs, 12 June 1995, Col 1560.

beginning of the case. This presented a further commercial prospect—arranging loans to pay the premiums at the generally high rates of interest characteristic of consumer loans in the UK. The scene was set for profiteering in which clients were encouraged to initiate personal injury cases, apparently at little or no risk to themselves. Defendants, for whom CFAs were rarely available or appropriate, often felt browbeaten into settling such cases, however spurious and unlikely to succeed in court, because of the costs of litigation.

This commercial opportunity was taken up most enthusiastically by claims companies, which had to work with solicitors where proceedings were required. The claims companies had the advantage of not being constrained by any code of professional conduct or ethics, nor were they regulated by any other body.[46] They could advertise freely, including cold calling, leafleting and approaching people on the street. They sold their own insurance packages, arranged loans through related companies at high interest rates to cover the premiums and employed their own expert witnesses (who often paid a referral fee to the company for the privilege of being a paid court expert witness). They also received referral fees from solicitors on their lists in return for the clients where proceedings had to be commenced. Many of the claims they handled were of small value (and doubtful legality) and the costs, both legal and insurance, far outweighed the value of the claim to the client but made a lot of money for the claims companies. Some solicitors failed to explain to their clients the nature of the agreements they had made with the claims companies and high success fees were charged for simple cases.

Clients were not advised on the reasonableness of the insurance premium or the loan for it. Some solicitors were in breach of the existing rules against referral fees, though this was generally obfuscated by calling such fees 'administration fees'. Clients were rarely informed of this fee and in any case understood little of the nature of the agreements they had entered into. Many were very distressed to find out that, even if they won their case, they would still have a loan to pay off in relation to their, often very expensive, insurance premium (where the premium was too high, the courts would not allow it to be recovered as costs from the other side and so the claimant had to pay it). Claimants who lost their cases, far from having 'no fee' to pay, were liable for sums often well over £1,000–2,000. These costs alone exceeded the estimated value of the damages that might have been recovered, as many of the cases involving minor injuries were worth only £1,000–2,000.

The situation had become scandalous and, unsurprisingly, led to extensive costs litigation by the unsuccessful defendants. This litigation was in part responsible for the insolvency of two of the largest claims companies[47]. An illustrative and leading case is *Sharratt v London Central Bus Co (No 2)*.[48] This case involved a number of PI cases against the London Central Bus Company handled by the claims firm The Accident Group (TAG).

---

[46] They now have to be registered and meet set conditions on their operation under the Compensation Act 2006 and the Compensation (Regulating Claims Management Services) Order 2006, SI 2006/3319. There were problems with 90% of the applications for registration. There are over 1,176 of such companies, twice as many as previously thought. Solicitors must not have dealings with unregistered companies. The Regulator of Claims Companies will pass to the SRA the names of any solicitors dealing with unregulated claims companies. See *Law Society Gazette*, 21 June 2006 and 22 February 2007.

[47] See *Re Claims Direct Test Cases* [2003] EWCA Civ 136; *Callery v Gray* [2002] 3 All ER 417.

[48] [2004] EWCA Civ 575, decision by costs judge Hurst upheld by the CA. Details of this case can also be found at the report of the No 1 case decided on a different point, [2003] EWCA Civ 718.

All the cases were settled with damages agreed at between £1,000 and 3,500. The costs, however, ranged from £2,100 to 4,800. The insurance premium was £840–997 (in 2000–2001). Solicitors involved in the cases paid a TAG subsidiary company a fee of £310 + VAT, apparently for investigations. The defendant bus company successfully argued that these were not reasonably recoverable costs. Judge Hirst held that the insurance premiums were too high for the risk and value of the cases. Moreover, he considered that the premiums covered services extraneous to the insurance. He therefore reduced the recoverable premiums to around £450. The payments made by solicitors were also held not to be recoverable as costs as they were in reality a referral fee proscribed by the professional conduct rules. The Claims Direct cases involved insurance premiums of £1,312, which for similar reasons was reduced to £621.

The other main issue that arose in these cases related to the duties of the solicitors involved. Under the prevailing regulations the client had to be given extensive information on the nature of the CFA contract and the client's potential liabilities. The advisor also had to investigate whether the client had some other way of funding the litigation, such as legal aid or existing insurance. In the TAG cases all this information and investigation was done by TAG and not the solicitor, who simply relied on TAG's employees doing the job properly. It was decided in *Sharratt (No 1)* that this could be acceptable. The solicitor could, in effect, delegate the duty to inform the client. However, the delegation would be acceptable only if the agent was properly appointed and provided an explanation to the client, as required under the regulations. Quite how this could be done by the unqualified agents of a claims company was not really explained.

Despite the above attempts by the courts to reign in the worst excesses of claims company practices (which has led to some bankruptcies amongst the companies themselves as the profits dwindled), it was obvious that the position was still not satisfactory. The Law Society did very little on the issue except to bewail the fact that claims companies were unregulated,[49] but this was required from 2007 and they were required to abide by certain conditions. Solicitors were forbidden from dealing with unregulated companies, the SRA frequently reminding them that to do so was a disciplinary matter. Further, the government repealed all the rather complex regulations on CFAs that had grown up since 1995 and told the Law Society to deal with the issue under the professional rules of conduct. Any CFA made after November 2005 is now regulated,[50] and the information is given to clients is contained in the Code. The inclusion in the Solicitors' Code is an indication that the rules are meant to protect the CFA client and not help the losing defendant avoid a legitimate costs order because the regulations have not been complied with.[51] In addition, it will

---

[49] The Law Society was represented in the *Sharratt* case (*Sharratt v London Central Bus Ltd* [2003] 4 All ER 590) in favour of the right to delegate the information duty to clients. The Law Society has, until November 2005, always taken the view that no new rules of professional conduct were needed to regulate conditional fees, which is odd in view of the fact the their introduction was so strongly opposed by many on ethical grounds.

[50] Courts and Legal Services Act 1990, as amended by the Access to Justice Act 1999 and by the Solicitors' Code of Conduct 2007, r 2.03.

[51] The courts have decided that a CFA is unenforceable only if there is a 'material' departure from the regulations, but that it is not necessary to show detriment to the CFA client in order to establish a material departure. See *Samonini v London General Transport Services Ltd* [2005] EWHC 90001; *Garrett v Halton BC* [2006] EWCA Civ 1017; *Crook v Birmingham CC* [2007] EWHC 1415. See also *Garbutt v Edwards* [2006] 1 All ER 553, where it was held that a failure to abide by the Code in providing costs estimates did not mean that the contract between solicitor

normally be easier, in the light of changing circumstances, to amend the Code than to change a statutory instrument.

Rule 2.03(2) requires solicitors acting under a CFA to give additional information to the client on costs. They must be informed in what circumstances they will be liable to pay their own solicitor and whether payment of those fees will actually be enforced. They must also be told of their right to seek assessment of those costs and whether the fees are being shared with any other organisation, such as a charity. The guidance adds little, except to remind solicitors that they must comply with the statutory requirements, which are that the contract must be in writing and the success fee not more than 100%. The client must also be advised of alternative funding mechanisms, such as legal aid and before-the-event insurance. Control of the success fee and other costs like insurance has been left to the courts and the CPR. The position on referral fees from claims companies is now governed by rule 9, as described in chapter 2.

CFAs were not, as might be expected, smothered in professional practice rules. The Law Society was keen to promote their use, organising the Accident Line scheme to provide insurance cover for the other side's costs in personal injury cases, and producing a model contract and a detailed guide. It recommends that solicitors should not charge a success fee which exceeds 25% of the amount recovered by the client. This does not, of course, mean that the total fee recovered by the solicitor will not exceed 25% of the sum recovered. It is for the courts to determine the success fee, and often much lower percentages will be chargeable. The model contract uses plain English to be comprehensible to the lay client, stating clearly the hourly rates, liability for disbursements and success fee. Clients terminating the agreement must pay basic costs to the solicitor, who can claim the success fee if the client goes on to win the case. The solicitor can terminate the agreement where the client fails to discharge his or her obligations,[52] or if the client rejects advice on settlement. In the latter case, costs, disbursements and, in certain circumstances, the success fee are payable by the client. The client might face a dispute in which they are at a considerable disadvantage when accused of being 'uncooperative' or 'misleading the solicitor'.

Not all solicitors act through Accident Line. An example of how the commercial system can work can be seen in the case of *Rogers v Merthyr Tydfil CBC*.[53] The solicitor was a member of the DAS insurance company panel—to whom he paid a referral fee for the business—and agreed to insure all his personal injury CFA clients through DAS. DAS provided ATE insurance cover through three staged premiums, which in this case totalled £4,860. The payment of the premiums by the claimant was deferred in the expectation that they would be paid by the defendant or, if necessary, from any recovered damages. The damages eventually agreed were £3,105. This was held to be a proportionate expense and recoverable from the defeated defendant. However, the court did rule that defendants should be notified that a particular insurance policy had been taken out and when phased

---

and client was unenforceable and therefore the indemnity principle in awarding costs still applied. For where the CFA is invalid and unenforceable costs orders can be made against the solicitors themselves, see *Myatt v NCB* [2007] 4 All ER 1094.

[52] To give instructions, not to mislead the solicitor, to be cooperative, submit to any necessary medical or other examinations and to pay disbursements as the case proceeds.

[53] [2006] EWCA Civ 1134.

premiums fell due. It can be clearly seen from this case that the real 'winners' were the lawyer (who recovered costs of £12,628) and DAS, who recovered the insurance premium in full and a referral fee from the solicitor. The client got £3,105 and the defendant council a huge bill of costs.

Speculative fees and *pro bono* work

A solicitor taking a case on a speculative basis agrees with the client that a fee will be payable only if the case is won, knowing that either the client will be in funds in that event or, more likely, that costs, including the solicitor's fees, will be ordered against, and paid by, the losing party. Such an agreement does not involve any uplift or percentage of the damages as in conditional or contingency fees. Speculative fees have been legal for years in Scotland, although the extent of use is unknown.[54] In England they were regarded as unlawful maintenance by the solicitor, smacking of ambulance chasing, but gained acceptance for clients who could not get legal aid on financial grounds.[55] Their legality was accepted by the Court of Appeal in *Thai Trading Company v Taylor*,[56] where it was held that

> there is nothing unlawful in a solicitor acting for a party to litigation agreeing to forgo all or part of his costs and disbursements if he wins.

Such costs can be recovered from the other side. The court considered that a speculative fee should not 'be regarded as contrary to public policy today, if indeed it ever was'.

Acting *pro bono* is not now regarded as illegal maintenance, and is in fact positively encouraged by the Law Society and the Bar.[57] The main risks are that the successful party's legal costs may not be recoverable from the other side or, where the case is lost, the costs of the defendant are imposed by the court on the plaintiff's lawyers. Some old cases mandated personal liability where the lawyers had not satisfied themselves that the client had a reasonable case. The law was clarified in *Tolstoy-Miloslavsky v Aldington*,[58] where it was held that the court had no jurisdiction to make a costs order against a solicitor solely on the ground that he acted without a fee and that, when so acting, a solicitor is not under an obligation to protect the other side from a hopeless case. He does not have to 'impose a pre-trial screen through which litigants must pass' before receiving free representation.[59] The only way in which a solicitor might be held personally liable for the other side's costs is under the wasted costs jurisdiction, a risk that applies to all cases, whether the lawyer acts without charge or for a fee.[60]

---

[54] In the debates in the House of Lords on conditional fees, it was said by Lord Allen that speculative fees are frequently used in Scotland: HL Debs, 12 June 1995 Col 1573.

[55] See H Genn, *Hard Bargaining: Out of Court Settlement in Personal Injury Actions* (Oxford, Clarendon Press, 1987); J Levin, above n 33.

[56] [1998] 3 All ER 65 CA.

[57] See chapter 6.

[58] [1996] 2 All ER 556.

[59] See also *Orchard v SE Electricity* [1987] QB 565, 572.

[60] See chapter 13 on wasted costs.

Commissions

Where a solicitor arranges an insurance policy, a pension, the purchase of shares or a similar transaction for a client, should he or she be allowed to receive a commission from the insurance company or other financial institution in the same way as other brokers? The prospect of a commission for the solicitor introduces a clear conflict between the duty to promote the client's best interests and the solicitor's interest in successfully selling something to the client. In view of core duty 1.04 to act in the best interests of clients, it might be thought that solicitors should be barred from receiving such commissions. This, however, is not the case; rule 2.06 allows solicitors to keep commissions of under £20. If it exceeds £20 and the solicitor tells the client how much it is, then the client can agree that the solicitor may keep it. There is no requirement for this information or consent to be in writing, though this would obviously be wise.[61] Any material excess on the original written calculation of the amount must be handed over to the client. The £20 rule is regarded as justified on the ground that the cost of the administrative work in accounting to the client would generally exceed the amount paid over. We doubt if anyone would accept such a justification from their bank in this era of computers. It represents a derogation from the normal law that a fiduciary or trustee shall not make a secret profit from his trust.

There is no specific requirement in the SRA's guidance on rule 2 that the client should be advised to take independent advice, for example where the commission is particularly significant in amount. However, elsewhere, in the guidance to rule 3 on conflict, it is stressed that the solicitor 'must insist that the client receives independent advice' in cases where a solicitor has a personal interest in a client's transaction.[62] It might be argued that these rules are not necessarily contrary to the interest of the client because, if the solicitor receives a commission in respect of the transaction, then his bill to the client may (but not must) be reduced. Nevertheless, many scandals in the financial services industry have, at their root, the desire of commissioned agents to represent that they are giving a client disinterested advice when in fact their advice is influenced by the commissions available. Disinterest is supposed to be the gold standard which distinguishes the advice of the professional lawyer from that of other types of agent. Allowing such commissions to be retained may therefore be regarded as dangerous to the long-term interest of the profession.

Negotiating fees

Except where they are fixed, as is the case with much legally aided work and some litigation, it is for the solicitor and client to agree the fee, subject to the possibility of assessment by the court. How should this be done? Do the professional conduct rules or other rules lay down any special provisions, or is this matter left to the parties under the normal rules of contract?

First, what information does the solicitor have to provide for the client on costs? Until 1991 there were no rules or specific legislation on this. In 1991 the Law Society promulgated

---

[61] R 2.05 guidance, para 59.
[62] R 3 guidance, para 45.

Written Professional Standards on Information on Costs, to supplement the introduction of rule 15 of the Solicitors' Practice Rules 1990. The current law is contained in the Solicitors' Code of Conduct 2007, rule 2 on client relations. This rule requires solicitors to ensure that clients are given

> the best information possible about the likely overall cost of a matter both at the outset and, when appropriate, as the matter progresses.

The solicitor must advise of the basis of their fees, when they may be increased and also any payments to be made to others (ie disbursements). They must explore with the client how payment is to be made, for example through legal aid, existing (before the event) or after the event insurance, or through some other third party such as a trade union. In the context of legal aid, the statutory charge should be explained, as must any contributions from the client and any liability for the other side's costs if the case is lost.[63]

Information on costs must be both clear and confirmed in writing.[64] The advice must be clearly expressed and regularly updated.[65] Solicitors will not be in breach of these requirements if they can demonstrate that it was inappropriate to meet all or some of them in the circumstances. The guidance stresses that the burden of proving this is on the solicitor, but, for example, it is accepted the client does not need the same information on costs for repeat work. The guidance also notes that there is much law on bills of costs: for example, there can be differences between contentious and non-contentious business, which must also be complied with. The new rules are part of the law and binding on solicitors, unlike the previous guidance which, it appears, was frequently disregarded.[66] Under the CPR, solicitors must inform clients about any costs order made against them within seven days.[67] They can advertise their fees provided they comply with the provisions of the Code rule 7 and the publicity is not be misleading or inaccurate, containing clear statements, for example, as to whether VAT and disbursements are included. The old rule that publicity must not make direct comparison with the charges of any other identifiable solicitor has been abolished.[68]

Controlling the amount charged

The ideal is, of course, to control fees before the work is done and not rely on challenging

---

[63] The courts require that this advice on the availability of legal aid be given where there is any dispute between client and solicitor over fees: *David Truex Solicitor v Kitchin* [2007] EWCA Civ 618 CA.

[64] Certain agreements on costs, non-contentious business agreements and agreements on costs in contentious matters must in any case be in writing under the Solicitors' Act 1974, ss 57 and59.

[65] R 2.03 guidance, para 27.

[66] See Research and Policy Planning Unit, *Quality of Solicitors' Practice Management Research Study No 10* (London, Law Society, RPPU, 1993); Ombudsman Annual Report 1995 and National Consumer Council Report, *Solicitors and Client Care* (London, NCC, 1994). There is a suggestion in *Garbutt*, above n 51, that a breach of the old Code does not make the contract between solicitor and client on fees unenforceable as a breach of regulations might have done.

[67] CPR 2007, r 44.2; see also Lord Woolf, *Access to Justice: Final Report to the Lord Chancellor on the Civil Justice System in England and Wales* (London, Lord Chancellor's Department, 1996) (hereafter Final Report) 79.

[68] Old Solicitors' Publicity Code, para 2(d).

them at the end. This was one of the aims of Lord Woolf[69] in relation to litigation, and the new CPR do make provision for costs orders to be made in the course of litigation and not just at the end. However, most controls on costs come after the event, in the form of a challenge to the rate or amount of the fees. The main way of challenging fees, apart from the complaints procedures dealt with in chapter 7, is assessment by the court under the considerably enhanced powers under the CPR. They can also be controlled by the court via the wasted costs jurisdiction and, in legally aided cases, are controlled by the LSC. These methods have not always been successful in controlling overcharging. It has proven particularly difficult to control the escalation of cost that has accompanied the introduction of conditional fee agreements. The gradual introduction of fixed fees, including success fees, in standard cases, by agreement between the representatives of the legal professions, the insurance industry (who of course bear many of the costs win or lose), the Civil Justice Council and the Ministry of Justice, may be the remedy.

Assessment by the court

In assessing costs, the court will be guided by the overriding objective stated in rule 1 of the CPR, which states, inter alia, that a case must be dealt with justly so as to ensure that costs are proportionate having regard to the value and complexity of the case and the financial position of each party.[70] This principle was central to Lord Woolf's report on which the rules are based and marks a basic change in attitude towards litigation which has developed since 2000 but has yet to reach full fruition.

The detail on costs is contained in rule 44 and its accompanying practice directions. There are two types of assessment:

(i)   the assessment of the winner's costs where they are to be paid by the loser as a result of a costs order at the end of the litigation; these can be assessed on a standard or indemnity basis and are known as party and party costs; and

(ii) the assessment of the lawyer's costs that are to be paid by his or her own client. These are known as solicitor and client costs. This assessment can be applied for by the client in both contentious and non-contentious business.[71]

The principles applied differ in the two types of assessment. When assessing the costs to be paid by the loser under (i) above, the court must decide whether to use the standard or the indemnity basis, the standard being the usual or default basis. The basic difference is that in standard assessments the costs must be proportionate to the matter in issue; those assessed on an indemnity basis need not be proportionate. In both the costs must be reasonable, but in assessments on the standard basis any doubt of reasonableness should be resolved in favour of the paying party whereas such doubts are to be in favour of the receiving party when assessed on the indemnity basis.

---

[69] See Final Report, ch 7, para 30.
[70] However, as Balcombe LJ commented in *Symphony Group v Hodgson* [1993] 4 All ER 143, 'there is only one immutable rule in relation to costs, namely that there are no immutable rules'.
[71] Solicitors' Act 1974, ss 68 and 70.

Costs on an indemnity basis are awarded only where there has been some culpability or abuse of process by the paying party.

In the assessment of solicitor and client costs under (ii) above, much will depend on the terms of the contract with the solicitor and what the client instructed the solicitor to do. In general, these costs are assessed on an indemnity basis, but if there is any doubt as to their reasonableness, it will be assumed that they are reasonable if they were approved by the client either expressly or impliedly.[72] In both cases the court will concern itself only with the costs that are specifically challenged and not evaluate the solicitor's bill as a whole unless this is asked for. In practice, assessment of solicitor and client costs has been rare. A major reason for this is that the client must pay the costs of assessment unless the bill is reduced by more than one-fifth.[73] Moreover, the solicitor must tell the client of the availability of assessment only before suing for the costs. The exception is the case of conditional fee arrangements, when such information must be contained in the agreement itself. Of course, party and party assessment, which is almost invariably applied for by the loser at the end of litigation, will also often act as a protection for the winning client. Few solicitors are happy to present their client with an enormous bill for work which a costs judge has decided was unnecessary. A third party who has paid, or is liable for, the costs can also apply for assessment but cannot apply for a remuneration certificate from the Law Society.[74]

Before 2000 the costs of interlocutory matters were postponed until the end of the case. At that stage the loser could face a bill inflated by purely tactical interlocutory proceedings. Lord Woolf considered that such costs should be awarded at the conclusion of the interlocutory proceedings and paid forthwith, and this has been embodied in the new rule 44.8. As Cook and Hurst remarked when the new system began, this rule will make clients

> realize that their lawyers have lost a battle and they will have to put their hands in their pockets and part with their money at an early stage in the proceedings.[75]

Moreover, where such a costs order has been made in relation to interlocutory proceedings, it must be paid within 14 days of the order, not at the end of the whole litigation.

Have the new civil procedure rules resulted in more reasonable costs for clients? In 2005 Zuckerman[76] argued that, while the litigation culture may have improved since 2000, the majority of costs are run up before litigation is begun and parties will be contractually liable to pay these costs to their lawyers. The weaker litigant is still under pressure to settle unfavourably. However, the courts have increasingly used principles in the CPR to make what is known as a protective costs order at an early stage in civil proceedings. This might have a greater effect on controlling escalating costs, as is shown in the case of *King v Daily Telegraph Group.*[77] In this libel case, run on a CFA with 100% success fee, the defendant newspaper would not get their costs paid even if they won because the claimant had no money and no after-the-event insurance. The likely costs would exceed £1 million, far in

---

[72] CPR, pt 48, r 48.8. There are special provisions in the Rules for conditional fee agreements and payments from the LSC in relation to legal aid: see rule 48.9.

[73] Solicitors' Act 1974, s 70(9).

[74] For details of such certificates, see below.

[75] M Cook and PT Hurst, *The New Civil Costs Regime* (London, Butterworths, 1999) 23.

[76] A Zuckerman, 'Costs Capping in CFA Cases' (2005) 24 *Civil Justice Quarterly* 1.

[77] [2005] 1 WLR 2282.

excess of the damages that would be awarded, which would be about £150,000. The defendants would be better off conceding the case than winning it. As was pointed out by Lord
Justice Brooke, the case was more valuable to the claimant's lawyers than to himself and
they had no incentive 'to advance their client's claim in a reasonable and proportionate
manner'.

The solution was for the court to make an order capping the costs early in the
proceedings and also determining recoverable costs early in the proceedings as described
above under CPR rule 44.8. This was the best method of controlling costs and should be a
first resort for the court.[78] To the argument that no advocate would take on the claimant's
case on such modest capped fees, Lord Justice Brook was unmoved; he considered that the
claimant's 'fate will be no different from that of a conventionally legally aided litigant in
modern times'. Whether capping will become the normal order in future—and whether it
will be the solution to escalating costs—remains to be seen.[79] The courts have been hesitant,
as in *R v Secretary of State for Trade*,[80] where it was said that they should be made only in
exceptional circumstances, and *Knight v Beyond Properties Ltd*,[81] where it was stated that
there must be evidence of extravagance which cannot otherwise be controlled. Cost-capping
orders have been available for some time in judicial review proceedings, largely because of
the need to allow issues of public importance to be litigated. In such cases the issue must be
one of public importance that the applicant has no private interest in. It must be fair and
reasonable to make the order. The rules are obviously meant to enable charitable or
campaigning bodies to bring judicial review proceedings without fear that the costs will
cripple their endeavours, and will apply particularly if their lawyers are acting *pro bono*.

Review by the Solicitors Regulation Authority

A costs review by the SRA is available only in relation to costs in non-contentious matters
where no non-contentious business agreement has been entered into.[82] As noted above,
clients rarely apply for court assessment of their solicitor's bills, probably because of the risk
of incurring further costs in so doing. The Law Society, now under the SRA, has long
provided a free service for clients reviewing bills under £50,000 in non-contentious matters.[83]
It is for the solicitor, at the request of the client, to apply for a review by the Law Society,
which will result in the issue of a remuneration certificate. The certificate will state what

---

[78] Other recommended methods were retrospective costs assessment and wasted costs orders; see para 105 of the
Judgment. The case applies to all litigation however funded, and not solely to CFAs.

[79] The approach has been approved by the House of Lords in *Campbell v MGN (No 2)* [2005] 4 All ER 793, 805.
In *Henry v BBC* [2005] EWHC 2503 it was held that cost capping cannot be retrospective and must be applied for
by the parties; it cannot be done on the initiative of the court.

[80] [2005] EWCA Civ 192.

[81] [2006] EWHC 1242.

[82] Under the Solicitors' Act 1974, s 57. See Solicitors' (Non-Contentious Business) Remuneration Order, cl 9(c). A
non-contentious business agreement is an agreement made in writing between solicitor and client on non-contentious business on remuneration. It must be signed by both. It may be sued upon and, as such, is subject to review on
taxation of costs. A client may be induced into making such an agreement without realising that by doing so he or
she forfeits the right to use the remuneration certificate procedure. This rule was criticised by the Legal Services
Ombudsman in his Annual Report (1996) 15.

[83] This limit was first introduced in 1994 by the Solicitors' (Non-Contentious Business) Remuneration Order,
ibid.

would be a fair and reasonable charge for the work covered by the bill. It will not increase the bill. A solicitor should inform his client of the right to apply for a remuneration certificate before suing or threatening to sue his client for the fees. He need not do this before sending the bill or making a further demand for payment.

Where the solicitor deducts the costs from money held on behalf of the client, and the client objects to the costs in writing within three months of delivery of the bill, the solicitor must inform the client of his right to apply for a remuneration certificate. The client has one month from being informed to exercise the right. A major condition requires that the client request a remuneration certificate to pay 50% of the costs plus VAT and disbursements in advance, but this can be waived by the SRA. The client cannot get a remuneration certificate after the expiry of the time limits or, most importantly, where the bill has already been paid,[84] nor can a remuneration certificate be obtained where a court has ordered an assessment of the bill. Failure by the solicitor to comply with the certificate may result in disciplinary proceedings. The SRA procedure is little used by clients compared to the numbers who, in surveys, express concern about solicitors' costs. About 2,000 bills are reviewed each year, perhaps because the procedure is little known to clients or because clients feel the SRA is unlikely to disagree with the solicitor on the matter of costs. In fact, about 60% of bills considered are reduced.

Wasted costs

The wasted costs jurisdiction under the Supreme Court Act 1981 section 51(6) as amended by the Courts and Legal Services Act 1990 is another method by which solicitors' and barristers' costs can be controlled at the behest of both their clients and the other side. It is mainly aimed at protecting third parties from inflated costs, and its a jurisdiction has greatly expanded in recent years. It is dealt with in detail in chapter 17.

Legally aided cases

The control of costs in legally aided cases rests, to a large extent, with the Legal Services Commission. Civil legal aid is provided through the Community Legal Services Commission and criminal through the Criminal Defence Service. Control of cost in civil cases is achieved through contracting with providing solicitors. They agree to provide a set number of case starts in a year for a fixed sum. Criminal costs are less successfully controlled through contracts, and this is now increasingly done through fixed fees for advocacy. The aims are both to control the quality of the work done and to prevent escalating costs. Successful unaided parties in civil cases rarely get their costs paid by the aided party or the CLS, so this control is important to them. It also protects assisted clients if they are paying a contribution or will be liable under the statutory charge. In some cases, however, the level of control may prevent lawyers from undertaking work that both they and their clients consider necessary and in the client's best interests, and proposals in 2007

---

[84] The exception is where the payment was made by deduction from client money held by the solicitor.

arising from the Carter Report on legal aid remuneration in criminal cases caused strikes by legal aid solicitors and barristers.

The process of assessment by the court also applies to legally aided cases. The legally aided client can take part in this process if he or she has an interest in the outcome. Such an interest may arise if the client is liable for a contribution or because the client is affected by the statutory charge. The costs of the assessment will be covered by the legal aid certificate.

Recovering fees from clients

Having negotiated the fee and dealt with any review or assessment, are there any special rules or guidance on enforcing the payment of the fee? In relation to solicitors, the relationship between lawyer and client is basically contractual and the general rules of contract normally apply. The contract can stipulate for payments on account, for example, and solicitors are free to sue if fees are not paid. There are, however, some special provisions, in particular relating to contentious business agreements.[85] Certain general rules are also more significant in lawyer–client relationships than in other relationships. Two in particular should be noted. First, there are rules conferring a lien over papers and property held by the solicitor where the fee is not paid. Secondly, the rules permitting a solicitor to refuse to do further work until he or she has been paid.

The solicitor's lien

The solicitor's lien enables the solicitor to retain papers and property belonging to the client pending the payment of the bill. The client must be informed about this at the outset of the case[86] The lien does not arise until a properly itemised bill has been delivered to the client. It applies to all papers, in the view of the SRA, not simply to those relating to the unpaid bill.[87] This power is not, of course, unique to solicitors; any person who has done work for another may retain the property on which the work has been done pending payment. However, the power is particularly effective in the case of solicitors as they frequently have possession of large sums of client funds. Holding on to papers will also make it difficult for the client to instruct another solicitor. The court has a discretion to order a solicitor to deliver up any documents in his custody.[88] It will normally do this where the client needs the documents for continuing litigation. An undertaking to restore the documents to the solicitor at the end of the litigation would normally be ordered. Further conditions might be imposed by the court, depending on the circumstances of the case. For example, in *Ismail v Richards Butler* the ex-client was required to provide further security for the payment of the outstanding bills.[89]

---

[85] Solicitors' Act 1974, ss 57(4) and 60(2).
[86] Solicitors' Code of Conduct 2007, r 2.03 (1)(e).
[87] See the *Law Society Gazette*'s answer to an ethics problem in August 1996. See also *Ismail v Richards Butler* [1996] QB 711.
[88] Solicitors' Act 1974, s 68.
[89] [1996] QB 711.

Suing for fees

In both contentious and non-contentious matters the solicitor cannot sue on the bill before one month has elapsed from its delivery to the client, unless the court gives permission. Where the bill relates to contentious matters the solicitor must always seek the leave of the court.[90] The client can ask for the bill to be assessed, but where a solicitor sues on the bill in contentious matters the court has the power to set aside the agreement on fees with the client, if it is unfair or unreasonable, and order assessment.[91] In non-contentious matters the solicitor cannot sue unless he has first informed the client of the right to apply for a remuneration certificate and the right to seek assessment. Solicitors are not therefore as free as other business people to sue customers because fees are not simply a matter of free negotiation with the client. In general, a client's failure to pay fees is a good reason to cease acting for the client, on reasonable notice.[92] The duties of confidentiality and legal privilege are not waived where the solicitor sues a client for fees.[93]

Looking after client funds

The rules on solicitor's accounts and the management of client funds have traditionally occupied many of the pages of the old Professional Practice Guide. Until comparatively recently, this area was also the only aspect of professional ethics forming a compulsory part of professional training. The rules, together with those on investment business, occupied over 260 pages of the 1999 edition of the Law Society Guide. This is not really surprising; it is vital that clients should have absolute confidence that solicitors will deal properly with their funds and that they will be compensated if not. The professional relationship would otherwise be jeopardised. It is significant that this area of professional practice has for along time been almost entirely based on binding rules made under the Solicitors' Act 1974; it was not left to discretionary guidance. The rules are now consolidated into the Solicitors' Accounts Rules 1998 and are not dealt with in detail,[94] but with reference to the general principles.

Accounting rules are needed both to ensure that solicitors act in the best interests of the client and to prevent the solicitor acting fraudulently or making a secret profit from a fiduciary relationship. They are also needed in purely practical terms to ensure that client funds are not confused with those of the solicitors' practice. This protects clients in the event of the solicitor's insolvency or other indebtedness. Finally, they are needed to ensure efficient and proper book-keeping systems in solicitors' offices. The Rules stress that

---

[90] Solicitors' Act 1974, s 61.

[91] Ibid

[92] Solicitors' Code of Conduct 2007, r 2.01(2). In non-contentious matters there must be an agreement with the client to make such payments in relation to fees (but not disbursements). In contentious matters a specific agreement is not required and a failure to make a payment on account is an acceptable reason for terminating the retainer on reasonable notice (Solicitors' Act 1974, s 65(2)).

[93] See chapter 11.

[94] The detail can be found in A Cordery, *Cordery on Solicitors* (London, Butterworths, 1995).

responsibility for adhering to the Rules lies with all the principals or partners of a firm; it cannot be delegated to one partner.[95]

The basic accounting system

The system laid down by the Rules relies on the requirement that two separate sets of accounts are maintained: the client account and the office account. In addition, there must be a controlled trust account to hold money that the solicitor receives as a sole trustee. Separate accounts ensure that the bank, building society or the solicitor cannot use the monies in one account for the purposes of the others, that is, funds in a client account cannot be used to satisfy the debts or expenses of the firm. The Rules then lay down precisely what monies must go into the client account and what to the office account, and what withdrawals may legitimately be made from both. Any money held or received by the solicitor on account of his client must be paid without delay into the client account, unless the client instructs otherwise. This includes money paid by the client for disbursements and payments on account of costs.[96] Where a single cheque consists of a mixture of client and office monies, the payment may be divided into each account or, if not, all of it must be paid into the client account.

Compliance rules

There are also rules designed to ensure compliance with the accounts rules. First, the SRA has the power to order that the books be inspected at random without giving any reason for the inspection.[97] This power overrides the confidence and privilege between solicitor and client, and the SRA need not reveal its reasons for such inspection. Secondly, annual accounts prepared by an accountant must be delivered to the SRA by the firm within six months of the end of the accounting period. Failure to do so, or lateness in doing so, may result in the refusal of a practising certificate.[98] All reporting accountants must be registered auditors. Their terms of engagement, which must be in writing, must incorporate the SRA's standard terms. The accountant now has to complete a standard form checklist for the SRA as well as producing a report. This provides greater assurance that the audit work has actually been done. Thirdly, breaches of the accounts rules may result in disciplinary procedures. Indeed, such breaches are the most common reasons for disciplinary complaints and penalties. A client who suffers as a result of any breach of these rules is protected by the Solicitors' Indemnity Fund, established under section 37 of the 1974 Act, on which see chapter 9.

Interest on client accounts

One issue relating to accounts has, in the past, been the subject of considerable controversy. What should be done with the interest earned on client accounts? In the absence of specific

95 Solicitors' Accounts Rules 1998, r 6.
96 *Ibid*, r 13.
97 Solicitors' Accounts Rules 1998, r 34.
98 Solicitors' Act 1974, ss 12 and 34, and Solicitors Accounts Rules 1998, r 35.

instructions to the contrary, most solicitors maintain one client account where all client funds are lodged. Individual clients may not have a large sum deposited with the solicitor, or sums may be in the account for a short period of time only. But the total amount in the account at any one time may be considerable, and interest will accrue on this balance. If the solicitor takes this interest, then he is unlawfully profiting at the expense of the clients. This was clearly held in *Brown v IRC*,[99] a case where the Inland Revenue wanted to charge a solicitor tax on interest in client accounts. The court pointed out that this money did not belong to the solicitor, to the surprise of solicitors in general. The Law Society, citing administrative difficulties produced by *Brown*, got section 33 inserted into the Solicitors' Act 1974 under which, *except as defined in the Rules*, a solicitor is *not* liable to account to the client for interest on client accounts.[100]

Rule 24 of the Solicitors' Accounts Rules 1991, made under section 33, appears to reverse the thrust of the section by stating that solicitors *shall* account to clients for any interest earned on deposits in separate designated client accounts. Where money is held in a general client account, again interest should be paid to each client, subject to the *de minimis* rule. Under this rule, sums of £20 or less need not be paid to the client, nor need interest be paid where money is held for only a short time. Thus, under rule 24(3), the solicitor need not account where he holds £1,000 of client's money for under eight weeks, £2000 for under four weeks, £10,000 for under two weeks and £20,000 for under one week. Even where the solicitor holds more than £20,000 for under one week, he need account only if it is 'fair and reasonable' in all the circumstances.[101] Where the solicitor holds funds as a stakeholder, for example a deposit in relation to a house purchase, then he must account for the interest to the person to whom the stake is paid.[102]

The Law Society justifies the rules on client account interest by reference to the same *de minimis* principle that applies to commissions (see above), under which a solicitor should not have to account to the client for sums around £20. However, of course, an amount which is *de minimis* to an individual client may not be *de minimis* when all clients are added together. It is not known how much solicitors benefit from interest on client accounts. In 1984 the Consumer Council issued a discussion paper on the issue.[103] They estimated, conservatively, that it then amounted to over £40 million a year. Since 1984, the rules have been tightened up in favour of clients, interest rates have declined and more use is now made of electronic money transfers. This means that less money is in fact held in client accounts. However, client interest is still being retained by solicitors. If it is still not feasible to account to each client, what should be done with it? In some jurisdictions, such as in Australia and in Ontario, Canada, a proportion of this interest is paid into a foundation managed by the Law Society and devoted to supporting a wide variety of charitable and *pro*

---

[99] [1965] AC 244.

[100] See Act s 33(3).

[101] R 24(3) (a) (ii).

[102] E 27(1). These Rules do not apply if a contrary arrangement is made in writing between the solicitor and client. Theoretically, therefore, the solicitor could ask the client to agree that all the interest earned in the client account should belong to the solicitor. However, the rules on conflict and client care would need to be complied with if this were proposed.

[103] National Consumer Council, *Whose Interest?: Solicitors and their Clients Accounts: A Discussion Paper* (London, National Consumer Council, 1984).

bono legal activities, such as educational scholarships, supporting law centres or libraries, research into the justice system and public interest advocacy centres. This was suggested for England and Wales by the Consumer Council in 1984, but nothing has come of it. Modern computing makes it possible and simple to calculate client interest and pay it to each individual client.[104] This is clearly in the client's best interest and it is therefore troubling that the rules have not been amended to reflect this.

Conclusion

Ensuring effective and fair control over the fees charged by lawyers is difficult, even for government and corporate clients. Complaints on costs form the majority of those made to the Law Society and the Legal Services Ombudsman. This is not surprising as there is an essential conflict of interest between a lawyer and client on the issue of the fee charged. The high cost of litigation is a key political issue and measures to control costs, such as wasted costs procedures, costs capping, and standard or fixed fees, are gaining ground because they are automatic and not the responsibility of the client.

---

[104] See A Evans, 'Professional Ethics North and South: Interest on Clients' Trust Funds and Lawyer Fraud. An Opportunity to Redeem Professionalism' (1996) 3 *International Journal of the Legal Profession* 281.

Part IV

WIDER OBLIGATIONS

Professional practice in law can be reconciled with virtue when professionals justify trust because of (i) a public pledge (ii) to promote the good of both individual clients and those in need (iii) while being committed to considering the good of other members of the community affected by service to clients.[1]

The expectation of social responsibility means that professions cannot be oblivious of the impacts of their actions. There must be a balance between the good they achieve for society by healing their clients' ills and the harm they do. Thus, the good of promoting client autonomy might conflict with the principle of non-malfeasance and, even, beneficence.

In some situation lawyers owe very clear duties to other third parties, the profession and the state. But, while clients may not constitute the limits of lawyers' ethical concerns, the extent of wider obligations are often not very clearly drawn, are unenforceable or are not enforced. We are concerned with the balance the lawyer is expected to achieve between the needs and rights of clients, third parties, the profession and society in general. In part IV we consider the obligations that lawyers owe to individual third parties, to collective third parties and to each other through the employment relationship.

The widest obligation expected of lawyers is public service. This is an ill-defined idea, but one interpretation is that lawyers are expected to carry out their work motivated not by making profit, but by the aspiration to promote justice. This gives rise to one of the oldest traditions of the legal profession, *pro bono publico*, or providing free legal services to those in need. This, though once voluntary and modest, has moved centre stage in recent years under the direction of large firms in the City of London, to the point that free service is becoming an expectation of lawyers.

---

[1] D Koehn, *The Ground of Professional Ethics* (London, Routledge, 1994) ch 4.

13

INDIVIDUAL THIRD PARTIES

The principle of fair play puts stringent conditions on the moral permissions an adversary game can mint.[1]

Introduction

This chapter examines the ethics and rules governing the way in which lawyers should deal with other individuals when acting on behalf of their clients, for example, solicitors and barristers on the other side, unrepresented opponents, other third parties who are affected by the transaction in question, such as beneficiaries under wills or trusts, and third parties paying for the legal work done for clients. Duties to the interests of society at large, or sections of it, are dealt with in the next chapter. Duties to third parties tend not figure large in the codes of ethics of legal professions. As we saw in chapters 1 and 9, it is sometimes asserted that the sole responsibility of the lawyer is to advance the interests of the client.[2] Even if this is accepted, it does not follow that the lawyer owes no duties to third parties. There are many such duties imposed on lawyers in order to advance the interests of the client. Examples are the duties owed by solicitors to the barristers they brief and vice versa. The personal responsibility imposed on solicitors to honour undertakings given to third parties are also intended to advance the efficiency and speed of legal business in the interests of clients, although they also protect the interests of the person to whom the undertaking has been given.

However, other duties owed to third parties can raise a conflict between the interests of the client and the interests of the third partly. Examples dealt with in this chapter include the duty not to take unfair advantage of the other side, duties to the Legal Services Commission in relation to legally aided clients and the wasted costs jurisdiction which, in effect, requires lawyers to consider the effect of their behaviour on the other side. The general duty of the advocate towards the court to act in the interests of justice can also present a conflict with the interests of the client.[3] It is therefore necessary to construct an ethic of the profession which encompasses three basic duties—loyalty to clients, candour towards the court and fairness towards third parties.[4]

---

[1] AI Applbaum, *Ethics for Adversaries: The Morality of Roles in Public and Professional Life* (Princeton University Press, 1999).

[2] See, eg T Schneyer, 'Moral Philosophy's Standard Misconception of Legal Ethics' (1984) *Wisconsin Law Review* 1529; J Leubsdorf, 'Three Models of Professional Reform' (1982) 67 *Cornell Law Review* 1021.

[3] This is dealt with further in chapter 14.

[4] See further LR Patterson, 'On Analysing the Law of Legal Ethics: An American Perspective' (1981) 16 *Israel Law Review* 28, 33.

General principles

The general principles governing solicitors were set out in paragraph 17.01 of the 1999 Law Society Guide. These principles are now contained in rule 10 of the 2007 Solicitors' Code of Conduct. Solicitors must not use their position to 'take unfair advantage of anyone either for [their] own benefit or for another person's benefit'.[5] This applies whether or not the action arises in relation to acting for a particular client. This principle, therefore, modifies the 'zeal' with which a solicitor may promote the interests of the client. The solicitor should not, at the behest of the client, take unfair advantage of another even if it is lawful to do so. Thus they should not receive or keep documents subject to an express condition if they are either unable or unwilling to abide by that condition.[6] They do not, however, have to correct any mistakes made by the other side and are free to take advantage of them.[7] Similarly, solicitors are not under an obligation to protect the other side by refusing to represent a client in a hopeless case; they need not impose a screen on the client's case before litigating. It is obviously difficult to draw a line between indulging in vexatious conduct and simply taking on a client's case even where it has a slim chance of success, as is exemplified in cases concerning wasted costs. The main constraint on the conduct of cases which are not vexatious or frivolous are the rules of court rather than the code of ethics. These allow considerable latitude.

Of course, everyone, including solicitors, has an obligation not to deceive or defraud as such acts are contrary to the law. If solicitors are subject to additional constraints, imposed by their professional ethics, these must be contained in the phrases referring to taking 'unfair advantage'. It must also be remembered that solicitors must not impugn public confidence in the profession under core duty 1.06. It is difficult to establish what conduct is meant to be covered here. In the 1999 Guide solicitors were told that they must not write 'offensive letters' to third parties, or behave offensively.[8] Good manners are required however appalling the solicitor or his client considers the other side to be.

The guidance to rule 10 advises solicitors not to send letters making claims that they know are 'not recoverable through the proper legal process'.[9] The implication of this guidance is that it applies only where some form of action is pending. In fact, it should apply to all letters or claims if it is to be consistent with the general principle of fairness. It is unprofessional to use the authority of the solicitor's role to bolster a claim which the solicitor knows, or should know, is not within the law and which therefore must be intended to frighten or pressurise the other side illegitimately. An example would be for a husband's solicitor to write to a wife demanding that she immediately vacate the matrimonial home owned by the husband. The law protects wives from summary eviction in such

---

[5] *Solicitors' Code of Conduct 2007* (London, Solicitors Regulation Authority, 2007) (hereafter Solicitors' Code) r 10.01. An example of taking unfair advantage for the solicitor's own benefit is where the solicitor is involved in a road accident and uses his position 'unfairly to harass or intimidate the other motorist' (guidance, para 1).

[6] Guidance to r 10.01, para 6(a). This also notes that so to do would 'diminish the trust the public places in you or the profession', contrary to core duty 1.06.

[7] See *Thames Trains Ltd v Adams* [2006] EWHC 3291 (QB) and *Thompson v Arnold* [2007] EWHC 1875 (QB).

[8] See N Taylor (ed), *The Guide to the Professional Conduct of Solicitors* (London, The Law Society, 1999) (hereafter the Law Society Guide) r 17.01, para 6 and r 19.01.

[9] Guidance to r 10.01, para 5.

circumstances and all solicitors know, or should know, this. The example given in the guidance is that in recovering a debt

> you should not demand from the debtor the cost of the letter of claim, since it cannot be said at that stage that such a cost is legally recoverable.

Another example relates to a change which was introduced into the costs regime in Employment Tribunals in 2001. Many employers (through their solicitors) routinely sent letters threatening costs applications where employees brought cases against them. These letters were, and are, clearly improper ,as costs are awarded in only limited and exceptional circumstances in Employment Tribunals in order to preserve their character as accessible to all, including the unrepresented employee.[10]

A case that provides an example within the scope of rule 10 is *Ernst & Young v Butte Mining Co.*[11] The court had approved a consent order setting aside a judgment by default and the defendants were permitted to serve a defence and counterclaim within a set time. The plaintiff's solicitor had the carriage (that is, drafting and issuing) of the order and, immediately after obtaining it, filed a notice to discontinue the action. This was intended to, and did, prevent the defendants from filing their counterclaim. It was held to be an abuse of process. The plaintiff's solicitors had misled the defendants as to their intentions and sought an unfair advantage by obtaining the defendant's agreement to their having the carriage of the order. Delivering judgement, Robert Walker J said:

> Heavy, hostile commercial litigation is a serious business. It is not a form of indoor sport and litigation solicitors do not owe each other duties to be friendly (so far as that goes beyond politeness) or to be chivalrous or sportsmanlike (so far as that goes beyond being fair). Nevertheless even in the most hostile litigation . . . solicitors must be scrupulously fair and not take unfair advantage of obvious mistakes . . . [This duty] is intensified if the solicitor in question has been a major contributing cause of the mistake.[12]

Rule 10 of the 2007 Rules also requires the solicitors not to take unfair advantage of that position for their own advantage, as well as that of clients. This applies whether or not they are acting for a client. The example given in the guidance is that if a solicitor is involved in a road accident he or she should not use his position to unfairly 'harass or intimidate the other motorist'.

---

[10] See *Gee v Shell UK Ltd* [2002] EWCA Civ 1479; P Plowden, 'Employment Tribunal Costs—Some Comfort for Applicants' [May 2004] *Legal Action* 28.

[11] [1997] 2 All ER 471.

[12] See *Haiselden v P & O Properties* [1998] All ER 180 (D), where the defendant realised that a case had been mistakenly set down for trial in the county court when it should have been dealt with as a small claim. The defendant did not alert either the court or the unrepresented plaintiff to this mistake. It was held that he was under an obligation not to take advantage of the mistake. See also *Vernon v Bosley (No 2)* [1997] 1 All ER 614 CA on the duty to inform the court of changed circumstances arising after the conclusion of the hearing.

Solicitors' relationships with other solicitors

Undertakings

The old principle 19.01 in the 1999 Law Society Guide required a solicitor to deal with other solicitors with 'frankness and good faith consistent with his or her overriding duty to the client'. This principle is not repeated in the 2007 Rules, though it could, presumably, come within the ambit of core duty 1.06. However, the most important issue, that of solicitors' undertakings, do feature in rule 10.05. Solicitors frequently give undertakings to the other side—to discharge mortgages, produce or return documents, hold monies to order, exchange contracts for the sale of land, etc. Much business could not be speedily or efficiently carried out without reliance on undertakings, and the rule governing such promises forms an important part of a solicitor's professional ethics. An undertaking is defined in rule 24.01 as:

> [A] statement made by you or your firm to someone who reasonably relies upon it, that you or your firm will do something or cause something to be done, or refrain from doing something.

Note that the definition applies to undertakings given to anyone, not just to other solicitors. It can be oral or in writing. Rule 10.05 requires a solicitor to fulfil an undertaking where it is given as a solicitor whether in the course of practice or outside it. An undertaking can in some circumstances be implied, as where a solicitor receives documents or money subject to a condition. He or she must return them if unwilling to abide by the condition. Undertakings must be fulfilled within a reasonable time.

A solicitor is personally bound by an undertaking and breach will prima facie be professional misconduct. The Solicitors Regulation Authority is rigorous about undertakings. They endure for as long as the solicitor remains on the roll, they cannot be unilaterally withdrawn. All partners are liable on the undertakings of each of them. The Law Society cannot specifically enforce the undertaking itself, though the court may be able to. The role of the court arose in the rather unsatisfactory case of *Twinsectra Ltd v Yardley and others*.[13] S, a solicitor for Yardley, had given an undertaking that he would pay out money received as a loan for Yardley only if it was to be used by him to acquire a property. S paid the money to L, also a solicitor acting for Yardley, having been assured by Yardley that the money would be so used. L then paid the money to Yardley without taking any steps to ensure that it was used for property purchase. No property was bought, the loan was not repaid and the lender sued L, amongst others, for acting in breach of trust and in breach of the undertaking not to pay the money out. The House of Lords dealt with the issue as one of breach of trust rather than specifically as a breach of a solicitor's undertaking. Having established that the transaction created a trust, the Lords went on to consider whether the breach by L was dishonest and he was thereby also liable for S's breach of undertaking. It was held that L was not dishonest despite the fact that he had 'shut his eyes' to the issue. Lord Hutton considered that L took a 'blinkered approach to his professional duties as a solicitor' but was not dishonest.[14] He and the majority of their Lordships appeared to expect a rather low

---

[13] [2002] UKHL 12.

[14] *Ibid*, para 22. A similar approach was taken in the case of *Bryant & Bench v The Law Society* (2007) *Law Society Gazette*, 24 January 2008, 28.

level of competence from a solicitor in this case. Only Lord Millett, dissenting, pointed out that L knew the terms of the undertaking given by S, but appeared to take the view that the breach of undertaking was solely S's responsibility. Lord Millett considered that L was civilly liable as an accessory to the tort of wrongful interference with the performance of S's fiduciary and contractual undertaking and also breach of trust.

The undertaking in *Twinsectra* was unusual, rather vague in its terms and probably therefore ultimately unenforceable, which may explain the decision in reality. Where there is a clear undertaking to receive money and not pay it out unless certain conditions prevail then a knowing breach of such an undertaking will normally be remediable as a breach of both the undertaking and a breach of trust. In relation to litigation, the court can exercise its inherent supervisory jurisdiction over solicitors and can order the performance of the undertaking, or award compensation if this is not possible. An illustrative case is *Udall v Capri Lighting Ltd*.[15] In this case the solicitor undertook orally to secure charges over the property of the directors of a company in favour of the plaintiff if the latter would adjourn judgment summonses he had obtained. The charges were not executed. Judgment was entered against the company, which then went into liquidation so that it could not be enforced. It was also impossible for the charges to be executed. The Court of Appeal held that failure to implement an undertaking was, prima facie, misconduct even where the solicitor had not acted dishonourably or could not implement it. The court could, in the exercise of its inherent jurisdiction, either order the implementation of the undertaking, where possible, or order compensation from the solicitor where it was not.[16]

Whatever the powers of the court, a failure to honour an undertaking can result in disciplinary proceedings against the solicitor. Compensation may be available through the firm's insurance or the Solicitors' Indemnity Fund (SIF). Unsurprisingly, the Solicitors Regulation Authority (SRA) is concerned that undertakings may be too easily given by solicitors, and be too vague in scope. Compensation for broken undertakings has in the past been a considerable drain on the SIF. Solicitors can also find themselves personally liable for them; for example, the SIF does not cover undertakings that amount to a bare guarantee for a client's financial obligations. The guidance points out that there is no obligation either to give or receive undertakings even where it might be in the client's interest to do so.[17] If given, they should be specific, confirmed in writing and realistic in the sense that a solicitor should not promise to do something that is not in his or her control. An undertaking is regarded as binding even if discharging it proves to be outside the control of the solicitor.[18]

Contacting an opposing party

Under rule 10.04, once a party is represented by a lawyer or licensed conveyancer (not just a solicitor, as was the case under the old principles), the opposing solicitor should not contact that party directly, except with the consent of that solicitor. This principle does not, however, prohibit client-to-client communications. Contacting witnesses is also allowed. The main

---

[15] [1988] QB 907.
[16] See also *Fox v Bannister* [1987] 1 All ER 737.
[17] Solicitors' Code, r 10.05 guidance, para 26.
[18] *Ibid*, guidance, para 38. See also *Citadel Management Inc v Thompson* [1999] 1 FLR 21.

exceptions to the rule are that contact can be made where the other solicitor has failed to communicate or pass on messages to their client or in exceptional circumstances. This rule may well be of practical importance as it prevents confusion and ensures that the other side's lawyer has all relevant communications. It also prevents any chance that a client might be personally pressurised by the opposing solicitor, which is inherent in the ethical rule to treat others fairly.

The guidance to this rule includes guidance on representing corporate clients (which is otherwise notably absent in either the new or the old rules). In the case of corporate clients, the 'client' is the employee or employees responsible for giving instructions. Therefore rule 10.04 does not prevent a solicitor from contacting other employees of the company directly. Such a course may, however, be hazardous: first, it may involve a breach of client confidentiality; secondly, it may put the employee in an invidious position, such as being asked to disclose information confidential to their employer. The contact should therefore not be made without advising the employer or their legal representative so that the employee can seek advice.[19]

Reporting other solicitors

Luban relates an incident in 1977 in which a senior lawyer in the US, 'an upright and courtly man', lied to an opponent to conceal discoverable documents, perjured himself to conceal the lie and, upon confessing the truth, resigned his job and spent a month in prison.[20] What is particularly interesting is the reaction of the associate who worked for the partner concerned who

> saw [the partner] lie and really couldn't believe it. And he just had no idea of what to do. I mean, he . . . kept thinking there must be a reason. Besides what do you do? The guy was his boss and a great guy.

The complicity of the associate was partly due to the ambiguity of the Americal Bar Association's model rule which permitted a subordinate lawyer to defer to a senior lawyer's reasonable resolution of an arguable question of professional duty. Luban argues that it is also the product of working in a large organisation, where lines of responsibility are confused and ambiguous, and can result in a gradual desensitisation to these issues.

In England and Wales disciplinary whistleblowing is not only allowed under the Public Interest Disclosure Act 1998, it is encouraged. Similarly, under the Solicitors' Code of Conduct 2007, rule 20.04 a solicitor must report to the SRA any serious misconduct by another solicitor, including, if a principal in the firm, misconduct by an employee of the firm. There is also a duty to report if there is 'reason to doubt the professional integrity of a solicitor' or if a firm is in serious financial difficulty which could put the public at risk. An employee should report such conduct of another employee to the principal or other director of the firm. The rule is intended to protect the public and the integrity of the profession, and seriousness should be construed in the light of this. Any conduct involving dishonesty or deception, or amounting to a serious arrestable offence, is construed as serious

---

[19] Guidance to r 10.04, para 21.
[20] DJ Luban, 'Milgram Revisited' (1998) 9 *Researching Law: An ABF Update* 1, 4.

misconduct. Misconduct can be reported on an anonymous basis.[21] The rule is subject 'where necessary' to the reporting solicitor's client's consent. The guidance states that this would be necessary if the report involved the disclosure of privileged or confidential information[22] of either the client or the other side. But the client may object in other circumstances; for example, he or she may well be loath to get involved in the unprofessional conduct of the other side's solicitor unless it impinges directly on their case. Indeed, such a report may delay matters or cause other problems to the client. There is no guidance on this.

Relationships with barristers

The primary relationship of the solicitor is with the client, but, of course, the solicitor will often brief a barrister on behalf of the client. How does this affect the relationship with the client? The 1999 Law Society Guide stated as a basic principle that a solicitor has a duty to brief appropriate counsel and should ensure themselves that counsel's advice does not contain any 'obvious errors'.[23] The courts require that solicitors should not follow counsel's advice blindly but continue to exercise their own judgement, especially where counsel is obviously or seriously wrong.[24] This raises the interesting possibility of solicitor and counsel presenting differing advice to the client, a position that only the client can resolve by deciding whose advice to accept. Relationships with barristers do not feature as such in the 2007 Rules, but the above principle is obviously still one of good practice.

Under the old principles a solicitor had a personal responsibility to pay the barrister's fees whether or not the client has put the solicitor 'in funds'.[25] This is not replicated in the new Rules, as it is possible now for a binding contract for the fees to be made and enforced in the usual way. In any case, a failure to pay might be a breach of core duty 1.06 not to diminish public trust in the profession. Solicitors should provide adequate instructions in good time. The solicitor, or a responsible representative, normally attends the barrister in court, with certain exceptions. The Law Society used to advise that 'careful judgement' is required on dispensing with attendance and suggested various situations where attendance is desirable even where a case falls within the exceptions: for example, where a client is a juvenile, is handicapped in some way or is a 'difficult character', or where a substantial sentence of imprisonment is likely.[26] This advice is obviously still good advice, even though it is not included in the 2007 Rules.

In criminal cases it is not uncommon for the barrister to return the brief at a late stage so that a substitute has to take over at the last minute. This can also happen in civil cases, though it appears to be less common. In such cases it will usually be desirable for a solicitor to attend court with the substitute barrister in order to protect the interests of the client.

---

[21] Solicitors' Code, r 20.04, guidance para22.
[22] *Ibid*, r 20.04 guidance, paras 23 and 28.
[23] Law Society Guide, ch 20, principle 20.05.
[24] See *Locke v Camberwell Health Authority* [1991] 2 Med LR 249; *Davy-Chiesman v Davy-Chiesman* [1984] 1 All ER 321; *Matrix Securities Ltd v Theodore Goddard* [1997] 147 NLJR 1847. See also, on wasted costs, *Tolstoy v Aldington* [1996] 2 All ER 556.
[25] Law Society Guide, principle 20.06.
[26] *Ibid*, 20.04 para 2.

The client may well wonder why two lawyers must be employed and paid for where one would do, and even more so where a last minute return of the brief results in the employment of a barrister unfamiliar with the case who has probably never met the client before the day of the hearing. Solicitors also find this a problem, as the following quotation shows:

> You get called to a case conference by the court at which the client is also required to attend, are you going to have to instruct a barrister to turn up and speak to the judge when you are the one who knows the case because the client says, well, you know my documents, and you know my witnesses, you have spoken to them, why do I need another person to come along and tell the judge what this case is about? Don't you know what the case is about? Clearly the answer has got to be we have got to do it ourselves.[27]

This leads to the more general issue of the division between solicitors and barristers. Is it in the interests of clients? The increase in the number of solicitor advocates since 1990 and the increase in the possibility of a client briefing a barrister directly suggests that in many cases both the professions and the government recognise that it is not. However, there are often good practical reasons for a solicitor to employ a separate advocate. A partner in a big City firm, or indeed smaller firms, is expected mainly to be a client 'getter and pleaser' and cannot be out of the office for days or weeks at a time undertaking advocacy. Advocacy is a special skill and needs constant practice, which few solicitors, other than those with specialist criminal practices which are organised to accommodate such work, can undertake in combination with running an office and attending to the demands of all their clients. In addition to these practical reasons, two other justifications are put forward in favour of the current rules. First, the existence of an independent bar enables even the smallest firm of solicitors to retain an expert advocate for their clients. As one solicitor expressed it:

> The great thing for small firms like us is what I have always said: we have on tap the best advocates without having to pay them a retainer or employ them and if we have the right case or the right fee, we can get the right person to do it.[28]

Even larger firms also appreciate the range of expertise available to them:

> A department . . . cannot have the pools of specialist expertise that may be available in a larger firm. What it does have of course is access to an independent bar, barristers numbering two thousand six hundred within half a mile of this office who are all, more or less, experts in particular fields and are all, more or less, trained advocates who do little else but.[29]

Secondly, the barrister is supposed to maintain a greater distance from the client than the solicitor in order to provide more objective and independent advice. This is the traditional role of the consultant in many other fields. It is not just that two heads may be better than one; it is also that the second head may not be so deeply involved with the details of the client's case and his expressed interests.

---

[27] J Flood, A Boon, A Whyte, E Skordaki, R Abbey and A Ash, *Reconfiguring the Market for Advocacy Services: A Case Study of London and Four Fields of Practice* (A Report for the Lord Chancellor's Committee on Legal Education and Conduct, 1996) (hereafter ACLEC Report) 101.
[28] *Ibid*, 186.
[29] *Ibid*, 129.

Whether, in order to achieve these benefits, it is necessary to maintain an entirely separate bar with its accompanying, though diminishing, restrictive practice rules is doubtful. The government was clearly not convinced when it introduced the wider rules on advocacy rights in both 1990 and 1998,[30] such that independence would thereby be impaired:

> independence is a matter of ethos, professional discipline and frame of mind, rather than a matter of how a lawyer is engaged or paid.[31]

Nor was it impressed with the alleged expertise of the bar in advocacy matters, pointing out the high number of returned briefs in criminal matters and the comparative inexperience of the junior bar.[32] Now, under the Legal Services Act 2007, it is proposed that mixed practices of barristers and solicitors will be permitted, with full advocacy rights for both types of lawyers. Moreover, it will be for the Legal Services Board to lay down the regulations for approving advocacy qualifications and rights. These rights will be attainable by many other professionals, such as legal executives or chartered surveyors, as well as members of the traditional legal professions. The traditional model—the client instructs a solicitor, who in turn briefs a barrister advocate/consultant—is becoming merely one of a number of models for delivering legal services.

Relationships with unrepresented parties

Where the other party is not represented by a solicitor, how should the solicitor deal with him or her? Solicitors tend to dislike dealing with laypersons, fearing that they will delay matters or not understand what to do. Do-it-yourself conveyancers often encounter this attitude. But unrepresented parties must be dealt with fairly under the obligation imposed by the Solicitors' Code of Conduct 2007, rule 10.01. There may be a conflict here between the best interests of the client and dealing with the unrepresented party 'fairly'. If the latter presents the solicitor with a badly drafted document, then they should be advised to seek legal advice; a solicitor should not seek to take advantage of the badly drawn document. Thus, as the guidance notes, rule 10.01 'limits your duty to act in the best interests of your client'. If the solicitor is inclined to deal with an unrepresented person helpfully, then care must be taken not to 'inadvertently create a contractual relationship with that party'.[33] Equally, the solicitor must beware of any possibility that a negligence claim might arise from the unrepresented party. In *Dean v Allin & Watts*[34] the unrepresented claimant, a car mechanic, had relied on the defendant's solicitor in relation to security for a loan he was making to the defendants. The advice was wrong and the solicitor, who knew the claimant

---

[30] Under the Courts and Legal Services Act 1990 and the Access to Justice Act 1998. See further chapter 19.

[31] *Rights of Audience and Rights to Conduct Litigation in England and Wales: The Way Ahead* (Lord Chancellors Consultation Paper, June 1998) para 2.9.

[32] Up to 75% of CPS instructions had been returned in a recent survey of nine Crown Court Centres; *ibid*, para 2.11.

[33] R 10.01 guidance, paras 2 and 3.

[34] [2001] All ER (D) 288. See article on the case by Jonathan Ross in 151 NLJ 960 (29 June 2001). See also *Hemmens v Wilson Browne* [1995] Ch 223, where there was no liability because the solicitors had advised getting independent advice.

was unrepresented, had not advised him to obtain independent legal advice. Moreover, at the time of the loan both parties had a mutual interest in ensuring that it was secured. It was held that a duty of care existed in this exceptional case and the solicitor was found liable to the unrepresented mechanic.

If the other party is represented or helped by an unqualified person, then the solicitor may decline to communicate with that representative if he or she is undertaking prohibited acts, and should report them to the Law Society. Prohibited acts include the provision of litigation, probate and conveyancing services whilst unqualified.[35] A fine line will have to be drawn sometimes between unlawful practice on the one hand and, on the other, communicating with someone who is lawfully assisting another with advice to help them represent themselves, such as a *McKenzie* friend[36] or an advice worker. However, lay representatives now have rights of audience in the Small Claims Court, the Lord Chancellor having granted this right under section 11 of the Courts and Legal Services Act 1990, and also in tribunals. Where relevant, these lay representatives can obtain the costs of representation. Such activity must be distinguished from acting as a solicitor. As Lord Justice Potter put it,

> The words 'acting as a solicitor' are limited to the doing of acts which *only* a solicitor may perform and/or the doing of acts by a person pretending or holding himself out to be a solicitor. Such acts are not to be confused with the doing of acts of a kind *commonly* done by solicitors but which involve no representation that the actor is acting as such.[37]

Other third parties affected by the transaction

A solicitor normally owes no professional duties, other than those of courtesy and fairness, to persons who are neither clients nor the other side, but who may be affected by the transaction. However, a duty of care under the law of negligence may arise, as is illustrated in the case of *Dean v Allin & Watts*, noted above. In 2005 a county court judge held that a solicitor owed a duty of care to a witness who was supporting the client. The case concerned a trainee solicitor who advised the witness that the latter could not be sacked if, in giving evidence in court, he admitted smoking at work. He was sacked and damages were awarded for negligence.[38]

There may also be a liability in negligence to the beneficiaries of wills or trusts made or administered by the solicitor. In *White v Jones*[39] the House of Lords held that a beneficiary could sue the deceased's solicitor in negligence. The case concerned the deceased's instructions to draw up a will. The matter was negligently delayed by the solicitors and the testator died before executing the will. As a result the beneficiary lost the bequest. It was held that it

---

[35] Solicitors' Act 1974, s 22 and Courts & Legal Services Act 1990, s 70. For the full list, see Solicitors' Code, r 20 guidance, para 10.

[36] *McKenzie v McKenzie* [1970] 3 All ER 1034. A McKenzie representative is a person who accompanies a litigant in court and gives them advice. Such a representative has no general right to address the court unless the court allows this. See also *R v Leicester City Justices* [1991] 3 ALL ER 935; *Re H* [1997] 2 FLR 423; *R v Bow County Court, ex parte Pelling* [1999] 4 All ER 751; *Noueiri v Paragon Finance Plc. The Times*, October 4 2001. Members of the Institute of Legal Executives have had advocacy rights in the lower courts in civil and family proceedings since the spring of 1998 and in the County Court since 2006 (The Institute of Legal Executives Order 1998, SI No 1077).

[37] Potter J in *Piper Double Glazing Ltd v DC Contracts (1992) Ltd* [1994] 1 All ER 177, 186 (emphasis added).

[38] See the *Law Society Gazette*, 1 September 2005, 4.

[39] [1995] 1 All ER 691.

was reasonably foreseeable that the negligence would cause such a loss. As neither the testator nor the estate had a remedy against the solicitor, the only way a remedy for the loss could be granted was to allow the intended beneficiary to make a claim. The House of Lords recognised that there were difficulties in reaching this decision (and two of their Lordships dissented). A solicitor normally owes a duty of care to clients only; no duty is owed to opponents in litigation or to the other side in conveyancing matters for example. Nor is there a duty of care to a prospective beneficiary of a client's disposition during that client's lifetime.[40] However, where the client is unable to obtain a remedy for the solicitor's negligence, as in *White v Jones*, a remedy should be provided for the beneficiary on the basis that 'the assumption of responsibility by the solicitor towards his client should be held in law to extend to the intended beneficiary'.[41] There is no conflict of interest in this type of case between the client and the third party; arguably, by allowing the action by the beneficiary, the duty of care owed to the testator is reinforced.

Where a solicitor accepts responsibilities to a third party by giving an undertaking, he or she may also be liable in negligence to that third party. An example of this arose in the matrimonial case of *Al-Kandari v Brown*.[42] The solicitor for the husband undertook not to release the husband's passport to him. On this basis, the husband was granted access to the children of the family. Due to the solicitor's negligence, the husband obtained the passport and managed to take his children out of the country. The wife sued in negligence and succeeded. The solicitors, in giving the undertaking, had

> stepped outside their role as solicitors for their client and accepted responsibilities towards both their client and the plaintiff and the children.[43]

Another route which might result in liability in negligence to a third party relates to a possible duty to warn such a party of a threat to life or injury. It would be a justifiable breach of the duty of confidentiality to a client to reveal information of this kind. Could a solicitor be held liable in negligence for a failure to warn an intended victim?[44]

Obligations to a third party paying the client's fees

The payment of fees by a third party used to be illegal under the old laws of maintenance. As noted in chapter 12, there were a number of reasons for this. One of them relates to the primary duty of the lawyer to the client and the possible conflict that may arise where the fees are paid by another. The lawyer may feel that a duty is owed to the fee payer which conflicts with the interests of the client. There is now no legal or ethical objection to the payment of

---

[40] See generally *Gran Gelato Ltd v Richcliff Ltd* [1992] 1 All ER 865; *Clark v Bruce Lance* [1988] 1 All ER 364; *Al-Kandari v Brown* [1988] 1 All ER 833.

[41] *White v Jones* [1995] 1 All ER 691, 710. See now *Carr-Glynn v Frearsons* [1998] 4 All ER 225, where a beneficiary under a will recovered from the deceased's solicitor's firm even though the estate also had a remedy against the firm. See also *Walker v Geo Medlicott* [1999] 1 All ER 685 and *Hooper v Fynmores* [2001] *Law Society Gazette*, 28 June 2001, 45.

[42] [1988] 1 All ER 833.

[43] *Ibid*, 836.

[44] In the US a psychiatrist was held to be negligent for failing to warn a murder victim of the murderous intentions of his patient, her former boyfriend: *Tarasoff v Regents of the University of California* [1976] 131 *Cal Rpter* 14. See further chapter 11.

fees by a third party. Common third party supporters of litigation include insurance companies, trades unions or other professional bodies, associations like the AA or RAC, charities and pressure groups. Similarly there may be an agreement for one side's fees to be paid by the other party, such as the landlord's costs of drawing up a lease being paid for by the tenant. Not only is there now no objection to such support, there are provisions under the Solicitors Act 1974, section 71 for such third parties to apply for assessment of costs. Rule 2.03 of the 2007 Code requires the solicitor to advise the client if the costs are covered by insurance or may be paid by another, such as an employer or trade union.

Obviously, regardless of who pays the costs, the solicitor's prime duty is to advance the best interests of the client, not of the funder. The same rule applies where a referral fee is paid by the solicitor for the introduction of the client. However, rule 10.02 of the 2007 Code does impose one duty for the benefit of the funder: it requires the solicitor to 'give sufficient time and information for the amount of your costs to be agreed or assessed' to the funder. This information should include the basis on which the fees are calculated. The terms of any funding arrangement may require the solicitor to inform the funder of the progress of the case—and the client will have to agree to this, as otherwise such reports would be a breach of confidentiality. This is normally an express contractual responsibility of the client in insurance contracts providing for legal expenses funding. However, it is primarily the client's responsibility to inform the insurance company and the solicitor should not do so without the client's consent.

Solicitors cannot in general enter into agreements with insurance companies giving them the right to act for a particular client. The client's freedom of choice of solicitor may not be restricted unless the terms of the policy fall within the Insurance Companies (Legal Expenses Insurance) Regulations 1990. These regulations allow restrictions on freedom of choice of solicitor except where there is a conflict of interest between insurance company and insured or in relation to an inquiry under the policy. This, however, may be an inaccurate interpretation of the Insurance Companies (Legal Expenses Insurance) Regulations 1990. Clause 5(4) of these Regulations states that

> The company shall . . . afford the insured the right to entrust the defence of his interests from the moment that he has the right to claim from the insurer under the policy, to a lawyer of his choice.

Clause 6 then goes on, rather unnecessarily, to state that the insured shall have freedom of choice of a lawyer 'to defend, represent or serve the interests of the insured *in any inquiry or proceedings*.'[45] Clause 6(2) makes clear that the insured always has a free choice of lawyer where a conflict of interest arises, a statement which is otiose if clauses 5(4) and 6(1) mean what they say.[46] It is very difficult to make sense of these Regulations, which were enacted to give effect to European Directive 87/344. That they are confusing, and that no clarification has been forthcoming, is perhaps a sign of how little legal assistance has been funded by insurance in this country until comparatively recently, though the market has greatly expanded in the last decade.[47] It should be noted that a solicitor employed by an

---

[45] Emphasis added.

[46] There are other exceptions to these rules laid down in reg 7.

[47] Little help is to be found in JA Holland (ed), *Cordery on Solicitors* (London, Butterworths, 1995), which simply states that any restriction on the freedom to chose a solicitor is unenforceable (para K 1088).

insurance company as an employed solicitor can act for an insured person provided the latter gives specific consent, the claim comes within the small claims limit in the county court, the case is not allocated to the fast or multi-track and it does not concern personal injuries.[48]

In many cases which are funded by insurance companies the insured client is a purely nominal client. For all practical purposes the case is managed by the insurance company, and the client may have little personal interest in its progress. Nevertheless, the theory is still that the solicitor should receive instructions from the insured client and is therefore responsible only to him or her. This theory is strained and has become further strained in the light of the decision in *Chapman v Christopher*,[49] which held that the insurance company's liability for the costs of the other side where the case is lost cannot be limited by the terms of the insurance contract with the nominal plaintiff where the company, in effect, managed and conducted the plaintiff's litigation. It was recognised in this case that the solicitor for the plaintiff was, in reality, being instructed by the insurance company. Where this is the situation, it may be arguable in a future case that the solicitor should owe certain duties to the insurance company, such as providing them directly with information on the progress of the litigation, in particular in relation to their liability for costs.

A further problem may arise in relation to the solicitor's duties where the funder withdraws funding or, more likely, tries to influence the conduct of the case by the threat of withdrawal of funding.[50] It is clear that the solicitor's duty is still to the client and not the funder, but equally the solicitor can withdraw from the case where it is clear that the client can no longer cover the fees and costs. This would be regarded as a 'good reason' for withdrawing from a case under the rule 2.01(2) of the Code, but reasonable notice of withdrawal would be required. In reality, therefore, the client may have no option but to agree to the terms of the funder with regard to the conduct of the case.

Obligations to the Legal Services Commission

The duty of lawyers to make reports on the progress of cases to the Legal Services Commission (LSC) could be regarded as a duty to society generally rather than to an individual third party. However, it seems convenient to deal with the issue in this chapter as the LSC is a particular example of a third party funder of litigation. Legal aid is now administered by the LSC, which is an arm's length agency of what is now the Ministry of Justice. As such, it raises ethical issues similar to those arising in the case of insurance, namely the possibility of a conflict of interest between the interests the client and the interests of the LSC. Issues can arise relating to the restriction on the client's right to free choice of solicitor and possible breaches of client confidence when the solicitor makes reports on the progress of the

---

[48] Solicitors' Code of Conduct 2007, r 13.06(2).

[49] [1998] 2 All ER 873.

[50] An example of this was reported by *Private Eye* on 15 April 2005. The Labour Party had provided the financial support for their councillors accused of election fraud and had retained solicitors on their behalf. The case became a political embarrassment, and the Party, and therefore the solicitors, withdrew their support one week before trial. The Councillors had to rely on a *pro bono* barrister who had not done any previous preparation for the case. The judge found the conduct of the Party and the solicitors 'inexcusable'.

case, or changes in the client's circumstances, to the LSC. Indeed, these ethical considerations were raised by opponents of legal aid when it was first introduced.

Notwithstanding these objections, where the overall best interests of the client were concerned, the balance lay in favour of the legal aid scheme. Traditionally, the basic principle was that the legally aided client should be treated in the same way as a privately paying client, subject to the specific provisions of the legislation. This principle was not statutory but was contained in note 7 to paragraph 5.01 of the 1999 Law Society Guide.[51] It is not contained in the new 2007 Rules. The principle remains a good one, however, even though in reality there are differences between the legally aided and the privately paying client because of the control the LSC can exercise over the cost and conduct of the case and the duties of the lawyers towards it.

Legal aid now is delivered by contracts made between the LSC and the supplier (which can be a solicitor or a not for profit organisation like a Citizens Advice Bureau). The client therefore does not have the same freedom as does a privately paying client to instruct his representative. These contracts provide for a specified number of cases (or matter starts) per year in specified areas of law (for example, family law, criminal law, welfare law). In general, the provider cannot give services to the client outside these areas (though there are some accepted 'tolerances' which permit help and advice in related areas of law in certain circumstances). Also, there are restrictions in the contract on the solicitor's freedom to use, for example, experts and interpreters, or to get paid for legal research. Thus the legally aided client may well not be offered or receive the kind of comprehensive or holistic service that the private client would be offered.

Work done under the contract must meet the test of 'sufficient benefit' to the client and be 'reasonable' in the eyes of the LSC, and the LSC audits the work done. The contract requires the solicitor to meet 'such level of performance, as measured by performance indicators, as we may require'. In addition, the contract requires both the LSC and the solicitor to 'work together in mutual trust and cooperation', but it recognises that this must be 'without prejudice to . . . your professional obligations in respect of clients'. The contract also specifically provides that the rules of the professional body must be abided by, in particular the Code of Conduct.

These provisions clearly indicate that the solicitor has a dual duty to both the client and the LSC. If he favours the client too much in preference to the LSC, then at the very least there will be a risk that he will lose the contract or not get it renewed when the next round of competitive tendering comes round. However, it is also of advantage to the client that the LSC requires an expert standard of work and also audits this—the client can have some confidence that the solicitor has expertise in the area of law concerned and is required to reach a minimum standard. The majority of the terms of the LSC contracts are concerned with fees and their payment. Fixed fees are set for standard procedures and solicitors are expected to deal with a set number of cases for a set overall payment. Obviously this affects the standard of work that can be done for particular clients—but this is also the case for privately paying clients whose resources are limited.

---

[51] See also, on solicitor's duties, O Hansen, *Legal Aid in Practice: the Guide to Civil and Criminal Proceedings* (London, Legal Action Group, 1993) 11.

The legally aided client cannot supplement the service received by offering private payment (though he can, of course, employ the solicitor in a private capacity for work which is not within the legal aid contract, provided he can afford to). The client does have a free choice of solicitor, provided the solicitor has a contract in the field of law, but there are restrictions on changing the solicitor once the client's case has been started. Any such change will have to be approved by the LSC and there will have to be a substantial reason for it, such as conflict of interest, not simply that the client does not get on with the solicitor or disagrees with the advice. A solicitor acting under a legal aid contract is under a duty to make reports to the LSC of information that would otherwise be confidential to the client. Monthly reports on completed cases must be sent to the LSC under the contract.

Solicitors must report suspected abuse of the scheme by the assisted person, reasons for any doubts that the action should be continued and other information on the conduct of the assisted person. The LSC must be given access to the files of clients and former clients. These reporting obligations are imposed both by law and by the contract. In theory, the solicitor should inform his client of these obligations at the start of the case and obtain client consent if the duties in relation to confidentiality are to be complied with. The 2007 Code is, however, silent on this issue. The LSC is also bound by client confidentiality in that it is not allowed to publish details relating to clients or use the information other than in relation to the administration of the scheme. Nevertheless it can get access to client details for research purposes and for client satisfaction surveys as well as for administrative purposes, so a considerable number of people will have access to the information both within and outwith the LSC.

The Bar also has duties to the LSC where acting for legally aided clients. However, the Code clearly states that, in supplying legally aided services, the barrister 'owes his primary duty to the lay client', but he must also abide by the provisions of the Access to Justice Act 1999 and related regulations in so acting.[52] In giving an opinion on an applicant's case, a barrister clearly has to act for both his client and the LSC. Counsel should set out any rival accounts of the facts so that the LSC can estimate the strength of the applicant's case. They must state whether a conference has been held to estimate the applicant's reliability as a witness, and suggest any limitations that should be imposed on the grant of funding.

Liability for wasted costs

A jurisdiction which has developed rapidly over the past few years is the wasted costs jurisdiction under the Civil Procedure Rules. Under it the lawyer may be ordered to personally pay the costs of the opponent or his own client. Insofar as it requires the lawyer to pay the costs of the other side, it provides a stark example of the solicitor (or barrister) having a duty to consider the interests of the other side as well as those of his or her own client. This creates a classic conflict between the lawyer's duties to the client, to the other side and to the court, and the proper administration of justice. This conflict is clearly illustrated in the cases decided under this jurisdiction.

---

[52] *Code of Conduct of the Bar of England and Wales* (London, Bar Standards Board, 8th edn, as amended, 2004) (hereafter the Bar Code) paras 303(c) and 304. See also Annex E.

The wasted costs jurisdiction now comes under the Supreme Court Act 1981, section 51(6), as amended by the 1990 Courts & Legal Services Act.[53] The latter Act was specifically directed at providing a remedy for people affected by unsatisfactory work by requiring that lawyers pay personally any costs run up as a consequence of that work. Under the Act the court may, at the instigation of either the client or the other side to the litigation, order the lawyer to pay the whole or any part of any wasted costs. Wasted costs are defined as costs incurred by a party as

a result of any improper, unreasonable or negligent act or omission on the part of any legal or other representative or any employee of such representative.[54]

At the time that the 1990 Act was being debated, the Law Society was very concerned that the jurisdiction would be used by the opposing side to intimidate or prevent a solicitor from acting properly for his client. It feared that the ethical duty to the court and to the administration of justice would be used as a tactical weapon against solicitors in the litigation process. As can be seen from the cases, this is exactly the issue with which the courts have had to grapple in exercising the wasted costs jurisdiction. It has also had to deal with the desire of the lawyers to evade the jurisdiction—also by resorting to other ethical principles such as legal privilege.

A leading case is *Ridehalgh v Horsefield*.[55] This was a consolidated appeal in six actions where the judge at first instance had made wasted costs orders against the solicitors and, in one case, a barrister. The facts of the six cases were very varied. They included a failure by a solicitor to ascertain that the workplace of the plaintiff suing for noise-induced hearing loss was not dangerously noisy and a failure to inform the other side that legal aid had been granted, which could have resulted in early settlement. The Court of Appeal, which allowed all the appeals, was therefore in a position to give general guidance on the jurisdiction. The Court decided that 'improper' conduct is constituted by a significant breach of a substantial duty imposed by a code of professional conduct, or by conduct which would be considered improper according to the consensus of professional opinion. 'Unreasonable' conduct is vexatious conduct designed to harass the other side rather than advance the resolution of the case. 'Negligent' conduct is a failure to act with the competence reasonably expected of a member of the profession.

The court was anxious that the wasted costs jurisdiction should not be used so as to require lawyers to 'filter out' unmeritorious cases. It was said that

A legal representative is not to be held to have acted improperly, unreasonably or negligently simply because he acts for a party who pursues a claim or defence which is plainly doomed to fail.[56]

It was argued that any other approach would conflict, in the case of barristers, with the 'cab-rank rule'. It would also discourage solicitors who respect the policy underlying that rule

---

[53] See ss 4, 111 and 112.
[54] Supreme Court Act 1981, s 51(7).
[55] [1994] 3 All ER 848.
[56] *Ibid*, Sir Thomas Bingham at 863a. See similarly *Locke v Camberwell HA* [1991] Med LR 249 and *C v C* [1994] 2 FLR 34.

from 'affording representation to the unpopular and the unmeritorious'.[57] This argument represents a confusion concerning the purpose of the cab-rank rule. It is aimed at ensuring that unpopular *people* or causes receive representation, not that unmeritorious *litigation* should be pursued. Sir Thomas Bingham recognised that it is not always easy to distinguish the case which is hopeless from the case which is an abuse of the process of the court, but stated that any doubt should be resolved to the benefit of the legal representative. A general statement from the Court of Appeal that bona fide actions aimed at bringing about a change in the law would not fall foul of the wasted costs jurisdiction would have been welcome.[58]

The House of Lords considered the jurisdiction for the first time in *Medcalf v Mardell*,[59] in which two barristers were alleged to have amended a notice of appeal to include allegations of fraud which, it appeared, had no basis in the evidence. The other side to the litigation then claimed wasted costs from the barristers to cover the costs of investigating and rebutting the fraud allegations. In the Lords the case was lost. The reasons were largely procedural, in that the barristers were unable to present evidence to rebut the claimant's case because they claimed to be bound by professional privilege in relation to the advice and counsel they had provided for their client. Where such a case was brought by the lawyers' own client, that issue would not, of course, arise, but where the claim was made by the other side, the Lords held that a wasted costs order would not normally be made unless there was clearly no possible defence to the claim even if the lawyers were not constrained by legal privilege. In addition, as in *Ridehalgh*, the summary nature of the jurisdiction was regarded as a problem because of the need to be fair to the lawyers involved. Save in the clearest case, applications against lawyers acting for an opposing party are unlikely to be apt for summary determination, since any hearing to investigate the conduct of a complex action is itself likely to be expensive and time consuming.

The desirability of compensating litigating parties who have been put to unnecessary expense by the unjustified conduct of their opponents' lawyers is, without doubt, an important public interest, but 'it is . . . only one of the public interests which have to be considered'[60]. Lord Hobhouse considered that the public interest to be protected was not that of the opposing party, to whom the barrister owes 'no duty', but the duty to the court.[61] The essentially punitive nature of the jurisdiction was recognised in *Harley v McDonald*, where it was suggested that, as such, it should be confined 'strictly to questions which are apt for summary disposal by the court', and that issues of negligence or professional conduct should be dealt with by court proceedings for negligence or by disciplinary proceedings rather than under the wasted costs jurisdiction.[62]

The courts are also well aware of another danger, originally pointed out by Lord Justice Balcombe in *Symphony Group v Hodgson*,[63] that an application to make the solicitor pay

---

[57] *Ibid*, 863f.

[58] The ruling in *Ridehalgh v Horsefield* reflects that in *Orchard v SE Electricity Board* [1987] 1 All ER 95 under the old costs jurisdiction.

[59] [2002] 3 All ER 721.

[60] *Ibid*, Lord Bingham, 734–5. See also *Harley v McDonald* [2001] 2 WLR 1749.

[61] *Ibid*, Lord Hobhouse at 741.

[62] [2001] 2 WLR 1749, paras 49–54. The court's gentle treatment of lawyers under this jurisdiction is further illustrated by *R v Staffordshire CC* [2007] EWHC 2441, where a wasted costs order was refused because it would have made the solicitor bankrupt, which was regarded by the court as disproportionate.

[63] [1993] 4 All ER 143.

wasted costs may be used as a way of getting round the fact that many successful unaided parties will not, at first instance, be able to get a costs order against a legally aided party or against the LSC.[64] It would, according to Sir Thomas Bingham, 'subvert the benevolent purposes of [the legal aid] legislation if such representatives were subject to any unusual personal risk'.[65] In the actual case of *Ridehalgh* the issue involved complex landlord and tenant legislation which both side's solicitors had misconstrued, as indeed had the judge at first instance. Unsurprisingly, therefore, it was held that the solicitors had not been negligent or careless in coming to their mistaken conclusions on the meaning of the legislation.

An example of a case where a wasted costs application was successful is *Tolstoy v Aldington*.[66] This case involved a lengthy and successful libel action brought by Lord Aldington against Count Tolstoy. Tolstoy sought to get the judgment set aside on the ground of fraud. His solicitors acted for him without fee, without having applied for legal aid[67] and without sending a letter before action. Tolstoy himself had been declared bankrupt and so, obviously, could not pay any costs awarded against him. The court found that the case was hopeless and struck it out as an abuse of process. Aldington therefore applied for a wasted costs order against the solicitors. He succeeded. In his judgment, Rose LJ stressed that acting without fee, even in a hopeless case, was not sufficient to justify an order.

The circumstances in *Tolstoy* were 'at least potentially vexatious'[68] and the proceedings were a collateral attack on the judgment of a court of competent jurisdiction. Rose LJ concluded that no solicitor could 'reasonably have instituted these proceedings'. In this case, counsel had signed the statement of claim. This astonished Lord Justice Rose, but no case against counsel was before the court. His Lordship stressed, however, that counsel's involvement did not exonerate the solicitors from their duty to exercise their own independent judgement in relation to the case.[69] Lord Justice Ward likewise concluded that the

> solicitors allowed themselves to be dragged outside that broad province where their actions could reasonably be said to further the ends of justice.[70]

Another example where a wasted costs order was made is *C v C*.[71] Here, a husband and wife, who were in dispute over financial provision on divorce, both applied for a wasted costs order against the wife's solicitor. The solicitor had failed to reconsider the case after it had become clear that the husband's assets were much less than originally thought. Expensive further investigations were made and information required of the husband. A Calderbank offer of £50,000 was rejected. The wife was eventually awarded £20,000, by which time her costs

---

[64] In *Kelly v South Manchester HA* [1997] 3 All ER 274, the court made a costs order against the Legal Aid Board under its discretionary powers in the Supreme Court Act 1981, s 51(1), holding that s 18 of the Legal Aid Act 1988 was not a 'complete code' in relation to costs orders against the Board. This jurisdiction would be exercised in exceptional circumstances only. Orders for costs against third party funders of litigation are frequently applied for but seldom awarded.

[65] *Ridehalgh v Horsefield* [1994] 3 All ER 848, 864c.

[66] [1996] 2 All ER 556.

[67] Which would have provided a screening process on the merits of the case.

[68] [1996] 2 All ER 556, 567c.

[69] See also *Davy Chiesman* [1984] 1 All ER 321; *Locke v Camberwell HA* [1991] Med LR 249.

[70] *Tolstoy*, above n 24, 572c.

[71] [1994] 2 FLR 34. See also *Woolwich Building Society v Fineberg* (1998) PNLR 216.

amounted to £60,000 and the husband's £70,000. A wasted costs order was made in respect of some of these costs on the grounds of unreasonableness and negligent conduct on the part of the solicitor.

Clearly, the wasted costs jurisdiction in civil cases shows that lawyers must not simply act as hired guns, but neither are they expected to act as a filter and ensure that only cases with a better than even chance of success are taken on. This is not always an easy distinction to make, but lawyers can take some comfort from the fact that comparatively few applications for wasted costs appear to have succeeded.[72] However, the main purpose of the jurisdiction is still not totally clear. Is it to punish lawyers for unreasonable or negligent conduct of the case or to compensate the other side (or the client) for having incurred unnecessary or excessive costs which cannot be recovered from any other source? It seems that the courts are primarily concerned with the former aim, but the latter also sometimes seems to be a consideration.[73]

Conclusion

As will be clear from this chapter, in general a lawyer's obligations to individual third parties are severely limited. While there are some rules which impose such obligations, these tend to be designed to facilitate legal transactions. The most notable exceptions, duties to the Legal Service Commission and the wasted cost jurisdiction, can be seen as attempts not to boost the ethical responsibility of lawyers to third parties as such, but to ensure the protection of public funds and to prevent frivolous litigation respectively. This underlines the argument that lawyers have considerable freedom in determining what they will do for clients and that it is in most cases very difficult either to limit or to police that freedom. The next chapter looks at the extent of the lawyer's duty towards society generally, or to sections thereof.

---

[72] See also *Re O (A minor)* [1994] 2 FLR 842; *R v Horsham DC & West Sussex CC* (1993) *New Law Journal* 22 October, 1477; *R v M* [1996] 1 FLR 750; *Re A Solicitor* [1996] 2 All ER 416; *Neill v DPP* (1997) *New Law Journal* 31 January, 136; *Re Boodhoo* [2007] 4 All ER 762.

[73] See further P Jones and N Armstrong, 'Living in Fear of Wasted Costs' (1994) *Civil Justice Quarterly* 208; H Evans, 'The Wasted Costs Jurisdiction' (2001) 64 *MLR* 51.

14

COLLECTIVE THIRD PARTIES

At the very least, the codes' silence on issues of general justice and the public interest as compared to the detailed regulation of matters such as how solicitors firms should be named, what matters can be referred to in lawyers' publicity, and the ownership and storage of documents, suggest that they are more important than questions of acting justly in regard to specific others, the general public or the environment.[1]

Introduction

Responsibility for collective third parties is broader than that considered in the previous chapter, which concerned identifiable and individual third parties with whom lawyers deal on behalf of their clients, such as the other side, their lawyers, witnesses and third party funders of litigation. It is in some ways a more difficult area for professional ethics because there is sometimes no individual to whom duties can be owed. Nevertheless, such wider obligations are well established. Indeed, the claim of lawyers to balance their self-interest or the interests of clients with the good of the wider community is one of the key claims of legal professionalism. Conceived of as part of the ethic of public service, this capacity also supports the case for self-regulation. The oldest example of such an obligation is the duty to the court, which is currently rapidly evolving. The duty to the court has long been recognised in case law, but it is now statutory and embodied in rules of court in a manner that barely existed before the introduction of the Woolf reforms of civil procedure in 2000. The field is also expanding to recognise the rights of other third party collectives, including the state, the general public or groups within the general public such as the employees, pensioners or shareholders of companies for whom they act.

This is an inchoate, though possibly developing, field in which many of the issues have been recognised only recently. It is, for example, the duties to the state and to the rule of law that are the central justification for current rules on reporting money laundering, or the duties of lawyers who act as special advocates in immigration cases. Arguably larger issues, however, such as environmental disasters, are sometimes perpetrated by corporations. These disasters may destroy communities and affect those far beyond the national sphere. Failure to take action, and failure to make specific rules on the issue, leads to the impression that the primary concerns of professions are the profession itself, its clients and the courts, rather than justice, morality or the wider community. Yet, despite recent extensions of the scope of

---

[1] D Nicolson and J Webb, *Professional Legal Ethics: Critical Interrogations* (Oxford University Press, 1999) 111.

lawyers' responsibilities, the imposition of new and more expansive duties on professionals is still highly controversial.

Frequently, new duties aimed at protecting wider collective interests constitute exceptions to established principles, such as the duty of confidentiality and the related duty of full disclosure to the client—ethical principles which are central to the traditionally formulated professional legal ethic. It is unsurprising, therefore, that it is this ethical duty of confidentiality which has been attacked most vociferously, both by government and by commentators who would like to impose 'whistleblowing' obligations on those most able to forestall wide social harm. It is more difficult, however, to formulate a new ethical approach that preserves both the legitimate expectations of the client to confidentiality and privacy in their affairs and also the public interest in detecting and punishing crime or preventing large-scale financial disaster, such as the collapse of a major company like Enron in the US, or environmental disaster resulting from polluting practices by a large corporate clients. If lawyers are to perform their traditional role in counselling and defending individual clients, can they also fill a policing role?

Third party collectives and the codes

Whilst the professional codes do contain some principles designed to protect the interests of individual third parties, they are either limited or almost silent about any duties to sections of the public or society at large. The Solicitors' Code of Conduct 2007, for example, is of little help, requiring only that solicitors act with integrity towards the courts and 'others' as well as their clients, and also 'not behave in a way which damages or is likely to damage the reputation or integrity of the profession'.[2] The latter is expressed negatively; there are no positive duties in the Rules to promote the interests of justice or access to it, and no duty to consider the impact of any action on the wider society. Yet, to the extent that society places trust in professions, it is allegedly because their members are assumed to be able to 'elevate the social good' above the narrow interests of their practitioner members and their clients.[3] There is a gesture towards this principle in the guidance to rule 1, which notes that ,where individual rules of conduct conflict, precedence is determined by the public interest, especially that of the administration of justice.[4] No examples are given to illustrate how this calculation should be done.

Despite the dearth of guidance from the Codes, lawyers do have some obligations to the wider community. The most obvious is mentioned in the Codes—the duty to the reputation of the profession as whole—but a raft of measures is being introduced, by statute and otherwise, that affects the way that lawyers do their jobs but are not mentioned in the Codes. There are duties to the state prescribed by legislation, such as the rules on money laundering, and also the new and troubling duties of special advocates in terrorism cases. But is there any positive duty to promote access to justice by, for example, acting without

---

[2] *Solicitors' Code of Conduct 2007* (London, Solicitors Regulation Authority, 2007) (hereafter Solicitors' Code) Core Duties r 1.

[3] R Abel (1988) *The Legal Profession in England and Wales* (Oxford, Blackwell) 27.

[4] Solicitors' Code, r 1 guidance, para 3.

charge for some clients?[5] How far should lawyers use their knowledge to prevent harm to others by informing the relevant authorities? There is a rather unclear power to breach confidence in order to prevent serious physical injury to individuals or the public at large, but should this extend to other kinds of harm? Finally, there is the question of how far lawyers representing organisations like companies have a duty to the members, shareholders or employees. We start here with one of the clearer codified obligations: that owed to the profession.

Examples of collective third party obligations

Obligations to the profession

An obligation not to damage the interests of the profession as a whole is well established in the rules. For solicitors it was embodied in rule 1 of the 1990 Rules, which required solicitors not to harm the 'good repute' of the profession. The Solicitors' Code of Conduct 2007, rule 1.06 requires solicitors not to behave so as to damage the 'reputation and integrity' of the profession or to diminish the trust the public places in it.[6] Similarly, the Bar Code states that barristers must not engage in conduct 'discreditable to a barrister' or likely to 'diminish public confidence in the legal profession or the administration of justice or otherwise bring the profession into disrepute'[7]. Of course, a breach of any of the more specific rules of conduct will also tend to bring the profession into disrepute, as will unlawful conduct, especially of a criminal nature. There is little guidance on what other behaviour is caught by these general rules.

Both codes attempt to regulate members' involvement in activities that might be disreputable in themselves. The Bar warns barristers that they must not engage, either directly or indirectly, in any occupation which might affect the reputation of the Bar adversely. The Solicitors' Code advises against behaviour 'within or outside' the profession which damages public trust in the profession. Presumably being involved in, say, the running of a massage parlour or sex shop (both legal activities) might come within this guidance. But what about running a betting shop, a pawnbrokers or a high-interest doorstep moneylender business? There is no clear guidance on other private conduct that might be generally regarded as odd, undesirable or unconventional although not criminal, such as open promiscuity, belonging to a bizarre religious sect or promoting currently unacceptable political beliefs. Presumably, it is not the behaviour itself but whether there is perceived to be harm to the reputation of the profession that is the acid test. Similarly, not even all criminal conduct will necessarily be regarded as bringing the profession into disrepute. If it were, any lawyer guilty of dropping litter, speeding or careless driving would also be subject to professional sanctions.

The activities most likely to bring censure are those that are permitted but heavily

---

[5] This issue is dealt with in chapter 15.

[6] Solicitors also have a duty to report to the SRA other solicitors in breach of their obligations. See further chapter 13.

[7] *Code of Conduct of the Bar of England and Wales* (London, Bar Standards Board, 8th edn, as amended, 2004) (hereafter the Bar Code), Para 301 and 301(iii). See also para 710.2(b) on advertising.

controlled, like advertising and statements to the press. Advertising used to be regarded as conduct bringing the profession into disrepute, but it is now accepted as normal. A breach of the advertising code, however, while it is now far less prescriptive than previously,[8] could attract sanctions. Similarly, statements made by lawyers of the press[9] in high-profile cases risk accusations that wild or inaccurate statements bring the profession into disrepute. This possibility might be used by the other side to censor press statements in their own interest as, for example, happened in the litigation arising from the Ladbrooke Grove rail crash. The solicitor for the relatives of the deceased issued a press release informing the press that the closing speech of their counsel would reveal 'shocking evidence of total mismanagement and utter callous disregard for safety' by the defendants, Railtrack, and similar statements. Railtrack complained to the Law Society that, not only were these comments a breach of the advertising code, but they also brought the profession into disrepute. After an 18 month investigation, in which the relatives' solicitor incurred considerable legal costs, it was decided that the press release, though regrettable, had broken no professional rules. The obvious conclusion is that some parties can restrict lawyers' statements to the press, depriving the public of knowledge of the details of legal proceedings and their wider implications.[10] This is especially troubling where one side has no way of reaching the press, other than through their lawyers, while the complaining side has the resources of a large institution or corporation.

Obligations to the state

Disclosing money laundering and suspected money laundering

Money laundering was described in 1993 by the Law Society as the process by which 'dirty money', the proceeds of crime, is handled so that the money appears 'to originate from a legitimate source'.[11] This definition is too narrow now because an attempt by anyone to hide the proceeds of any crime 'in such a way that the authorities cannot trace the proceeds back to the original crime' falls within the definition, and an offence could therefore be committed inadvertently by solicitors.[12] The most infamous example is of Michael Renton, a partner in a South London criminal practice, convicted of laundering some of the 30 million pounds stolen in the Brinks Mat gold bullion robbery. Overseas accounts were used to launder the money and produce profits from property transactions.[13] Concern that sophisticated criminal clients could use lawyers, and the protection afforded by the rules on confidentiality and legal privilege, in order to make arrangements for laundering the proceeds of crime, in

---

[8] See chapter 9.

[9] The professional conduct rules on this are dealt with in chapter 9 at p 194.

[10] For an account of this case, and also another against Peter Herbert, a barrister, in relation to a case of race discrimination against the CPS, see C Dyer, *The Guardian*, 9 January 2002.

[11] Law Society Guidance 1993, para 2, reproduced in JA Holland (ed), *Cordery on Solicitors* (London, Butterworths, 1995).

[12] See P Camp, *Solicitors and Money Laundering* (London, The Law Society, 2004) 4. This is a good source of the detail of the current law and how solicitors should cope with it. However, new regulations came into force on 15 December 2007, and reference should be made to the Law Society Guidance made on these regulations and other statutory changes which came into force on 26 December 2007 but were not fully available at the time of writing.

[13] P Lashmar, 'Grassing on the Client', *The Guardian*, 29 March 1994.

particular the proceeds of drug trafficking and terrorism, led to legislation against money laundering and a major inroad into the duty of confidentiality and privilege.

The original provisions were contained in the Criminal Justice Act 1988, section 93A,[14] the Drug Trafficking Offences Act 1994 and the Prevention of Terrorism (Temporary Provisions) Act 1989. Money laundering is an international problem. and the provisions of the Criminal Justice Act and the accompanying Money Laundering Regulations were enacted partly as a response to the European Council Directive 91/308/EEC, which requires disclosure of suspicious transactions by credit and financial institutions.[15] The obligation on lawyers to break client confidentiality therefore applies throughout the European Union. The current provisions are contained in the amended Proceeds of Crime Act 2002 and its associated Money Laundering Regulations 2007, which came into force at the end of 2007. What follows is an overview of the main provisions regarding money laundering,[16] excluding circumstances linking this activity to terrorism.[17]

It is a criminal offence for a person, including a solicitor, to enter into or become concerned

> in an arrangement which he knows or suspects facilitates (by whatever means) the acquisition, retention, use or control of criminal property by or on behalf of another person.[18]

Criminal property is broadly defined in the 2002 Act as

> a person's benefit from criminal conduct or it represents such a benefit (in whole or in part and whether directly or indirectly).[19]

Criminal conduct includes any offence in the UK, or conduct that would be an offence in the UK if it had occurred there.[20] Thus, if a solicitor knows or suspects that a client is buying a house with money that originated from a criminal offence but nevertheless carries on doing the conveyancing, he or she will be guilty of the offence.[21] It is of considerable practical importance to lawyers undertaking any kind of transaction to consider the possibilities of illegality.

If, in the context of family litigation, a solicitor forms the view that one of the parties has

---

[14] Inserted by the Criminal Justice Act 1993, s 29.

[15] A challenge to the directive was launched by the Bar in Belgium, France and Poland under Art 6 of the ECHR. See *Law Society Gazette*, 21 July 2005, 1.

[16] The basic law in the Proceeds of Crime Act 2002 and the Terrorism Act 2000 as amended by the Amendment Regulations 2007/3398 apply to all solicitors (and other professionals).The Money Laundering Regulations 2007/2157 replaced the 2003 Regulations and were enacted in response to the Third EU Money Laundering Directive 2005. These apply only to solicitors who undertake investment business and are registered and therefore regulated under the Financial Services Act 1986. For further details, see the Law Society Guidance on its website and the book by Camp, above n 12.

[17] There are separate offences in relation to terrorism and in relation to property to be used for terrorist purposes (which might not be criminal property under the Proceeds of Crime Act 2002) falling under the Terrorism Act 2000, as amended. See Camp, *ibid*, 27 and 60.

[18] Proceeds of Crime Act 2002, s 328.

[19] S 340(3).

[20] While there are no restrictions on the nature of the offence now, indictable offences only were caught under the previous legislation.

[21] A solicitor who acted for an estate agent who he 'trusted' in selling a house that had been undervalued was jailed for six months. The house was being sold by drug traffickers. The solicitor claimed he had committed an error of judgement, but the Court of Appeal stated that 'society demands a high degree of professionalism from solicitors': *Law Society Gazette*, 9 November 2006, 4.

unlawfully evaded paying his VAT bills, is he concerned with an 'arrangement' relating to 'criminal property'? A first decision under the Act suggested that this was the case,[22] but a subsequent Court of Appeal case, *Bowman v Fels*,[23] restored the equilibrium of the legal profession. In *Bowman*, a case on the ownership of the home after a relationship breakdown, the solicitor suspected that the defendant had included the costs of the renovation of the home in his business account and his VAT returns. He therefore reported this to the National Criminal Intelligence Service (NCIS) under section 328, causing considerable disruption to the civil proceedings. It was held that the ordinary conduct of litigation was not covered by the definition in section 328; it was not becoming involved in an arrangement involving criminal property. Any other decision, said the court, would prejudice the right to a fair trial under Article 6 of the European Convention on Human Rights (ECHR).

The main defence to an accusation under section 328, or to other related offences under sections 327 and 329, is that the solicitor made an authorised disclosure of the suspected money laundering to an authorised person or body. Such disclosures are therefore mandatory. It is here that the major issue arises in relation to the rules on confidence and professional privilege. Under section 330 a disclosure must be made in prescribed circumstances. These circumstances, broadly, are that the solicitor[24] knows, suspects or has reasonable grounds for suspecting another of money laundering, that this knowledge came to him or her in the course of business in the regulated sector,[25] and that the disclosure is made to the prescribed persons and in the prescribed format. To be an effective defence to the offence of money laundering, the disclosure must be made before the solicitor has committed the offence. Where the disclosure is required, irrespective of its role as a defence in any criminal proceedings, it must be done as soon as practicable. Disclosure is normally made to the police (normally to the NCIS), a customs officer or a nominated officer in the firm (who then makes the disclosure to the public authorities). Failure to disclose where required by the Act is itself an offence.

The Act also makes provision for voluntary disclosures under section 337, which deals with what is known as a 'protected disclosure'. These may be made wherever, in the course of business, the discloser knows, suspects or has reasonable cause to suspect another of money laundering. Solicitors who make such a disclosure in relation to a client are not regarded, under section 337(1), as having acted in breach of the rules relating to privilege or confidentiality, or in breach of contract. They cannot therefore be successfully sued by the client for making such disclosures. Where a disclosure is required by law, solicitors can offer the defence of legal professional privilege to the offence of failure to disclose. Under section 330(6) a professional legal adviser may be able to claim that the information came to him under privileged circumstances. This defence, however, will not apply if the information was given to the solicitor by the client with the intention of furthering a criminal purpose. The defence is elaborated in section 330(10). Privilege is defined, for the purposes of this Act, in

---

[22] *P v P (Ancillary Relief: Proceeds of Crime)* [2003] EWHC Fam 2260, [2004] 1 FLR 193.

[23] [2005] EWCA Civ 226.

[24] These laws are not confined to solicitors, but we are dealing with solicitors only here.

[25] This phrase has a very complex definition, on which see Camp, above n 12, 45. Broadly, it covers work relating to investments, which will include holding property on trust, holding documents of title, managing and advising on investments, and all activities undertaken by most solicitors.

a similar way to that of the Police and Criminal Evidence Act,[26] namely, it covers information from, or given to, a client seeking legal advice from the adviser or in connection with legal proceedings.

A solicitor refusing to make a required disclosure of suspected money laundering may therefore, if prosecuted, plead privilege as a defence. This will succeed only if all the conditions are complied with. However, a solicitor may think that discretion is the better part of valour and decide to make a disclosure of money laundering by a client or other person, whether voluntary or mandatory. If this is done, the solicitor is protected under section 337 from any claim by the client (or anyone else) for breach of the duty of confidentiality or professional privilege, whether that duty arises under common law, statute, professional rules or contract. Sceptics may well feel that this means that solicitors have the best of both worlds. Failure to disclose may be justifiable under the rules of legal professional privilege, but, if a disclosure is made, the client cannot complain that the disclosure is in breach of his rights under those same rules of privilege. It should also be noted that solicitors may have a conflict of interest in such cases. Do they act so as to protect themselves from potential criminal prosecution or do they act in the best interests of their client by refusing to disclose and pleading privilege? If they do decide to 'shop' their client, a further issue is whether a solicitor continues to represent that client. Apart from the fact that the client is likely to fire the solicitor anyway, it is difficult to see how a solicitor could continue to act in these circumstances. There is a clear conflict of interest between client and solicitor as well as a loss of confidence that would undermine the lawyer and client relationship and therefore justify the withdrawal of the solicitor from the case.

Should a solicitor who is considering reporting a suspicion of money laundering inform the client that this is what he is going to do? Here the solicitor must beware of two further offences. The first, known as tipping off, is making a disclosure that 'is likely to prejudice any investigation', which might be made following the money laundering disclosure.[27] This offence now applies only to solicitors regulated under the Financial Services Act as described below. It can only be committed once the solicitor knows or suspects the money laundering disclosure has been made. The second is committed if, knowing or suspecting that an investigation is about to be or is being conducted, any disclosure is made which is likely to prejudice the investigation.[28] Therefore a solicitor should be very careful before warning a client (or any other person) that money laundering is suspected. It can be done only after a disclosure has been made and it must not be done in such a way as to prejudice its proposed or actual investigation. Clearly, while both legal advice and litigation privilege protects solicitors in this context,[29] they may find themselves making some difficult and fine distinctions when considering their options regarding disclosure.

In addition to the above statutes, the Money Laundering Regulations 2007 apply to firms conducting relevant investment business within the Financial Services Act 1986 and

---

[26] On this, see chapter 11.
[27] S 333.
[28] S 342.
[29] See ss 333(3) and 342(4). It is not proposed to detail the provisions here, but it should be noted that the privilege defence also applies to the disclosure provisions under the terrorism legislation.

'relevant business' within Regulation 2(2), which covers a wide variety of financial and related activities. Not all solicitors conduct such business—for example, firms that specialise in criminal law will not—but most firms who deal with clients' commercial, tax or property affairs will, as will those who give more mainstream financial and tax planning advice. These regulations require solicitors to ensure that their firm's employees are trained to recognise and handle suspicious transactions, that clients' identities (and also those of certain beneficiaries of trusts) are adequately checked, that internal reporting procedures are set up and that certain records of transactions are maintained for five years. The requirement to keep records enables an audit trail of transactions to be followed. The regulatory authorities have extensive supervisory and inspection powers, and can also resort to various civil and criminal penalties for failure to adhere to the regulations. The requirement that firms verify a client's identity before proceeding with any financial trans-action[30] applies even to what may appear to be mundane transactions such as domestic house purchase. The stringent obligations imposed on lawyers to encourage detection seems calculated to render excuses such as 'I didn't know or understand what was going on' or 'it wasn't me, it was my staff' less sustainable, as the solicitor in *Francis and Francis v Central Criminal Court* discovered.[31]

The laws on money laundering were greatly expanded in scope by the Proceeds of Crime Act 2002. The provisions represent a major inroad into the conventional professional approach, which emphasised client confidentiality and lawyer independence from the law enforcement machinery of the state. The rules were again extended in December 2007 in response to a third directive from the European Union. Although the Law Society opposed certain aspects of this extension,[32] similar, and often wider, rules have been introduced in Europe and the US. Lawyers are thereby recruited as 'gatekeepers' to the enforcement of the law, particularly in the area of financial and corporate fraud, crimes which notoriously are difficult to detect and enforce. As Odby notes, lawyers were perceived as using their skills to facilitate corporate wrongdoing, most notably in relation to the collapse of the Enron Corporation in the US, resulting in the loss of billions of dollars to creditors, investors and pensioners of the corporation.

The fact that Enron and similar scandals might have been prevented by the lawyers acting for the corporations is not by itself, however, a clear-cut reason for imposing wider responsibilities in the professional codes. While their activities might have been cloaked in the veil of legal privilege and client confidentiality, it is arguable that the existing duties in professional practice rules towards third parties (or justice) are weak and unenforced. Therefore it is necessary to impose legal obligations on solicitors personally in order to protect the public interest.

---

[30] For full details, see the guidance published by the Law Society and also see Camp, above n 12, ch 9.

[31] See chapter 11.

[32] See *Law Society Gazette*, 18 January 2007. The dispute related to obligations on solicitors to investigate persons having beneficial ownership of property under trusts and the like. The duties of investigation are said to be vague in scope and costly to carry out. Some positive response by the government to the Law Society's lobbying was achieved. They also succeeded in excluding non regulated solicitors from the tipping off criminal penalties. See Law Society press release, December 2007.

Lawyer gatekeeper liability is the very antithesis of the traditional adversarial paradigm. Here client interests are relegated to the background and the paramount public interest is . . . the general public interest in the prevention of crime.[33]

Odby considers that the dawn of such broad collective third party obligations should cause the professional bodies to redraft their professional rules, but, as yet, this has not happened.

Disclosing details of tax avoidance schemes

Another recent attempt by the government to impose gatekeeping obligations on lawyers concerns tax avoidance schemes. So far, in the UK, lawyers have been more successful in resisting these proposals than they have been in slowing the imposition of money laundering regulations. Under the Finance Act 2004, the promoters and users of certain types of tax avoidance schemes created after 2004 are required to disclose their details to the Inland Revenue. The duty to disclose applies only to 'schemes or arrangements', not routine tax advice. The aim is to allow the Inland Revenue to obtain advance warning of new tax schemes being promoted by the financial services industry so that they can attempt to circumvent them in advance by new regulations or litigation. While the duty of disclosure is imposed on the promoters of the schemes, professionals are likely to be caught. Accountants and financial advisers are clearly covered, but, on the face of it, so are lawyers.[34]

Where professionals are under a duty to disclose tax avoidance schemes, it overrides the normal rule of confidentiality to clients but not legal professional privilege,[35] as persons subject to legal professional privilege are not to be included within the definition of 'promoter' of the schemes. For lawyers, therefore, it will be important to be able to establish that the details of the tax avoidance scheme were devised for the client in the context of legal advice covered by legal privilege. In this context, the House of Lords decision in the *Three Rivers* case, discussed in chapter 11, makes establishing this less difficult than did the Court of Appeal's decision in the same case.[36] However, although the lawyer may not have a duty of disclosure, the client himself does have a personal duty to disclose the scheme to the Revenue within five days of the first transaction forming part of the scheme. The lawyer clearly has a duty to his client to advise him of this. Presumably, if a wider conception of lawyers' duties in their relationships with clients is taken seriously, lawyers should also counsel reluctant clients to make disclosure.

---

[33] A Odby, 'Lawyers as "Gatekeepers": the Impact of Preventative Anti Money Laundering Obligations on the Legal Profession in England and Wales (PhD Thesis, University of Westminster, 2006); see also A Odby 'The European Union and Money Laundering: The Preventive Responsibilities of the Private Sector' in I Bantekas (ed) *International and European Financial Criminal Law* (London, LexisNexis Butterworths, 2006), discussing the money-laundering regime created by EU legislation, including the Third Directive.

[34] A promoter is anyone whose business or profession involves tax services and who designs or promotes a notifiable tax scheme.

[35] Finance Act 2004, s 314. Amendment regulations make this clear: Tax Avoidance Schemes (Promoters, Prescribed Circumstances and Information) Amendment Regulations 2004/2613. The rules came into force in November 2004. Accountants not unnaturally consider that this exemption gives lawyers an unjustified commercial advantage.

[36] See Finance Act 2004 and The Tax Avoidance Schemes Regulations made under the Act for the full details. See also 154 NLJ 1608 (29 October 2004). A similar scheme applicable to stamp duty tax avoidance schemes came into force on 1 August 2005.

Special advocacy

Special advocacy represents another example of the recruitment of lawyers by the state to protect its interests at the expense of those of the client.[37] The role arises from the desire to protect national security, mainly in asylum deportation cases which involve allegations of terrorism or threats to national security. The Special Immigration Appeals Commission, created in 1997, has rules which allow the hearing to be held in private, in the absence of the appellant and his chosen lawyer. In this way, the case is dealt with without revealing the state's evidence to the appellant or his lawyer and with very limited rights of cross-examination, a procedure that obviously violates normal rules of procedural justice. The rules also provide for the appointment by the Attorney General of special advocates to represent the interests of the appellant. There is a pool of about 20 such advocates, mainly barristers, and they are security vetted. This procedure has been extended to cases whereby foreign nationals are certified as being terrorism suspects, for the removal of citizenship and detention pending deportation. It has also been extended in a rather ad hoc fashion to other courts and tribunals dealing with national security issues, such as the Proscribed Organisations Appeal Commission and the Pathogens Access Appeal Commission. A further extension is to the ordinary courts, using their powers to regulate their own procedures, although such extensions have given rise to dissenting judicial opinions.[38]

The role of the special advocate is to review sensitive evidence and make representations to the tribunal on behalf of the appellant at the closed hearing. Special advocates are instructed to act in the interests of the appellant, but must not reveal any of this sensitive evidence to the appellant. So seriously is this taken that the special advocate is even forbidden from communicating with the applicant after the information has been revealed, a precaution designed to prevent inadvertent leakage. The advocate is therefore acting for the appellant 'but without instructions and sometimes, even, consent'.[39] The advocate is a lawyer who

> cannot take full instructions from his client, nor report to his client, who is not responsible to his client and whose relationship with the client lacks the quality of confidence inherent in any ordinary lawyer–client relationship.[40]

This represents the antithesis of the conventional relationship of lawyer and client and, of course, is contrary to numerous professional conduct rules for both branches of the profession.

Special advocates are appointed by the state, 'the client' has a very limited choice restricted to members of the panel and the advocate works to detailed rules laid down by the state. The fundamental objection, however, is that the role cannot be reconciled with acting independently in the best interests of the 'client', except in the very limited sense that it may be better to have a shackled lawyer than no lawyer at all. The duty of disclosure to

---

[37] A Boon and S Nash, 'Special Advocacy: Political Necessities and Legal Roles in Modern Judicial Systems' (2006) 9 *Legal Ethics* 101. The relevant legislation is the Special Immigration Commission Appeals Act 1997 and the Procedure Rules 2003, as extended by the Anti-terrorism, Crime and Security Act 2001 and the Nationality Immigration and Asylum Act 2002.

[38] See Lords Bingham and Steyn in *Roberts v Parole Board* [2005] UKHL 45.

[39] Boon and Nash, above n 37, 101.

[40] Lord Bingham in *R v H; R v C* [2004] UKHL 3.

the client is compromised and therefore so is the duty to take instructions from the client. Although the role of special advocate drives a coach and horses through the Bar's Code of Conduct, the Bar Council nominates suitable candidates and makes no special provision in its rules. Since the role of special advocate is not consistent with normal professional conduct standards, it is arguable that it should not be accepted by members of the Bar. The legal profession should also oppose the further extension of the system or it will surely begin to undermine the ethics of the profession in a far wider category of cases than now. At the very least it must be clearly recognised that special advocates are in reality agents or employees of the state and not lawyers representing the interests of their detainees.

Duty to the court

The duty to the court has traditionally applied to advocates. According to Lord Justice Brooke in *Copeland v Smith*,[41] the justice system of England and Wales 'has always been dependent on the quality of the assistance that advocates give to the bench' and this also permits the state to avoid 'having to incur the cost of legal assistance for judges'. This particular collective duty therefore imposes a responsibility on clients to save the state money by paying their lawyers to inform its courts of its own laws! It is, however, not a duty that is unduly onerous to the profession. Lord Justice Brooke also said that the need to keep up to date encompassed only the material to be found in generalist law reports, such as the Weekly or All England Reports, and not specialist reports.[42] Whether the latter comment is still valid must be open to question in the light of current sophisticated search engines and websites covering the law. The duty to the court is now, presumably, subsumed within section 42 of the Access to Justice Act 1999, which imposes a wider duty to 'act with independence in the interests of justice' on all those with authorised rights to conduct litigation.[43] Under the existing law and rules of conduct, constraints on the lawyers' duty to act in a client's best interests are numerous. It remains to be seen whether they will expand under the new statutory duty.

A limited interpretation of the duty to the court is an obligation to comply with rules of court and rules of professional conduct even if so doing conflicts with lawyers' other obligations, such as those owed to the client. Such duties constitute a major limitation to the notion that the lawyer's sole or even main duty is to promote the client's interests. Not only does the lawyer have a duty not to mislead the court or allow others to do so; there is also a positive duty to disclose certain information even if it assists the case of the other side.[44] Solicitors and barristers must bring to the court's attention any documents or procedural irregularities if failure to do so might result in the court being misled.[45] A lawyer whose client wishes to or does mislead the court must normally withdraw from representing him or her (although the lawyer should not explain to the court or anyone else why he is withdrawing as this would breach litigation privilege). Equally, a lawyer should not make allegations of fraud in pleadings or in court unless he or she has some evidence supporting

---

[41] [2000] 1 All ER 457.
[42] *Copeland v Smith* [2000] 1 All ER 457 CA, 462–3.
[43] See chapter 19.
[44] Solicitors' Code, r 11.01 and the guidance thereto; Bar Code 708(c).
[45] Solicitors' Code, r 11.01(2): Bar Code 708(d).

those allegations[46], nor should contentions or arguments be made in documents or in court which the advocate does not consider to be 'properly arguable'. All relevant cases and statutory material must be revealed, however unhelpful to the client, and the obligation is ongoing for the duration of litigation.[47]

Duties to the public at large

The extent to which lawyers should be responsible to 'the public', rather than to the state or government, is a hotly contested issue. What are lawyers' responsibilities where they hold client information which, if revealed, may help to prevent environmental, public health or financial disasters?[48] It is clearly acceptable to disregard the basic duty of confidentiality in order to alert the relevant authorities if a client is about to commit an act which is likely to result in serious personal injury or death. But the position is less clear if the danger is to the environment, or a threat to property or finances. A lawyer cannot be involved with or promote a client's future illegal or criminal conduct, and must withdraw from representing the client in such a case. However, should the lawyer inform any person or body that the illegal conduct or crimes are planned? The issue of financial risk was thrown into sharp relief by cases in the US relating to the Savings and Loan scandal (the Kaye Scholar affair) and later to the collapse of the Enron Corporation. These incidents raise significant questions about the balance to be struck between duties to clients and wider duties to sections of the public, such as shareholders, employees and pensioners, and also public regulatory agencies. The specific issue in both cases was whether a duty of candour is or should be owed to such third parties on matters of public importance. One consideration in debating such issues is the implications of imposing such a duty in relation to the duty of confidentiality owed to clients.

Financial risks

The Kaye Scholer affair

The Kaye Scholer affair is complex, but is outlined here based on an article by Simon.[49] It concerns a US bank, Lincoln Savings and Loan, which was liquidated with a loss of $3.4 billion to the US federal banking and insurance system. Banking agencies, when sifting through the confidential records of the defunct bank, found documents suggesting that its

---

[46] *Medcalf v Mardell* [2002] 3 All ER 721. Solicitors' Code, r 11.01(3); Bar Code 704(c). See discussion in chapter 13 at p 281.

[47] *Copeland v Smith* [2000] 1 All ER 457 CA.

[48] In relation to the environment, the Convention on Access to Information, Public Participation in Decision-Making and Access to Justice in Environmental Matters (United Nations Economic Commission for Europe, 1998), also known as the 'Aarhus Convention', imposes obligations on public authorities to disclose environmentally sensitive information (see A Osborn, 'Environment Law in Public Hands', *The Lawyer*, 20 October 1998, 11). This creates circumstances in which in-house and external lawyers employed by corporations could be subject to considerable conflicts in advising clients.

[49] WH Simon, 'The Kaye Scholer Affair: The Lawyer's Duty of Candor and the Bar's Temptations of Evasion and Apology' (1998) 23 *Law and Social Inquiry* 243. This account is based on this article.

lawyers, Kaye, Scholer, Fierman, Hays & Handler ('Kaye Scholer'), had reason to suspect that the firm had systematically misled the regulatory authorities about the activities of its client bank over a three-year period. Had the firm not done so, numerous dubious transactions and substantial losses of publicly underwritten insurance money would probably have been prevented. Simon's analysis of the conduct of the lawyers was based on allegations made in the pleadings.[50] These showed active participation by the lawyers, including the provision of misleading information to the regulator, in many of the transactions.

To Simon, the key ethical issue raised by the case was whether a lawyer has an obligation to withdraw where he knows that he cannot act for the client without furthering a client's fraud.[51] This begs a number of questions concerning not only the definition of 'fraud', but also what the lawyers knew about it and about the respective responsibilities of government and bureaucrats for the debacle. At the ethical level, a major issue is whether the lawyers had perceived what was happening and, if so, how they should have perceived their obligations.[52] What was the obligation of the lawyers to disclose information to third parties such as the regulatory body? Were the lawyers subject to a minimal obligation, for example an obligation not to mislead explicitly, or did they have a more onerous obligation, namely to fulfil the client's obligation of full disclosure under the banking regulations or, at least, to withdraw from representation if the client refused to authorise them to do so?

The regulator's first argument for the higher duty was based on the fact that the firm had actively 'interposed' itself between the regulator and the client by insisting that the regulator should deal directly with the law firm. The second argument was based on the alleged existence of a general duty to disclose regulatory evasion by clients. Simon agrees with the first argument but regards the second as less plausible, even in the context of the strict regulatory regime, which clearly operated in the public interest to ensure the probity of the financial system. Because of the difficulty in drawing general principles from the case, Simon suggests that an intermediate standard should be applied, whereby the lawyer would be prohibited from directly or indirectly misleading conduct and 'from providing any services substantially related to active unlawful client conduct'.[53]

The legal establishment defended Kaye Scholer on the ground that its lawyers were bound by the duty of confidentiality not to disclose details of their client's actions. It was argued that not only was the duty of confidentiality more binding in this case because the firm was instructed in anticipation of litigation instigated by the regulator, but also that the assertions made to the regulator were in the nature of arguments rather than statements of fact. Simon offers a compelling demolition of these arguments[54] and particularly that relating to confidentiality. One of the key arguments for confidentiality is that it encourages clients to disclose planned wrongful conduct so that the lawyer can dissuade them from the proposed course of action.[55] For Simon, the failure of the Kaye Scholer lawyers to do this, and the nature of the arguments raised by the legal establishment in

[50] *Ibid*, 247–51.
[51] *Ibid*, 244. The lawyer should withdraw under professional rules in England and Wales.
[52] DC Langevoort, 'What Was Kaye Scholer Thinking?' (1998) 23 *Law and Social Inquiry* 297.
[53] Simon, above n 49, 255.
[54] *Ibid*, 270–3.
[55] *Ibid*, 281.

their defence, raises serious questions about the profession's ethics and, hence, its capacity to regulate itself.[56]

There can be disagreements with Simon on points of detail. For example, in relation to confidentiality, clients sometimes legitimately need to explore the limits of legality.[57] Possibly Simon's expectation that the American Bar Association and other bar institutions would do anything other than defend Kaye Scholer was naive; lawyers had, long ago, abandoned all but a pretence of serving any wider interest than that of clients.[58] The behaviour of the lawyers and their organisations was, therefore, outrageous but not surprising. The debate rumbles on, both the issues and their wider implications being in considerable dispute. It illustrates the inherent difficulty of establishing a clear standard for the disclosure of information which may cause wrongful and avoidable loss to others.[59] What the Kay Scholer affair and the reaction to it also illustrate is the wider problem of squaring the client-focused ethics of lawyers with expectations of virtue associated with professionals. Gordon, for example, blames the Kaye Scholer affair, and the US bar's response, on the

> uncontrolled expansion of libertarian ideology into lawyers' common consciousness—to the point where lawyers have come to feel genuinely affronted and indignant when any authority tries to articulate a public obligation of lawyers that may end up putting them at odds with clients. We have no public obligations, they claim; we are private agents for private parties (though at the same time they claim privileges and immunities that ordinary citizens don't have); our loyalties to clients must be absolute and undivided. In this libertarian mood, they tend to characterise the framework of law as some alien other—'the government,' the 'cops' the 'regulators'—an adversary that they are entitled to outwit and frustrate with every trick in the book.[60]

While the philosophy attributed to lawyers was stretched by the Kaye Scholer affair, it is near to breaking point following the Enron scandal.

The Enron scandal

The role of lawyers in the collapse of the energy giant Enron in the US in 2001 has resulted in almost as much ethical soul searching in the US as did the Watergate scandal. One of the

---

[56] The New York Supreme Court, the disciplinary authority, found no grounds for professional discipline. Nevertheless, judgments worth billions of dollars are outstanding against the key figure at the bank and his associates. Kaye Scholer have themselves been subject to injunctions and compensation orders for over $40 million in an out-of-court settlement of the regulatory authority's claim.

[57] S Pepper, 'Why Confidentiality?' (1998) 23 *Law and Social Inquiry* 331,

[58] JR Macey, "Professor Simon on the Kaye Scholer Affair: Shock at the Gambling at Rick's Palace in Casablanca" (1998) 23 *Law and Social Inquiry* 323.

[59] Miller argues that Simon's 'onerous standard' is that which currently applies and that the difficulty with the case was the unproven nature of the allegations. Even the payment by Kaye Scholer to settle the case is not suggestive because the regulatory body obtained an order freezing the firm's assets and effectively stopped them from trading. Settlement, Miller argues, could therefore be seen as the only prudent course for the firm: GP Miller, 'Kaye Scholer as Original Sin: The Lawyer's Duty of Candor and the Bar's Temptations of Evasions and Apology' (1998) 23 *Law and Social Inquiry* 305. It is also arguably an oppressive and unethical tactic by government lawyers doubtful about their ability to prove the charges: see KR Fisher, 'Neither Evaders nor Apologists: A Reply to Professor Simon' (1998) 23 *Law and Social Inquiry* 341; Macey *ibid*; WH Simon, 'Further Thoughts on Kaye Scholer' (1998) 23 *Law and Social Inquiry* 365.

[60] RW Gordon, 'A Collective Failure of Nerve: The Bar's Response to Kay Scholer' (1998) 23 *Law and Social Inquiry* 315.

major issues that arose from this was whether and, if so, how far the lawyers acting for Enron owed a duty to safeguard the interests of the shareholders at large, the employees and possibly the pensioners of Enron, and, even more widely, the community at large. All these groups were harmed or placed at risk in numerous ways by the collapse into bankruptcy of a megacorporation. Should the lawyers have blown the whistle on the illegal activities of the firm so as to alert regulatory authorities such as the Securities and Exchange Commission (SEC), thereby preventing the total collapse of Enron or at least minimising the losses to shareholders and employees? If so, how is this to be reconciled with their duty to their client, Enron, in particular in relation to their duty of client confidence? This was a similar debate to the Kaye Scholer affair but involved a significantly greater corporate collapse.

It is necessary to summarise the facts of the Enron collapse to illustrate the issues.[61] Enron was a giant energy corporation that became more concerned with making even larger amounts of money by trading in financial contracts connected with their energy assets rather than from actually providing that energy. Many of these financial arrangements involved creating a multitude of partnership organisations, the main aim of which was to allow a sanitised version of the corporation's accounts to be presented to the public. This gave a totally false impression of the corporation's security and solvency. The arrangements also made a lot of money for the individual executives involved in their creation, including at least one of the in-house lawyers employed by the corporation. Much of this was clearly not only unlawful but criminally fraudulent, and has resulted in convictions of senior managers involved. An Enron insider, not a lawyer, finally revealed the fraud and the corporation collapsed, resulting in the loss of the loss of 4,000 jobs and $70 billion of savings and shares.

Lawyers were involved in many facets of the Enron scandal. First,

attorneys all played an important role in the process of drafting and certifying disclosure statements, and advising whether the legal and accounting requirements governing [the partnership organisations] had been met.[62]

Secondly, senior lawyers in the corporation, presented with evidence of malpractice, failed to investigate or take any action. Thirdly, an outside firm of lawyers was implicated in some of the illegality, yet also agreed to undertake, at the request of Enron itself, an investigation into the process once questions were asked about the probity of the way the company was being run. The firm was therefore investigating its own work and was clearly in a position where its interest conflicted with those of other third parties. Unsurprisingly, the report that resulted from the firm's investigation was short, exculpatory and dismissive. Finally, once it was clear that a government investigation and litigation was likely to ensue, one of Enron's senior employed lawyers began to shred the evidence and actively presented a misleading press release on Enron's position.

It is clear that many of the lawyers involved had broken a variety of accepted ethical norms and had also been involved in the promotion of fraud. The senior lawyer who had

---

[61] For good brief accounts, see D Rhode and P Paton, 'Lawyers, Ethics and Enron' (2002–3) 8 *Stanford Journal of Law Business and Finance* 9; E Wald, 'Lawyers and Corporate Scandals' (2004)7 *Legal Ethics* 54.

[62] Rhode and Paton, *ibid*, 15.

shredded evidence had attempted to frustrate a federal investigation, but had acted contrary to a basic ethical rule of the profession on the destruction of evidence. It appears, however, that little or no disciplinary activity by the professional organisations has been put in train. Quite apart from the question of enforcement of professional obligations, the question also arises as to whether the ethical rules governing the lawyers prioritised too highly the duty to the client, putting that above all other duties, including the duty to the wider public to warn of illegal activity which could have catastrophic consequences. In other words, should the lawyers have broken their client's confidence and warned the SEC that its rules were being broken or that fraud was being perpetrated? Equally, should the lawyers have used their skills to invent far-fetched arguments designed to 'sprinkle the transactions with holy water'[63] on behalf of the company, knowing of their very doubtful legality and that they were intended to present sanitised and misleading company accounts?

If the Enron lawyers' conduct was acceptable, then clearly lawyers' ethics paid no heed to the real interests of the company as a whole. It was put at high risk of collapse whilst the managers made considerable private gains at the company's expense. The wider public interest in the proper regulation of companies was equally ignored. But there is also the third issue of the lawyers' duty to maintain their independence from, inter alia, their clients. It was clear that the Enron lawyers, both in-house and external, identified with the chief executive officers (CEOs) of the organisations and were not acting independently of their interests.[64] The CEOs were purporting to act on behalf of the corporation and had authority to give the lawyers instructions. But, arguably, the corporation as a whole was the 'real' client and its interests were different from those of the CEOs.[65] At the very least, it had an interest in continuing to survive and meet the expectations of its shareholders. As Gordon notes,

> The company they advised is now facing at least seventy-seven lawsuits . . . At best, the lawyers were closing their eyes to the risk of disaster; at worst they were helping to bring it on.[66]

As noted in relation to the Kaye Scholar affair, one of the justifications put forward by the profession itself for the client confidentiality rules is that they enable lawyers to alert their clients to any illegality and help to prevent it. The Enron Corporation as a whole did not get the benefit of their lawyers' performance of this role. The attitude of both the CEOs of Enron and its lawyers seemed to be that legal obligations were to be got round or evaded if at all

---

[63] See RW Gordon, 'Professionalisms Old and New, Good and Bad' (2005) 8 *Legal Ethics* 24.

[64] It appears that for the outside firm employed, Vinson & Elkins, Enron was its largest client and also that many of its employees had taken jobs with Enron as in-house counsel. It is often asserted that big City solicitors' firms in England and Wales also identify more with their corporate clients than with the legal profession as a whole or the Law Society as its regulatory body.

[65] See WH Simon, 'Whom (or What) Does the Organisation's Lawyer Represent? An Anatomy of Intraclient Conflict' (2003) 91 *California Law Review* 57' MC Regan,' Professional Responsibility and the Corporate Lawyer' (2000) 13 *Georgetown Journal of Legal Ethics* 197; R Gordon, 'A New Role for Lawyers? The Corporate Counsel after Enron' (2003) 26 *Harvard Journal of Law & Public Policy* 195.The only recent case in England and Wales in which the issue of 'who is the client?' arose in a corporate context is *Three Rivers v Bank of England*, where the House of Lords refused to rule on it. In the Court of Appeal it was decided that documents prepared by the Bank of England's employees and sent to their lawyers were not privileged because they (the employees) were not clients and therefore litigation privilege did not arise.

[66] Gordon, above n 63, 1192.

possible; the law was 'seen as merely an imposition and a nuisance',[67] not as a guide to conduct. However, it can be forcibly argued that

> a corporate agent acting unlawfully no longer represents the corporation, and the corporation's lawyer owes him no loyalty, and no duty of zealous representation.[68]

If it is accepted that corporate lawyers have no duty actually to conceal illegality, then it is necessary to spell out what such a lawyer's ethical duties are, and in particular how and to whom he should 'blow the whistle'. At the very least, the lawyer should have an obligation to alert those higher up in the corporation's hierarchy that such illegality, or suspected illegality, is being perpetrated. The Sarbanes-Oxley Act 2002, passed by the US Senate in response to the Enron scandal, requires lawyers to report material violations of securities laws or breaches of fiduciary duty to the corporation's general counsel, then to its CEO and then to the board of directors. There is no statutory obligation, however, to alert the SEC. Only such an obligation might have saved Enron from the activities of its board. The ethical codes of the legal professions in England and Wales do not address these issues at all. Corporate clients do not even appear in the index of the vast 1999 edition of The Guide to the Professional Conduct of Solicitors, nor are they dealt with in the trimmer Solicitors' Code of Conduct 2007.

The environment and the future

The way that lawyers have coped with the moral choices facing them in major financial and political scandals does not give grounds for optimism concerning the future of the planet. While not trivialising financial scandals, risks to the environment are arguably more serious and long term, affecting future generations unable to take action now to prevent them. Many regard it as shocking that lawyers who are aware that their clients or employers habitually cause illegal pollution or are planning activity that will precipitate ecological problems, such as illegal deforestation overseas, currently have no clear duty to take action to prevent it. In fact, it is arguable that they would breach client confidence to do so. According to Nicolson and Webb, these are important public-face ethical issues which could be regulated without undue difficulty, such as 'whistle-blowing to prevent harm to health, safety and the environment',[69] but such action would raise collateral issues.

The argument against imposing a whistleblowing obligation on lawyers who become aware of their clients' threat to collective third party interests concerns the potential of the lawyer to offer wise counsel. If lawyers were forced to blow the whistle, it would encourage polluters to keep the information from their lawyers or to change lawyers frequently so that none of them get to know fully of their business. In that case, lawyers would lose the

---

[67] Ibid, 1197. The attitude to legal rules seems to be that of Holmes's 'bad man' rather than that of the official who internalises the law as an indication of what should be done as described in HLA Hart's Concept of Law (Oxford, Oxford University Press, 1961). Nancy Rapoport also attributes the behaviour of the Enron lawyers and similar cases to the 'eat what you kill' philosophy of large firms, the work ethic that constitutes a 'race to exhaustion, a race to sloppiness, and a race to malpractice', with no countervailing ethic within the work environment. See N Rapoport, 'The Curious Incident of the Law Firm that did Nothing in the Night' (2007) 10 Legal Ethics 98.

[68] Above n 63, 1206.

[69] Nicolson and Webb, above n 1, 111.

potential to bring moral pressure to bear to prevent these harms. To support the argument that lawyers should be left free to offer wise counsel, however, it would help to have evidence that such counselling is being undertaken effectively. The difficulty is that such evidence is never likely to be produced precisely because it was given in conditions of confidence while the evidence of scandal is more publicised. At the very least, therefore, the duty to offer counsel to avoid harm could be made more explicit. If, however, a duty to avoid collective third party harms were to be imposed, it would be important that it were framed to impact on transaction work and in such a way as to avoid impinging on litigation privilege. Corporations charged with offences in relation to collective harms are still entitled to effective representation, although they should not be represented by lawyers implicated in causing the very harm that is the subject of litigation. It would be sensible, however, for any future rules on this to clarify that lawyers involved in pre-litigation activity precipitating such harm should not act on the grounds that this would be a conflict of interest.

Conclusion

It is clear that more work is needed on the ethical duties of lawyers to society at large or to sections of it. It is an undeveloped area in the codes and such duties that have been created recently have been piecemeal and statutory. They have not been rooted in a general theory of the ethics of the profession, but have been imposed on the profession by the government in response to perceived threats such as terrorism or money laundering. The professions have generally opposed them and have sometimes successfully limited their scope, but these developments still raise serious concerns that lawyers are being co-opted to do the state's business, rather than independently represent clients. One particular example of this, special advocates, is difficult to defend at all, while the money laundering responsibilities of lawyers now appear sensible. What is clear from this is that once one state of affairs is seen to be natural, the government will always want more, as the attempt to require solicitors to give advance notice to the Inland Revenue of tax avoidance schemes illustrates. It is necessary to develop some robust theory with which to evaluate future attempts.

One line of approach is to make a distinction between the duties of lawyers in criminal cases, which are clearly not only adversarial but also involve the protection of individual human rights when faced with prosecution by the state, and those in civil cases. Rules developed in the criminal context should not automatically be assumed to be appropriate in all civil disputes. In particular, the duties of corporate lawyers, both to the corporation as a whole and the regulatory bodies in particular, need greater analysis, not least because lawyers in corporations are under potentially greater pressure from their client—their employer—than lawyers in private practice. Large corporations have greater ability than private individuals to harm individuals, society and the environment, and often cannot achieve their dubious aims without the assistance of lawyers. Moreover, lawyers can design schemes so as to make corporate activities appear legal or to conceal their illegality from the authorities. It is inappropriate to apply to them the criminal model of the lawyer–client relationship and to treat corporations as though they were flesh-and-blood human beings facing conviction and punishment for past misdeeds. Their lawyers should have, Nicolson and Webb propose, a discretion to 'weigh up the values of confidentiality against the gains to be had from whistle blowing'.[70]

There is an equal need to define the scope of the corporate lawyer's duties so as to allow them, in certain circumstances, to take into account the interests of the shareholders or employees, where they are concerned that the officials who are instructing them are acting so as to endanger the interests of these groups in favour of their own. However, the most striking lesson to emerge from the corporate scandals in the US is the failure of the professional regulatory bodies to take disciplinary proceedings against the lawyers, even where it was clear that existing ethical rules, such as those relating to the promotion of criminal conduct or relating to conflict of interest, have been breached. The message seems to be that ethical rules will be enforced only against the proverbial 'little man' while the professional elite will not be pursued. If the profession continues to take this attitude to breaches of its own codes, it is to be expected that the state will resort increasingly to legislation to control its members.

[70] *Ibid*, 267–8.

15

PUBLIC SERVICE

It is demonstrably true that today the sharpest critics of the legal profession and the administration of justice are judges, lawyers, and teachers of law. It is historically true that the great
legal reforms of the twentieth century have been devised, fought for, and established by lawyers. Often they have been opposed by too many members of the profession; often they have
won the day only by securing public support; but the fact remains that the constructive leadership came from within the profession itself.[1]

It is pretty hard to find a group less concerned with serving society and more concerned with
serving themselves than the lawyers.[2]

Introduction

Roscoe Pound offered an often-quoted definition of a profession as

a group of men pursuing a learned art as a common calling in the spirit of public service—no
less a public service because it may incidentally be a means of livelihood.[3]

Despite this assumed relationship between public service and professionalism,[4] it is difficult
to pin down. Professional rules of conduct rarely formalise or state positively public service
obligations.[5] Therefore, although such obligations may be keenly felt and observed, they are
somewhat ephemeral and perhaps easily changed or reconceived. Most conceptions of 'public
service' are about eschewing self-interest, particularly making money, as the raison d'être of
professional practice. Recently, providing services free of charge to those who cannot afford
to pay, or *pro bono publico*, has achieved a high profile as the expression of this commitment,
promoted by the profession and government alike. *Pro bono publico* is the new face of public

---

[1] R Pound, *The Lawyer from Antiquity to Modern Times: with Particular Reference to the Development of Bar Associations in the United States* (St Paul, MN, West Publishing 1953) X.

[2] F Rodell, 'Goodbye to Law Reviews' (1936) 23 *Virginia Law Review* 38, 42.

[3] Pound, above n 1, 5.

[4] AT Kronman, 'Living in the Law' in D Luban (ed), *The Ethics of Lawyers* (Aldershot, Dartmouth Publishing,
1994) 835 (the deployment of skill without concern for public interest makes a person a legal technician, not a good
lawyer); N Strosen, 'Pro bono Legal Work: For the Good of not only the Public but also the Lawyer and the Legal
Profession' (1992–3) 91 *Michigan Law Review* 2122; HT Edwards, 'A Lawyers' Duty to Serve the Public Good' (1990)
65 *New York University Law Review* 1148; R Abel, *The Legal Profession in England and Wales* (Oxford, Blackwell,
1988) 27; A Flores, 'What Kind Of Person Should A Professional Be' in A Flores (ed) *Professional Ideals* (Belmont,
CA, Wadsworth Publishing, 1988) 1.

[5] *Solicitors' Code of Conduct 2007* (London, Solicitors Regulation Authority, 2007) core duty 1.06 states that a
solicitor shall not 'behave in a way likely to diminish the trust the public places in you or the profession', but note
that this is expressed negatively. Rules rarely impose positive duties to promote the legal profession.

service, but the demand for such legal services by the state may be the price the profession has to pay for any continuing monopoly, making demonstrable forms of public service a new overhead of professional practice.

Conceptions of public service

Pound saw the very act of maintaining a profession, and thereby the integrity of lawyers, the legal process and the rule of law, as a public service. He observed that, whenever lawyers had been discouraged or had been weakly organised, from ancient Rome to the American frontier, abuse was rife and the public interest suffered.[6] Beyond this, Pound cited various ways that the bar associations in the US had abjured self-interest and contributed to the public good. First, professionals, unlike businessmen, were not competitive with each other; if a lawyer discovered something

> useful to the profession and so to the administration of justice through research or experience he publishes it in legal periodicals . . . It is not his property.[7]

Secondly, professionals, unlike other employees, did not go on strike, thus putting their public obligations before their personal self-interest. Thirdly, professionals acted collegially with each other, advancing the science of jurisprudence, promoting the administration of justice, upholding the honour of the profession of law and establishing cordial relations among the members of the bar.[8] Pound's notion of public service was subtle and elusive in terms of demonstrable public benefit. Since the Second World War the profession's ability to abjure self-interest and operate in the public interest has increasingly been called into question.

Signs that the legal profession was falling in the public's esteem were evident in a survey of respondents using agencies in three London boroughs in 1967–1968.[9] It revealed a broadly positive perception of lawyers, with many thinking that they charged fair prices, were honest, and gave both rich and poor equal attention. The seeds of a future decline in professional standing were evident in the contradictory perceptions that lawyers would do anything to help their clients and often overcharged. Negative perceptions grew in the succeeding decades, when the credibility of the public service claim was increasingly queried. Whether this was due to the worldwide growth of consumerism,[10] better information or increased contact with professions by ordinary people is immaterial. By 1987 the Law Society's own research showed that, compared with similar occupations, solicitors were only perceived as less dishonest and avaricious than estate agents.[11] The decline of public

---

[6] Pound, Above n 1, XXV and 40.

[7] *Ibid*, 6 and 10.

[8] *Ibid*, 14.

[9] B Abel-Smith, M Zander and RB Ross, *Legal Problems and the Citizen: A Study in Three London Boroughs* (London, Heinemann Educational, 1973) 249.

[10] In the US, the President and Chief Justice rebuked the profession for its low public standing, which opinion polls suggested was due to its 'greedy and self serving' image. HC Petrowitz, 'Some Thoughts About Current Problems in Legal Ethics and Professional Responsibility' (1979) 6 *Duke Law Journal* 1275.

[11] J Jenkins, E Skordaki and CF Willis, *Public Use and Perception of Solicitors' Services* (London, The Law Society, 1989) 10.

service in legal practice was commented on in one of the key works on the sociology of the professions, where it was attributed to the advent of legal aid.[12] The theory was advanced that public funding of access to justice had caused wider notions of public service to give way to an ethic of dedicated service to individual clients. At the same time, changes in the legal services market, extreme competitiveness between the wealthiest firms and threats of strike action by legal aid lawyers threatened Pound's genteel conception of public service.

The reformulation of the public service ideal came from an unlikely source. In 1999 the the Access to Justice Act was enacted, partly prompted by the government's irritation at the Law Society's campaign against cuts in legal aid, which had included expensive newspaper advertising. Section 46 of the Act was intended to prevent the profession using members' funds for political purposes and restricted the purposes for which the income from practising certificates could be used. This can be read as the government's perception of the public service role of the legal profession. The approved purposes are:

> formulating and implementing rules and regulations, developing and disseminating guidance, recommendations and other guidance contributing to the control, government and direction of the profession and the way it practises (including the definition, review and supervision of professional conduct and work), participation in the legislative process in relation to proposals relevant to the organisation and conduct of the profession, law reform work falling outside this, support for pro bono, furtherance of human rights and development of international relations.[13]

The list leaves much scope for debate. For example, does the permitted 'law reform work' leave any scope for future campaigns against government policy?[14] Similarly, what does furthering human rights encompass? Action using members' practising certificate fees would presumably offend the section, however central to the profession's interest the cause— defending natural or procedural justice, for example. It is, however, notable that the list contains *pro bono*, an ancient tradition of lawyers working for poor clients without pay, perhaps the only item that takes the list beyond the conventional. This fact conceals a long and occasionally tempestuous history between government and the profession on the nature and place of free legal services in a strategy for access to justice.

Access to justice and free legal services

The roots of the *pro bono publico* tradition run deep and its origins are obscure. It may have developed from bans on legal representatives accepting fees in ancient Rome and dark age Europe.[15] It may have been connected with the fact that both the medical and legal professions assumed responsibility for their areas of expertise from the clergy and, with them,

---

[12] See G Mungham and PA Thomas, 'Solicitors and Clients: Altruism or Self Interest?' in R Dingwall and P Lewis (eds), *The Sociology of the Professions: Lawyers, Doctors and Others* (Basingstoke, Macmillan Press, 1983).

[13] The Access to Justice Act (1999), s 46(2)b as extended under s 46(3)(a).

[14] While a campaign on legal aid may be considered part of a public service remit for a legal profession, the primary ethical concern of which should be justice, it obviously crossed the line so far as the government was concerned.

[15] Pound, above n 1, 52. In the Middle Ages a gift was permitted (*ibid*, 55 and 68).

charitable responsibility for the poor and the dispossessed.[16] A possible route was through a right to sue *in forma pauperis*, whereby courts could assign lawyers to act for litigants without a fee.[17] The court's motive was not necessarily charitable, since matters progress more swiftly and efficiently with presentation by those familiar with rules of evidence and of court. Such practises would explain the fact that the literal translation of *pro bono publico* is 'for the good of the state', rather than 'for the good of the public' or community, as is often assumed today.[18]

There was no serious consideration of the accessibility of legal services as an issue of policy before the twentieth century. In the sixteenth and seventeenth centuries litigation was commonplace,[19] but, subsequently, judicial discouragement of free representation[20] and professional disdain for 'low grade' work caused a decline of *pro bono publico*. In civil cases, the ancient laws against maintenance, supporting litigation in which one had no legitimate interest, and champerty, sharing damages, discouraged lawyers supporting impoverished litigants. There was a change of attitude to free work for the poor in the later Victorian era, with the Victorian professional middle class adopting the *noblesse oblige* traditions of the aristocracy.[21] By the beginning of the twentieth century, a confused and contradictory case law had evolved to the point where lawyers were reasonably safe acting without expecting payment, provided the proceedings were not frivolous and vexatious.[22] The volume of free work conducted by the legal profession is not known, but was probably low.

Attempts to introduce limited legal aid in the early twentieth century were undermined by the professional bodies' concern to stamp out 'a black market in legal aid' conducted on a contingency basis.[23] By 1914 working class demands for the right to divorce led to the introduction of the Poor Persons Procedure, whereby solicitors and barristers provided their services free.[24] The demand for assistance led to the establishment of a large office, but, because in some cases solicitors charged expenses, a committee was established to consider the procedure. In 1919 the Lawrence Committee decided to drive out the profiteers and to

---

[17] JA Brundage, 'Legal Aid for the Poor and the Professionalisation of Law in the Middle Ages' (1988) 9 *Journal of Legal History* 169.

[18] A right to sue *in forma pauperis* was established by statute in 1495 but probably has earlier origins: JM Maguire 'Poverty and Civil Litigation' (1923) 36 *Harvard Law Review* 361. A similar example of court-assigned advocates is the dock brief in criminal trials, whereby the judge asks an advocate to appear for an unrepresented defendant: WR Prest, *The Rise of the Barristers: A Social History of the Bar 1590–1640* (Oxford, Clarendon Press, 1986) 22.

[18] JW Bellacosa, 'Obligatory *Pro Bono* Legal Services: Mandatory or Voluntary? Distinction Without a Difference' (1991) 19 *Hofstra Law Review* 744.

[19] In the late sixteenth and seventeenth centuries, litigation was more widespread than at any time until the 1970s, and probably over 75% of litigants were 'non-gentlemen'. M Burrage, 'From a Gentleman's to a Public Profession' (1996) *International Journal of the Legal Profession* 45, 47.

[20] T Goriely, 'Law for the Poor: The Relationship between Advice Agencies and Solicitors in the Development of Poverty Law' (1996) 3 *International Journal of the Legal Profession* 215, 217.

[21] This comprised disinterested service and the continuing desire to distance oneself from low-grade work and payment that might be seen as 'money grubbing'. H Perkin *The Rise of Professional Society: England since 1880* (London, Routledge, 1989).

[22] J Levin 'Solicitors Acting Speculatively and Pro Bono' (1996) 15 *Civil Justice Quarterly* 44.

[23] See B Abel-Smith and R Stevens, 'Legal Services for the Poor' in *Lawyers and the Courts: A Sociological Study of the English Legal System 1750–1965* (London, Heinemann, 1967) 135, 146 and 158. They use the word 'commission', but it is clear that what the Law Society were seeking to abolish was contingency and speculative work by solicitors.

[24] T Goriely 'Gratuitous Assistance to the "Ill-dressed": Debating Civil Legal Aid in England and Wales from 1924 to 1939' (2006) 13 *International Journal of the Legal Profession* 41.

make the procedure more inaccessible,[25] but demand continued to exceed the supply of services. The Law Society feared that anything less than a free service might result in officials being appointed to handle cases, and a second Lawrence report reaffirmed the principle of free legal service[26] and recommended that the Law Society administer the scheme, which it did from 1926.

Between the two world wars a gap opened up between the professional elite in the Law Society and practitioners conducting the Poor Persons' Procedure. The elite held a conception of public service that eschewed profit and recognised a social obligation to those less fortunate, while many regional solicitors demanded that the scheme be formalised and payment made. The Bar held a relaxed attitude on these matters, bordering on indifference, perhaps because the scheme had marketing potential for independent advocates building a clientele.[27] The Bar favoured a free scheme but solicitors' resistance to the Poor Persons' Procedure and demands for payment, particularly in Wales, laid the ground for the Rushcliffe Committee in 1945. This led to the implementation of its recommendation for a legal aid scheme after the Second World War.[28] Conscious of the implications of managing legal aid in relation to its independence from the state, the Law Society's embrace of the scheme was out of fear that something worse might be imposed.[29]

The Legal Aid Scheme, as the Law Society feared, changed the legal profession's relationship with and attitude to low-paying work. Accepting responsibility for 'poor persons law', and doing it for profit, put the profession in potential conflict with the voluntary advice sector. The Law Society was adamant that legal aid should not support advice bureaux, and the London centres only survived with support from the London County Council.[30] This ambivalence was reflected in restrictions imposed on solicitors working as volunteers for advice centres, ostensibly because free work amounted to advertising and the unfair attraction of business.[31] By the 1960s various gaps in legal aid provision, notably in employment and other tribunals that did not award lawyers costs, were partly filled by advice agencies and law centres. The 'sympathetic lay advice' became more specialised and expert,[32] but the solicitors' anxiety about it was allayed when they perceived

---

[25] T Goriely, 'Civil Legal Aid in England and Wales 1914 to 1961: the Emergence of a Paid Scheme' (PhD thesis, University College London, 2003).

[26] The committee upheld a moral obligation, in return for the monopoly in the practice of law, to offer legal services to those who could not afford to pay, provided this did not place an unnecessary burden on practitioners. See Goriely, above n 24; see also AA Paterson, 'Professionalism and the Legal Services Market' (1996) 1(2) *International Journal of the Legal Profession* 137, 160, note 19.

[27] Instructions under the Poor Persons Scheme had the obvious benefit for barristers of advertising their services to solicitors and potential lay clients attending court. The Bar had objected to the presentation of divorce petitions in the county courts because they wanted to preserve barristers' exclusive advocacy rights under the poor persons procedures. It also objected to poor persons cases being concentrated on specific days because the barristers would not then have a wider audience. Goriely, above n 25.

[28] *Ibid.*

[29] The Law Society resisted the establishment of state employed and salaried lawyers. Goriely, above n 20, 224; JS Auerbach, *Unequal Justice: Lawyers and Social Change in Modern America* (New York, Oxford University Press, 1976).

[30] Above n 25.

[31] M Zander, 'Restrictions on Lawyers Working for the Poor' in *Lawyers and the Public Interest: A Study of Restrictive Practices* (London, Weidenfeld & Nicolson, 1968), 238.

[32] Above n 25, 220–1.

that the advice sector provided points of access[33] and screened out weak or unprofitable cases.[34] The thawing of the relationship between the advice centres and the profession was symbolised by the formation of the Free Representation Unit (FRU) in 1972, by a group of Bar students wishing to represent welfare benefit claimants.[35] By 1977 an agreement had been reached whereby, provided they did not encroach on areas such as personal injury and crime, the Law Society would grant waivers to solicitors working in law centres from certain practice rules. Reporting in 1988, the Marre Report acknowledged that

> It is no longer possible to consider only the two branches of the legal profession when considering the supply of legal services.[36]

From the late 1980s, the government tried to reduce the legal aid budget by raising the eligibility threshold.[37] The resulting increase in litigants in person[38] was a considerable burden on the courts[39] and evidence of a decline in access to justice. The Law Society, now representing a profession swollen by legal aid revenues and espousing a credo of access to law, launched a campaign against legal aid cuts. The government, stung by criticism from all sides, actively considered ways of addressing the problem. The Thatcher government's strategy had been to force reforms that might reduce the legal profession's market control. The Labour government opted for encouraging the advice sector to compete with lawyers, building upon what had become recognised as superior expertise in many areas of welfare law.[40] Advice agencies were a cornerstone of the government's plan for a Community Legal Service and were invited to bid for legal aid franchises. This policy campaign was accompanied by a political campaign against lawyers, criticising them for encouraging litigation, for charging high fees and for not doing enough free work.

The politics of *pro bono*

While in opposition, the Labour Party legal affairs spokesman, Paul Boateng, had threatened wealthy law firms with a 'framework for them' to make a contribution to 'the traditional duty

---

[33] Advice agencies tend to provide advice to low-income groups particularly on social security, housing, family and consumer law. A 1986 survey by the Advice Services Alliance recorded that, nationwide, there were 896 Citizens Advice Bureau service points, 354 generalist independent advice services, 142 generalist advice agencies serving specific groups (eg young people), 55 independent housing advice service points, 25 money advice service points and 14 immigration advice service points. Training Committee of the Law Society *The Recruitment Crisis* (London, The Law Society, 1988) 17.

[34] Above n 25, 233–7.

[35] FRU pamphlet (undated) 1.

[36] Lady Marre CBE, *A Time for Change: Report of the Committee on the Future of the Legal Profession* (London, General Council of the Bar and Council of the Law Society, 1988) (the Marre Report) paras 5.28 and 6.8; see also B Abel-Smith, M Zander and R Brooke, *Legal Problems and the Citizen: A Study of Three London Boroughs* (London, Heinemann Educational, 1973) 217.

[37] Goriely, above n 25, citing (at note 9) J Plotnikoff and R Woolfson, *Report of Study into Reasons for Refusal of Offers of Legal Aid* (London, Legal Aid Board, 1996).

[38] A working party chaired by Lord Justice Otton in 1995 noted that, in March 1995 alone, there were 4,258 litigants in person in actions in the High Court, an increase from one in ten to one in three since 1989/90.

[39] They absorbed disproportionate court time and were less successful than represented parties. *The Times*, 7 July 1995; J Ames, 'Rescuing DIY Litigants', *Law Society Gazette*, 26 July 1995.

[40] Green form bills for areas of 'social welfare' law for 1975–6 were £27,000 or 11% of the total. By 1994–5 this had risen to £468,000, or 30% of the total.

and responsibility of lawyers as a profession to the proper and equitable administration of justice'. Widely taken to mean that *pro bono* work would be made a condition of practice, by late 1994 he was proposing a levy on the 'private legal profession to supplement public resources'.[41] Whilst opposing this, the Law Society established a Pro Bono Working Party, which reported in 1994.[42] It recommended that solicitors should not be subject to a mandatory professional obligation to provide free legal services, stressing that the profession should not ameliorate or redress, by the provision of free services, the growing legal need created by declining legal aid budgets. It also suggested abandoning the term *pro bono publico* in favour of the potentially ambiguous 'voluntary legal services'. It did, however, make six proposals for stimulating the involvement of solicitors in *pro bono* activity, including publishing a policy statement encouraging solicitors, creating a free representation advice agency and establishing a trust fund to receive voluntary funds to support *pro bono* activities.[43]

In 1995, in a speech to the London Solicitors' Litigation Association, Boateng suggested a mutual responsibility for access to justice, promising that Labour would invest in the 'legal infrastructure' if lawyers tackled the 'Spanish practices and customs' that contributed to the £1.6 billion legal aid bill. Martin Mears, then president of the Law Society, criticised the policy of urging *pro bono* work on lawyers, suggesting that 25% of small firms earned less than £10,000 a year.[44] By the end of 1996, progress was reported on only one of the Working Party's six proposals, concerning representation at tribunals. Boateng wrote to the new President of the Law Society, Tony Girling, threatening 'alternatives of a statutory nature, if necessary'.[45] Anticipating proposals for a levy in Labour's consultation paper *Justice Indeed*, Boateng wrote to the Law Society and the Bar Council offering collaboration on a 'public–private partnership',[46] but by December 1996 he revisited the idea of legislation to force solicitors to do more *pro bono* work.[47] During the passage of the Woolf reforms and the Access to Justice Bill in 1998, the Lord Chancellor, Lord Irvine, cited the profession's failings on *pro bono publico* in defending his far-reaching reforms.[48]

Individuals disappointed with progress on the Law Society's Pro Bono Working Party Report convened an open meeting in 1996, resulting in the formation of the Solicitors' Pro Bono Group (SPBG). It was not until September 1998 that the Law Society's Council adopted a weak motion, instigated by the SPBG, that:

> Recognises the value of solicitors providing voluntary services, and emphasises the valuable contribution which they already make to the community by providing their professional ser-

---

[41] 'Labour Suggests Levy to Support Legal Assistance', *The Lawyer*, 27 September 1994, 3; 'Labour Eyes US *Pro Bono* Model', *The Lawyer*, 8 November 1994, 2; 'Labour Creates Future Vision', *Law Society Gazette*, 22 February 1995, 68.

[42] Report of the Law Society's Pro Bono Working Party, 1994 (and see *The Times*, 9 October 1995).

[43] R Abbey and A Boon, 'The Provision of Free Legal Services by Solicitors: A Review of the Report of the Law Society's Pro Bono Working Party' (1995) 2 *International Journal of the Legal Profession* 261.

[44] 'Hard Labour?' *The Times*, 7 November 1995, 35.

[45] The model might be the American Bar Association's projects in Chicago, which provide resources from private practice for specific projects, already copied in 600 locations in the US. '*Pro bono* Wrangle', *Gazette* 93/46, 13 December 1996, 6.

[46] *Ibid.*

[47] 'Boateng in Threat to Impose *Pro bono* Rules', *The Lawyer*, 10 December 1996, 1.

[48] Eg franchising and block contracting of legal aid to advice bureaux, Criminal Defence and Community Legal Service.

vices and skills to support community and charitable projects;

Welcomes the successful launch of the Solicitors' Pro Bono Group and declares its support for the Group and the work which it does

Encourages solicitors and firms to become members of the Solicitors' Pro Bono Group and to work together and with the Solicitors' Pro Bono Group towards greater coordination of *pro bono* effort; and

Recognises clearly that voluntary legal services work is not and never can be a substitute for a properly funded legal aid scheme.[49]

This period, however, marked the high water mark of the Law Society's efforts on *pro bono*. In 1998 it also supported the creation of the Young Solicitors' Group Annual Pro Bono Awards.[50] The following year Kamlesh Bahl, then Vice President of the Law Society, suggested the adoption of an aspirational *pro bono* target,[51] allowing continuing professional development points and the allocation of the whole of the Law Society's challenge fund (£50,000) to develop local *pro bono* projects. The Law Society trust also made a contribution of £90,000, spread over two years, to the Solicitors' Pro Bono Group.[52]

The government's attack on the profession's record on *pro bono* continued unabated,[53] and Lord Philips of Sudbury lamented the lack of ammunition to counter the 'drip, drip of denigration from government spokesmen' in the House of Lords.[54] The Law Society claimed a good record of solicitors providing free services, although the evidence for this was sketchy at best. In common with other legal professions,[55] neither the Bar nor the Law Society collected data on free services.[56] The evidence that did exist was either contradictory or suggested that the free work done was neither significant nor widespread.[57] In a Law Society survey of solicitors in 1989, 41% claimed to carry out 'public service work for which [they] did] not charge fees' but the majority performed one hour or less work a week.[58] In 1993

---

[49] Law Society Council Minutes, 24 September 1998.

[50] J Ames 'Do the Right Thing', *Gazette* 97/30, 27 July 2000.

[51] Possibly to be calculated as a number of hours of *pro bono* work per solicitor or a target calculated as a percentage of gross fees (*Law Society Gazette*, 6 November 1999).

[52] *Gazette*, 20 January 1999, 4.

[53] In a House of Lords debate Lord Irvine reported that the fees of barristers and Queen's Counsels (QCs) and their claims on the legal aid fund, were impeding access to justice. The quoted levels (£1 million per annum) were only true of top commercial silks, although leading criminal silks specialising in fraud and child care cases could earn £200,000–300,000 per annum, largely from legal aid. See *The Guardian*, 15 July 1997, 1; C Dyer, 'Law Chief Fires Fresh Volley on "Fat Cat" Lawyers', *The Guardian*, 10 December 1997. In June 1998 the clerk to the Parliaments refused to sanction legal aid bills presented by QCs for work in the House of Lords. See C Dyer, 'On Trial: A System That Makes QCs Rich', *The Guardian*, 3 June 1998. In March 1999 Andrew Dismore, solicitor and Labour MP, asked a parliamentary question about the relevance of *pro bono* work to appointment as a QC.

[54] A Philips, 'Want of Experience', *The Gazette*, 28 April 1999.

[55] The American Lawyers' Annual Survey of large firm contributions, dates only from 1990. M Galanter and T Palay, 'Public Service Implications of Evolving Firm Size and Structure' in RA Katzmann (ed), *The Law Firm and the Public Good* (Washington, DC, The Brookings Institute, 1995) 41.

[56] Even after this, the Law Society's panel survey found that 68% of firms kept no record of time spent: Research and Policy Planning Unit, *Panel Study of Solicitors' Firms* (London, The Law Society, 1997).

[57] In 1976 the Royal Commission on Legal Services estimated that 3,300 solicitors supported advice agencies by offering free services (*The Royal Commission on Legal Services Report*, Cmnd 7648 (1979) para 2.21), but an independent survey of 59 Law Centres found 369 wholly or partly qualified lawyers, less than 1% of the solicitors then holding practising certificates, offering voluntary services. See L Hiscock and G Cole, 'The Motivation, Use and Future of Volunteer Lawyers in Law Centres' [1989] *Journal of Social Welfare Law* 404.

[58] G Chambers and S Harwood, *Solicitors in England and Wales: Practice, Organisation and Perceptions* (London, The Law Society, 1991).

the Law Society's Pro Bono Working Party undertook a survey of 123 local Law Societies, but only 32 responses were received and none of the respondents held records or monitored *pro bono* work in any way. Yet the report claimed that many local societies were 'aware that local practitioners were active in assisting Citizens Advice Bureaux on a rota basis'.[59] The Law Society appeared unclear on what constituted free services and, conscious that many members were suffering an often disastrous decline in legal aid income, uncertain whether they should be providing them at all.

Although no concerted action had been taken to improve the quality of *pro bono* data for the profession as a whole, the Law Society attempted a publicity offensive. In 1997 it issued a press release, based on a Law Society Research Unit study, claiming that 70% of 460 surveyed firms provide legal advice to private individuals whose cases fell outside the scope of legal aid. It noted that only 11% provided no such services. The release also claimed that solicitors in private practice contributed an annual average of 37 hours of services

> free of charge or at a rate substantially below that normally charged either during the firm's time or during [their] own.[60]

On this basis, the Law Society claimed that

> value of pro bono work by solicitors is the equivalent to a cash gift to good causes of at least £124 million a year.[61]

This claim did not tally with any of the previous research. A possible explanation for the discrepancy is the confusion introduced by the Law Society Working Party's attempt to drop the term *pro bono publico* in favour of 'voluntary legal services'. This had opened the door to counting irrecoverable fees or undercharged services, cases handled for 'a rate substantially below that normally charged', unsuccessful conditional fee cases, time spent on friends and acquaintances, loss leaders for existing clients and even bad debts.[62]

During this time, the Bar had a relatively easy ride from the government, possibly because it was seen to be actively involved in promoting *pro bono publico*. In 1989, in response to Green Papers, the Bar warned that the implementation of the government's proposals would in fact diminish the public service work performed by solicitors and barristers, but nevertheless undertook to encourage barristers to do *pro bono* work and to expand the Free Representation Unit both in London and in other major centres.[63] Since its formation, the FRU had expanded its work to embrace a range of tribunals for which legal aid was not available, aiming to provide representation equal to that available through legal aid.[64] In 1992, 2,063 cases were referred to the FRU by Citizens Advice Bureaux and Law

---

[59] Report of the Law Society's Pro Bono Working Party (London, The Law Society, 1994) Annex C, para 1.

[60] J Jenkins, *Law Society Omnibus Survey 2: Report 5: Pro Bono Activities Conducted by Private Practice Solicitors* (London, The Law Society, 1997).

[61] Law Society news release, 'Solicitors Give at Least £124 Million of Free Legal Help a Year', 27 January 1998. This figure was based on volunteer hours claimed by 1,113 interviewees multiplied by an unspecified charging rate.

[62] A Boon and A Whyte 'Something for Nothing?: The Provision of Legal Services *Pro Bono Publico*' (London, University of Westminster, 2001).

[63] General Council of the Bar, *The Quality of Justice: The Bar's Response* (London, Buttwerworths, 1999).

[64] FRU is authorised by the Bar Council in relation to each of the tribunals in which its representatives appear.

Centres, and barristers appeared in 1200 cases, but this has fallen since.[65] The FRU employed administrators and a solicitor to prepare the more complex cases.[66] In 1993 the FRU appealed to barristers in London and the South East to assist by launching its 'Chamber Scheme'.[67] This was supported by the Bar Council, and in 1995 the chairman, Peter Goldsmith, took cases himself to encourage more senior barristers to supplement volunteer Bar students[68] and pupils.[69]

The resurgence of *pro bono publico*

There was a marked change of attitude in relation to *pro bono publico* in 1996. That was the year that the Bar Pro Bono Unit (BPBU) was formed as an independent charity[70] supplementing a number of other schemes.[71] Barristers were asked to donate two or three days a year to free work. Despite being described as 'far too modest',[72] at least this was a target. Since its formation, the BPBU has increased its capacity,[73] and in 1997 took on 44% of the cases referred to it, though half of these cases involved just giving advice. Some significant cases involved more substantial assistance, including a case brought by a pensioner against the National Grid over the alleged use of £47 million of pension fund money to make redundancy payments.[74] In 2000, Bar in the Community was launched to recruit barristers to the management committees of voluntary organisations.[75] In 2002 the BPBU set up a solicitors' panel of 11 firms, including most of the 'magic circle', for cases that needed a solicitor as well as barrister.[76] The Unit received a major grant from the Bar in 2001, but still raises some of its

---

[65] FRU currently handles around 700 cases a year: 300 employment, 300 social security benefits and the rest criminal injury compensation and immigration; C Tulloch, 'Thirty Five Years of "Poverty Law"', *Independent Lawyer*, November 2007, 11.

[66] Funding was provided by the Bar Council (33%), the Inns of Court (26%), covenants from individual barristers (20%), subscriptions from referral agencies and income from training days. See *Counsel*, 'FRU—The Bars Contribution' [April 1994] *Counsel* 23.

[67] D Conn, 'A Matter of Principle' [July 1993] *Counsel* 18, notes that by 1993 the FRU had 2,400 clients—an increase of 25% over the previous year.

[68] The Inns of Court Law School provides a Bar Vocational Course option for those wishing to work at FRU. See N Duncan, 'FRU and the Bar Vocational Course', *New Law Journal*, 5 November 1993.

[69] There was a decline in the number of cases for which FRU representation could be found from 1,682 in 1994 to 1,394 in 1995: M Phelan, 'Effective Access to Justice' [April 1996] *Counsel* 16.

[70] V Sims, 'Pro Bono at the Bar' (1998) 4 *Amicus Curiae* 21.

[71] This was in addition and complementary to existing schemes, especially the regional schemes run on the Northern Circuit, Western Circuit and Wales and Chester Circuit, and the schemes run by subject area Bar Associations, eg the Employment Law Bar Association Scheme, the Planning Bar Association's Free Advocacy Scheme and Environmental Legal and Mediation Service. *Ibid.*

[72] Phelan, above n 69.

[73] In 1996 it had 282 volunteers and 171 requests for help. In 1997 it was reported that 720 barristers of differing levels of seniority, including 120 QCs, had agreed to provide at least three days a year to *pro bono publico* work. This represented less than 10% of the practising Bar. By 1998 it was reported that the number of participating barristers had increased to 800, including 130 QCs, of which almost 600 were based in London. Fifty legal specialisms were represented. In 1998 the FRU handled 1,600 cases a year and Bar Pro Bono Unit provided assistance in 400: S Solley and R D'Cruz 'Deliverance from Death Row?' [October 1998] *Counsel* 22. In 2002 it had 886 requests and 1,220 barristers registered; see Sims, above n 70; S Weale and C Dyer, 'Heard the One About the Lawyer Who Works for Nothing…', *The Guardian*, 11 June 2002.

[74] C Dyer, 'On the Lawyers Who Work for Free', *The Guardian*, 15 July 1997, 17.

[75] Bar Pro Bono Unit Annual Report 2000–2002.

[76] 'BPBU Creates Solicitor Panel', *The Lawyer*, 28 January 2002.

overheads independently. It earned praise from the government for its work and for publishing records of the its work.

The meeting that led to the formation of the SPBG was also held in 1996, led by Andrew Philips, partner in a large solicitors' firm specialising in charities law, and Caroline Knighton, head of Business in the Community Professional Firms Group. Despite the aim of promoting *pro bono* work among solicitors generally,[77] building relations with Citizens Advice Bureaux and Law Centres and establishing a nationwide referral system[78], the initial target was large firms, a number of which paid the start-up costs. By 2000, the Solicitors' Pro Bono Group had 130 firms and other members, including 40% of the top 50 law firms.[79] The focus on large firms was understandable because of their high levels of organisation and resources,[80] but also because elite lawyers tend to be concerned with the image and status of the profession. Although the SPBG's publicity materials emphasised the advantages, mainly 'business' advantages, of participation, it is clear that large firms had varying degrees of engagement with *pro bono publico.*

A study conducted in large London law firms between 1990 and 1994 found little interest, though several firms claimed 'substantial pro bono programmes'.[81] A survey of the 100 largest national firms in 1994 also found a mixed picture.[82] Six firms had a policy on *pro bono* work conducted by the firm and four assigned work to firm members. Twenty-seven firms claimed to perform work exceeding £10,000 in value per annum, but eight said they undertook no *pro bono* work whatsoever. The same was probably true of the 39 firms that did not respond. Advisory work at Citizens Advice Bureaux (CABx) and Law Centres, conducted by trainees, was the major area of activity. Senior personnel tended to deal with appeals to the Judicial Committee of the Privy Council in capital cases or with cases from organisations such as Business in the Community or Liberty. By 1994 a small number of firms had appointed in-house *pro bono* coordinators and begun vying for recognition as leaders in the field, but the SPBG undoubtedly increased the profile and efforts of large firms. LawWorks, adopted as its operating name, also described a partnership between the SPBG and the Law Centres Federation to match lawyers with advice centres.

By 2000 the atmosphere had changed in relation to solicitors' pro bono. In 2001 the SPBG reported recruiting 500 volunteers to LawWorks, mainly from large firms.[83] By 2006 it had set up 55 free clinics in CABx and council buildings, and helped 26,000 clients a year, not supported by legal aid, in new areas like bankruptcy.[84] A new scheme, LawWorks for Community, aimed to match up senior solicitors and in-house lawyers with community groups needing commercial advice. Also in 2001, 13 of the top 20 firms had *pro bono* coordinators, and many claimed to be performing thousands of hours of free work.[85] A

[77] 'Solicitors Vote for Boost to *Pro Bono*', *The Lawyer*, 12 November 1996, 1.

[78] The Solicitors Pro Bono Group brochure (undated).

[79] M Swallow, 'Who is Behind *Pro bono?*', *The Lawyer*, 27 September 1999.

[80] RA Katzmann, 'Themes in Context' in Katzmann, above n 55.

[81] M Galanter and T Palay, 'Large Law Firms and Professional Responsibility' in R Cranston, *Legal Ethics and Professional Responsibility* (Oxford, Clarendon Press, 1995) 201.

[82] A Boon and R Abbey, 'Moral Agendas: *Pro Bono Publico* in Large Law Firms in the United Kingdom' (1997) 60 *Modern Law Review* 630.

[83] L Hickman 'Pro Plus', *Gazette* 98/28, 12 July 2001.

[84] C Dyer 'Win or Lose, no Fee: Pro Bono Week Promotes Free Legal Services', *The Guardian*, 5 June 2006, 14.

[85] In 2001 Alan and Overy claimed 12,232 hours and Clifford Chance 18,000 hours per annum: Hickman, above n 83.

survey of 1,000 lawyers found that 70% claimed to be undertaking *pro bono* work and 38% of firms had an organised programme. Firms with over 100 partners were the least likely to be organised, although lawyers from these firms were often found to contribute.[86] The SPBG won a £700,000 award from the government to allow corporate lawyers to offer free advice by email. David Lock of the Lord Chancellor's Department said that although it was no substitute for publicly funded assistance, it would complement the work of the Community Legal Service.[87] It won a £350,000 grant from the government to establish a website through which lawyers could answer questions raised by CABx and similar organisations,[88] and sponsored projects training corporate lawyers to deal with welfare type areas, providing non-litigation advice to small charities and encouraging *pro bono* by law students.[89] Expanding its reach beyond London with projects in Leeds and the Midlands,[90] the College of Law promised to provide clinics at its branches in collaborations with regional firms.[91]

Part of the reason for the increased interest of large firms was a changed social climate in relation to voluntary work in the corporate sector. The Labour governments of the 1990s accepted the inevitability of scaled-down social welfare commitments, resuscitating private philanthropy as part of a social philosophy built on individualism, responsibility and materialism.[92] Labour's compromise with 'market fundamentalism',[93] the so-called 'third way', envisaged a strong civil society enshrining rights and responsibilities, and strong communities built upon shared responsibility and devolved power.[94] This effort involved reversing the decline of voluntary activity occurring over the previous 90 years[95] such that 'volunteering' was seen as 'an act of citizenship'.[96] Closer examination of the social and environmental credentials of large companies, the need to attract, motivate and retain high quality staff, and the instigation of campaigns of corporate social responsibility stimulated more charitable and community work,[97] meeting the requirement of company benefit.[98] It was sold to the corporate sector as an act of self-interest, a means of ameliorating the social threat posed by the disenfranchised 'underclass' and building communities safe for business. It was sold back to the profession partly through the efforts of Business in the Community

---

[86] *Ibid.*

[87] *Gazette* 98/03, 18 January 2001.

[88] Hickman, above n 83.

[89] S Bucknall 'Pro Bono—Meeting the Challenge' (2001) 151 *New Law Journal* 389; A Cox 'Something for Nothing', *Legal Week*, 18 October 2001.

[90] N Rovnick 'SPBG Midlands Launch Sparks Pro Bono Fever', *The Lawyer*, 5 November 2001; N Rovnick 'Solicitors' pro Bono Group goes for national coverage with Leeds project', *The Lawyer*, 28 January 2002, 6.

[91] Rovnick 'SPBG Midlands', *ibid*; 'Wragges and College of Law Team Up', *The Lawyer*, 16 July 2001.

[92] B Jordan, *The Common Good: Citizenship Morality and Self-interest* (Oxford, Basil Blackwell, 1989).

[93] G Soros, *The Crisis of Global Capitalism: Open Society Endangered* (London, Little Brown, 1998).

[94] T Blair, *The Third Way: New Politics for the New Century* (London, The Fabian Society, 1998) 6.

[95] R Hoggart, *The Way We Live Now* (London, Chatto & Windus, 1995).

[96] *Ibid*, 2 and 14.

[97] A MORI survey in 2006 found that 58% of employees in the UK thought that companies' social responsibility was important, probably partly because this enhances their self-image and esteem. S Brammer 'Feel-good Factories', *The Guardian*, 21 January 2006.

[98] Corporate charitable donations were forbidden except for the benefit of the company. See Bowen LJ in *Hutton v West Cork Railway Company* (1883) 23 Ch D 654, 673; CM Slaughter, 'Corporate Social Responsibility: a New Perspective' (1997) 18 *The Company Lawyer* 313. Cause related marketing is an acknowledged technique for establishing a brand. H Pringle and M Thompson, *Brand Spirit: How cause related marketing builds brands* (Chichester, John Wiley & Sons, 1999).

(BITC), formed in 1981 following an Anglo-American conference on the private sector's role in urban regeneration. This initiative penetrated mainstream commercial life as 'a public way to deliver socially responsible brand values'[99] following a high-profile campaign in 1990 asking leading companies to donate 1% of pre-tax profits.[100] BITC brought the idea of employee volunteering to large firms through its Professional Firms Group, formed in 1989, and by 1996 over 200 firms had joined, including 40 law firms.[101]

Large law firms had increasingly adopted corporate identity but had been slow to accept the new 'corporate responsibility' being urged on their corporate clients. In solicitors' firms *pro bono* was a matter of individual conscience.[102] The increasing financial success of corporate law firms from the late 1980s was notable, probably causing some, encouraged by the SPBG, to influence their lawyers to do more free work. Some corporate clients dropped law firms without *pro bono* programmes from their panels. In March 1999, British Aerospace announced such a policy, stating:

> British Aerospace has a vision. We have five corporate values and one of those is partnership with the community. We want our law firms to be aligned to our values, to have a similar culture to our culture.[103]

When Zurich Financial Services joined the SPBG it announced that it would be demanding a commitment to *pro bono* from its external lawyers.[104] One corporate lawyer said that four other clients had recently insisted on evidence of commitment to *pro bono* as part of tenders for their legal work.[105] It is also likely that, along with direct pressure of this kind, large firm lawyers were absorbing the normative values of the volunteering culture in client corporations.[106] By early 2001 three legal departments in large corporations had committed to providing *pro bono* services and two required that their law firms did so.[107] The success was modest, however.

Another factor influencing large firms was the increased presence of US law firms in the City. In 2000 the Law Society hosted an American Bar Association (ABA) seminar on promoting *pro bono* in a global environment.[108] In 2001 firm leaders met to discuss the provision of joint programmes. Although offering advice on English law was a longer-term goal, they committed themselves to a variety of community schemes. [109] One US firm appointed a full-time *pro bono* officer.[110] A 2004 survey of commercial firms found that,

---

[99] N Hill, 'Market Ethics', *The Guardian* (*Society* supplement), 19 May 1998, 85 quoting Peter Mandelson.

[100] 'The Giving List: FTSE 100 Givers', *The Guardian*, 25 November 2002, 4. Amongst the 100 or so leading contributors the percentage rose to 0.95% in 2002, but the 1990s ended as it had begun, with the top 400 firms making community contributions of 0.42% of pre tax profits.

[101] The professional firms agreed to provide up to £5,000 worth of their professional services for specific projects at no charge.

[102] E Nosworthy, 'Ethics and Large Law Firms' in S Parker and C Sampford (eds), *Legal Ethics and Legal Practice* (Oxford, Clarendon Press, 1995) 70.

[103] *The Lawyer*, 3 November 1998, 13.

[104] D Jordan, 'Zurich In-house Demands Firms Commit to *Pro bono*', *The Lawyer*, 4 October 1999.

[105] *Ibid.*

[106] WW Powell, 'Fields of Practice: Connections between Law and Organisations' (1996) *Law and Social Inquiry* 959.

[107] 'Ford Credit Links Up with Lovell's for Prince's Trust Pro Bono Work', *The Lawyer*, 19 February 2001.

[108] S Forsythe and Y Waljiee, 'UK Pro Bono Meets US', *The Lawyer*, 24 July 2000, 14.

[109] C Smith 'US Firms in London Set to Launch Joint Initiative on Pro Bono Work', *The Lawyer*, 12 February 2001.

[110] J Baxter, 'White and Case Hires First Pro Bono Officer', *Legal Week*, 15 March 2001, 2.

while hours had generally increased since 2001, UK firms were behind their US counterparts operating in the UK.[111] Despite this, it was also clear that many of the large firms were serious enough about *pro bono* to export it to overseas offices,[112] countries[113] and continents.[114]

Large firms engaging with *pro bono* were sometimes greeted with suspicion. Large firms often made a play of *pro bono* in their brochures, suggesting that their efforts might be a marketing ploy. The trade press also offered generally positive coverage,[115] probably fuelling this perception. Then there was a feeling that free work might be loss leader for the more entrepreneurial firms, a feeling not allayed when a spokesman for Freshfields, following the firm's selection as legal consultants to Green Globe, an environmental pressure group said,

> We are happy to provide the service on a *pro bono* basis because it is a very good way of accessing a huge market which we think we are uniquely well placed to serve.[116]

Hostility from high-street firms was sometimes palpable, a former President of the Law Society remarking that

> if a big City firm is doing a certain amount of *pro bono* work this has far less value for ordinary people than *pro bono* work by High Street practices which are geared up for everyday problems.[117]

The feeling that large firms may not be sincere converts to *pro bono* was given some credence when the New York office of Clifford Chance came bottom of a national survey in *American Lawyer* measuring associate satisfaction. Among their complaints contained in a memorandum to the partners was their 'deplorable animosity' to *pro bono* work. Clifford Chance eventually responded by including the performance of *pro bono* work as one of seven criteria for promotion.[118]

Despite some tension in the relationship between lawyers and *pro bono*, there was a strong lead from the government in 2002 when the new Attorney General, Lord Goldsmith, the founder of the Bar Pro Bono Unit, launched the Attorney General's Pro Bono Co-ordinating Committee, which he also chaired. The committee's remit was to promote, develop and coordinate the national effort.[119] The group also comprised the Solicitor-General, representatives of the profession and various *pro bono* interest groups, including a *pro bono* envoy, former President of the Law Society Michael Napier, who had special responsibility for the provinces. With this encouragement, the branches collaborated

[111] J Bartle, 'UK Firms Pro Bono Efforts Put to Shame by US Counterparts', *The Lawyer*, 4 October 2004, 4.

[112] Following a merger with a German firm, Lovells announced it was spreading its *pro bono* practices to the Berlin office: 'Pro Bono Export', *Gazette* 97/32, 17 August 2000.

[113] A team of associates with a US firm conducted an analysis of Zimbabwean legislation clamping down on voting rights for the International Bar Association Human Rights Institute (K Hobbs 'Shearmans in Pro Bono Anti-Mugabe Endeavour', *The Lawyer*, 25 March 2002, 13.

[114] Allen and Overy developed a European-wide child protection project with the Belgian charity Child Focus, based on its network of offices. N Rovnick 'A&O Launches Pro Bono First with Pan-European Work for Child Focus', *The Lawyer*, 25 March 2002.

[115] Eg N Rovnick 'Cobetts Consolidates its Pro Bono Initiatives', *The Lawyer*, 15 October 2001; J Hobson, 'Lawyers Give Helping Hand', *The Times*, 19 October 1999; C Dyer, 'A Bono Fide Freebie', *The Guardian*, 3 June 2003.

[116] 'Freshfields to do Free Work for Fresh Fields', *The Lawyer*, 22 November 1994, 3.

[117] J Smerin, 'For Love Not Money' (1995) 92/38 *Law Society Gazette*, 25 October 1995, 1.

[118] N Rovnick 'Clifford Chance New York Puts Pro Bono on Associates' Agenda', *The Lawyer*, 3 February 2003, 3.

[119] Press release from the Atorney General's Chambers, 23 April 2002; V MacCallum, 'Lord Goldsmith Unveils Pro Bono Drive to Coordinate Work across the Country', *Gazette* 99/17, 25 April 2002.

to launch National Pro Bono Week in 2002 to celebrate and encourage *pro bono*.[120] In 2003 Napier announced three initiatives: a protocol endorsed by the committee, a focus on law student activity and a national *pro bono* website.[121] The second of these initiatives met a hurdle when, in 2005, the Higher Education Funding Council for England and Wales rejected the idea of funding law schools to provide students with *pro bono* experience, but the numbers of institutions providing services were relatively high.[122] Nevertheless, a survey conducted for the Law Society in 2007 showed a 6% increase in solicitors doing *pro bono* work, albeit with a halving of average hours donated.[123] At a time when old-fashioned public service motivation, like a determination to do legal aid work, may be in decline, *pro bono* is filling the gap.[124]

Interests and motivations

The fact that large firms were the focus of the resurgence of *pro bono* among solicitors is not surprising. US research shows that the opportunity for *pro bono* participation is often seen as a 'life-style reward', and is used to attract and keep staff.[125] The ability to afford *pro bono* explains the strong correlation between successful firms, measured by size, number of associates and gross revenue, and the high volume of *pro bono publico* work performed.[126] The success of some large firms in internally promoting *pro bono* has, however, changed its character.[127] First, in firms that are committed to *pro bono*, there has been a shift from informal, individual action towards organised, corporate provision of mass services.[128] Secondly, because it is now aligned with corporate volunteering, in which non-contentious lawyers and support staff might participate, the emphasis may have shifted from conventional representation to corporate charitable activity of a general kind. Thirdly, because community-based, environmental or social welfare work can alienate corporate clients, some interests may be under-represented.[129] Fourthly, there is some indication that the largest group of *pro bono* participants in large firms are trainees.

---

[120] 'Power of Pro Bono', *Gazette* 99/17, 25 April 2002.

[121] M Napier 'Delivering Hope on Pro Bono', *Gazette* 100/13, 3 April 2003, 13.

[122] S Browne 'A Survey of Pro Bono Activity by Students in Law Schools in England and Wales' (2001) 35 *The Law Teacher* 33.

[123] N Goswami, 'Survey Reveals Fifty Per Cent Slump in Individual Pro Bono Hours', *The Lawyer*, 12 November 2007, 4.

[124] The value of work to the community appeared at the bottom of the list of important factors in choosing employment for both males and females. L Norman, *Career Choices in Law: a Survey of Law Students, Research Study 50* (London, The Law Society, 2004) 24.

[125] Galanter and Palay, above n 55, 127; E Levenson 'A Nice Package', *The Lawyer*, 5 November 2001, 31. Some commercial firms, including 'magic circle' firms, publish details of their *pro bono* activities targeted at law students; see The Solicitors' Pro Bono Group, *A Guide to Law Firm Pro Bono Programmes in England and Wales* (London, SPBG, 2004).

[126] Galanter and Palay, above n 55, 43.

[127] A Boon and A Whyte '"Charity and Beating Begins at Home": The Aetiology of the New Culture of Pro Bono Publico' (1999) 2:2 *Legal Ethics* 169.

[128] *Ibid*; see also S Cummings, 'The Politics of Pro Bono' (2004) 52 *UCLA Law Review* 1.

[129] The Federalist Society of the US demonstrated outside the ABA's annual conference in New York to alert clients to the causes their lawyers were supporting: J Ames, 'Do the Right Thing' *Gazette* 97/30, 27 July 2000; see further E Wentworth, 'Barriers to Pro Bono: Commercial Conflicts of Interest Reconsidered' in C Arup and K Laster, *For the Public Good: Pro Bono and the Legal Profession in Australia* (Annandale, NSW, Federation Press, 2001) 166.

The fact that trainees in large firms are often enthusiastic about *pro bono* may be explained both by youthful idealism and the advantages it offers them. Large firms often offer junior lawyers little contact with clients and *pro bono* increases the sense of engagement with practice for young lawyers, helping them to develop skills,[130] enhancing their status and self-image, and admitting them to the rank of 'front-line' professionals admired by the public.[131] Similar effects may be experienced by students, offering a path for the expansion of educational *pro bono* services. This assumes that mandating *pro bono*, or clinical, work at law school makes practitioners more likely to remain involved, or creates sympathetic attitudes to those needing free legal services.[132] If the case for the activity is the benefit to the trainee, the profession must be careful. Legal services *pro bono publico* only warrants praise when justice for the client is the primary consideration. The common position is that free work should be performed to the same standard of service that a paying client should receive.[133] Because many trainees have little practice experience, their deployment invites the criticism that they are learning at the expense of clients who cannot afford 'real lawyers'. Whether or not these criticisms are valid,[134] it is important that firms and the profession do not merely encourage, but support young lawyers providing such services.

A report for the Nuffield Foundation published in 2001 examined some of the core diffi-culties facing the profession over *pro bono*. It recommended that it seize the opportunity presented to 'rebuild the connection between legal professionalism and public service'.[135] The report proposed a definition of *pro bono* work that the professional bodies could include in their rules, expanding the traditional conception to include transaction and community work, but excluding dubious categories and charitable activity without a legal dimension. It suggested that they accredit suitable activity and find ways that *pro bono* might complement new funding mechanisms likes CFAs, by having lawyers agree in advance to contribute recovered costs to *pro bono* charities. It also advocated stimulating a *pro bono* culture by encouraging Law School clinical work.[136] Some of these recommendations were pursued by the Attorney-General's Pro Bono Committee,[137] while others were ignored.[138]

---

[130] See generally DW Hoagland, 'Community Service Makes Better Lawyers' in Katzmann, above n 55 (working for the poor with limited resources sharpens decision-making powers and increases sensitivity to the human dimension of complex problems).

[131] A Abbott, 'Status and Status Strain in the Professions' (1981) 86 *American Journal of Sociology* 819, 819. A less kind view is that it allows liberal corporate lawyers 'to feel a little better about themselves': S Scheingold and A Bloom, 'Transgressive Cause Lawyering: Practice Sites and the Politicization of the Professional' (1998) *International Journal of the Legal Profession* 209, 221.

[132] LA McCrimmon, 'Mandating a Culture of Service: Pro Bono in the Law School Curriculum' (2003–4) 14 *Legal Education Review* 53.

[133] Para 22 of The Law Society's Pro Bono Working Party Report suggests that imposing a requirement for *pro bono publico* work is counter to the Law Society's role in promoting 'high standards of integrity, a high quality of work and guaranteed compensation when things go wrong'.

[134] In reality, trainees are more likely than their seniors to have recent exposure to welfare law and, as the YSG awards show, young lawyers in large firms produce innovations which others can develop or follow. Katzmann, above n 55, 12; EE Lardent, 'Structuring Law Firm Pro Bono Programmes: A Community service Typology' in RE Katzman (ed), *The Law Firm and the Public Good* (Washington, DC, The Brookings Institute, 1995), 59, 87.

[135] Boon and Whyte, above n 62, 11.

[136] *Ibid*.

[137] When the availability of conditional fee agreements called into question the need for *pro bono*, Michael Napier argued that the fees recovered should be contributed to *pro bono* charities: M Napier, 'Access to Justice, Human Rights and the Role of the Pro Bono Lawyer', paper for the Commonwealth Law Conference 2005.

[138] Launching the Attorney General's Pro Bono initiative, the press release included work done at reduced cost. News release, Attorney General's Chambers, 23 April 2002.

The professional bodies have, arguably, the strongest incentive for high profile public activity like *pro bono*. Public support for institutions is strongly influenced by knowledge of and respect for those institutions,[139] and *pro bono* is a very obvious source of acclamation. The solicitors' and barristers' professional bodies both have a somewhat ambivalent attitude to it, partly for fear that formal commitments might fail, but officially because of concerns about standards[140] and public funding for legal services.[141] Such fears are certainly not unfounded. The Law Society's anxiety about accepting *pro bono* obligations were vindicated when a judge in a family case told solicitors that they should act *pro bono* when costs limits imposed by the Legal Services Commission were exceeded.[142] Yet, while neither branch proposes a practice rule regarding *pro bono*, both have joined with the Institute of Legal Executives, the SPBG and the Bar's Pro Bono Unit to promote National Pro Bono Week and define standards.[143] The Bar Council contributes £60,000 to the Bar Pro Bono Unit annually, 50% of its operating costs. With funding from the Inns of Court, the BPBU is housed in the Bar Council administrative offices and it offers secondments to members of certain firms of solicitors.[144] The Law Society, however, has apparently tired of supporting the SPBG financially,[145] a decision that may prove to be short-sighted. When the future of professional monopoly is so finely balanced, gratuitous access to justice may be the price. When the state seeks evidence that professions continue to serve the public interest, *pro bono publico* is a symbol of their 'conscientious administration of trust'.[146]

It is no coincidence that the *pro bono* efforts of lawyers are now a worldwide issue in common law jurisdictions[147] and beyond.[148] Legal professions would be ill-advised to vacate this stage when it is has such potent ideological force. This leaves the question of what form the profession's efforts should take. Clearly there are competing interests. There are those who argue that the provision of legal services for the poor would benefit from removing the established professions from them.[149] While lawyers' interest in providing such services may

---

[139] A Sarat, 'Support for the Legal System' in WM Evan (ed), *The Sociology of Law: A Social-Structural Perspective* (New York, Free Press, 1980) 167.

[140] John Buckingham, head of litigation at Shakespears, said 'any government should be making sure that the rates of the legal aid fund are in good order, not telling lawyers what they should be doing': Smerin, above n 117.

[141] The Working Party's report stated that any obligation to provide voluntary legal services to the poor had been reduced by the impact on high-street firms of declining income from legal aid and conveyancing. It argued that legal aid firms made a significant contribution *pro bono publico* because legal aid rates were less than the private rate for work. A Bradbury, 'Solicitors Rally for UK Pro Bono Scheme', *The Lawyer*, 15 October 1996, 1, claimed 'the legal aid factor is largely responsible for the fact that there is no national *pro bono* scheme, even though 75% of firms do *pro bono* work'. See also N Maley, 'Bar and Law Society Warn Pro Bono Work is "No Substitute" for Legal Aid', *The Lawyer*, 10 October 1995, 2. The Bar Council also asserted to the need to maintain a proper system of legal aid (*Quality of Justice*, above n 63, paras 2.28 and 2.32).

[142] S Allen, 'Act Pro Bono if Cash Runs Out, Judge Tells Solicitors', *Gazette* 98/07, 15 February 2001.

[143] 'Power of Pro Bono', *Gazette* 99/17, 25 April 2002; V MacCallum 'Attorney-General Unveils Protocol that Sets Out Key Elements of Pro Bono Work', *Gazette* 100/13, 3 April 2003, 4; M Napier 'Delivering Hope on Pro Bono', same issue, 13.

[144] BPBU Annual Review 2005.

[145] Towards the end of 2004 the SPBG was desperately seeking funds to support its operating costs, which the Law Society refused to supplement.

[146] Boon and Whyte, above n 62.

[147] Arup and Laster, above n 129.

[148] F Regan, 'How and Why is Pro Bono Flourishing: A Comparison of Recent Developments in Sweden and China' in Arup and Laster, *ibid*, 148.

[149] A Southworth, 'Taking the Lawyer Out of Progressive Lawyering' (1993) 46 *Stanford law Review* 213.

be to prevent others gaining a toehold on the legal services market, expecting them to supply full access to justice may be too ambitious. The Nuffield Report suggested that the profession should focus on the quality of *pro bono*, rather than the quantity: because *pro bono* services are unlikely to make up for a lack of public funding, the profession should not aim to ensure that all lawyers do a little, but rather that what is done is genuinely useful. In particular, it should concentrate on cases that will advance social welfare and rights generally by creating new law.[150] In so doing, the profession may find itself in uncomfortable political territory, such as arguing for benefits for social groups or intervening against prevention of terrorism legislation.[151] This is unlikely to be what the government had in mind when it urged *pro bono* on the profession, but in the modern world, it may be the most appropriate way of fulfilling an iconic tradition.

Conclusion

It is far from certain whether legal *pro bono publico* can continue to flourish without stronger support from the profession and broader grass roots support. It is not yet established as a professional obligation, recent high levels of activity being somewhat tenuously built on the current support of charismatic individuals and elements at the elite end of the profession. Free services will doubtless continue to be provided for a variety of reasons, but whether they can or should provide satisfactory access to justice is moot. Some lawyers have particular incentives to offer such services. Large firm domination of the market place may accentuate inequalities in access to justice,[152] and the profession's relationship with the state may be eased by assistance on this issue.[153] Providing such services for the wrong reasons, for marketing purposes for example, impugns the motives to such an extent that it is not an ethical act.[154] Advocates of *pro bono* tend to argue that the motive does not matter, that the reasons why people do good are complex and unknowable,[155] and that what matters is that the work is done.[156] Nevertheless, the profession should arguably do more to preserve the integrity of *pro bono* by defining such work more closely and controlling references in firm brochures and publicity. One of the main advantages of the involvement of the professional bodies would be to address the delicate balance between ethics and commercialism[157] and ensure that *pro bono publico* publicity is used sensitively and to promote the profession as a whole.

[150] See, eg establishment of a panel of barristers to take cases to the European Court of Human Rights: N Rovnick, 'Liberty Sets Up Human Rights Pro Bono Unit', *The Lawyer*, 22 October 2001.

[151] Law Society press release, 'Undermining Human Rights across the World in the War against Terror', 15 November 2005.

[152] Galanter and Palay, above n 55, 40.

[153] Paterson, above n 26, 155.

[154] See Nosworthy, abve n 102, 71; CS Rhee, '*Pro Bono*, Pro Se' (1996) 105 *Yale Law Journal* 1719, 1724.

[155] C Menkel-Meadow, 'The Causes of Cause Lawyering: Toward an Understanding of the Motivation and Commitment of Social Justice Lawyers' in A Sarat and S Scheingold, *Cause Lawyering: Political Commitments and Professional Responsibilities* (Oxford University Press, 1998) 31 argues this position in proposing that *pro bono publico* should simply be labelled 'mixed-motive altruism'.

[156] For further discussion, see M Ridley, *The Origins of Virtue* (Harmondsworth, Penguin, 1997) 21; M Waters, 'Collegiality, Bureaucratization, and Professionalization: A Weberian Analysis' (1989) 94 *American Journal of Sociology* 945.

[157] Nosworthy, above n 102, 71.

16

EMPLOYMENT

Psychologists, organization theorists, and economists all know that the ethics of ethical decision-making change dramatically when the individual works in an organisational setting. Loyalties become tangled and personal responsibility gets diffused. Bucks are passed and guilty knowledge bypassed. Chains of command not only tie people's hands, they fetter their minds and consciences as well. Reinhold Niebuhr called one of his books *Moral Man, Immoral Society*, and I suggest for students of ethics no topic is more important than understanding whatever truth the title contains.[1]

Introduction

The employment relationship is a key ethical relationship, not merely in supporting ethical conduct, but in terms of how relationships of power are managed by, and in relation to, practitioners. The relationship of lawyers to the organisation to which they belong[2] is one that begins in a state of some ambiguity. Both branches stipulate a period of supervised induction by established and approved practitioners, during which the trainee undertakes work and receives payment, but which may not result in subsequent employment. The shortage of training and employment opportunities and the allocation of the best of these to social and educational elites raise the spectre of discrimination as an ethical issue[3] since the profession is obliged to have due regard to the need to eliminate unlawful discrimination and promote equality of opportunity and good relations between different racial groups.[4] In the case of barristers, the period of training does not formally constitute employment, although, to outward appearances, there are similarities. In the case of solicitors, training is employment, although ordinary employment rights, like security of employment, do not accrue. Many solicitors and barristers, however, remain at the place where they train, sometimes throughout their careers.

Training

The purpose of lawyers' work-based training is seldom articulated clearly, although inculcating ethics is implicit. Until relatively recently, solicitors' articled clerks paid a premium for

---

[1] DJ Luban, 'Milgram Revisited' (1998) 9(2) *Researching Law: An ABF Update* 1, 4.
[2] The basic requirements of practice are covered in chapter 2.
[3] See generally, P Thomas (ed), *Discriminating Lawyers* (London, Cavendish Publishing, 2000).
[4] Race Relations Amendment Act 2000; 'Opinion—Janet Paraskeva' (2002) 16 *The Lawyer*, 11 March 2002, 19.

their training,[5] and their experience was variable. Any ethical values absorbed flowed from the fact of professional servitude, but these may have been significant. Burrage laments the replacement of five year articles of clerkship by two years for graduates as the main route into the solicitors' branch.[6] The longer route meant that entrants were highly committed and motivated, the 'hardship, drudgery and semi-servitude' encouraged an appreciation of membership and the time served offered a thorough induction into the ethical community.[7] In contrast, the primary interest of university law schools—cognitive development—undermined respect for rules of etiquette, practice and ethics, leading to declining responsibility for the 'collective honour of the profession'.[8]

Solicitors

Solicitors train in the workplace for two years, and firms must behave cautiously and reasonably to avoid claims for unfair dismissal.[9] Under the training contract, trainee solicitors (trainees) must receive a minimum salary, unless the Law Society agrees to waive payment.[10] The training regime begun in the 1990s introduced stricter controls, requiring firms to observe a code of conduct incorporating monitoring and appraisal of trainees.[11] Firms can take trainees only if they offer experience in four different departments, or 'seats', a measure which precluded many small and niche firms from offering training. Under this regime, training contract requirements are subjected to closer monitoring by the Solicitors Regulation Authority.[12] Programmes can be declared unsatisfactory, recommendations can be made for improvements or firms can be prevented from taking on trainees. These increased demands led many large firms to appoint directors of education and training to supervise induction, provide staff development[13] and mentor trainees. Smaller firms sometimes grouped together to provide some of these advantages, but the net affect was often a diminution of the time that partners themselves devoted to their traditional training role.[14] Many firms claimed that the changes had shifted the balance against taking trainees.[15]

---

[5] By the late 1960s a premium for articles was demanded by only 5% of firms and most paid small salaries, the Law Society recommending an 'allowance' rather than a living wage. E Cruikshank, 'Surviving Hard Times', 100/32 *Law Society's Gazette*, 23 August 2003, 22.

[6] Attention to articles was almost non-existent until the Solicitors Act 1922 made part-time attendance at law school for one year compulsory for articled clerks. E Cruikshank, 'Building a Profession', 100/25 *Law Society's Gazette*, 26 June 2003, 32.

[7] M Burrage, 'From a Gentleman's to a Public Profession' [1996] *International Journal of the Legal Profession* 45, 68.

[8] *Ibid*, 72.

[9] See the Employment Relations Act (1999) and A Coles, 'Training contracts under the microscope' *Law Gazette* 22 September 1999.

[10] Law Society Education and Training Unit, *Training Trainee Solicitors: The Law Society Requirements* (July 2007) pt 3.

[11] *Ibid*.

[12] Solicitors Regulation Authority *Annual Report 2006/7*, 10.

[13] Firms employing these increased from 4 to 96 between 1987 and 1990. Firms attracted recruits by showing that they took training seriously, developing in-house PSC and CPD programmes, more participatory formats and new topics, eg marketing. EH Greenebaum, 'Development of Law Firm Training Programs: Coping with a Turbulent Environment (1996) 3 *International Journal of the Legal Profession* 315, 318–19, 331 and 345.

[14] The Law Society, *The Recruitment Crisis: A Report by the Training Committee of the Law Society* (London, The Law Society, 1988) para 11(c).

[15] Before the changes, solicitors and trainees agreed that the first year of traineeship was of equal benefit to firm and trainee, but that the second year benefit was mainly for the firm. K Economides and J Smallcombe, *Preparatory Skills Training for Solicitors* (London, The Law Society, 1991) 16.

The Legal Practice Course (LPC) usurped the assumed aims of workplace learning, introducing entrants to work tasks and inducting them into the ethos of the profession, but it led to a marginal enhancement only in ethical training. The main increase was in the Professional Skills Course (PSC), launched at the same time as the LPC for those in training contracts.[16] The PSC comprises communication and advocacy skills, financial and business skills and client care,[17] and an ethics component with a minimum tuition time of 12 hours.[18] Despite the review of the training scheme in 2000, the Law Society's guidance to trainees raised few expectations regarding ethics, beyond the PSC, in the training contract.[19] Guidance issued in 2007 continued in the same vein, providing lists of skills and subjects to which the trainee must be exposed, and providing for reviews, appraisal and 'guidance', but barely mentioning ethics, even in an extensive list of trainee responsibilities.[20] Goriely and William's research on the Law Society's new training regime observed that 'on the job' training was still regarded as the most important element of a solicitor's education.[21] It suggested, however, that supervision was often little more than sharing a room with a more senior person. Supervisors often found it difficult to articulate what the process of training involved and their rotation undermined the continuity of pastoral care. Few supervisors of trainees had read the *Guide to the Professional Conduct of Solicitors*, regarding it as a reference work rather than an integral part of working life. Trainers and trainees were dismissive of the PSC, except for the advocacy component, and trainees regarding the day spent on professional conduct as a 'token gesture'.[22]

During the 1990s, both the Bar and the Law Society sponsored research, longitudinal or cohort studies, following groups of students into practice.[23] The Law Society's longitudinal study found that three-quarters of trainees were satisfied with the work experience provided in training, but the majority had little choice of training contract and 14% were unhappy with the type of firm they were in.[24] Goriely and Williams suggested that large firms recruit

---

[16] Firms must provide 72 hours (12 days) of study leave and pay the course fee.

[17] Law Society Training Regulations (1990).

[18] Originally, Ethics and Client Responsibilities, but renamed Client Care and Professional Standards in the relaunch of the PSC in 2000 (*ibid*, 64).

[19] Law Society, *A Trainee Solicitor's Guide to Authorisation* (Redditch, Law Society Monitoring and Training Department, 2000).

[20] It recommends that trainees record any professional conduct issues that may have arisen in their training contract record. *Training Trainee Solicitors*, above n 10, s 4, and see s 8 for trainee responsibilities

[21] T Goriely and T Williams, *The Impact of the New Training Scheme: Report on a Qualitative Study* (London, The Law Society, 1996).

[22] *Ibid*.

[23] The Bar cohort study covered three years from the vocational course taken in 1989/90, through pupillage in 1991 to practice in 1993. See J Shapland, V Johnston and R Wild, *Studying for the Bar* (Sheffield, Institute for the Study of the Legal Profession, 1993); J Shapland and A Sorsby, *Starting Practice: Work and Training at the Junior Bar* (Sheffield, Institute for the Study of the Legal Profession, 1995) 90. The solicitors' cohort study comprised six surveys beginning with second year undergraduate law students, then third year students, the vocational year, and practical training and concluding with members working as qualified solicitors. See D Halpern, *Entry Into the Legal Professions: The Law Student Cohort Study Years 1 and 2* (London, The Law Society, 1994) ch 9 (first survey); M Shiner and T Newburn, *Entry Into the Legal Professions: Law Student Cohort Study Year 3* (London, The Law Society, 1995) (second survey); M Shiner, *Entry into the Legal Professions: The Law Student Cohort Study Year 4* (London, The Law Society, 1997) (third survey); M Shiner, *Entry into the Legal Professions: The Law Student Cohort Study Year 5* (London, The Law Society, 1999) (fourth survey); E Duff, M Shiner, A Boon and A Whyte, *Entry into the Legal Professions: The Law Student Cohort Study Year 6* (London, The Law Society, 2000) (fifth survey).

[24] Shiner, *Year 4, ibid*, ch 6.

trainees with a view to their long-term development, whereas small firms use them for routine tasks like photocopying.[25] The cohort study revealed a disturbingly high incidence of harassment and bullying, themes also reflected in calls to the Trainee Solicitors' Group helpline,[26] but found a nuanced picture of the advantages and disadvantages of training in a commercial firm or high-street practice. Many trainees in high-street firms resented their onerous caseloads, expectations of early contributions to profitability and inadequate supervision, but others welcomed the responsibility and appreciated the opportunity to develop.[27] Nor did trainees in large or commercial firms find training perfect.

In commercial firms, retention rates tend to be high[28] and turnover rates for assistant solicitors relatively low[29] because of the high cost of training. Special measures, apart from salary rises,[30] are often taken to keep staff, such as providing mentors to discuss problems with.[31] Some large firms think creatively about the 'training package', prioritising personal development.[32] Nevertheless, City firm trainees complained of their inability to choose the kind of work they did, inadequate exposure to clients and lack low-level work on which to practise. Moreover, because of concern with profitability, the advantages of large firms come at a cost. The most common is the demand for more 'billable hours', increasing the pressure towards unethical practises such as 'padding', inflating the hours billed.[33]

The Training Framework Review proposes retaining two years of work-based learning as a prerequisite for practice, but envisages that it will not necessarily be based at a single firm, or at a firm at all, provided it is under the supervision of a solicitor. It advocates tighter procedures for monitoring and review, with regular appraisal and completion of a reflective journal and a centrally administered test, possibly involving ethics questions, to be completed before the end of the work-based learning period. Many of the details have yet to be resolved and increased administrative burdens risk reducing training opportunities. Proposals to extend the range of potential training organisations and lift the training contract requirement of providing four seats may offset any deficit.[34]

---

[25] Above n 21.

[26] Of the 1,162 calls received between 1 August 2003 and 12 March 2004, 52% the largest substantive category (51) concerned problems in the training contract, 14 inadequate training and 12 disclosing convictions to the Law Society (*Trainee Solicitors' Group Helpline Review*, August 2003–March 2004). Problems with the training contract rose to around 270 for the year March to March 2004–5, with trainees in both surveys complaining of bullying and sexual harassment (*Trainee Solicitors' Group Helpline Review*, March 2004–March 2005).

[27] A Boon, 'From Public Service to Service Industry: the Impact of Socialisation and Work on the Motivation and Values of Lawyers' (2005) 12 *International Journal of the Legal Profession* 193.

[28] Retention rates in the top 50 law firms average 70%. G Charles, 'Retention Rates for Top 50 Firms Promise Stability for Trainees', *The Lawyer*, 25 October 2004, 2).

[29] In 2005, for example, the average assistant solicitor turnover rate in the top 50 firms was 14%: H Morris and E Quinn, 'Top 50 Law Firms' Assistant Turnover Rate Hits 14%' [October 2005] *Lawyer 2B* 1.

[30] Higher associate salaries are increasingly paid because of competition in the City, including with US firms. J Wilson, 'Young City Lawyers Pay Price for Salary Rise', *The Guardian*, 7 August 2000, 3.

[31] J Harris, 'Herbies Asks Associates to Stay as More Jump Ship', *The Lawyer*, 31 October 2005, 3.

[32] E Levenson, 'A Nice Package', *The Lawyer*, 5 November 2001, 31.

[33] DR Richmond, 'The New Law Firm Economy, Billable Hours and Professional Responsibility' (2000) 29 *Hofstra Law Review* 207.

[34] J Eldred, 'How to Put Recruits through their Paces', 99/34 *Gazette* 5 September 2002, 21.

Barristers

Before commencing training, a barrister must be called to the Bar, a process that involves signing a Declaration and Undertaking,[35] falsification or breach of which constitutes professional misconduct.[36] Any period of pupillage must be registered before commencement, and there is detailed guidance intended to maximise the benefits of the experience.[37] An intending barrister's pupillage is divided into the non-practising six months, the 'first six', and a practising six months, , the 'second six'.[38] Both may be served with organisations other than chambers but must be spent with a pupil supervisor[39] who has received appropriate training,[40] is approved by the Bar Council and whose obligations to the pupil barrister are set out in the Bar Code.[41] The first six is intended to be spent working on the supervisor's cases, reading and researching, and the second six working on one's own account. All pupillages should involve training in professional conduct and etiquette, and practical experience of advocacy, conferences, negotiation and legal research.[42] Pupils must attend advocacy training[43] and the Advice to Counsel course. They must complete a checklist at the end of their first and second sixes, which must be confirmed by the pupil supervisor and retained by chambers for three years for review and monitoring by pupillage review panels.

In 1989 the Bar Council accepted the principle that pupils should receive a wage, but three committees failed to settle an acceptable rate or mechanism for implementation. Then there were concerns that some pupils fell within the Minimum Wage Act in 1998, but *Edmonds v Lawson*[44] established that pupillage is a binding contract for education and training and not an apprenticeship or contract of employment, and was outside the scope of the Act.[45] The Court of Appeal noted that, while barristers were self-employed, it was beneficial to chambers to have talented and hard-working members, just as it was beneficial to the pupils to prove themselves worthy of tenancy in a flourishing set. In 1998 a Bar working party recommended implementation of a subsidy to pupils[46] and in 2000 it was decided to pay all pupils £10,000. There was anxiety that this, and increasing regulation,

---

[35] *The Consolidated Regulations of the Inns of Court and the General Council of the Bar (as at October 1 2001)* (London, General Council of the Bar, 2001) para 24(a).

[36] *Ibid*, para 24(c). The Standard Declaration of Call requires declosure, inter alia, of criminal offences and other matters 'which might reasonably be expected to affect the mind of a Bencher of the Inn considering your application'. An applicant must also declare that 'so long as I remain a barrister I will observe the Code of Conduct' (*ibid*, sch 5).

[37] See Bar Council, *Pupillage File 2007/08* (London, Bar Standards Board, 2007), available at http://www.barstandardsboard.org.uk/ (last accessed 1 April 2008).

[38] *The Consolidated Regulations*, above n 35, pt V, para 41.2. Both or either six can be in private or employed practice.

[39] A Pupil Master must be entered on the Bar Council's register and, unless approval is given, may only take one pupil at a time. *The Consolidated Regulations, ibid*, paras 47 and 48.

[40] *Ibid*, paras 48.6 and 48.7.

[41] Para 804. This requirement has applied to employed barristers since 2003.

[42] Bar Council, *Pupillage File*, above n 37, s 2.3.

[43] Weaknesses in advocacy must be reported to pupil supervisors and may be taken into account before signing the pupil's certification form which confirms satisfactory completion of pupillage.

[44] (2000) QB 501; (2000) 2 WLR 1091; (2000) ICR 567; (2000) IRLR 391.

[45] *Edmonds v Lawson, ibid*, established that pupillage does not require a pupil to do anything that is not conducive to his own training and development.

[46] S Pye, 'Cash Crisis and Poor Prospects for Young Bar', *The Lawyer*, 20 October 1998.

would stop chambers taking pupils,[47] but after a reduction in the already short supply, numbers of pupillages have steadily risen[48] and few applications to waive payment are approved.[49]

Responsibility for the quality of pupillage falls on heads of chambers. They must take all reasonable steps to make proper arrangements, including drawing up a chambers pupillage policy, making an annual return to the Bar Council, and appointing a Pupillage Training Principal to take responsibility for pupils and pupillage arrangements. The Bar has long been concerned about the quality of pupillage, however. Four reports between 1994 and 1996 led to the conclusion that the problem lay not in the structure or written guidance, but in the implementation of pupillage guidelines.[50] The resulting *Guide to Good Practice in Pupillage* distilled and presented the lessons of the Bar Cohort Study, rejecting the idea that there was one model, but recommending that chambers put in place 'safeguards'.[51] These included pupillage committees, agreed induction procedures, policies on allocating and controlling the flow of paperwork to pupils, and periodic review of and feedback on performance.

Experience

While the work of lawyers in many areas of the legal system has not been extensively researched, work in the early years of practice has been explored in longitudinal studies of cohorts of students conducted for the profession. While the research suggests general satisfaction with early careers, a stream of research suggests that some experience 'a nasty shock'.[52] In the mid-1990s a survey of trainees and recently qualified lawyers found a 'considerable level of disquiet', attributed 'to debt, lack of job security and the quality of supervision and training'.[53] The fifth solicitors' cohort survey found that 6% said they would not be working as a solicitor or barrister in five years, while 18% were not sure. The high levels of investment in legal careers combined with high attrition rates is a cause for concern, particularly given persistent allegations that the profession remains a white,

---

[47] The Bar Cohort Study had already noted that modest requirements on chambers to improve the experience of pupils might affect willingness to offer pupillage and that it may be necessary to make taking pupils a professional responsibility for larger chambers.

[48] The numbers commencing their first six in 2001–2 was 812, compared with 518 over the same period in 2003–4. In the year ending 30 September 2007, 527 first six and 563 second six pupillages were registered (Bar Standards Board Education and Training Department).

[49] Between 2002 and 2004 there were 72 applications for unfunded, 11 for unadvertised and 56 for unfunded and unadvertised pupillages. Permission was granted for 6 unfunded, 9 unadvertised and 22 unfunded and unadvertised (of which 14 were for overseas students intending to return home on completion).

[50] *Report of the Professional Standards Committee Pupillage Working Party* (London, Bar Council, 1994) (Mallins Report); *Report of the Working Group on Pupillage* (London, Bar Council, 1995) (Hooper Report).

[51] Shapland and Sorsby, above n 23.

[52] P McDonald, '"The Class of '81"—A Glance at the Social Class Composition of Recruits to the Legal Profession', 9 *Journal of Law and Society* 267.

[53] R Moorhead and F Boyle, 'Quality of Life and Trainee Solicitors: a Survey' (1995) 2 *International Journal of the Legal Profession* 217, 218.

middle-class, male preserve,[54] with the Bar perhaps more exclusive[55] than the more socially inclusive solicitors.[56]

Equal opportunities is a burning political issue for professions. With social cohesion dependent on equal opportunity and fair distribution of privilege, access is an ethical issue,[57] with attention focused particularly on processes, like training, prescribed for entry.[58] The profession can adopt progressive policies,[59] appoint equal opportunities officers and sponsor research into disadvantage, but can influence individual employment decisions only indirectly. There is mounting pressure to keep in step with social trends, to ensure professional legitimacy by reflecting the composition of society and encouraging access to law by the whole community.[60] The Langlands report made many recommendations for maintaining levels of entry to the professions, arguing for broader entry, flexible entry routes, including for people changing careers, and provision of equal access by employers.[61]

Data suggest that both branches of the legal profession have made giant steps to becoming more representative of wider society,[62] but some sectors are bastions of privilege. Those from less advantaged backgrounds may get a foot on the professional ladder, but it is often the social elite that control the highest earning jobs in law. Despite the changing composition of the student body, advice on the business advantages of diverse workforces and rule 6 of the Solicitors' Code of Conduct 2007,[63] designed to prevent discrimination in firms, elite legal employers are reluctant to look beyond Oxbridge,[64] thereby also recruiting a large proportion of privately educated lawyers.[65] There are rational explanations for why Oxbridge students succeed at interview or at the Bar,[66] for example, firms and chambers

---

[54] Women were refused access to the bar and the solicitors' branch before the First World War. See chapter 8 n 17 and, for a fuller account, see MJ Mossman, *The First Women Lawyers* (Oxford, Hart Publishing, 2006).

[55] The numbers qualifying for practice at the Bar were contained by an 'invisible' process of selection which prioritised 'ascribed' characteristics, such as social class. The expense of training and the requirement that non-graduates sit examinations in Latin and Greek were effective controls on the numbers of barristers. C Glasser, "The Legal Profession in the 1990s: Images of Change" (1990) 10 *Legal Studies* 1.

[56] H Kirk, *Portrait of a Profession: A History of the Solicitor's Profession, 1100 to the Present Day* (London, Oyez Publishing, 1976).

[57] The ethical connotations of this social vision include promoting individual autonomy in career choices and securing social justice by providing equality of opportunity.

[58] C Thomson, 'Fairness for All', *The Lawyer*, 20 May 1997 (student supplement page vi).

[59] See N Taylor (ed), *The Guide to the Professional Conduct of Solicitors* (London, The Law Society Publishing, 1999) ch 7 (anti-discrimination rules and model policy); General Council of the Bar, *Code of Conduct of the Bar of England and Wales* (London, General Council of the Bar) para 204.1 and Annex Q, Summary of the Equality Code for the Bar; P Thomas, 'Introduction' in Thomas, above n 3, xivff.

[60] W Twining 'Access to Legal Education and the Legal Profession: a Commonwealth Perspective' in R Dhavan, N Kibble and W Twining (eds), *Access to Legal Education and the Legal Profession* (London, Butterworths, 1989).

[61] A Langlands, *The Gateways to the Professions Report* (London, Department for Education and Skills, 2005).

[62] See, eg B Cole, *Trends in the Solicitors' Profession: Annual Statistical Report 1999* (London, The Law Society, 2000), but see B Cole and J Sidaway, 'Job's Worth', *Gazette* 93/40, October 1996.

[63] M Burch, 'Survival of the Fittest' *The Lawyer* 10 December 2007, 24; T Foster, 'Culture Vultures', *The Lawyer*, 10 December 2007, 25.

[64] L Twigg, *Analysis of Combined 1998/1999/2000 PACH Statistics*—we are grateful to the Education and Training Committee of the General Council of the Bar for permission to cite this research.

[65] In 2005 research by the Sutton trust showed that judges, and solicitors and barristers in leading commercial practices were overwhelmingly privately educated and from Oxbridge and Russell Group universities. *Sutton Trust Briefing Note: The Educational Backgrounds of the UK's Top Solicitors, Barristers and Judges* (June 2005); F Gibb, 'The Route to the Top Law Jobs is Disturbingly Familiar', *The Times: Student Law*, 24 May 2005.

[66] There are long-standing arguments about the inherent virtue of public schools and Oxbridge that might justify high representation. See generally H Glennerster and R Pryke, 'The Contribution of the Public Schools and

may value those recruits who can access networks in the key financial and business institutions.[67] Yet, Goriely and William's research into recruitment for training contracts concluded that the key question for solicitors in choosing trainees was 'are they one of us?',[68] an approach that explains statistical indications of discrimination.[69] While selection for elite parts of the profession may reflect rational recruitment policies,[70] the result is that social privilege is seen to be self-sustaining.[71] Indirect discrimination, selection by reference to criteria that some groups cannot meet, is particularly problematic when qualification depends on finding a firm or chambers to offer training. After a recruitment crisis in the late 1980s,[72] there have generally been many more seeking qualification than there are training pupillages, and traineeship is a pressure point.[73] Employers who take applicants from ordinary backgrounds on work placements often find that they could be 'one of us',[74] but the legal profession has yet to demonstrate that it has overcome the assumption that one particular type of person is automatically better than another.[75]

As barriers to access are removed, new problems are discovered. Gender, for example, is no longer a significant barrier to initial entry,[76] although both race[77] and class[78] remain

Oxbridge: 1 "Born to Rule'" in J Urry and J Wakeford (eds), *Power in Britain* (London, Heinemann Educational Books, 1973) 213 and, in relation to law, V Bermingham and J Hodgson, 'Desiderata: What Lawyers Want From Their Recruits' (2000) 35 *The Law Teacher* 1.

[67] See, eg G Hanlon, *Lawyers, the State and the Market* (Basingstoke, Macmillan Press, 1999) 113 (corporate counsel instructing university friends on smaller matters).

[68] Above n 21.

[69] M Shiner, 'Young Gifted and Blocked! Entry to the Solicitor's Profession' in Thomas, above n 3, 87.

[70] Thomas argues that the practice of selecting only from elite institutions may be promoted as 'sound recruitment policies' (n 3 above, xvi), while contributors to his volume on discriminating lawyers urge providers of legal education to examine their priorities in providing opportunities to part-time students: see AM Francis and IW McDonald 'All Dressed Up and Nowhere to Go? Part-time Law Students and the Legal Profession' in Thomas, *ibid.*

[71] Historically, senior lawyers in elite firms ensured that their children attended elite universities. J Slinn, *A History of Freshfields* (London, Freshfields, 1984); J Slinn, *Linklaters and Paines—The First One Hundred and Fifty Years* (London, Longman, 1987).

[72] In 1988 the Law Society reported a recruitment crisis, particularly in local government, in the CPS, and in private practice in the North East, parts of the North West and the Midlands '. . . even firms in the City of London report difficulties', above n 14.

[73] In 1995 there were 9,849 applications to study the LPC and a total of 6,921 full-time and 954 part-time places; 7,800 students studied the LPC but only 4,063 training contracts were registered with the Law Society that year. A Sherr and L Webley, 'Legal Ethics in England and Wales' (1997) 4 *International Journal of the Legal Profession* 109, 112.

[74] Above n 21.

[75] The Lord Chancellor's right to appoint 'a friend', former Herbert Smith lawyer Garry Hart, as a special adviser was upheld by the Court of Appeal on the grounds that appointment from close circles of family, friends and acquaintances was 'not likely to constitute indirect discrimination'. T Branigan, 'Irvine Has the Right to Employ a Friend', *The Guardian*, 23 November 2001, 14.

[76] Numbers of women rose steadily to become the majority admitted as solicitors in 1993/4 (E Skordaki, "Glass Slippers and Glass Ceilings: Women in the Legal Profession" (1996) 3 *International Journal of the Legal Profession* 7, 10 and 11), and they currently account for around 60% (see generally A Sherr, 'Coming of Age' (1994) 1 *International Journal of the Legal Profession* 3, 4).

[77] In relation to barristers, see the Barrow Report (Final Report of the Committee of Inquiry into Equal Opportunities on the Bar Vocational Report *Equal Opportunities at the Inns of Court School of Law* (1994); Shapland and Sorsby, above n 23.

[78] In relation to solicitors, see above n 21, 16 and n 23 generally.

significant. Debt and discrimination are the most likely reasons for this.[79] Most law students have to pay off quite heavy loans from their earnings as lawyers,[80] but a serious decline in levels of legal aid, particularly for criminal work, has depressed opportunities and salaries in High Street firms, often forcing students towards the commercial sector for training,[81] where they then decide to stay.[82] The shortage of trainees in legal aid work led the Legal Services Commission to recommend sponsorship of tuition fees for the LPC and training contracts in return for a commitment of two years' post-qualification work.[83] The Commission thought that the proposal would benefit ethnic minority trainees and others from disadvantaged backgrounds because they were more likely to find training contracts with High Street practices.[84] This view about the employment of ethnic minority students is borne out by the evidence which suggests good progress towards proportionate representation of ethnic minorities,[85] but continuing disadvantage in some legal careers. Those that are successful are likely to be employed in-house rather than in private practice,[86] and those in private practice tend to be found in the smaller, high-street firms rather than in the elite commercial firms and chambers.[87] While this may reflect the aspirations and preferences of some ethnic minority students,[88] it is also due to the recruitment practices of employers in the commercial sector, where the cohort study found representation of ethnic minorities to be poor.[89]

Many organisations recruit early to secure 'high flyers', and are forced to look for earlier qualifications, such as 'A' levels, rather than later qualifications, such as degree classification.[90] This, together with a culture that is tolerant of unequal methods of selection,[91]

---

[79] L Norman, *Career Choices in Law (A Survey of Law Students) Research Study 50* (London, The Law Society, 2004).

[80] Forty-five per cent owed debts of between £5,000 and £15,000 and 27% between £15,000 and £25,000, which over 90% aimed to pay off by salary (*ibid*, 29).

[81] Although around 60% of law students were interested in a career in legal aid work, only 21% thought they would be likely to do so given the associated career prospects, eg the differences in salary and working conditions (*ibid*, 41–4); R Moorhead, 'Legal Aid and the Decline of Private Practice: Blue Murder or Toxic Job?' (2003) 11 *International Journal of the Legal Profession* 159.

[82] A survey of young solicitors, where 41% of respondents worked in the City of London, showed 51% interested in business and commercial affairs, 18% in civil litigation and little interest in any other kind of practice (*ibid*, 24).

[83] Announced in Legal Services Commission Consultation Paper, *Developing Legal Aid Solicitors, 2002*, together with incentives to barristers to work in immigration and asylum.

[84] *Ibid*, 3.

[85] Of the 104,543 solicitors with practising certificates in 2006, 44,394 were women and 9,471 from ethnic minorities. B Cole, *Trends in the Solicitors' Profession: Annual Statistical Report 2006* (London, The Law Society, 2006).

[86] Fifty-five per cent of ethnic minority solicitors on the roll hold practising certificates and 78% of those with practising certificates are in private practice. In contrast, 83% of white or European solicitors on the Roll in 1996 held practising certificates, and approximately 82% of solicitors holding practising certificates are in private practice.

[87] The fourth solicitors' cohort survey found the City commercial and large provincial firms' recruitment practises worked against ethnic minorities and new university students and that their starting salaries were lower (Shiner, *Year 4*, above n 23.

[88] Minority ethnic group students are more likely to want to practise in small firms than white students and less likely to want to go to large firms (above n 58, 58).

[89] For analysis of a similar issue in the US, see D Wilkins and G Mitu Gulati, 'Why Are There so few Black Lawyers in Corporate Law Firms: an Institutional Analysis' (1996) 84 *California Law Review* 493.

[90] H Rolfe and T Anderson, *The Recruitment of Trainee Solicitors* (London, The Law Society, 2002) s 3.

[91] These include appointing applicants direct to the firm, or relatives, or those produced by recruitment consultants. A Boon, L Duff and M Shiner, 'Career Paths and Choices in a Highly Differentiated Profession: The Position of Newly Qualified Solicitors' (2001) 64 *The Modern Law Review* 563.

including nepotism and favouritism,[92] advantages groups with social capital.[93] Since major firms of solicitors often fund the vocational courses of those they have offered training contracts, the fairness of recruitment practices takes on great importance.[94] Other employers achieve similar results by recruiting from elite universities. These and other forms of recruitment indirectly discriminate, but are common practice in the graduate recruitment market for elite corporate jobs outside law.[95] Recruiters to the professions are aware of this. When the Bar attempted to mitigate unfair recruitment practices by introducing a clearing system, some chambers simply opted out of the process. Further, while a recent survey showed that nearly 70% of lawyers favoured hiring former comprehensive school students, between 30 and 40% were opposed to different forms of diversity monitoring.[96]

Post qualification practice

After the period of training, lawyers are subject to the same legal duties as other employers. It is arguable, however, that professional organisations should observe higher ethical standards in relation to employees than non-professional employers. The substance of any such additional standards is largely undefined. The expectations of professional entrants are a yardstick. For example, it is generally accepted that incentives for professional work include good salary, support, opportunities and breadth of work, while disincentives to entering or remaining in a job or profession include low status, poor work life balance, stress,[97] emotional exhaustion and unmet career expectations.[98] Intending lawyers are attracted by the intrinsic interest of work, security of employment, long-term salary prospects and availability of jobs,[99] all reasonable expectations of a professional career. An ethical issue that arises is that, if entrants are likely to find that this promise of professionalism will be broken, should they be informed and, if so, on whom does moral responsibility for this fall: the profession, the educators[100] or the employers?

---

[92] A President of the Law Society argued that it is not discriminatory when a small firm did not intend to take a trainee but made 'an exception for the son or daughter of one of its partners or valuable clients'. M Mears, letter to *Law Society Gazette*, 29 November 1995.

[93] The third cohort study, above n 23, showed that academic achievement, attending elite universities and having relatives in the profession were positive factors in obtaining a training contract, whereas ethnicity and social class were negative factors.

[94] *The Legal Services Consultative Panel Advice to the Secretary of State on The Legal Profession: Entry, Retention and Competition* (May 2005), available at http://www.dca.gov.uk (last accessed 25 March 2008).

[95] Many blue chip companies select by targeting promotion at the institutions they want to recruit from and by screening for high UCAS points scores. D Williams, 'Degrees of Separation', *The Guardian: Rise*, 21 January 2006, 3.

[96] K Williams, 'Firms Rail against Diversity Monitoring', *The Lawyer*, 10 September, 2007.

[97] Department for Education and Skills, *Literature Review in Relation to 'Gateways to the Professions'* (London, DfES, 2005) ch 3.

[98] I Houkes, PPM Janssen, J de Jonge and AB Bakker, 'Specific Determinants of Intrinsic Work Motivation, Emotional Exhaustion and Turnover Intention: a Multisample Longitudinal Study' (2003) 76 *Journal of Occupational and Organisational Psychology* 427.

[99] Above n 27.

[100] For example, educational providers may have a responsibility to do more to improve their prospects of some disadvantaged groups, like part time students; Francis and McDonald, above n 70, 41.

Terms and conditions

Lawyers' earnings are widely diverse. Partners share the profits of the firm after deducting the overheads, including staff salaries, carrying the risk that they get less from the business than employees on fixed salaries. The large commercial solicitors' firms generally pay the highest salaries to newly qualified staff, often higher than those of the partners in some legal aid firms. The sixth solicitors' cohort study found significant differences in newly qualified salaries, from £20,000 in high-street firms to £50,000 in the City. Some of the partners of the larger corporate and commercial firms can expect to earn £1million per annum. In smaller firms, particularly those relying on legal aid, partners allegedly struggle to earn more than £30,000 per annum. Barristers' earnings depend on the briefs they attract. At the junior end of the Bar it is notoriously hard to build a practice and small incomes are the norm, particularly for legal aid practitioners.[101] At the other end of the scale, the earnings of many Queen's Counsels (QCs) exceed £1million per annum, including some whose main paymaster is the legal aid fund. The status of QC, once achieved, is deemed by the Office of Fair Trading as being of questionable value to consumers. The widely held perception that new QCs achieve an unjustified leap in earnings is not necessarily true; solicitors are likely to select more senior QCs and it may be many years before a new QC can command top rates. Nevertheless, the Carter Review of Legal Aid Procurement, which recommended a shift in the allocation towards the junior Bar, should ensure a fairer distribution of public money.

Different systems for rewarding staff inside organisations also have an ethical dimension. The most frequently discussed is the use of the traditional lockstep method of dividing partnership profits rather than merit or bonus schemes.[102] Under lockstep systems, partners move towards taking a full profit share incrementally, reducing their incentive to work. This has led to the introduction of managed lockstep systems, where progression is not automatic and there is even the possibility of demotion. Some British firms have moved in recent years to more merit-based systems,[103] particularly following mergers with US firms. Most of the larger, commercial firms have adopted bonus schemes by 'top slicing' the profits and allocating them to high-performing staff. Such systems can also be used to lure 'stars' from other firms. One ethical issue is the fairness of the method for deciding pay, whether by patronage of a senior partner or by merit. Deciding on merit can involve focusing on crude measures like bills or income generated and clients attracted, often measured in an elaborate but objective points system.[104] The problem with merit systems is that they can encourage inter-partner rivalry, partners hogging the most profitable work and wrangles over who should get the credit for bills.[105] However, lockstep and pension provisions may fall foul of discrimination law.[106]

Security of employment is one of the traditional benefits and expectations of

---

[101] A Gillan, 'Car Mechanics Overtake Barristers' Hourly Rate', *The Guardian*, 17 February 2006, 5.

[102] M Chambers and R SenGupta, 'The Mystery of Lockstep' (2000) 39 *Commercial Lawyer* 23.

[103] A Mizzi, 'Stepping Stone to Revolution' (2001) 98/01 *Law Society's Gazette*, 10 January 2001, 14.

[104] M Moore, 'Merit Marks' (2003) 147 *Solicitors Journal* 371.

[105] P Hodkinson and A Novarese, 'Fakes and Ladders', *NIOS—Legal Week*, 17 March 2005.

[106] R Rothwell, 'Age-old Problem' (2005) 102/07 *Law Society's Gazette*, 17 February 2005, 18; P Jeanneret, 'Law Firms Feel Their Age' (2006) 156 *New Law Journal* 277; C Binham, 'Freshfields Girds Itself for Age Discrimination Fight', 26 *The Lawyer*, 7 July 2007.

professional life. It is again in the commercial firms where the idea of inexorable progression to the top of the professional tree has been most challenged. Gallanter and Pallay coined the phrase 'tournament of lawyers' to describe the internal race to partnership in large US law firms.[107] Firms recruit too many lawyers at the bottom of the firm and then select those who distinguish themselves in the succeeding years for partnership. This promotes a culture of competition and long hours, and puts a premium on individual profitability and the ability to attract and retain elite clients.[108] Menkel-Meadow suggests that the quality of life permitted by law firms is an ethical issue[109] and, more specifically, that the treatment of employees, including requiring overlong hours, is itself an ethical issue.[110] Lee raises similar concerns regarding the emergence of the tournament of lawyers in large firms in the UK.[111] He questions the policy of 'up or out', whereby solicitors who do not achieve partnership are asked to leave or, feeling their position untenable, choose to leave. Lee is concerned that those not heading for partnership are not told this in case they are demotivated.[112] This, he suggests, offends the Kantian injunction that people are to be treated as ends and it also undermines the ethical principles of individual autonomy and fairness.[113] Lee's concern, therefore, is with the way firms operate the policy rather than the policy itself, security being one of the key promises of professionalism. In the US the tournament model has given way to 'two-tier partnerships', where some lawyers remain associates and never make partner,[114] a system perhaps preferable to 'up or out', but one that challenges the collegial assumptions of the traditional law firm model.[115]

The insecurity of professional employment is reflected in data on retention of trainees in large firms. In 2004, one in five newly qualified lawyers, some 288 people, left the top 50 solicitors' firms on completion of their training contract, about the same as in the previous year.[116] Some trainees choose to leave, usually to do the kind of work they want,[117] but many are let go. If, as is claimed, it costs £150,000 to train and produce a lawyer, the wasted investment of £43 million indicates a high-stakes gamble by firms and entrants. The insecurity continues, however, into later employment. The trade press is replete with stories

---

[107] M Galanter and T Palay, *Tournament of Lawyers: Growth and Transformation of the Big Law Firm* (Chicago University Press, 1991); M Galanter, 'Old and in the Way: the Coming Demographic Transformation of the Legal Profession and its Implications for the Provision of Legal Services' (1999) *Wisconsin Law Review* 1081.

[108] Some large firms expect associates to bill 2,420 hours per annum, which, assuming four weeks' holiday, represent 10 hours chargeable time for every working day.

[109] C Menkel-Meadow, 'Portia Redux: Another Look at Gender Feminism, and Legal Ethics' in *Legal Ethics and Legal Practice: Contemporary Issues* (Oxford, Clarendon Press, 1995) 24.

[110] *Ibid*, 55.

[111] R Lee, '"Up or Out"—Means or Ends? Staff Retention in Large Firms' in Thomas, above n 3, 183.

[112] *Ibid*, 195.

[113] He asks 'whether the solicitors are accorded sufficient respect and the necessary autonomy to make appropriate career choices in the face of confused messages and misinformation about their progress and prospects' (*ibid*, 187).

[114] W Henderson, 'An Empirical Study of Single-tier versus Two-tier Partnerships in the Am Law 200' (2006) 84 *North Carolina Law Review* 1691.

[115] E Lazega, *The Collegial Phenomenon: The Social Mechanisms of Cooperation Among Peers in a Corporate Law Partnership* (New York, Oxford University Press, 2001); J Flood, 'Partnership and Professionalism in Global Law Firms: Resurgent Professionalism?' in D Muzio, S Ackroyd and J Chanlat, *Redirections in the Study of Expert Labour: Established Professions and New Expert Occupations* (Houndmills, Palgrave Macmillan, 2007) 52.

[116] G Charles, 'Retention Rates at Top 50 Firms Promise Stability for Trainees', *The Lawyer*, 25 October 2004, 2.

[117] Some trainees appear to be aware of the difference between the remunerative corporate and finance work and 'knowledge area' and choose the latter, preferring to leave if they are not available (above n 27).

of firms 'clearing out' groups of lawyers and of whole departments changing firms. The marketisation of legal services has loosened the bonds of the employment relationship, introducing instability and uncertainty. This reflects changes in the employment market generally, which has become more insecure since the 1980s.

Job satisfaction

Numerous studies show that a high level of job satisfaction is the key promise of profession-alism. Most entrants are attracted to areas that stimulate them intellectually or emotionally, like human rights or criminal law, rather than corporate or commercial law.[118] While surveys record high levels of job satisfaction for solicitors, law jobs are notable for being amongst those that many graduates find boring.[119] The favoured areas may be more interesting academic subjects, and they are also notable for offering a role helping people in crisis and allowing some personal autonomy in doing the work.[120] Over 42% of women leaving the profession were disappointed that their expectations regarding the value of the work to the community were not met.[121] Some commercial firms are so specialised that they do not have work offering this public service element.[122] Their young employees often seek *pro bono* projects in order to do such work. High-street practices often offer these features, but not the pay available in larger firms.[123] This may explain why newly qualified solicitors find that the most satisfying work is in 'knowledge' areas, often specialist litigation, and the most hospi-table firms are medium-sized commercial and larger high-street firms with a broad base of work, including commercial.[124] These firms potentially provide a balance of the intrinsic and extrinsic rewards that are becoming elusive in the extremes of the legal services market. It is probably no coincidence that they also tend to be traditionally organised, along the lines of the classical model.

Helping clients is also attractive to aspiring professionals, not least because professional autonomy is part of the helping role. The consumer society, however, replaces 'clients' with 'customers', and customers are likely to get angry when they cannot have what they think they have paid for. Young lawyers often find that, rather than gratitude, clients express resentment at paying fees for receiving remedies they think they are entitled to anyway. Increased emphasis on client satisfaction also impinges on autonomy and changes the

---

[118] The fifth survey of the solicitors' cohort study (above n 23) showed a close relationship between levels of subject interest and areas of law in which they desired to work, including family, crime, benefits and personal injury. Human rights and EU law had a disproportionately high level of interest compared with numbers of trainees who worked or might expect to work in them, whereas commercial areas, including commercial property and business and commercial affairs, had low levels of interest compared with numbers expecting to work in them. M Shiner, *Year 5*, above n 23, 32–3.

[119] In a Law Society survey, 69.5% of male and 64.6% of female solicitors express overall job satisfaction: *Working Lives Survey 2005–6* (London, The Law Society, 2006). J Carvel, 'Graduates Find Prized Jobs Boring, Say Survey', *The Guardian*, 27 July 2006, 8.

[120] Above n 27.

[121] Above n 79, 96.

[122] City trainees are more likely to find work uninteresting and to be dissatisfied with their breadth of experience than those in high-street or large provincial firms (above n 27).

[123] Fifty per cent of prospective solicitors were interested in legal aid work but only 8% were likely to pursue this given the career prospects (above n 79, 31).

[124] Above n 27.

emotional balance in the relationship between lawyer and client. Hochschild's finding that workers in certain service jobs involve 'emotional labour', involving emotional display and exhaustion,[125] can also be extended to professionals.[126] Competition with solicitors for advocacy work has put pressure on young barristers to cultivate professional and lay clients, demands they prepare themselves to meet by vocational training.[127] Indeed, the Bar cohort study found that one-third of young barristers reported interpersonal problems with their clerks,[128] solicitors,[129] clients or relatives.[130] Young solicitors in big commercial firms also seem to be at risk. They are subject to close control by clients whose business is worth millions of pounds, whose loyalty depends on personal relationships and who employers would do almost anything to please.

Employers have a statutory duty to ensure, so far as is reasonably practicable, the health, safety and welfare of their employees. Breach of the duty to provide a safe system of work can constitute negligence,[131] and a particular risk in professional workplaces is stress. Various factors have contributed to the general increase in workplace stress since the 1980s.[132] There are many theories to explain why this has happened, but competition seems a likely candidate. Across a range of occupations intrinsic work motivation is associated with challenging tasks, but emotional exhaustion is caused by a high workload and the lack of social support.[133] New demands, like attracting and keep clients, have been generated by competition, and old demands, like turning over work, have been exacerbated. This has created a culture of long hours[134] and insecurity,[135] in many ways the opposite of the promise of professionalism. This may explain US research suggesting that levels of depression, alcoholism and other drug dependency among lawyers are almost double that of the population as a whole[136] and UK evidence that lawyers suffer more stress in the workplace than other professions, including doctors.[137] While stress may arise in all types of legal work, most of the writing on lawyers' workplace stress concerns large firms.

---

[125] AR Hochschild, *The Managed Heart: Commercialisation of Human Feeling* (Berkeley, CA, University of California Press, 1983).

[126] CA Wellington and JR Bryson, 'At Face Value? Image Consultancy, Emotional Labour and Professional Work' (2001) 35 *Sociology* 933.

[127] LC Harris, 'The Emotional Labour of Barristers: An Exploration of Emotional Labour by Status Professionals' (2002) 39 *Journal of Management Studies* 553.

[128] Particularly in the allocation of work and knowing how to deal with them (Shapland and Sorsby, above n 23, 70).

[129] *Ibid*, usually over poorly prepared instructions.

[130] *Ibid*, often when a case had not turned out well.

[131] *Walker v Northumberland County Council* (1995) 1 All ER 737.

[132] The Health and Safety Executive defines stress as 'the adverse reaction people have to excessive pressures or other types of demands placed on them'.

[133] Houkes *et al*, above n 98.

[134] The cohort study found that just over a quarter in high-street firms, 40% in large provincial and 56% in City firms worked over 50 hours a week (Sixth survey 41).

[135] A director of the legal healthcare charity SolCare observed that, between 1997 and 1999, the subject of the majority of calls received had switched from alcohol to stress. '. . . there is a culture in the legal profession that says if you aren't stressed you're not working properly. We've had calls from people who were certain they'd lost their jobs because they had complained about their workloads.' H Syedain, 'Stressed Out—but Quids in?', *The Observer*, 11 July 1999.

[136] P Goodrich, 'Law-induced Anxiety: Legists, Anti-lawyers and the Boredom of Legality' (2000) 9 *Social and Legal Studies* 143.

[137] Above n 135.

Job satisfaction may also have been affected by the decline of collegiality in professional organisations. Sommerlad suggests that the decline in conveyancing income and increased commercialisation have had particular impact on the job satisfaction of legal aid practitioners and women[138] because funding constraints and franchise auditing mechanisms have put financial constraints on client contact, limited professional autonomy and created a climate of 'denigration and distrust' for public sector professionals. Specialisation also has a negative impact on relationships by reducing the common work experience of employees and, therefore, the extent to which they have interests in common. Whereas workers in service industries with demanding and abusive customers cope by sharing problems with co-workers,[139] professional cultures may be becoming more individualistic and less supportive. This is a particular concern because collegiality reinforces professional values and customer pressure undermines the 'professional detachment' that characterises professional autonomy.

Diversity

Embracing diversity is a recent response to the culture of rights. Potential entrants assume that the professions, as ethically orientated public bodies, are in the vanguard of such initiatives. In fact, of course, professions also have conservative tendencies and often follow social trends rather than lead them, as the history of women lawyers illustrates. Women were only admitted as solicitors after the First World War[140] and have only been admitted in equal numbers to men in the last 20 years. In one study a quarter of solicitors holding practising certificates were women, but many were working part-time or were unemployed.[141] Large solicitors' firms were notable for taking equal numbers of men and women trainees, but women's pay begins to slip quite quickly compared with men.[142] Although it takes time to reach the top of an organisation, some of the patterns have already become established.[143] So, for example, relatively few women progress to partnership.[144] Successful women in US law firms typically come from higher social groups than their male counterparts, suggesting at least a gender component and at worst sex-based barriers to female progression.[145]

There are different theories explaining occupational segmentation on gender lines. Supply-side theories suggest that women seek work roles consistent with motherhood or, perhaps less contentiously, that men are more likely to aspire to partnership at an earlier

---

[138] H Sommerlad, 'Managerialism and the Legal Profession: a New Professional Paradigm' (1995) 2 *International Journal of the Legal Profession* 159.

[139] M Korczynski, 'Communities of Coping: Collective Emotional Labour in Service Work' (2003) 10 *Organization* 55, 57.

[140] The first woman was admitted as a solicitor in 1922. See Mossman, above n 54, ch 3, 118.

[141] H Sommerlad, 'The Myth of Feminisation: Women and Cultural Change in the Legal Profession' (1994) 1 *International Journal of the Legal Profession* 31.

[142] Cohort Study 5, above n 23.

[143] Female recruitment had broadened in the late 1980s and there are currently signs that it may be doing so again in the large law firms. Gibb, above n 65.

[144] It was 1998 before the arrival of the first woman senior partner in a top 100 law firm (*The Lawyer*, 20 October 1998, 3). Women make up half of newly qualified lawyers but only 15% of partners. See R Verkaik, 'Women Lawyers Suffer Pay Bias', *The Independent*, 6 September 1999; Sommerlad, above n 141, 34.

[145] D Rhode, "Perspectives on Professional Women" (1988) 40 *Stanford Law Review* 1163.

stage. Research suggests that females are more likely to seek intrinsic interest and work of value to the community,[146] while males are more interested in long-term salary prospects. This is reflected in the fact that males tend to seek the higher-status business areas of practice, while women prefer to work on family and relationship problems, or conveyancing and wills. These choices often affect progression since firms are more likely to reward and promote employees making higher financial contributions.[147]

Demand-side theories explain women's apparent failure to flourish in solicitors' firms by pointing to occupational structure, exclusionary mechanisms or gender stereotypes operating in the workplace.[148] Gilligan's theory that men and women have different moral orientations[149] means that male-led organisations may have a rational and legalistic culture[150] whereas those led by women would make allowances for individuals.[151] Therefore, the culture of long hours and the focus on the importance of generating business[152] lead to the subordination of women in large firms[153] and general hostility to motherhood.[154] The cohort study and later research done by the Law Society bears this out.[155] Female solicitors were seen to earn less than men, were more dissatisfied with partnership opportunities, long hours and the work/life balance,[156] and were significantly more likely to have considered leaving the profession. It may take a long time for increasing numbers of women in the law office to lead to 'feminisation' of the workplace[157] as organisational norms tend to be resistant to revision by new practitioners, however great their numbers.[158]

There are small signs that the situation is not that bleak and that, in the longer term, legal practice may change. There are more women partners and women associate solicitors

[146] Above n 79, 45.

[147] A similar phenomenon occurs in large firms, where women often decide to work in 'knowledge areas' like employment litigation, rather than in the corporate and commercial departments from which partners tend to be drawn (above n 26).

[148] H Sommerlad and P Sanderson, 'The Legal Labour Market and the Training Needs of Women Returners in the United Kingdom' (1997) 49 *Journal of Vocational Education and Training* 45.

[149] According to C Gilligan, *In a Different Voice: Psychological Theory and Women's Development* (Cambridge, MA, Harvard University Press, 1982), men's judgements are based on an ethic of rights whereas women's flow from the desire to avoid pain, a so-called ethic of care. See also N Noddings, *Caring: A Feminist Approach to Ethics and Moral Education* (Berkeley, CA, University of California Press, 1999).

[150] C Menkel-Meadow, 'Portia in a Different Voice: Speculation on a Women's Lawyering Process' (1984) 1 *Berkeley Women's Law Journal* 39.

[151] R Auchmuty, 'The Fiction of Equity' in SS Hunt and H Lim (eds), *Feminist Perspectives on Equity and Trusts* (London, Cavendish, 2001) 1.

[152] P Sanderson and H Sommerlad, 'Professionalism, Discrimination, Difference and Choice in Women's Experience in Law Jobs' in Thomas, above n 3, 155, 161.

[153] *Ibid*, 182.

[154] Women who took a career break to raise families were unlikely to make partnership and, when firms laid off solicitors, those affected were disproportionately women. J Ames, 'Late Bloomer' , 90/12 *Law Society Gazette*, 24 March 1993, 10.

[155] J Siems, *Women Solicitors Volume I: Equality and Diversity* (London, The Law Society, 2004); L Duff and L Webley, *Women Solicitors Volume II: Equality and Diversity* (London, The Law Society, 2004).

[156] *Ibid*, vol I, 119.

[157] Skordaki, above n 76; Sommerlad, above n 141.

[158] It has been argued that the addition of women to male environments does not change 'violent' ways of doing things. A Giddens, *Modernity and Self-identity: Self and Society in the Late Modern Age* (Cambridge, Polity Press, 1991) 229–30.

in the large national firms than in City firms,[159] suggesting that the elite are not leading on this issue. There is greater awareness of the issues and willingness to tackle them.[160] A recent diversity league table showed that in two firms in the top 100 over one-third of the partners were women, and all the top 10 firms had more female than male associates.[161] Measures to address disadvantage, such as mentoring support for women to encourage more to aim for partnership,[162] may help. They do not address the reality that many firms see long hours as an indication of commitment and as a pre-requisite of progression.[163] The objection that these are gendered social constructions of merit and commitment are unlikely to change this.[164] If women are to compete for partnership on equal terms with men, they need opportunities to generate a client base and the leeway to accommodate motherhood, which involves changing attitudes in practice and in the private sphere.[165]

Despite the Bar's different organisational context, it has also struggled to accommodate the aspirations of women. Women are not represented proportionately as judges or QCs, perhaps because of earlier difficulties in establishing practices.

Flood, in 1983, remarked that, in most cases, the clerk's criteria for allocating work

> accord with those of the Bar, with a strong reluctance to accept women and members of eth-
> nic minorities as tenants in chambers.[166]

Since then, disadvantage of a different kind has emerged. The Bar cohort study found that 40% of women entering the Bar suffered sexual harassment at work[167] and 70% of women claimed to have encountered sexual discrimination in their careers.[168] Twenty-six percent of barristers felt that sexual discrimination was a major problem at the bar.

The problems of ethnic minorities in legal employment appear almost as a postscript, because they are present in such small numbers in the elite sectors. This is, however, an area where City firms might perform better than the large national firms, if only because of the London demographic. The increased presence of many US firms in the City may also bring about change there.[169] Data on diversity of the top 100 solicitors' firms suggests that ethnic minority partners usually constitute less than 5% of partners, and they comprise an average of around 10% of associates in the 10 most ethnically diverse firms, whereas Clifford

---

[159] The top firm in a 2006 Diversity League Table of the top 100 firms was Shoosmiths, with 40% female partners and 59% female associates. Clifford Chance were the first City firm, with 18.6% female partners and 51.3 female associates. S Hoare, 'National Firms Shame City Giants in Diversity Stakes', *The Lawyer*, 27 March 2006, 1.

[160] When a solicitor sent a partner an email expressing the hope that a departing black secretary could be replaced by a 'busty blonde', the Office for the Supervision of Solicitors investigated the incident as a breach of the Law Society's conduct rules: *The Lawyer*, 4 March 2002, 5.

[161] The highest was Keoghs, with nearly 66%, and the lowest Clifford Chance, with 51.3% (above n 159).

[162] H Begum, 'Freshfields to Kick Off Female Buddy Scheme', *The Lawyer*, 20 February 2006, 1.

[163] Sommerlad, above n 141, 36–9.

[164] H Sommerlad and P Sanderson, *Gender, Choice and Commitment: Women Solicitors in England and the Struggle for Equal Rights* (Brookfield, VT, Ashgate Publishing, 1998).

[165] *Ibid.*

[166] JA Flood, *Barristers' Clerks: The Law's Middlemen* (Manchester University Press, 1983) 132.

[167] Based on a survey of 822 students entering practice: Shapland and Sorsby, above n 23, table 5.3, 71; see also B Hewson, 'A Recent Problem', *New Law Journal*, 5 May 1995, 626.

[168] Shapland and Sorsby, *ibid*, 74–5.

[169] In 1999 the Association of Corporate Counsel, representing in-house lawyers in the US, made a statement on behalf of 300 of the largest companies stating that they gave weight to the promotion of diversity in the workplace in appointing outside counsel.

Chance had 5.5% ethnic minority partners and 17% ethnic minority associates.[170] There is particular pressure to account for partnership profiles and the factors that lead to ethnic minorities being under-represented.[171] The Bar also has difficulties. In the Bar cohort study, 24% thought that racial discrimination was a major problem at the Bar.[172] More recently, it was suggested that barristers' clerks systematically deprive black pupils of work, and that senior barristers do not tackle the problem because the clerks operate in their interests.[173]

Opportunity

Providing equality of opportunity is obviously a key to diversity, but opportunity issues also arise independently at almost every stage of employment. Entrants may expect an opportunity to establish a financial base, to enjoy broad employment opportunities and access to the full menu of professional work, and have a wide choice of working environments. All of these promises require qualification. The Bar cohort study confirmed the trend noted in the Goldsmith Report of declining work levels,[174] less serious than anticipated, with 20% finding it difficult to manage financially,[175] possibly leading to them leaving the Bar. The sixth solicitors' cohort study found that movement between sectors and types of firm was extremely rare, and that newly qualified solicitors were usually limited to the type of firm where they trained and, often, the type of work they performed there. Finally, the loss of small firms has decreased the diversity of the profession and reduced the kind of working environment that may be preferred by women lawyers.[176]

Employee duties

The duties of employees of legal businesses are largely defined by law, but there are some that may arise independently as a consequence of the professional relationship. The most obvious are competence, diligence, honesty and loyalty. Competent performance is a basic obligation of employees, hence the requirements for continuing professional development as a condition of practise.[177] The aim of these requirements is the active engagement in personal development rather than the passive and reluctant attendance at dull and unimaginative

---

[170] Above n 159.

[171] A Department of Constitutional Affairs junior minister, David Lammy, endorsed investigation of minority ethnic representation at senior levels of firms, alleging that ethnic minority recruits were often channelled into the 'knowledge areas' of work and therefore missed out on partnership. M Mullally, 'A Step Forward', Legal Director, 17 August 2004.

[172] Shapland and Sorsby, above n 23, 25.

[173] See T Growney, 'Bar to Equal Opportunity', The Guardian, 27 May 1997. See also the Bar Diversity Code recommending that chambers monitor work distribution: Bar Council, Equality and Diversity Code for the Bar (London, Bar Council, 2004) 103.

[174] Attributed to more tenants, less magistrate's court work and more solicitors doing minor court appearances themselves.

[175] Attracting work was only a major problem for 16% in London and for 8% in the provinces.

[176] Above n 152, 161.

[177] Compulsory continuing education began in 1985 for those in the period of three years post-qualification but has since been extended to all practitioners. The requirement has been 16 hours per annum for solicitors since November 2001.

lectures,[178] but some lawyers inevitably regard continuing professional development (CPD) as a burdensome imposition. The Law Society has attempted to make its compulsory CPD, the 'Best Practice Course', taken in solicitors' third year following admission, relevant by providing 'a reference manual of basic management techniques suitable for application to private practice',[179] but the CPD undertaken has minimal quality requirements. Some analysts feel that more could be done with CPD in terms of ethics education, and there are certainly arguments that lawyers in mid-career might benefit from a reacquaintance with the basic principles.[180]

Newly qualified barristers must undertake the New Practitioners' Programme, comprising 45 hours of accredited CPD, including at least nine hours of advocacy training and three hours of ethics,[181] enabling new practitioners to identify those situations which raise ethical problems, understand the principles that govern professional conduct and apply these principles to given situations. Courses are required to incorporate discussions of the three basic duties of the Code of Conduct:

the overriding duty to the court, the duty to act in the client's best interests and duties to third parties and may deal with client care and the cab rank rule . . .[182]

Chambers are 'authorised providers' under the scheme and are

specifically encouraged to offer the ethics component of the programme, because chambers are regarded as particularly suited to the small group discussions essential to effective ethics teaching.[183]

On completion of the New Practitioners' Programme, barristers must undertake the Established Practitioners' Programme, comprising 12 hours of CPD a year. Failure to comply with these requirements may lead to a reference to the Professional Conduct and Complaints Committee.

Duties of loyalty to employers and clients are compromised by legislation,[184] but the increasingly insecure legal employment market affects employee loyalty. Sennett's study of work in the US suggests that insecurity has undermined the promise of a career, a

---

[178] K Rockhill, 'Mandatory Continuing Education for Professionals: Trends and Issues' (1983) 33 *Adult Education* 106.

[179] R Steele, 'The Best Practice of Management' (1991) 20 *The Law Society's Gazette* 29 May, 21.

[180] CPD is too often professional updating, providing an experience of dubious value which is the antithesis of 'self-directed learning' (CO Houle, *Continuing Learning in the Professions* (San Francisco, CA, Jossey-Bass Publishers, 1980) 266). It may be possible to incorporate ACLEC's proposal for a sustained postgraduate course incorporating professional responsibility issues with Schon's advocacy of a significant intellectual component in developing high levels of professional skill (DA Schon, *Educating the Reflective Practitioner: Toward a New Design for Teaching and Learning in the Professions* (London, Jossey-Bass Publishers, 1987) 312) and his proposal that the best place for this is in the professional's 'mid-career' phase (342).

[181] This applies to all barristers commencing practice on or after 1 October 1997. 'Practice' includes working as an employed lawyer. *The Continuing Professional Development Regulations (2001)*, paras 1–2.

[182] The Professional Standards Committee of the bar provides a model ethics syllabus for such courses and the Inns, Circuits and some specialist Bar Associations provide accredited programmes. *Ibid*, 2–3.

[183] *The New Practitioners' Programme* (London, Continuing Education Unit, General Council of the Bar, 1997) 3 and 4.

[184] In relation to loyalty and the conflict with statutes relating to money laundering and 'whistleblowing', see further chapter 14.

well-made road, as an antidote to aimlessness and personal failure.[185] A consequence of this is that the importance of character in employment has diminished. Character, 'the personal traits which we value in ourselves and which we seek to be valued by others', in employment[186] develops over time as a result of emotional experience, and is expressed in loyalty. It results in mutual commitment, the pursuit of long-term goals and delayed gratification for the sake of a future end. Sennet observes that the short-term focus, demand for continuous change and erosion of mutual commitment and trust in employment relationships are inimical to loyalty, commitment, purpose and resolution, which are the foundations of character. The shifting orientation of many organisations to flexible, short-term and routinised work encourages emphasis on personality, which is superficial. Ethicality is a feature of character and Sennett's analysis is a timely warning for the legal profession.

Conclusion

The employment relationship has seldom been seen as producing ethical issues for lawyers, but it is important on many levels. The decline of small practices, the increasing success of large firms and their success in 'converting' trainees into practising professionals have seen the production of new lawyers shift towards commerce. Among the affects are that law, with its base of small organisations, is disadvantaged in retaining a substantial share of its undergraduate base[187] and a decline in the careers that were once a key promise of legal professionalism. There has been some disenchantment and the loss of significant numbers of potential recruits. Aspects of the problem have been treated as issues, but the profession has responded slowly to meeting this challenge by recruiting more broadly from those who do desire legal careers. Despite progress, accommodating diversity remains a challenge for the legal profession.

---

[186] R Sennett, *The Corrosion of Character: The Personal Consequences of Work in the New Capitalism* (New York, WW Norton, 2000) 120.

[186] *Ibid*, 10.

[187] Department for Education and Skills, *Literature Review in Relation to 'Gateways to the Professions'* (London, DfES, 2005) ch 4.

Part V

DISPUTE RESOLUTION

Litigation is central to how lawyers are perceived, even when it is not the main, or any, part of what they do. Ways of resolving disputes are culturally and socially determined,[1] and lawyers had a central role in fashioning the justice system in England and Wales, championing its excellence as a guarantor of citizens' rights. They also have an interest in preserving it, since it represents the way they choose to do the business of litigation. These interests and perspectives are potentially at odds with the government's interest in the efficiency of the civil litigation system, which is political and financial. An efficient and fair litigation system facilitates the access to law that underpins a rights-based society[2] and attracts international commercial 'forum shoppers' who pay handsomely for dispute resolution services.

The adversary system tests truth by a clash of opposing views umpired by the court. For many years cost and delay were endemic features of adversarial justice,[3] and were used as tools by lawyers to attain client goals. The decline of legal aid led to a search for better ways of processing claims and reducing costs,[4] and to growing interest in alternative dispute resolution (ADR). The Civil Procedure Rules resulting from Lord Woolf's overhaul of the civil justice system made greater use of ADR as an adjunct to trials. The introduction of an alternative to adversarial justice brought a new range of ethical issues for lawyers. But the CPR had implications for the ethics of lawyers beyond ADR, as Lord Woolf sought a new spirit of cooperation in conducting litigation.

These issues are tracked through four areas: the litigation process, negotiations, advocacy and the role of lawyers in ADR as advisors, representatives and 'third party neutrals'. These chapters represent different processes for resolving disputes, all revolving around the central process of litigation. Some are rich in a mixture of regulation, including rules of litigation, professional ethics and court judgments, while negotiation is, controversially and despite its great practical importance, almost beyond professional ethics.

---

[1] S Roberts, *Order and Dispute* (Harmondsworth, Penguin, 1979).

[2] The 1988 White Paper stated 'social exclusion would increase, and the rule of law would be threatened, if less well-off people, as a class were effectively excluded from justice'. Lord Chancellor's Department, *Modernising Justice: The Government's plans for reform of legal services and the courts* (London, Lord Chancellor's Department, 1998).

[3] Despite differences in the legal systems of the US and the UK, both systems generate concern at 'the cost, delay and inaccessibility of the legal process, the high level of unmet legal need, the range of unprotected interests, the frequency of professional incompetence, neglect, incivility and adversarial abuse and the inadequacy of institutional response'. DL Rhode, 'Ethics by the Pervasive Method' (1992) 42 *Journal of Legal Education* 31.

[4] Lord Mackay of Clashfern, 'Access to Justice: The Price' (1991) 25 *The Law Teacher* 96.

17

LITIGATION

Jarndyce and Jarndyce still drags its dreary length before the Court, perennially hopeless . . . The one great principle of English law is, to make business for itself.[1]

Introduction

Litigation is seen as a defining activity of lawyers. While it does not provide the largest revenues of most solicitors' firms, and possibly even some barristers' chambers, the capacity for conducting litigation remains the norm. Further, both branches of the profession retain a stranglehold on work in the courts, although litigants may act in person. Solicitors' long-standing monopoly on the initiation and conduct of litigation and barristers' monopoly of advocacy in higher courts have been breached in law,[2] but practice is slow to change. The initial signs were that private practitioners in both branches of the profession would stick to their traditional work,[3] but this reluctance to cross boundaries is expected to increasingly break down. This chapter looks at both criminal and civil litigation, although the primary focus of this chapter is civil, while chapter 19 looks primarily at crime. First, though, it is necessary to sketch the system.

The litigation system

The blueprint for the court system was drawn in the nineteenth century, when the county courts and the Supreme Court were established. The Supreme Court now consists of the High Court, the Court of Appeal and the Crown courts.[4] Crown courts hear serious criminal cases and appeals, with less serious cases, applications for bail and for search warrants,[5] and some civil matters being heard in magistrates' courts.[6] The county court and High Court civil jurisdictions largely overlap, but the High Court hears the higher value and more complex cases. The High Court is split into three divisions: Family, Queen's Bench and Chancery. The

---

[1] C Dickens, *Bleak House* (London, Bradbury and Evans, 1853), chs 1 and 39.
[2] That is, with some solicitors acquiring higher rights of audience and some barristers the right to conduct litigation.
[3] A Boon and J Flood, 'Trials of Strength: The Reconfiguration of Litigation as a Contested Terrain' (1999) 33 *Law and Society Review* 595.
[4] The county courts were created in 1846 and the Supreme Court in the 1870s.
[5] Magistrates' courts hear around 95% of the million annual criminal trials.
[6] For a fuller account of the criminal system, see the report of Auld LJ, *A Review of the Criminal Courts of England and Wales* (London, Stationery Office, 2001), particularly ch 3.

jurisdictions of Chancery and Queen's Bench overlap but, despite a growing Chancery interest in commercial litigation, its main work includes bankruptcy, estates and mortgages. The Queen's Bench division deals with the bulk of tort and contract cases. In some specialist areas, such as employment, tribunals operate outside the court structure with their own rules of procedure, although appeals may be to the High Court, for example, on points of law. The state funds the civil litigation system, employing a range of legal personnel, including judges drawn from private practitioners with advocacy experience. Most magistrates are part-time volunteers without legal qualification, being advised on the law by a justice's clerk. A much smaller number of district judges and deputy district judges must have seven years' experience of advocacy before appointment.[7] There are obvious differences in the courts, parties and processes of criminal and civil litigation, and in the ethics of each system.

The litigator's responsibility for the administration of justice

Litigators were recently placed under a statutory duty to the court to act with independence in the interests of justice and comply with the rules of conduct of their professional body, a duty overriding any obligation the lawyer owes (other than under the criminal law) if it is inconsistent with them.[8] The separation of these responsibilities is consistent with the development of the duty to the court under the common law prior to the legislation, where the ethics and codes provided a starting point for defining the duty but were not definitive. The courts' inherent jurisdiction to secure the proper administration of justice is a summary jurisdiction,[9] meaning that any charge against a lawyer arises out of the case and should be capable of being put to the lawyer in simple terms. Pleadings or discovery should not normally be required, and the proceeding should not be complicated or overlong.[10] A number of outcomes are possible when there is a breach of the duty to the court, including an order for a new trial, an order for costs against one of the lawyers and reporting the lawyers to the relevant disciplinary body.

The principle underpinning the duty to the court was further complicated by the different positions of solicitors, who, as officers of the court, were subject to its disciplinary jurisdiction,[11] and barristers, who were not officers of the court but owed a duty to the court as advocates and had immunity from negligence actions brought by their own clients. The distinctions are now largely irrelevant, particularly with the mixing of roles between the branches,[12] but this historical background, together with the unpredictability in the issues,

---

[7] There are 28,000 lay magistrates serving 600 local justice areas and around 105 district judges.

[8] Courts and Legal Services Act 1990 s 28(2A) (rights to conduct litigation) as amended by the Access to Justice Act (1999) s 42.

[9] Per Lord Wright in *Myers v Elman* [1940] AC 282, 319.

[10] *Harley v McDonald* [2001] 2WLR 1749.

[11] *Abraham v Jutsun* [1963] 2 All ER 402.

[12] In *Brown & anor v Bennett and others* [2002] 2 All ER 273 it was held a barrister could be liable for wasted costs arising from settling documents and advising clients and in *Medcalf v Mardell and others* (*The Times*, 2 January 2001) barristers were held liable for wasted costs having pleaded allegations of fraud in grounds of appeal that could not be substantiated. The case was reversed in the Lords on the facts and also because it could not be dealt with summarily. However, the basic principle remains; see [2002] 3 All ER 721.

the way they arise and the remedy sought, affects the conception of the duty, creating a rather ragged jurisprudence. These confused disciplinary and compensatory functions of the court have been further complicated by their intersection with court rules and legislation.

An early important case in defining the litigation duty in modern times is *Myers v Elman*.[13] In an action against five defendants for fraudulent conspiracy, the solicitors of one of the parties was held liable for a third of the costs of the case because of having filed an inadequate affidavit verifying a client's list of documents. The House of Lords, reversing the Court of Appeal's decision for the solicitor,[14] made five important points. First, the disciplinary jurisdiction over solicitors was separate from that required to make a wasted costs order. Secondly, a disciplinary finding requires serious professional misconduct, but a wasted costs order does not. Thirdly, the wasted costs jurisdiction derives from the duty to the court to promote justice. Fourthly, it is not necessary to find conduct justifying striking a solicitor from the roll to make a wasted costs order. Fifthly, the jurisdiction is compensatory and not merely punitive. The separation of the duty to the court and the right to make wasted costs orders is important, but they are linked by a common concern over the conduct of lawyers.

By the time of the next important cases, a collection of applications for wasted costs orders going under the name of the first case *Ridehalgh v Horsefield and anor*, the conduct for which lawyers could be penalised had been defined in legislation as that which was 'improper, unreasonable or negligent'.[15] Interpreting this section, the court found 'improper' conduct was

> a significant breach of a substantial duty imposed by a relevant code of professional conduct or conduct which the consensus of professional opinion, including judicial opinion, considered improper.

Unreasonable conduct was said to be that which was vexatious or harassing rather than that intended to advance resolution of the case. Negligence was not coterminous with the tort, but simply failure to achieve the competence reasonably expected of a member of the profession. The court considered that, in any case, it was quite possible that the conduct complained of would be improper, unreasonable and negligent. For any such breaches, lawyers were only to be punished by costs orders when their conduct was directly causative of wasted costs.[16] In *Re A Barrister* it was observed that where a court finds improper conduct but no wasted costs, it may refer the lawyer to the relevant disciplinary body, or to the legal aid authorities if appropriate.[17] As this implies, the lawyer's ethical failings are secondary to the court's enquiry into whether an abuse has prejudiced the administration of justice and, if so, what remedy is appropriate.

As is clear from these cases, the litigation duty to the court and the wasted costs jurisdiction are closely related but separate. They spring from similar but subtly different policy

---

[13] *Myers v Elman*, above n 9.

[14] The Court of Appeal considered he could not be personally liable in costs because the work had been done by his managing clerk.

[15] Courts and Legal Services Act 1990, s 4 substituting Supreme Court Act 1981, s 51(6).

[16] *Ridehalgh v Horsefield and anor* [1994] Ch 205.

[17] *Re a barrister (wasted costs order) (No 1 of 1991)* [1993] QB 293.

objectives. The rationale for the lawyer's duty to the court is that it is imposed, not for the benefit of the parties, but with the underlying purpose of ensuring that lawyers act properly,[18] thereby protecting the administration of justice. The wasted costs jurisdiction is primarily concerned that litigants should not be unjustifiably prejudiced in costs by the conduct of their opponent's lawyers.[19] In exercising the wasted costs jurisdiction, the court aims to hold in the balance the competing public interest that lawyers should not be deterred from pursuing their clients' interests by fear of costs orders against them. The professional codes are often quoted and discussed in judgments, but they do not define the duty. Lawyers may be punished in costs for conduct that is unethical or merely negligent, but can only be reported for the former. They may also be highly unethical in how they conduct their litigation but escape punishment by a wasted costs order if their conduct has not caused wasted costs. Ethics codes are not necessarily an issue with wasted costs orders, but they tend to be central with the duty to the court.

The duty to the court in litigation potentially affects every area of ethics. A conflict of interests may arise, for example, when there is a possibility that the lawyer may be called as a witness.[20] The clearest cases occur in the context of advocacy,[21] where the lawyer's failure may result in a new trial. These cases are examined elsewhere.[22] Ipp[23] suggests that coherence can be brought to the English and Australian cases by organising them in four categories, including those involving wasted costs. The first, duties of disclosure, includes the advocate's duty to the court. The others are conducting cases expeditiously,[24] avoiding abuse of process and avoiding corrupting the administration of justice.[25] However, as the rationale for the duty to the court is the propriety of lawyer conduct, and since the wasted costs jurisdiction encompasses conduct beyond the 'improper', it is unclear whether coherence of principle can be achieved by lumping all of the cases under the duty to the court. It is, nevertheless, important that the courts can review lawyer conduct and take appropriate action as necessary, since honest and fair behaviour is needed if an adversary system is to function effectively. In civil matters, for example, justice may be prejudiced if full disclosure is not made. When each side provides the other with details of documents harmful to their case, including any for which privilege is claimed, lawyers must not be complicit in their clients' concealment or destruction of harmful material. Similarly, how far it is acceptable to go in 'preparing' witnesses is an issue that arises daily, and with new significance with increased use of witness statements as evidence in chief. The litigator's duty applies equally to civil and criminal proceedings, although it will arise in different ways because of the different nature of the proceedings.

---

[18] Per Sir Thomas Bingham MR in *Ridehalgh v Horsefield*, above n 16.
[19] *Ibid.*
[20] *Re Recover Ltd (in liquidation) Hornan v Latif Group SL and others* [2003] EWHC 536 (Ch).
[21] D Pannick, *Advocates* (Oxford University Press 1992) 105.
[22] See chapter 19.
[23] D Ipp, 'Lawyers' Duties to the Court' (1998) 114 *Law Quarterly Review* 63.
[24] *Brennan v Brighton BC* (*The Times*, 24 July 1996).
[25] Above n 23, 65.

Criminal litigation

Justice requires that those accused of crimes receive fair treatment, including expedition in bringing charges, processing,[26] and a 'fair and public hearing . . . including an adequate defence'.[27] A person has the right

> to defend himself in person or through legal assistance of his own choosing or, if he has not sufficient means to pay for legal assistance, to be given it free when the interests of justice so require.[28]

Criminal prosecutions are brought by the Crown Prosecution Service (CPS), headed by the Director of Public Prosecutions. It services the casework of local police forces. Since 2003, the CPS, rather than the police, have made the decision whether to charge a suspect,[29] although police and CPS often work together in Criminal Justice Units to prepare cases for court. The CPS employs many solicitors and barristers as caseworkers and advocates, and instructs private practitioners as advocates. The Legal Services Commission was responsible for establishing the Criminal Defence Service.[30] Although this is currently a network of preferred suppliers, mainly solicitors' firms, a public defender service to complement the CPS, using directly employed lawyers, currently exists in a very few centres but is unlikely to be extended.

The relationship of the state to criminal prosecution and defence is controversial, because of the potential for abuse by the state. As state employees, prosecutors may be under pressure to meet targets that private practitioners would not. This may affect their judgement on particular issues and encourage them to cut corners in order to meet targets. Using state-employed lawyers for criminal defence creates an obvious conflict of interest, but the payment of private practice barristers through legal aid is expensive. Legal aid payment rates have fallen to such an extent that a threat of a strike by criminal defence barristers in the summer of 2005 was only averted by the promise of a review by Lord Carter of Coles. The Carter report proposed reducing the number of small solicitors' firms allowed to do criminal legal aid work and cutting the fees paid to the top end of the criminal bar, redistributing them to barristers doing 1–10 day cases in the Crown courts.[31] This does not seem likely to reverse the long-term pattern of decline, since criminal barristers will not even have the prospect of remunerative years as a QC to compensate for earlier penury.[32]

The ethics of lawyers in criminal matters is of fundamental importance because of the need to balance human and civil rights, that is, the rights of the individual and the protection of society. The struggle to find this balance is clearly played out in criminal

---

[26] Human Rights Act (1998), Art 5 (right to liberty and security).

[27] Human Rights Act (1998), Art 6 (fair trial), para 1.

[28] *Ibid*, para 3(c).

[29] Criminal Justice Act (2003), s 28 and Sch 2.

[30] Administration of Justice Act (1999), s 12.

[31] Government figures published prior to the review showed that in 2004–5 one barrister had been paid £1.18 million from legal aid and the next 10 highest made more than £600,000 each. Barristers at the lower end of the scale had not seen their rates rise since 1997. C Dyer, 'Shakeup in Legal Aid Will Put End to £1m-a-year Earnings', *The Guardian*, 10 February 2006, 16.

[32] Lord Carter noted England and Wales has the highest per capita spending on criminal legal aid in the world. Attributing this to payment by the hour, he proposed fixed fees for all except the most complex, where individual rates will be negotiated, and introducing more competition between lawyers.

advocacy, considered in chapter 19. The best-known professional ethical issue for the defence lawyer is the client who admits guilt to the lawyer but wants to plead 'not guilty'. Requiring the prosecution to prove their case is the proper response to this dilemma. It is quite consistent with the duty to the court for the defence to subject the prosecution case to intensive investigation and present a case consistent with the facts and the defendant's plea. The proper assessment of the facts increases the chances of correct verdicts and, where conviction results, leads to a sentence proportionate to the crime[33] and the surrounding circumstances, such as the conduct of the accused after the event. These advantages are considered to be worth the possibility that the guilty are occasionally not convicted.

The process of criminal law is subject to stringent procedural requirements, imposed mainly on prosecution lawyers. The decision to prosecute, for example, is taken according to criteria in the Code for Crown Prosecutors,[34] which imposes a two-stage test: whether the evidence offers a realistic prospect of conviction and, if so, whether the public interest requires a prosecution. On indictments and in some summary cases, both sides are under duties of openness laid out in the Criminal Procedure and Investigations Act 1996. Evidence detrimental to the prosecution case, including details of adverse witnesses, must be divulged to the defence, except where public interest immunity is confirmed by the court.[35] The accused must serve a defence statement setting out the nature of the defence, details of any alibi and those elements of the prosecution case that are contested.[36] A review of the criminal courts by Auld LJ favoured using conduct codes and disciplinary and costs sanctions to force defence lawyers to comply exactly with these requirements.[37] An area of ethical difficulty is plea bargaining, a process whereby a lighter sentence is accepted in return for a guilty plea and sanctioned by the judge before the plea is entered. The subject commands a significant ethical literature in the US, but the official position in the UK is that plea bargaining does not happen.[38] Courts can take into account the timing and circumstances when guilty pleas are entered in sentencing, but must state in open court the reasons for any discounted sentence.[39]

Numerous studies in both the US and the UK question the diligence and competence of criminal defence lawyers. One reason is disillusionment; lawyers find that their clients tend to be guilty and this corrodes their determination to construct a defence or set out to test the prosecution evidence.[40] McConville et al found that:

> Almost all our respondents came to see criminal defence practices as geared, in cooperation with the other elements of the system, towards the routine production of guilty pleas. A

---

[33] A Ashworth, 'Ethics and Criminal Justice' in R Cranston (ed), *Legal Ethics and Professional Responsibility* (Oxford, Clarendon Press, 1995) 146.

[34] Issued under s 10 of the Prosecution of Offences Act 1985.

[35] Criminal Procedure and Investigations Act (1996), s 3(a).

[36] Criminal Procedure and Investigations Act, s 5.

[37] Auld Report, above n 6, paras 115–84 and 194–205.

[38] In *R v Turner (Frank Richard) (No 1)* [1970] 2 QB 321, the Court of Appeal held that judges cannot indicate what sentence they have in mind, but may indicate that, regardless of what plea is entered, the sentence will take a particular form.

[39] Powers of Criminal Courts (Sentencing) Act 2000, s 152. Significant discounts on sentence are usually given for guilty pleas especially where made at the earliest opportunity. See further C Flood-Page and A Mackie, *Sentencing Practice: An Examination of Decisions in the Magistrates' Court in the Mid-1990s* (London, Home Office, 1998).

[40] See Flood-Page and Mackie, *ibid*, 137.

minority of them found this to be a source of injustice for clients and of disillusionment for themselves, given their earlier expectations of the defence solicitors' role in an adversarial system.[41]

Another factor could be the financial rewards in criminal defence, which may not attract the most able or motivated lawyers. Poor profitability may also explain discontinuous representation, whereby different staff are assigned to deal with different stages of a case. This must undermine the individual lawyer's commitment and sense of responsibility for a client, but a recent study discovered it to be quite common.[42] An ancillary problem to delay caused by inefficiency is tactical delay. Delay may cause a case to be dismissed, cause witnesses' nerves to fray or recollections to dim and dissipate the victim's commitment. All of these factors help the defendant, but are increasingly frowned upon. Auld also wanted the costs of pre-trial hearings necessitated by failure to comply with timetables to be followed by public reprimands and reporting of offending lawyers to the professional body and Legal Services Commission.[43]

Civil litigation

Lord Woolf's reform of civil litigation, represented in the Civil Procedure Rules 1998 (CPR), introduced in April 1999, sought a change in ethos for the system. It is important to understand the common elements of the old and the new processes so as to understand the strategic and ethical choices lawyers faced before and after the changes. The framework and timescales for conducting the different stages of civil litigation are provided by voluminous rules, laying down what must be done unless the court permits otherwise. Litigation begins with the court issuing proceedings brought by the claimant setting out details of the claim. After a defence is filed, both sides can seek further particulars or issue notices to admit facts. When the formal exchange of pleadings is complete, the parties provide lists of those documents that are or were in their possession that are likely to be relevant to the issue in question. Inspection and exchange of any documents that are not privileged follows. Completion of all these formal steps means that the case can be listed for trial. Automatic timetables and standard directions for the conduct of the cases govern more routine matters. The timetable of more complex cases may be interrupted by appearances at court where officials give 'directions' tailored to the circumstances of the case. Either way, the considerable lengths of time required to prepare a case allow lawyers the opportunity to deploy strategies and tactics. Litigation is expensive and out of the reach of most people's personal finances. Litigation strategies generally involve psychological pressure on the opponent, manipulating the key variables of unpredictability, delay and cost.

The allocation of costs is an important element in litigation strategy. The English system is that, at the court's discretion, the loser pays the winner for work necessarily performed. Costs are fixed, or assessed, by the court after the event, so that if the claimant's lawyer does

---

[41] *Ibid*, 71.

[42] M McConville, J Hodgson, L Bridges and A Pavlovic, *Standing Accused: The Organisation and Practices of Criminal Defence Lawyers in Britain* (Oxford, Clarendon Press, 1994) 41.

[43] Auld, above n 6, para 220.

more work than necessary, those costs may be disallowed. Similarly, the delaying defendant, forced only by the claimant's applications to comply with the rules, might have to pay more costs. The exception to the principle that the loser should pay the winner's costs arises when the defendant is willing to settle the claim but the claimant demands more money than is on offer. In this situation, the defendant can make a firm offer to settle or pay the sum into court.[44] If the claimant recovers less than that amount at trial, the court usually orders defendants to pay claimants' costs only up to the date of payment in, and claimants to pay their own and defendants' costs from that date. This substantially increases the risk of litigation for claimants, because the main expense of most actions is the trial stage, and they may be under pressure to avoid the risk and settle for less than their claim is worth. Conditional or 'no win, no fee agreements' impose on claimants' lawyers the risk of not succeeding in litigation[45] and is an additional incentive to win at all costs.

Different types of litigant have different tactical options. Certain kinds of defendant may consider declaring bankruptcy, but this possibility appeals to only a few with little to lose.[46] At the other end of the scale, instructing all the specialist lawyers in a field at different times, so that they cannot appear against you under conflict of interest rules, is an option available only to top corporations. The costs of legally aided clients are paid, win or lose, and their opponents are unlikely to recover costs against them. Litigants' circumstances therefore affect their attitude to risk. When one of the parties is a large organisation, no one person in the organisation stands to gain or lose from litigation and the personal risk to individuals is small. People in organisations are more likely to be litigation 'repeat players' and be untroubled by the process. Individuals, particularly those funding litigation themselves, are more likely to be risk averse, and anxious to avoid cost and trouble where possible.[47] This means that, in most situations, organisations are content to let litigation run its course while individuals want it to end. This creates pressure to settle on lawyers acting for individuals which does not affect those acting for organisations.

The cost, risk and annoyance of court proceedings are inevitable features of litigation. They are factors that can be used strategically by litigators, but can be difficult to control. Claims that are issued for an ulterior or malicious purpose are abuses of process. A party pursuing them is potentially in contempt of court, and lawyers knowingly issuing such claims are potentially in breach of their duty to the court. But while some ulterior purposes may be obvious—a claim for gambling debts when all of them were unlawful, for example[48]—unmeritorious claims are not always so easily identified, and outlawing them is difficult.[49] The court's inherent jurisdiction over behaviour is likely to be invoked and wasted costs orders made, but only in relatively extreme cases. Lawyers must be wary how they use the possibility of such sanctions, since threatening applications for wasted costs

---

[44] CPR pt 39.

[45] Courts and Legal Services Act 1990 as amended by the Access to Justice Act 1999, s 27.

[46] See RE Kagan, 'The Routinization of Debt Collection: An Essay on Social Change and Conflict in the Courts' (1984) 18 *Law and Society Review* 323.

[47] M Galanter, 'Law Abounding: Legalisation Around the North Atlantic' (1992) 55 *Modern Law Review* 1, 20.

[48] Gambling debts are irrecoverable for reasons of public policy. In *R v Weisz* [1951] 2 KB 611 a claim for an alleged gambling debt was issued so as to use that fact to cause embarrassment to the defendant.

[49] Lord Pearce said in *Rondel v Worsley* [1969] 1 AC 191, 275 that it would be deplorable, and injurious to the cab-rank rule, if lawyers were to be sanctioned for pursuing hopeless cases (cited in *Ridehalgh v Horsfield* by Bingham MR).

orders may itself be intimidation and improper. Alerting the other side that its conduct may have crossed the line is acceptable.[50] Nevertheless, the possibility that lawyer behaviour might be sanctioned is ever-present, and changes in the ethos of litigation bring new possibilities for penalties.

Litigation fields

Approximately half of all civil disputes involve damage to vehicles, divorce, accident or injury and unpaid debts.[51] The majority involve minor issues and ordinary people, and are settled. Litigation, when it occurs, is usually a prelude to negotiation; trials may occur because lawyers have miscalculated the risks or engaged in a strategy that misfires[52] rather than because of a point of principle. Outcomes in settled cases might be affected by the parties' relationship, funding arrangements and the incidence of costs, the availability of insurance or other means of offsetting liability for damages and costs, the distribution of authority to settle as between claimants and others (for example, insurers), and differences in success rates between fields.[53] A crucial ethical issue for a litigation system is the balance it seeks to achieve between trial and settlement. Prior to the Woolf reforms, a generally laissez-faire approach prevailed, with the ethos of litigation varying between fields. This can be illustrated by looking at two areas: personal injury, where lawyers were criticised for not being adversarial enough, and family, where they were criticised for being too adversarial.

Personal injury

Personal injury victims are numerous and many specialist firms practise in this area. It is generally held that personal injury victims have little control over their lawyers, whether or not the lawyers are specialists.[54] Over the years, there have been numerous concerns expressed about lawyers' incompetent handling of personal injury litigation and their manipulation of the system for their own advantage.[55] The conventional view used to be that

---

[50] *Orchard v South Eastern Electricity Board* [1987] QB 565.

[51] National Consumer Council and the BBC Law in Action Programme, *Seeking Civil Justice: A Survey of People's Needs and Experiences* (London, National Consumer Council, 1995) 15.

[52] SR Gross and KD Syverud, 'Getting to No: A Study of Settlement Negotiations and the Selection of Cases for Trial' (1991) 90 *Michigan Law Review* 319.

[53] Gross and Syverud found that success rates California superior court jury cases varied greatly between and within 'fields': 42.1% in road traffic cases based on negligence, 29.2% in medical negligence, 92% in employment cases and 71.4% in real estate cases, differences attributable to the factors determining which cases were brought to trial (*ibid*, 338).

[54] TM Swanson, 'A Review of the Civil Justice Review: Economic Theories Behind the Delay in Tort Litigation' [1990] *Current Legal Problems* 185, 202–4; DR Harris, M Maclean, H Genn, S Lloyd-Bostock, P Fenn, P Corfield and Y Brittan, *Compensation and Support for Illness and Injury* (Oxford, Clarendon Press, 1984) 124; H Genn, *Hard Bargaining: Out of Court Settlement in Personal Injury Actions* (1987) 7; DE Rosenthal, *Lawyer and Client: Who's in Charge* (New York, Russell Sage, 1974).

[55] *The Report of the Committee on Personal Injuries Litigation*, Cmnd 3691 (1968), the Winn Committee—firms underestimate complexity of personal injury work; *Report of the Personal Injuries Litigation Procedure Working Party* (The Cantley Report), Cmnd 7476 (1979)—problems of delay laid at door of inexperienced solicitors; *Report of the Royal Commission on Civil Liability and Compensation for Personal Injury* (The Pearson Report), Cmnd 7054 (1978); *Report of the Review Body on Civil Justice*, Cmnd 394 (1988)—personal injury litigation is a major cause of public

a claimant's lawyer should proceed as quickly as possible,[56] getting the case to court before the defendant made a payment in.[57] If the claimant's lawyers conceal the details of the claim until late in the day, accurate payment in is more difficult. The defendant's incentive to negotiate and avoid escalation of costs[58] is counterbalanced by the withdrawal of those victims without funding or the stomach for a long or expensive fight. In the 1980s, research criticised general practice solicitors 'dabbling' in personal injury work for being duped by defendants' delaying tactics, not preparing cases properly in expectation of settlement and settling for less than cases were worth.[59] Specialist firms, who were said to eschew negotiation and swiftly pursue litigation, were held up as paragons of virtue.[60]

When the Law Society established its Personal Injury Panel in the early 1990s,[61] applicants were required to be committed to 'the expeditious pursuit of proceedings and the readiness to go to trial if need be'.[62] Guidance notes sent out to prospective members of the panel by the Law Society asserted that:

> It is essential that personal injury personal specialists approach the majority of their personal injury cases on the basis that the case will reach trial and not be settled. Panel applicants are expected to demonstrate a commitment to take appropriate cases to a full hearing.[63]

This stance carried the implication that 'litigation first' was an ethical approach, not least because it required competence to implement. There was also a suspicion that the panel's validation of litigation as the primary means of dispute resolution was motivated by a degree of self-interest. The leading firms that dominated the panel were supporting an approach to litigation that would inevitably increase costs,[64] while 'kite marking' their own expertise and excluding non-members from access to clients referred by the Law Society's 'Accident Line' service.

Despite the Personal Injury Panel's endorsement and the advocacy of some specialist firms, it was doubtful that the 'litigation first' strategy was routinely employed by the

---

concern because delay saps the morale of plaintiffs and causes them to accept low sums. See also J Phillips and K Hawkins, 'Some Economic Aspects of the Bargaining Process: A Study of Personal Injury Claims' (1976) 39 *Modern Law Review* 497; Genn, *ibid*; M Joseph, *Lawyers Can Seriously Damage Your Health* (London, Michael Joseph, 1985).

[56] See also R James, 'Delay and Abuse of Process' (1997) 16 *Civil Justice Quarterly* 289.

[57] Swanson, above n 54, 198, note 24 and 200, note 13

[58] If a defendant thinks a claim is worth £25,000–30,000 it is cost effective to pay £30,000 now, when costs are £1,000, rather than £27,500 later, when costs are £10,000. Swanson, *ibid*, 197, note 24.

[59] Genn, above n 54, 166.

[60] S MaCaulay and E Walster, 'Legal Structures and Restoring Equity' (1971) 27 *Journal of Social Issues* 173; Genn, *ibid*, 97–123.

[61] Delay, incompetent claims handling and the risk that inexperienced solicitors would be exploited by experienced opponents were all cited as reasons for establishing the panel. It was noted that personal injury cases accounted for 10% (£17.8 million) of the total paid under the solicitors' indemnity fund in 1991. E Gilvarry, 'Council Backs PI Panel' (1992) 89/27 *The Law Society's Gazette*, 15 July 1992, 4.

[62] D Skidmore, *Drawing the Line: A Report on the Law Society's Personal Injury Panel* (1993), an explanatory note by the Personal Injury Panel Chief Assessor accompanying the applicant's questionnaire.

[63] The Law Society, *The Personal Injury Panel—Notes for Guidance* (London, The Law Society, undated). Applicants were required to have 'actively supervised at least sixty personal injury instructions in the five years prior to the application or at least thirty six personal injury instructions in the three years prior to application' (*Rules and Procedures for the Law Society's Personal Injury Panel*, undated).

[64] This issue is considered generally by P Cane, *Atiyah's Accidents Compensation and the Law* (London, , Butterworths, 1993); Genn, above n 54, 83–96.

majority of expert litigators[65] or, indeed, by insurance companies.[66] In fact, there was evidence from small studies that some adapted their strategy according to the type of claim.[67] They aimed to settle small-value claims, which comprised the vast majority of most personal injury litigators' caseloads. Insurance companies were happy to dispose of most of these quickly to keep costs low, even if liability was in doubt, once reputable lawyers had written a letter before action. Large claims were, however, a different matter. They were more likely to go to court, with interest awarded from the date proceedings were issued. It made sense to incur as many litigation costs as possible before the defendant made payment in to court. Expert litigators might depart from these rules occasionally. For example, where a particular insurance company had been unreasonable in the past, a claimant's solicitor might issue proceedings as early as possible and avoid negotiations. If, as seems likely, these patterns were common, experts determined which litigation strategy to use in a particular case, rather than assuming 'one size fits all'.

Family

Family disputes are another area where litigation strategy has ethical implications. In these proceedings, an aggressive adversarial approach might exacerbate tensions in the relationship between the parties. There may also be competing considerations, such as financial arrangements, the welfare of children and the desire of some divorcing couples to use litigation to avenge past wrongs by causing ex-partners suffering.[68] This gives rise to serious ethical considerations, such as separating financial and contact issues as far as possible. Unfortunately, the record of family lawyers has not always been exemplary. Until recently, many family lawyers approached the work in a spirit of confrontation. In the early 1990s, one specialist observed that opposing lawyer often acted 'as if war had broken out . . . you could not send your client their letters'.[69]

The current social and political consensus is that acrimonious divorce is in neither party's best interests, particularly when the welfare of any children of the family is an important criterion in many family matters. Although legislative policy has moved towards 'no fault' divorce,[70] making proceedings less fraught, scope for friction remains. During the 1990s, a transformation occurred in family work, largely as the result of the success of the

---

[65] Research into the conduct of asbestosis litigation found that expert plaintiff lawyers offered 'reasonable opposition', rather than fierce competition, so that they were able to give and receive the benefits of 'professional courtesy' from those defendants' representatives they dealt with regularly. R Dingwall, T Durkin and WLF Felstiner, 'Delay in Tort Cases: Critical Reflections on the Civil Justice Review' (1990) 9 *Civil Justice Quarterly* 353, 363.

[66] Lord Chancellor's Department, *Civil Justice Review: Personal Injury Litigation* (London, Lord Chancellor's Department, 1986) para 67.

[67] A Boon, 'Cooperation and Competition in Negotiation: The Handling of Civil Disputes and Transactions' (1994) 1 *International Journal of the Legal Profession* 109 and 'Ethic and Strategy in Personal Injury Litigation' (1995) 22 *Journal of Law and Society* 353.

[68] *Ibid*; see also RH Mnookin and L Kornhauser, 'Bargaining in the Shadow of the Law: The Case of Divorce' (1979) 88 *Yale Law Journal* 950.

[69] A Boon, 'Litigation Solicitors' in P Hassett and M Fitzgerald (eds), *Skills for Legal Functions II: Representation and Advice* (London, Institute of Advanced Legal Studies, 1992).

[70] The Divorce Reform Act 1969 introduced divorce based on a period of separation rather than behaviour (two years with both parties' consent and five if one party did not consent). It is still necessary to allege a matrimonial 'offence' in all other cases.

Solicitors' Family Law Association, now called Resolution, which was formed in order to promote constructive solutions to family breakdown.[71] Resolution's broad-based membership contradicts the view that family lawyers exacerbate disputes. In the late 1990s, the government promoted family mediation over the conventional negotiation and adjudication model, proposing that it be compulsory in divorce proceedings.[72] The last significant divorce legislation, the Family Law Act 1996,[73] was underscored by the government's belief that lawyers caused conflict and acrimony.

The Act originally proposed a regime in which parties were first dissuaded from divorce and then required to mediate,[74] and this over-reliance on conciliation and mediation at the expense of negotiation and adjudication was averted only by the strong advice of the Law Commission.[75] Mediation pilot projects had poor take-up,[76] with a significant minority of those going through the process evincing an even stronger inclination to see a solicitor.[77] Meanwhile, Eekelaar et al found little evidence that the behaviour of divorce solicitors conformed to official stereotypes.[78] The adversarial approach was certainly in the armoury of lawyers with a wealthy clientele, but the dominant ethos of publicly funded work in particular was like social work or general practice. The government tended to conclude that, because some cases are costly and slow, lawyers should be excluded and mediation promoted. Such solutions were misguided and contrary to the evidence[79] that divorce solicitors generally tried to diminish conflict between the parties.[80]

Litigation strategy

As has been noted previously, various civil litigation strategies are used in English courts. Some lawyers push their cases into court as quickly as they can, others use the escalating cost of litigation to create a better bargaining climate for negotiation and yet others try to settle cases quietly without litigation. Others use a variety of approaches, using litigation as a backdrop, albeit a necessary one, to the process of settlement. Is any approach more or less

---

[71] Resolution, arguably the lead body for divorce lawyers, was formed in 1982 by central London family law solicitors. The two Law Society family law panels adopt Resolution's code of practice.

[72] Based on the Law Commission Report, *The Ground for Divorce* (Law Commission No 192, 1990).

[73] The Act allowed parties to apply for divorce nine months (or 15 months where there are children) following an allegation of marriage breakdown by one party. Much of the Act has never been brought into force.

[74] The Act required that applicants for legal aid for divorce had to attend an 'information meeting', the underlying purpose of which was to dissuade parties from divorcing (J Eekelaar, M Maclean and S Beinart, *Family Lawyers: The Divorce Work of Solicitors* (Oxford, Hart Publishing, 2000) 3). Another innovation was a meeting with a mediator with a view to denying legal aid if the matter was deemed appropriate for mediation Family Law Act 1996, s 29. Legal aid is only available in divorce proceedings for ancillary relief (division of property, financial provision, children).

[75] See *The Ground for Divorce*, above n 72; Eekelaar *et al, ibid*, ch 1.

[76] A Ogus, M Jones-Lee, W Cole and P McCarthy, 'Evaluating Alternative Dispute Resolution: Measuring the Impact of Family Conciliation on Costs' (1990) 53 *Modern Law Review* 57, 59.

[77] *Home Office Supporting Families: A Consultation Document* (1998) paras 4.31–33; Lord Chancellor's Department, Information Meetings and Associated Provisions within the Family Law Act 1996: Summary of Research in Progress (1999), cited in Eekelaar *et al*, above n 75, 10.

[78] Eekelaar *et al, ibid*.

[79] *Ibid*, 28.

[80] The lawyers observed in the study were, however, members of Resolution (*ibid*, 32).

ethical than the others? Since a number of factors are in play, it is tempting to say that it depends on the circumstances and competing considerations of fairness. It is unfair to the client not to pursue a case expeditiously, but it is unfair to third parties to run up costs unnecessarily. There is a balance to be struck between competitive litigation strategies, like 'litigation first', and cooperative ones, like negotiation. Can a lawyer have a general strategy of litigation that ensures that cooperative and competitive behaviours are balanced and appropriate?

Game theory models strategic behaviour when 'two or more individuals interact and each individual's decision turns on what that individual expects the others to do'.[81] In a famous example, the 'prisoner's dilemma', two players decide whether to 'cooperate' or 'defect', with each ignorant of the other's choice,[82] points being awarding depending on the outcome.[83] In a one-off encounter in the prisoner's dilemma, or when the other player's propensity for defection is known, the rational decision, given the reward structure, is to defect.[84] Cooperation is the rational strategy when the game is repeated. This is because the pay-off structure rewards cooperation over the longer term. This proposition was comprehensively proven in a competition to find the best strategy for repeat playing the prisoner's dilemma, organised for computer programmers, mathematicians and gamers. Each entry played other programs 100 times.[85] The most successful strategy was called 'Tit for Tat'. Its strategy was simply to cooperate on the first move and then mirror the opponent's previous move, an approach that can be described as conditional cooperation.

Some key features of the strategy are worth emphasising. Tit for Tat does not randomly offer or return to cooperation; it requires that an opponent who first defects 'apologises' for defection by first returning to cooperation. Most other strategies are intelligent enough to realise that continuing defection is mutually assured destruction and return to cooperation. Translating 'Tit for Tat' into human behaviour suggests that people should begin relationships by being cooperative; they should punish uncooperative behaviour in equal measure; and they should return to cooperation if they receive an 'apology', provided that it offers future cooperative behaviour; this strategy should be open and transparent to the parties they are dealing with. It is held that this is as true of life as it is of litigation and, indeed, that the cooperation it elicits is the foundation of ethical behaviour.[86] The ethical problem for

---

[81] DG Baird, RH Gertner and RC Picker, *Game Theory and the Law* (Cambridge, MA, Harvard University Press, 1994) 1.

[82] The game represents a situation where two criminal accomplices kept apart (the prisoners) have to decide whether or not to talk to the authorities and implicate each other or remain silent and hope that their co-defendant does likewise. Their decisions are, therefore, to cooperate (ie with each other, by remaining silent) or to defect (ie to implicate their accomplice).

[83] The payoffs depend on the strategic decision taken and are numerical. If both cooperate they receive three points each. If one defects and the other does not, the defector gets five points and the cooperator nil. If they both defect, they get one point each. These pay-offs mirror the theoretical pay-offs of the bargaining model whereby cooperation is a proxy for integrative bargaining and defection a proxy for competitive bargaining. The total rewards for a cooperative approach is six points, albeit shared equally, whereas the total reward for mutual defection is only two. However, there is a massive pay-off for defection against a cooperating opponent, where the defector grabs five points, the highest possible individual score.

[84] This guarantees one point. There is no way of retrieving unreciprocated cooperation and, on an isolated occasion, there is no way of predicting how the other accused will react.

[85] R Axelrod, *The Evolution of Co-operation* (London, Penguin, 1984).

[86] M Ridley, *The Origins of Virtue* (Harmondsworth, Penguin, 1997) ch 3.

some lawyers is the adversarial system's demand for the aggressive pursuit of client's goals, particularly in litigation.

It is arguable that conditional cooperation is in the interests of clients generally because, by maintaining reasonable relations with insurers and other lawyers, litigators are able to settle appropriate cases speedily. The success of 'Tit for Tat' suggests that the routine use of 'litigation first' is unwise for litigators, particularly in fields requiring frequent contact with other lawyers or industry professionals like insurance representatives. A lawyer consistently 'defecting', by using 'litigation first', for example, must expect at least lack of trust. At worst, they may expect that their opponents will punish them if they can, by routine payment into court, for example. In theory, constantly facing such reprisals may undermine a litigator's ability to achieve the best results for future clients. In practice, cooperation is almost certainly the best strategy for settling large numbers of cases cheaply,[87] where sensible discussion usually leads to amicable settlement.

Lawyers employing conditional cooperation must ensure that their relationships with opponents do not become too 'cosy', but that is the essence of professionalism. The strategy calls for high-level strategic decision making and, because of this element of discretion, it is consistent with high traditions of professionalism. The ethical dilemma it courts is inconsistency with the adversarial ethos, under which duties are owed to clients in particular, not in general. Conditional cooperation is not designed to take advantage of any weakness or mistakes of the other side and is not, therefore, in the best interests of the client who would benefit. Lord Woolf helpfully pointed out that the overriding objective of the justice system is justice, implying the need to balance fairness to clients and to others. This tipped the ethical balance towards conditional cooperation. Woolf envisioned a new landscape for procedural justice, operating in the traditional adversarial context, in which people would be encouraged to start litigation 'only as a last resort'[88] and where litigation would be 'less adversarial and more cooperative'.[89]

The Woolf reforms

Lord Woolf's review of civil litigation aspired to a system understood by the public and available at reasonable cost.[90] He accepted that the existing system was costly and slow, and that lawyers exacerbated its faults by their behaviour.[91] In the High Court, for example, cases proceeded with only a bare outline of the claim established. Proceedings could be launched without the claimant's lawyer having fully investigated the claim, and weak cases could drag on in the vague hope of a 'nuisance payment'. Defendants' lawyers might delay, hoping that claimants would lose their nerve or be unable to meet their lawyer's requests for costs on

---

[87] Discussed by RJ Condlin, 'Bargaining in the Dark: The Normative Incoherence of Lawyer Dispute Bargaining Role' (1992) 51 *Maryland Law Review* 1, 57.

[88] *Access to Justice*, Final Reports to the Lord Chancellor on the Civil Justice System in England and Wales (London, Stationery Office, July 1996) 4, paras 8 and 9.

[89] *Ibid*, 5.

[90] *Access to Justice*, Interim and Final Reports to the Lord Chancellor on the Civil Justice System in England and Wales (London, Stationery Office, June 1995 and July 1996).

[91] Interim report (*ibid*) 7, 12 and 13.

account, or that witnesses would disappear before trial. Despite timetables for the various stages to be completed, there was often no pressure on either side to move swiftly, and delay was common and sometimes tactical. Piecemeal reforms had tried to increase efficiency and place tighter constraints on lawyers' discretion,[92] but Lord Woolf's brief was to examine the civil litigation system as a whole and expand access to justice without additional public expenditure.[93] His proposals, implemented in April 1999 with the new CPR, were radical by the standards of its predecessors, bringing together a host of ideas in a 'big bang'.[94]

The CPR increased the transparency of the system, starting with the simple step of insisting that claimants clearly state their case[95] and that defendants give reasons for denying liability.[96] Pre-action protocols force lawyers to disclose information early on, enabling defendants to value claims more accurately.[97] The CPR established timetables and mechanisms for information exchange, disclosure and agreeing a joint expert that, while not compulsory, could lead to costs penalties if not followed. The aim was to better inform parties before litigation, avoiding the cost of proceedings where settlement was possible and avoiding delay where it was not. The aim of promoting settlement was furthered by modifying the principle that costs follow the event except in exceptional circumstances. A new rule required that the court consider the conduct of the parties, their success in different parts of the case and offers to settle not complying with the rules on payment into court, in exercising the discretion to award costs.[98] The relevant conduct included the period before the litigation and covers the reasonableness of all parts of the claim and the manner in which it was pursued. A string of early cases established that aggressive litigants, those leaving 'no stone unturned' or those in any way acting unreasonably, faced costs sanctions.[99] Further, the court could take into account offers to settle made in the period before commencement of litigation in judgments on costs,[100] putting pressure on the claimant to settle at the earliest opportunity. While a payment into court under part 36 was normally required to put the claimant at risk on costs once proceedings were on foot, the courts proved willing to take into account other serious offers to settle.[101]

---

[92] Prior to the Courts and Legal Services Act 1990 there was a considerable overlap in jurisdiction of the High Court and the county courts. Lawyers often preferred the High Court because of its quicker procedures and generous fee scales. The Act placed responsibility on lawyers for assessing the suitability of the case for the venue, giving courts better oversight of the decision and the right to change the venue.

[93] Woolf Final Report, above n 89, 3, para 5 (and the 'substantial risk' that the existing system undermines 'our competitive position in relation to other jurisdictions').

[94] Using different court 'tracks' according to gravity and complexity was presaged by the small claims courts, created in 1973. Automatic directions existed in personal injury claims. The idea of more active case management by courts had been introduced by a practice direction in 1995.

[95] The court can strike out a case disclosing no reasonable grounds (CPR, r 3.4(2)a).

[96] Defendants must deny, admit or require proof of each allegation (CPR, r 16.5(1)(a)–(c)).

[97] Protocols followed consultation with representatives of the legal profession and related industries for personal injury, medical negligence and housing cases. Pre-action discovery had existed in personal injury, because plaintiffs sometimes needed information from the defendant in order to formulate their claim. Woolf favoured extending this to all cases, but the step has not actually been taken.

[98] CPR, r 44.3(4)(a)–(c).

[99] CPR, r 44.3(5) and see *Phonographic Performance Ltd v AEI Rediffusion Music Ltd* [1999] 2 All ER 299; *Firle Investments v Datapoint International Ltd* [2001] EWCA Civ 1106; *Mars UK Ltd v Teknowledge Ltd (No 2)* (1999) *The Times*, 8 July 1999.

[100] CPR, r 36.14.

[101] *Crouch v Kings Healthcare NHS Trust and Murry v Blackburn NHS Trust* [2004] All ER (D) 189 (Court of Appeal).

While procedural changes made aggressive litigation tactics less feasible, one of the key strategies of the new regime, judicial case management, shifted the responsibility for controlling bigger and more complex cases from lawyers to judges. Judges were to take a much more proactive role, forcing the pace of cases and facilitating settlement by encouraging mediation.[102] One of the most important principles introduced by the CPR was proportionality: matching procedures to the sums involved, the importance of the case, the complexity of the issues and the financial positions of the parties.[103] To this end, the court structure was reconfigured, with both sides completing an allocation questionnaire as soon as defence was filed so that the court could place cases on one of three tracks:[104] the small claims track was for cases valued at less than £5,000, a fast track for those valued between £5,000 and £15,000, and multi-track for cases valued over £15,000.[105]

Different venues and procedures governed each track. Fast-track cases could be dealt with in a county court or the High Court, as appropriate. The fast track incorporated fixed timetables, aimed at reducing the complexity, length and cost of proceedings, and a fixed cost regime. Once the case had been allocated to the small claims track or the fast track, the timetable was relentless and difficult to change, including a trial date fixed 30 weeks later. Trial hearings were kept to one day by expedients such as dispensing with openings by lawyers and having witness statements stand as evidence in chief. Experts could only be called at the court's discretion[106] and the order was likely to be that they be jointly appointed, except for multi-track cases.[107] Multi-track cases were to be heard in the High Court only and subject to individual case management by the judge.[108] Directions most suited to the particular case were made following allocation to the multi-track.

The ethics of civil litigation

The CPR swept away the previous system, and the aims of the civil litigation system were newly articulated. Dealing with cases justly was conceived as ensuring equality of the parties, saving expense, ensuring expedition and fairness, and allocating appropriate resources. Decisions must be just and predictable, litigants must be treated fairly, appropriate procedures must be provided and cases must be processed speedily.[109] An important goal was to change the litigation culture. The courts' responsibility to manage cases actively included, inter alia, encouraging the parties to cooperate in conducting the proceedings,[110] the parties and their representatives being under the duty of 'helping judges' with furthering the

---

[102] The allocation questionnaire allows parties to seek a month's stay of the operation of the timetable to allow for settlement efforts (CPR, r 1.4(2)(e)).

[103] Proportionality was reflected in fee scales but did not usually affect procedure. In over 40% of claims for £12,500 or less the costs exceeded the amount in dispute.

[104] CPR, rr 26.3 and 26.5.

[105] CPR, r 26.6.

[106] CPR, r 35.4.1.

[107] CPR, r 32.1 gives the court a general discretion to control evidence by deciding the issues requiring evidence, the nature of the evidence and the way it is placed before the court. Joint experts (see CPR, rr 35.7 and 35.8) owe an overriding duty to the court rather than the party paying their bill (CPR, r 35.3).

[108] CPR, r 29.

[109] CPR, r 1.1(2)

[110] CPR, r 1.4(2)(a).

overriding objective.[111] Contemporaneously, the right to conduct litigation was subject to duties to the court to act with independence in the interests of justice and to comply with the rules of conduct of the authorising body,[112] such duties to 'override any obligation which the person may have (otherwise than under the criminal law) if it is inconsistent with them'.

The courts went a considerable distance in construing the CPR in light of the 'overriding objective' of doing justice.[113] Litigants were less likely to be denied access to the courts for technical procedural breaches,[114] could be expected to help the other side correct technical errors[115] and could expect to be criticised for correspondence that might antagonise.[116] It was quickly established that parties could not be prevented from hiring expensive lawyers because their opponents could not afford to,[117] although the courts did show some interest in restraining the escalation of costs where an applicant showed that they had exercised restraint.[118] Following criticism of lawyers' behaviour by the BCCI working party interim report as 'unattractive', the Lord Chancellor, Lord Falconer, outlined plans to replace lawyers who delayed cases.[119]

The new CPR can be regarded as a success because it had an immediate and dramatic impact by reducing the workload of the High Court.[120] If the 'missing cases' were brought in a county court or settled because of the new protocols, Woolf would be further vindicated. The transparency enforced by pre-action protocols and part 36 offers were a constraint on 'litigation first' tactics and speculative actions, and may have led to more settlements before proceedings were issued. Reform can also have unforeseen negative consequences. Speeding up cases reduces time for preparation, favouring wealthy clients whose lawyers can mobilise resources quickly[121] and therefore potentially increasing inequality. The front-loading of preparation imposes investigation and disclosure costs, even on cases that might have settled without going to court.[122]

If, in some cases, the CPR reduced the quality of justice and increased cost, Lord Woolf was unrepentant. He argued that it is right to deter claimants who cannot muster the evidence to proceed, claiming that 'the courts should not be used merely as part of the tactical equipment of a macho lawyer'.[123] This suspicion of lawyers, the reason for interfering with the negotiation and adjudication system, and the control and discretion of lawyers also risked negative consequences. The costs regime virtually excludes lawyers from

---

[111] CPR, r 1.3.

[112] Administration of Justice Act 1999, s 42(2) amending s 28 of the Courts and Legal Services Act 1990 (rights to conduct litigation granted by an authorised body).

[113] *Totty v Snowden* [2002] 1 WLR 1384, [34].

[114] *Chilton v Surrey County Council* (1999) LTL 24/6/99.

[115] *Hertsmere Primary Care Trust v Estate of Rabindra-Anandh* (2005) *The Times* 25 April 2005.

[116] *King v Telegraph Group Ltd* (2004) *The Times*, 21 May 2004.

[117] *Maltez v Lewis* (1999) *The Times*, 4 May 1999.

[118] *McPhilemy v Times Newspapers Ltd* [1999] 3 All ER 775.

[119] If they acted for the defendants, the judge would report them to the Legal Services Commission, which could then ask the defendant to find another lawyer. N Goswami, 'Falconer: Tardy Litigators will be Fired', *The Lawyer*, 4 June 2007.

[120] A reduction in workload of up to 80%. R Musgrove, 'Unified Civil Jurisdiction' in *Civil Justice Council: Annual Report 2004*.

[121] C Glasser, 'Civil Procedure a Time for Change' in R Smith (ed), *Shaping the Future: New Directions in Legal Services* (London, Legal Action Group, 1995).

[122] M Zander, 'The Government's Plans on Civil Justice' (1999) 61 *Modern Law Review* 382.

[123] J Fleming, 'Trying Woolf', *Law Society Gazette*, 28 April 2000, 18.

the county courts, penalising those who need a lawyer to pursue a claim.[124] Reducing cost does not necessarily lead to increased usage[125] and may encourage a new range of undesirable tactics. The absence of potential costs penalties may encourage 'nuisance claims'. Small businesses may find that a regime of low costs encourages chronic debtors to defend claims.[126]

While litigation lawyers were seen both as a target of and an impediment to the Woolf reforms,[127] most welcomed the CPR,[128] perhaps too readily. Opponents of the reforms drew on the trenchant critique of mediation and settlement developed in the US.[129] The law can be distorted when companies can afford to lose money, setting precedents based on facts favourable to their businesses.[130] So-called 'irrational' claimants can counterbalance this distortion of the system if their cases are not funnelled into mediation.[131] Those with an eye on this bigger picture argued that it was a mistake of link justice with access and a bigger mistake to create a dispute resolution model aiming for quick and easy determinations, at the expense of a policy implementation model, where courts produce standards for governing society.[132] While proportionality is a rational principle, it is inevitable that compromises are made, both procedurally[133] and in the accuracy of judgments.[134] Other critics, like Mr Justice Lightman, argued that the reforms were too limited because the system could not be fixed. In any adversarial model, he argued, expense is inevitable. Lawyers must keep abreast of increasingly voluminous case law and analyse, collect and present evidence. The skill and training required ensures that the cost of civil litigation remains high.[135] The only solution was to implement the inquisitorial system, relying even more on the skill and training of judges rather than that of lawyers generally.

Attempts to deflect parties from litigation and establish other means of dispute resolution are not new. In the 1930s, in the US, the ABA Canons of Professional Ethics were hostile to litigation, providing that

> Whenever the controversy will admit of fair adjustment, the client should be advised to avoid or to end the litigation[136]

---

[124] R Smith, 'The Changing Motive of Legal Aid', in Smith, above n 121, 209.

[125] J Baldwin, *Monitoring the Rise of the Small Claims Limit: Litigant's Experiences of Different Forms of Adjudication* (London, Lord Chancellor's Department, 1997) 74.

[126] T Aldridge, 'Downside of Procedural Reform', *Solicitors Journal*, 29 November 1996, 1142.

[127] See generally, AAS Zuckerman and R Cranston (eds), *Reform of Civil Procedure: Essays on Access to Justice* (Oxford, Clarendon Press, 1995) and particularly AAS Zuckerman, 'Reform in the Shadow of Lawyers' Interests', 75.

[128] A MORI poll published in April 2000 showed that 80% of solicitors were happy with the CPR.

[129] See, eg O Fiss, 'Against Settlement' (1983) 93 *Yale Law Journal* 1073, 1076; D Barnhizer, 'The Virtue of Ordered Conflict: A Defense of the Adversary System' (2001) 79 *Nebraska Law Review;* and see further chapter 18.

[130] J Robins, 'Food for Thought', *The Lawyer*, 6 September 2004, 19.

[131] FB Cross, 'In Praise of Irrational Plaintiffs' (2000) 86 *Cornell Law Review* 1.

[132] N Armstrong, 'Making Tracks' in Zuckerman and Cranston, above n 127, 97; D O'Brien, 'Blood on the Tracks: The Woolf Report and Substantive Justice (1998) 3 *Contemporary Issues in Law* 17.

[133] R Thomas, 'A Code of Procedure for Small Claims: A Response to the Demand for Do-it-yourself Litigation' (1982) 1 *Civil Justice Quarterly* 52, discussing the small claims procedures of the County Courts and the extent to which they meet the demand for access to justice in relation to small claims.

[134] O' Brien, above n 132.

[135] Mr Justice Lightman, 'The Civil Justice System and the Legal Profession—The Challenges Ahead' (2003) 22 *Civil Justice Quarterly* 235.

[136] Canon 8 of the ABA's 1936 Code. See GC Hazard, 'The Future of Legal Ethics' (1991) 100 *Yale Law Journal* 1239.

and that

> It is unprofessional for a lawyer to volunteer advice to bring a lawsuit, except in rare cases
> where ties of blood, relationship or trust make it his duty to do so.[137]

The 1983 Model Rules of Professional Conduct abandoned these admonitions, imposing no
constraints on litigators beyond those imposed by the procedures for the conduct of
litigation.[138] This neutral stance, where no strategy of negotiation was encouraged or
discouraged, was formerly that of the English rules of court. The litigation strategy most
consistent with the new CPR appears to be conditional cooperation.

Justice reconceived

In many civil areas, conditional fee agreements are now the norm, and in personal injury they
may be regarded as a success. The exclusion from legal aid of a number of areas, including
business and consumer disputes and inheritance and probate, is more problematic,[139] raising
the political stakes of increasing access to justice by reducing the cost of litigation and
increasing the accessibility of courts. Citizens Advice Bureaux and Law Centres receive direct
and indirect support, mainly for civil legal work in areas of marginal interest to the legal
profession, such as welfare law.[140] The Woolf reforms opened up the wider question of the
potential of courts for achieving social justice as well as legal justice. No longer a question of
the thorough and fair resolution of a presented dispute, they hinted at the system's responsibility for unmet legal need, the 'justiciable cases' lying below the surface of the official
statistics. It is likely that many people with good cases in law do not know that they have a
good case, or do know but choose not to pursue it.[141]

Factors such as the educational background of potential claimants, their financial and
emotional resources, and the availability and type of advice all affect rates of claim. So, too,
does the type of case. For example, those with problems arising from employment, divorce
or separation, or residential property ownership are significantly more likely to seek advice
than those with money problems, landlord and tenant problems or consumer problems.[142]
The importance of the problem, its intractability and its impact on the prospective parties'
relationships with others are factors in seeking advice, and taking advice has a positive

---

[137] Canon 28 (*ibid*, 1262).

[138] *Ibid*, 1263. Although, in the context of litigation in the 1930s the rules could be seen to be an attempt to curtail
actions between the wealthy and business classes (*ibid*, 1256).

[139] T Goriely, P Das Gupta and R Bowles, *Breaking the Code: the Impact of Legal Aid Reforms on General Civil
Litigation* (London, Institute of Advanced Legal Studies, 2001).

[140] The first Law Centre was established in the UK in 1970. See National Consumer Council, *Ordinary Justice:
Legal Services and Courts in England and Wales: A Consumer View* (London, HMSO, 1989); M Galanter, 'Law
Abounding: Legalisation Around the North Atlantic' (1992) 55 *Modern Law Review* 1, 12; Lady Marre CBE, *A Time
for Change: Report on the Committee on the Future of the Legal Profession* (London, The General Council of the Bar,
The Law Society, 1988) ch 9.

[141] LF Felstiner, RL Abel and A Sarat, 'The Emergence and Transformation of Disputes: Naming, Blaming,
Claiming' (1980–1) 15 *Law & Society Review* 630.

[142] H Genn *Paths to Justice: What People Do and Think About Going to Law* (Oxford, Hart Publishing, 1999) 135.

impact on resolution.[143] Nevertheless, a large proportion of justiciable problems are dealt with without legal proceedings or other formal process.[144]

The relatively low level of recourse to courts is not the only blemish on contemporary society's claim to be just. Research into users and potential users of the civil justice system uncovered the fact that many claimants have ancillary problems, perhaps including legal claims, not currently dealt with by the courts.[145] Statistically, these problems form clusters varying according to geographical and demographic differences.[146] The four main problem clusters are:

1. Family problems, including domestic violence, divorce, relationship breakdown and disputes concerning children.
2. Homelessness, often linked with unfair police treatment and action taken against a respondent.
3. Medical negligence and mental health.
4. Consumer transactions, money and debt, employment, neighbours, rented housing, personal injury, owned housing, welfare benefits, thinking of taking legal action. Within this, there is a core cluster incorporating consumer, money and debt, neighbour and employment problems.[147]

Fewer than half of respondents reporting justiciable problems reported multiple problems, but around 73% of justiciable problems fell within one of the clusters. The demographic predictors for some clusters suggest that middle age is a reliable indicator for problem cluster 1, as being young is for clusters 2 and 4. Experiencing multiple problems in more than one cluster was rare.

The government is keen to understand problem clusters because of the link with social exclusion[148] and the potential to use legal services in building community capacity to tackle problems and renew neighbourhoods.[149] Effective points for advice and problem solving might prevent problems escalating and multiplying, assist the development of diagnostic tools for advisers and facilitate targeting of social programmes and public legal services. The underlying problem of school truancy, for example, may well stem from family breakdown, arising from health problems, in turn linked to unsafe housing or working conditions.[150] While dealing with such issues is not the usual role of the civil justice system, many of the problems that form clusters are presented there and it provides an existing network with good geographic distribution. Courts could become multi-agency centres dealing with wider

---

[143] *Ibid*, 252.

[144] About 8 out of 10 justiciable cases are resolved, successfully or unsuccessfully, in this way (*ibid*).

[145] *Ibid*.

[146] P Pleasence, H Genn, NJ Balmer, A Buck and A O'Grady, 'Causes of Action: First Findings of the LSRC Periodic Survey' (2003) 30 *Journal of Law and Society* 11.

[147] P Pleasence, NJ Balmer, A Buck, A O'Grady and H Genn, 'Multiple Justiciable Problems: Common Clusters and Their Social and Demographic Indicators' (2004) 1 *Journal of Empirical Legal Studies* 301.

[148] A 'shorthand term for what can happen when people or areas suffer from one or a combination of linked problems such as unemployment, poor skills, low incomes, poor housing, high crime environments, bad health and family breakdown' (*Legal and Advice Services: A Pathway to Regeneration* (DCA and Law Centres Federation) 7).

[149] *Ibid*, 34.

[150] *Ibid*, 33.

social issues rather than just legal disputes. This is perhaps a foretaste of the emergence of a comprehensive or transformative law movement, first identified in the US.

According to Daicoff, the transformative law movement reflects nine converging vectors: collaborative law, restorative justice, procedural justice, transformative mediation, therapeutic jurisprudence, problem-solving courts, preventative law, holistic justice and creative problem solving.[151] These movements intersect in two areas:

> First, they seek to optimise the well-being of the people involved in the legal matter by maximising their emotional health, the quality of their personal relationships, their moral development or their social integration. Second, they encourage the lawyer and client to focus on more than just the client's rights and duties (or the economic bottom line). This second feature is the 'rights plus' approach, which considers such factors as the client's wishes, goals, desires, needs, resources, emotions, relationships, values, morals and beliefs.[152]

Although lawyers are increasingly unwelcome in small claims, claimants are usually unconfident of pursuing remedies unaided.[153] If courts were to be pivotal in such a system, they should probably intersect with the Community Legal Service,[154] particularly advice services, but possibly with wider social services. Recent developments include initiatives such as duty solicitor schemes in County Courts and the award of a quality mark at three levels, information (libraries, job centres, GP surgeries), general help (Citizens Advice Bureaux) and specialist (solicitors, Law Centres). Lawyers working in the system could find their roles changing, with an expectation that they take a 'holistic' approach to the problems of clients, making themselves aware of the agencies and mechanisms capable of assisting their clients with their non-legal problems.

Conclusion

The popular image of adversarial justice is the barrister's confrontational courtroom manner and an expectation of competitiveness. The government's search for efficiency in the litigation system is justified by its role in promoting an effective economy and a respect for law, and by its investment through legal aid. The role of lawyers in litigation is adapting to new requirements for cooperation as the system changes to achieve the overriding objective of justice. The goal of justice has, however, been reconceived as a matter of access rather than as one of quality. One consequence is that the lawyers' concern with process is denigrated to pave the way for increased judicial control of proceedings. Procedures have been introduced to increase transparency and facilitate settlement. In the process, the ethical landscape has changed considerably, reducing the scope for lawyers to use procedure and delay to further clients' interests. It comes with new dispute resolution mechanisms, like mediation, as part of a strategy to make access to justice more community based, less formal and less

---

[151] S Daicoff, 'Resolution without Litigation: Are Courtrooms Battlegrounds for Losers?' (Oct/Nov 2003) 20 *GPSolo Magazine* (ABA General Practice and small firm section).

[152] *Ibid*, 2.

[153] The Law Society Strategic Research Unit, *Injury Victims' Experiences of Bringing a Lower Value Personal Injury Claim with the Benefit of Legal Advice and Representation* (London, The Law Society, 2006).

[154] The Community Legal Service is seen as a key element in tackling social exclusion (above n 148).

legalistic.[155] It is arguable that the new spirit of cooperation provides a better ethos for litigation, but the implicit tempering of the adversarial spirit affects the way that lawyers interpret their role and the ethical obligations they are under. This also affects the way lawyers approach the key litigation tasks of negotiation and advocacy and respond to mediation in their mainstream work.

---

[155] SE Merry, 'The Social Organisation of Mediation in Nonindustrial Societies: Implications for Informal Community Justice in America' in RL Abel (ed), *The Politics of Informal Justice, Volume 2: Comparative Studies* (New York, Academic Press, 1982) 17.

18

NEGOTIATION

When lawyers fall out! It would make a great ITV series. You'd see CCTV coverage of them hitting each other viciously with their pink-ribboned 'bundles' before going back to the robing room for a laugh and a smoke. That's the way I feel about Tony Blair and Michael Howard. I picture them slapping each other on the back in private, having long forgotten whose client had just gone down for 15 years.[1]

Introduction

Negotiation, in ordinary speech, is a process of seeking agreement by discussion. The form of legal negotiation differs considerably according to context. In commercial matters, the terms of agreement, from the sale of goods to the transfer of companies, are agreed through negotiation. In conveyancing, lawyers must agree dates for exchange of contracts or completion of the transaction. A matter may be settled by a single telephone call, or follow intermittent exchanges or uninterrupted discussions lasting several days. It may be based on a standard contract or follow years of formal and informal information exchange. The agreement may be bounded by well-established conventions or be completely novel.[2] Negotiating deals of various kinds is a central part of most lawyers' work, in the contexts of both transactions (non-contentious proceedings) and disputes (contentious proceedings).[3] In civil actions, negotiation, rather than adjudication, determines the outcome in the majority of cases. Unlike advocacy, legal negotiation usually occurs in private, unmonitored by the court. Even clients sometimes are unsure of what happened when their lawyers met. In no other area of legal representation is the conduct of lawyers as important to clients or the ethics of lawyers more tested and difficult to verify.

Despite the practical importance of negotiation to lawyers, it is relatively unregulated. No rules of conduct for either the bar or solicitors explicitly govern negotiation, although some, such as obligations to treat third parties fairly, and relevant professional virtues, like honesty,

---

[1] S Hoggart, 'Grandest Grandee Sets Gold Standard for Rage', *The Guardian*, 29 April 2004, 2.

[2] The word 'negotiation' sometimes describes a broad process including all interactions between parties. Hence, Galanter describes the process of litigation and settlement as 'litigotiation': M Galanter, 'Worlds of Deals: Using Negotiation to Teach about Legal Process' (1984) 34 *Journal of Legal Education* 268. Bargaining 'generally describes a narrower process including attempts to reach agreement, face to face': DA Lax and JK Sebenius, *The Manager as Negotiator: Bargaining for Cooperation and Competitive Gain* (New York, Free Press, 1986). For simplicity we distinguish here between 'litigation' and 'bargaining'.

[3] See generally on this distinction DG Gifford, *Legal Negotiation: Theory and Applications* (St Paul, MN, West Publishing, 1989) 38; MA Eisenburg, 'Private Ordering through Negotiation: Dispute Settlement and Rulemaking' (1976) 89 *Harvard Law Review* 637.

frankness and integrity, must apply. Yet, even where such requirements exist as general principles of conduct for lawyers, it is not clear whether they apply to negotiation. Whereas other important activities—litigation and advocacy, for example—are subject to sophisticated rules of procedure, the 'unwritten rules' of negotiation are intuitive and obtuse. Add to this the fact that most negotiation takes place in private without formal reporting and it seems likely that ethical norms are 'violated with . . . confidence that there will be no discovery and no punishment'.[4] This may be deliberate so that lawyers can, invoking Donald Schon's famous metaphor, descend into 'the swamp' of practice and progress the messy business of solving client conflicts in the real world. With the attenuation of the adversarial ethic in litigation generally, there is an argument that negotiation should be invested with norms of fairness in the public interest. As part of the litigation process, it is subject to the litigator's duty to the court to act with independence in the interests of justice and comply with the rules of conduct of their professional body.[5]

Theories of negotiation

A voluminous literature on the theory of dispute bargaining[6] suggests that, while certain patterns may be universal[7] in both transactions and disputes, the difference between distributive and integrative approaches is fundamental.[8] Distributive approaches assume a fixed resource: a gain for one side implies a loss for the other. Integrative approaches seek, to a greater or lesser degree, to satisfy both parties' interests. Despite the wide range of contexts in which negotiation takes place, there are said to be only two kinds of negotiating problem, reflecting the above approaches. The first is a problem of distribution. This may involve the allocation of rights to a resource, such as a commodity or company, or settling the price of something, such as the value of a legal claim for compensation. In this kind of problem the resource is usually fixed or finite; more for one party means less for the other. There is, ultimately or relatively, a winner and a loser, a situation sometimes called a 'zero sum' negotiation.

The other kind of negotiation problem may have more integrative potential, allowing exploration of the possibility of meeting needs in ways that do not require distribution

---

[4] CB Craver, *Effective Legal Negotiation and Settlement* (Charlottesville, VA, Michie, 1993).

[5] See Courts and Legal Services Act 1990, s 28(2A) (rights to conduct litigation) as amended by the Access to Justice Act (1999), s 42; see also chapter 17.

[6] Summaries of much of the theoretical work can be found in GT Lowenthal, 'A General Theory of Negotiation Process, Strategy and Behaviour' (1982) 31 *Kansas Law Review* 69; C Menkel-Meadow, 'Toward Another View of Legal Negotiation: The Structure of Problem Solving' (1984) 31 *UCLA Law Review* 754. For criticisms of the theory applied to practice, see RJ Condlin, 'Cases on Both Sides: Patterns of Argument in Legal Dispute-Negotiation' (1985) 44 *Maryland Law Review* 65. Empirical work includes G Williams, *Legal Negotiation and Settlement* (St Paul, MN, West Publishing, 1983); SR Gross and KD Syverud, "Getting to No: A Study of Settlement Negotiations and the Selection of Cases for Trial" (1991) 90 *Michigan Law Review* 319; M Heumann and JM Hyman, 'Negotiation Methods and Litigation Settlement in New Jersey: "You Can't Always Get What You Want"' (1997) 12 *Ohio State Journal on Dispute Resolution* 253.

[7] P Gulliver, *Disputes and Negotiations: A Cross-cultural Perspective* (New York, Academic Press, 1979).

[8] Gifford, above n 3. See also HL Ross, *Settled Out of Court: the Social Process of Insurance Claims Adjustment* (Chicago, IL, Aldine, 1970).

between the parties to the negotiation. An 'integrative solution' is one that allows both parties to meet their needs without cost.

These different kinds of negotiating problems suit different processes. For example, if the problem is distributive, the outcome is likely to reflect the aspirations of the negotiators, which may overlap to create a 'settlement zone'. Since neither side knows the other side's settlement zone, one tactic is to create a narrow range of possible settlement; demand a large share of the fixed resource and refuse to compromise. Whether or not such a negotiator is successful in getting that share depends on the relative strength of the parties' bargaining positions. If the problem is susceptible to integrative solutions, however, success depends on how well the potential of the situation is explored and the range of possible solutions revealed.

If the nature of a problem is unclear, there is a risk of using the wrong approach to resolving it. This proposition is often illustrated by the tale of two children arguing over the last orange in the fruit bowl. Neither is prepared to give it up and their argument brings the intervention of a wise adult, who quickly establishes that one child wants the sections of the orange to eat while the other wants the skin as a cake ingredient; both can have exactly what they want. A problem that the children interpreted as distributional was susceptible to an integrative solution. The reason that the solution was obscure to the children was because their competitiveness obscured the possibilities offered by a problem-solving approach based on needs analysis and creative problem solving. Legal problems are seldom susceptible to such a neat solution.

Many legal negotiations have both distributional and integrative features. If, for example, a solicitor is considering joining a firm, the type of work he or she will do and the kind of experience he or she will get are important, and will perhaps play a greater role in the negotiation than higher pay. How flexible the firm could be on these issues may be unexplored. Sometimes distributive issues dominate negotiations and obscure attention to needs and integrative potential. Even where interests may appear to be opposed it may be possible to improve outcomes by understanding the different values that each party places on the subject matter.[9] For integrative situations a 'problem-solving' orientation is preferable. The focus is on identifying the parties' underlying needs and objectives, finding ways to meet those needs directly and, whether or not this is possible, expanding the resources available to add value.

If the exact parameters of legal negotiation are unclear, there must be doubt as to the best approach in any particular situation. Williams identifies two styles of bargaining used in legal negotiation: competitive and cooperative. Cooperative approaches are consistent with both distributional and integrative strategies, but a competitive approach is suited only to problems of distribution. Cooperative negotiators seek 'fair' agreements and 'communicate a sense of shared interests, values and attitudes using rational logical persuasion as a means of cooperation'.[10] The competitive or 'adversarial' style is characterised by the pursuit of one-sided gains and attempts to dominate the negotiating relationship. Condlin observes that:

---

[9] Menkel-Meadow, above n 6, 795.
[10] Williams, above n 6, 53.

cooperative argument consists of non-coercive rational analysis in which the objective is to teach another about the truth of one's substantive claims. This effort stops when the listener understands, or when the claims have been shown to be false . . . Competitive argument consists of rhetorical psychological manoeuvring designed to coerce an adversary, sometimes subtly and sometimes not, into deferring to one's view when, if fully informed he would not or should not. The objective is manipulation not understanding. Efforts to persuade stop when the adversary agrees to do as one wishes.[11]

The cooperative negotiator seeks to build a shared sense of interests, values and attitudes, using logical persuasion to reach an agreement fair to both sides.[12] Small concessions are offered in order to build trust and, realising that reconciliation of fiercely opposed positions demands compromise, to seek a reasonable settlement.

Given the different orientations of competitive and cooperative negotiators, the prospects of success in a simple distributive negotiation favour the competitive negotiator: the lion's share of a fixed resource is likely to go to the person making extreme demands and few, if any, concessions.[13] Since cooperative negotiators seek a fair settlement, their 'settlement zone' lies between fair settlement and the competitive negotiator's extreme demands. While a competitive negotiator is more likely to get the best of a distributive argument, the conclusion that lawyers should always use competitive negotiation is too simplistic. Competitive bargaining tends to have fundamental weaknesses as a process.

While competitive and cooperative negotiators tend to proceed by 'positional' bargaining, they do so with very different orientations towards settlement. At the extreme, competitive negotiators pretend that they are indifferent to settlement. To the extent that they appear willing to consider it, they demand an unrealistic share of the distribution. They make few offers or counter-offers, and may even deliver a 'take it or leave it' ultimatum. Negotiators of this type run a very high risk that the negotiation will break down. They also miss the opportunity to explore the integrative potential of the situation. If, for example, the parties foresee a long-term business or personal relationship, a focus on issues of distribution may impede exploration of other issues, including how their long-term relationship could be made to work better. Maximising integrative potential is achieved by a problem-solving approach in which basic, underlying interests are identified, understood and explored, and creative solutions to meeting these needs are proposed and tested. This process is best conducted in a constructive spirit and a cooperative approach, enabling the parties to identify the best interests of the parties and the optimum deployment of their resources and capabilities to meet those needs.[14]

Fisher and Ury popularised a method of negotiation using cooperative and integrative approaches which they claim is resistant to the pressure exerted by competitive negotiators.

---

[11] See Condlin, above n 6.

[12] Williams, above n 6, 53. It is possible to use such a strategy with positional bargaining, but its effectiveness against a competitive approach is questionable.

[13] Rigid commitments at or near the other side's minimum acceptable settlement point is a basic tenet of competitive negotiation and the discovery of that point is the fundamental aim of competitive strategy. See GT Lowenthal, 'A General Theory of Negotiation Process Strategy and Behaviour' (1982) 31 *Kansas Law Review* 69. Condlin, above n 6, argues that taking 'positions' is common to all negotiation, and the only objection relates to the manner in which positions are advanced. However, differences in the nature of positions, and the stage at which they are adopted, also indicate strategy.

[14] Menkel-Meadow, above n 6.

'Principled negotiation' assumes that the aim of negotiation is a fair and reasonable agreement, efficient in expression and operation, and improving, or at least not harming, any continuing relationship between the parties.[15] It focuses on interests, rather than positions, seeks creative solutions, resolves distributive problems by identifying appropriate objective criteria and reduces the interpersonal friction which sometimes accompanies competitive approaches. It builds on the cooperative style, encouraging attention to long-term relationships between parties. It advocates never playing the 'positional game' favoured by competitive negotiators by always insisting on the use of objective criteria to resolve distributive problems. By exploring the parties' interests, the principled negotiator may find unexpected ways of satisfying them. If one party values early payment, it may be that this can be arranged, albeit at the cost of something he values less. In addition to crafting low-cost solutions to identified needs, exploring interests also facilitates 'expanding the pie'. A clearer understanding of the other side's interests may help in identifying offers we can make to them which are of value to them and no cost to us—for example, where one side can provide the other with valuable marketing or promotional opportunities without incurring extra cost. If both sides approach a negotiation in this spirit, agreement is more likely. Both negotiators recognise an obligation to consider the other side's interests and to produce an agreement maximising the advantages of the interaction for both sides.

Proponents of principled negotiation argue that it offers superior outcomes to a competitive, distributional one.[16] This seems unlikely, at least theoretically. The best outcome possible for a party, at least in a situation where there is a simple distribution of resources, is more likely to be achieved by a competitive strategy with high demands and little movement towards the initial offer. Therefore, it may be argued that a competitive approach and positional bargaining trumps principled negotiation as a strategy of choice for lawyers because it serves their client's best interests in achieving the best possible distribution of resources. The theory that the obligation to pursue their client's best interests requires a consistently competitive approach must, however, be qualified by the theoretical insights drawn from game theory, previously considered in the chapter on litigation.

Just as the idea of conditional cooperation can be translated to litigation strategy, it can be applied to negotiation. First, be 'nice'; never defect first. Second, be provocable; do not suffer betrayal of trust without reprisal. Third, forgive; return to cooperation when the other side indicates a willingness to do so. Finally, be transparent; do not conceal or be unpredictable. Conditional cooperation appears to be a good fit with principled negotiation. It is unlikely that lawyer negotiators would tolerate 'hard bargaining' in those they deal with repeatedly without devising strategies to counteract it. If a negotiator continued to make unreasonable demands, their opponents would probably refuse to enter negotiation or perhaps refuse to continue the process.

---

[15] R Fisher, W Ury and B Patton, *Getting to Yes: Negotiating Agreement Without Giving In* (London, Century Business, 2nd edn, 1992).

[16] R Fisher, 'Fisher's Response to Jim White' [1984] *Journal of Legal Education* 120, commenting on criticisms of 'Getting to Yes', says 'Students have now taught me that there are categories of negotiations where positional bargaining is the best way to proceed. On single issue negotiations among strangers where the transaction costs of exploring interests would be high and where each side is protected by competitive opportunities, haggling over positions may work better than joint problem solving. A typical case would be negotiating a sale on the New York Stock Exchange.'

The theoretical advantages of integrative bargaining and the implications of game theory for strategic choices in negotiation make a powerful case for principled negotiation as the negotiation approach most consistent with the ethical commitments to honesty and integrity. Principled negotiation also promotes core ethical principles, such as promoting individual autonomy, beneficence, non-maleficence and justice.[17] By seeking to meet people's needs, principled negotiation respects individual autonomy; by attempting the expand the 'negotiating pie', it supports beneficence; by not taking advantage of the other side, it respects the principle of non-maleficence; by identifying objective criteria for resolving distributional issues, it seeks to do justice. The proposition that principled negotiation best fits with the ethical obligations of lawyers to act with integrity in professional life is subject to an important qualification. Lawyers are obliged to pursue their client's best interests. It can be argued that the cooperative style at the core of principled negotiation, with its pursuit of compromise, is inconsistent with such an obligation. Therefore, while recognising that the theory offers some useful insight into negotiation, it is necessary to see how it translates to practical legal contexts.

Theory into action

Despite the fact that principled negotiation seems to offer lawyers the best prospect of meeting their ethical obligations, research suggests that lawyers tend not to use it. An overview of research in the US[18] and the UK[19] suggests that legal negotiation is usually a routine activity, conducted over the telephone, using a positional process[20] and at fairly 'low intensity'.[21] Cultural factors are the most likely explanation for this commonality. Positional approaches are easy and familiar; a 'market place' haggle is a recognised way of transacting business. What is noticeable, however, is that, although positional, the exchange is often cooperative rather than competitive[22] and unlikely to be allied to a problem-solving approach, or to have other features of principled negotiation.[23] Gifford reasons that lawyers entering a negotiation first decide whether to be competitive and, if this approach is rejected, then consider whether to use a cooperative approach or an integrative one.[24] The chosen strategy may then change depending on the approach of the other side. Some contextual factors, such as lack of competence in the negotiator, the high complexity of cases or the lack of authority of either party to negotiate, may constrain the choice of strategy.

---

[17] TL Beauchamp and JF Childress, *Principles of Biomedical Ethics* (New York, Oxford University Press, 5th edn, 2001).

[18] M Galanter, 'The Federal Rules and the Quality of Settlements: A Comment on Rosenberg's, The Federal Rules of Civil Procedure in Action' (1989) *University of Pennsylvania Law Review* 2231, 2236.

[19] M Murch, 'The Role of Solicitors in Divorce Proceedings' (1977) 40 *Modern Law Review* 625 for solicitors and J Morison and P Leith, *The Barrister's World and the Nature of Law* (Milton Keynes, Open University Press, 1992).

[20] A Boon, 'Competition and Cooperation in the Handling of Disputes and Transactions' [1994] *International Journal of the Legal Profession* 109.

[21] Menkel-Meadow, above n 6.

[22] Williams, above n 6; Morison and Leith, above n 19, 121.

[23] Heumann and Hyman, above n 6, found that US litigation lawyers used positional bargaining in 71% of cases and a 'problem solving' approach in only 16% of cases.

[24] DG Gifford, 'A Context-based Theory of Strategy Selection in Legal Negotiation' (1985) 46 *Ohio State Law Journal* 41.

Many of the accounts of bargaining by lawyers suggest that the type of legal negotiation has a big impact on bargaining strategy. Positional bargaining is buttressed in some areas of work by the use of standard form contracts, which reduce the scope of negotiation. It can also act as a cover for incompetence, such as lack of familiarity with the file. An example of this is a 'war story' told by a practitioner about when he was a novice. His supervising partner instructed him that nothing in the client's standard form agreement could be changed, and he concluded a deal on the terms of the agreement although he understood hardly any of its contents. He achieved this by responding 'it's not negotiable' to every proposal by the other side.[25] The use of standard form contracts in a particular area of work quickly creates expectations and reduces the scope for innovation and change. Gifford notes that claiming lack of authority to shift an offer is a tactic of competitive bargaining often used by negotiators acting on behalf of insurance companies. This severely limits the potential for integrative bargaining.[26]

Another factor supporting positional bargaining is the sheer scale and complexity of the issues.[27] Sale of companies is a case in point. A solicitor may be negotiating in a team of 20, some of whom come from another firm, each with responsibility for part of the deal. A participant lawyer might contribute a specialist input to the negotiation often unaware of what constraints the company operated under or, indeed, of anything about their business. An employment and pension practitioner explained that his instructions were limited, that he would simply be told:

> You can let go of everything else provided this stays in; its horsetrading. You don't really explore the needs of the other side . . . The client is saying 'This is what we want—get on and do it' . . . If you kept calling up saying 'this is where we are, what do you think?' they'd soon get fed up.[28]

While contextual factors may change considerably between areas of work, some factors are consistent between areas of work. In contentious business, an important factor is the background of litigation and the incidence of costs. Avoidance of the costs of trial is a powerful incentive to settle, particularly as the loser ordinarily shoulders the whole costs burden.

Relationship pressures on lawyers are another piece of the legal negotiation jigsaw. Lawyers specialising on opposite sides of the same area of work may develop a friendly relationship that they may prefer not to damage by hostile negotiations. Research on plea-bargaining criminal cases[29] and personal injury settlement[30] in the US found a strong

---

[25] Above n 20.

[26] Gifford, above n 24.

[27] For work on the growth of litigation complexity, see PH Lindblom and GD Watson, 'Complex Litigation—a Comparative Perspective' (1993) 12 *Civil Justice Quarterly* 33.

[28] Above n 20.

[29] Plea bargaining, arrangements where defendants negotiate a discount on sentence for a guilty plea, are frowned on in the UK (see chapter 17). Sudnow's US research paints a dismal picture of public defenders' conduct of plea bargaining (not wanting trials, not fighting to win), arguing that plea bargaining should be restricted to 'normal crimes': D Sudnow, 'Normal Crimes: Sociological Features of the Penal Code in the Public Defender's Office' (1965) 12 *Social Problems* 255; see also AS Blumberg, 'The Practice of Law as Confidence Game: Organizational Cooptation of a Profession' (1967) 1(2) *Law and Society Review* 15; M Heumann, 'A Note on Plea Bargaining and Case Pressure' (1975) 9 *Law and Society Review* 515.

[30] See, eg Ross, above n 8.

tendency for defence lawyers and plaintiff lawyers to value their relationship with prosecutors or insurance company representatives over those with their clients. Where
negotiation takes place 'in the shadow of the law', as in divorce and personal injury work, it
is natural that the lawyers' negotiations should rehearse the evidence, arguments and applicable law. Ultimately, however, the rationales of the lawyer as advocate and the lawyer as
negotiator are different. The duty of the advocate is to advance the client's case within the
limits of the law. For the negotiator, trial outcome is only one of a number of factors to be
considered. The duty of the negotiator is to achieve a settlement that reflects the client's
preferences in terms of substantive outcome, cost and timing. The relevance of these factors
depends on the client, the area of work and the circumstances of the particular case.

Negotiation is the primary means of settling personal injury litigation. The principle
focus of bargaining is monetary and, although there may be issues such as the type or
timing of payments,[31] there are no obvious integrative features in the bargaining situation.
In the bulk of personal injury litigation—motor accidents and accidents at work, for
example—insurers indemnify the defendant, minimising the impact on any continuing
relationship between the parties. Despite the large sums sometimes at issue, research
suggests that personal injury bargaining is relatively crude[32] 'horse trading'.[33] The use of
aggressive litigation tactics is a typical 'hard bargaining' tactic designed to elicit offers and
stop the escalation of costs. Family conflict offers legal negotiators very different challenges
from personal injury cases. In divorce proceedings, lawyers may have to deal with the
parties' bitterness and resentment, and sometimes grief, while distributing matrimonial
property and future income and dealing with access to children. The different impact of
costs may also play a part. Costs are rarely awarded in divorce cases, and even the successful
legally aided have to face the statutory charge. This produces strong financial incentives to
settle to limit reduction of the matrimonial pot.

The abandonment of government plans to marginalise lawyers in divorce proceedings,
because they were thought to ferment conflict and acrimony, has been rare victory for
lawyers in recent years. Lewis identified a number of assumptions reflected in the consultation paper and the White Paper published before the 1996 Act.[34] These include the belief
that lawyers geared negotiation towards achieving the best deal and increased tension and
conflict between parties; that communication between lawyers and clients is distorted and
causes anger in the other party; and that lawyers disrupt mediated agreements. He found
that the research evidence contradicted this, with many, though not all, divorce solicitors
doing a good job in difficult circumstances. Eekelaar et al noted that, although successive
governments have continued to base family policies on the belief that mediation offers
better solutions than the conventional negotiation and adjudication model, extensive
consideration of the practice of divorce solicitors found little evidence that their behaviour
is confrontational or exacerbates conflict in family cases.[35]

---

[31] Eg a structured settlement.

[32] See H Genn, *Hard Bargaining: Out of Court Settlement in Personal Injury Actions* (Oxford, Clarendon Press,
1987) 134.

[33] Ross, above n 8 (but see Fisher *et al*, above n 15 and Menkel-Meadow, above n 6).

[34] P Lewis, *Assumptions about Lawyers in Policy Statements: A Survey of Relevant Research* (Lord Chancellor's
Department, 2000). Note that much of the 1996 Act on divorce never came into force.

[35] J Eekelaar, M Maclean and S Beinart, *Family Lawyers: The Divorce Work of Solicitors* (Oxford, Hart Publishing, 2000).

Lawyers who think that their client's best interests are not served by conflict may first have to convince the client that this is so. Perhaps that is why Sarat and Felstiner's study of divorce lawyers in the US found that most tried to manage their client's perceptions and expectations, laying the foundation for their acceptance of settlement terms.[36] Divorce solicitors also raise or deflate their client's expectations, according to their view of what the law offered.[37] Ingleby noted that divorce solicitors rarely challenged their client's preferences for outcomes and sought early settlement when possible. By doing so, they controlled the decision making in cases, managed caseloads more effectively and maintained collegial relations with other solicitors.[38] They also realised that settlement was more easily achieved before litigation and believed that consensual agreements had a better chance of enduring. While Ingleby found that divorce lawyers used the twin tracks of litigation and negotiation, he did not record a single case of the financial settlement being decided by the judge. Davis's research found that, leaving aside consent orders that are approved by judges to prevent the possibility of future applications for variation, less than 5% of divorce cases are adjudicated.[39]

The family lawyers' group, Resolution, publishes a code of practice instructing members to

encourage the attitude that a family dispute s not a contest in which there is a winner and a loser, but rather that it is a search for fair solutions.[40]

The code states:

You should encourage your client to see the advantages to the family of a constructive and non-confrontational approach as a way of resolving differences. You should advise, negotiate and conduct matters so as to help the family members settle their differences as quickly as possible and reach agreement.[41]

Although many family matters do not come to court, this is an area in which litigation still offers the final recourse. Yet the code tells solicitors to 'avoid using words or phrases that suggest or cause a dispute when there is no serious dispute'.[42] Eekelaar *et al* found that most of the negotiation in their sample was principled,[43] although it met this definition only by virtue of seeking objective criteria, rather than by being integrative. Nevertheless, they concluded that, with regard to the sums in issue, the outcomes and the costs, 'the way the legal process handles these matters is broadly satisfactory from the point of view of the

---

[36] A Sarat and WLF Felstiner, 'Law and Strategy in the Divorce Lawyer's Office' (1986) 20 *Law and Society Review* 93. See also J Griffiths, 'What Do Dutch Lawyers Actually Do in Divorce Cases?' (1986) 20 *Law and Society Review* 135.

[37] Above n 35.

[38] R Ingleby, *Solicitors and Divorce* (Oxford University Press, 1992).

[39] G Davis, J Pearce, R Bird, H Woodward and C Wallace, *Ancillary Relief Outcomes: A Pilot Study for the Lord Chancellor's Department* (Bristol, University of Bristol, 1999).

[40] Resolution Code of Practice, s 4. Interestingly, Resolution's introduction also use the 'war' analogy 'it is best for the whole family if the proceedings are conducted in a constructive and realistic way rather than in the midst of a war zone' (http://www.divorceguideuk.co.uk/9–0.htm).

[41] *Ibid*, s 2.

[42] *Ibid*, s 4.

[43] Above n 35, 123–5.

clients'.[44] The difficulty with the great tide of cooperative dispute resolution engulfing family matters concerns its limits. Counselling clients to forego their day in court may impinge on their personal autonomy. Divorce is still firmly located within the adversarial model, yet the ethical picture for family lawyers is confused.[45]

Condlin and others have pointed out the basic incoherence of the lawyer's role in litigation and settlement.[46] The marked differences in approach to negotiation between solicitors specialising in family law and those specialising in personal injury work illustrates the difficulty in devising meaningful regulations for divergent areas of practice. In personal injury and family law, the current ethos of negotiation is a reaction to criticism of the past practice of lawyers in the respective areas. Personal injury lawyers were criticised for weak negotiating tactics and welcomed encouragement to make hard bargaining tactics a core of their practice. In contrast, family lawyers have moved towards a more cooperative ethos, taking responsibility for persuading their clients to follow.

Lawyers' ethics in legal negotiation and settlement

The application of theories of negotiation to work in different legal contexts, suggests many areas where ethical issues are raised. These include the duty of diligence and the definition of the client's best interests, responsibilities to others with whom one negotiates, lawyers and non-lawyers, and the issue of the reputation of the profession and how it is best protected. Before considering the regulatory possibilities it is necessary to examine the balance between the duty of diligence in negotiation and responsibilities to third parties.

Diligence

The starting point of any discussion of the duty owed by lawyers to clients in negotiation is the issue of client autonomy. Since lawyers act in a client's name, it follows that they should respect that client's wishes. Lawyers must consult clients before negotiating to discover how the client's interests can best be served. This is, however, an ongoing responsibility, since a lawyer is in no position to know how the client values different possibilities, or to evaluate creative solutions suggested by the other side. Discovering the client's wishes may extend to the means as well as the ends of negotiation. The continuing growth of ethical investments suggests that many people are motivated not merely by maximising gain; some clients may be troubled by the fact that their lawyer is using dubious tactics in representing them. Subordinating the lawyer's choice of method to the client's instructions, either in general or for the specific negotiation, promotes the client's autonomy at the expense of the lawyer's.

Respecting client autonomy also raises the issue of whether clients should be present in negotiations. With integrative bargaining there may be a considerable advantage to this. Only clients can reflect on their own wants and preferences, and decide that solution A is

---

44 *Ibid*, 147.
45 L Webley, 'Divorce Solicitors and Ethical Approaches—The Best Interests of the Client and/ or the Best Interests of the Family?' (2004) 7 *Legal Ethics* 230.
46 RJ Condlin, 'Bargaining in the Dark' (1992) 51 *Maryland Law Review* 1.

better than solution B in satisfying those interests. A lawyer may feel constrained in their behaviour by the presence of a client, perhaps feeling that it limits their flexibility. It may, however, represent the 'official position', since much of the guidance given to lawyers suggests that they take clear instructions and advice at the outset of a matter, but do not deal with what should happen thereafter.[47] It is perhaps no surprise that clients often hear of a negotiated offer to settle their claim only after the negotiation has taken place. Respecting client autonomy regarding the goals and methods of negotiation has considerable disadvantages for lawyers. One problem is that the client's preference may result in the lawyer having to use a style of negotiation that he or she is uncomfortable with. Another is that consultation makes the process more long-winded, complicated and, potentially, costly.

It might be argued that taking instructions for the conduct of negotiation is not always necessary. Choice of negotiation strategy is, arguably, within the sphere of autonomous professional activity for lawyers or because the cost of taking instructions is not justified given the sums at issue. Assuming, however, that lawyers are sometimes justified in negotiating without specific instructions, what is the minimum commitment that their professional ethics require? The general duty of diligence, as manifest in the specific obligation to act in a client's best interests, requires that lawyers do not sell a client short. Seeking a settlement that serves the client's best interests may not require integrative bargaining in every situation, but there must be many occasions when the interests of clients are better served by a problem-solving strategy than by a positional strategy.[48] If positional bargaining is indicated by the circumstances, lawyers should only accept a settlement that, from the client's perspective, is reasonable and can be justified by objective criteria. Where proceedings are issued or contemplated, the objective criteria of reasonable settlement reflect the likely outcome of litigation, although the full value of the claim might be discounted for a degree of litigation risk.

If a client expects it, is a lawyer obliged to use a highly competitive positional approach, notwithstanding that, like the family lawyers, his ethical obligation is also to persuade the client against this strategy? Should he behave contrary to norms of integrity or honesty if this will increase the client's gain? These issues account for much of the literature on the ethics of bargaining, mostly from the US and concerned with the proposition that bargaining is a partisan activity carried out under the umbrella of 'zealous advocacy'.[49] Then, if a case can be made for this in some areas of work, like personal injury, and professional rules tend not to distinguish between contexts, 'zealous advocacy' must be justified in whatever area of work the lawyer is instructed. Our argument in the first edition of this book was that the English profession's emphasis on best interests rather than 'zealous advocacy' is a significant difference from the ethical stance of US attorneys. This difference

---

[47] See, eg the Personal Injury Accreditation Scheme: criteria and guidance notes Practice Management Standard F4.a(i) and (ii), available at http://www.sra.org.uk/documents/solicitors/accreditation/personal-injury-guidance.pdf (last accessed 28 March 2008). The Family Law Panel Advanced Knowledge and Skills criteria emphasises more diverse factors, eg 'the client's emotional state', 'underlying issues' and 'keeping the [case] strategy under review' (Element 2(i)).

[48] Menkel-Meadow (above n 6) argues that competitive approaches encourage rigidity and potential stalemate and allow for 'closed or limited problem solving'.

[49] D Luban, *Lawyers and Justice: An Ethical Study* (Princeton University Press, 1988).

has been emphasised by the shift in policy towards encouraging compromise and proportionality in litigation.[50] Dare, however, argues that, irrespective of jurisdiction, lawyer zeal can be interpreted as meaning only 'mere zeal' rather than the 'hyper zeal'. Mere zeal he links with a type of commitment we have called diligence; he claims that only 'hyper zeal' is associated with underhand tactics,[51] and it is this form of zeal that is sometimes advocated in the US literature.

Eekalaar et al noted that divorce lawyers, often reluctantly, pursued client wishes that they thought were dubious or excessive. They concluded that they should generally be entitled to do so, partly because they were sometimes successful against expectations, and partly because lawyers should not have too much power to prejudge outcomes.[52] They also considered that such positions should be advanced moderately, and that a retainer might be justifiably terminated for cause, partly because the other party would be caused unnecessary expense by unjustified claims.

Treating the other side fairly

An obligation to treat the other side fairly may coexist with a duty of diligence owed to clients. There are two possible dimensions to such an obligation. The first concerns any duty owed to the client represented by the opposing lawyer. There is no specific obligation to ensure that a negotiated settlement meets their needs or satisfies their interests, although there are theoretical arguments why it should aim to do so. How far a lawyer is entitled to recognise an obligation to the other side to some extent depends on the extent of the duty of diligence to one's own client, discussed above. Some commentators argue that a situation of unequal resources between the parties may justify ethically the weaker side using tactics that would otherwise be deemed unfair.[53] That is, however, not a widely accepted position. The second dimension of treating the other side unfairly concerns behaviour in the negotiation itself, where the use of underhand tactics may breach rules demanding certain virtues, such as honesty, or other norms associated with standards of professional courtesy or collegiality.

Among the underhand tactics sometimes associated with competitive bargaining is deception. The essence of positional and competitive bargaining is to mislead the other side on the 'bottom line', their minimum or maximum settlement figure.[54] The rules of litigation, which support substantive competitiveness, are sometimes taken by practitioners to support 'stylistic competitiveness' of this kind that, while ethically dubious, is not prescribed.[55] While, in the absence of fraud or actionable misrepresentation, this deception

---

[50] If, for example, the courts are anxious that litigation costs are proportionate to the sum in issue, the efforts employed in negotiation must be proportionate also.

[51] T Dare, 'Mere Zeal, Hyper-zeal and the Ethical Obligations of Lawyers' (2004) 7 *Legal Ethics* 24.

[52] Above n 35, 88.

[53] Eg the argument that lawyers need not be truthful where deception is a norm of bargaining or where there is a power imbalance between the parties and the deceitful lawyer acts for the weaker side. WH Simon, 'Ethical Discretion in Lawyering' (1988) 101 *Harvard Law Review* 1083, calls this the test of relative merits. See also Gifford, above n 3, 134; RB McKay, 'Ethical Considerations in Alternative Dispute Resolution' (1990) 45 *The Arbitration Journal* 15, noting that although the ABA's Model Rules of lProfessional Conduct (r 4.1) prohibit making a false statement of material fact, estimates of value are not treated as material facts (at 19).

[54] Occasionally, of course, the opening bid is also the final offer, but this is either very much the exception or not a negotiation at all, but an ultimatum.

[55] See generally Lowenthal, above n 6.

may not give rise to legal remedies, it may be considered a breach of obligations such as honesty or candour that, ideally, exist between professionals.[56] Yet 'bluffing' of this kind has been defended from a number of positions. If positional bargaining is accepted in professional circles, only a fool would conduct it by telling the other side immediately the minimum payment he would accept.

In the US it has been argued that lying on behalf of clients is consistent with the zealous advocacy promoted by the American Bar Association's (ABA's) model code, although a different standard is now provided for negotiation:[57]

> As advisor, a lawyer provides a client with an informed understanding of the client's legal rights and obligations and explains their practical implications. As advocate, a lawyer zealously asserts the client's position under the rules of the adversary system.[58]

Assuming a responsibility an obligation of zealous advocacy, academics had argued that

> effectiveness in negotiations is central to the business of lawyering and a willingness to lie is central to one's effectiveness in negotiations.[59]

Nevertheless, the large literature defending deception in bargaining generally can be seen as a defence of bluffing, which in turn can be seen part of the process of concession exchange rather than outright deception.[60] If misleading is acceptable in some situations, the rationale can easily be extended to other issues, blurring the 'bright line' between the ethical and unethical and creating uncertainty. The risk, of course, is that a culture of deception encourages larger and worse lies.[61] The Solicitors' Code of Conduct 2007 contains a rule about dealing with third parties, the most relevant section of which, rule 10.01, states that

> you must not use your position to take unfair advantage of anyone either for your own benefit or for another person's benefit.[62]

It is not clear how this applies to negotiation, although lying would usually be seen as unfair. To unpick the ramifications of 'unfair advantage' it is necessary to refer to the old code, which, while problematic, raised the issues more explicitly.

Later editions of the Guide contained two rules apparently more relevant to negotiation than the current rule 10.01. The first was a principle obliging solicitors to 'act towards other solicitors with frankness and good faith consistent with the overriding duty to the client'.[63] This may have been intended to apply primarily to negotiation, since 'good faith' is linked

---

[56] Note 1 to Principle 19.01 reminds solicitors that 'any fraudulent or deceitful conduct by one solicitor to another will render the offending solicitor liable to disciplinary action in addition to the possibility of civil or criminal proceedings'.

[57] There is considerable literature in the US on whether the lawyer's duty to her client obliges her to take a partisan, and therefore competitive, stance in negotiation. Much of this work is reviewed by Condlin, above n 46. See also DE Rosenthal, *Lawyer and Client: Who's in Charge* (New York, Russell Sage, 1974); WH Simon, 'Visions of Practice in Legal Thought' (1984) 36 *Stanford Law Review* 469; JP Heinz, 'The Power of Lawyers' (1983) *Georgia Law Review* 891 and C Fried, 'The Lawyer as Friend: The Moral Foundations of the Lawyer-Client Relationship' (1976) 85 *Yale Law Journal* 1060.

[58] *Model Rules of Professional Conduct 2004* (Chicago, IL, American Bar Association, 2002) preamble, para [2].

[59] GB Wetlaufer, 'The Ethics of Lying in Negotiation' (1990) 76 *Iowa Law Review* 1219.

[60] C Provis, 'Ethics, Deception and Labor Negotiation' (2000) 28 *Journal of Business Ethics* 145, 148.

[61] DJ Luban, 'Milgram Revisited' (1998) 9 *Researching Law: An American Bar Foundation Update* 1, 4.

[62] *Solicitors' Code of Conduct 2007* (London, Solicitors Regulation Authority, 2007) r 10.

[63] Principle 19.01, *The Guide* (London, The Law Society, 8th edn, 2004) 359.

with honesty in bargaining and the refusal to seek an unconscionable advantage.[64] Frankness could have meant that information supplied was to be accurate, although it might also mean that negotiation should only be attempted where there is a genuine intention of achieving settlement. Subjecting the duty to the client's 'overriding interest' could be read as excusing lying for the client. Uncertainty was compounded by a second principle stating that:

> Solicitors must not act, whether in their professional capacity or otherwise, towards anyone in a way which is fraudulent, deceitful or otherwise contrary to their position as solicitors. Nor must solicitors use their positions as solicitors to take unfair advantage for themselves or another person.[65]

The positive duties of frankness and good faith owed to other solicitors contrasts with the negative duties, not to be fraudulent or deceitful 'towards anyone'. A literal interpretation could prohibit competitive positional bargaining by solicitors, the basis of which is deceit and the goal of which is to take unfair advantage. Assuming, however, some kind of cultural exception for the low level deceit, or bluffing, employed in positional bargaining, the obligations to be frank and to act in good faith rule out more extreme deception. Where the line was intended to be drawn is unclear.

A rare chance to explore the scope of the duties of frankness and good faith, and what is meant by not taking unfair advantage, is provided in *Thames Trains Ltd v Adams*.[66] Mr Adams, a US citizen, had suffered serious injuries in a train crash for which the plaintiffs were liable. Thames Trains' solicitors had paid US $9.3 million into court when Adams's solicitor, Ms C, rang them proposing that their clients increase the sum to US $10 million. She was told that no further monies were available, but Thames Trains' solicitors contacted their clients who in fact agreed to offer a further US $500,000. This was communicated to Ms C by telephone, who accepted. What Thames Trains' solicitors did not know, and Ms C did not tell them, was that, when Ms C was told that no more money was available, she had instructed another solicitor in her firm to send a fax accepting the US $9.3 million in court. The fax was not seen by Thames Trains' solicitors because of an internal computer problem. On discovering the earlier fax, Thames Trains sought to set aside the consent order recording the terms of settlement, claiming mistake, estoppel and unconscionable conduct by Ms C. They argued that her failure to inform them of the earlier offer was a breach of her duty to act towards other solicitors with frankness and good faith.

Nelson J held that, under ordinary law, the fax was an offer to settle that could be withdrawn at any time, but was Ms C's conduct unconscionable and sufficient to upset the agreement? The judge thought it significant that it was only after agreeing to accept the additional US $500,000 that Ms C checked and discovered that the fax had been sent. Therefore, it would have been a breach of her duty of confidentiality to her client had she

---

[64] HC Black, JR Nolan, JM Nolan-Haley, *Black's Law Dictionary: Definitions of the Terms and Phrases of American and English Jurisprudence, Ancient and Modern* (St Paul, MN, West Publishing Company, 1990) 693: 'honestly and with no ulterior motive'. *Central Estates (Belgravia) Ltd. v Woolgar* [1971] 3 All ER 647, 649 per Lord Denning MR quoted in JB Saunders *Words and Phrases Legally Defined* (1989) vol 2, 321. 'Good faith bargaining' is a labour law concept meaning coming to the table with an open mind and sincere desire to reach agreement (Black *et al*).

[65] Principle 17.01, *The Guide* (8th edn) 346.

[66] *Thames Trains Ltd v Adams* [2006] EWHC 3291.

revealed, during the conversation about an increased offer, her willingness to accept the sum in court. The judge felt that his decision was 'counter-intuitive' because the duty of frankness between solicitors and litigants is one that courts should promote. In all the circumstances, however, Ms C's duty to the administration of justice, or as an officer of the court, did not require her to correct her opponent's misapprehension. The underlying reasoning of the case is that a solicitor need not be frank with another solicitor about an intention to settle and may remain silent on a material matter, including a misapprehension that the other solicitor is under, where speaking out would not be in the client's interests. The judge did say, however, that had he found that there was a duty on Ms C to speak, she would have been estopped from asserting the higher settlement. This distinction, between positively misleading and misleading by silence seems at odds with the duty in advocacy not to mislead the court.

Thames Trains Ltd v Adams provides an insight into the pragmatic nature of personal injury negotiation. It appears that Ms C may have had instructions to accept the sum in court were the attempt to obtain an increase to fail, or at least knew she would get them. When it was put to her in cross-examination that her client had no plans to travel to England for a trial she answered 'I remain silent'. Similarly, her opponent sought instructions for an increased payment having stated that no more was available. None of this was considered particularly remarkable by counsel or the judge. It was conceded by counsel for Ms C that she would have been under a duty to answer a direct question about her intentions regarding the payment in, but argued that, even had she fallen foul of the frankness requirement by lying, her professional misconduct would be insufficient to overturn the consent order. Nelson J helpfully offered an opinion as to what she should have done, 'as a matter of courtesy', in the telephone call when she was offered the increase. As soon as she realised that she was to be offered more money, she should have said that she had sent a fax accepting the sum in court, but now that she realised that more money was available, that offer was withdrawn. Of course, the case may then have had a different outcome since Thames Trains' solicitors may not have proceeded with the offer.

The Law Society's current Code of Conduct is an advance only by virtue of avoiding the contradiction in the old. It barely mentions negotiation[67] and does not provide much guidance of direct relevance. The two principles on dealing with third parties are replaced by a rule that solicitors 'must not take unfair advantage of anyone either for your own benefit or for another person's benefit'.[68] This eradicates the difference between dealing with solicitors and other third parties, and omits the 'overriding interest of clients' exception when dealing with lawyers. The rule also leaves many questions, not least why the previous distinctions were considered irrelevant. Since the new rule applies to 'anyone', it applies to solicitors' dealings with lawyers. In that respect, it is buttressed in its application to negotiation by the core duty not to damage the reputation or integrity of the profession; lawyers who are not frank, do not act in good faith or who are fraudulent and deceitful risk bringing their profession into disrepute.[69]

---

[67] Except that rule 10.02 says that solicitors negotiating payment of their costs must give with the other side sufficient time and information.

[68] *Solicitors' Code of Conduct 2007* (London, The Law Society 2007) r 10.01.

[69] *Ibid*, r 1.06.

The new rule may have brought clarity to one area of dealing with solicitors. Rude and bullying behaviour, a tactic used by some negotiators, would appear to taking unfair advantage. Other rules impose a general duty on solicitors to report the 'serious misconduct' of another solicitor or where their professional integrity is doubted[70] and it might be expected that such behaviour would produce complaints. Given the previously low levels of reporting,[71] this may be optimistic. It is unknown whether even extreme examples of negotiation misbehaviour are what the Law Society has in mind, but it is an advance that the obligation to report serious misconduct is no longer subject to a client's consent.

Guidance in the new solicitors code potentially applying to negotiation is the statement in the notes to rule 10 that 'it would be unfair to demand anything that is not recoverable through the proper legal process'.[72] The example given refers to a letter of claim, but the example is not exhaustive. It is debatable that canvassing extra-legal solutions, a key element of integrative bargaining, would constitute a 'demand'. Nevertheless, it is unfortunate that the question arises, particularly since the rules in general seem to reflect the new spirit of cooperation. That this should not be more explicit, if intended, is unfortunate given that the field has been mired in concerns about the obligations and limits of adversarialism and zealous advocacy. Competitive positional bargaining may, in some practitioners' minds, stand in place of a court trial. There is no reason why this should be so. Transferring the norms of advocacy to bargaining risks blighting settlement practices with the disadvantages of court processes: cost, time and the narrowness of possible outcomes. Freeing lawyers of their misapprehension may require clearer guidance on expectations.

The idea that integrative bargaining represents an ethical leap forward is supported by analysis suggesting that bargaining practices have a pattern of evolution from a warrior concept based on self-interest and opportunism, through mercantile and civil styles. This progression is marked by increasing recognition of the rights of the other to expect benefits from the exchange and, therefore, the necessity for cooperation. The most recent stage of this evolution, the constructive concept, embraces willingness to explain and explore all interests on the basis of reciprocity.[73] This stage of bargaining evolution recognises the potential of integrative bargaining and links to theorists like Habermas, who identifies the importance of exploring shared values through argumentation,[74] and Kohlberg, who charts stages of moral development towards non-arbitrary social cooperation.[75] It is only recently that the long-term effectiveness of 'defection' or whether a profession should explicitly sanction lying on behalf of clients has been raised.[76] This may explain why neither the Bar

---

[70] Solicitors' Code of Conduct 2007, r 20.04(a) and (c).

[71] The 1990 edition of *The Guide* contained a similar principle (Principle 19.04), but that edition showed that only 33 allegations of impropriety of any kind were made by solicitors against fellow solicitors in 1986 and 45 in 1987. Similar data did not appear in subsequent editions.

[72] Above n 68, guidance to r 10, note 5.

[73] W French, C Häßlein, R van Es, 'Constructivist Negotiation Ethics' (2002) 39 *Journal of Business Ethics* 83.

[74] See eg J Habermas, *Communication and the Evolution of Society* (trans by T McCarthy) (Boston, MA, Beacon Press, 1991).

[75] L Kohlberg, 'Stages and Sequence: The Cognitive Development Approach to Socialisation' in DA Goslin (ed), *Handbook of Socialisation Theory and Research* (Chicago, IL, Rand Mcnally, 1969).

[76] Condlin, above n 46, 68–86; LE Fisher, 'Truth as a Double-edged Sword: Deception, Moral Paradox, and the Ethics of Advocacy' (1989) 14 *The Journal of the Legal Profession* 89.

nor the Law Society deals explicitly with standards in bargaining in their guidance to the profession.

Regulatory possibilities

There are a number of difficulties in directly regulating negotiation. The first lies in reaching consensus about what constitutes ethical, or even appropriate, behaviour in this sphere of activity, given (i) the different models of bargaining that may be appropriate and (ii) the large range of situations potentially subject to bargaining. Despite this, in the US at least, there are periodic calls for effective regulation[77] despite the fact that the ABA's model rules are already more explicit than the English equivalents.[78] A rule on negotiation could marry the obligations of honesty and candour in relation to material facts with obligations

— to explore with clients their perceptions of their interests;
— to seek a settlement where that is in the client's best interests; and
— to seek a settlement which satisfies the client's interests as far as possible and which is fair and reasonable to both sides.

Such a move would be consistent with continuing attempts to make litigation more transparent and less vulnerable to manipulation. If such proposals seem destined to fall on sceptical ears in a profession that prides itself on a pragmatic approach to business in an adversarial setting, it is therefore worth reviewing the main arguments for such a shift.

Improving outcomes for clients

Principled approaches to litigation and bargaining, which depend on honesty and problem solving, offer a more coherent theoretical basis for the lawyer's role in dispute resolution, not only because they are often more effective, but also because they harness the 'power of legitimacy'.[79] Conducted properly, problem-solving bargaining is more rigorous and resistant to exploitation than an adversarial approach based on positional strategies. There is research evidence, for example, that providing the other side with too much information is potentially dangerous against a competitive negotiator but that modest information provision improves outcomes, even when unreciprocated.[80] This supports the idea that lawyers in civil dispute resolution should be required to cooperate with each other and with non-lawyer representatives of other parties.[81] While principled negotiation improves potential outcomes for

---

[77] RR Perschbacher, 'Regulating Lawyers' Negotiations' (1985) 27 *Arizona Law Review* 75; AR Rubin, 'A Causerie of Lawyer's Ethics in Negotiation' [1975] *Louisiana Law Review* 577; WW Steele Jr, 'Deceptive Negotiating and High-toned Morality' (1986) 39 *Vanderbilt Law Review* 1387.

[78] Model rule 4.1 states that a lawyer shall not knowingly (a) make a false statement of material fact or law to a third person or (b) subject to rules on client confidences, fail to disclose a material fact to a third person so as not to assist a criminal or fraudulent act.

[79] Indeed, Condlin argues that the most valuable contribution made by principled negotiation to cooperative strategy is the legitimacy added by the injunction 'yield only to principle, not pressure' (above n 46, 26).

[80] L Thompson, 'Information Exchange in Negotiation' (1991) 27 *Journal of Experimental Social Psychology* 161.

[81] *Ibid*, 93. Indeed, this is the ethic contained in the Code of Conduct for Lawyers in the European Community. This states that the corporate spirit of the profession requires a relationship of trust and cooperation between

particular clients—those with integrative problems—it can also be argued that supporting and promoting a culture of integrative bargaining would improve the position of clients generally. The main reason for this is that it would increase trust between lawyers.

Cooperation between negotiators is crucial in producing the best possible outcomes to integrative bargaining. Trust is vital to cooperation and generally benefits markets by facilitating agreement and reducing transaction costs. The current situation, where there are no definitive rules of bargaining for lawyers, is inimical to an environment of trust. In each interaction, the protagonists are unsure what to expect, and this breeds excessive caution and results in poor solutions for clients in the long term.[82] Moreover, the control mechanisms proposed by game theory are too crude because conditional cooperation involves punishing each defection. In theory, the transaction costs of those with a bad reputation are increased as others deal with them cautiously or not at all, making them uncompetitive and likely to fail in the market. This process may, however, take a long time to work through, particularly if the protagonists are in frequent contact and general reputation does not operate to make others wary of the defecting negotiator. In the meantime, some clients of the lawyer who is 'punished' for defection in negotiations continue to suffer. A lawyer may be unfair to future clients by being unreasonable on behalf of a present client. The balance of the argument therefore seems to be to regulate to promote an environment of trust between legal professionals. The ethical value of fairness would seem, logically, to trump client autonomy on this issue and candour promotes trust most effectively when there is a perceived commitment to shared ethical norms.[83]

Enhancing professionalism

A regulatory commitment to principled negotiation may also serve to enhance professionalism. On the issue of deception, for example, principled negotiators need not disclose all information but should make it clear that they are not doing so and why.[84]

Thurman argues that ambiguity in the model rules should be eradicated:

> Maintaining moral sensitivity and awareness is crucial to the practice of law. The profession must resist inroads on the lawyer's commitment to the truth, and take steps to correct rules that lessen this commitment. The unique role lawyers occupy in our society and their position as officers of our judicial system require that their word be trusted. More is required of a

---

lawyers for the benefit of their clients and in order to avoid unnecessary litigation. It can never justify setting the interests of the profession against those of justice or of those who seek it'. Law Society Guide 1999, 218, para 5.1.1 of the Code.

[82] See generally RA Johnson, *Negotiation Basics: Concepts, Skills and Exercises* (London, Sage Publications, 1993) 77; Condlin, above n 46.

[83] C Provis, 'Ethics, Deception and Labor Negotiation' (2000) 28 *Journal of Business Ethics* 145, citing, inter alia, N Luhmann, 'Familiarity, Confidence, Trust: Problems and Alternatives' in D Gambetta (ed), *Trust: Making and Breaking Cooperative Relations* (Oxford, Blackwell, 1988); W Ross and J La Croix, 'Multiple Meanings of Trust in Negotiation Theory and Research: A Literature Review and Integrative Model' (1996) 7 *The International Journal of Conflict Management* 314.

[84] R Fisher and WL Ury, *Getting to Yes: Negotiating Agreement Without Giving In* (Boston, MA, Houghton Mifflin, 1981) 140.

lawyer than the custom of the marketplace, than bargaining in a bazaar, or in playing poker. Lawyers must feel that theirs is a worthy role and an honourable profession.[85]

It has been argued that implicit exceptions for 'bluffing' should be abandoned as they are likely to lead to unintended violations, compromise the position of lawyers as officers of the court or lead to a decrease in necessary levels of trust and cooperation.[86]

Caveats

The consensus of the bargaining literature is moving inexorably towards the conclusion that integrative bargaining must be promoted on ethical grounds. There are, however, some important caveats to register. Principled negotiation should produce outcomes very similar to those produced by mediation. Research in the US suggests that lawyers are more likely to be cooperative, although not necessarily more effective at problem solving, in a mediation context.[87] This may reflect a consensus among lawyers that negotiations between represented parties should be adversarial unless the parties have agreed to mediation.[88] The distinction between negotiation and mediation is one that both lawyers and their clients may wish to retain. Imposing a duty to be principled may give an advantage to those who are unprincipled. There may also be an increase in transaction costs, such as insurance, if tighter regulation of negotiation gave rise to legal actions and remedies.[89]

Several research studies suggest that caution must be exercised before accepting that cooperative styles of negotiation are ethically superior to competitive styles. One study found that ethical idealists, those most likely to follow rules of conduct, were more assertive in negotiation than ethical relativists, who bent the rules believing that ends justify means. However, the idealists were also more likely to be competitive and less likely to identify integrative possibilities.[90] In an experiment by Kim et al, negotiators who received positive feedback on their effectiveness[91] became more competitive, while those receiving negative feedback on competence not only became less competitive, but were also less able to identify mutually compatible interests. Surprisingly, people were significantly more likely to behave

---

[85] RF Thurman, 'Chipping Away at Lawyer Veracity: The ABA's Turn toward Situation Ethics in Negotiations' [1990] *Journal of Dispute Resolution* 103, 115.

[86] See generally S Bok, *Lying: Moral Choice in Public and Private Life* (New York, Vintage Books, 2nd edn, 1999); Thurman, *ibid*.

[87] EE Gordon, 'Attorney's Negotiation Strategies in Mediation: Business as Usual? (2000) 17 *Mediation Quarterly* 377.

[88] Critics suggest that 'principled negotiation' has less value when there are no continuing relationships to consider, and that objective criteria are persuasive rationalisations for positions and warnings of the consequences of failing to reach agreement are just subtle threats. See JJ White, 'The Pros and Cons of Getting to Yes' (1984) 34 *Journal of Legal Education* 115. Fisher, above n 16, and Menkel-Meadow, above n 6, 829, acknowledge the limitations on a problem solving strategy when dealing with negotiators who have the leverage to achieve their goals by the exercise of power.

[89] AM Burr, 'Ethics in Negotiation: Does Getting to Yes Require Candour?' [May/July 2001] *Dispute Resolution Journal* 10.

[90] JT Bana and JM Parks, 'Lambs among Lions? The Impact of Ethical Ideology on Negotiation Behaviors and Outcomes' (2002) 7 *International Negotiation* 235.

[91] Negotiators negotiated with previous negotiating partners having been told by those partners that on the past negotiation they had found them to be either good or poor negotiators or ethical or unethical negotiators. PH Kim, KA Diekman and AE Tenbrunsel, 'Flattery May Get You Somewhere: The Strategic Implications of Providing Positive vs. Negative Feedback about Ability vs. Ethicality in Negotiation' (2003) 90 *Organizational Behavior and Human Decision Processes* 225.

ethically having been told that they had been experienced as unethical in the previous negotiation. If they had been told that they appeared ethical, they behaved less ethically thereafter. This effect was attributed to the fact that that, having been experienced as unethical, a negotiator is more likely to consider that their bluffing is transparent and to stick to the truth as closely as possible, and vice versa. While the finding on improved performance may reflect a mistaken impression of what constitutes competence, the finding on ethicality reinforces the point that more is usually necessary to encourage ethical negotiation than simply enacting rules.

Greater attention to negotiation in education and training would be a necessary part of changing the culture of bargaining for lawyers. Both the solicitors' and barristers' vocational courses teach negotiation and some courses offer mediation as an option. The course materials for most of the courses are light on bargaining theory and do not clearly separate integrative and positional bargaining. At present, these courses tend to conflate problem-solving methods of bargaining and more adversarial styles. This deepens confusion regarding the lawyer's obligations and makes it more difficult for problem solving to take root in the legal culture. Revising the adversarial ethic in civil litigation, including establishing a different culture of negotiation, may be a long-term project for the profession.

Conclusion

The existence of different kinds of negotiating problems and different defensible models of negotiation complicates the task of defining an appropriate ethic of negotiation for lawyers. To suggest that an approach may be ethical in some circumstances but not others is a difficulty if it is not possible to specify the circumstances. Given that a distributive problem implies loss or gain for each party, success in resolving a distributive problem is inextricably linked with the distribution, a classic zero sum game in which success is securing a larger share of a scarce resource. In contrast, success in a negotiation involving mainly integrative features and few, if any, distributive problems depends on identifying the potential for integration and maximising that potential for the benefit of both parties.

These differences raise the question of whether lawyers should have a consistent approach to negotiation or be accomplished in different styles of negotiation and deploy each selectively as the situation demands. Serving the best interests of the client suggests that competence in different styles of negotiation is required unless, as many have suggested, lawyers commit themselves to integrative bargaining in all circumstances. The advantage of this is that some methods of integrative bargaining, such as principled negotiation, advocate cooperative approaches to negotiation which are more consistent with collegial obligations and expectations of integrity than more adversarial styles. The disadvantage is that many clients, particularly the rich and powerful, want lawyers to be adversarial in all circumstances. Imposing a culture of cooperation in bargaining may prove deeply unpopular with lawyers and clients alike.

19

ADVOCACY

It should be remembered that if counsel fails to appear the opposing counsel will take his place and in the best of faith adduce the facts and state the law that he must meet and overcome. Here is 'priesthood'.[1]

Introduction

Advocacy involves the professional presentation of another's case or point of view, which may or may not coincide with the advocate's personal convictions.[2] All lawyers are advocates in this sense. 'Advocacy services' has a more restricted meaning,[3] and is concerned with court appearances, broadly conceived, but usually adversarial.[4] The criminal trial is the model, because the rights of criminal defendants are sacrosanct, demanding the rigorous testing of evidence. Even here, however, the advocate's power and control is offset by a duty to the court, cutting across partisan obligations to clients. The existence of this duty partly rests on the classical role of the English judge, umpire in a clash of champions and affording advocates autonomy in exposing flaws in evidence and presenting legal arguments. Unclear of the details of the case and the advocate's instructions, judicial intervention could be totally misconceived.[5] This model has, however, been undermined in the civil sphere, with advocates' autonomy somewhat curtailed by the judicial case management and cost penalties introduced by the Civil Procedure Rules.

Jurisdiction

Until 1990, advocacy in higher courts was the preserve, and the raison d'être, of the Bar, the rationale for the split profession and a recurring source of friction across its divide.

---

[1] B Hollander, *The English Bar: The Tribute of an American Lawyer* (London, Bowes, 1964).

[2] See R Audi, 'The Ethics of Advocacy' (1995) 1 *Legal Theory* 251.

[3] The Courts and Legal Services Act defines 'advocacy services' in connection with 'a right of audience in relation to any proceedings, or contemplated proceedings' (s 119).

[4] 'Court' means: (i) any court of record (the House of Lords, the Court of Appeal, the High Court, the Crown Court, county courts, magistrates' courts, coroners' courts); (ii) any tribunal which the Council on Tribunals is under a duty to keep under review; (iii) any court-martial; and (iv) a statutory inquiry within the meaning of s 19(1) of the Tribunals and Enquiries Act 1971, although the Solicitors' Code (r 24—interpretation) is more succinct.

[5] M Frankel, 'The Search for the Truth: An Umpireal View' (1975) 123 *University of Pennsylvania Law Review* 1024.

Solicitors had day-to-day contact with clients and instructed barristers to appear in court,[6] often even when they had rights of 'audience', and were expected to be represented in court for the duration of the case. The Bar Code now allows barristers instructed by professional clients to appear without those clients being present with the court's permission,[7] provided the interests of the lay client and the interests of justice are not prejudiced, and even allows them to interview witnesses and take proofs of evidence in such circumstances.[8] Accordingly, it is rare nowadays for a solicitor to be in court with a barrister, particularly in legally aided work.[9] The Bar has been ever sensitive to changes in the advocacy market,[10] but its foundations were shaken when the Courts and Legal Services Act 1990 allowed new bodies to apply for the right to grant their members rights of audience.[11] Bodies are required to demonstrate that they had rules of conduct 'appropriate in the interests of the proper and efficient administration of justice',[12] effective mechanisms for enforcing them and the propensity to do so.[13] The Law Society, whose members could, until then, appear only in the county courts, magistrates' courts and tribunals, could grant rights of audience in higher courts to solicitors in private practice from 1993.[14] The Law Society created a new Code for Advocacy, based on the Bar Code, to supplement its Guide. The advocacy code was repealed by the Solicitors Code of Conduct 2007,[15] which includes its main points in rule 11 and the guidance thereto.[16]

There were several justifications for restricting advocacy rights, but the primary one is market based. First, newly qualified barristers must undertake a wide variety of advocacy work to survive, graduating from minor cases to serious cases as their experience and

---

[6] On the duty to provide proper, competent instructions, see S Payne, 'Instructing Counsel' in S Payne (ed), *Instructing Counsel* (Croydon, Tolley Publishing, 1994) 3–4.

[7] *Code of Conduct of the Bar of England and Wales* (London, Bar Standards Board, 8th edn, as amended, 2004) (hereafter Bar Code) para 706.

[8] Bar Code, para 707.

[9] See also *The Role of Barrister in Non-Solicitor Cases*, available at http://www.barcouncil.org.uk/guidance/ (last accessed 28 March 2008), which takes account of the Court of Appeal decision, *Agassi v Robinson* [2005] EWCA Civ 1507, *The Times*, 22 December 2005.

[10] Solicitors were given audience in the county courts when introduced in 1834, leading to a decline of the Bar on the circuits. A Thornton, 'The Professional Responsibility and Ethics of the English Bar' in R Cranston (ed), *Legal Ethics and Professional Responsibility* (Oxford, Clarendon Press, 1995) 53, 57.

[11] The Minister of Justice approves applications to become authorised to grant rights of audience from professional bodies under s 27 (sch 4, pts 1–5), competition authorities (sch, 4 pts 1–3) and an advisory panel (sch 4, pts 1–7), currently the Legal Services Consultative Panel (Access to Justice Act (1999), s 35), Courts and Legal Services Act, s 29 and sch 4 (as amended).

[12] *Ibid*, s 17(3)d.

[13] Courts and Legal Services Act 1990, s 17(3)b(i)–(iii).

[14] As an authorised body under the Courts and Legal Services Act 1990, s 27 and by virtue of the Solicitors Act 1974, s 2, ILEX had existing rights to appear in chambers in county courts and the High Court. It became an authorised body for advocacy in civil and family proceedings in open court in the county and magistrates' courts in 1998. It is applying for rights to appear in criminal proceedings in the magistrates' courts and in some interlocutory proceedings in the High Court. Patent agent litigators have rights of audience in the Patents County Court and limited rights in the High Court. The Institute of Trade Mark Attorneys has the right to conduct litigation in the High Court and county courts.

[15] *Solicitors' Code of Conduct 2007* (London, Solicitors Regulation Authority, 2007) (hereafter Solicitors' Code) r 25.01(g).

[16] Original requirements, such as organising practices to support advocacy, maintaining libraries and ensuring that employees are aware of obligations arising under the Solicitors' Advocacy Code (para 3.1) were not included.

reputations permit. Solicitors' practice arrangements may restrict regular experience and the variety of advocacy they undertake. Secondly, barristers, as independent practitioners, are not paid a guaranteed salary, and a successful career depends on performance, durability and often a large slice of luck. Solicitors have the cushion of a salary and might survive as advocates despite poor performance. Thirdly, barristers are selected by discerning professionals, whereas solicitor advocates are selected by their firms on behalf of clients. Fourthly, there are differences in primary training, with barristers taught a greater range and given more experience of advocacy. The slow uptake of advocacy rights by solicitors is attributed to the qualification procedures and also to economic, structural and cultural forces operating on solicitors.[17] Despite the opening up of the advocacy market, most solicitors outside of the commercial firms have stuck to their traditional roles. The same is largely true of barristers, despite licensed and public access[18] allowing barristers to appear in court without a solicitor in certain circumstances.[19]

Qualification and training

Barristers who complete all stages of their education and training are called to the Bar. They can then offer advocacy services in all courts, provided that they are working in the office of a qualified person.[20] When they have maintained a practice for three years they can offer advocacy services in all courts.[21] After three years' practical experience of advocacy,[22] solicitors can apply to take one of two routes to satisfy the approved regulations and obtain higher rights of audience. First, a Higher Courts qualification may be granted under regulation 4 of the Higher Courts Qualification Regulations to solicitors with 'appropriate judicial or higher court advocacy experience'[23] as defined in schedule 1 to the Regulations.[24] Those without such experience must take the second route and

> satisfy the Society that they are suitably experienced and suitably qualified to exercise rights of audience in the proceedings relating to the qualification for which they have applied.[25]

---

[17] Most solicitors' firms were not geared up for advocacy in higher courts and most did not want it in-house. See A Boon and J Flood, 'Trials of Strength: The Reconfiguration of Litigation as a Contested Terrain' (1999) 33 *Law and Society Review* 595; M Zander, 'Rights of Audience in the Higher Courts in England and Wales Since the 1990 Act: What Happened?' (1997) 4 *International Journal of the Legal Profession* 167.

[18] Courts and Legal Services Act 1990. Under licensed access, organisations or individuals with specific legal expertise can be licensed by the BSB to instruct barristers directly in those areas. The licence covers advice or representation or both, permitting licensees to instruct barristers either on their own affairs or on behalf of their clients. Available at http://www.barcouncil.org.uk/about/instructingabarrister/licensedaccess/ (last accessed 28 March 2008).

[19] See further A Heppinstall, 'Public Access to the Bar is Good for All' (2005) 155 *New Law Journal* 1360; L Sinclair, 'Licensed Access: Opportunity or Blind Alley?' (2005) 155 *New Law Journal* 895.

[20] See chapter 16 for a discussion of deferral of call.

[21] The Courts and Legal Services Act preserved the existing rights of audience of barristers in all courts and of solicitors in lower courts, and approved the Bar Council's arrangements for training advocates.

[22] The Higher Courts Qualification Regulations (1992), Reg 2 (Applications).

[23] Reg 4(a).

[24] 'Additional steps' may be required, including gaining more advocacy experience, submission of references, the passing of the appropriate test and the passing of the appropriate course (sch 1(2)).

[25] Reg 5(i).

Evidence of 'suitable experience' relates to 'the range,[26] frequency, regularity[27] and quality'[28] of advocacy experience[29] in the 'recent past'[30] and must be supported by two references.[31] If successful, the solicitor is issued a certificate of experience and eligibility to proceed[32] to either the Test of Evidence and Procedure in the Higher Criminal Courts and/or the Test of Evidence and Procedure in the Higher Civil Courts.[33] Passing the test is normally[34] a prerequisite of attending the appropriate course(s).[35] The structure, content and assessment methods of the course, which is intensive and difficult, are set out in schedule 4 to the Regulations.[36] Preliminary reading may be sent to participants, who may be required to leave the course if they 'clearly have not read it'.[37] The minimum duration of the course is 34 hours, of which 17 hours 'should be spent on oral and written practical exercises'.[38] These exercises form the basis for assessing whether the participant is competent to conduct advocacy in the relevant courts.[39] The criteria for performance assessment are not currently published.

Although both vocational courses now include advocacy, procedure and evidence, the Bar requires extensive coverage, while the LPC includes an advocacy component of equal weighting to the other skills taught on the course and is assessed on the basis of competence.[40] Following the Legal Practice Course (LPC), solicitors undertake further advocacy

---

[26] The Criminal Proceedings Qualification requires that a solicitor has appeared in the normal range of magistrates' court criminal work: 'bail applications, adjournment applications, committals, summary trials and guilty pleas, including summary offences, either way offences and indictable offences' (sch 2(5)); for the Civil Proceedings Qualification, 'a full range of county court work, including interlocutory applications, pre-trial reviews and hearing involving final orders of judgement, including contested trials' is necessary (sch 2(6)); and for the All Proceedings Qualification, mixed experience, not as extensive as for each of the other two qualifications, is important (sch 2(7)).

[27] A minimum of 20–25 appearances a year before courts and tribunals (sch 2(3)), but shortages of opportunities in regions (sch 2(8)) or areas of practice (sch 2(9)) or 'career breaks, job changes, illnesses or disabilities' may be taken into account (sch 2(10)).

[28] Those lasting for a number of hours or days carry more weight (sch 2(4)), as does higher court experience as an instructing solicitor (sch 2(11)).

[29] Sch 2(1).

[30] In the two years preceding the application (sch 2(2)).

[31] 'From those who have first hand experience of the solicitor's advocacy work and whose standing as members of the judiciary, the court service or the legal profession would enable them to offer informed opinions' (sch 2(1)).

[32] Reg 5(ii).

[33] Reg 6(1).

[34] Reg 6(5).

[35] The Higher Criminal Courts Advocacy Training Course or the Higher Civil Courts Advocacy Training Course, in each case provided by authorised and monitored providers (Reg 6(2)).

[36] Participants prepare an action for trial, develop a case presentation strategy, identify admissible evidence to be used in the presentation of a case and make submissions concerning the admissibility of evidence, examine, cross-examine and re-examine witnesses effectively and in accordance with the rules of evidence, demonstrate a sound understanding of ethical requirements, formulate and present a cohesive argument based upon facts, general principles and legal authority in a structured, concise and persuasive manner, analyse personal and other advocates' performances to assess their effectiveness and identify the action necessary to deal with identified weaknesses, and draft pleadings relevant to the conduct of proceedings in the relevant courts, including applications for leave to appeal and notices of appeal.

[37] The course specification includes ethics sources and practical exercises.

[38] Sch 4(3).

[39] Sch 4(4).

[40] The Legal Practice Course and the Professional Skills Course (PSC) were introduced at the same time as higher rights. The PSC had a bias towards advocacy at the expense of the solicitor's traditional skill of negotiation, but there was still criticism that the standard of advocacy achieved is often low because of lack of time.

training in the Professional Skills Course, although it is understood that trainees have to be extremely poor to fail advocacy. In response to the challenge from solicitor advocates, the Bar increased substantially the focus on advocacy training, marshalling the very considerable resources of the Inns and circuits to provide additional support. Following the Elias Working Party in 2001, significantly more hours were devoted to advocacy on the Bar Vocational Course (BVC),[41] covering a greater range of trial tasks.[42] The BVC also assesses all skills, including advocacy, on a graded basis, thereby identifying outstanding potential.

The Collyear and Dutton reports were influential on advocacy training at the Bar, suggesting that barristers needed more advocacy exposure than previously because of the dearth of smaller cases and proposing that the Inns combine to provide training.[43] It also noted the oddity that advocacy, the skill that distinguishes the Bar, is not assessed after the BVC. This was offered as a reason why 3–5% of pupils on subsequent advocacy training were unfit to represent clients in court.[44] The report led to an increase in the hours of advocacy training undertaken by pupils from 9 to 12 hours and assessment, leading to the award of a certificate of competence in a number of areas.[45] The hours of training for newly qualified barristers on the New Practitioners' Programme[46] were increased from six to nine. The diverse training provided by the Inns and circuits were brought together under one organisation, the Advocacy Training Council, which was to standardise materials and training of instructors. This increasing divergence in the time devoted to advocacy training is unlikely to stave off solicitors' attempts to equalise the rights regime. Although the Bar's advantage survived Lord Irvine's consultation on higher rights published in June 1998,[47] the Solicitors Regulation Authority consulted on the issue in 2007. The conclusion was that the formal requirement that solicitors obtain higher rights should be abolished, to be replaced by advice to solicitors to undertake training.[48] Although their current regime is onerous, its total abandonment would leave solicitors seriously adrift of the Bar in the training required for advocates.

[41] BVC providers are encouraged to teach advocacy to groups of no more than six.

[42] This required 50–60 hours of advocacy training, delivered in 12 sessions, with two advocacy assessments covering written arguments, interventions from the bench and witness handling, comprising 20% of the course mark. Mr Justice Elias, *Report of the BVC Respecification Working Party* (January 2001).

[43] Sir John Collyear, *Blueprint for the Future* (London, General Council of the Bar, 1999); Timothy Dutton QC, *Advocacy Training at the Bar of England and Wales: Organisation, Delivery and Outcomes* (London, General Council of the Bar, 2002).

[44] Dutton, *ibid*, para 85.

[45] The Advocacy Certificate covers case analysis, use of skeleton arguments, oral submissions, examination in chief and cross-examination. The Advocacy Working Party, *Report of Assessment of Advocacy* (February 2004) (Dutton 2).

[46] This applies to all barristers commencing practice on or after 1 October 1997. 'Practice' includes working as an employed lawyer, as per The Continuing Professional Development Regulations 2001, paras 1–2.

[47] *Rights of Audience and Rights to Conduct Litigation in England and Wales: The Way Ahead* (London, The Lord Chancellor's Department, 1998); 'Solicitors Celebrate as Govt Sweeps away Bar Monopoly', *The Lawyer*, 30 June 1998.

[48] The SRA will try to introduce such a regime at the end of 2008, following discussions with the Ministry of Justice and the judiciary.

Personal duties

Competence

Protecting advocates from the consequences of their own incompetence was once considered an important goal of public policy[49] even when they acted against their client's express wishes.[50] Long usage was invoked as a justification,[51] but ethical arguments held sway in the decision to sustain immunity from suit. The first was that cases might not be conducted 'fearlessly and independently' if clients could launch collateral attacks on judgments by suing their advocates. The second was that the integrity of the cab rank rule would be undermined if barristers had an incentive to avoid litigious clients. Consequently, courts would only grant new trials where there was suspicion that flagrantly incompetent advocacy caused injustice.[52] In *Hall v Simons*,[53] however, the House of Lords in 2000 abolished advocates' immunity in both criminal and civil proceedings. It was argued that there were adequate safeguards against collateral attacks on judgments in the considerable practical difficulty in bringing actions[54] and the courts' option of striking out. Lord Steyn thought that the 'critical factor'[55] was whether removing immunity would undermine professional ethics, particularly 'the willingness of barristers to carry out their duties to the court',[56] but, considering that immunity was by no means universal in other jurisdictions,[57] he concluded that advocates were in no greater ethical peril than other professionals.[58]

Hall v Simons has highlighted the importance of advocates refusing cases they are not competent to handle. The Bar Code imposes on barristers a requirement not to accept any

---

[49] In *Rondel v Worsley* [1969] 1 AC 191 the House of Lords confirmed advocates' immunity from clients' actions in negligence in conducting trials, or work so intimately connected with trials that it constituted a preliminary decision on the conduct of the case, eg preliminary work such as drafting pleadings. Lord Upjohn, however, thought that immunity should cover letters before action onwards.

[50] *R v Gantam* [1988] CLY 574 (allegedly incompetent cross examination). See also *R v Ensor* [1989] 1 WLR 497 (decision by counsel not to apply for separate trials where defendant charged on two counts of rape where the defence to both was the absence of sexual intercourse and consent); *R v Swain* (1988) CLR 109.

[51] *Rondel v Worsley*, above n 49; *Somasundaram v M Julius Melchior* [1988] 1 All ER 129 (action for negligence against solicitor who persuaded defendant to plead guilty to imprisonment and assault of his wife. Civil actions attacking final judgments were contrary to public policy, even where the advice was not protected from immunity); *R v Roberts* [1990] Crim LR 122 (counsel's decision not to introduce medical evidence not a valid ground of appeal, even if wrong, unless there was flagrantly incompetent advocacy; once a court announced a decision it regards itself as *functus officio*). See also *Munster v Lamb* (1883) 11 QBD 558, holding that immunity could be claimed when defamatory attack by an advocate was malicious, not negligent. For a case where liability in negligence was established, see *Acton v Pearce* [1997] 3 All ER 909.

[52] *R v Ensor* [1989] 1WLR 497. Tactical decisions, even if they may be mistaken, were not grounds for retrial: see *Telfer v DPP* (1996) 160 JP 512.

[53] *Arthur J S Hall & Co (a firm) v Simons, Barratt v Ansell and others (trading as Woolf Seddon (a firm), Harris v Scholfield Roberts & Hill (a firm) and another* [2000] 3 All ER 673.

[54] See also B Malkin, 'In the Firing Line', *The Lawyer*, 3 September 2001.

[55] *Hall v Simons*, above n 53, 681h–j.

[56] *Ibid* 678f.

[57] Australia and New Zealand followed *Rondel v Worsley*, above n 49, but European countries, where the duty to the court was less extensive, had no immunity. US prosecutors and defenders in a few states had immunity but not in Canada. Lord Steyn regarded Canada as important since *Rondel* was considered in *Demarco v Ungaro* (1979) 95 DLR (3d) 385, concluding that fears that actions against barristers would undermine the public interest were 'unnecessarily pessimistic' (683a).

[58] Where an AIDS-infected patient asks a consultant not to reveal his condition to others, the ethical dilemma is as difficult as those facing barristers (682b).

task which: (i) he knows or ought to know he is not competent to handle; (ii) he does not have adequate time and opportunity to prepare for or perform; or (iii) he cannot discharge within a reasonable time having regard to the pressure of other work,[59] and there are strong cultural expectations concerning the kinds of case appropriate for barristers of different experience.[60] Barristers must also consider whether they can handle the work adequately given time and other constraints.[61] The Solicitor's Code for Advocacy required solicitors to consider whether a particular brief was consonant with their experience[62] and whether or not their firm was the most suitable to conduct the case, but the Solicitors Code of Conduct 2007 has relegated these matters to guidance.[63]

There is also a performance dimension to what constitutes competent advocacy and conceptions of this shift over time. This is very clearly illustrated by attitudes to lengthy presentations of the case, which can be characterised as thoroughness or verbosity, depending on perspective. Hollander, an overseas commentator on the English Bar, appreciated the latitude that English advocates possessed:

> Patience and thoroughness is the rule of the Bar and the Court; time is never more than a passing consideration and counsel are permitted to exhaust the argument . . . no warning light and cutting short as in the U.S. Supreme Court—'Justice is seen to be done'.[64]

The thorough, honest and skilful presentation of cases saves court time and reduces expense,[65] but, while the Bar distinguishes thoroughness from verbosity,[66] not all barristers can. The Royal Commission on Criminal Justice noted that the best barristers are outstanding, many are very good but a small number are 'incompetent, prolix and poorly prepared'.[67] On the civil side, control over lengthy advocacy was one of the aims of Lord Woolf's proposals for judicial case management, although it is not always successful.[68] This new emphasis on economical delivery is now reflected in the Bar Code[69] and the training of

---

[59] Bar Code, para 701.

[60] Overstretching the capabilities of junior members could be disastrous for a referral profession.

[61] Para 701 provides a practising barrister: (c) must read all briefs and instructions delivered to him expeditiously; (d) must have regard to the relevant Written Standards for the conduct of Professional Work (which are reproduced in Annex H of the code); (e) must inform his professional client forthwith and subject to para 620 return the instructions or the brief to the professional client or to another barrister acceptable to the professional client: (i) if it becomes apparent to him that he will not be able to do the work within a reasonable time after receipt of instructions; (ii) if there is an appreciable risk that he may not be able to undertake a brief or fulfil any other professional engagement which he has accepted.

[62] *Ibid*, para 4.3.1.

[63] Guidance to r 11, note 4.

[64] B Hollander, *The English Bar: The Tribute of an American Lawyer* (London, Bowes, 1964).

[65] R Pound, *The Lawyer from Antiquity to Modern Times: with Particular Reference to The Development of Bar Associations in the United States* (St Paul, MN, West Publishing, 1953) 27.

[66] A boy, asleep in the well of the court, fell and broke his neck. The barrister speaking at the time was, in the spirit of 'comradely humour', indicted by the Circuit 'for murder with a certain dull instrument to wit a long speech of no value' (Pound, *ibid*, 127).

[67] A Owen, 'Not the Job of a Judge', *The Times*, 6 December 1994, 39.

[68] Mr Justice Tomlinson's post-BCCI working party's interim report singled out an 80 day opening speech in that case as 'wasted': N Goswami, 'Falconer: Tardy Litigators will be Fired', *The Lawyer*, 4 June 2007.

[69] 'A barrister . . . must in all his professional activities be courteous and act promptly conscientiously diligently and with reasonable competence and take all reasonable and practicable steps to avoid unnecessary expense or waste of the Court's time' (Bar Code, para 701(a)).

advocates generally.[70] The Bar's continued existence may very well depend on barristers demonstrating that they offer greater efficiency and economy in delivering advocacy services.

Neutrality

While barristers and solicitor advocates have different codes, the Law Society based its code on relevant sections from the Bar Code, so examples from one were echoed in the other. As a result of the reworked new brevity of the Solicitors Code, differences are emerging. The Bar Code continues to list extensive circumstances of 'professional embarrassment' in which instructions must be refused,[71] whereas the solicitors are less detailed. The Bar Code also details circumstances in which barristers must return briefs,[72] but the detailed instructions previously in the Solicitors Code for Advocacy have virtually been have abandoned.[73] The Bar Code also identifies situations where barristers may withdraw, for example where their professional conduct is impugned or for another substantial reason,[74] but they must explain the reason to their client.[75] Similar advice is, again, omitted from the Solicitors Code.

A situation that is often misunderstood is that where an advocate represents someone who has confessed guilt to his lawyer but wants to plead 'not guilty'. Representing such a client is not forbidden by either code, a situation that often surprises lay people. The first, formal response to the imagined dilemma of the 'guilty client' is the duty of neutrality, part of which is the principle that all defendants are entitled to representation. The underlying policy rationale is that it would be inefficient if advocates had to withdraw in the light of admissions of guilt, forcing their clients to find new representation. The second, slightly technical, argument is that it is not the advocate's position to decide who is guilty and who innocent, but for the judge or jury, and an argument that does not convince the advocate may convince others. The third, more ethical, line is that, if the client admits guilt or something that may seem damning to his case, the advocate may still act so long as he does not mislead the court. This means that the advocate must not put the case on a basis contrary to the admission or allow the client to give perjured evidence.[76]

Both codes require advocates to withdraw in cases when clients instruct them to mislead the court,[77] but this does not extend to 'misleading' not guilty pleas. The Bar Code does not deal with this situation explicitly,[78] but the Solicitors Code comes close when it advises that

---

[70] AA Majid, 'The Art of Advocacy: An Indispensable Skill for Common Law Advocates' (2005) *European Journal of Legal Education* 39.

[71] Para 603.

[72] Eg legal aid wrongly obtained by false or inaccurate information and the client refuses to remedy situation (608(c)); becoming aware of a document that the client refuses to disclose (608(e)); or having accidentally read a document 'belonging to another party by some means other than the normal and proper channels' where they would thereby be embarrassed in the discharge of their duties by their knowledge of the contents of the document provided that they may retire or withdraw only if they can do so without jeopardising the client's interests (608(f)).

[73] But see Solicitors' Code, guidance to r 11, paras 15 and 16 (withdrawal in light of client perjury or inconsistent statements presented as false evidence).

[74] Bar Code, para 609.

[75] *Ibid*, para 610(a).

[76] See, especially, Solicitors' Code, r 11, guidance note 12(c).

[77] Bar Code, para 608 (d); Solicitors' Code, r 11.01(1).

[78] See rr 603 (c) and 608(d). The latter only requires withdrawal when the client will not authorise disclosure the duty to the court requires him to make.

a solicitor need not stop acting when clients make inconsistent statements, except where they offer false evidence.[79] Therefore, representation can be provided on a not guilty plea provided the defence is technical or merely requires the Crown to prove its case. In these circumstances, evidence should not be presented that is intended to establish the client's innocence.[80] Obviously, such a course is risky ethically because there are a number of ways in which such defences can cross the ethical line. The more common circumstances are dealt with under the section dealing with the duty to the court.

Independence

The independence of advocates is a multi-faceted and iconic institution. The separation of advocacy from other legal roles—for example, the decision to prosecute or the task of case preparation[81]—is fundamental to the Bar's unique modus operandi and ethos.[82] It has various manifestations in the Bar Code,[83] the most specific alluding to three main areas of independence: from conflicts of interest, from the state and from pressure brought by clients and judges.[84]

There are many potential conflicts of interests for, and pressures on, advocates. Accepting presents is one of the more obvious situations to avoid.[85] More insidious conflicts of interest arise when barristers are over-dependent for instructions from a restricted range of solicitors. In such cases, they may be more susceptible to pressure to bend rules at a client's request. Solicitors face a different conflict of interest when their firm does not offer the particular advocacy services the client needs. The guidance in the Solicitors Code suggests that they are required to consider referring the client to someone with more experience and skill, outside the firm if appropriate.[86] This is a real test of ethics, since there is bound to be anxiety about sending clients to competitors.

The most significant manifestation of the independence of the advocates is their freedom from the influence of the state. This was the subject of debate in articles by Freedman and

---

[79] Solicitors' Code, r 11, guidance note 16.

[80] Advocates testing the prosecution case must not overstep the line by putting the case of the accused through questions to witnesses. If the matter put was not raised by the accused after he was charged with the offence, the judge is entitled to make a so-called adverse inference direction to the jury under s 34 of the Criminal Justice and Public Order Act 1994. See *R v Webber* 2004 UKHL 1; S Nash, 'Drawing Inferences from Positive Suggestions Put to Witnesses: *R v Webber*' (2004) *International Journal of Evidence and Proof* 50.

[81] This was raised by the Bar Council in opposition to Crown Prosecutors being granted higher rights (see Thornton, above n 10, 62).

[82] The Bar's response to the 1989 Green papers asserted that its strength lay 'in its independence, and in the "cab-rank" rule, made possible by the independence of barristers in private practice as sole practitioners'. General Council of the Bar, *The Quality of Justice: The Bar's Response* (London, Butterworth, 1989) paras 2.3–2.4.

[83] Bar Code, para 104 states that the general purpose of the Code is to provide requirements and rules and standards of conduct appropriate in the interests of justice and in particular: '(a) in relation to self-employed barristers to provide common and enforceable rules and standards which require them . . . (i) to be completely independent in conduct and in professional standing as sole practitioners'.

[84] 'A barrister must not: (a) permit his absolute independence integrity and freedom from external pressures to be compromised; . . . (c) compromise his professional standards in order to please his client the Court or a third party, including any mediator.' Bar Code (as amended 23 March 2005), para 307. Formerly echoed in para 2.6 of the Law Society's Code for Advocacy, but not part of the Solicitors' Code, r 11.

[85] Bar Code, para 307(b): '[must not] do anything (for example accept a present) in such circumstances as may lead to any inference that his independence may be compromised'.

[86] Solicitors' Code, guidance to r 11, note 4.

Noonan in the US in the 1970s. Freedman argued that the adversarial system demands 'zealous advocacy' on behalf of criminal defendants, requiring defence lawyers to discredit witnesses known to be telling the truth, allow witnesses who would commit perjury to give evidence and advise clients in a way that enables them to give perjured evidence.[87] Noonan challenges Freedman's conception of trials as 'battles', arguing that the advocate's duty is to assist the judge in making an impartial, wise and informed decision; to seek to establish the truth;

> the advocate plays his role well when zeal for his client's cause promotes a wise and informed decision of the case.[88]

Justice demands proper assessment of the facts, increasing the chance of correct verdicts and, where conviction results, a sentence proportionate to the crime.[89]

The virtues of the adversarial system in orchestrating the clash of two 'versions of the truth' have long been debated,[90] but Freedman sees in it a natural defence against oppression absent in civil systems. The state has massive power and resources at its disposal and so its interests 'are not absolute, or even paramount', and indeed, it must be constrained whenever possible. The best way of doing this is to ensure that

> the defendant is at least afforded that one advocate, that 'champion against a hostile world', whose zealous allegiance is to him or her alone.[91]

From this perspective, 'zealous advocacy' is a bulwark against state oppression, and the willingness to advance a client's case without fear of public, governmental or professional disapproval, is its bedrock.[92] In Freedman's account, therefore, the independence of the legal profession, expressed in its alignment with individuals against the state, is the key, not only to an effective state system of justice, but to effective democracy.[93]

The trend in England and Wales over the last 200 years has been towards the containment of 'zealous advocacy', at least of the stripe advanced by Freedman. A significant transition occurred between 1820 and 1850, following Brougham's oft-quoted expression of counsel's obligation to defend clients by 'all expedient means'.[94] Infamous cases of counsel asserting their client's innocence while being aware of their guilt[95] led to the control of

---

[87] See MH Freedman, 'Professional Responsibility of the Criminal Defence Lawyer' (1966) 64 *Michigan Law Review* 1469; W Simon, 'The Ideology of Advocacy: Procedural Justice and Professional Ethics' (1978) 29 *Wisconsin Law Review* 30, 34.

[88] J Noonan, 'The Purposes of Advocacy and the Limits of Confidentiality' (1966) 64 *Michigan Law Review* 1485; Simon, *ibid*.

[89] A Ashworth, 'Ethics and Criminal Justice' in R Cranston (ed), *Legal Ethics and Professional Responsibility* (Oxford, Clarendon Press, 1995) 146.

[90] George Bernard Shaw characterised this as ' [t]he theory . . . that if you set two liars to exposing each other, eventually the truth will come out'. Quoted in MJ Saks, 'Accuracy v Advocacy: Expert Testimony Before the Bench' [Aug/Sept 1987] *Technology Law Review* 43.

[91] *Ibid*, 48.

[92] SL Jacobs, 'Legal Advocacy in a Time of Plague' (1993) 21 *Journal of Law Medicine and Ethics* 382.

[93] 'There is only one way to keep the law "trustworthy"—only one way to keep the bureaucrats honest, and to make the law work, that is, by making sure that there is an independent Bar, prepared to challenge government action and to do so as zealously and effectively as possible.' MH Freedman, 'Are There Public Interest Limits on Lawyers' Advocacy?' (1977) *The Journal of the Legal Profession* 47, 54.

[94] See chapter 1.

[95] A Watson, 'Changing Advocacy: Part One' (2001) 165 *Justice of the Peace* 743.

rhetoric[96] and reinforcement of the duty to the court.[97] The English legal profession has never adopted the phrase 'zealous advocacy', although recent academic discussion has proposed an obligation on advocates as 'mere zeal', diligence, rather than the 'hyper zeal' promoted by Freedman.[98] Today, therefore, the formal position in England and Wales tends more towards Noonan's theory of the purpose of the system than Freedman's and, therefore, to Noonan's interpretation of the advocate's role.

Advocates' duties to clients

For both branches of the profession the advocate's duty is a part of the general duty to protect the client's best interests and act in good faith. This is balanced by the duty to the administration of justice, conventionally expressed as a duty the court, which sometimes requires actions conflicting with clients' interests. The advocate's control of the strategic presentation of the case creates a grey area between following the client's wishes and wider duties, on which issue the Bar states unequivocally that the duty to the court prevails.[99] On fundamental issues advocates must expect to obtain instructions and disqualify themselves if they cannot in conscience follow them, but conflict between the duty to the court and the duty to the client is avoidable in most situations by the simple precaution of describing to the client what the duty to the court permits the advocate to do. There is no breach of a legal[100] or ethical duty if an advocate refuses to call a witness the client wants to be heard but who is likely to damage the client's case. Nor must an advocate run a point considered unarguable. In both cases, as in other cases where the client requires unethical conduct, the advocate can explain why he must refuse and what the options are, including the client's right to sack that advocate.[101]

Assuming that advocate and client are agreed on the conduct of the case, the remaining question concerns the limits on the advocate's behaviour. Both advocacy codes speak of acting 'fearlessly'. This presumably goes beyond not acting merely to please colleagues or officials.[102] It is not clear, but it is presumed from this and the tenor of the code generally

---

[96] Bar Code, para 708(b): '[a barrister] must not unless invited to do so by the Court or when appearing before a tribunal where it is his duty to do so assert a personal opinion of the facts or the law'.

[97] Bar Code, paras 302 (misleading the court) and 708(b) (asserting guilt or innocence of clients) are attributable the arguments advanced by William Forsyth in *Hortensius or the Advocate, an Historical Essay* (1849). See Watson, above n 95.

[98] T Dare, 'Mere Zeal, Hyper-zeal and the Ethical Obligations of Lawyers' (2004) 7 *Legal Ethics* 24; M Blake and A Ashworth, 'Ethics and the Criminal Defence Lawyer' (2004) 7 *Legal Ethics* 167.

[99] 'Duties of an Advocate to the Court' supplementary memorandum by the General Council of the Bar (Ev 01d) to the Joint Committee on The Draft Legal Services Bill (Minutes of Evidence), particularly number 5, 'Difficult Cases'.

[100] Lord Steyn in *Hall v Simons*, above n 53, stated 'The mere doing of his duty to the court by the advocate to the detriment of the client could never be called negligent' (para 683b).

[101] In *R v G* [2004] 1 WLR it was held that a court could not require a barrister to give an undertaking not to disclose to a client information discovered in a hearing he was entitled to attend. In *R v Davis* [2006] EWCA Crim 1155, however, advocates were given the option of cross-examining concealed witnesses or being able to see the witness and not describing them to their clients. The barrister could observe the duty to both court and client by seeking instructions that would allow him to see the witness without telling the client. If the client could not accept the restriction, the witness would remain obscured from the barrister's view.

[102] '. . . and do so without regard to his own interests or to any consequences to himself or to any other person (including any professional client, or intermediary or another barrister)'. Bar Code, para 303(a).

that advocates must resist oppressive judging. Excellent advocates have considerable scope for assisting clients without infringing the letter of the code. The duty to the court does not impinge on a clever advocate overcoming less able or less experienced opponents and, although advocates may not venture an opinion on the innocence of their client, the best are praised for conveying this confidence in their manner.[103]

Advocates' duties to witnesses

One of the key skills of advocacy is cross-examination of the other side's witnesses. This is intended to test and expose flaws in the witnesses' accounts, thereby indicating who is telling the truth.[104] The strategies range from limiting the impact of witnesses[105] to discrediting them completely.[106] Techniques for discrediting include questioning that sets out to attack their credentials or character and to confront, fluster, confuse and entrap them. The process involves using mainly closed and leading questions[107] to control the witness and elicit limited responses consistent with the advocate's own 'theory of the case'.[108] The behaviour associated with this technique would, in any other context, be regarded as bullying behaviour. While all these tactics are legitimate, there are limits to the treatment that witnesses can be expected to take and there are, increasingly, limitations imposed on advocates intended to protect third parties, like witnesses. Some limitations apply to all witnesses and others apply only to special categories.

Freedman's conception of trials as battles is out of favour, but his propositions regarding the implications of the adversarial paradigm remain the acid test of the ethical limits of advocacy. His first proposition is that opposing witnesses must be discredited even when 'known' to be truthful.[109] In *Rondell v Worsley* Lord Reid puts it a different way, stating that:

> every counsel has a duty to his client fearlessly to raise every issue, advance every argument, and ask every question, however distasteful, which he thinks will help his client's case. But . . . counsel . . . must not lend himself to casting aspersions on the other party or witnesses for which there is no sufficient basis in the information in his possession.[110]

---

[103] D Pannick, *Advocates* (Oxford University Press, 1992) 154.

[104] R Audi, 'The Ethics of Advocacy' (1995) 1 *Legal Theory* 251, 276.

[105] There are weaknesses in eye witness testimony that can exploited without attacking witness integrity. See EF Loftus, *Eyewitness Testimony* (Cambridge, MA, Harvard University Press, 1996).

[106] A Boon, *Advocacy* (London, Cavendish Publishing, 2nd edn, 1999).

[107] The use of leading questions stems from prohibitions on defence closing speeches in criminal trials, thus forcing counsel to explain their case to the jury through their questions. D Cairns, *Advocacy and the Making of the Adversarial Criminal Trial 1800–1865* (Oxford, Clarendon Press, 1998) 31.

[108] Boon, above n 106.

[109] Freedman, above n 87, illustrates his argument with the example that the judge may, mistakenly, permit an honest witness to give irrelevant testimony. See also Pepper, who asserts that a challenge to a truthful witness is permissible in all circumstances: S Pepper, 'The Lawyers' Amoral Ethical Role: A Defense, A Problem and Some Possibilities' [1986] *American Bar Foundation Research Journal* 613. While Freedman argues that the opposing lawyer may then be obliged to discredit the witness, rather than the testimony, Noonan, above n 88, argues that the advocate must trust the judge to exclude such testimony. A lawyer, he says, must not pre-empt the role of the judge or jury in assessing the truth.

[110] Above n 49.

The English codes contain only general limitations on the treatment of witnesses, providing that advocates cannot ask questions to scandalise, vilify, insult or annoy[111] or impugn a witness in a speech unless that witness has had a chance to answer the allegation in cross-examination.[112] Nor can they make a defamatory aspersion on a witness's conduct or accuse them of a crime unless such allegations go to a matter in issue.[113] The 'matter in issue' could be anything material to the lay client's case that appears to be supported by reasonable grounds, including the credibility of the witness. Therefore, even under English rules, a 'truthful' witness might be legitimately attacked on the grounds that they are not qualified to venture an opinion, did not perceive events correctly or misremembered what they saw.

There are special cases where cross-examination of witnesses is highly problematic, including cases involving children, people with learning difficulties and rape victims.[114] While all these examples present serious issues, the low conviction rate for those accused of rape is a continuing blot on the reputation of the courts,[115] causing the Attorney-General to mandate prosecutors to support alleged victims of rape at all stages of the case.[116] It is, however, difficult to balance their rights against those of the accused within the structure of the adversarial trial, particularly when a bullying style of cross-examination is the norm. There have been attempts to control cross-examination, in recognition that some questioning risks impairing the rights of victims. One example is where the accused elects to conduct their own defence, the subject of a claim against the UK that was settled before it could be heard by the European Court for Human Rights.[117] Subsequently, measures were introduced to prevent cross-examination of protected witnesses,[118] including rape complainants, by the accused in person.[119] Defendants in person could 'abuse the rules in relation to relevance and repetition which apply when witnesses are questioned'.[120] Courts were required to appoint, as advocates, lawyers chosen either by the accused or, in default, by the court, to cross-examine the victim.[121] It is often said, however, that victims can suffer almost as much from the questioning of lawyers as from that of the accused.

Representing a defendant on a rape charge where the defence is consent is a minefield for advocates. There is often no independent evidence to corroborate the account of either party, so it is one person's word against another. Alleged victims are often subject to long

---

[111] Bar Code 708(g), Solicitors' Code 11.05(a).

[112] Bar Code 708(i), Solicitors' Code 11.05(c).

[113] Bar Code 708(j), Solicitors' Code 11.05(d).

[114] L Ellison, 'The Mosaic Art?: Cross Examination and the Vulnerable Witness' (2003) 21 *Legal Studies* 353.

[115] Conviction rates fell from 33% in 1977 to 5.29% in 2004. See further C Dyer, 'Judges Try to Block Rape Reforms', *The Guardian*, 23 January 2007, 1; R Ford, '"Betrayal of Justice" as Rapists Walk Free', *Timesonline*, 30 March 2006.

[116] The Rt Hon Lord Goldsmit,h *Statement by the Attorney-General—The Prosecutors' Pledge* (London, Office of the Attorney-General, 2006); L Ellison, 'Witness Preparation and the Prosecution of Rape' (2007) 27 *Legal Studies* 171, 185.

[117] The victim was brutally raped over a period. The accused cross-examined her for 6 days, wearing the same clothes used in the attack, and she was later admitted to hospital. *JM v United Kingdom* Application No 41518/98 (unreported, 28 September 2000) (ECHR); *The Lawyer*, 29 October 1996. See also *R v Ralston Edwards* [1997] EWCA Crim 1679 (3 July 1997).

[118] Youth Justice and Criminal Evidence Act (1999), s 35.

[119] *Ibid*, s 34.

[120] *R v Milton Brown* [1998] EWCA Crim 1486 (6 May 1998).

[121] Youth Justice and Criminal Evidence Act (1999), s 38.

cross-examination by defence advocates,[122] a popular strategy being to undermine the victim's credibility by focusing on their past sexual history in order to present them as promiscuous and, therefore, more likely to have consented. One legislative attempt to control the practice having failed,[123] the Youth Justice and Criminal Evidence Act 1999, section 41[124] now limits the introduction of sexual history to behaviour around the time of the alleged rape, or to rebut prosecution evidence about the sexual behaviour of the complainant. Strict time limits apply[125] and full explanations are required when applications are late. Research conducted to establish the impact of the legislation found a suspiciously high level of cases where the victim's sexual history was admitted into evidence[126] and many cases where there was no application in writing before the trial. Lawyers were said to connive at this because the defence suffered no penalty by applying late, did not have to prepare the required written notices and put the victim under maximum pressure. The research concluded that many victims were subject to inappropriate cross-examination on their sexual history as a result of the devious tactics of defence barristers and the ignorance of some judges. Even recently, barristers admitted to poring over medical records 'for dirt-digging opportunities', one saying 'When I'm defending it's no holds barred'.[127]

When defence lawyers circumvent the rules introduced to protect the autonomy and rights of victims, it suggests that Freedman's assertion about advocates' perceptions of their duty is accurate. They may be supported by the judiciary, which criticises defendants but absolves their advocates of responsibility for the way they conduct their cross-examination.[128] The impression created is that advocates must present whatever case the client wants, even if their own judgement differs,[129] yet the Bar Code places the responsibility for the conduct of proceedings in court squarely on the advocate.[130] In reality, the path in problem areas is more often negotiated. The persistence of hostile tactics supports the impression that some lawyers, including some members of the judiciary, are resistant to attempts to assist possible rape victims. When due process produces unjust, even unconscionable, results, the cry is that there is no better system, combative advocacy is its best feature and the challenge is to convince the public of these facts.[131] It is unclear whether the

---

[122] In one infamous case, a victim was cross-examined for 30 hours over 12 days on behalf of multiple defendants.

[123] Sexual Offences (Amendment) Act (1976).

[124] S 41: '(1) If at a trial a person is charged with a sexual offence, then, except with the leave of the court, (a) no evidence may be adduced, and (b) no question may be asked in cross-examination, by or on behalf of any accused at the trial, about any sexual behaviour of the complainant.'

[125] Applications to admit evidence of sexual behaviour is required within 28 days of committal, providing a summary of the evidence, details of the questions to be asked and explaining how it falls into the exceptional categories. Crown Court Rules 1982 (as amended), r 23D.

[126] The study covered a three-month period in 2003 and 400 rape cases before the Crown courts in England and Wales. Applications to introduce sexual history were made in almost one quarter of cases and were successful in two-thirds of these. L Kelly, J Temkin and S Griffiths, *Section 41: An Evaluation of New Legislation Limiting Sexual History in Rape Trials* (London, Home Office, June 2006).

[127] F Abrams, 'Haunted by the Past', *The Guardian* (G2), 29 May 2001, 16.

[128] Mr Justice Boal, delivering convictions for a gang rape, said to the defendants, 'outrageous suggestions were put to her (the victim) on your instructions. You, not your counsel, added insult to injury and heaped further humiliation on her.' See *The Guardian*, 24 August 1996 and 5 and 7 September 1996.

[129] See, eg Pannick, above n 103, 92–3.

[130] Bar Code, para 708(a) provides that a practising barrister, when conducting proceedings at court, 'is personally responsible for the conduct and presentation of his case and must exercise personal judgement upon the substance and purpose of statements made and questions asked'.

[131] Pannick, above n 103, 166–9.

promised training course for barristers involved in rape cases, aimed at ensuring that they deal with the issues more sensitively,[132] will resolve the problem.

Advocate's duty to the court

The advocate's duty to the court counterbalances privileges such as the right to maintain client confidentiality[133] and is one of the few explicit exceptions to client loyalty. So fundamental to the integrity of the adversarial system is this duty that the legislative enactment of the advocate's duty[134] is separate from a similar duty imposed on litigation generally.[135] As with the duty on litigators, the advocate's duty, to act with independence in the interests of justice, is coupled with a duty to follow the rules of the body granting the advocacy rights. The separation of the duties to assist in the administration of justice and to follow the code suggests that the court's jurisdiction over the conduct of advocates is not circumscribed by the profession's interpretation of its ethical responsibilities. Therefore, assuming the wasted costs jurisdiction is part of the duty to the court, a barrister may be held responsible for costs wasted by inadequate presentation.[136] Nevertheless, it is likely to be the baseline or starting point of judicial interpretation. The legislation follows closely the formulation in the Bar Code, whereby:

> A practising barrister has an overriding duty to the Court to ensure in the public interest that the proper and efficient administration of justice is achieved: he must assist the Court in the administration of justice and must not deceive or knowingly or recklessly mislead the Court.[137]

Although the Solicitors Code does not refer to a duty to the court,[138] both codes draw on the Bar's conception of that duty; a duty to disclose relevant authorities, points of law that may have eluded an opponent, to point out procedural irregularities and not to make submissions considered not to be properly arguable.[139] The Solicitors Code is arguably more explicit, at least in the guidance to rule 11, in that it spells out the line that solicitor advocates should take in some of the more difficult points emerging from case law,[140] considered below. A

---

[132] A Travis, 'Barristers and Judges Accused of Undermining Rape Reform', *The Guardian*, 21 June 2006.

[133] The Marre Report, for example, stated that: 'Because of the doctrine of legal professional privilege, which shields from outside eyes what passes between a lawyer and his client, the observance by the lawyer of his duty to the court is of particular importance.' Lady Marre CBE, *A Time for Change: Report on the Committee on the Future of the Legal Profession* (London, The General Council of the Bar, The Law Society, 1988) para 6.6.

[134] Courts and Legal Services Act 1990, s 27(2A) (rights of audience), as amended by the Access to Justice Act 1999, s 42(1): 'Every person who exercises before any court a right of audience granted by an authorised body has (a) a duty to the court to act with independence in the interests of justice; and (b) a duty to comply with rules of conduct of the body relating to the right and approved for the purposes of this section; and those duties shall override any obligation which the person may have (otherwise than under the criminal law) if it is inconsistent with them.'

[135] See chapter 17. The need for a separate section for advocacy may be because barristers could argue that they are not caught by a provision relating to litigators.

[136] *Ibid.*

[137] Bar Code, para 302.

[138] The Law Society Code for Advocacy contained a similar formula to para 302 (para 2.3(b)), but r 11 of the Solicitor's Code does not (but see the rule for a general duty to the administration of justice).

[139] Bar Code, para 708.

[140] Solicitors' Code, r 11, guidance notes 12–17.

potential problem is that detailed examples potentially circumscribe the duty. However, since the legislation separates the obligation to follow codes from the obligation to promote the administration of justice, the duty to the administration of justice, if not the duty to the court, is broader than the code. It could, for example, embrace an obligation of deference and courtesy to the judge and the judicial institution, a matter not expressly mentioned in the codes.[141]

While the duty to the court potentially covers the whole process of litigation, including the interface with advocacy itself, the discussion here focuses on the trial process. While there is a public interest in protecting the integrity of litigation in general, the conduct of those producing evidence in court has special significance. This is reflected in the judge's power to punish witnesses delivering perjured testimony. Freedman argues that such powers do not determine the duty of the advocate. He suggests, for example, that an advocate might be ethically justified in permitting perjury to achieve a just result.[142] The profession in England and Wales takes a stricter and more conventional line on the issue, illustrated in the Marre report:

> A lawyer may not, directly or indirectly, lend himself knowingly to any false story being put before the court. If he is asked to do so, he must immediately cease to act for the client.[143]

The cases are a little more ambiguous, but this principle clearly emerges from them.

The difference between the position expounded by Freedman and that taken by the English courts may, in part, reflect cultural differences in trial presentation. If US legal documentary or fiction is to be believed, the presentational aspect of trials is accepted. Therefore, 'witness preparation' is overt and detailed, whereas it has always been frowned on in England. The Bar Code states that barristers must not devise facts that will assist in advancing the client's case,[144] or rehearse, practice or coach a witness in relation to the evidence they will give.[145] Indeed, a recent Court of Appeal decision attempted to stop a growth industry in witness programmes, distinguishing between witness familiarisation, which is allowed, and witness preparation, which is not.[146] Familiarisation includes informing witnesses about the court, the sequence of events and the role of the personnel, whereas witness preparation programmes must not take place in relation to specific trials or refer to similar fact patterns. The Bar issued advice of its own, stating that witnesses may be told how to perform their role—to listen, answer questions, speak clearly and slowly, and avoid irrelevant comment.[147] It has also advised that, when instructed to prepare witness statements, barristers should ensure that it is the witness's account that is recorded, but, more contentiously perhaps, can draw attention to evidence conflicting with what the

---

141 S Ginossa, 'The Lawyer's Divided Loyalties: An Introductory Note' (1981) 16 *Israel Law Review* 1.

142 This is contradicted by cases decided under US state laws. For example, in *McKissick v United States* 379 F 2d 754 (5th Cir 1967) admission of perjury to attorney was good cause for withdrawal from case; the attorney would be subject to discipline if he continued the defence without reporting to the court; in *Dodd v Florida Bar* 118 So 2d 17 (Fla 1960) advising several persons including client to perjure themselves warranted disbarment. See GC Hazard, 'The Future of Legal Ethics' (1991) 100 *Yale Law Journal* 1239, 1257.

143 The Marre report, above n 133, para 6.6.

144 Para 704.

145 Para 705(a).

146 *R v Momodou* [2005] EWCA Crim 177.

147 Bar Standards Board website (last accessed July 2007).

witness is saying and point out that a court would find a particular point difficult to accept. The line between familiarisation and preparation is highly debatable in an area of fine but significant cultural differences.[148]

While fabricating evidence is proscribed, the position where an advocate is silent when misleading evidence is presented is less clear. Decisions over the past 50 years suggest the courts may be moving towards a more demanding standard. Such decisions typically arise in applications for a new trial because the court has been misled, or disputes over costs, where the conduct of the advocate—whether it was permitted and what was its affect—is central. Although the conclusion may not affect the advocate personally, it is possible that disciplinary sanctions may also follow the court's decision.[149] The cases therefore define the scope of the duty as perceived by judges at particular times. The imprecise nature of the duty not to mislead was suggested by dictum in *re Mayor Cooke*, [150] where it was said that:

> it was a part of [a lawyer's] duty that he should not keep back from the Court any informa-tion which ought to be before it, and that he should in no way mislead the court by stating facts which were untrue . . . How far a solicitor might go on behalf of his client was a question far too difficult to be capable of abstract definition , but when concrete cases arose every one could see for himself whether what had been done was fair or not.[151]

The 'concrete cases' revealed that the courts were prepared to extend the duty beyond the advocate 'stating facts which were untrue', although with difficulty. The first category of case is where advocates allow witnesses giving evidence to conceal facts about themselves that creates a misleading impression.

In *Tombling v Universal Bulb Company Limited*[152] the application for a new trial focused on the behaviour of the plaintiff's counsel. He had conducted an examination-in-chief of a witness and established his home address, his previous employment as a prison governor and his subsequent employment, without referring to the fact that the witness was at the time of the trial serving a prison sentence for a driving offence. The Court of Appeal refused to set aside the decision of the court below because it was not satisfied that awareness of this fact would have affected the outcome of the trial. It was not attracted by the argument that the perpetration of a trick by counsel,[153] even if proven, should itself be a basis for ordering a new trial. This decision is, of course, irrelevant to the ethical question of whether the counsel should have questioned the witness in such a way as not to raise the issue of his convictions. This is far more problematic.

Somervell LJ felt that counsel was probably not under any duty to disclose the witness's convictions, but that it would have been better had the plaintiff's counsel not led the plain-tiff's evidence in the way he had. Denning LJ would have been disposed to order a new trial

---

[148] Ipp, for example, suggests that witnesses in general can be shown the oral evidence of other witnesses (D Ipp, 'Lawyers' Duties to the Court' (1998) 114 *Law Quarterly Review* 63, 91), but a Scottish case criticised the practice of letting any but the client to see evidence (*Ian Smith Watson v Student Loans Company*, available at http://wwwscotscourts.gov.uk (last accessed July 2007)).

[149] Hilbery, for example, talks of the sanction being a reprimand from the judge followed by ostracism by 'his' peers for repeat offenders: The Hon Sir M Hilberry, *Duty and Art in Advocacy* (London, Stevens & Sons, 1946) 21.

[150] *In re G Mayor Cooke* (1989) 5 Times Law Reports 407.

[151] *Ibid*, 408.

[152] [1951] 2 The Times Law Reports 289.

[153] Presumably presenting the witness as more credible than he in fact was.

had there been any improper conduct by the successful party. But, he said, there was nothing improper in the conduct of the plaintiff's counsel. Had the questions been put to the witness with the intention of misleading the Court, it would have been a different matter. His Lordship was, however, satisfied that it had not been put with that intention. Singleton LJ took a less forgiving line, saying that, regarding the conflicting duties owed by advocates,

> in this case counsel thought only of his duty to his client to the exclusion of the duty which he owed to others, and, in particular, that which he owed to the court.[154]

He would have ordered a retrial on the basis that this witness's evidence was material to establishing the plaintiff's case. Further, he said, there was a need to see that courts should be above suspicion and parties should feel that they had a fair deal. It is clearly not an easy task to unpick the ethical and tactical decisions made by an advocate. Had the evidence been material and a new trial ordered, it is difficult to see how the administration of justice, or the duty to the court, would have been served by defending the advocate's right not to present a truthful picture.

In *Meek v Fleming*,[155] a case with broadly similar facts, the decision went the other way and a retrial was ordered. This was an action in which witness credibility was central—a civil action by a journalist claiming damages for an uncorroborated assault by a senior police officer. The defendant's counsel, a QC, took full responsibility for concealing from the court the fact that his client had been demoted for a deception in a court of law in the course of his duty as a police officer. At the trial the defendant had been deliberately dressed in civilian clothes and was addressed as 'Mister' throughout, yet his status and seniority had clearly been material factors in the trial. It was held that to uphold the decision at first instance would be a miscarriage of justice. Holroyd Pearce LJ accepted Denning LJ's argument in *Tombling* that the intention of the advocate was material. The instant case, he said, was different from *Tombling* in that the court was deceived as a 'premeditated line of conduct'.[156] Wilmer LJ said that counsel's decision had 'involved insufficient regard being paid to the duty owed to the court and to the plaintiff and his advisers'.[157]

The second category of case covered by the duty not to mislead the court involves facts known to the advocate that are not presented in evidence. In *re Mayor Cooke* it was said that the duty to the court should embrace documents that might be material to the way the evidence is perceived. The judge said:

> [if counsel] were to know that an affidavit had been made in the cause which had been used and which, if it were before the Judge, must affect his mind, and if he knew that the judge was ignorant of the existence of that affidavit, then if he concealed that affidavit from the Judge he would fail in his duty . . . if he were to make any wilful misstatement to the judge he would be outrageously dishonourable.[158]

---

[154] *Ibid*, 296.
[155] [1961] 2 QB 366.
[156] *Ibid*, 379.
[157] *Ibid*, 383.
[158] *Ibid*, 408.

Vernon v Bosley (No 2)[159] presented analogous circumstances to those described in *re Mayor Cooke*. The case is interesting for the light it throws on the issue of how, in practical terms, the duty to the court can be reconciled with loyalty to the client and, specifically, the obligation to respect client confidentiality and autonomous decision making.

The plaintiff had been awarded substantial damages for nervous shock resulting from the death of his two daughters. Following the first instance judgment, the defendant's counsel received copies of a judgment in proceedings relating to unconnected family proceedings. This suggested that the plaintiff had substantially recovered by the time the judgment was delivered in his claim for shock but, obviously, the damages would be greater had his condition persisted. Stuart-Smith LJ held that there should have been disclosure to the defendant of the fact of his recovery, because litigators should not mislead the court or opponents. Misleading the court was broader than giving evidence known to be untrue, but included leading the court to believe that circumstances which were once true had not changed when they clearly had. The duty continued until the judge had given judgment.

In *Vernon v Bosley (No 2)*, Stuart-Smith LJ gave examples of instances where an advocate may be silent while the court was misled. Where a barrister knows of his client's previous convictions he is not under an obligation to disclose them, but must not then assert the good character of his client. Similarly, he is not bound to call evidence which did not support his case. However, where evidence had been presented of material facts which were known to be untrue, counsel had an obligation to advise his client to make disclosure. If the client refused this advice,

> it was not, as a rule, for counsel to make the disclosure himself, but he could no longer continue to act.

The integrity of the process would be somewhat protected by the non-appearance of the plaintiff's counsel, even in the absence of a positive duty on the advocate to break the obligation of confidentiality to the client; the plaintiff's solicitor, the defendant's advisers and also the judge would be alerted to the fact that something was amiss.

Evans LJ, dissenting, sought to blame the plaintiff's expert witnesses, who had given evidence in both sets of proceedings. Plaintiff's counsel, he said, did not mislead the court or act improperly in any way. He was particularly concerned at the implications where expert witnesses, having given their evidence, changed their minds. Thorpe LJ argued that the current reform of civil justice must include 'strengthening the duty to the court'. He argued that counsel would know instinctively or intuitively that a course of action felt wrong and that, in such cases, he should not follow it. His Lordship suggested that the correct course of action was for plaintiff's counsel to make disclosure to the opposing counsel in order to avoid the likelihood that injustice would be done.[160] Thorpe LJ's judgment is notable for its invocation of 'ordinary morality' as a guide to behaviour, when lawyers are normally guided by the specific morality of their adversarial role.

The third category of case does not affect evidence at all, but falls within the wider conception of the duty to uphold the proper administration of justice. A case that saw a similar evocation of principle as those *in re Mayor Cooke* and *Vernon v Bosley* is *Haiselden v*

---

[159] [1997] 1 All ER 614.
[160] See D Pannick, 'When Counsel Should Come Clean', *The Times*, 14 January 1997.

P&O Properties,[161] where a litigant in person commenced an action for damages for personal injury in the county court. The sum involved required the court to enter the case for arbitration, where no costs would be awarded. In error, the case was put on the path to trial, where the plaintiff was at risk of costs if the case was lost. The error remained undetected, the plaintiff lost the case and costs were awarded against him. On appeal to the Court of Appeal, Thorpe LJ said that the defendants' advocate had:

> very creditably and candidly informed us that at all stages the defendants perceived the advantage to themselves of the error of the court service . . . They thought that they would win on liability; they did not want an arbitration determination; they wanted determination by trial so that they had the prospect of recovering the costs of their defence. Accordingly they took advantage of the judicial error and felt able to do so because they considered that it was still arguable that some administrative notice of reference to arbitration needed to be issued. They comforted themselves by saying, 'if and when such a notice is issued we will then apply to the judge *inter partes* for a ruling rescinding the reference to arbitration.[162]

The plaintiff succeeded in having the order for costs set aside on the basis that there should never have been a trial. There was no hint of criticism in the judgment of the advocate, who, realising the court's mistake, had allowed the process of trial to continue. The narrow principle, therefore, is that an advocate must not allow a legal process to commence or continue on an incorrect footing, for example, where there is a misapprehension as to jurisdiction. The basis of this rule is that this compromises the proper administration of justice. The value of *Haiselden v P&O Properties* in this discussion, however, lies in illustrating courts' expanding willingness to find that they have been misled.

The principles that appear to unite the English decisions on the duty to the court is that advocates should not present partial evidence on an issue when they and only they know that the court would regard it as a fact material to the way the proceedings are conducted. This seems too broad, however. There is no duty to point out to an opponent, unless it is a litigant in person, that they may have made a tactical error in running their case, even though this could affect both process and outcome.[163] If advocates are obliged to paint a full picture of every element of their evidence, it might overly restrict how they present their client's version of the facts. After all, the adversarial system works on the premise that each side reveals the fault lines in the other's case. It is safer to contain *Tombling* and *Meek*, and possible to do so, on the basis that the concealed fact related to the way the advocate presented the witness to the court, not how they gave evidence-in-chief. Since the credibility of witnesses is a vital tool for evaluating their evidence, this presentation is crucial. The other cases can be classed as failures to point out procedural irregularities, and therefore only tangentially connected to the advocate's duty.

The Bar Code has been content to leave the problems raised by the cases as part of the general duty to the court, thus ensuring that the duty remains flexible. The new Solicitors Code takes a more direct approach. In addition to the familiar prohibitions on concealing documents that come to light in proceedings, allowing false evidence to be led or

---

161 [1998] All ER (D) 180, [1998] EWCA Civ 773.

162 [1998] EWCA Civ 773, 7.

163 Eg where counsel notices a break in continuity that may be the basis of a successful 'half time submission'.

influencing witnesses,[164] it advises solicitors to ensure that clients adopting different names are not seeking to deceive the court and to ensure that judges are aware of relevant document filed in the proceedings.[165] The trend in the cases is towards a more onerous conception of the advocate's duty to the court, consistent with the broad duty to the administration of justice rather than a narrow obligation not to mislead. The most recent proposal is that advocates be obliged to advise judges on their sentencing power, following cases where unlawful convictions have been quashed.[166] Increasing the obligations of advocates is somewhat inconsistent with the trend towards greater judicial control of cases.[167] The courts have approached the cases discussed by asking two questions: did the advocate deliberately mislead the court and did this affect the outcome of the case? It is interesting that this link should be made, since it suggests that the decisions hinge on the ethical failing of the advocate when the question should be whether a retrial, or some other order, is necessary in the interests of justice.[168] Confusion is heightened by the fact that the court is sometimes at pains to point out that, while it was misled, the advocate had behaved ethically.

Conclusion

Advocacy is the distinguishing activity of lawyers and remains the source of considerable prestige and status, leading to tension between the Bar and the Law Society. The long-term future of the Bar depends on its continued excellence, economy and efficiency in providing advocacy services, but the current arrangements may not survive sustained pressure from the government to rationalise the legal services market. The arguments for a separate Bar include the specialist coverage it offers and the high standards it achieves. Implicit in its standards is the ability to balance duties to clients and to the courts. This has been reinforced by the introduction of a general duty for advocates to act with independence in the interests of justice. It is not clear whether this heralds a new and more onerous conception of the duty to the court, but, even before the legislative initiative, a trend towards a stricter interpretation of the duty to the court was evident in judicial decisions. This is consistent with the move towards cooperative litigation instigated by the Civil Procedure Rules. The tensions of managing the limits of adversarial roles are one of many reasons why so-called Alternative Dispute Resolution has been welcomed. The promise of 'win–win' solutions to disputes appears to offer escape from the deep conflicts, of interests and ethics, attendant on adversarial justice.

---

[164] Solicitors' Code, r 11, guidance note 12.

[165] *Ibid*, guidance notes 13 and 14.

[166] C Dyer, 'Law Chief Justice Urges Advice for Judges on Sentencing Limits', *The Guardian*, 15 January 2007, 15.

[167] As noted in *Hall v Simons*, above n 53, continental jurisdictions, eg Germany, tend not to oblige advocates to refer the court to adverse authorities (682f).

[168] In *Visham Boodoosingh v Richard Ramnarace* [2005] UKPC 9, for example, there was no consideration of whether lawyers were implicated in their clients' attempt to deceive the court.

20

ALTERNATIVE DISPUTE RESOLUTION

Why . . . are lawyers, in essence, such obscure men? Why do their undoubted talents yield so poor a harvest of immortality? The answer, it seems to me . . . is their professional aim and function [is] not to get at the truth, but simply to carry on combats between ancient rules.[1]

Introduction

Most common law jurisdictions have sought ways of avoiding the cost and delay of litigation by exploring the use of Alternative Dispute Resolution (ADR), particularly mediation, to supplement or replace it. ADR is seen as part of a social and political movement towards 'informalism'.[2] It is a response to the criticism that litigation is too formal, conflictual and slow, but also to the perception that disputes are more complex or that society applies legal machinery to problems that are really economic, social or political.[3] ADR processes appear to provide an answer. They can be tailored to a variety of conflict types, disputes or parties.[4] The growth of ADR raises many questions for lawyers. Should lawyers compete for ADR business? Should they seek a role in regulating it? If the answers to these questions are affirmative, what are the implications for the way they work, bearing in mind their professional ethic based on adversarial assumptions?

Defining ADR

There are a wide range of processes embraced by ADR, including arbitration, mediation, conciliation, mini-trial,[5] arbitration,[6] expert determination[7] and hybrids combining features

---

[1] HL Mencken, 'Editorial' [January 1928] *American Mercury* 35, 36.

[2] See generally RL Abel, 'The Contradictions of Informal Justice' in RL Abel (ed), *The Politics of Informal Justice: The American Experience* (New York, Academic Press, 1982).

[3] This may be a reaction to more complex disputes, multiple parties, a high level of interdependency between parties and issues, and polycentricity (interlinking of issues, unclear linkages and poor understanding of issues by parties). DP Emond, 'Alternative Dispute Resolution: A Conceptual Overview' in DP Emond (ed), *Commercial Dispute Resolution: Alternatives to Litigation* (Aurora, Canada Law Books, 1989) 1, 14.

[4] P Gulliver, *Disputes and Negotiations: A Cross-Cultural Perspective* (New York, Academic Press, 1979); WF Felstiner, RL Abel and A Sarat, 'The Emergence and Transformation of Disputes: Naming, Blaming, Claiming' (1980–1) 15 *Law and Society* 631 and particularly at 640–1.

[5] A shortened, full trial presented to senior executives of the parties to the dispute, or a retired judge, to clarify legal and factual merits—often as a precursor to negotiation. See JF Davis and LJ Omlie, 'Mini Trials: The Courtroom in the Boardroom' (1985), 21 *Willamette Law Review* 531; BC Hart, 'Alternative Dispute Resolution:

of one or more methods. The unifying feature is that a third party helps to resolve the dispute. Since this is essentially what a judge does, and given that ADR often embraces formal and binding processes not very different from those of courts, we must consider the two main ways in which ADR is 'alternative'. In arbitration, expert determination or mini-trial the similarities to trial are strongest, the parties agreeing to substitute a third party for a judge provided by the state and to accept the decision.[8] The parties agree to accept the outcome in advance and the process often follows state adjudication closely, frequently allowing recourse to the courts. The motive for the parties in using these 'alternative' processes is to reduce litigation costs or to provide a swifter outcome to disputes and specialist adjudicators. There is however, also more flexibility than courts would normally allow, so that parties can agree the forum and rules of procedure in advance. This group of processes are 'alternative' in the sense that both the parties opt to use them, rather than one being coerced, and they are not state sponsored.[9]

A second group of ADR processes is different to court trials, mainly because the parties are not committed to a formally binding conclusion unless they both agree. In mediation and conciliation, for example, a third party brings together the disputants, aiming to facilitate understanding of differences, resolve them if possible and create a better relationship. The outcome may be novel, or non-legal, solutions, including acceptance or accommodation of problems.[10] Conciliation may leave the process there, as when a couple with marital problems decide to continue their relationship. The focus of mediation, however, is often settlement of a more material dispute, as where they decide to part and divide marital property.

There are different aspirations for mediation, and hence different kinds, including facilitative, evaluative and transformative, each with distinct philosophies and methods.[11] They share the advantage over court processes in promoting understanding of the causes of conflict, including cultural differences. From this understanding, mediation encourages consideration of a wider range of solutions, allowing outcomes that reflect the values and priorities of the parties. In these respects, the goals and techniques of mediation are identical to those of a problem-solving negotiation, the difference lying in the crucial role of the third party.[12] Mediators facilitate a fuller understanding by the parties of the other side's perceptions, circumstances and feelings, and promote rational communication and

---

Negotiation, Mediation and Minitrial' (1987) *FICC Quarterly* 113; C Ervine, *Settling Consumer Disputes: A Review of Alternative Dispute Resolution* (London, National Consumer Council, 1993) 12.

[6] A non-judicial proceeding in which awards tend to be binding, final and enforceable in the courts. BH Goldstein, 'Alternatives for Resolving Business Transactions Disputes' (1983) 58 *St John's Law Review* 69; MP Reynolds, *Arbitration* (London, Lloyd's of London Press, 1993) pt 1; BJ Thompson, 'Commercial Dispute Resolution: A Practical Overview' in Emond, above n 3, 89, 91.

[7] Parties to a contract jointly instruct an 'expert' to make a binding decision. J Kendall, 'Simpler Dispute Resolution', *Solicitors Journal*, 29 November 1996, 1152.

[8] See, eg, in relation to expert determination, *Mercury Communications Ltd v Director of Telecommunications* [1996] 1 All ER 575; [1996] 1 WLR 48 and Arbitration Act 1996, s 9(2).

[9] GC Hazard, 'Court Delay: Toward New Premises (1986) 5 *Civil Justice Quarterly* 236.

[10] R Young, 'Neighbour Dispute Mediation: Theory and Practice' (1989) 2 *Civil Justice Quarterly* 319.

[11] Eg transformative models treat conflict as a tool of personal growth, while others downplay stress.

[12] C Menkel-Meadow, 'Lawyer Negotiations: Theories and Realities: What We Learn from Mediation' (1993) 56 *Modern Law Review* 361.

negotiation.[13] They can take a more proactive role than the parties could, encouraging them to clarify values and identify possible joint gains, bringing about and sustaining dialogue when deadlock threatens, reminding both sides of the advantages of agreement and persuading and cajoling them.

ADR—An Ethical Dispute Resolution Process?

Because of its holistic approach to conflict and its cooperative assumptions, mediation can be presented as an ethically superior system of dispute resolution to trial. Parties agree the process, and the informality that often results affords opportunities for the participation of the lay client in the process. Unlike courts, which follow their own rules, mediation changes how the parties regard their situation and can adapt the process accordingly. Unlike courts, which impose solutions, mediation promotes agreements freely arrived at with full knowledge of legal and practical alternatives, encouraging compliance with the outcome.[14] These features are seen to be consistent with the aims of plural liberal society. Procedural flexibility increases the chance of accommodating the different interests and perceptions that individuals bring to disputes, and freedom of choice is consistent with the obligation of the liberal state to promote individual agency and personhood.[15] Mediation also promotes key ethical values. The capacity to increase client participation stimulates client choice, and therefore individual autonomy. The generation of solutions encourages exploration of mutual benefit, creating the possibility of satisfaction, and therefore 'justice', for both sides. These features make processes like mediation attractive as inexpensive, accessible and community-orientated forms of dispute resolution, making justice achievable for all.

Debates about the ethicality of ADR arose from the mixed experience of the proliferation of schemes in North America during the 1980s.[16] Court congestion was substantially reduced and settlements increased.[17] The accountability of representatives and third party neutrals was effectively secured and state-sponsored schemes absorbed accommodation and other overheads. Some argued that these gains were so important that compulsion was justified to overcome widespread ignorance of disputing alternatives.[18] Many critics strongly opposed state co-option of ADR, particularly mediation, to court processes. They argued that compulsory participation eroded the crucial, consensual nature of ADR and the vital

[13] M Roberts, 'Who is in Charge? Reflections on Recent Research on the Role of the Mediator' (1992) 14 *Journal of Social Welfare and Family Law* 372, 374–6. See generally A Bevan, *Alternative Dispute Resolution* (London, Sweet & Maxwell, 1992); JM Haynes, *Alternative Dispute Resolution: Fundamentals of Family Mediation* (Horsmonden, Old Bailey Press, 1993).

[14] There is often greater compliance with mediation agreements than with court orders. CA McEwen and RJ Maiman, 'Small Claims Mediation in Maine: An Empirical Assessment' (1981) 33 *Maine Law Review* 237.

[15] A Wellington, 'Taking Codes of Ethics Seriously: Alternative Dispute Resolution and Reconstitutive Liberalism' (1999) 12 *Canadian Journal of Law and Jurisprudence* 297.

[16] M Galanter, 'Law Abounding: Legalisation Around the North Atlantic' (1992) 55 *Modern Law Review* 1, 11.

[17] DR Hensler, 'What We Know and Don't Know about Court Administered Arbitration' (1986) 69 *Judicature* 270; WK Edwards, 'No Frills Justice: North Carolina Experiments with Court Ordered Arbitration' (1988) 66 *North Carolina Law Review* 395; AJ Pirie, 'The Lawyer as a Third Party Neutral: Promise and Problems' in Edmond, above n 3, 27, 35.

[18] SB Goldberg, ED Green and FEA Sanders, *Dispute Resolution* (Boston, MA, Little Brown, 1985) 490.

intimacy, reciprocity and permanence of the social context.[19] In some circumstances, compulsion could be abusive.[20] The increased formality of court-annexed schemes can lead to reduced client participation,[21] stronger pressure to settle,[22] less participant satisfaction and fewer durable agreements.

Others opposed bringing ADR into the court system because it did not promote ethical goods. They argued that mediation is 'second rate' or 'compromise' justice, and that its outcomes are likely to reflect financial or psychological power inequalities between parties.[23] Judges can compensate for inequality,[24] but the absence of powers of compulsion means that mediators cannot. Whereas commercial parties might agree to mediate in advance, there was no justification for denying the choice of ordinary disputants. Moreover, deflecting individual legal challenges into informal routes reduced the number of court cases and legal precedents, slowing the rate of social change and contradicting the rights ethos of liberalism.[25] ADR, they said, undercuts substantive law, permitting parties to reach solutions that ignore public standards[26] and the interests of third parties. The result was an uncertain environment that encourages disputation.[27] During the 1990s, similar doubts about mediation's claims to ethical superiority arose in the UK.[28]

The Range of ADR

There are many private ADR systems operating in the UK, particularly in the commercial sphere. Efficient dispute resolution services support the business and commercial infrastructure, and the use of a country's dispute resolution forums boosts its invisible earnings. The UK has a mixed record. Despite having widely admired judges, and attracting a good share of international litigation, it was one of the last major countries to adopt the

---

[19] TB Carver and AA Vondra, 'Alternative Dispute Resolution: Why it Doesn't Work and Why it Does' (1994) 72(3) *Harvard Business Review* 120; J Auerbach, *Justice Without Law? Resolving Disputes Without Lawyers* (Oxford University Press, 1983).

[20] FE Raitt, 'Informal Justice and the Ethics of Mediating in Abusive Relationships' (1997) *Juridical Review* 76.

[21] See generally RL Abel, 'The Contradictions of Informal Justice' in Abel, above n 2; Auerbach, above, n 19.

[22] R Dingwall, 'Empowerment or Enforcement? Some Questions about Power and Control in Divorce Mediation' in R Dingwall and J Eekelaar (eds), *Divorce Mediation and the Legal Process* (Oxford, Clarendon Press, 1988); JDD Smith, 'Mediator Impartiality: Banishing the Chimera' (1994) 31 *Journal of Peace Research* 445.

[23] Poor parties cannot pay for expert preparation of the case, cannot predict the outcome of adjudication and are under financial pressure to settle (O Fiss, 'Against Settlement' (1983) 93 *Yale Law Journal* 1073, 1076; N Fricker and J Walker, 'Alternative Dispute Resolution: State Responsibility or Second Best?' (1994) 13 *Civil Justice Quarterly* 29). Informality may encourage unreasonable behaviour (R Delgado, C Dunn, P Brown, H Lee, and D Hubert, 'Fairness and Formality: Minimizing the Risk of Prejudice in Alternative Dispute Resolution' (1985) *Wisconsin Law Review* 1359).

[24] Auerbach, above n 19.

[25] Fiss, above n 23, 1075; Emond, above n 3, 24–5.

[26] MA Scodro, 'Arbitrating Novel Legal Questions: A Recommendation for Reform' (1996) 105 *The Yale Law Journal* 1927.

[27] Ervine, above n 5, 16.

[28] S Roberts, 'Mediation in the Lawyers' Embrace' (1992) 55 *The Modern Law Review* 258; R Dingwall and D Greatbatch, 'Who is in Charge? Rhetoric and Evidence in the Study of Mediation' (1993) 15 *Journal of Social Welfare and Family Law* 367; M Roberts, 'Who is in Charge? Effecting a Productive Exchange between Researchers and Practitioners in the Field of Family Mediation' (1994) 16 *Journal of Social Welfare and Family Law* 439; R Dingwall and D Greatbatch, 'Family Mediation Researchers and Practitioners in the Shadow of the Green Paper: A Rejoinder to Marion Roberts' (1995) 17 *Journal of Social Welfare and Family Law* 199.

UN-sponsored model code for arbitration.[29] The Arbitration Act 1996 was introduced to revise an inadequate regulatory framework[30] and boost the credentials of the UK as a centre for international arbitration.[31] The Act was intended to provide the parties with the maximum flexibility to design their own proceedings[32] without intervention by the court, except in limited circumstances. Although London's Centre of International Arbitration has gained ground on its major rivals in Paris and Stockholm, critics argue that it was a mistake to preserve any role for the courts to review decisions.[33] In a rapidly evolving global market for services, impediments to swift solutions must be removed. At the other end of the commercial scale, mediation is often used for handling consumer complaints, but not necessarily with high levels of satisfaction.[34]

ADR has also become increasingly significant in the public sphere. Conciliation in divorce proceedings predates the Second World War.[35] It grew in significance from the 1960s, when a sixfold increase in the rate of divorce[36] saw unofficial annexation of such schemes to some county divorce courts and magistrates' domestic courts. Although lawyers were often blamed for fuelling conflict in family disputes, conciliation was popular with solicitors,[37] a greater problem being lack of funding and formal structures. The Family Law Act 1996 proposed to introduce mediation for divorce,[38] but the legislation, due to come into force in 2000, was scrapped after pilots.[39] Since the mid-1970s, ADR began to increase with conciliation in trade union disputes, through the medium of the Arbitration and Conciliation Advisory Service, and the so-called 'arbitration', in fact a relaxed judicial process, used for small claims in the county courts.[40] In construction disputes, ADR was given statutory foundation, becoming the norm rather than the alternative,[41] a recognised adjunct of court process. In the Commercial Court scheme, established in 1994, parties could be directed to settle by 'ADR orders'. These limited uses of ADR were not just widely

---

[29] UNCITRAL Model Law on International Commercial Arbitration 1985 (as amended).

[30] 'Fair, Speedy and Cost Effective Resolutions of Disputes', *Solicitors Journal*, 23 February 1996.

[31] It was hoped that the UK would 'retain pre-eminence in the field of international arbitration, a service which brings this country very substantial amounts indeed by way of invisible earnings': Saville LJ, chair of the Departmental Advisory Committee of the Department of Trade and Industry, quoted in M Rutherford, 'Arbitration Act Update', *Solicitors Journal*, 22 November 1996, 1125. See further, PR Ellington, 'The New Arbitration Act 1996' (1998) 3 *Amicus Curiae* 14.

[32] The Act contains mandatory and non-mandatory provisions (see s 4). Those dealing with conduct of proceedings (ss 33–95) were mainly non-mandatory. S York, 'Privatisation of Disputes' (1996) 140 *Solicitors Journal* 1153.

[33] 'Global Warring', *Law Society Gazette*, 2 November 2000, 32.

[34] The processes were sometimes seen as unfair. See *Out of Court: A Consumer View of Three Low Cost Trade Schemes* (London, National Consumer Council, 1991).

[35] See also A Ogus, M Jones-Lee, W Cole and P McCarthy, 'Evaluating Alternative Dispute Resolution: Measuring the Impact of Family Conciliation on Costs' (1990) 53 *Modern Law Review* 57, 59.

[36] Conciliation schemes were set up by local professionals, lawyers, social workers and probation officers.

[37] Lady Marre CBE, *A Time for Change: Report on the Committee on the Future of the Legal Profession* (London, The General Council of the Bar, The Law Society, 1988) (hereafter the Marre Report) para 11.10; in relation to labour disputes, see R Singh, 'Dispute Resolution in Britain: Contemporary Trends" (1995) 16 *International Journal of Manpower* 42.

[38] Based on the Law Commission Report, *The Ground for Divorce* (Law Commission No 192, 1990).

[39] It added approximately £150 to the cost of settling a child dispute (Ogus *et al*, above n 35, 73).

[40] Ervine, above n 5, 8.

[41] Under a procedure established by the Housing Grants Construction and Regeneration Act (1996) parties can seek interim or non-binding adjudications by legal or construction professionals that usually resolve the dispute. M O'Callaghan, 'The Best Alternative', *The Lawyer*, 10 September 2001, 39.

accepted; many consumers expressed a preference for ADR over court-based dispute resolution.[42]

Lord Woolf's review of the civil justice system in 1996 proposed an increased role for ADR.[43] The Civil Procedure Rules (CPR) introduced in 1999 required that judges encourage parties to use ADR if appropriate. They were also to facilitate the use of the procedure as part of their active case management and in pursuit of the overriding objective of dealing with cases justly.[44] The pre-action protocols required the parties to consider ADR and allowed judges to stay proceedings for up to a month for mediation to take place, even where the parties did not request it.[45] Costs rules were used to penalise parties for unreasonable behaviour in litigation, including those refusing or obstructing mediation.[46] A Community Legal Service Fund covering litigation and mediation costs[47] replaced legal aid, and assistance could be refused where parties had unreasonably failed to try mediation first.

With enthusiastic encouragement by judges and masters, the introduction of mediation initially had a dramatic impact. With a drop of 37% in cases filed in the Queen's Bench Division by 2001 and a rising number of cases being referred to mediation, it appeared that ADR would be a great success. The number of cases going for ADR then declined.[48] Further, it was suggested that the falling numbers of cases going to trial was not attributable to ADR, but to the more cooperative culture created by the CPR generally, and to the pre-action protocols and part 36 offers to settle.[49] The government persevered, announcing that it would include ADR clauses in standard contracts.[50] The Lord Chancellor's Department announced in March 2001 that ADR would be used to replace litigation wherever possible. In 2004 the Lord Chancellor's Department agreed with the Treasury to use ADR to reduce county court and High Court cases by 200,000 cases, or 10%, to reduce log jams and cost.[51]

A patchwork of court-annexed mediation pilot schemes was established alongside the CPR, and evaluations showed that they were relatively successful.[52] They varied in their

---

[42] Three-quarters of respondents would have preferred some form of ADR to the process of civil litigation they had actually experienced. Six out of ten personal injury or divorce case parties would have preferred mediation. Less than one in ten favoured a full trial as the best means of resolving their dispute. *Seeking Civil Justice* (National Consumer Council, 1995) 11.

[43] Lord Woolf, *Access to Justice* (Final Report) (London, HMSO 1996) 4–12.

[44] CPR, r 1.4.

[45] A stay of one month follows if all parties request it in the allocation questionnaire or where the court considers such a stay appropriate (CPR, rr 26.4(1) and (2)).

[46] CPR, rr 44.3(4) and (5).

[47] Access to Justice Act (1999).

[48] The 468 disputes referred to CEDR in 1999 was down to 338 by 2001, according to J Ede, 'It's Good to Talk—Rather than Sue', *The Times*, 26 November 2002, 7; M Lind, 'ADR and Mediation—Boom or Bust', *New Law Journal*, 17 August 2001, 1238; H Genn, 'Solving Civil Justice Problems: What Might be Best?', paper for the Scottish Consumer Council on Civil Justice, 19 January 2005.

[49] J Peysner and M Seneviratne, *The Management of Civil Cases: the Courts and the post-Woolf Landscape* (London, DCA, 2005).

[50] 'Government Pledges to Opt for ADR', *The Lawyer*, 26 March 2001, 2.

[51] B Malkin, 'LCD Pledges to Cut Costs as Govt Pushes Mediation Plan', *The Lawyer*, 15 March 2004, 4.

[52] Voluntary schemes were established in the Central London County Court (1996) and Court of Appeal (Civil Division) (1997) and in Birmingham (2001), Leeds (2000) and Manchester (2000). See Genn, above n 48; L Webley, P Abrams and S Bacquet, *Evaluation of the Birmingham Court-based Civil (Non-family) Mediation Scheme* (London, DCA, 2006); S Prince, *An Evaluation of the Effectiveness of Court-based Mediation Processes in Non-family Civil Proceedings at Exeter and Guildford County Courts* (London, DCA, 2006); S Prince, *An Evaluation of the Small Claims Dispute Resolution Pilot at Exeter County Court* (London, DCA, 2006).

remit between the different county courts, dealing with small claims in one and fast and multi-track claims in others, but were similar in approach. A common pattern was three-hour mediation slots allocated to parties volunteering to mediate or directed to do so by the court. All dealt with significant volumes of cases—around a third of the cases issued in the period of the studies. All dealt mainly with contractual claims, but some dealt with housing repairs and personal injury. They all had relatively high settlement rates and satisfaction levels from both solicitors and parties. Some parties experienced pressure to settle from mediators, but they did not necessarily resent this and there were generally clear savings of court time. Two schemes, a small claims support service and a small claims mediation scheme, were effective in achieving settlements by using telephone 'shuttle diplomacy'.[53] This raises questions about the need for 'formal' mediation in all cases, and justifies interest in a more holistic approach to defining issues and dispute resolution processes. One of the longest standing schemes had mixed results, however. The Automatic Referral to Mediation scheme at Central London County Court evoked a high rate of objection and 'opt out', and added between one and two thousand pounds to the cost of unsettled cases.[54] A parallel voluntary scheme was relatively unpopular, particularly for personal injury cases, and settlement rates were disappointing, at less than 50%.

ADR AND LAWYERS' ETHICS

Lawyers are natural pioneers, or colonisers, of ADR and, given the opportunity, are often prominent among ADR practitioners. They have certain advantages: legal knowledge, a facility with complex information and familiarity with negotiation. This background enables them to balance the value of informal outcomes against the likely result of legal processes. Lawyers can provide basic protections in forums that lack guarantees of fairness. A legal perspective is also helpful in neutralising the emotions and moral connotations that accompany blame, dealing with which is one of the crucial barriers to settlement.[55] Non-lawyer mediators may have difficulty in encouraging attribution and acceptance of blame, but it is lawyers' natural territory. Despite this natural facility, lawyers may have ethical problems that other third party neutrals do not, particularly in mediation, where parties may be confused about a lawyer's role as a neutral and expect legal advice as part of the process.

The issue of lawyers' participation in ADR and the accompanying tendency to legalism is controversial. Some suggest that the lawyer's role in mediation could be enhanced by giving legal advice to both parties in each other's presence.[56] Since their expertise puts lawyer mediators in a good position to secure fair agreements, it is also suggested that they should be ethically obliged to do so, and to seek solutions maximising the benefits to the parties.

---

[53] Craigforth, *Evaluation of the Small Claims Support Service Pilot at Reading County Court* (London, DCA, 2006); M Doyle, *Evaluation of the Small Claims Mediation Service at Manchester County Court* (London, DCA, 2006).

[54] H Genn, P Fenn, M Mason A Lane, N Bechai L Gray D Vencappa, *Twisting Arms: Court Referred and Court Linked Mediation under Judicial Pressure* (London, Ministry of Justice, 2007).

[55] MJ Borg, 'Expressing Conflict, Neutralising Blame, and Making Concessions in Small-claims Mediation' (2000) *Law and Policy* 115.

[56] LL Riskin, 'Toward New Standards for the Neutral Lawyer in Mediation' (1984) 26 *Arizona Law Review* 329.

An obligation to achieve fairness addresses the possibility that mediators will put settlement before other possible goals of mediation. An obligation to maximise benefits would not just apply to processes, but might also put a premium on legal competence. For example, a mediator might be expected to see the potential for a tax advantage flowing from a settlement structure. The more common view, however, is that providing or advising the parties to take independent legal advice is a further barrier to settlement which, like cooling off periods after signing the mediated settlement, are heavy handed and antithetical to the aims of mediation.[57] In fact, many observers, including lawyers, downplay the scope of legal expertise in ADR, preferring instead to emphasise the importance of facilitation,[58] and suggesting that deep-seated flaws in the legal psyche make lawyers inappropriate participants.

There are many arguments why the legal mindset may be unwelcome in ADR. It is sometimes argued that lawyers have attitudes, values and tendencies, instilled through their professional ethos, ethics and education, which are antithetical to ADR. Their relationships with clients may be paternalistic, encouraging dependency, leading them to make assumptions about their client's best interests and obstructing informed decision making.[59] Lawyers are also criticised for their litigious orientation, seen as an unsuitable basis for problem solving. Arguing forcefully for their client's view is irreconcilable with the role of 'healers of human conflict'[60] required in mediation and conciliation. Another criticism of lawyers' involvement in ADR is that they are used to working towards narrow goals in the form of judicial remedies, damages and injunctive relief, and towards negotiation outcomes that mirror them. Finally, lawyers are wedded to the process rather than the solution, leading to the 'juridification' of processes and delay.[61]

It is sometimes argued that the unsuitability of lawyers for ADR is overplayed. US research suggests that lawyers are more likely to use integrated problem solving in mediation than in negotiation, suggesting that mediation can be used by lawyers without jeopardising the adversarial system.[62] For lawyers to make the transition to the environment of ADR, however, they must modify any paternalistic, competitive and aggressive traits. It is also necessary to develop different attitudes and qualities and learn new skills, attitudes and techniques. Among the capacities required for ADR are empathy, genuineness, listening and probing, which, together with creativity and foresight, analysis, advice, explanation and cooperation, constitute the core skills of counselling.[63] If one adds to these the skills of strategy, persuasion and conciliation, they constitute the core skills of problem-solving negotiation. Adding respect for client autonomy, and the acceptance of individuals as

---

[57] *Ibid.*

[58] The NCC asserts that a 'mediator without legal knowledge is definitely preferable to a lawyer who is deficient in mediation skills'. Ervine, above n 5, 34.

[59] A Gutmann, 'Can Virtue be Taught to Lawyers?' (1993) 45 *Stanford Law Review* 1759.

[60] W Burger, 'Isn't There a Better Way?' (1982) 68 *American Bar Association Journal* 274.

[61] J Flood and A Caiger, 'Lawyers and Arbitration: The Juridification of Commercial Disputes' (1993) 56 *Modern Law Review* 412; N Gould and M Cohen, 'ADR: Appropriate Dispute Resolution in the UK Construction Industry' [1988] *Civil Justice Quarterly* 103.

[62] EE Gordon, 'Attorney's Negotiation Strategies in Mediation: Business as Usual?' (2000) 17 *Mediation Quarterly* 377.

[63] RM Bastress and JD Harbaugh, *Interviewing, Counseling and Negotiating: Skills for Effective Representation* (Boston, MA, Little Brown, 1990) 5.

rational problem-solving entities, completes the intellectual and attitudinal toolkit required for ADR.[64] To this might be added the skills of conducting an informal but orderly proceeding and skills in dealing with people.[65]

None of the skills that underpin successful engagement in ADR are given a high profile in the education of lawyers in the UK. Mediation itself is, at best, an optional course on degrees or professional courses. If lawyers are serious about ADR, they need to pay more attention to training.[66] It can be argued that the timing of education and training in ADR presents a dilemma: leaving it too late risks entrenching the adversarial mindset, but teaching adversarial and cooperative skills simultaneously risks students becoming cynical and seeing legal practice as 'mastery of the arts of interpersonal manipulations'.[67] This may be overstating the scale of the problem for a profession that already accommodates a range of dispute prevention and resolution techniques in its armoury. In any event, rather than hide the contradictions inherent in a role that embraces negotiation and advocacy simultaneously, it may be better to give lawyers a more sophisticated education in 'the morality of influence'.[68]

The Legal Profession and ADR

Abel argues that lawyers, judges and officials are predisposed to be suspicious of ADR, preferring the high-status cases they are trained to handle, but see potential in the new order once 'alternatives' are created.[69] This is, to some extent, the English experience in relation to mediation, whereby ADR has had both supporters and detractors in the profession. Elite sectors, such as business lawyers, are often among the chief proponents of arbitration or other methods,[70] probably because some clients prefer informality and the flexibility of 'customised dispute resolution'[71] and the lawyers can control the process more effectively and develop remunerative sidelines as representatives or arbitrators. Lawyers outside the commercial sphere tend to be ambivalent about ADR, perhaps because one of its selling points is that it is quick, cheap and does not need them, or because they are uncomfortable about the shift in the balance of power in their relationship with their clients.[72] Cynicism is not borne out by research, suggesting that lawyers are not hostile to ADR, but think the time

---

[64] SC Grebe, 'Ethics and the Professional Family Mediator' (1992) 10 *Mediation Quarterly* 155; DP Joyce, 'The Role of the Intervenor: A Client Centred Approach' (1995) 12 *Mediation Quarterly* 301.

[65] RB McKay, 'Ethical Considerations in Alternative Dispute Resolution' (1990) 45 *The Arbitration Journal* 15, 22.

[66] The second report of the Law Society Courts and Legal Services Committee (June 1992) proposed a syllabus for an introductory course on ADR. See Ervine, above n 5, 26 and, further, M Minnow, 'Some Thoughts on Dispute Resolution and Civil Procedure' (1984) 34 *Journal of Legal Education* 284.

[67] PD Carrington, 'Civil Procedure and Alternative Dispute Resolution' (1981) 34 *Journal of Legal Education* 298.

[68] P Brest, 'The Responsibility of Law Schools: Educating Lawyers as Counsellors and Problem Solvers' (1995) 58 *Law and Contemporary Problems* 6.

[69] Abel, above n 2.

[70] Y Dezalay, 'The Forum should Fit the Fuss: the Economics and Politics of Negotiated Justice' in M Cain and CB Harrington (eds), *Lawyers in a Postmodern World: Translation and Transgression* (Buckingham, Open University Press, 1994) 155.

[71] Eg in disputes between international corporations, where parties want to agree a third party neutral with known skills and detachment.

[72] L Mulcahy, 'Can Leopards Change their Spots? An Evaluation of the Role of Lawyers in Medical Negligence Mediation' (2001) 8 *International Journal of the Legal Profession* 203.

and expense of ADR is not justified by the returns, particularly given the fillip the Woolf reforms gave to inter-party negotiation.[73]

Even before Lord Woolf proposed the expansion of court-annexed mediation, the profession had welcomed the involvement of lawyers in mediation[74] with relatively few qualms.[75] The seventh edition of *The Guide* in 1996 advised that solicitors could offer ADR services, defined as acting as a third party neutral, as part of their practice or as a separate business.[76] Three other principles were laid out in the ADR chapter. Solicitor mediators were required to inform clients that they would be independent and impartial, would not advise either party, would avoid conflicts of interest and would recommended to follow a code of practice.[77] It also suggested that

> solicitors wishing to offer ADR services should undertake appropriate training and work with one of the bodies providing training and a regulatory framework.[78]

The ADR chapter in the seventh edition of *The Guide* also included a specimen code, said to be for civil and commercial disputes, but possibly requiring adaptation for family matters.[79] It provided that the mediator's role is to 'help parties to work out their own principles and terms for the resolution of the issues between them', continuing:

> the mediator may meet the parties individually and/or together and may assist the parties for example: by identifying areas of agreement, narrowing and clarifying areas of disagreement; defining the issues; helping the parties to examine the issues and their available courses of action; establishing and examining alternative options for resolving any disagreement; considering the applicability of specialised management, legal, accounting, technical or other expertise; and generally facilitating discussion and negotiation, managing the process and helping them to try to resolve their differences.[80]

The rejection of a more 'legal' conception of the lawyer mediator role, implicit in this formulation and the official reports,[81] conveyed conventional positions against evaluating options,

---

[73] Genn, above n 48.

[74] The Beldam Committee (*Report of the Committee on Alternative Dispute Resolution* (General Council of the Bar, 1991)) endorsed using lawyers as mediators. The Law Society Family Law Committee proposed draft Standards of Practice for lawyer mediators, and a family court, with annexed conciliation services, was welcomed by the Marre Committee (Marre Report, above n 37, paras 11.16 and 11.19).

[75] A Law Society report in 1991 suggested that ADR would be inappropriate in cases where issues of principle of a public nature were involved, where there were power imbalances between parties or where ADR was used as a tactic, for example to delay litigation (H Brown, 'Alternative Dispute Resolution', prepared for the Law Society's Courts and Legal Services Committee, July 1991).

[76] N Taylor (ed), *The Guide to the Professional Conduct of Solicitors* (London, The Law Society, 7th edn, 1996), ch 22.

[77] *Ibid*, para 22.04.

[78] *Ibid*, para 22.01.4.

[79] Note to 22.04. The specimen, 'Mediation—specimen code of practice—practice information' appears as Annex 22A, 375 of the *Law Society Guide* (7th edn).

[80] Specimen code of practice 1.5.

[81] The Beldam Committee also perceived mediation to be largely faciliative and left these questions unanswered (S Roberts, above n 28, 260).

[82] Abel, above n 2; Auerbach, above n 19; D Greatbach and R Dingwall, 'Selective Facilitation: Some Preliminary Observation on a Strategy used by Divorce Mediators' (1990) 28 *Family and Conciliation Court Review* 1; R Dingwall, 'Empowerment or Enforcement? Some Questions about Power and Control in Divorce Mediation' in Dingwall and Eekelaar, above n 22; and discussion by Roberts, above n 13, 377*ff*, criticising the methodology.

pressuring parties to accept them,[82] or other ethically compromising behaviour in pursuit of the 'right' result.[83] The view of lawyer mediators as facilitators, 'consciously unobtrusive and non-directive',[84] was also reflected in the panel codes, which, by the eighth edition of *The Guide*, had replaced the specimen code.[85] Members of the panels had to agree to be bound by these,[86] but the generalist model mediation code had disappeared, apparently leaving solicitor mediators who were not panel members without regulation or guidance.

As mediation schemes were piloted in the county court, the early indications were that lawyers were reluctant to recommend pilot mediation schemes, and take-up was low.[87] Lawyers apparently believed that mediation was only suited to litigants in person,[88] preferring their 'known litigation strategies' for their own clients.[89] Lord Woolf's proposal to extend the use of mediation[90] precipitated a massive increase in the numbers of mediators and providers of mediation services. The Law Society introduced a Civil and Commercial Mediation Panel in Autumn 2001[91] and a Dispute Resolution Section in 2006 to represent the common interests of litigators and mediators, and to 'influence the increasingly complex legal and commercial environment'.[92] A few organisations trained mediators, including some lawyers, and undertook mediations, but the number of mediators was disproportionate to the number of cases. The use of lawyers as representatives varied between schemes and types of case.[93]

The disparity between mediators and cases was predictable. As often happens in new markets in mediation, a group of super mediators, typically male lawyers, emerged, snapping up the plum cases.[94] The apparent proliferation of services and lack of work led to calls for stricter regulation to control numbers and supplement the providers' kite mark quality systems.[95] The Law Society was uninterested in regulating mediators generally,[96] probably because this would involve regulating non-lawyers.[97] The increasing numbers of competing organisations and unaffiliated mediators may have been theoretically desirable

---

[84] Bevan, above n 13, 33.

[85] Roberts, above n 13, 383.

[86] Taylor, above n 76, ch 22.

[86] Civil and Commercial Mediation Panel: Criteria and Guidance Notes (Version 4, November 2006) 4, Law Society's Code of Practice for Family Mediation (Version 2, September 2005) 5.

[87] A pilot out-of-court mediation scheme in Bristol, backed by the Law Society, had only 24 cases in its first year, only two of which reached the mediation stage. York, above n 32.

[88] H Genn, *The Central London County Court Pilot Mediation Scheme: Evaluation Report* (Lord Chancellor's Department, 1998) and above n 54.

[89] L Tsang, 'Research Finds Solicitors are Hostile to Mediation Scheme', *The Lawyer*, 4 August 1998, 2.

[90] Ervine, above n 5, 35.

[91] Accreditation standards for the panel were worked out with the leading providers, with practitioner members requiring 65 hours of experience and training over two years.

[92] Law Society press release, 27 February 2006.

[93] See the evaluations of the court-annexed pilot schemes (above n 52).

[94] C Baar and RG Hann, 'Mandatory Mediation in Civil Cases: Purposes and Consequences', paper for the Hart Workshop, Institute of Advanced Legal Studies, London, 2001.

[95] The number of providers increased from less than 10 before 1999 to around 60 after. The major provider, the Centre for Effective Dispute Resolution, increased its commercial caseload from 462 in 1999/2000 to 467 in 2000/2001. G Chadwick, 'Finding its Feet', *The Lawyer*, 10 September 2001, 33; A Glaister, 'ADR: Quality not Quantity' (2000) 144 *Solicitors Journal* 1024.

[96] D Jones, 'The Men from the Boys', *The Lawyer*, 10 September 2001, 37.

[97] Although ADR Group, a leading ADR service provider, requires non-lawyer members to subscribe to the Law Society Civil and Commercial Panel Code.

for ADR; the expansion of 'the universe of recognized conflicts' tends to produce new groups of practitioners with new methodologies,[98] making it difficult to embrace all in one framework of practice. The result is considerable scope for differences in approach, the absence of agreed standards, except in some areas of work,[99] and no common ethic for the mediation field.[100]

Lawyers' roles in relation to ADR

Despite the absence of a single ethical code for different areas of ADR, all lawyers are increasingly affected by ADR, whether offering general advice or participating in an alternative process in the capacity of a representative or third party neutral.

Advice and dispute prevention

ADR must be considered when advising on disputes because of the 'heavy obligation to resort to litigation only if it is really unavoidable'.[101] Therefore, whether or not clients explicitly seek advice on ADR, they are under a duty to consider non-litigious options for resolution[102] and may be penalised in costs for any unjustified failure to consider mediation. This covers the period before litigation even commences[103] as well as circumstances when the court directs mediation.[104] Therefore, while the Court of Appeal held that compulsory mediation contravenes Article 6 of the Human Rights Act (1998), and even denied a presumption in favour of mediation, reasonableness of refusal to mediate will be judged against the nature of the case, the merits of the case, the cost of mediating and the prospects of success at mediation.[105] The solicitors' and bar codes impose no duty to consider ADR,[106] even in relation to the basic standard required by the courts, but the case law ensures that it is part of the general duties of competence and diligence to include ADR in initial advice, even when litigation is not immediately contemplated.

---

[98] W Warfield, 'Some *Minor* Reflections on Conflict Resolution: The State of the Field as a Moving Target' [2000] *Negotiation Journal* 381.

[99] The Forum of Insurance Lawyers and the Association of Personal Injury Lawyers agreed to cooperate to promote common standards of mediation and establish a joint panel of mediators in those personal injury cases for which mediation was suitable. J Fleming, 'PI Mediation Boost', *Gazette* 97/25, 22 June 2000, 5.

[100] See further R Dingwall, 'Divorce Mediation—Market Failure and Regulatory Capture', paper for Liberating Professions Conference of the Institute for the Study of the Legal Profession, Sheffield, July 1995; A Boon, R Earle and A Whyte, 'Regulating Mediators?' (2007) 10 *Legal Ethics* 26.

[101] Per Lord Woolf in *Cowl and Others v Plymouth City Council* Times Law Reports, 8 January 2002, para 27.

[102] In *Dunnett v Railtrack* PLC [2002] EWCA Civ 303 the defendants made the plaintiff what they considered a reasonable offer in settlement of her claim in negligence and rejected ADR because they did not want to increase their costs. They were denied their litigation costs when the plaintiff's claim failed.

[103] The court is entitled to take an unreasonable refusal into account, even when it occurs before the start of formal proceedings (see r 44.3(5)(a) of the Civil Procedure Rules 1998). Thus, when the other side suggests mediation before litigation begins, the court can scrutinise the reasons for refusal; see *Burchell v Bullard and others* [2005] EWCA Civ 358.

[104] *Hurst v Leeming* [2002] EWHC 1051 (Ch); *Leicester Circuits Ltd v Coates Bros PLC* [2003] EWCA Civ 333; *Royal Bank of Canada Trust Corporation v Secretary of State for Defence* [2003] EWHC 1479 (Ch).

[105] *Halsey v Milton Keynes NHS Trust* [2004] EWCA Civ 576. For further cases and discussion, see K Dreadon, 'ADR Post-Halsey: Recent Amendments to the CPR Further Encourage Mediation' [May 2006] *The In-House Lawyer* 75; Genn *et al*, above n 54, 14–20.

Lawyers might also advise on mediation issues even though they were not originally instructed to do so in connection with a specific dispute. Before disputes arise, lawyers may insert a dispute resolution clause into an agreement, requiring consideration of the best model and forum for the types of dispute that might arise. Legal advice may also be required after processes such as mediation. Some codes counsel that parties should not reach agreement without taking legal advice,[107] or mediators may suggest this in the particular circumstances of the case. Subjecting mediated outcomes to legal scrutiny may subvert the ethical principle of promoting client autonomy, and lawyers should be wary of substituting their own preferences for the party's.[108] Therefore, when lawyers are asked to review proposed mediation agreements in this way, they should be sensitive to the distinctive aims of mediation in the specific context, and consider both the interests of the party and their position in law in framing their advice.

Representative responsibilities

Acting as a representative in a mediation may be one of the most difficult roles for lawyers and the option should be considered carefully,[109] since the client could appear in person. The specimen code that originally appeared in *The Guide* had more general emphasis, but the panel codes that replaced it exclusively focused on solicitors as mediators rather than as representatives, leaving solicitor representatives in mediation without assistance from education, guide or code. [110] This is unfortunate, since acting as a representative requires lawyers to depart from the familiar legal role. Some may need to be cautioned that the adversarial mindset must be left behind. Tactics, such as using ADR to delay proceedings, are against the spirit of mediation, could breach the primary duty to the client to act in his interests and may be an abuse of process.

If they appear as representatives, lawyers must demonstrate ordinary standards of competence and possess a level of appreciation and skill to enable them to properly represent their client's interests.[111] They may also be bound by conventional ethics relating

---

[106] Contrast the situation in the US, where many state bar codes contain a rule obliging lawyers to identify the objectives or means of representation and advise which dispute resolution methods are most appropriate, given the client's preferences and the nature of the problem (S Widman, 'ADR and Lawyers Ethics' (1994) 82 *Illinois Bar Journal* 150). In both Texas and Colorado, lawyers are under specific obligations to advise clients regarding the availability and/or advisability of ADR (T Arnold, 'Reviewing Ethics Issues in Mediation' (1995) 19 *ALI-ABA Course Material Journal* 53; MJ Breger, 'Should an Attorney be Required to Advise a Client of ADR Options?' (2000) 13 *Georgetown Journal of Legal Ethics* 427). This may be regarded as a minimum obligation; it could be even more extensive under some formulations. Carrington, above n 67, suggests that representatives should be under a duty to consider explicitly a range of actors, including the qualifications and status of third party neutrals, the information on which the process is to be based and the cost of gathering it.

[107] The specimen code (paras 6.2 and 6.3) suggests that parties may consult legal advisers to formalise draft heads of agreement or for advice before entering a binding agreement based on the mediation.

[108] SC Grebe, 'Ethics and the Professional Family Mediator' (1992) 10 *Mediation Quarterly* 155.

[109] The options are to allow no lawyers or only lawyers, or to permit lawyers at the option of parties. The last of these, recommended by Beldam (s 14, 10), may be least likely to facilitate agreement (S Roberts, above n 28, 260).

[110] This contrasted with the American Bar Association Standards of Practice, which distinguishes between the mediator role and traditional legal advisor (Marre Report, above n 37, para 11.8).

[111] In a business setting they must be aware of the commercial context of the dispute, the interests of the party in a continuing relationship, the potential for mutually beneficial agreement and so on (see Thompson, above n 6, 90).

to litigation, for example on disclosure of evidence.[112] Unless timing is prescribed by rules of court, it will be necessary to consider at which point in litigation mediation should take place or, if negotiation has been attempted, whether it should take place at all. They must seek to assist the third party neutral mediator in finding the best way to handle the dispute and not disrupt the process. A lawyer must persist with mediation even if he or she considers the initial proposals to be inadequate,[113] particularly as the court may disagree that the effort is a waste of time, and use costs to punish withdrawal. One of the vexed issues around mediation is whether clients and representatives should attend all meetings together. The Law Society's specimen code of conduct for mediation envisaged solicitors taking part in discussions or meetings without the parties being present,[114] but the result may be that a veil of secrecy descends over parts of the process. Lawyers should consider the implications of unaccompanied participation by them or their clients, from the possibility of misapprehension to breach of natural justice, and at least warn clients of the risks.[115]

Lawyers as neutral third parties

'Neutral third party' is an omnibus term covering the central role in ADR processes, whether as arbitrator, mediator or conciliator. Many professional groups can be used here, depending on the area of work.[116] Sometimes, multi-disciplinary teams are formed,[117] particularly when perspective is a critical determinant, such as when gender[118] or cultural issues[119] arise. The ethical principles binding third party neutrals are clear and probably also underpin legal decisions. They include duties of honesty, integrity, neutrality, impartiality, candour with the parties, avoidance of conflicts of interest, fees and fee arrangements.[120] On the use of legal expertise in the role of mediator, the solicitors' codes tread a middle course: the parties can be assisted in understanding the principles of law applicable and their application in the specific circumstances, but should not be advised on their rights or how they might be translated into settlement terms.[121]

---

[112] *Yoldings v Swann Evans (A firm)* [2000] All ER (D) 1633 (Technology and Construction Court) (solicitors failed to notify arbitrator or other side of discovery of order form showing the incorporation of respondent's standard terms into contract).

[113] See *Colt International Ltd v Tarmac Construction Ltd* (1996) *Arbitration and Dispute Resolution Law Journal* 328 (application by party to remove arbitrator for bias or incompetence).

[114] Specimen code, above n 79, para 5.1.

[115] M Simmons, 'Mediators Offer Little Value', *The Lawyer*, 13 March 2000, 33.

[116] In the construction industry, for example, lawyers are a minority of those who appear as arbitrators. Flood and Caiger, above n 61, 414, suggest that the percentage of lawyers appointed in construction disputes in 1991 was less than 10%.

[117] In family mediation, solicitors and social workers sometimes work together on all issues (Roberts, above n 13, 373).

[118] G Davis and M Roberts, *Access to Agreement: A Consumer Study of Mediation in Family Disputes* (Milton Keynes, Open University Press, 1988).

[119] S Shah Kazemi, 'Family Mediation and the Dynamics of Culture' (1996) 6 *Family Mediation* 5.

[120] T Arnold, above n 106.

[121] Civil and Commercial Code of Practice, commentary on s 1.

The duties of third party neutrals

This section considers the ethical responsibilities applying to third party neutrals. The sources of the duties, whether regulatory or ethical, are various. The authority and duties of arbitrators, for example, are found in the arbitration agreement, the law of the specified juris-diction, the rules of the arbitrator's organisation, where these are incorporated in the agreement, and the rules of the profession.[122] The duties that usually emerge from these sources include obligations to ensure efficiency and the integrity of the fairness of the process, and to behave consistently within the role. Common themes in mediators' codes of conduct are disputant self-determination, informed consent, impartiality and neutrality. There are many differences between different types of ADR and, often, differences within jurisdictions. A fundamental example relates to orientation. In mediation, a mediator may be justified in ignoring a lawyer's legal submissions when a client is asserting an alternative agenda,[123] whereas in arbitration it could be negligent to do so.

The highly developed case law around the arbitrator's role provides useful insights into how the key areas of competence, neutrality and confidentiality may apply to other forms of ADR. Like arbitrators, mediators are subject to civil liability, for example for breach of contract, breach of fiduciary duty or professional negligence. When case law is developed it will almost certainly be based on the ethical principles set out in codes of conduct. Solicitors who wish to be mediators will find relatively little assistance in the code of conduct, but they may fall under either the codes of practice of the Law Society's Civil and Commercial Mediation Panel or the Code of Practice for Family Mediation. Both panels require that members agree to comply with their codes as a condition of membership.[124]

Competence

The power, and therefore the competence to act as third party neutral, varies according to the ADR process concerned.[125] The common law is the arbiter of competence, and the courts may determine whether the requirements of the agreement are met.[126] The consequence of incompetence could be removal of the third party neutral or an action for negligence or breach of contract.[127] Incompetence may be easier to determine with arbitration because there is no universally accepted description of the mediator's role. So, because mediation is usually voluntary and terminable at any time,[128] the incompetence of the third party neutral may result in the breakdown of the process, but not in any liability for that event.

---

[122] See, eg the International Bar Association, *Rules of Ethics for International Arbitrators*, available at www.ibanet.org (last accessed 29 March 2008), which suggest a clause for incorporation into the Arbitration Agreement.

[123] See Mulcahy, above n 72, 216.

[124] Civil and Commercial Mediation Panel: Criteria and Guidance Notes (Version 4, November 2006), 3; Law Society's Code of Practice for Family Mediation (Version 2, September, 2005), introduction.

[125] In Med/Arb, for example, a third party neutral attempts to mediate between the parties but, in default of agreement, can make an arbitral award (Thompson, above n 6, 92).

[126] *Pan Atlantic Group Inc and Others v Hassneh Insurance Co of Israel Ltd* (1992) *Arbitration and Dispute Resolution Law Journal* 179 (where an arbitrator loses a position proscribed by the arbitration agreement he may still retain the competence to act).

[127] For a discussion of exemption clauses in mediation agreements, see Bevan, above n 13, 33.

[128] Specimen code of practice, above n 79, para 1.2.

Among the basic requirements of third party neutrals are the level of knowledge and experience demanded by a dispute.[129] For example, if third party neutrals are responsible for advising the parties on the most appropriate process, they must be able to distinguish the different processes.[130] Thereafter, the competence depends on the process in use. Arbitrators must apply the law unless the parties agree otherwise and the particular jurisdiction permits this. Mediators should be capable of exploring the interests of the parties, the most suitable options for satisfying those interests, and the costs and benefits of these options. Some models may require a more proactive approach, such as proposing packages or mechanisms for reaching agreement, taking steps towards 'operationalising' the agreement, and evaluating and monitoring enforcement procedures.[131]

Neutrality and impartiality

Neutrality, as is obvious, is a fundamental requirement for selection as a third party neutral, whereas impartiality relates to later behaviour.[132] Where it is difficult to find an arbitrator who is seen as neutral to all sides, as in international matters,[133] a panel of three arbitrators may be appointed.[134] The duty of neutrality requires that any possible conflict of interest be disclosed at the outset. There may be a legal challenge if the arbitrator does not disqualify himself for a conflict of interest, but such a conflict must be material,[135] timely[136] and have proper foundation.[137] In contrast, the duty of impartiality means that those acting as arbitrators, mediators or conciliators must not be seen to lean towards either side. It is

---

[129] Inexperience at the level may cause delay and increased cost and be more likely to be subject to appeal (Thompson, above n 6, 117).

[130] This is a feature of some codes of conduct. See Bevan, above n 13, 36–60 and 34–5, citing the Centre for Dispute Resolution (Denver, Colarado Code of Professional Conduct for Mediators); Roberts, above n 13, 382.

[131] CW Moore, *The Mediation Process: Practical Strategies for Resolving Conflict* (San Francisco, CA, Jossey Bass Publishers, 1986) 14, cited by Pirie, above n 17, 41.

[132] A dictionary definition (Neutrality: 1. 'not supporting or assisting either side in a dispute or conflict . . . impartiality, not favoring one more than another . . .' in *Oxford Paperback Dictionary* (Oxford University Press, 1979)) implies that neutrality is a pre-existing state whereas partiality may develop. See also Roberts, above n 13, 376.

[133] J Epstein, H Gabriel, R Garnett and J Waincymer, *Practical Guide to International Commercial Arbitration* (Dobbs Ferry, NY, Oceana Publications, 2001).

[134] One panel member is nominated by each side to interpret local laws and customs and to ensure that all arguments are heard, and a neutral third is appointed by agreement or nominated by an institution either under the arbitration agreement or otherwise.

[135] In *Kuwait Foreign Trading Contracting and Investment Co* (Paris, Court of Appeal 1991 (1993) *Arbitration and Dispute Resolution Law Journal* pt 3) the claimant's application for annulment on the ground that a barrister arbitrator was from the same chambers as a barrister instructed by one of the parties was insufficient connection for a conflict of interest. There had to be 'material' or 'intellectual' connections with one of the parties. An English barrister's membership of chambers did not create 'common interests or any economic or intellectual interdependence among its members' because the sharing of chambers was not a material connection.

[136] In *Fletamentos Maritimos SA v Effjohn Internation BV* (1996) LTL 21/2/97 an arbitrator had provided a witness statement highly critical of the applicants' solicitor, and failed to formally disclose the possible conflict. The attempt to remove him failed because the court only had jurisdiction to correct procedural errors in extreme cases, the applicants' attention had been drawn to the issue by their solicitor earlier in the proceedings and there was no evidence of impartiality.

[137] In *Bremerhandelsqueseuschaft mbh v ETS Soules etc cie & Anar* (1985) FTCR 4.5.85, an application by a commodity seller for the removal of the director of a commodity house from the Board of Appeal was refused because nothing in the individual's record suggested bias towards buyers rather than sellers.

sometimes suggested that lawyers may face a problem in this respect: because their training encourages them to evaluate and balance merit, they cannot resist taking sides.[138] While judges seem to clear this hurdle, lawyers should bear it in mind. This is an area in which arbitration practice is well established, acting as an example for other ADR processes.

Arbitration

In arbitration, impartiality is central and protected by procedures requiring the arbitrator to observe a judicial distance from the parties.[139] An arbitrator can suggest that the parties should explore settlement but should not participate unless this is allowed by the *lex arbitri* and agreed to by the parties. Judicial review may be available on the grounds of the arbitrator's misconduct, such as bias or a failure to apply the principles of natural justice,[140] and appeals may be allowed when agreed procedures are not followed.[141] A decision can be overturned and an arbitrator removed for bias if, on the evidence adduced and arguments made, the decision was unfair[142] or the arbitrator's conduct was unreasonable viewed from the perspective of a reasonable man.[143] Particular problems surround evidence. Unlike a judge in most circumstances, arbitrators usually have the power to call witnesses, and must use their own knowledge and experience in interpreting evidence. They must be careful not to use that experience to supply evidence that the parties have not chosen to supply themselves,[144] because that 'would be discarding the role of an impartial arbitrator and assuming the role of an advocate for the defaulting side'.[145]

Different jurisdictions have different tests for challenging or removing arbitrators where doubts about impartiality emerge during proceedings. Such doubts may be raised by unreasonable conduct, such as lack of openness, but mere procedural errors are insufficient.[146] Therefore, arbitrators should not communicate with either party in the absence of the other

---

[138] AJ Pirie, 'The Lawyer as Mediator: Professional Responsibility Problems or Profession Problems?' (1985) 63 *Can. Bar Review* 378; but see AT Kronman, *The Lost Lawyer: Failing Ideals of the Legal Profession* (Cambridge, MA, Belknap Press, 1993) 113, suggesting that the 'case method' requires students to constantly shift perspective from that of judge to advocate.

[139] In *Road Rejuvenating and Repair Services v Mitchell Water Board and Another* (1990) *Arbitration and Dispute Resolution Law Journal* 46 it was said 'Arbitrators are not mediators. It is not their function to deal directly with disputants where legal representatives are retained.'

[140] HJ Kirsh, 'Arbitrating Construction Disputes' in Emonds, above n 3, 175, 180.

[141] *Oakstead Garages Ltd v Leach Pension Scheme (Trustees) Ltd* [1996] 24 EG 147. Appeal allowed against the decision of the arbitrator in a rent review who had told parties that he would inspect relevant comparable properties but failed to do so. See also *Mabanaft GBMH v Consentino Shipping Company SA* [1984] 2 Lloyd's Reports 191: an arbitrator's decision based on a theory not raised with the applicants. Held to be an issue of fact and degree whether a party should have an opportunity to deal with such points.

[142] *The Ellisar* [1984] 2 Lloyds Rep 84, approved in *Town Centre Securities Plc. v Leeds City Council* (1985) *Arbitration and Dispute Resolution Law Journal* 54.

[143] In *Tracomin SA v Gibbs Nathaniel (Canada) and Anor* (1985) FTCR 1.2.85, an arbitrator was observed sitting behind one party's counsel, apparently giving instructions. The reasonable man would think that the arbitrator was in the enemy's camp and that there was a real likelihood of bias.

[144] In *Top Shop Estates Ltd v C Domino* (High Court 1984) (1992) *Arbitration and Dispute Resolution Law Journal* 47, an arbitrator's award was overturned, inter alia, on the ground that he gathered evidence without the consent or knowledge of the parties, including conducting a 'pedestrian court' without the knowledge of the parties, and accepted unsupported evidence without affording an opportunity to challenge his interpretations.

[145] Lord Denning MR in *Fox v PG Wellfair Ltd* [1981] 2 Lloyds' Report 514.

[146] In *L/S A/S Gill Brakh v Hyundai Corporation* (1987) ILR 2.11.87 it was held that an error in admitting evidence did not by itself amount to misconduct by an arbitrator.

unless the exchange concerns administrative matters only. In cases of alleged bias, there must be evidence of actual bias going beyond mere suspicion. In *Christopher Alan Turner v Stevenage Borough Council*, an application to remove an arbitrator for bias was rejected merely because one side had complied with his request for interim payment but the other had not.[147] The Australian case, *Road Rejuvenating and Repair Services v Mitchell Water Board and Another*, is on the other side of the line, an arbitrator being removed for clearly partial behaviour in relation to both evidence and conduct.[148]

Other ADR processes

Neutrals in ADR processes other than arbitration must also be impartial and avoid conflicts of interest. Rules against acting for former clients are not uncommon in lawyers' mediation codes.[149] The conflicts of interest section of the solicitors' code prevents solicitor mediators acting for former parties to mediation where they acted as mediator, or in connection with a matter for which they or their firm was instructed.[150] They may, however, act for former or present clients with the consent of both parties.[151] Most models of mediation stress the need for the mediator to be even-handed. As in arbitration, mediators must be particularly cautious about private meetings with the parties and about passing on information discovered in such meetings.[152] Even making recommendations to avoid breakdown of the mediation at the request of the parties may compromise neutrality.[153] This general approach usually means that mediators cannot redress inequalities between the parties,[154] although it is sometimes argued that some contexts require this to ensure a fair agreement.[155] The Law Society's mediation panel codes take the conventional view on impartiality as a 'fundamental principle' and one mentions, in commentary, that personal views of the substance of the negotiations must not be allowed to affect this.[156] Somewhat contradictorily, both also have a section on 'dealing with power imbalances', which envisage a proactive role for mediators in addressing these situations.[157]

---

[147] (1997) EGCS 34.

[148] The arbitrator, the second defendant, had accepted into evidence hearsay and irrelevant material damaging to the plaintiff. He arrived for a meeting driven by an officer of the first defendant. The court held that this was an 'inexcusable alignment of an arbitrator with one party'. Supreme Court of Victoria, Nathan J (1990) *Arbitration and Dispute Resolution Law Journal* 46.

[149] Rules vary in the USA and Canada, but mediators are often prohibited from acting in mediations involving former clients and/or are prohibited from acting for either party in the future. See Pirie, above n 17, 45, discussing the rules published in British Columbia and by the ABA.

[150] *The Law Society's Code of Conduct and Recognised Body Regulations* (London, The Law Society, 2005) paras 3.06(a) and (b).

[151] *Ibid*, para 3.06(c).

[152] Arnold, above n 106, 63.

[153] It is generally seen as preferable to advise parties 'as to the desirability of seeking further assistance from professional advisers such as lawyers, accountants, expert valuers or others' (Civil and commercial, ss 5.4 and 5.5; and see Thompson, above n 6, 92).

[154] Bevan, above n 13, 34.

[155] In family conciliation, for example, the third party neutral may be expected to counteract attempts by a stronger party to exploit the weaker: Divorce Reform Proposals (1990) Law Commission para 5.34, cited by Roberts, above n 13, 373.

[156] Code of Practice for Civil and Commercial Mediation, s 3 and commentary to s 3.

[157] Law Society's Code of Practice for Family Mediation, s 6.2: 'if power imbalances seem likely to cause the mediation process to become unfair or ineffective, the mediator must take appropriate steps to try and prevent this' and if 'power imbalances cannot be redressed adequately' must end the mediation (s 6.4). See also Civil Panel, s 6.

Confidentiality and privilege

Effective ADR is often dependent on full disclosure of oral or documentary information,[158] so it is vital that the admissions and concessions a party makes against their interest are protected. Confidentiality and privilege refer to two different areas of protection. Confidentiality refers to a client's expectation that anything divulged to another party will not be disclosed in any context, whereas privilege means that it cannot be produced in court. Therefore, there may be circumstances where one applies but not the other, as where a third party neutral is not required to give evidence in court of what has transpired in mediation or conciliation but may be under an obligation to breach confidence, as where there is a physical threat to another party from one of the participants. The justification for attaching confidentiality and privilege to material produced with a view to settlement is twofold. [159] First, there is a public policy interest in encouraging settlement and protecting settlement negotiations, in whatever form they take, usually conveyed by using the words 'without prejudice' in communications to that end. Secondly, there is the express or implied agreement of the parties that their communications for that purpose be protected.

Conciliation

It is well established that privilege from production attaches to communications during the course of family conciliation[160] and proceedings under the Children Act (1989).[161] Conciliation privilege may no longer rely on the 'without prejudice' formula, having developed into a new head based on the public interest in promoting the stability of marriage.[162] The effect is that neither advisors nor conciliators can be compelled to give evidence of what has transpired in conciliation. The privilege extends from the parties, if they attempt conciliation themselves, to their advisors, including lawyers[163] or other official parties, like probation officers or priests, or even private individuals appointed as conciliators.[164] There are exceptions to the general principle against non-disclosure: where negotiation was not genuine or where the parties consent to disclosure. In such cases, a third party neutral cannot themselves claim privilege.[165] Privilege may also be lost if the evidence concerns potential harm to a child, or a risk of such harm in future. Even here, however, the circumstances must be exceptional, the judge exercising discretion in deciding whether protecting the child outweighs the public interest in preserving the confidentiality of attempted conciliation.[166]

---

[158] Discussion and agreement are generally the means of verifying information but, although mediation processes seldom require the parties to produce specific relevant documents, disclosure may resolve misunderstandings (see, eg mediation specimen code, para 4.2).

[159] *Rush & Tompkins Ltd v GLC* [1989] AC 1280; *Cutts v Head* [1984] Ch 290; *Unilever plc v Proctor & Gamble Co* [2000] 1 WLR 2436.

[160] *La Roche v Armstrong* (1922) 1 KB 485.

[161] Children Act, s 1(1); see also *Practice Direction (Family Division: Conciliation)* [1992] 1 WLR 147.

[162] See Lords Hailsham and Simon in *D v National Society for Prevention of Cruelty to Children* [1978] AC 171.

[163] *Henley v Henley* [1955] 1 All ER 590.

[164] *McTaggart v McTaggart* [1949] P 94; *Mole v Mole* [1951] P 21; *Theodoropoulas v Theodoropoulas* [1964] P 311.

[165] *McTaggart v McTaggart, ibid.*

[166] *In re D (Minors)* [1993] Fam 231.

Mediation

Unlike, possibly, family conciliation, the confidentiality and privilege from production in court enjoyed by mediation continues to be based on the protection of 'without prejudice' communication and the mediation agreement.[167] Using the formula is not decisive,[168] the court being entitled to consider the purpose and nature of the discussion, and its relevance to settlement of the same dispute for which privilege is claimed.[169] The court is also entitled to consider whether it is fair and just to allow the use of such material in litigation[170] and to explore whether settlement was reached.[171] A case illustrating the difficulty in linking litigation and the mediation process is *Robert Aird and Karen Aird v Prime Meridian Ltd*,[172] where one of the parties to a court-annexed mediation wanted to use a joint experts' report prepared at the direction of the judge in the continuing litigation. The other part resisted this on the ground that they, and their expert, had understood that it would be privileged. The Court of Appeal held that the joint expert statement complied with CPR rule 35.12, having been agreed by both sides, and was not a mediation document privileged from production.

While courts in the UK, and abroad, have asserted the importance of protecting the secrecy of settlement,[173] uncertainty surrounds the security of mediation. This has led to suggestions that no notes or records should be kept of confidential discussions,[174] but this would not prevent mediators being asked questions about what they could remember. The Law Society's specimen code went further than the panel codes on the confidentiality issue, stating that:

> all discussions and negotiations during the mediation will be regarded as evidentially privileged and conducted on a 'without prejudice' basis, unless such privilege is waived by the parties by agreement, either generally or in relation to any specific aspect'; nor is such information to be referred to in any 'subsequent proceedings.[175]

The code optimistically states that no party can require the mediator to give evidence, or have access to a mediator's notes,[176] but a court refusing to recognise 'mediator privilege' could put a mediator at risk of contempt of court. The Law Society's panel codes avoid this risk by providing that mediators will not disclose information discovered in the course of mediation except with the consent of the parties, where such matters are already public, where persons are at risk or where there is an overriding obligation in law to disclose.[177]

Confidentiality principles can be put to the test when mediators discover that an agreement they facilitated was based on false information or bad faith. The normal

---

[167] *Smith Group plc v Weiss* [2002] All ER 356 (ChD) (inclusion of material gathered in mediation in a list of documents is not a waiver of their privileged status).

[168] Bevan, above n 13, 31.

[169] *Muller v Linsley & Mortimer, The Times*, 8 December 1994; *South Shropshire District Council v Amos* [1986] 1 WLR 1271; *Rediffusion Simulation v Link-Miles* [1992] FSR 196; see also J McEwan, 'Without Prejudice: Negotiating a Minefield" (1994) 13 *Civil Justice Quarterly* 133.

[170] *Smith Group v Weiss*, above n 167.

[171] *Brown v Rice* [2007] All ER 252.

[172] [2006] EWHC 2338 (TCC), [2006] EWCA Civ 1866.

[173] *Hall v Pertemps Group* [2005] All ER (D) 15.

[174] BE Larson and SB Hansen, 'Ethics in ADR' (1992) 22 *The Brief* 14.

[175] Specimen code, above n 79, 2.3.

[176] *Ibid*, para 2.3.

[177] Civil and Commercial Code, s 7.2, Family Code, s 7.1.

assumptions regarding the ethicality of keeping confidences are then turned on their head. In such circumstances, it has been suggested that a mediator should try to persuade the parties to rectify the problem and, if this fails, to withdraw.[178] Whether this is sufficient for ethical integrity is debatable. It is arguable that the mediator is obliged to bring the irregularity to the attention of those outside the process. At one end of the scale they might be expected to report crimes,[179] but the only risks usually canvassed in codes relate to averting the risk of bodily harm.[180] Codes are often vague about whether other situations might also be exceptional, as where the family panel code refers to 'public policy considerations' or rules of evidence rendering 'privilege inapplicable'.[181] It remains unclear whether mediators are under an obligation to breach the confidentiality of the process when they discover they have been gulled by the fraudulent presentation of evidence.

Conclusion

Government policy has offered lawyers a new role in dispute resolution at a time when civil litigation appears to be in decline. Lawyers participating in ADR as neutral third parties, arbitrators, mediators, conciliators or representatives in such process require different skills to those required in their adversarial role. They are also subject to different ethical rules, many of which are unclear, contradictory or unresolved. For example, while the legal profession has leaned towards the facilitative model for its codes, there may be competing pressures when ADR is offered as an adjunct to court processes, with potential blurring of the adversarial and facilitative roles. Lawyers representing clients in ADR processes require a good understanding of the potential of ADR and legal education probably needs to change accordingly. The ethics of the work change also, with far more emphasis on cooperation and facilitation of the client's goals. It is unclear how far the traditional ethic of lawyers, based as they are on an adversarial tradition, will accommodate or survive this wave of cooperative influence.

---

[178] Bevan, above n 13, 32.

[179] Assisting in negotiating a settlement could be treated as being 'concerned' in an arrangement for the purposes of committing an offence under the Proceeds of Crime Act (2002), s 328, giving rise to an obligation to inform the National Criminal Intelligence Service: *P v P (Ancillary Relief: Proceeds of Crime)* [2003] EWHC Fam 2260, [2004] 1 FLR 193. Clients cannot be informed of this disclosure if ongoing investigations might thereby be prejudiced.

[180] Family Panel Code 7.6.

[181] *Ibid.*

EPILOGUE

The last decade has been a period of continuous change for the legal profession. Although there has been constant pressure on the professional bodies to reconceptualise their role in the delivery of legal services, the scale of change has not been as seismic as might have been imagined. Some changes predicted in the Epilogue of the first edition of this book have stalled, some are still in progress and yet others have proceeded more quickly than expected.

It is too early to say whether a paradigm shift is occurring in law as a result of information and communications technology.[1] Despite some bold new forms of legal service[2] the growth of online services has not yet developed to the point that consumers are liberated from lawyers.[3] Therefore, although access to legal information may become more widespread, awareness of what to do with it remains fundamental. The technological revolution has and will continue to assist advice agencies to compete with lawyers in welfare areas, but some mediation between knowledge and consumers is required. It is too soon to know whether the potential for technology to spawn a 'self help revolution' in the market for legal services has receded.[4] Technology has undoubtedly contributed to the continuing 'routinization' of legal work,[5] but it also increases the scope of what individuals can do, provided they have the skills. In the future we might expect a greater range of legal professionals to take on tasks previously considered the preserve of the others. Thus, solicitors will embrace advocacy and barristers will seek neutral roles in a burgeoning dispute resolution market. Advice agencies will take more complicated cases further under legal aid franchises, and they or similar institutions may open up what Susskind identifies as latent legal markets. Such developments offer both an opportunity and a threat to the profession.

The Woolf reforms, and the new Civil Procedure Rules, showed that adversarialism could survive tempering by an obligation on the parties to cooperate in avoiding litigation. As many had argued, the partisan obligation to clients has ever been constrained, the only issue being where the line is drawn. This has now been clarified by subjecting lawyers to a

---

[1] R. Susskind, *The Future of Law: Facing the Challenges of Information Technology* (Oxford, Clarendon Press 1998).

[2] www.axiomlegal.com.

[3] T Purcell, 'Technology's Role in Access to Legal Services and Legal Information' in R Smith (ed), *Shaping the Future: New Directions for Legal Services* (London, Legal Action Group, 1995) 66.

[4] FS Mosten, 'The Unbundling of Legal Services: Increasing Legal Access' in Smith, *ibid*, 47.

[5] The vision of the future promoted by Susskind is obviously dominated by the large corporate solicitor's firm. Whether such developments will affect the individual client (in particular, the accused client) is doubtful. Susskind also notes that the use of IT brings us 'to the brink of an entirely new era of mankind, very few philosophers or social commentators have explored the [ethical] ramifications in the depth that it surely merits' (above n 1, 69). Neither does he explore them. Computerisation clearly raises some immediate ethical problems, eg, of confidentiality and of the personal responsibility of IT package users for negligence, etc.

statutory duty to the administration of justice in litigation and advocacy, effectively providing a clear bottom line for the duty to the court. This, though, does not take us to the position where 'danger to the state or public duty may supersede the duty of the agent to his principle'.[6] Such inroads as there are to the duty of confidentiality are provided by statute, as with money laundering, rather than the professional codes, which arguably should go further.[7] Using the law to help clients market a potentially lethal drug[8] arguably remains within the realm of lawyer's role morality; the administration of justice leaves such moral issues to courts.

The cooperative spirit that mediation engenders might appear to symbolise the nail in the coffin of adversary values. While the growth of mediation has stalled, it appears to have taken root. The main reason for this appears to be that many of those entering the court system seek a decision, not a compromise. There does, however, appear to be a beneficial byproduct of mediation moving more mainstream, in the involvement of clients in their cases. The process of mediation is therefore easing a path towards participative decision making and greater individual autonomy for clients in their relationships with lawyers. This is a potentially important shift away from lawyers determining clients' objectives and tactics,[9] to trying to modify them in the light of ethical and other considerations. This, together with the increased emphasis on *pro bono publico*, might be the basis of a new conception of the public service ideal, the assumption of which no longer automatically cloaks professional practice.

By far the greatest changes to professional ethics in the past 10 years have emanated from what appeared to be an attempt by the government to bring the legal profession to heel by ending self-regulation. Clementi's halfway house, especially since it is situated on the way to the last chance saloon, will be a driver for de facto fusion of the profession, with common codes for lawyers in legal disciplinary practices playing the role of Trojan horse.[10] The cab rank rule, for example, might not survive mass migration to the new business firm. Yet the separation of regulatory and representative functions, and the bolstering of the former by much increased lay representation on professional committees, is a compromise between Johnson's models of self-regulation and consumer control.[11] It potentially preserves what is best about the idea of self-regulation, expertise, accountability and ownership while providing useful counterbalances.

Regulatory oversight will also provide broader perspectives and, potentially, a fillip to professional regeneration. Whether the Legal Services Act will head off further interference from the government depends on performance on a number of fronts, not least ethics. The Law Society's long-running review of its code and a similar venture recently announced by the Bar suggest that the profession is warming to the task. Whether they will be able to retain codes separate from each other, as alternative business structures take root, is

---

[6] Lord Findlay in *Weld-Blundell v Stephens* [1920] AC 596, cited in Bankes LJ in *Tournier v National Provincial and Union Bank of England* (1924) 1 KB 461.

[7] See M Brindle and G. Dehn, 'Confidence, Public Interest, and the Lawyer' in R Cranston (ed), *Legal Ethics and Professional Responsibility* (Oxford, Clarendon Press, 1995) 115.

[8] MH Freedman, 'Are There Public Interest Limits on Lawyers' Advocacy?' (1977) *The Journal of the Legal Profession* 47, 52–3.

[9] JP Heinz, 'The Power of Lawyers' (1983) 17 *Georgia Law Review* 891, 897.

[10] D Clementi, *Review of the Regulatory Framework for Legal Services in England and Wales—Final Report* (London, Legal Services Review, 2004) paras 25, 111.

[11] TJ Johnson, *Professions and Power* (London, Macmillan Press, 1972) 13.

debateable. When it is commonplace for barristers and solicitors to work alongside each other the logic of distinct codes will become more difficult to sustain. Such a transformation will also bring about changes in the conception of professionalism in organisations. It is unclear whether relationships of trust, within and between organisations, will be as easily sustained by more corporate forms of governance[12] and more regulatory means of securing compliance.

Were the differences between the bar and solicitors to diminish even further we might expect a change in their relationship. Among the many possible models for that relationship is that the Bar remains an advocacy and advice profession, but one open only to solicitors who have already established themselves as advocates. In the meantime, renewed enthusiasm for the subject of ethics will be reflected in the gradual increase of ethics in the professions' education requirements. This began in a small way with the vocational stage but, with the Training Framework Review, could become more pervasive. Moreover, it may be that some in the professional bodies are beginning to rediscover the power of ethics. By offering a broad structure of effective and ethical regulation, legal professions have the possibility of controlling the market by offering competitors space within their regulatory frameworks.[13] Legal services are a complex business and only the fit for purpose should survive. Therefore, the rise of different business forms need not be a threat to the viability of a common ethics, provided professions are flexible in looking for solutions, as the Bar showed in adapting their ethics code to embrace employed lawyers.

The future of the professional ethics of lawyers is, however, no longer a parochial concern. Globalisation of the world economy, the process of European harmonisation[14] and the regulation of international trade and investment all fuel the international practice of law,[15] currently dominated by the Anglo-American law firms,[16] often as multi-national practices.[17] These tend to be concentrated at the international centres of finance (London, New York and Tokyo), of arbitration (London and Paris) and of government (Brussels, Luxembourg and Strasbourg).[18] The increasing mixing of professions undertaking the same professional work may be thought to pose a serious challenge to professional ethics, but it appears that the lawyers engaged in these spheres are characteristically resourceful. Resolving complex disputes between national jurisdictions, and sometimes without commonly agreed procedures, calls for the parties to create new rules and procedures, so-called 'private ordering'.[19] They have even solved problems such as fulfilling a public

---

[12] J Flood, 'Partnership and Professionalism in Global Law Firms: Resurgent Professionalism?' in D Muzio, S Ackroyd and J Chanlat, *Redirections in the Study of Expert Labour: Established Professions and New Expert Occupations* (Houndmills, Palgrave Macmillan, 2007) 52.

[13] A Boon, J Flood and J Webb, 'Postmodern Professions? The Fragmentation of Legal Education and the Legal Profession' (2005) 32 *Journal of Law and Society* 473.

[14] Eg harmonising European professional qualifications; see *Christine Morgenbesser v Consiglio dell'Odine degli avvocati di Genoa* (Case C-313/01) [2003] All ER (D) 190 (Nov).

[15] R Badinter, 'Role of the International Lawyer' (1995) 23 *International Business Lawyer* 505.

[16] Of the 100 leading world firms by turnover, 75 are from the US and 17 from the UK, but the average revenue of the latter is 21% higher than their US counterparts (The Lawyer, *Global 100: The World's Largest Law Firms 2006*).

[17] RL Abel, 'Transnational Legal Practice' (1993–5) 44 *Case Western Reserve Law Review* 737.

[18] *Ibid*, 743.

[19] J Flood and E Skordaki, 'Normative Bricolage: Informal Rule-making by Accountants and Lawyers in Mega-insolvencies' in G Teubner (ed), *Global Law without a State* (Aldershot, Dartmouth, 1997) 109.

service role,[20] with US lawyers in London participating in, and even taking a lead on, *pro bono publico* and diversity issues.

The internationalisation of the Anglo-American professional model also has a political dimension. The trend of globalisation is the spread of liberal democracy as the universal model of world government,[21] with the rule of law at the forefront. The active participation of legal professions in this process moves the market theory of professionalisation from the national to the international sphere,[22] but the English professional bodies have contradictory, and sometimes contrary, tendencies. In continental terms, English lawyers are seen as highly specialised, competitive and particularly aggressive in international markets. They are keen to deregulate and relatively open-minded, for example, on multi-disciplinarity. Yet the profession as a whole is also conservative, seen to resist the logic of European harmonisation, particularly as regards such distinctive features as the split profession and the maintenance of distinct jurisdictions for England and Wales, Scotland and Northern Ireland.[23]

Despite the perception that the English profession is not geared up for internationalisation of the legal services market, there is a complex domestic regulatory framework. Part of this is to comply with the European directive providing that European lawyers can practice in another European Union state under their home title, without integrating into the local profession.[24] Much of the rest provides for more integrated 'multi-national legal practice'. The framework for this is provided by the Courts and Legal Services Act 1990, section 89 and schedule 14.[25] There are two types of multi-national legal practice: multi-national partnerships (MNPs) and other recognised bodies. Multi-national partnerships must include at least one partner who is a solicitor or a European lawyer registered with the Solicitors Regulation Authority (SRA) and at least one partner who is a Registered Foreign Lawyer (RFL),[26] but must not include a partner which is a recognised body. Recognised bodies are companies, or limited liability partnerships (LLPs) incorporated by registration,[27] accepted by the SRA as suitable to provide the professional services offered by solicitors or lawyers of other jurisdictions which include one member, shareowner or director who is an RFL.

The complex arrangements for incoming lawyers controls their participation in international practice, for example in relation to partnerships with solicitors, or in restricting their right to do reserved work, like litigation or immigration work. RFLs who become partners in an MNP, a member of a recognised body that is an LLP or director of a recognised body

---

[20] Abel, above n 17, 743 and 749.

[21] The role of financial institutions in promoting government according to the rule of law is suggestive. For example, the European Bank of Reconstruction and Development will only lend money to countries committed to promoting the rule of law.

[22] TC Halliday and L Karpik , *Lawyers and the Rise of Western Political Liberalism: Europe and North America From the Eighteenth to Twentieth Century* (Oxford, Clarendon Press/New York, Oxford University Press, 1997) 349.

[23] K Gromek-Broc, 'The Legal Profession in the European Union—A Comparative Analysis of Four Member States' (2002) 24 *Liverpool Law Review* 109.

[24] A Registered European Lawyer registered under the Establishment of Lawyers Directive 98/5/EC.

[25] See also the Administration of Justice Act 1985, s 89 and sch 2, and the European Communities (Lawyers' Practice) Regulations (2000).

[26] A Registered Foreign Lawyer registered with the SRA under the Courts and Legal Services Act 1990, s 9.

[27] Under the Limited Liability Partnerships Act (2000).

that is a company, become subject to the Solicitors' Code of Conduct.[28] The arrangements also preserve, so far as possible, the distinctiveness of solicitors' practice. So, for example, a solicitor in an MNP with limited liability, created under the law of another state, cannot be a partner if that partnership has an office in England and Wales. Overseas lawyers not subject to the Establishment Directive need not register with the SRA or be subject to solicitors' regulation provided they practice, for example, under their home title. A section in the Solicitors Code of Conduct explains how the core duties of the code extend to overseas practice.[29]

The growth of international practice has stimulated attempts to harmonise ethics codes. The Council of the Bars and Law Societies of the European Union (CCBE) Code of Conduct for Lawyers in the European Community applies to the cross-border activities of lawyers within the European Community.[30] The express purpose of the code is to 'mitigate the difficulties which result from the application of double deontology' arising from 'the continued integration of the European community and the increasing frequency of the cross-border activities of lawyers within the community'.[31] The Code is offered for adoption by local bars and law societies, and urges members to take it into account 'in all revisions of national rules of deontology or professional practice with a view to their progressive harmonisation'.[32] In the meantime, it suggests that disputes between lawyers from different member states be settled 'in a friendly way' if possible or, if not, referred to the lawyers' own bars or law societies for the purpose of mediation.[33]

The second code governing international practice is the International Code of Ethics published by the International Bar Association (IBA).[34] This

> applies to any lawyer of one jurisdiction in relation to his contacts with a lawyer of another jurisdiction or to his activities in another jurisdiction.

It has also been adopted by the Law Society, presumably intended to apply in situations or countries where neither its own code nor the CCBE code applies. The IBA also publishes General Principles of Ethics as a yardstick for members to judge their rules of conduct. Many provisions of the IBA Code are subject to national codes, for example, in relation to advertising and soliciting, and the delegation of work to non-qualified personnel.[35] The IBA limits the purpose of its code to being a guide to what the IBA considers to be a desirable course of conduct by all lawyers engaged in the international practice of law, although it reserves the right to 'bring incidents of alleged violations to the attention of relevant organisations'.[36]

John Toulmin QC, a former president of the CCBE, asserts that the differences between

---

[28] Solicitors' Practice Rules (1990), A(2), 18(2)(fc) and (fd).

[29] Solicitors Regulation Authority, *Solicitors' Code of Conduct* (London, Solicitors Regulation Authority, 2007) r 15.

[30] That is, lawyers of the European Union and the European Economic Area as they are defined by the Directive 77/249 of 22 March 1977: Council of the Bars and Law Societies of the European Union, *Code of Conduct for Lawyers in the European Community* (Brussels, CCBE, 1998, as amended 2002) para 1.4.

[31] *Ibid*, para 1.3.1.

[32] *Ibid*.

[33] Para 5.9.

[34] International Code of Ethics of the International Bar Association (1988).

[35] *Ibid*, paras 8 and 20.

[36] *Ibid*, preamble.

the US and Western Europe are minimal. They are, he says, 'like two trains on the same track with the US train in the lead',[37] creating the possibility of a worldwide code based on the US model rules, the Japanese Code and the CCBE Code. Areas of incompatibility, secrecy and confidentiality, advertising, conflicts of interest and contingency fees, are, he argues, 'greater in theory than they are in practice'.[38] The need for such a code is debatable. The present CCBE Code is even shorter than the new Solicitors' Code of Conduct 2007, with the consequence that more detail would need to be explicated before international legal professions could be brought in line. The CCBE's ambivalence in relation to the differences between its members[39] reflects inevitable cultural differences that brief codes of professional ethics must struggle to resolve. Indeed, it is even arguable that transnational legal work should remain deregulated. If the main justification of professional ethics is protecting clients from the consequences of information asymmetries, it is arguable that the market for international legal services does not need them; it favours the client rather than the lawyer.[40] As to the possibility of increasing globalisation bringing less savvy citizens within the sphere of international markets, there are contradictory trends. Countries re-erecting barriers to free trade suggest that globalisation may stall[41] while new international systems of dispute resolution possibly herald increased legal activity.[42]

Efforts to internationalise legal professional ethics often meet scepticism. They are regarded as either largely symbolic or a reflection of wider trends in international business,[43] themes that fit within a wider trend identified by Picciotto. He suggests that an internationalist ruling class emerged between 1915 and 1975 based on corporate liberalism and transatlantic unity.[44] The inadequacy of the international state system in regulating business led to the growth, since the 1960s, of 'international economic soft law',[45] including codes of conduct for international business. These codes were largely symbolic:

---

[37] J Toulmin, 'A Worldwide Common Code of Professional Ethics?' 15 *Fordham International Law Journal* 673.

[38] *Ibid*, 16; and see, regarding Japan, K Economides, 'Anglo-American Conceptions of Professional Responsibility and the Reform of Japanese Legal Education: Creating A Virtuous Circle?' (2007) 41 *The Law Teacher* 155.

[39] 'The particular rules of each Bar or Law Society arise from its own traditions. They are adapted to the organisation and sphere of activity of the profession in the Member State concerned and to its judicial and administrative procedures and to its national legislation. It is neither possible nor desirable that they should be taken out of their context nor that an attempt should be made to give general application to rules which are inherently incapable of such application. The particular rules of each Bar and Law Society nevertheless are based on the same values and in most cases demonstrate a common foundation' (above n 34, para 1.2.2).

[40] Abel, *above n* 17, 762, argues that powerful jurisdictions, with major international business, should negotiate the lowering of foreign barriers. He does, however, propose that each jurisdiction should establish a register of foreign lawyers practising in that jurisdiction, areas of reserved practice and disciplinary proceedings, and facilitate the requalification of foreign lawyers. He urges that foreign jurisdictions should not try to regulate fees of overseas lawyers and that contingency fee arrangements should be permitted and home disciplinary proceedings should apply at the instance of clients.

[41] J Gray, *False Dawn: The Delusions of Global Capitalism* (London, Granta, 1998); P Kennedy, 'Coming to Terms with Contemporary Capitalism: Beyond the Idealism of Globalisation and Capitalist Ascendancy Arguments' (1998) 3 *Sociological Research Online*.

[42] P Ruttley, 'The WTO's Dispute Settlement Mechanism' [1997] *Amicus Curiae* 4.

[43] A Boon and J Flood, 'The Globalisation of Professional Ethics: The Significance of lawyers International Codes of Conduct' (1999) 2 *Legal Ethics* 29.

[44] S Picciotto, 'The Control of Transnational Capital and the Democratisation of the International State' (1998) 15 *Journal of Law and Society* 58, 64.

[45] *Ibid*, 70.

a reaction to and an attempt to contain the growing criticisms of and actions against transnational corporations from the 1960s onwards.[46]

The international codes of legal professions can be seen be seen in similar light; the emulation by commercial lawyers of their organisational counterparts in business.

Halliday and Karpik see deeper motives for legal professions seeking international solidarity. They argue that a number of factors have eroded lawyers' engagement with political liberalism, both in the UK and on the continent.[47] In the UK, for example, it took increasing attempts at state control of the legal profession to stimulate political resistance and attempts to mobilise public opinion.[48] The relative failure of these campaigns was arguably reflected in the failure of the public service ideal, but legal professions need not accept that the political sphere is not their province. They have a continuing role in guarding civil society and the rule of law from the increasing power of the state and the periodic inclinations of the government to deprofessionalise legal services. Worldwide alliances of professional associations might yet provide important checks on the accumulation of state power in the service of trade and corporations, providing channels of communication with similar groups in other countries[49] and preserving the professional ideal.

The movement towards international ethics rules may be theoretically more satisfying, and more effective, if it aimed to unify the different strata of national professions. Advocates of harmonisation acknowledge that large firm lawyers in New York or Chicago have more in common with those in similar firms in London or Brussels than with sole practitioners in their own jurisdictions. So, for example, it makes more sense to have an international code for criminal defence lawyers than it makes to have a single national code for all lawyers. But such international reformulation must negotiate the ideologies of domestic professions and they are deep rooted. Therefore, the codes recycle the renegotiated international consensus of what lawyers represent. Like the codes of the legal profession in England and Wales, for example, the CCBE code espouses a grand vision of lawyers' social functions:

> In a society founded on respect for the rule of law the lawyer fulfils a special role. His duties do not begin and end with the faithful performance of what he is instructed to do so far as the law permits. A lawyer must serve the interests of justice as well as those whose rights and liberties he is trusted to assert and defend and it is his duty not only to plead his client's cause but to be his adviser. A lawyer's function therefore lays on him a variety of legal and moral obligations (sometimes appearing to be in conflict with each other) towards:
> the client;
> the courts and other authorities before whom the lawyer pleads his client's cause or acts on his behalf;

---

[46] *Ibid*, 71.

[47] Lawyers in these different countries have located themselves in different relationships to the state, so that in England, for example, overseas observers saw professional self-government as a pillar of civil society and a bulwark of liberal political society (Halliday and Karpik, above n 22, 8).

[48] *Ibid*, 38.

[49] Johnson, above n 11, 14, quoting KS Lynn, *The Professions in America* (Boston, MA, Houghton Mifflin, 1967) 653.

438   EPILOGUE

the legal profession in general and each fellow member of it in particular;
the public for whom the existence of a free and independent profession, bound together by
respect for rules made by the profession itself, is an essential means of safeguarding human
rights in face of the power of the state and other interests in society.'[50]

While this familiarity is welcome to those seeking coherence to the professional ethics of
lawyers, some are sceptical of the effort. McBarnett argues that the rhetoric of the rule of law
is inconsistent with the role of business lawyers, whose advice to corporations—on tax
avoidance, for example—obviates rights and renders them ineffective.[51] Therefore, in order
to claim legitimacy for international codes, elite groups must remain in professional unity
with groups of lawyers who actively support the rule of law at national level: lawyers working
in the fields of criminal defence, civil liberties or welfare law. At the same time, these groups
are more likely to face financial, language and geographical difficulties in transposing
national modes of organisation to the international level.[52] Harmonisation of the professional ethics of lawyers is likely to remain a long-term ideal, albeit one pursued with vigour
by elite lawyers.[53]

Conclusion

Anticipating the consequences of the Legal Services Act 2007, the legal profession has
increased lay involvement in its regulatory processes. The appointment of a regulator will see
further inroads into the principle of self-regulation. These moves are not necessarily negative,
however, since more external involvement will probably have a positive impact on the ethical
performance of the profession and may forestall more government control. The existence of a
regulator and the pressure towards homogeneity promised by Alternative Business Structures
could lead to further convergence of the branches or, possibly, further splits into groups of
practitioners with more homogenous interests. These developments might increase the
prospect of collaboration of diverse groups of lawyers across national boundaries, particularly with the European drive to harmonisation of employment regimes. Although diverse
national grouping may yet see their interests best served by national solidarity within traditional boundaries, internal fragmentation and international harmonisation might facilitate
meaningful international codes of professional ethics. Alternatively, the appointment of a
super-regulator may also increase the process of 'legalising' the professional codes so that
they become a code of public law, enforced by normal adjudicative processes.[54] A more
regulatory emphasis would raise questions about the ethical dimension of professionalism
and how it might be pursued and developed. Lawyers developing a 'regulatory mindset',
whereby traditional ethical commitments becomes rules to be steered around, is something

---

[50] Above n 30, para 1.1 (The function of the lawyer in society).

[51] D MacBarnet, 'Law, Policy and Legal Avoidance: Can Law Effectively Implement Egalitarian Policies?' (1998) 15
Journal of Law and Society 113, 118–19.

[52] Above n 44.

[53] See generally TC Halliday and L Karpik, 'Postscript: Lawyers, Political Liberalism, and Globalization' in Halliday
and Karpik, above n 22, 349.

[54] GC Hazard, 'The Future of Legal Ethics' (1991) 100 *Yale Law Journal* 1239, 1241.

that should be avoided if possible. The upside of the legal profession's position is that it still controls disciplinary processes and, most importantly, education and training. There are, however, many issues that need to be addressed in that respect, at both the academic and vocational stages and beyond.[55]

---

[55] A Boon, 'Ethics in Legal Education and Training: Four Reports, Three Jurisdictions and a Prospectus' [2002] *Legal Ethics* 34; A Boon and A Whyte, 'Looking Back: Analysing Experiences of Legal Education and Training' (2007) 41 *The Law Teacher* 169.

INDEX